Off to Work™ with Office 97

LABYRINTH
PUBLICATIONS

(800) 522-9746

Trademarks, Copyright

ISBN 1-887281-39-8
Revision 2.0

Labyrinth Publications Product Listing

	Title & Description	ISBN
	Discover the Internet with Netscape Navigator 3.0	1-887281-30-4
Win 95	Laying a Foundation with Windows 95	1-887281-10-X
Win 95	Crowd Control - (Windows 95 Desktop Control Software) *(25 or more computers)*	
Office 97	Off to Work with Microsoft Office 97	1-887281-39-8
Office 97	Off to Work with Word 97	1-887281-33-9
Office 97	Word 97 Quick Course – Part 1	1-887281-38-X
Office 97	Off to Work with Excel 97	1-887281-32-0
Office 97	Excel 97 Quick Course – Part 1	1-887281-37-1
Office 97	Off to Work with PowerPoint 97	1-887281-41-X
Office 97	Off to Work with Access 97	1-887281-43-6
Office 97	Off to Work with Outlook 97	1-887281-45-2
AutoGrade	AutoGrade – Word 97	
AutoGrade	AutoCheck – Word 97	
AutoGrade	AutoGrade – Excel 97	
AutoGrade	AutoCheck – Excel 97	
Office 95	Mastering the Essentials of Microsoft Word 7.0	1-887281-13-4
Office 95	Word 7.0 Quick Course	1-887281-18-5
Office 95	Mastering the Essentials of Excel 7.0	1-887281-19-3
Office 95	Excel 7.0 Quick Course	1-887281-06-1
Other	Mastering the Essentials of Microsoft Word 6.0	1-887281-05-3
Other	Mastering The Essentials of WordPerfect 6.1	1-887281-04-5
Introduction to Computers	Computer Fundamentals 3.1 (Windows 3.1 Version)	1-887281-12-6
Introduction to Computers	Computer Fundamentals 95 (Windows 95 Version)	1-887281-17-7
Introduction to Computers	Learning Microsoft Works through Fun Projects 3.0 *(Version 3.0 for Windows 3.1)*	1-887281-00-2
Introduction to Computers	Learning Microsoft Works through Fun Projects 4.0 *(Version 4.0 for Windows 95)*	1-887281-08-8
Introduction to Computers	Welcome to the World of Computers 3.0 *(Includes Computer Fundamentals 3.1 and Microsoft Works 3.0)*	1-887281-01-0
Introduction to Computers	Welcome to the World of Computers 4.0 *(Includes Computer Fundamentals 95 and Microsoft Works 4.0)*	1-887281-09-6
DOS	Take Charge of Your PC *(Includes DOS and the Hardware & Software chapters from Fundamentals)*	1-887281-02-9

Table of Contents

Unit Two – Word 97 51

Unit One

Windows 95

1 Windows 95 Basics

Objectives:

- Understand operating system concepts
- Power up a computer
- Use a mouse
- Start programs and switch between programs
- Minimize, maximize and restore windows
- Move and size program windows
- Create files using WordPad and Paint
- Open and save files
- Use pull-down menus and dialog box controls
- Understand multitasking concepts
- Print documents
- Shut down Windows 95

The Project – A Drawing Contest

In this lesson, you will use WordPad and Paint - two of Windows 95's built-in programs - to create a drawing and cover letter for an art contest. This project is designed to introduce fundamental computer skills in a fun and enjoyable way. By the end of this project, you should feel comfortable using Windows 95, working with Windows programs and creating and saving documents. The letter and drawing are shown below in the WordPad and Paint program windows.

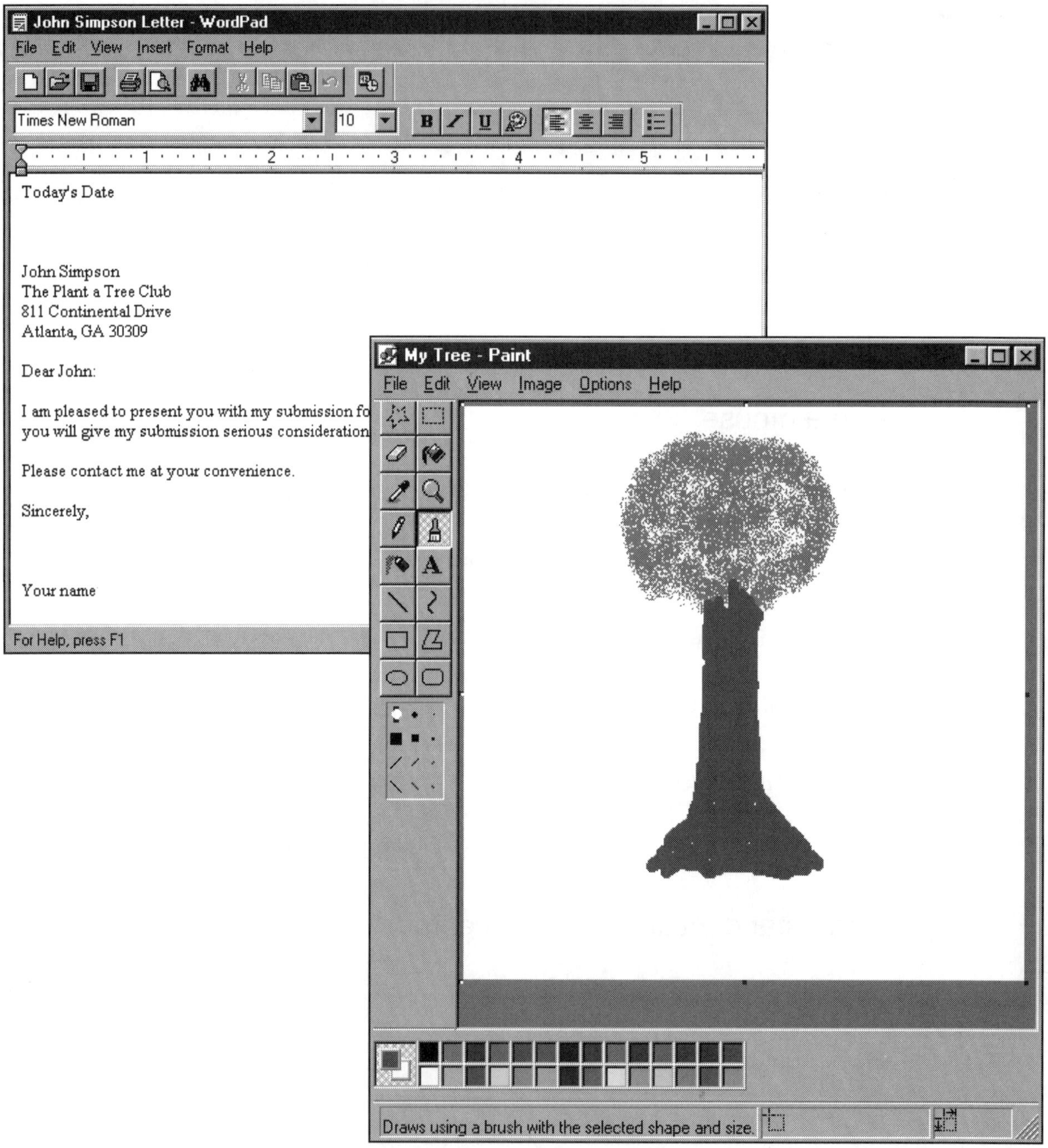

What is Windows 95?

Windows 95 is an **operating system**. Every computer must have an operating system to be able to function. An operating system is responsible for many tasks including the following.

- **File management** - The operating system stores files on disks and retrieves them from disks when a user or program requests them. The operating system knows where the files are located on the disks and it knows where to locate the files when they are needed.
- **Memory management** - The operating system loads programs into RAM (Random Access Memory). The operating system also stores user data in RAM as it is entered into the system. The operating system manages RAM for all programs on the system.
- **Program management** – Windows 95 is a **multitasking** operating system. A multitasking operating system allows many programs to run at the same time. Windows 95 manages the programs and ensures they have adequate RAM and other system resources. It also lets you switch between programs and copy information between them.
- **Interface to the hardware** - The operating system provides an interface between the user, the programs and the hardware. The operating system manages input and output activities. These activities include receiving keyboard and mouse input from the user and outputting data to the monitor.

Windows 95 provides a graphic user interface

A Graphic User Interface (GUI) lets you interface or communicate with the computer through graphic symbols, pictures, and other visual elements. You use a mouse or some other pointing device to interact with a Graphic User Interface.

Windows 95 is a big improvement over windows 3.1

Windows 3.1 is the predecessor of Windows 95. Windows 3.1 is not a true operating system because it is dependent upon DOS (Disk Operating System). Windows 3.1 provides a Graphic User Interface while DOS handles file management and other operating systems tasks. Windows 95 is independent of DOS and therefore has much greater capability than Windows 3.1. In particular, Windows 95 brings the following enhanced capabilities to personal computers.

- **32-bit performance** - Windows 95 allows programs to run faster because it takes full advantage of high-speed modern processors such as the Pentium.
- **True multitasking** - Multitasking lets you run many programs at the same time. For example, with Windows 95, you can print a long report in one program while sending e-mail with another program.
- **Improved GUI** - Windows 95 has a vastly improved interface that makes it much easier to use.
- **Long filenames** - Windows 95 lets you assign filenames of up to 255 characters. This is a huge improvement over Windows 3.1/DOS, which restricted filenames to eight characters or less.
- **Plug & Play** - Windows 95 simplifies the installation of hardware devices through its Plug & Play compatibility. Plug & Play recognizes new hardware devices and automatically installs the necessary software to make the devices run.

Powering Up a Computer

You power up a computer system by switching on the various components. You must switch on the system unit, monitor, printer and other components. The system unit is the box that houses the motherboard, disk drives and other devices. The computer goes through a start up procedure known as the boot process after it is switched on.

Using a surge protector

If the components are connected to a surge protector, then you can switch them on by flipping the power switch on the surge protector. This works fine for most personal computer systems. On some systems, however, components such as the monitor must be switched on before the system unit. This lets the system unit recognize the components as it boots up.

Remove diskettes from the disk drives first

You should remove all diskettes from the disk drives before switching on the power. Your system will give you an error message if diskettes are in the drives. You can insert your diskettes after the Windows 95 desktop appears.

Hands-On 1.1 – Power up the computer

Use the following steps if you are a new computer user and your computer is not powered up.

1. Remove any diskettes from the drives.
2. If your components are connected to a surge protector, then switch on the surge protector and the surge protector light should light up.
3. Switch on your monitor, printer, and other peripheral devices.
4. Switch on your system unit.

   Your system will "boot up." After approximately one minute the Windows 95 desktop or logon dialog box will appear. You will learn how to log on on the following page.

Logging On

Windows 95 may require you to log on before you can begin working. A logon dialog box appears if your system requires you to log on. The logon dialog box will prompt you to enter a **user name** and **password**.

User names and passwords

A user name and password can be important if other people use your computer. Windows 95 lets you customize the desktop (you will learn about the desktop on the next page) and other Windows 95 settings. Your user name displays your customized desktop when you log on.

Hands-On 1.2 – Log on

You can skip this exercise if your system does not require you to logon.

1. Ask your instructor for a user name and password and write them in the spaces below.

   User name: ____________________

   Password: ____________________

   In the next step, you will enter your user name and password. You can move between the User name and Password boxes by tapping the Tab *key on the keyboard. Also, your password will appear as asterisks as you type it in. Be careful not to make spelling mistakes when entering your user name and password.*

2. **Enter your user** name and **password** into the logon dialog box as shown in the example below.

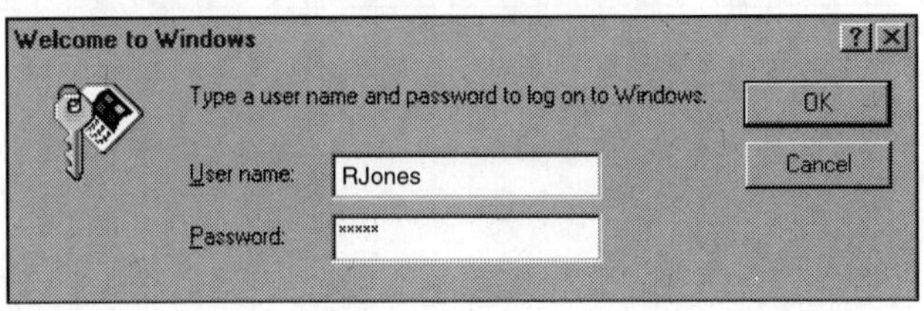

3. **Tap** the Enter key on the keyboard and the Windows 95 desktop should appear.
   A Welcome dialog box may also appear.

4. If the Welcome dialog box appeared, then **tap** the Esc key at the top left corner of the keyboard.
   The Welcome dialog box will close.

The Windows 95 Desktop

The Windows 95 desktop appears immediately after the boot up and/or logon process is complete. The desktop provides the workspace for all activities in Windows 95. Program windows, icons and other elements appear on the desktop. The following illustration discusses the major desktop elements.

Programs run in program windows (although you will not see any program windows at this point).

Desktop icons provide access to common Windows 95 features.

You can place folders, program icons, and shortcuts on the desktop. This lets you easily access the items you use most often.

The Start button and Taskbar make it easy to start programs and switch between them.

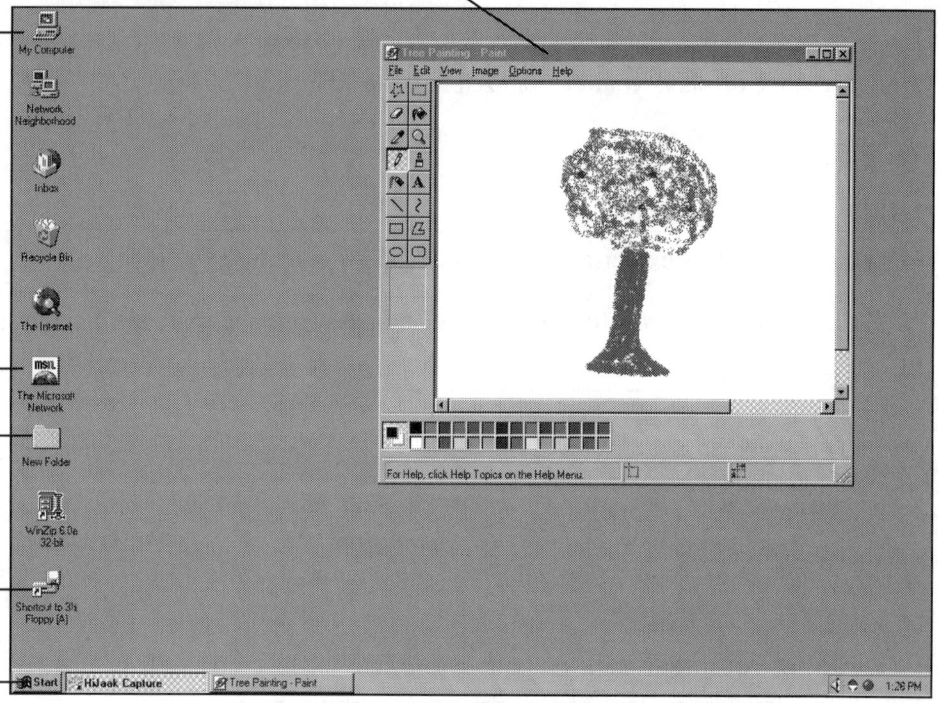

Using a Mouse

A mouse is a small hand held device that lets you interact with Windows 95 and other programs that use a graphic user interface. The mouse lets you point to screen objects and issue commands. Most mice have two buttons as shown in the following illustration.

This is the primary button for right-handed mouse users. It is used for most actions.

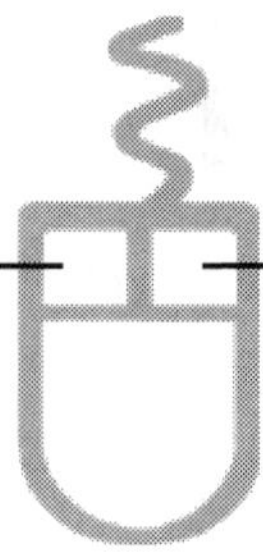

This is the secondary button for right-handed mouse users. It is only used for right-clicking.

The primary and secondary mouse buttons

The primary mouse button is used for most actions. As shown above, the primary button is the left button on mice that are designed for right-handed users. Windows 95 lets you reverse the primary and secondary mouse buttons. This may be necessary for left-handed users who are using a mouse that is designed for right-handed users.

The mouse pad

A mouse pad is a foam pad on which the mouse is moved. A ball rotates on the bottom of the mouse as it slides across the pad. This rolling action causes the mouse pointer to move on the screen. You can slide the mouse along a tabletop but the ball may not track well. The mouse pad has just the right amount of friction to ensure proper tracking.

Mouse talk

The following terminology is used to describe common mouse actions.

Term	Meaning
Point	Position the mouse pointer on a screen object.
Click	Press and release the primary mouse button.
Double-click	Click the primary mouse button twice in rapid succession.
Drag	Press & hold the primary mouse button while sliding the mouse.
Right-click	Press & release the secondary mouse button.

Hands-On 1.3 – Use the mouse

In this exercise, you will use the mouse to click, double-click and right-click.

1. Position the mouse pointer on the Start button at the bottom left corner of the desktop. Make sure you point at the center of the button as shown in the following illustrations.

The pointer is too high

The pointer is too low

The pointer is just right

2. Keep the mouse pointer on the Start button, then gently **press and release** ("Click") the **left mouse button**.

   The Start menu will appear as shown below. The Start menu lets you start programs, use online Help, find files and perform other functions.

3. Use the following steps to display the Accessories menu.

❷ ***Slide*** *the mouse pointer to the right and point at* ***Accessories****. The Accessories menu will appear as shown here. You will use several of the accessories later in this lesson.*

❶ ***Slide*** *the mouse pointer up the Start menu to* ***Programs*** *and the Programs submenu will appear as shown here. Your Programs menu will most likely have different programs than shown here. A submenu appears whenever you point to a menu option that has a right-pointing triangle.*

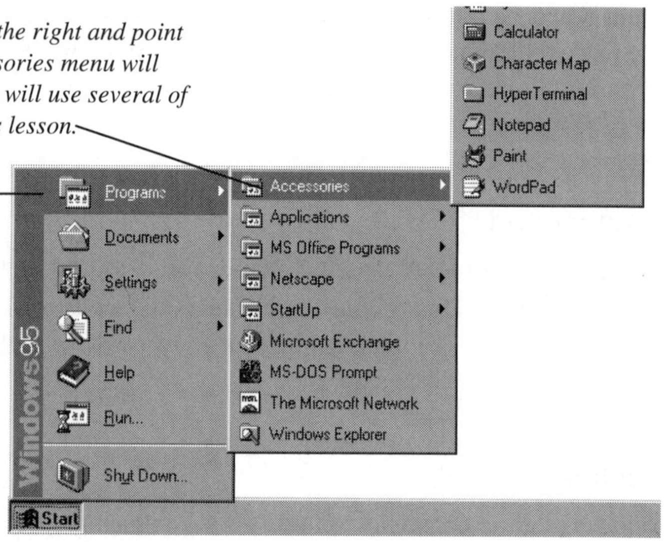

4. Now **close** the menus by positioning the mouse pointer in an open part of the desktop and **clicking**.

   You can always close an open menu by clicking outside of it.

Try right-clicking and double-clicking

5. Position the mouse pointer in an open part of the desktop and **click** the **right mouse button**.

   A context-sensitive menu similar to the following example will appear. Right-clicking is an effective technique to use in Windows 95 and Windows 95 programs because it displays context-sensitive menus. Context-sensitive menus contain commands that are likely to be needed by the user at the screen location where the user clicks.

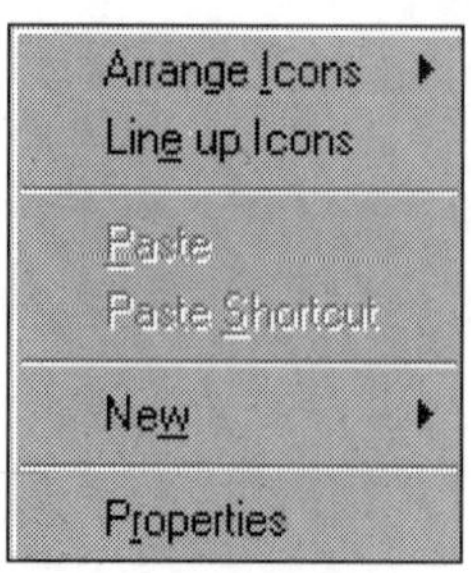

A context-sensitive menu

Continued...

6. Close the menu by clicking with the **left** mouse button in an open part of the desktop.

7. Locate the My Computer  icon on the desktop.

8. Position the pointer on the My Computer  icon and **double-click** the left mouse button.

   Make sure you keep the mouse pointer on the icon while you rapidly click the button twice. My Computer is a Windows 95 tool that lets you browse through the disk drives and other information storage devices on your computer system. My Computer also lets you browse devices that are located on a network (if your computer is connected to a network). My Computer can also be used to create folders, copy files and perform other administrative tasks. In the next lesson, you will learn how to work with files and folders.

9. Use the following illustration to explore the My Computer program window.

*This is the **Title bar**. It displays the name of the program.*

*This is the **Menu bar**. You can issue commands by choosing them from the pull-down menus on the menu bar.*

*This is a **toolbar**. Most programs have toolbars with buttons. You can issue commands by clicking buttons.*

This is the main part of the program window where you "get your work done."

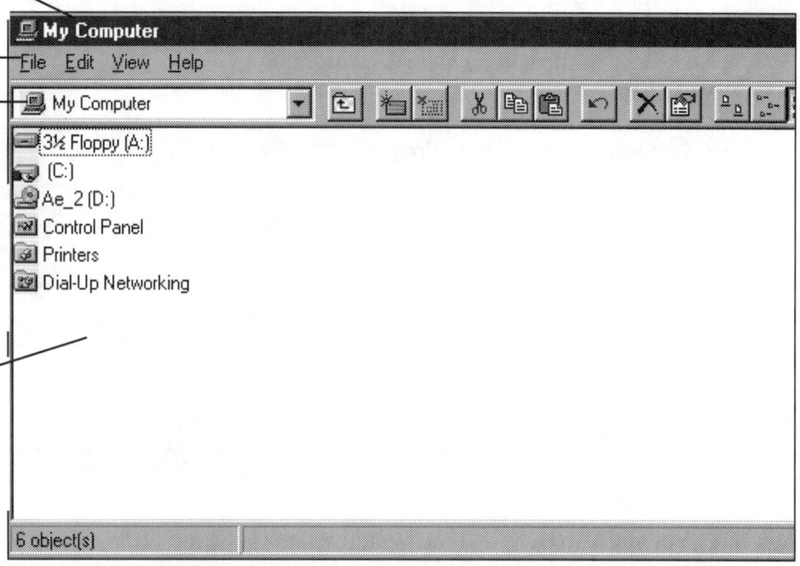

10. Now use the following step to close the My Computer program window.

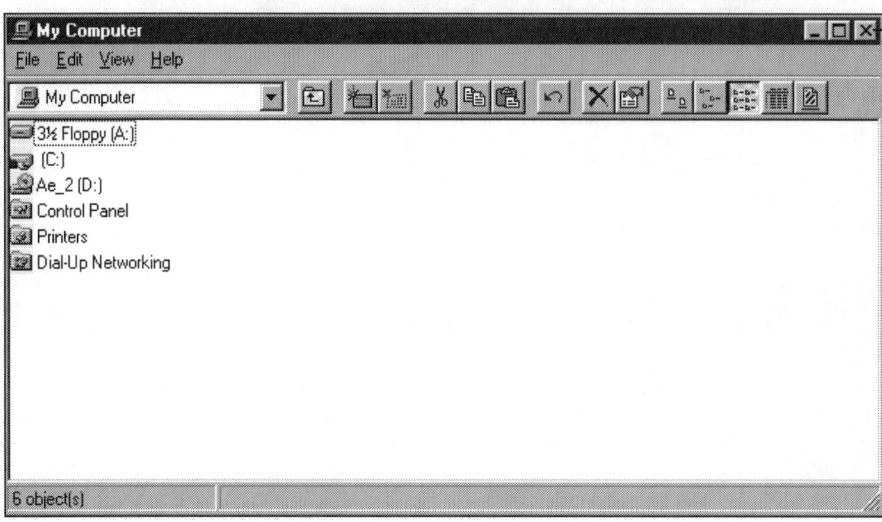

➊ ***Click** the Close*  *button at the top-right corner of the window. The Close button can always be used to close program windows.*

Starting Programs

You can start a program by clicking the Start button and choosing the desired program from the Programs menu. You can also start a program by double-clicking a desktop icon for the program (if a desktop icon exists). In the previous exercise, you started My Computer by double-clicking a desktop icon.

Hands-On 1.4 – Start WordPad

In this exercise, you will start a program named WordPad. WordPad is an entry-level word processing program that can be used to create letters and other simple documents. In a later exercise, you will use WordPad to compose a letter.

1. **Click** the Start button and use the following steps to start WordPad.

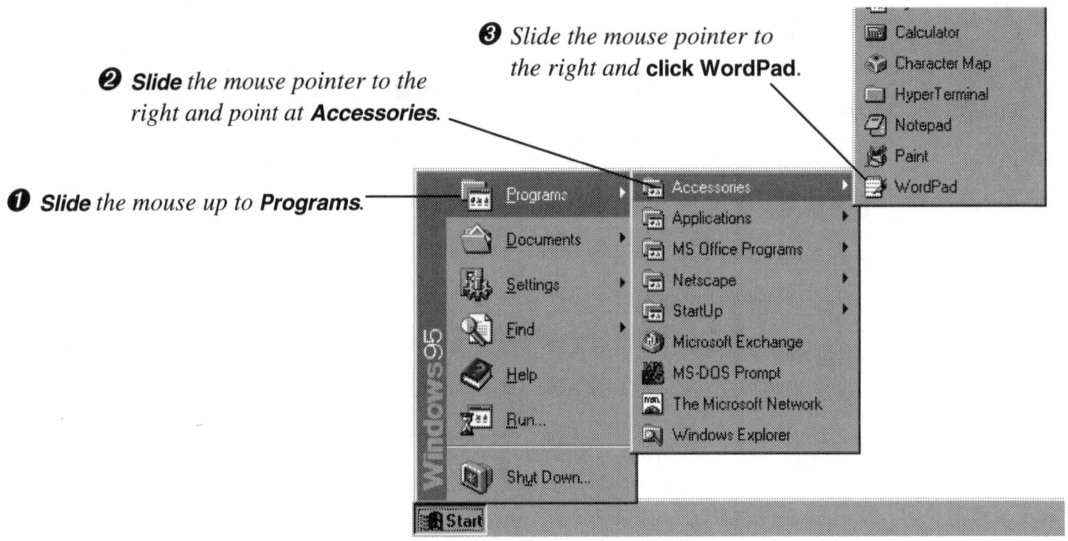

2. Notice that the WordPad window has the same elements as the My Computer window.

   The elements include the Title bar, Menu bar and one or more toolbars. Leave the WordPad window open because you will continue to use it.

Quick Sizing Buttons

Every program window has quick sizing buttons located at the top right corner of the window. The quick sizing buttons are described in the following table.

Button	Description
Minimize	Removes the program window from the desktop but keeps the program running. Clicking the program button on the Taskbar restores the program window.
Maximize	Expands the program window until it covers the desktop. Only the maximized program and the Taskbar are visible.
Restore	Restores a program window to the size it was set to before it was maximized. A restored window covers only a portion of the desktop.
Close	Removes a program from RAM and the desktop.

Hands-On 1.5 – Use quick sizing buttons

1. Notice the WordPad [Document - WordPad] button next to the Start button on the Taskbar.
   The button is recessed (pushed in) because WordPad is the active program. A button appears on the Taskbar for each running program.
2. Look at the top-right corner of the WordPad window and there will be three quick sizing buttons.
   The left quick sizing button is always Minimize and the right button is always Close. The middle button will be either Restore or Maximize. The Restore and Maximize buttons never appear together. The Restore button is displayed when the window is maximized and the Maximize button is displayed when the window is restored. A restored window covers only part of the desktop.
3. If the middle-sizing button is the Maximize button, then click it.
   At this point, the WordPad window will be maximized. Only the WordPad window, the Taskbar and the Start button should be visible.
4. **Click** the Minimize button on the WordPad window.
   The window vanishes but the button [Document - WordPad] is still visible on the Taskbar.
5. **Click** the WordPad [Document - WordPad] button on the Taskbar and the window will reappear.
   You can always restore a minimized window by clicking that program's button on the Taskbar.
6. **Click** the Restore button and the window will occupy only part of the desktop.
7. Finally, **click** the Maximize button.
   You will enter text into the WordPad window in the next exercise.

Creating Files

You create documents by using application programs like WordPad. Documents are entered into the computer's RAM memory as you create them. However, the contents of RAM are erased whenever the computer is turned off. For this reason, you must save documents onto a diskette, hard disk or other storage device if you want to save them for later use. The word **file** is used to describe any document that has been saved onto a storage device. A typical hard disk drive will have thousands of files stored on it.

The Save and Save As Commands

Most Windows programs provide two commands that let you save documents. The **File→Save** command saves the current document onto a disk. If the document had previously been saved, then the previous version is replaced by the new edited version. If the document is new, then a Save As dialog box appears. The Save As dialog box lets you name the document and specify the disk drive and folder that you wish to save the document to. You can also use the **File→Save As** command to make a copy of an existing document by saving the document under a new name.

Save your documents frequently

One important lesson to learn is to **save your documents frequently!** Power outages and careless accidents can result in lost data. The best protection is to save your documents every 10 or 15 minutes and after making significant changes.

Windows 95 supports long filenames

All programs that are designed to work with Windows 95 support long filenames. You can use up to 255 characters when naming files in a Windows 95 program. This is a huge improvement over the 8-character limitation that was imposed by earlier versions of Windows and DOS. You can also use spaces, hyphens -, underscores _ and other characters in Windows 95 filenames.

Hands-On 1.6 – Type a letter in WordPad and save it as a file

1. Notice the flashing vertical insertion point in the WordPad window.

   You can begin typing the moment WordPad is started. Text in inserted in the WordPad window at the insertion point location. In a moment, you will type a letter in the WordPad window. Use the BackSpace key on the keyboard if you make typing mistakes. The BackSpace key deletes the character to the left of the insertion point.

2. Now type the letter shown on the following page tapping Enter only in the locations indicated.

   WordPad will automatically wrap the line in the main paragraph without you needing to tap Enter.

Continued...

Today's Date [Enter]
[Enter]
[Enter]
[Enter]
John Simpson [Enter]
The Plant a Tree Club [Enter]
811 Continental Drive [Enter]
Atlanta, GA 30309 [Enter]
[Enter]
Dear John: [Enter]
[Enter]
I am pleased to present you with my submission for your 1997 Plant a Tree Day logo competition. I hope you will give my submission serious consideration. [Enter]
[Enter]
Please contact me at your convenience. [Enter]
[Enter]
Sincerely, [Enter]
[Enter]
[Enter]
[Enter]
Your name

Save the file

3. Insert your exercise diskette into the disk drive.

Ask for assistance if you are unsure how to insert a diskette.

4. Use the following illustration to issue the Save command.

❶ ***Click File*** *on the WordPad menu bar and the File menu will drop-down as shown here.*

❷ ***Slide*** *the mouse* ***down*** *and* ***click Save*** *on the File menu. The Save As dialog box will appear. Dialog boxes such as Save As are often displayed when you issue commands. Dialog boxes let you set options prior to completing a command. Continue with the steps on the following page where you will name the file and complete the command.*

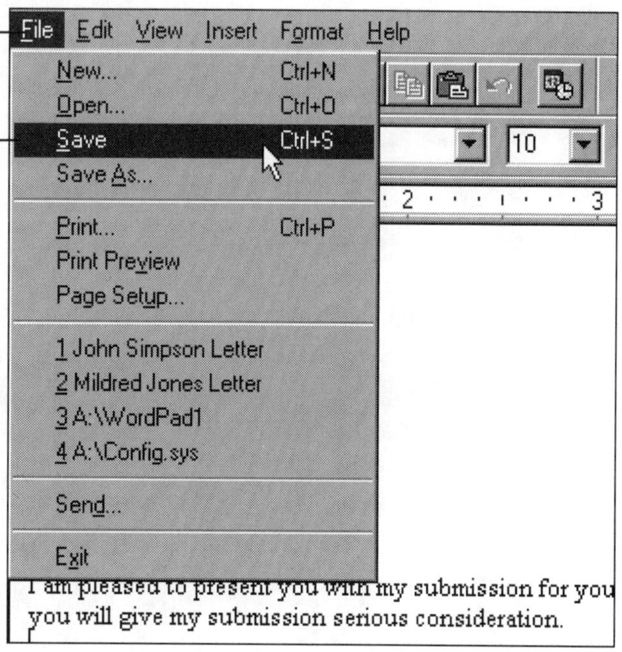

Continued...

5. Use the following illustration to complete the save.

❶ ***Click here*** *and choose the disk drive with your exercise diskette. It is most likely 3 ½ Floppy [A:]. Your exercise diskette may already contain files as shown here.*

❷ *Notice that WordPad proposes the name Document in the File name box. The name Document may also be highlighted or "selected."*

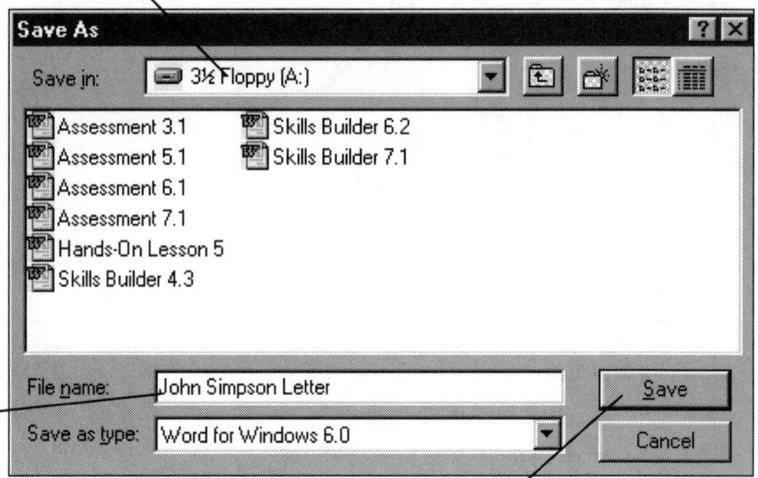

❸ ***Click*** *in the File name box to the right of the name Document.* ***Use*** *the* ***Backspace*** *key on the keyboard to delete the name Document and then* ***type*** *the name* ***John Simpson Letter*** *as shown here.*

❹ ***Click*** *the* ***Save*** *button. The light on your diskette drive will light up and the drive will spin as the file is saved.*

The WordPad window will remain open with the John Simpson letter displayed.

A Closer Look at Pull-Down Menus

Pull-down menus are used frequently in Windows programs to initiate commands. Almost all windows programs use pull-down menus. There are several symbols that appear on pull-down menus that you should be familiar with. The following illustration discusses the symbols on WordPad's File pull-down menu.

Notice that each command on the menu bar and pull-down menu has one underlined letter. You can use the **Alt** *key on the keyboard and the underlined letters to initiate commands. This is accomplished by* **pressing & holding** *the* **Alt** *key and* **tapping** *the* **underlined letter** *of the desired command on the menu bar. Once a menu is pulled-down, you can tap the underlined letter of the desired command on the pull-down menu (without holding the Alt key). In other words, you can initiate commands without using the mouse.*

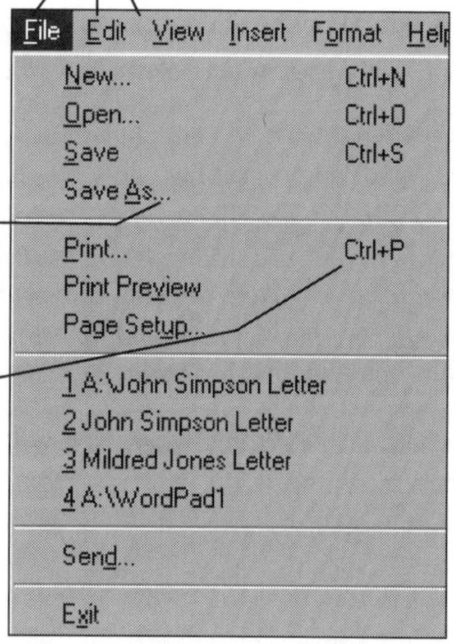

Notice that some commands have three dots ... after them. These dots are known as an **ellipsis**. *An ellipsis indicates that a dialog box will appear if the command is chosen.*

Notice that keystrokes (such as Ctrl + P) are displayed to the right of some commands. These keystrokes are known as **shortcut keys**. *You can initiate the indicated command (without using the pull-down menus) by pressing the shortcut keys. This is convenient for issuing frequently used commands.*

Hands-On 1.7 – Edit the letter and save it under a new name

In this exercise, you will edit the name in the delivery address section of the letter. You will then save the modified letter under a new name. You will use the **File→Save As...** command to accomplish this. The Save As command lets you save a document under a new name.

1. Use the following steps to edit the delivery name in the letter.

Today's Date

John Simpson
The Plant a Tree Club
811 Continental Drive
Atlanta, GA 30309

Dear John:

❶ *Position the mouse pointer just to the right of the name John Simpson and* **click** *the left mouse button. The flashing insertion point should be positioned to the right of the name Simpson as shown here.*

❷ **Tap** *the* **BackSpace** *key on the keyboard until the name John Simpson is deleted.*

❸ *Now* **type** *the name* **Mildred Jones**.

Continued...

Save the new letter

In the next step, you will be instructed to choose File→Save As... from the menu bar. In this course, the right arrow → symbol is used to separate the components of a command. Also, feel free to display the Save As dialog box by using the **Alt** key on the keyboard and the underlined letters in the command names as discussed on the previous page. This is an alternative method that you can always use if you have difficulty using the mouse.

2. Choose **File→Save As...** from the menu bar.

   The Save As dialog box will appear and the name John Simpson Letter should be selected in the File name box.

3. **Type** the name **Mildred Jones Letter** and it will replace the name John Simpson Letter.

4. **Click** the **Save** button on the dialog box to complete the save.

   Your exercise diskette now has WordPad documents named John Simpson Letter and Mildred Jones Letter.

5. Now close the WordPad program window by choosing **File→Exit** from the menu bar.

   Almost all Windows programs have commands such as File→Save and File→Exit. This commonality between programs is one of the many benefits that Windows provides. The commonality makes it easier to learn new programs. By the way, you could also have closed WordPad by clicking the Close  *button at the top-right corner of the WordPad window. As you have seen thus far, Windows programs provide a variety of ways to issue commands.*

6. Now continue with the next topic where you will learn to open an existing document.

Opening Documents and Making Changes

You can issue an Open command to use a document that has been saved onto a storage device. The Open command copies the desired file into the RAM memory and displays the document on the screen. You can then view the document and make the desired editing changes.

Most Windows programs let you open documents with a **File→Open** command or by clicking an Open button on a toolbar. In the following exercise, you will use a toolbar button in WordPad to open the Mildred Jones Letter document. This document was saved to your exercise diskette in the previous exercise.

Hands-On 1.8 – Open the Mildred Jones letter

Start WordPad

1. **Click** the Start button.
2. **Slide** the mouse up to **Programs**.
3. **Slide** the mouse to the right and then up to **Accessories**.
4. Choose **WordPad** from the Accessories menu.

Open the document

5. **Click** the Open button on the WordPad toolbar.

   It is possible that the WordPad toolbar will not be displayed. If it is not displayed, then choose View→Toolbar from the menu bar to display it.

6. Use the following steps to open the file named Mildred Jones Letter.

❶ *If necessary, click here and choose the disk drive that your diskette is in. It is most likely in 3 ½ Floppy [A:].*

❷ *Choose the **Mildred Jones Letter** file by clicking it.*

❸ ***Click** the **Open** button.*

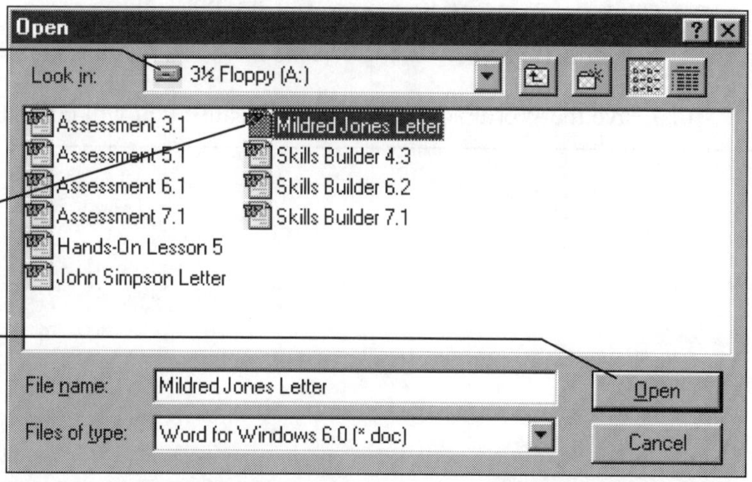

The letter will appear in the WordPad window. This document is now in RAM memory and it is being reflected on your screen.

7. **Notice** that the salutation Dear John needs to be changed to Dear Mildred.

   You will make this change in the next few steps. After making the change, you will save the letter again to update the changes on your diskette.

Continued...

8. Use the following steps to edit the salutation.

Today's Date

Mildred Jones
The Plant a Tree Club
811 Continental Drive
Atlanta, GA 30309

Dear John:

❶ *Position the mouse pointer just to the* **left** *of the name John in the salutation and* **click** *the left mouse button. The flashing insertion point should be positioned to the left of John as shown here.*

❷ ***Tap*** *the* ***Delete*** *key on the keyboard* ***four times*** *and the name John will be deleted. The Delete key deletes the character to the right of the insertion point.*

❸ *Now type the name* ***Mildred****.*

Save the change

In the next step, you will save the change you just made by clicking the Save button on WordPad's toolbar. The Save button automatically updates changes to a document that has previously been saved. Most programs have a Save button. The Save button provides the same result as choosing File→Save from the menu bar.

9. **Click** the Save button on WordPad's toolbar.

Your diskette drive should "come alive" as the file is updated.

10. Leave the WordPad window open because you will continue to use it.

Moving and Sizing Program Windows

You can move and size program windows. This allows you to adjust the position and size of windows as desired. A window must be restored (not maximized) before it can be moved or sized. You will move and size the WordPad window in the following exercise.

Working with Scroll Bars

Scroll bars appear in windows when the amount of text in a document exceeds the size of the window. The scroll bars let you scroll through a document and thus view the entire document.

Hands-On 1.9 – Move and size the WordPad window and use scroll bars

The WordPad window should be maximized from an earlier exercise.

1. **Click** the Restore button near the top-right corner of the WordPad window.
   The window will be reduced in size and occupy a portion of the desktop.
2. Use the following steps to move and size the WordPad window.

❶ *Position the mouse pointer on the blue Title bar and* ***press & hold*** *the* ***left mouse button.***

❷ ***Drag*** *the window to a new location on the desktop and* ***release*** *the mouse button.*

❸ *Position the mouse pointer on the* ***left edge*** *of the window and a double-headed arrow will appear.*

❹ ***Press & hold*** *the left mouse button while you* ***drag*** *the double-headed arrow to the left. The width of the window will increase. Dragging is a mouse action that you will use often.*

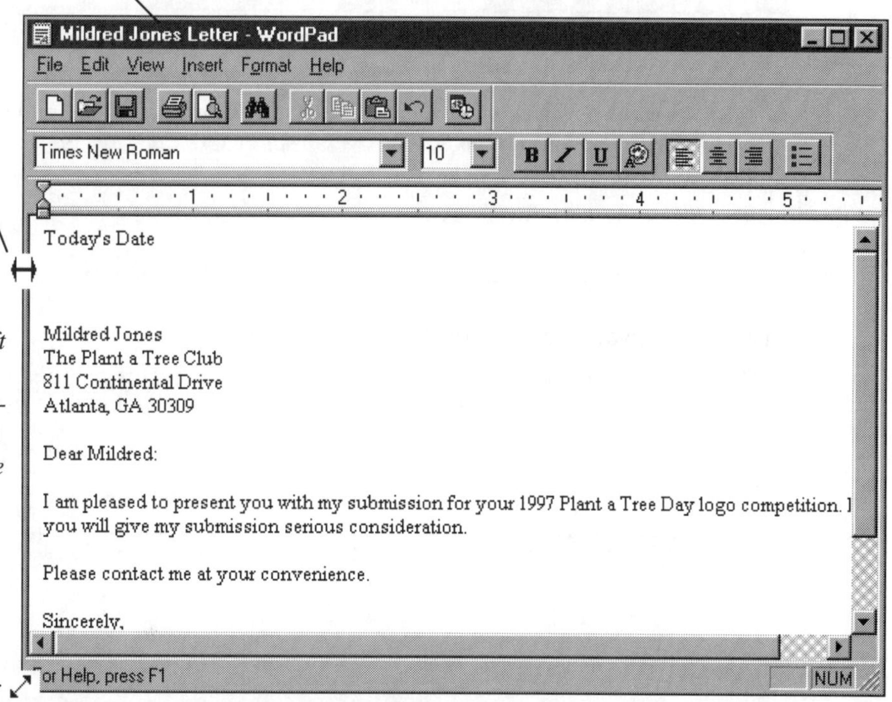

❺ *Now* ***drag any corner*** *of the window to change both the width and height together. Scroll bars will appear in the window (as shown here) once the window is too small to display the entire document.*

3. Take a few minutes to practice moving and sizing the window.
   You can use these techniques with all windows.

Continued...

4. If necessary, adjust the size of the WordPad window until scroll bars appear as shown below.

5. Use the following illustration to scroll through the document.

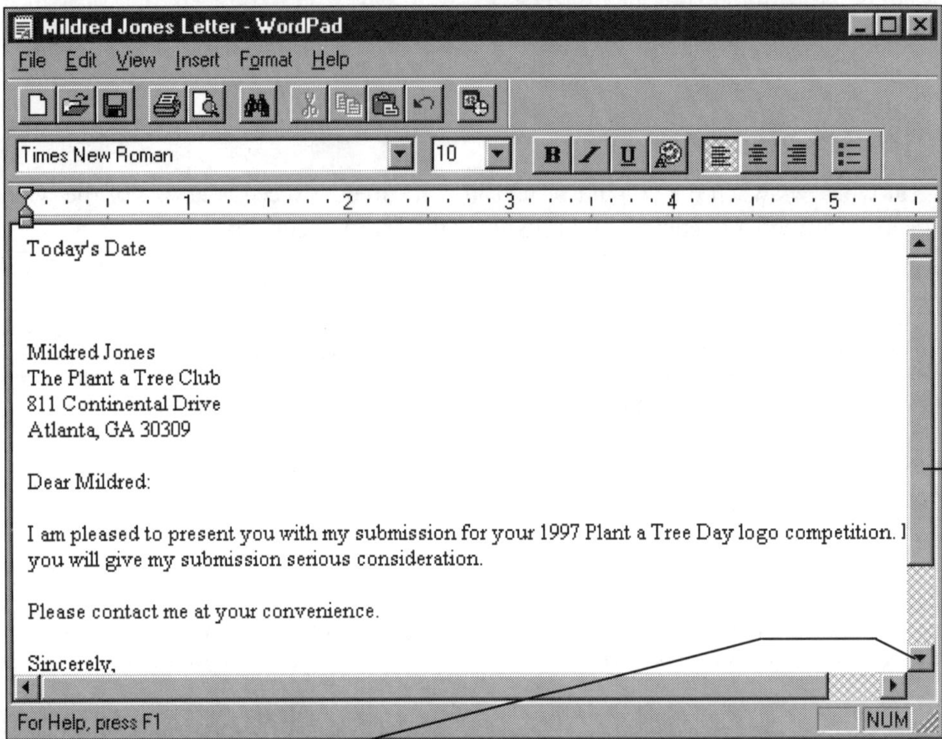

❶ ***Click** the **scroll down** button on the vertical scroll bar several times. The document will scroll one line each time you click the button.*

❷ ***Drag** this scroll box up or down to rapidly scroll through the document.*

6. Try using the horizontal scroll bar at the bottom of the window.

7. Try clicking in an open part of the scroll bar between the scroll box and the up or down buttons.

   This useful technique will scroll one screen at a time. This technique is especially useful if you are reading a long multi-page document on your screen. You can rapidly browse through the document one screen at a time.

8. Leave WordPad open because you will continue to work with it.

Multitasking

One of the most important benefits of Windows 95 is it allows you to run multiple programs simultaneously. The ability to run multiple programs simultaneously is known as multitasking. For example, with Windows 95 you can download files from the Internet, print a long document and type a letter in a word processor all at the same time. You use the Taskbar to easily switch between multitasked programs. This is accomplished by clicking the desired program button on the Taskbar.

Hands-On 1.10 – Start Paint and switch between programs

In this exercise, you will open a program named Paint. Paint lets you design colorful drawings using your mouse and your imagination.

Start Paint

1. **Click** the Start button and **slide** the mouse up to **Programs**.
2. **Slide** the mouse to the right and then up to **Accessories**.
3. Choose **Paint** from the Accessories menu.

   The Paint program will start. As you can see, there are a several useful programs on the Accessories menu.

4. If Paint is not currently maximized, then **click** the Maximize button on the Paint window.

   Paint will occupy the entire desktop and WordPad will no longer be visible. However, you can tell that WordPad is still running because the WordPad button is still visible on the Taskbar. Notice that the Paint button is pushed-in on the Taskbar. This indicates that Paint is the active program.

Switch between programs

5. **Click** the WordPad button on the Taskbar to activate WordPad.
6. Now **click** the Paint button on the Taskbar to activate Paint.

   Notice how easy it is to switch between running programs with the Taskbar.

7. **Click** the Restore button on the Paint window.

   The Paint window will occupy a portion of the desktop. At this point, both Paint and WordPad should be restored. You should be able to see a portion of both program windows. You can always move and size restored program windows to allow you to view multiple programs simultaneously.

8. **Click** anywhere in the WordPad program window to make WordPad active. If the WordPad window isn't visible, then click the WordPad button on the taskbar.

   You can make a program active by clicking anywhere in the program window.

9. **Click** the Close button on the WordPad window and click Yes if WordPad asks you to save the changes to the document.
10. Now **click** the Maximize button on the Paint window.

    You will continue to work with Paint.

Dialog Boxes

Dialog boxes let you set options and controls prior to issuing a command. There are a variety of controls that you will encounter in dialog boxes. The following illustrations discuss the various dialog box controls.

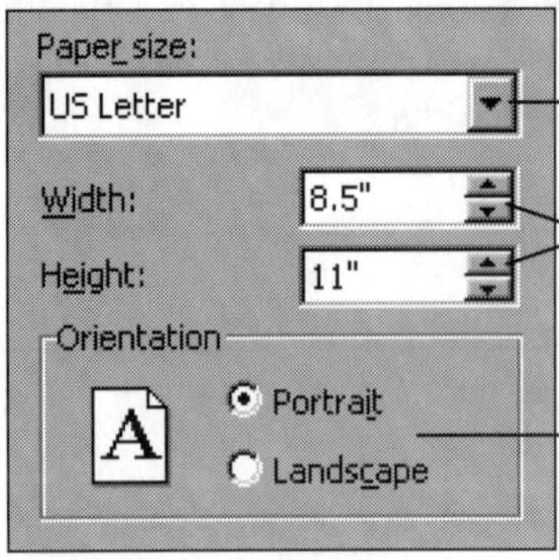

Drop-down buttons provide a list of options to choose from.

Spinner bars let you increase or decrease a setting one increment at a time.

Radio buttons let you choose one option. Only one radio button can be chosen for a given set of options.

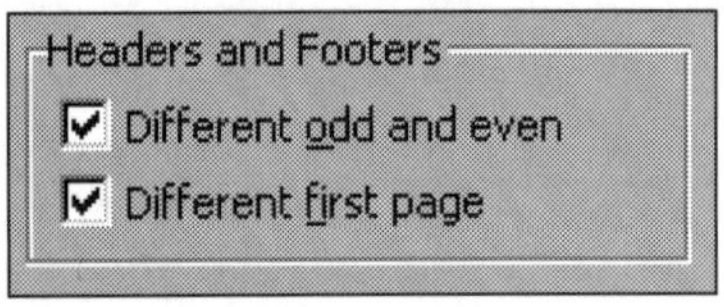

Check boxes let you choose more than one option. You can check as many boxes as desired.

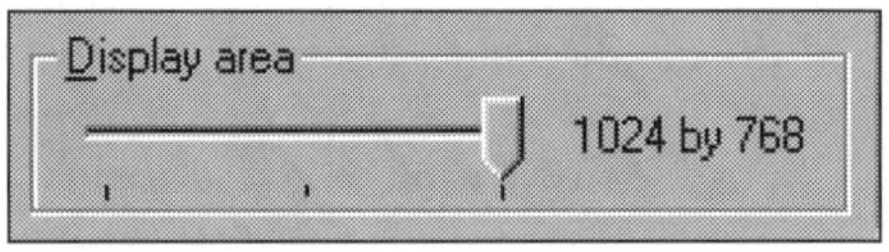

Slider bars let you adjust a setting by dragging a bar.

Hands-On 1.11 – Set options in Paint

In this exercise, you will use dialog boxes to set two options in the Paint program. The options you set will reduce the size of the Paint file that you will save to your exercise diskette. This is necessary because the Paint program produces graphics files. Graphics files occupy a large amount of disk space when compared to text files. One Paint file would occupy your entire diskette if you were not to make the settings discussed in this exercise.

1. Choose **Image→Attributes...** from the Paint menu bar.

   You will use this dialog box to specify the drawing size. The drawing size impacts the file size.

2. Use the following steps to set the drawing size. Make sure you do the steps in order (1, 2, 3…).

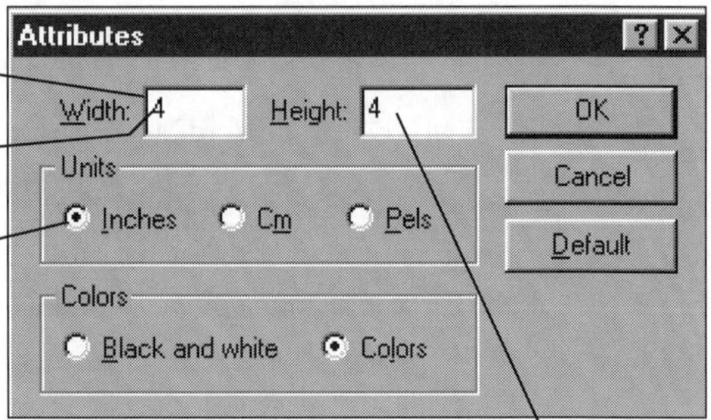

❷ **Click** *in the Width box.*

❸ *If necessary, use the Delete or Backspace keys to delete the measurement that is in the box and then* **type 4** *as shown here.*

❶ *If necessary,* **click** *the* **Inches** *radio button to set the units of measurement to inches.*

❹ **Tap** *the* **Tab** *key on the keyboard. The insertion point will move to the Height box and the measurement in that box will become selected. The Tab key can be used in many dialog boxes to move from one field to the next.*

❺ **Type 4** *as shown here.*

Continued...

3. **Click** the **OK** button on the dialog box.

   The image size will be set to 4" by 4". In the next few steps, you will save the empty drawing to your exercise diskette. You will use a drop-down button on the Save As dialog box to set the Save As Type. Most programs have a Save As Type option that lets you specify the type of file you wish to create. In the Paint program, you use the Save As Type option to determine the amount of color information that is stored in the file. You will reduce the amount of color information to conserve space on your diskette.

4. Choose **File→Save** from the menu bar.

5. Use the following steps to set the Save As Type and save the file.

❶ *If necessary, click here and choose the disk drive that your diskette is in. It is most likely in 3 ½ Floppy [A:].*

❷ *Type* ***My Tree*** *as the filename.*

❸ *If necessary, click anywhere in the Save as type box and choose 256 Color Bitmap.*

❹ ***Click*** *the* ***Save*** *button.*

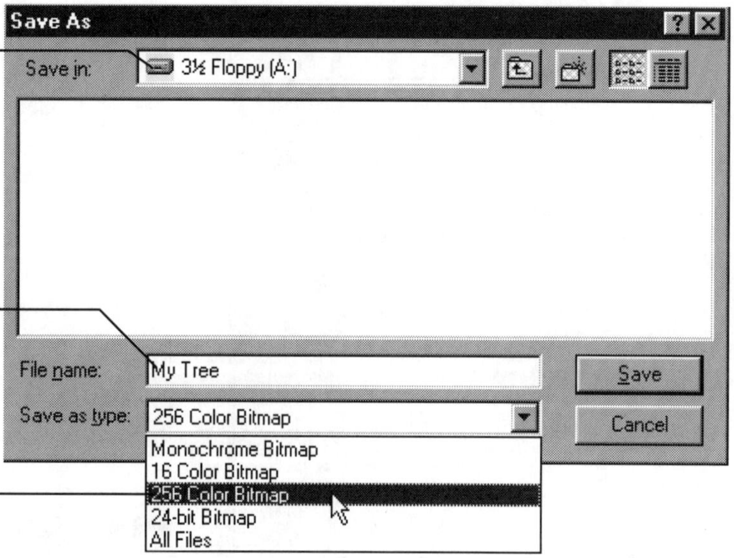

Continued...

Create your tree

In the remainder of this exercise, you will use Paint's drawing tools to create a drawing of a tree. Feel free to experiment with the various tools and make sure you have fun.

6. Use the following steps to choose a drawing tool and color and to begin drawing.

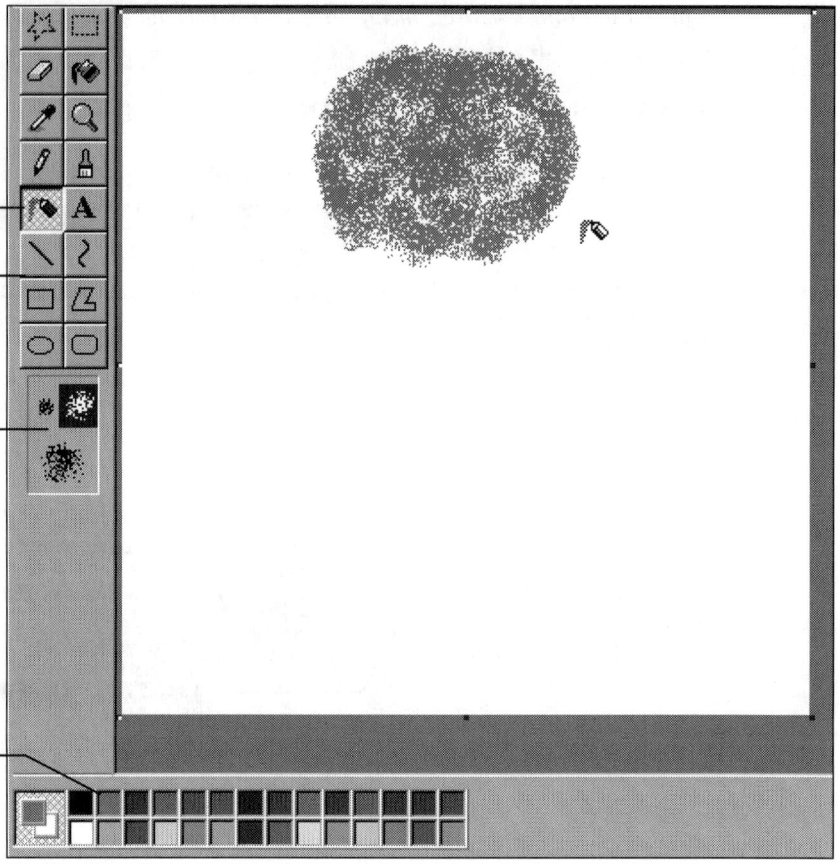

❶ *Choose the Airbrush tool by clicking this button.*

❷ *Choose a spray pattern.*

❸ *Choose a color.*

❹ *Position the mouse pointer in the drawing area and it will have a spray can shape as shown above.*

❺ **Press & hold** *the left mouse button while you swirl the mouse around. The Airbrush tool will spray paint wherever you drag the mouse.*

❻ *Continue spraying paint until you have a treetop like the one shown above.*

7. If necessary, **click** the Eraser tool on the Paint toolbar.

The mouse pointer will become a sqaure □. You can drag the square over a painted area to remove paint/color from the area. The Eraser tool can be used to help clean up a drawing.

Continued...

8. Use the following steps to add a trunk to the tree.

❶ *Choose the Brush tool by clicking this button.*

❷ *Choose a brush pattern.*

❸ *Choose a color.*

❹ **Drag** *the mouse up and down in the drawing window to complete the tree shown in this illustration.*

9. Choose **File→Save** (not Save As) from the menu bar to save the changes to your drawing.

You will print your drawing in the next exercise.

Printing

Almost all Windows programs have a **File→Print** command or a Print button on a toolbar that you can use to print your documents. The **File→Print** command usually displays a dialog box that lets you choose the printer and other options. A document with color (such as a Paint drawing) will only print in color if you have a color printer. Otherwise, the colors will print as shades of gray.

Hands-On 1.12 – Print the drawing

1. Choose **File→Print...** from the menu bar.
2. Take a moment to study the dialog box options and then **click OK**.

   After a brief pause, your drawing will be printed. Graphics (such as your drawing) usually take longer to print than text documents like the WordPad letters you created earlier.
3. Feel free to enhance your drawing by experimenting with the other Paint tools.
4. When you have finished experimenting, **click** the Close button on the Paint window.

   If you made changes to the drawing since the last time you saved it, then Paint will ask if you want to save the changes. ***Click Yes*** *if you wish to save the changes and* ***click No*** *if you want to discard the changes. At this point, the Paint window should be closed.*
5. Now continue with the last topic in this lesson.

Shutting Down Windows 95

You should always use Windows 95's Shut Down command prior to switching off your computer system. The Shut Down command closes all programs and performs other "housekeeping" tasks. You can also use the Shut Down command to restart the computer without switching off the power. You issue the Shut Down command by **clicking** the **Start** button and choosing **Shut Down**.

Hands-On 1.13 – Shut down Windows 95

In this exercise, you are instructed to restart the computer with the Shut Down command. In the future, you should ask your instructor for the proper shut down procedure in your computer lab.

1. Remove your exercise diskette from the disk drive.

   You must remove diskettes from the drive prior to starting or restarting the computer.
2. **Click** the Start button and choose **Shut Down...** from the Start menu.
3. **Click** the **Restart the computer?** option button.

   In the future, you should use the ***Shut down the computer?*** *option when you have finished using the computer and you wish to switch it off. Windows 95 displays a message telling you it is safe to turn off the computer when you use this option.*
4. **Click** the **Yes** button and the computer system will restart.

   Now continue with the end-of-lesson questions and exercises.

Concepts Review

True / False

1. Windows 95 is responsible for file, memory and program management. 1. T F
2. Windows 95 provides a graphical user interface. 2. T F
3. You double-click by pressing the secondary mouse button twice in rapid succession. 3. T F
4. You can start a program by clicking the Start button and choosing the desired program from the Programs menu. 4. T F
5. The File→Open command is used to save a document to a diskette. 5. T F
6. Filenames can have up to 255 characters in Windows 95. 6. T F
7. Scroll bars are used to maximize restored windows. 7. T F
8. Windows 95 is a multitasking operating system. 8. T F
9. You can choose as many radio buttons as desired when setting options for a feature. 9. T F
10. You should always shut down Window's 95 prior to switching off the computer system. 10. T F

Multiple Choice

1. Which of the following buttons restores a window?
   a) 
   b) 
   c) 
   d) 
   ( )

2. Which of the following buttons maximizes a window?
   a) 
   b) 
   c) 
   d) 
   ( )

3. Which keyboard keys are used to pull-down menus without using the mouse?
   a) The Alt key and the underlined letter of the desired menu command.
   b) The Ctrl key and the underlined letter of the desired menu command.
   c) The Shift key and the underlined letter of the desired menu command.
   d) You cannot pull-down a menu without the mouse.
   ( )

4. Which of the following techniques is used to move a program window?
   a) Maximize the window and drag the Title bar.
   b) Restore the window and drag the Title bar.
   c) Minimize the window and drag the Title bar.
   d) Drag a corner-sizing handle.
   ( )

5. Which of the following commands can be used to print in most programs?
   a) File→Save
   b) File→Open
   c) View→Print
   d) None of the above.
   ( )

Skills Builder 1.1 – Use the Calculator

This Skills Builder will show you how to use the Windows 95 Calculator program.

1. **Click** the Start button and slide the mouse up to **Programs**.
2. Slide the mouse to Accessories and chose **Calculator**.
3. Use the following illustration to add two numbers.

❶ *If necessary, click the View menu and choose Standard to display the Standard calculator style shown here. The View menu also lets you choose a Scientific calculator style.*

❷ *Click any of the number buttons on the calculator or tap any number keys on the keyboard.*

❸ *Click the Plus + button on the calculator or tap the plus + key on the keyboard.*

❹ *Click or type any numbers and then click or tap the equal = button/key.*

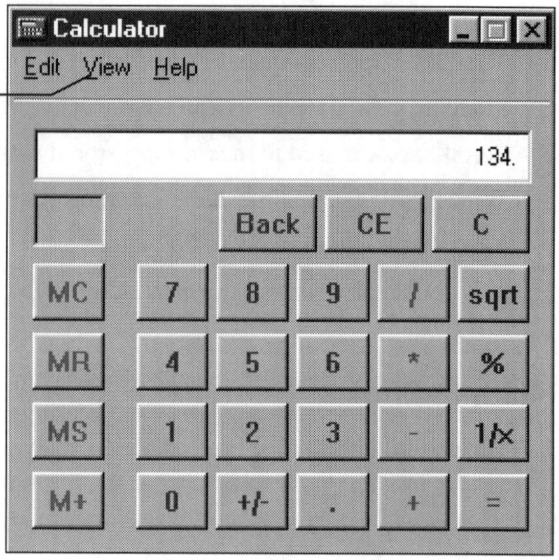

4. Feel free to experiment with the calculator.
5. **Click** the Minimize button to minimize the calculator.
6. **Click** the Calculator button on the Taskbar to restore the calculator.
   Notice that you can hide the calculator when you are not using it and display it when you need it. This technique is used often when working with multiple programs.
7. Feel free to experiment with the calculator.
8. Close the calculator when you have finished experimenting and continue with the next Skills Builder exercise.

Skills Builder 1.2

1. Start the WordPad program.
2. Type a To Do list of the things you need to do this week.
3. Save your list to your exercise diskette using a descriptive name. Keep in mind that you can use any number of characters in the filename including spaces.
4. Feel free to print your To Do list.
5. Close WordPad and save any changes (if WordPad gives you that option).

Skills Builder 1.3

1. Start the Paint program.
2. Choose **File→Save** from the menu bar.
3. Set the Save as type (at the bottom of the dialog box) to 16 Color Bitmap.
   This setting will significantly reduce the size of the file.
4. Save the empty drawing to your exercise diskette with the name **My House**.
5. Use your investigative skills, your creativity and a lot of trial and error to draw a house. Try to include objects such as doors, windows, a roof and perhaps landscaping.
6. Feel free to print your drawing.
7. **Close** Paint and **save** any changes (if Paint gives you that option).

2 Windows Explorer and Online Help

Objectives:

- Use online Help
- Understand file management concepts
- Use Windows Explorer
- Set view options and sort files
- Expand and collapse folders
- Display folder contents
- Create and delete folders
- Select multiple files
- Move, copy and delete files
- Use drag and drop
- Use cut, copy and paste

The Project – Organizing Your Exercise Diskette

In this lesson, you will use Windows 95's online Help to get help on various topics. You will also use a powerful file management tool named Windows Explorer to organize the files on your exercise diskette. The Windows Explorer program window is shown below. The right side of the window shows the files on your exercise diskette and the two folders that you will create in this lesson.

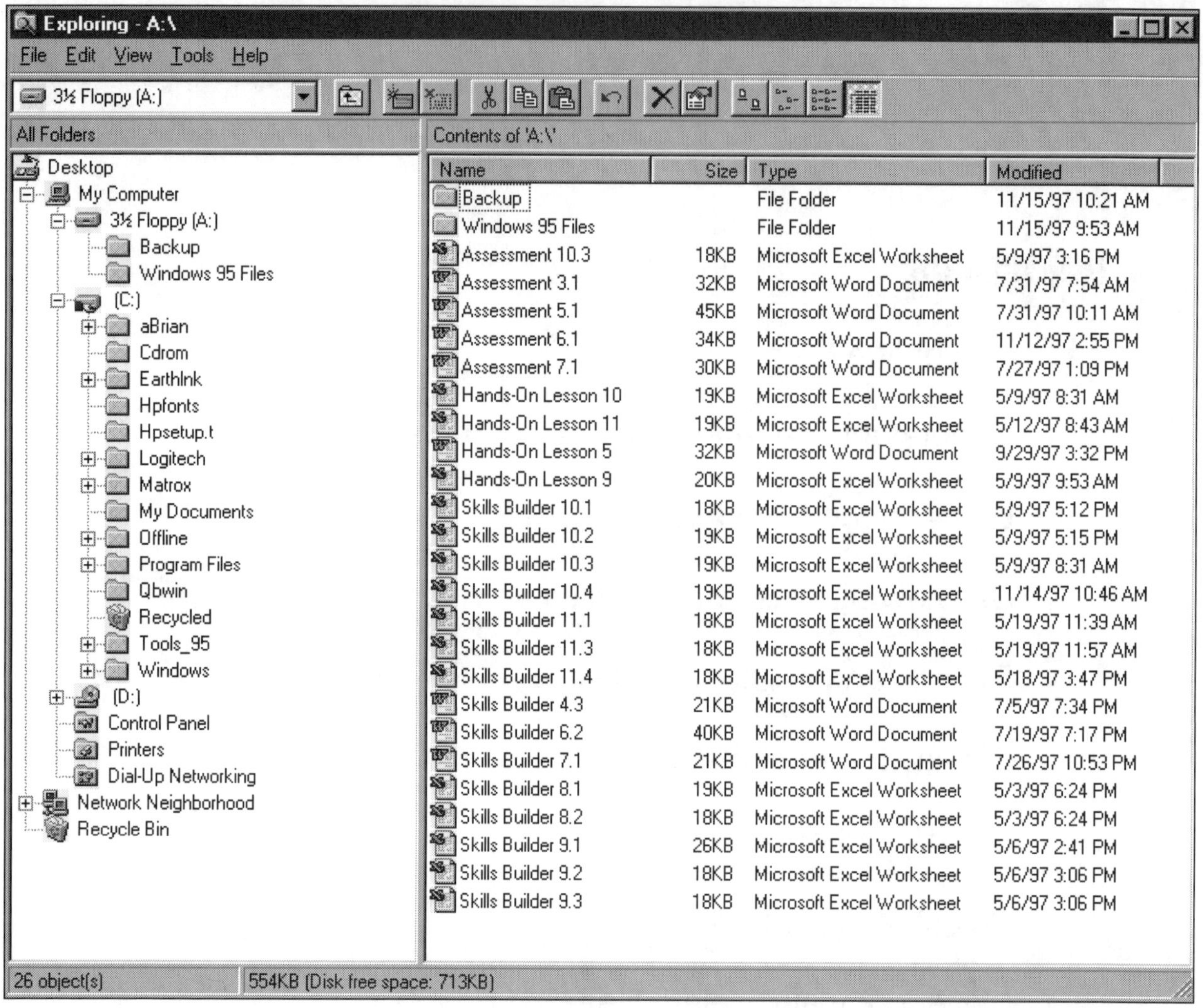

Using Online Help

Windows 95's online Help puts a complete reference book at your fingertips. Help is available for just about any topic you will ever need. It is important that you know how to use online Help because Microsoft and other software publishers no longer provide reference manuals with their software. The reference manuals are now integrated into online Help.

The key to online Help is finding the desired Help topic

Your goal when using online Help is to locate a Help topic. The Help feature provides several methods that you can use to locate topics. All Help topics have keywords that identify them. For example, a Help topic that discusses copying files can probably be located by using the keywords **copying files**. Regardless of which method you use, the goal is to locate a topic. Once you locate the desired topic, you can display it and follow the instructions in the topic.

Help is consistent across Office applications and Windows 95

Online Help works the same way in Windows 95, Excel, Word and other Microsoft applications. The following table describes the various search methods that can be used to locate Help topics.

Search Method	Description
Contents	The Contents method is useful if you are trying to locate a topic but you aren't really sure how to describe it. The Contents method lets you navigate through a series of categories until the desired topic is located.
Index	The Index method lets you locate a topic by typing keywords. An alphabetically indexed list of topics is displayed from which you can choose the desired topic. This method is most useful if you know the name of the topic or feature that you need assistance with.
Find	The Find method searches inside of the Help topics for the keywords you enter. This provides an in-depth search and lets you locate topics that you may not be found using the other search methods.

Hands-On 2.1 – Experiment with online Help

Use a Contents search

1. **Click** the Start [Start] button and choose **Help** from the Start menu.
2. Use the following illustration to explore the Help dialog box.

❶ *Notice the tabs at the top of the dialog box. Clicking a tab displays a new set of options. Make sure the **Contents** tab is chosen.*

❷ *Notice the closed and open book icons. A closed book opens when you double-click it displaying other books or Help topics. You can locate Help topics by double-clicking books until the desired topic is located (but don't do it).*

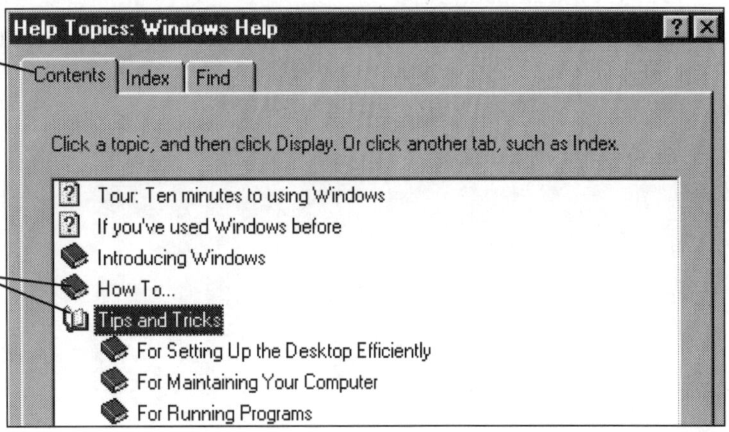

Continued...

3. Use the following illustration to locate and display a Help topic on copying files.

❶ ***Double-click*** *the* ***How To...*** *closed book and it will open as shown here.*

❷ ***Double-click*** *the* ***Work with Files and Folders*** *closed book.*

❸ *Notice the Question Mark icons in front of the items in the book. These items are Help topics.*

❹ ***Double-click*** *the* ***Copying a file or folder*** *Help topic and a Help screen will appear.*

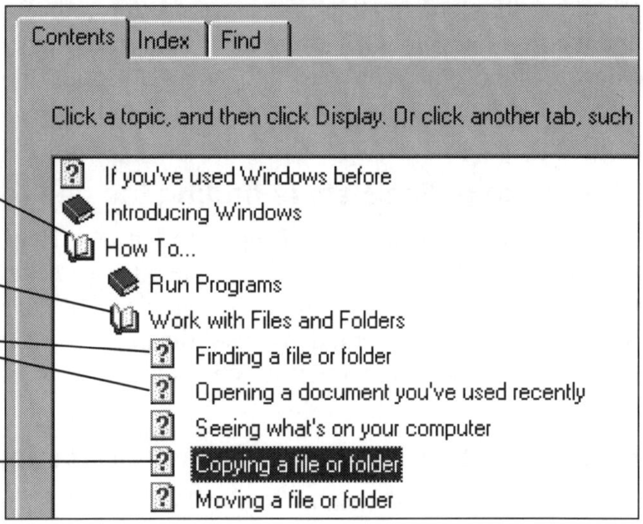

4. Use the following illustration to explore the Help screen.

❶ *Take a few moments to read the information in the Help screen. Notice there are specific instructions on how to copy files and folders.*

❷ ***Click*** *the* ***Help Topics*** *button to redisplay the Help Topics dialog box. Notice that the Help screen remains open. Help screens are designed to "stay on top" so that you can continue working while reading the Help topic.*

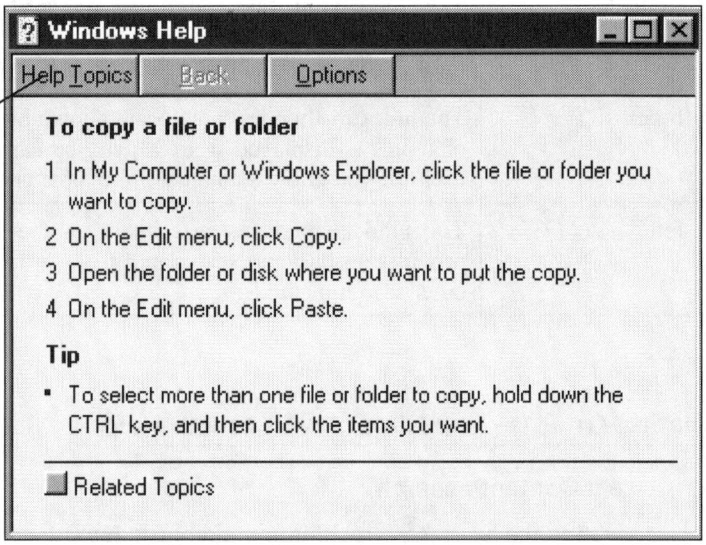

Use an index search

In the next few steps, you will use an index search to locate the same copying files and folders Help topic. This will show you two different ways to locate the same Help topic. The index search method lets you locate topics by typing keywords.

5. Use the steps on the following page to locate the Help topic.

Continued...

❶ ***Click** the **Index** tab.*

❷ *Type **copying** here. Notice that a list of topics on copying is displayed.*

❸ ***Double-click** the **files or folders** topic and a list of topics on files and folders will appear.*

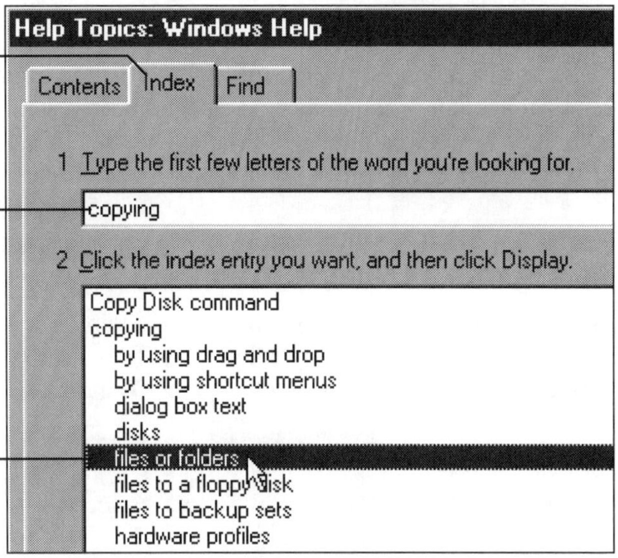

6. Use the following illustration to display the Help screen.

❶ ***Double-click** the **Copying a file or folder** topic and the same yellow Help screen will be visible. As you can see, Windows 95 gives you a variety of ways to locate Help topics.*

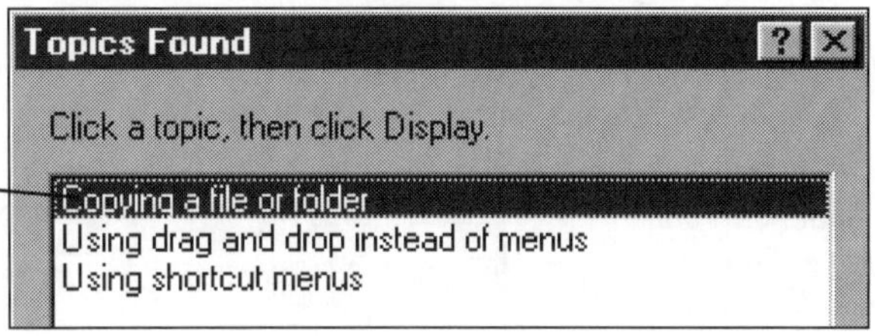

7. **Click** the Close button at the top-right corner of the Help screen.

8. Take 15 minutes to experiment with the Help feature. Try using both the Find and Contents search methods. Experiment and explore until you are comfortable using Help.

9. If necessary, **close** all Help dialog boxes and screens and continue with the next topic.

Windows Explorer

Windows Explorer is a powerful tool that lets you manage the files and folders on your computer system. File management is an important skill to master with modern computer systems. This is because a modern computer system can have thousands of files. You risk losing important documents if you do not use proper organization and file management techniques.

File System Organization

In Windows 95, files are organized in a hierarchical system. Disk drives and storage devices are at the top of the hierarchy followed by folders and files. The following illustration discusses the Exploring program window and the organization of a typical Windows 95 computer system.

Notice that the Exploring window has a menu bar and toolbar like other program windows.

C: is the hard drive.

These folders are under the hard drive. Folders can contain other folders, program files and user files.

The Program Files folder has been expanded and there are several folders under it. You expand a folder by clicking the plus + sign in front it.

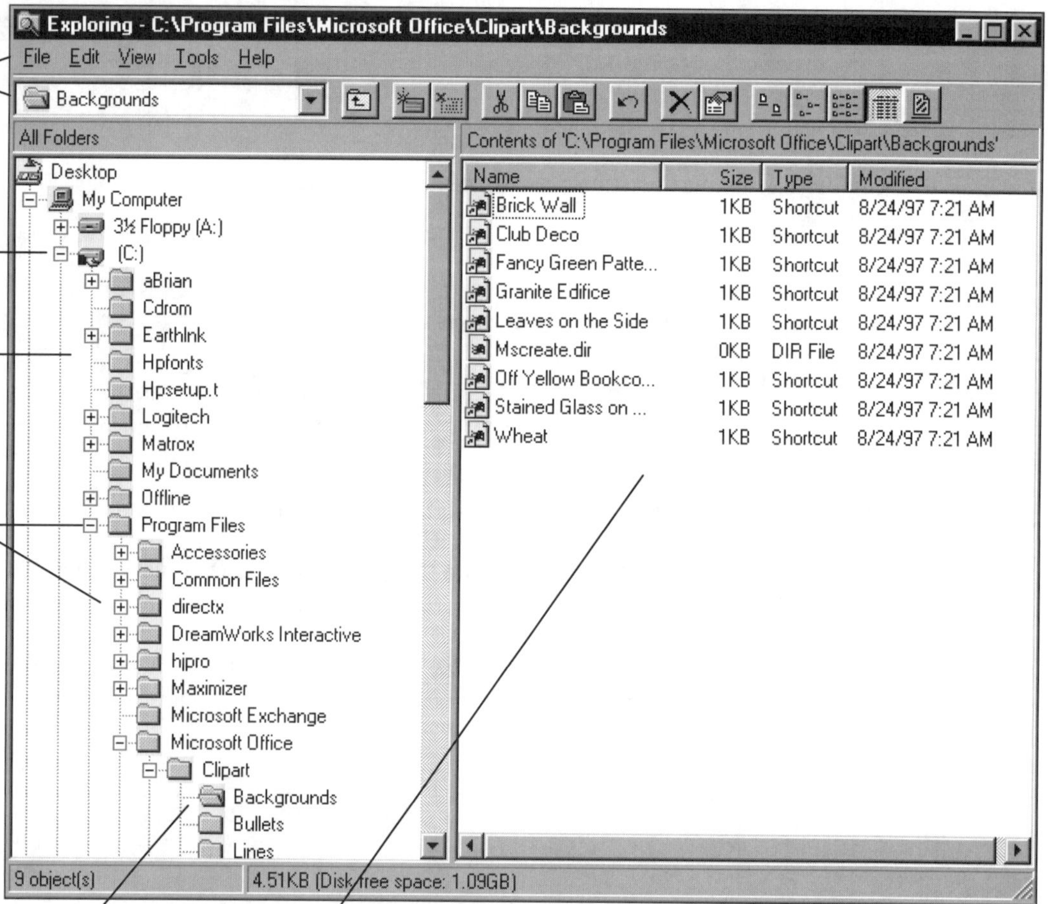

The Backgrounds folder is opened and its contents are displayed in the right pane of the Exploring window. You open a folder by double-clicking it. The right pane always displays the contents of the open disk drive or folder.

Starting Windows Explorer

You can start Windows Explorer using any of the following techniques.

1. **Click** the **Start** button, **choose Programs** and then **choose Windows Explorer**.
2. **Right-click** the **Start button** and **choose Explore**.
3. **Right-click** the **My Computer** icon on the desktop and **choose Explore**.

Hands-On 2.2 – Start Windows Explorer and maximize the window

1. Use the following illustration to start Windows Explorer.

   ❶ *Position the mouse pointer on the Start button and* **click** *the* **right mouse button** *(right-click).*

   ❷ *Use the* **left mouse button** *to choose Explore from the pop up menu.*

2. **Click** the Maximize button on the Exploring program window.

3. Take a few moments to study the Exploring window.

   In the next exercise, you will expand and collapse folders in the window until your window looks similar to the illustration on the previous page.

Expanding and Collapsing Folders

You can expand a folder in the left pane of the Exploring window by clicking the plus + sign in front of the folder. You collapse a folder by clicking the minus – sign in front of the folder. All subfolders are displayed when you expand a folder. All subfolders are hidden when you collapse a folder. Expanding and collapsing folders lets you view the folder hierarchy in various ways. You can open a folder by clicking it in the left pane. The contents of an open folder are displayed in the right pane.

View Options in the Exploring Window

You can view the files and folders in the right pane of the Exploring window in various ways. This is accomplished with the four view buttons on the right end of the Exploring toolbar.

Hands-On 2.3 – Expand and collapse folders and change the view

1. Use the following illustration to expand and collapse folders.

❶ *If necessary, use the scroll bar in the left pane to scroll up until the hard drive icon is visible.*

❷ *If necessary, click the plus + sign in front of the hard drive icon to expand the hard drive. However, your system will have different folders than shown here.*

❸ *If necessary,* **scroll down** *until the* **Program Files** *folder is visible. This folder should be present on your system.*

❹ **Click** *the plus + sign in front of the Program Files folder to expand the folder.*

❺ *Now* **click** *the minus - sign in front of the folder to collapse it.*

❻ *Take five minutes to practice expanding and collapsing folders on the hard drive.*

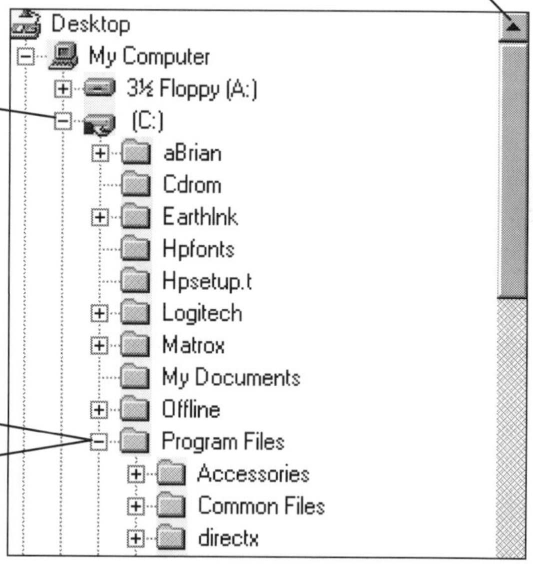

2. Use the following illustration to display the contents of a folder in the right pane.

❶ *Expand and collapse folders until the* **Accessories** *folder is visible below the Program Files folder as shown here.*

❷ **Click** *the* **Accessories** *folder. The folder will open and files and folders will appear in the right-pane of the Exploring window.*

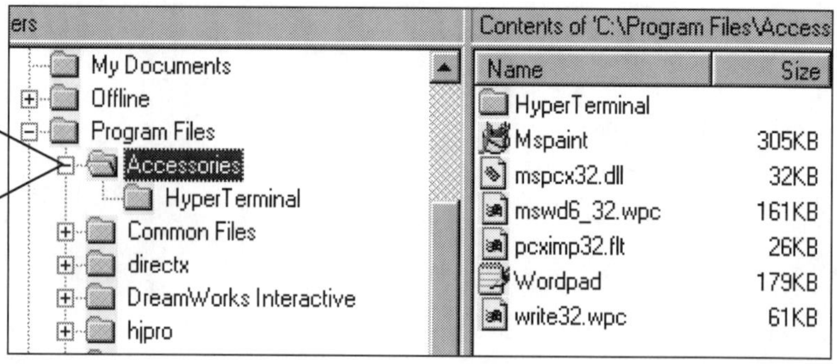

Continued...

3. Use the following illustration to change the view in the right pane.

❶ ***Click** the **Large Icons** button and a large icon will represent each file in the Accessories folder. Keep in mind that your folder may have different files/icons than shown here.*

❷ *Now **click** the **Details** button and the right pane will display the name, size, type and date that each file was last modified.*

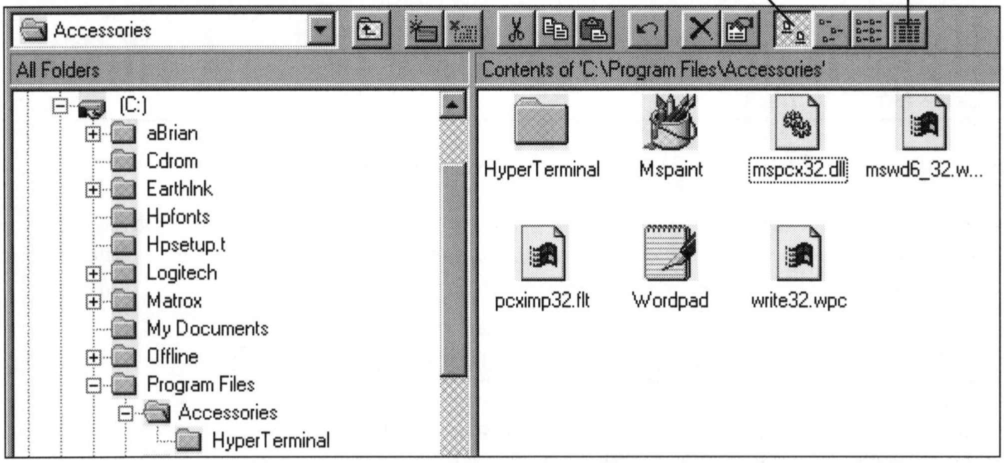

4. Now use the following illustration to display the contents of your exercise diskette.

❶ *Scroll to the top of the left pane and **click** the **3 ½ Floppy [A:]** icon. The files shown in this illustration should be visible in the right pane. Most of these files were placed on your exercise diskette for this course.*

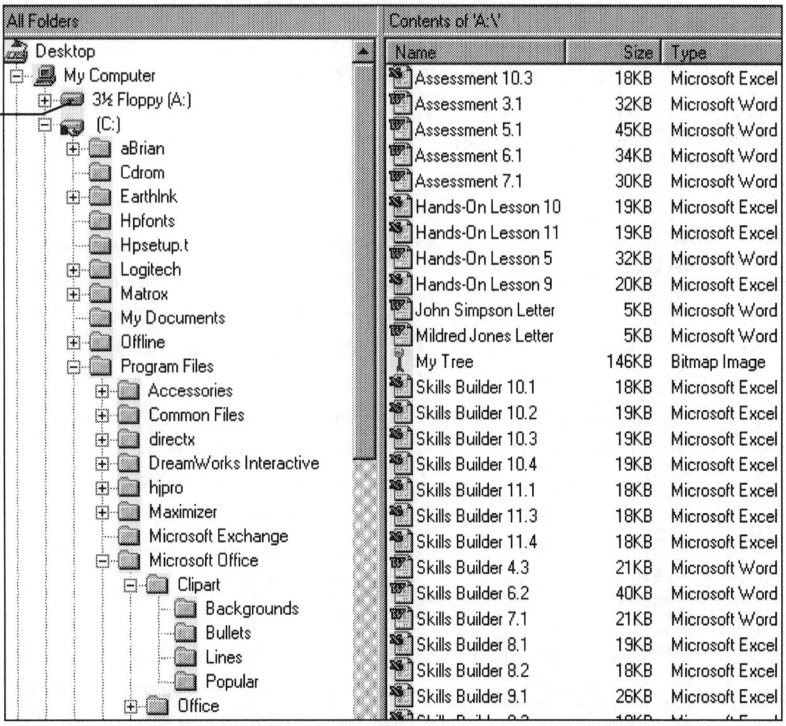

Do you see the My Tree, John Simpson Letter and Mildred Jones Letter files that you created in the previous lesson. If so, then you successfully saved those files in the previous lesson.

5. Take five minutes to practice expanding, collapsing and opening folders.

Sorting the View

You can sort the files in the right pane of the Exploring window by clicking the Name, Size, Type and Modified headings at the top of the columns. For example, clicking the Name heading sorts the files by Name whereas clicking the Size heading sorts them by size. If you click the same column heading twice, then the files are sorted in descending order. Folders always appear at the top or bottom of the sorted list.

Hands-On 2.4 – Sort the files

1. Use the following illustration to sort the files in various ways.

❶ ***Click** the **Size** button to sort the files by size.*

❷ ***Click** the **Size** button again to sort the files in descending order (largest to smallest) by size.*

❸ *Try clicking the other column headings.*

❹ *Finally, **sort** the files **by Name** as shown here.*

Name	Size	Type	Modified
Assessment 10.3	18KB	Microsoft Excel Worksheet	5/9/97 3:16 PM
Assessment 3.1	32KB	Microsoft Word Document	7/31/97 7:54 AM
Assessment 5.1	45KB	Microsoft Word Document	7/31/97 10:11 AM
Assessment 6.1	34KB	Microsoft Word Document	11/12/97 2:55 PM
Assessment 7.1	30KB	Microsoft Word Document	7/27/97 1:09 PM
Hands-On Lesson 10	19KB	Microsoft Excel Worksheet	5/9/97 8:31 AM
Hands-On Lesson 11	19KB	Microsoft Excel Worksheet	5/12/97 8:43 AM
Hands-On Lesson 5	32KB	Microsoft Word Document	9/29/97 3:32 PM
Hands-On Lesson 9	20KB	Microsoft Excel Worksheet	5/9/97 9:53 AM
John Simpson Letter	5KB	Microsoft Word Document	11/14/97 6:32 PM
Mildred Jones Letter	5KB	Microsoft Word Document	11/14/97 6:34 PM
My Tree	146KB	Bitmap Image	9/19/97 10:02 AM
Skills Builder 10.1	18KB	Microsoft Excel Worksheet	5/9/97 5:12 PM
Skills Builder 10.2	19KB	Microsoft Excel Worksheet	5/9/97 5:15 PM
Skills Builder 10.3	19KB	Microsoft Excel Worksheet	5/9/97 8:31 AM
Skills Builder 10.4	19KB	Microsoft Excel Worksheet	11/14/97 10:46 AM
Skills Builder 11.1	18KB	Microsoft Excel Worksheet	5/19/97 11:39 AM
Skills Builder 11.3	18KB	Microsoft Excel Worksheet	5/19/97 11:57 AM
Skills Builder 11.4	18KB	Microsoft Excel Worksheet	5/18/97 3:47 PM
Skills Builder 4.3	21KB	Microsoft Word Document	7/5/97 7:34 PM
Skills Builder 6.2	40KB	Microsoft Word Document	7/19/97 7:17 PM
Skills Builder 7.1	21KB	Microsoft Word Document	7/26/97 10:53 PM
Skills Builder 8.1	19KB	Microsoft Excel Worksheet	5/3/97 6:24 PM
Skills Builder 8.2	18KB	Microsoft Excel Worksheet	5/3/97 6:24 PM
Skills Builder 9.1	26KB	Microsoft Excel Worksheet	5/6/97 2:41 PM
Skills Builder 9.2	18KB	Microsoft Excel Worksheet	5/6/97 3:06 PM
Skills Builder 9.3	18KB	Microsoft Excel Worksheet	5/6/97 3:06 PM

File Management with Windows Explorer

Windows Explorer lets you manage the files and folders on your system. You can create and delete folders, move and copy files and perform other administrative tasks. You will learn all of these techniques throughout the remainder of this lesson.

Creating and Renaming Folders

Folders are the tools that you use to organize your system. You can create folders on floppy disks and hard disks. You can also create subfolders, which are folders within folders. In fact, there is no practical limit to the number of subfolder levels that you can have. On a well-organized computer system, all files are placed in folders with descriptive names. This allows you to easily locate the files at a later time.

In Windows Explorer, you create folders by opening (clicking) the disk drive or folder that you wish to place the new folder under. Then, you choose **File→New→Folder** from the Exploring menu bar. You rename a folder by clicking once on the folder in the right pane, pausing for one or two seconds, clicking again and then typing a new name.

Hands-On 2.5 – Create folders

The contents of your diskette should be visible in the right pane from the previous exercise.

Create folders

1. Choose **File→New→Folder** from the Exploring menu bar.

   A New Folder *icon will appear at the bottom of the file list. Notice the insertion point is flashing within the selected phrase New Folder. Windows 95 is waiting for you to type a descriptive name for your new folder. You use the same naming rules for folders as you do with filenames.*

2. **Type** the name **WordPad** and then **click outside** of the new folder to complete the change.

3. Use the technique in steps 1 and 2 to create another new folder named **Paint**. You may notice that the position of the New command has moved down on the File menu.

Rename folders

4. **Click** once on the **WordPad folder**.

5. **Pause** for one or two seconds and then **click** the folder **again**.

   The insertion point will be positioned in the folder name and the folder name will be selected.

6. Type the name **WordPad Files** and then **tap** the Enter key.

   You can complete a name change by tapping Enter or by clicking outside of the folder.

7. Now rename the Paint folder to **Paint Files**.

8. **Click** the Name heading **once or twice** until the WordPad Files and Paint Files folders are at the top of the column.

Moving and Copying Files and Folders

Windows Explorer lets you move and copy files and folders from one folder or disk drive to another. This lets you organize your system and make copies of important files.

Selecting Multiple Files

You can select a range of files by clicking the first file and then pressing & holding the **Shift** key while clicking the last file in the range. All files between the first file and last file will be selected. You can select a random assortment of files by pressing & holding the **Ctrl** key while clicking the desired files.

Hands-On 2.6 – Practice selecting files

The contents of your exercise diskette should still be visible from the previous exercise.

1. Use the following illustration to select a range of files in the right pane of the Exploring window.

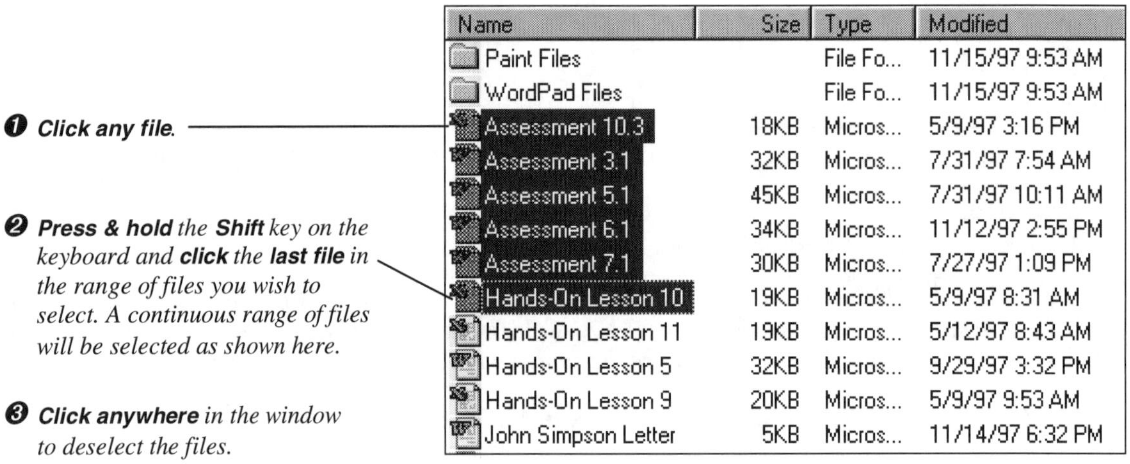

2. Use the following illustration to select a random group of files.

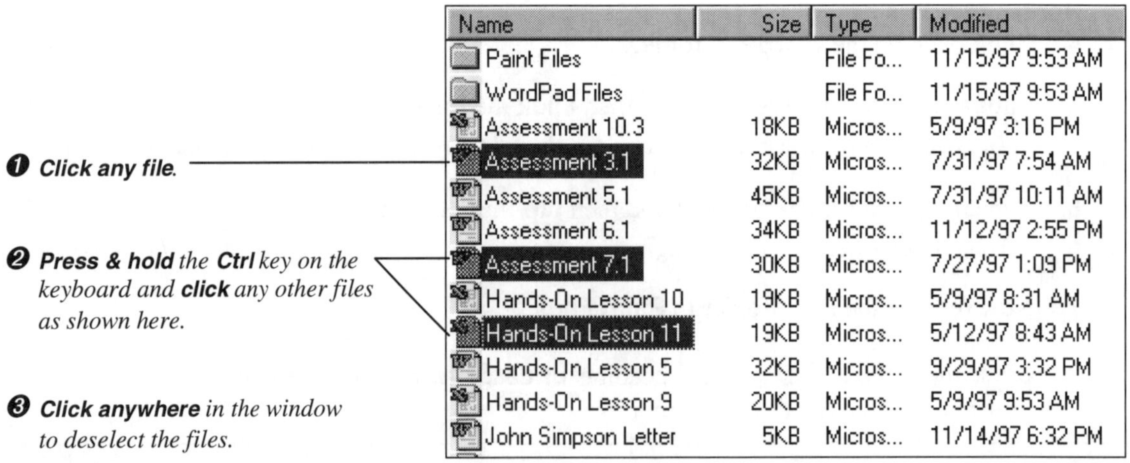

Using Drag and Drop to Move and Copy Files

You can move and copy files by dragging the desired files with the mouse and dropping them in the desired destination folder or disk drive. This is usually accomplished by dragging from the right pane of the Exploring window to the left pane. The following rules and procedures can be used when dragging and dropping.

- The file(s) are moved if the source and destination folders are on the same drive. If you wish to copy file(s) and the source and destination folders are on the same drive, then press & hold the **Ctrl** key while dragging and dropping.
- The file(s) are copied if the source and destination folders are on different drives. If you wish to move file(s) and the source and destination folders are on different drives, then press & hold the **Shift** key while dragging and dropping.

Hands-On 2.7 – Use drag and drop

In this exercise, you will use the drag and drop technique to reorganize the files on your diskette. You will drag and drop in the right pane of the Exploring window and between the right and left panes. You must have the John Simpson Letter, Mildred Jones Letter and My Tree files on your diskette. These files were created in the previous lesson. Also, the WordPad Files and Paint Files folders should be on your diskette from an earlier exercise in this lesson.

1. Use the following steps to move the My Tree file into the Paint Files folder.

❶ *Position the mouse pointer on the* ***My Tree*** *file and* ***press and hold*** *the* ***left mouse button****.*

❷ ***Drag*** *the mouse up until the pointer is over the Paint Files folder as shown here.*

❸ ***Release*** *the* ***mouse button*** *and the file will be moved to the Paint Files folder.*

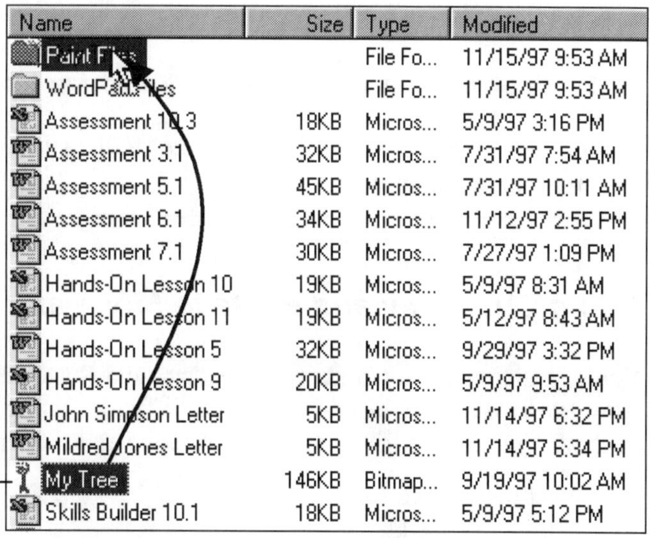

The My Tree file should no longer be visible in the right pane.

Verify that the file has been moved

2. **Double-click** the Paint Files folder in the right pane. The Paint Files folder will appear opened in the left pane and the My Tree file will appear in the right pane as shown below.

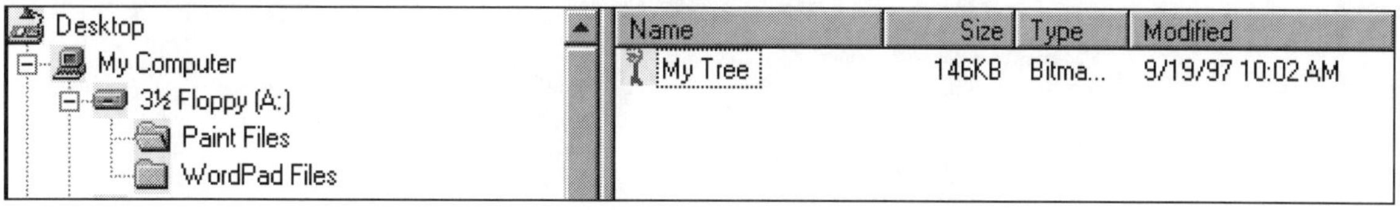

Continued...

Move two files at once

3. Display the contents of your exercise diskette in the right pane by **clicking** the 3½ Floppy (A:) icon in the left pane.

4. Use the following illustration to move the John Simpson Letter and Mildred Jones Letter files to the WordPad Files folder.

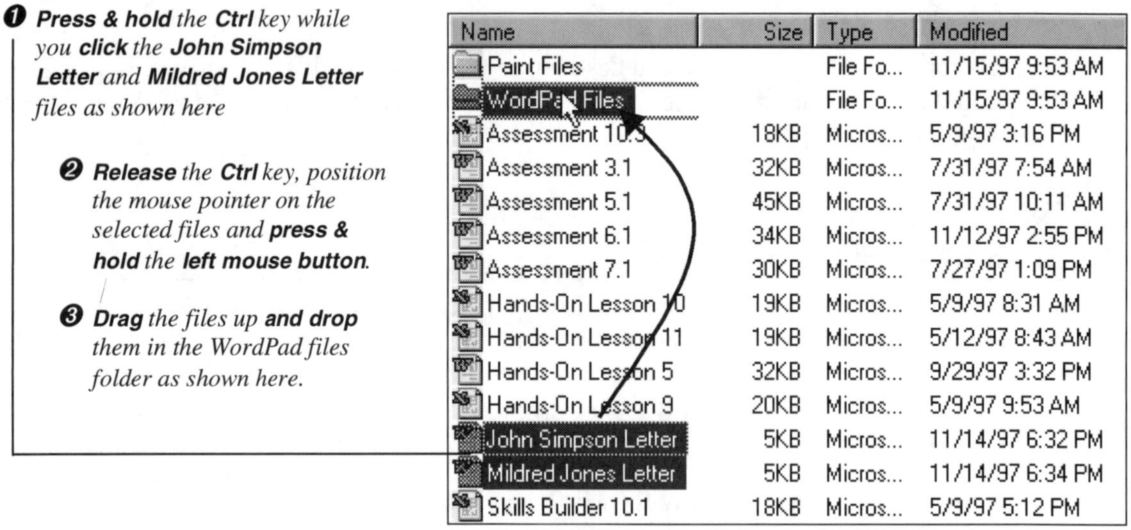

5. **Double-click** the WordPad Files folder to verify that the files have been moved.

6. Display the contents of your exercise diskette in the right pane by **clicking** the 3½ Floppy (A:) icon in the left pane.

Using Cut, Copy and Paste to Move and Copy Files

You can also use the Cut, Copy and Paste buttons on the Exploring toolbar to move and copy files. Many beginners who have difficulty using the mouse prefer using the cut, copy and paste method. You use the following steps to move and copy files with cut, copy and paste.

– Select the desired files

– Click the Cut button if you want to move the files or the Copy button if want to copy them.

– Navigate to the desired destination folder and double-click the folder to open it.

– Click the Paste button.

Deleting Files and Folders

You can delete files by selecting the desired files and clicking the Delete button on the Exploring toolbar. The **File→Delete** command can also be used to delete selected files. You can use the same technique to delete a folder and all of the subfolders and files within the folder.

The Recycle Bin

When you delete files from the hard disk, Windows 95 moves the files from the folder they were located in to the Recycle Bin. The files remain in the Recycle Bin until you empty the Recycle Bin at a later time. This provides you with a recovery mechanism in case you need to restore a file that has been accidentally deleted. However, files that are deleted from diskettes are not moved to the Recycle Bin. Files are permanently deleted when you delete them from diskettes. You can restore files from the Recycle Bin by double-clicking the Recycle Bin icon on the desktop, selecting the desired files and issuing the **File→Restore** command.

Hands-On 2.8 – Delete a folder

In this exerise, you will consolidate the Paint and WordPad files into one folder. You will delete the remaining folder from your exercise diskette. The contents of your exercise diskette should be displayed in the right pane from the previous exercise.

Move a file from one folder to another

1. **Double-click** the Paint Files folder in the right pane.
2. Use the following steps to move the My Tree file from the right pane to the WordPad Files folder in the left pane. This will move the file into the WordPad Files folder.

❶ ***Drag*** *the* ***My Tree*** *file to the WordPad Files folder in the left pane and* ***drop*** *it in the folder as shown here.*

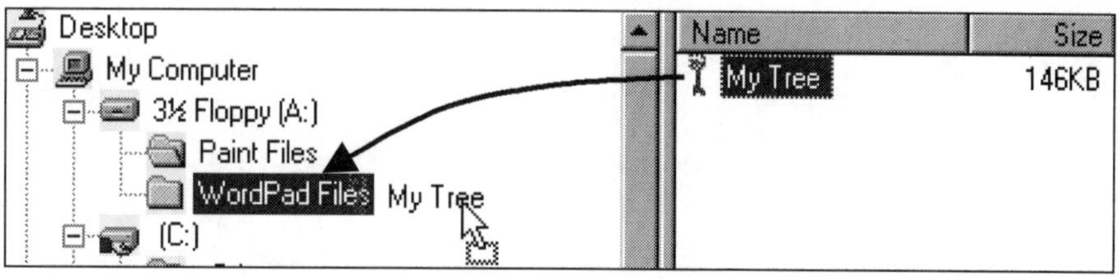

3. Notice that the right pane is now empty and the Paint Files folder is open in the left pane.

   The right pane is empty because the Paint Files folder is open (and empty) in the left pane. The right pane always reflects the contents of the open folder in the left pane.

4. **Click** the Up One Level button on the Exploring toolbar.

   This button moves you up one folder level in the hierarchy. Since the Paint Files folder was open, you will be moved up to the top of the diskette hierarchy. The entire contents of the diskette should once again be displayed in the right pane.

Delete the Paint Files folder

5. **Click** the Paint Files folder in the left pane.
6. **Click** the Delete button on the Exploring toolbar.
7. **Click Yes** on the dialog box that appears to confirm the folder deletion.

   The WordPad Files folder will open and its contents will be displayed in the right pane.

Continued...

Rename the WordPad Files folder

8. Display the contents of your exercise diskette in the right pane by **clicking** the 3½ Floppy (A:) icon in the left pane.

9. **Click** the WordPad Files folder in the right pane.

10. **Pause** one or two seconds and then **click** the folder **again**.

    The folder name will become selected.

11. Type the new name **Windows 95 Files**.

12. **Click outside** of the **folder** to complete the name change.

13. Now **double-click** the Windows 95 Files folder and the John Simpson Letter, Mildred Jones Letter and My Tree files should all be in that folder.

14. Finally, display the contents of your exercise diskette 3½ Floppy (A:).

15. Feel free to experiment with the topics you have learned in this lesson. However, do not to delete any of the files on your exercise diskette because you will need them throughout this course.

16. When you have finished experimenting, **close Windows Explorer** by clicking the Close button at the top-right corner of the window.

Concepts Review

True / False

1. A contents Help search lets you locate Help topics by typing keywords. 1. **T F**
2. Windows Explorer lets you view the files and folders on your system. 2. **T F**
3. Windows 95 organizes files and folders in a hierarchical manner. 3. **T F**
4. Expanding a folder displays the contents of that folder in the right pane. 4. **T F**
5. Collapsing a folder hides the subfolders of that folder in the left pane. 5. **T F**
6. The Ctrl key can be used to randomly select a group of files. 6. **T F**
7. Folders can have subfolders within them. 7. **T F**
8. Files are copied when they are dragged to a different folder on the same disk drive. 8. **T F**
9. Files are sent to the Recycle Bin when they are deleted from diskettes. 9. **T F**
10. Files in the Recycle Bin can be restored with the File→Restore command. 10. **T F**

Multiple Choice

1. Which of the following methods can be used to start Windows Explorer?
   a) Click the Start button, choose Programs and then choose Windows Explorer.
   b) Right-click the Start button and choose Explore.
   c) Right-click the My Computer icon on the desktop and choose Explore. ( )
   d) All of the above.
2. Which of the following techniques is used to expand a folder in the left pane?
   a) Click the plus + sign to the left of the folder.
   b) Click the minus – sign to the left of the folder.
   c) Double-click the folder. ( )
   d) None of the above.
3. Which of the following buttons displays a detailed view in the Exploring window?
   a) 
   b) 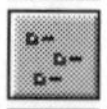 ( )
   c) 
   d) None of the above.
4. Which command is used to create a new folder?
   a) File→New→Folder.
   b) File→Folder→Create.
   c) Click the New Folder  button. ( )
   d) All of the above.
5. If a filename is already selected in the Exploring window, then which key could be used to select a block of files while clicking just once?
   a) Shift
   b) Alt
   c) Ctrl ( )
   d) None of the above.

Skills Builder 2.1

1. **Click** the Start button and choose **Help** from the Start menu.
2. **Click** the **Index** tab in the Help Topics dialog box.
3. Start typing the search phrase **recycle bin** and you will notice that the phrase Recycle Bin appears after you type the letters recy.
   You usually only need to type the first few characters of the desired search phrase.
4. **Double-click** the **emptying** topic that appears.
5. Read the topic and then close it by clicking the Close button.
6. Use the Index search method to get Help on the following topics.
   - Start menu→tips→Adding a program to the Start or Programs menu
   - Windows Explorer→changing the way items are displayed.
   - Copying→files or folders→Using shortcut menus.

   These Help topics will give you tips and alternatives to the methods you have already learned.

Use the Contents search method

7. Display the Help Topics dialog box and **click** the **Contents** tab.
8. **Double-click** the **Tips and Tricks** book.
9. Locate five different Help topics in the books under Tips and Tricks and take the time to open the Help topics and read them.
10. Experiment with Help until you are confident that you can find topics when the need arises.

Skills Builder 2.2

1. **Start Windows Explorer** and display the files on your exercise diskette in the right pane.
2. **Sort** the files **by size** so that the files with the smallest size are on the top of the list.
3. **Create a folder** on your exercise diskette named **Backup**.
4. **Select** the **three smallest files** on your diskette.
   The first three files should be selected (highlighted).
5. **Click** the Copy button on the Exploring toolbar.
6. **Double-click** the **Backup** folder.
   The Backup folder should be open in the left pane and the right pane should appear empty.
7. **Click** the Paste button on the Exploring toolbar.
   The three files you had selected should appear in the right pane of the Exploring window.
8. **Click** the Up One Level button on the Exploring toolbar.
   The three files that you had selected should still be visible at the top level of your exercise diskette. The files were copied so they now appear in two locations.
9. **Close** the Exploring window.

Unit Two

Word 97

3 Creating and Editing Business Letters

Objectives:

- Create various styles of business letters
- Select and edit text
- Use editing tools including Undo and Redo
- Save documents
- Open documents
- Use the Show/Hide button
- Exit from Word

What is Microsoft Word?

Microsoft Word is a program that makes word processing a pleasure instead of a chore. Word's powerful suite of tools let you focus on content instead of on formatting. There are tools to assist you in virtually every aspect of document creation. For these and many other reasons, Word is the most widely used word processing program in both homes and businesses.

Why Use Word?

Word provides a number of important features and benefits that make it a smart choice to use.

1. **IntelliSense Technology** - Word's IntelliSense technology includes automated tools to assist you in creating, editing and formatting documents. This speeds up the process of creating and formatting documents, so that you can focus on content.
2. **GUI** - Word's Graphical User Interface is so easy to use that even beginning computer users find it simple. The interface reduces the need to memorize commands and it will make you more productive.
3. **Writing Tools** – Word 97 has powerful new writing tools including automatic grammar checking and spell checking as you type. These and other tools will help you improve your writing skills.
4. **Widely Used** - Word is the most widely used word processing software. Word is the right choice if you are trying to develop marketable skills and find employment.
5. **Integration with Other Office Programs** - Word is part of the Microsoft Office suite of programs which also include Excel, Access and PowerPoint. The ability to exchange data with these programs is one of the most powerful and attractive features of Word.

It's Time to Learn Word!

It's time to put your fears behind and learn this wonderful program. You will be amazed at the power and simplicity of Word and how easy it is to learn. The knowledge you are about to gain will give you a marketable skill and make you the master of Word.

Starting Word 97

There are several ways to start the Word 97 program. You should have some Windows 95 experience before proceeding. The three most common methods for starting Word are listed below.

- Click the Start button and choose Microsoft Word from the Programs menu.
- Click a desktop shortcut for the Word program (if a shortcut is on the desktop).
- Click the Microsoft Word  button on the Microsoft Office toolbar (if it is displayed).

Hands-On 3.1 – Start Word

In this exercise, you will start the Word program.

1. Start your computer and the Windows desktop will be displayed.
2. **Click** the Start 

button and choose **Programs**.
3. Choose **Microsoft Word** from the Programs menu.

   The Word program will load and the document window shown below will appear. Don't be concerned if your document window appears different from this example.

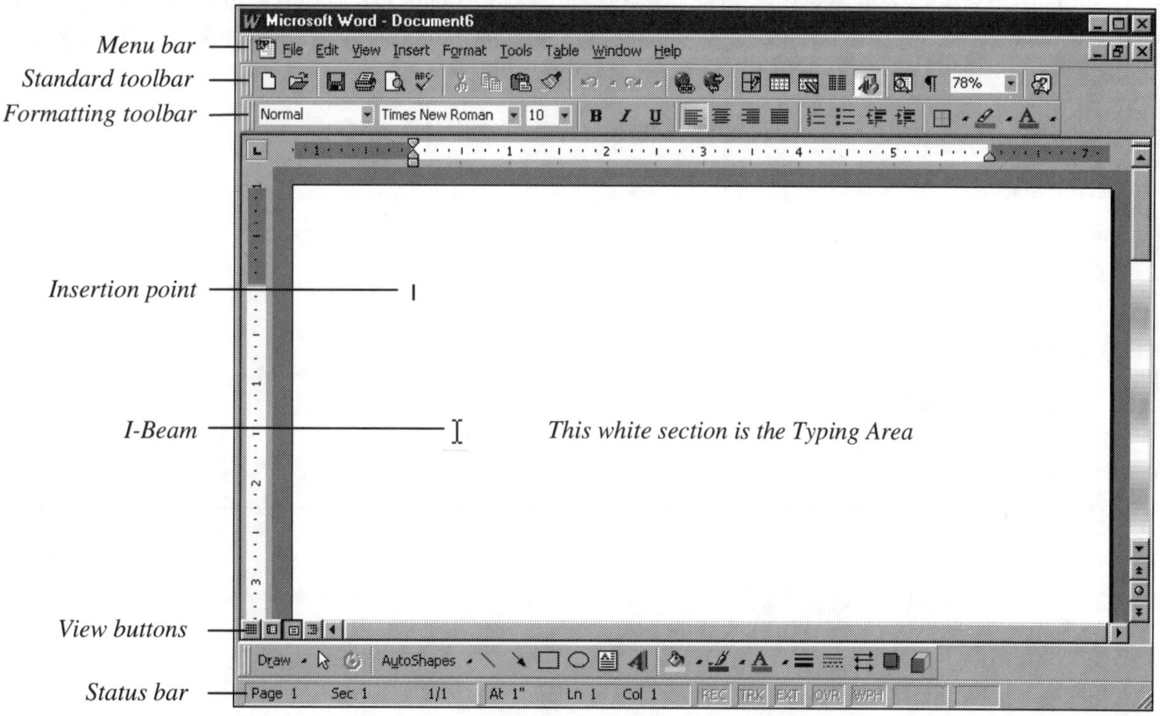

The document window is the place where you type information into Word. The document window lets you access Word commands and it can be customized to suit your particular needs. You will learn how to modify the document window at a later time.

The Project – Creating and Editing a Business Letter

In this lesson, you will create the block style business letter shown below. You will learn how to format and set up various styles of business letters. You will also learn basic techniques for entering and editing text, saving documents and using Word commands.

Today's Date

John Smith
811 Fairview Drive
Belleville, IL 64320

Dear John:

Thank you for your interest in Zephron Industries. Unfortunately, we are unable to offer you a job at this time.

Jane Alexander indicated you are qualified for the position with one exception, you lack Word 97 for Windows skills. I am sorry to deny you this very high paying position, but as you know, Word 97 is the hottest thing since sliced whole wheat bread was first invented.

John, please contact me as soon as you have learned Word 97.

Regards,

Bill Brown
Manager, Human Resources

Xx:Hands-On Lesson 3

Business Letter Styles

Overview

There are a variety of acceptable business letter styles. The style discussed below is a traditional **block style** letter with minimal formatting. All business letter styles contain the same or similar elements but with varied formatting.

Block Style Letter

*The **date** is positioned two to six lines below the letterhead or approximately 2" from the top of the page.*

*The **inside address** appears next. Tap Enter four times between the date and inside address.*

*The **salutation** appears next. Tap Enter twice between the inside address and salutation. Use a **colon** after the salutation. You can change the formality of the letter by using words such as Mr. in the salutation.*

*The **body** of the letter comes next. Single space within paragraphs and double space between paragraphs.*

*Use Enter four times between the **complimentary close** and **signature block**. Use a **comma** after the complimentary close. Acceptable complimentary closes include Regards, Best regards, Sincerely and several others.*

2" or two to six lines below letterhead

Date

John Smith
811 Fairview Drive
Belleville, IL 64320

Dear John:

Thank you for your interest in Zephron Industries. Unfortunately, we are unable to offer you a job at this time.

Jane Alexander indicated you are qualified for the position with one exception, you lack Word 97 for Windows skills. I am sorry to deny you this very high paying position, but as you know, Word 97 is the hottest thing since sliced whole wheat bread was first invented.

John, please contact me as soon as you have learned Word 97.

Regards,

Bill Brown
Manager, Human Resources

Xx:Hands-On Lesson 3

Enclosure: Test results

__Reference initials__ may be positioned two lines below the signature block. They may include the typists and/or author's initials. This example also includes the file name (Hands-On Lesson 3). Including the file name can help you locate the file at a later time. Other elements such as an enclosure notation may be placed below the reference initials as shown here.

Modified Block Style Letter

The modified block style has the same elements and spacing between paragraphs as the block style. However, the date, complimentary close and signature block begin at the center of the lines as shown in the following example.

Begin the date at the center.

Begin the complimentary close and signature block at the center.

Date

John Smith
811 Fairview Drive
Belleville, IL 64320

Dear John:

Thank you for your interest in Zephron Industries. Unfortunately, we are unable to offer you a job at this time.

Jane Alexander indicated you are qualified for the position with one exception, you lack Word 97 for Windows skills. I am sorry to deny you this very high paying position, but as you know, Word 97 is the hottest thing since sliced whole wheat bread was first invented.

John, please contact me as soon as you have learned Word 97.

Regards,

Bill Brown
Manager, Human Resources

Xx:Hands-On Lesson 3

Enclosure: Test results

AMS Simplified Style Letter

The American Management Society (AMS) simplified style omits the salutation and complimentary close. However, a subject line is included below the inside address and the signature block is modified as shown below.

Tap Enter three times before and after the subject line. Type the subject line in uppercase.

Tap Enter four times between the last paragraph and the signature line. Tap Enter twice after the signature line.

Date

John Smith
811 Fairview Drive
Belleville, IL 64320

EMPLOYMENT APPLICATION

Thank you for your interest in Zephron Industries. Unfortunately, we are unable to offer you a job at this time.

Jane Alexander indicated you are qualified for the position with one exception, you lack Word 97 for Windows skills. I am sorry to deny you this very high paying position, but as you know, Word 97 is the hottest thing since sliced whole wheat bread was first invented.

John, please contact me as soon as you have learned Word 97.

BILL BROWN, MANAGER, HUMAN RELATIONS

Xx:Hands-On Lesson 3

Enclosure: Test results

Entering Text

You can begin typing the moment Word is started. Text is inserted into the document at the flashing **insertion point**. If you continue to type when the insertion point reaches the end of a line, then Word automatically wraps the line and begins a new line. You can also use Enter to begin a new line or when you want to insert a blank line in the document.

AutoComplete and Other Automated Features

Word 97 has a number of new features to assist you in entering text and creating business documents. AutoComplete recognizes certain phrases such as dates and company names and offers to complete them for you. You accept a phrase that AutoComplete proposes by tapping the Enter key. You can increase the number of phrases that AutoComplete recognizes by adding new AutoText entries to the system. You will learn more about AutoComplete and AutoText later in this course. For now, you will use AutoComplete to enter today's date in a business letter.

Hands-On 3.2 – Begin typing a business letter

A new document window should be visible from the previous exercise.

Use AutoComplete to enter today's date

1. Type today's date but stop typing when AutoComplete displays a yellow date tip as shown below.

   The example below uses the date April 4, 1997 but you should type today's date. Also, AutoComplete may not display the date tip. This is because AutoComplete may not be set up to automatically display tips. You will learn how to configure AutoComplete later in this course.

   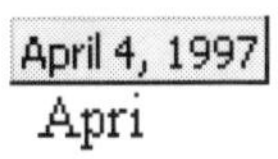

2. If AutoComplete displays the date tip, then tap Enter to complete the date. Otherwise, complete today's date by typing it.

   You can always accept an item that AutoComplete proposes by tapping Enter.

Use the Enter key and complete the inside address and salutation

3. **Tap** the Enter key **four** times.

   Notice the Enter key pushes the insertion point down each time that you tap it. You always insert new blank lines in a document by tapping enter. You should always tap Enter a minimum of four times after typing the date in a business letter. ***In this course, you should always tap Enter four times after the date!***

4. Now type the inside address and salutation as shown on the following page.

   Only tap Enter in the locations indicated. The Office Assistant should appear when you tap Enter after typing the salutation. The Office Assistant is discussed on the following page.

Continued...

Today's Date Enter
Enter
Enter
Enter
Mr. Smith Enter
811 Fairview Drive Enter
Belleville, IL 64320 Enter
Enter
Dear Mr. Smith: Enter
Enter

The Office Assistant

The Office Assistant is a new interactive Help tool in Microsoft Office 97. The Office Assistant monitors your activities and provides suggestions whenever it assumes you need assistance. The Office Assistant recognizes certain actions and phrases (such as salutations that begin with the word Dear). The Office Assistant should have appeared when you tapped Enter after typing the salutation (but it's OK if it didn't).

5. If the Office Assistant just appeared as shown below, then **click** the **Cancel** button to close it. If it didn't appear, then continue with the next step.

   You will work with the Office Assistant in the next lesson.

Continued...

6. Now complete the remainder of the letter as shown below. Only tap Enter in the indicated locations. Use the BackSpace key to correct any typing mistakes. Your letter may look different from this example because the text may wrap differently. Word 97 automatically checks spelling and grammar as you type. Word underlines words and phrases in red or green that it thinks are incorrect. For now, ignore any red or green underlining that appears.

Today's Date Enter
Enter
Enter
Enter
Mr. Smith Enter
811 Fairview Drive Enter
Belleville, IL 64320 Enter
Enter
Dear Mr. Smith: Enter
Enter
Thank you for your interest in Zephron Industries. Unfortunately, we are unable to offer you a job at this time. Enter
Enter
Jane Alexander said you were qualified for the position with one exception, you lacked Word 97 for Windows skills. Enter
Enter
I am sorry to deny you this very high paying position, but as you know, Word 97 is the hottest thing since sliced whole wheat bread was first invented. Mr. Smith, please contact us as soon as you have learned Word 97. Enter
Enter
Regards, Enter
Enter
Enter
Enter
Bill Brown Enter
Manager, Human Resources

Saving the Letter

One important lesson to learn is to **save your documents frequently!** Power outages and careless accidents can result in lost data. The best protection is to save your documents every 10 or 15 minutes and after making significant changes. It is recommended that you understand the concepts of files, folders and pathnames before attempting this exercise. These and many other essential Windows 95 concepts are discussed in Labyrinth Publications, ***Laying a Foundation with Windows 95*** textbook.

The Save and Save As Commands

Word provides several commands that let you save documents. The **Save** command saves the current document onto a disk. If the document had previously been saved, then Word replaces the previous version with the new edited version. If the document is new, then Word displays the **Save As** dialog box. The Save As dialog box lets you name the document and specify the disk drive and folder that you wish to save the document to. You can also use Save As to make a copy of an existing document by saving the document under a new name.

Word 97 supports long filenames

Microsoft Word 97 supports long filenames. You can use up to 255 characters when naming a file in Word 97. This is a huge improvement over the 8-character limitation in some previous versions of Word.

Hands-On 3.3 – Save the letter

In this exercise, you will save the letter that was created in the previous exercise. Your instructor will most likely want you to save your documents onto the exercise diskette that is provided with this course. You will most likely be saving documents onto the A: or B: disk drives.

1. Choose **File→Save...** from the menu bar and the **Save As** dialog box will appear.
2. Use the following steps to save the letter.

❶ ***Click here*** *and choose the disk drive with your exercise diskette. It is most likely 3 ½ Floppy [A:].*

❷ *Notice that Word proposes the first part of the date as the name. Word always proposes the first line of text as the filename.*

❸ *Type the name* **Hands-On Lesson 3** *and it will replace the proposed name. (If you switched disk drives, then you may need to click in the File name box, delete the proposed name with the Delete and/or Backspace keys, then type the new name.)*

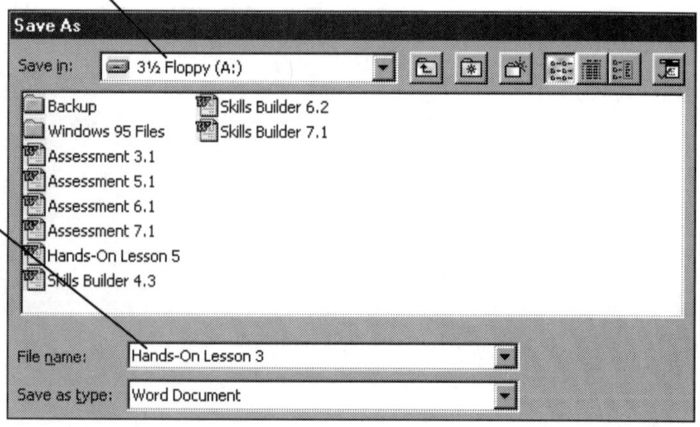

❹ ***Click*** *the* ***Save*** *button.*

Notice the letter was saved and it remains on the screen. You will continue to use the letter throughout this lesson.

Scrolling and Repositioning the Insertion Point

Scroll bars let you browse through documents. However, scrolling does not move the insertion point. You must click the mouse in the document to reposition the insertion point. The vertical scroll bar is on the right side of the document window and the horizontal scroll bar is at the bottom of the document window. Scroll bars also appear in many dialog boxes. The following illustration shows the scroll bars and their components.

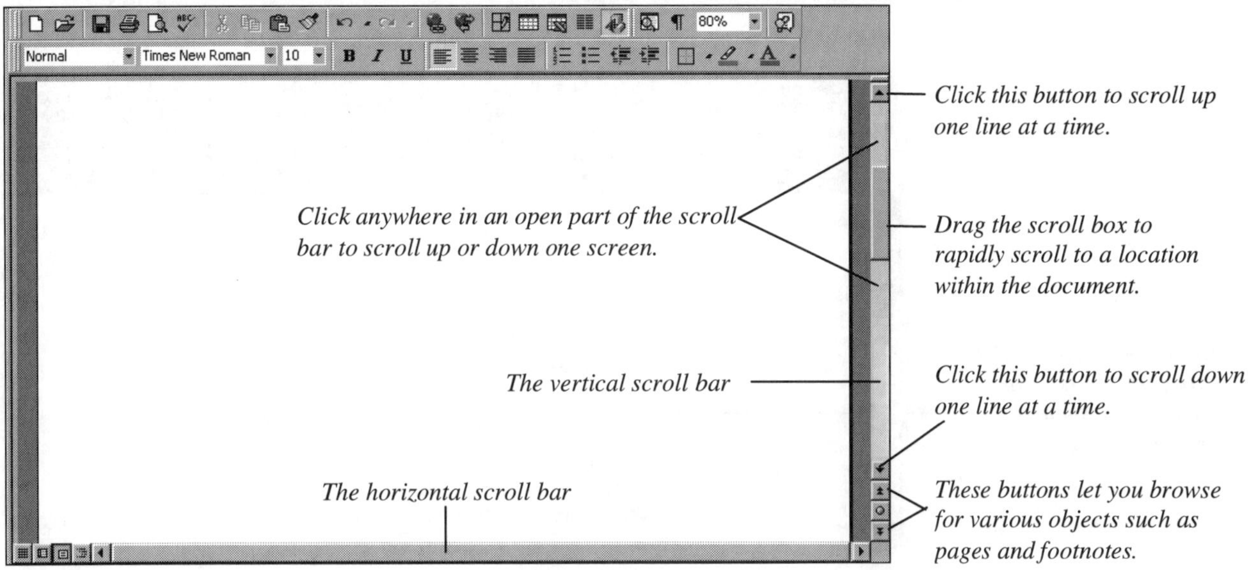

Hands-On 3.4 – Scroll and reposition the insertion point

In this exercise, you will use the scroll bars to browse through the letter.

Scroll down and then up

1. **Click** the Scroll Down button **5 times**.
   Notice the document scrolls down but the insertion point does not move.
2. **Click** the Scroll Up button until the date is visible at the top of the letter.

Reposition the insertion point

3. Slide the mouse and the pointer will have an I-Beam I shape when it is in the typing area.
   The pointer must have this I-Beam shape before the insertion point can be repositioned.
4. **Click** the I-Beam anywhere on the **date** and the blinking insertion point will be positioned there.
5. Move the I-Beam into the **left margin** area and it will become an arrow.
   This arrow ***should not*** *be present if you are trying to reposition the insertion point.*
6. Position the I-Beam on the **first line** of the address just in front of the word **Mr.,** then **click** the left mouse button.
   The insertion point should be positioned just in front of Mr. If a black background appears behind the text, then you have accidentally selected the text. Selecting is discussed later in this lesson, but for now, you can deselect the text by clicking the mouse pointer outside of it.
7. Take a few minutes to practice scrolling and repositioning the insertion point.

The Show/Hide Button

The Show/Hide ¶ button on the Standard toolbar displays or hides all nonprinting characters in a document. Nonprinting characters are inserted whenever you tap Enter, Spacebar, Tab etc. Showing the symbols enables you to see where these characters have been inserted. It also makes it easier for you to edit the document. The following illustration shows the Show/Hide button and the symbols that are inserted whenever the Spacebar and Enter key are tapped.

The Show/Hide button has been turned on.

These symbols are called paragraph marks. They are inserted whenever Enter is tapped.

The dots between words are inserted whenever the Spacebar is tapped.

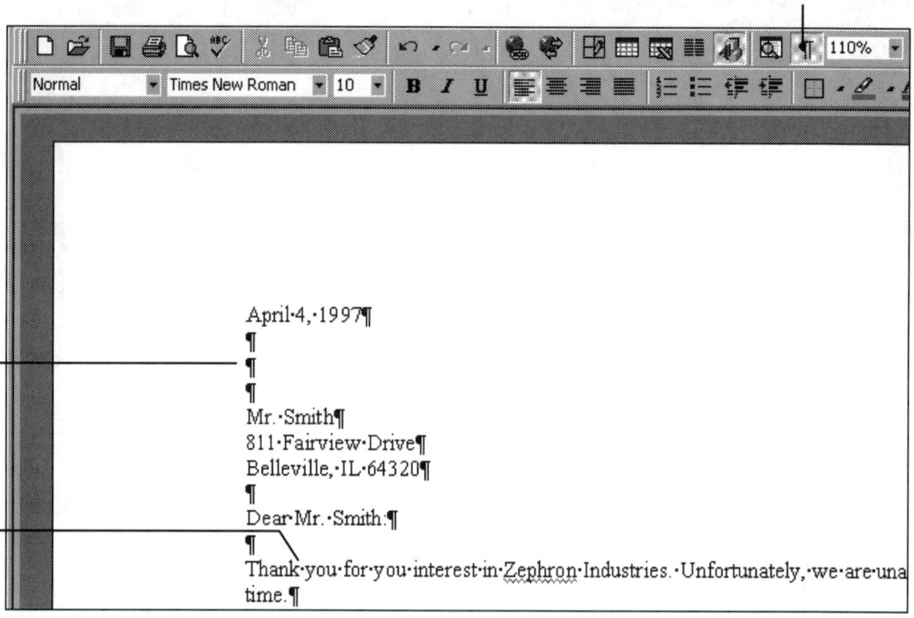

Hands-On 3.5 – Use the Show/Hide button

---

1. **Click** the Show/Hide ¶ button once or twice until the Paragraph Mark ¶ and Spacebar • symbols appear.

   You will work with these symbols throughout this course. Remember that it is usually beneficial to show the symbols especially when you are making changes to a document.

Undo and Redo

Word's Undo button lets you easily reverse your last editing action(s). You can reverse simple actions such as accidental text deletions or you can reverse more complex actions such as margin changes. You can Undo most commands or actions, however, there are a few commands which cannot be undone such as printing and saving files.

Word also has a Redo button that reverses Undo. Use Redo when you Undo an action but then decide that you want to go through with that action after all. You will probably love Redo if you have a difficult time making up your mind.

The arrow buttons to the right of Undo and Redo let you Undo or Redo multiple actions. You can Undo or Redo an almost unlimited number of actions! You will use Undo, Redo and the arrow buttons soon.

Inserting and Deleting Paragraph Marks

Paragraph marks ¶ play an important role in the Word program. A paragraph mark is inserted into a document whenever the Enter key is tapped. Paragraph marks create space between paragraphs and they affect the appearance and format of the document.

Paragraph marks can be deleted

You will need to delete paragraph marks as you create and edit documents. For example, you may want to combine two paragraphs together. You can delete paragraph marks with the Delete and Backspace keys as discussed in the following table.

This key	Deletes
Delete	Character or paragraph mark to the right of the insertion
BackSpace	Character or paragraph mark to the left of the insertion

Hands-On 3.6 – Insert and delete paragraph marks

In this exercise, you will restructure several paragraphs in the letter. You will also add reference initials and the filename to the letter. The paragraph mark symbols should be displayed from an earlier exercise. Remember to click Undo if you make mistakes in this exercise.

Combine the second and third paragraphs

1. Position the insertion point in front of the paragraph mark at the end of the second main paragraph as shown in the following illustration.

Position the insertion point here by clicking the I-Beam just in front of the paragraph mark.

Jane·Alexander·said·you·were·qualified·for·the·
Windows·skills|¶
¶
I·am·sorry·to·deny·you·this·very·high·paying·pc

2. **Tap** the Delete key once.

   The paragraph mark to the right of the insertion point will be deleted. The mark below the paragraph will immediately move up to take its place. Notice that the gap between the paragraphs is no longer a double space.

3. **Tap** the Delete key again and the paragraphs will be joined together.

4. **Tap** the SpaceBar once to create space between the two sentences in the combined paragraph.

   The combined paragraph should look like the following example.

> Jane Alexander said you were qualified for the position with one exception, you lacked Word 97 for Windows skills. I am sorry to deny you this very high paying position, but as you know, Word 97 is the hottest thing since sliced whole wheat bread was first invented. Mr. Smith, please contact us as soon as you have learned Word 97.

Split the combined paragraph into two paragraphs

5. Position the insertion point in front of the word Mr. in the last sentence of the paragraph.

6. **Tap** Enter **twice** to push the sentence **Mr. Smith...** down and form a new paragraph.

   Notice the two paragraph marks that were inserted when you tapped Enter.

Continued...

Add reference initials and the filename to the letter

Many business letters include the typist's initials and the filename below the signature block. This makes it easy to identify the typist and locate the file at a later time.

7. **Click** to the right of the title, **Manager, Human Resources** at the bottom of the letter.

8. **Tap** Enter **twice** to create a double space below the title.

9. Type **Xx:Hands-On Lesson 3** where Xx is your initials.

   For example, type jp:Hands-On Lesson 3 if your name is Jane Peterson. Word will capitalize your first initial because Word identifies it as the first word in a sentence. Word's AutoCorrect feature automatically makes these and other changes.

10. **Click** the Save button on the Standard toolbar.

    The Save button automatically updates the changes to a document that has been previously saved. You should use this button frequently to save changes to your documents.

11. Feel free to experiment with inserting and removing paragraph marks.

    Use the Undo button after making each change and make sure the final state of your document closely matches the example below. You will continue to edit this document throughout this lesson.

Today's Date

Mr. Smith
811 Fairview Drive
Belleville, IL 64320

Dear Mr. Smith:

Thank you for your interest in Zephron Industries. Unfortunately, we are unable to offer you a job at this time.

Jane Alexander said you were qualified for the position with one exception, you lacked Word 97 for Windows skills. I am sorry to deny you this very high paying position, but as you know, Word 97 is the hottest thing since sliced whole wheat bread was first invented.

Mr. Smith, please contact us as soon as you have learned Word 97.

Regards,

Bill Brown
Manager, Human Resources

Xx:Hands-On Lesson 3

Inserting Text

Word makes editing text a pleasure instead of a chore. You can insert, delete and replace text and Word will automatically reformat the lines and paragraphs for you.

Hands-On 3.7 – Inserting text

In this exercise, you will edit the letter. You will change all occurrences of **Mr. Smith** to **Mr. Jack Smith**. You will do this by inserting the word **Jack** in front of **Smith**.

1. Move the insertion point to the inside address (at the top of the letter) in front of the **S** in **Smith**.
2. **Type** the word **Jack** and **tap** the SpaceBar once.
3. Move through the document and change all occurrences of **Mr. Smith** to **Mr. Jack Smith**.
   You will need to reposition the insertion point for each change.

Overwriting Text

Insert is the default editing mode in Word. In insert mode, existing text moves to the right as new text is typed. This makes room for the new text. You have been working in insert mode thus far. In overwrite mode, existing text is replaced as new text is typed. You can switch between insert and overwrite modes by double-clicking the OVR button on the Status bar.

Hands-On 3.8 – Overwriting text

In this exercise, you will change all occurrences of **Jack Smith** to **John Smith**. You will do this by overwriting the word **Jack**. This is the only time that overwrite mode is used in this book.

1. Position the insertion point in the inside address in front of the **J** in **Jack**.
2. **Double-click** the OVR button on the Status bar at the bottom of the screen as shown below.

Double-click the OVR button and the letters OVR will become highlighted. This indicates that Word is in overwrite mode.

3. **Type** the word **John** and Jack should be replaced by John.
4. Change all occurrences of **Jack** to **John**.
   There is no need to double-click OVR to accomplish this. Simply position the insertion point in front of the word Jack and type John over Jack.
5. **Double-click** the **OVR** button when you have finished.
   The letters OVR will be dimmed on the status bar.
6. **Click** the Save button to update the changes.

Selecting Text

Word makes it easy to **select** text. You can move, copy, delete, format and perform numerous other operations on selected text. There are many ways to select text with both the mouse and the keyboard. This section will focus on selecting with the mouse.

Selected text is displayed in reverse video

Selected text is always displayed in white on a black background. This is referred to as **reverse video**. There are several examples of selected text in the illustration shown below.

Keyboard Selecting

You can select text by pressing and holding the Shift key while using the arrow keys to move the insertion point. Text is selected whenever the Shift key is held and the insertion point is moved.

Left Margin Arrow Selecting

Word makes it easy to select lines, paragraphs or an entire document. This is accomplished by clicking or dragging the selection arrow in the left margin as demonstrated in the following exercise.

Hands-On 3.9 – Left margin arrow selecting

1. Use the following steps to select text.

   ❶ *Place the mouse pointer to the left of the date and it will have this shape.* ***Click*** *the* ***left mouse button*** *to select the entire line.*

   ❷ ***Click here*** *to select the salutation. Notice that the date becomes* ***deselected****.*

   ❸ *Select this paragraph by* ***double-clicking*** *in front of it. Notice that the salutation becomes* ***deselected****.*

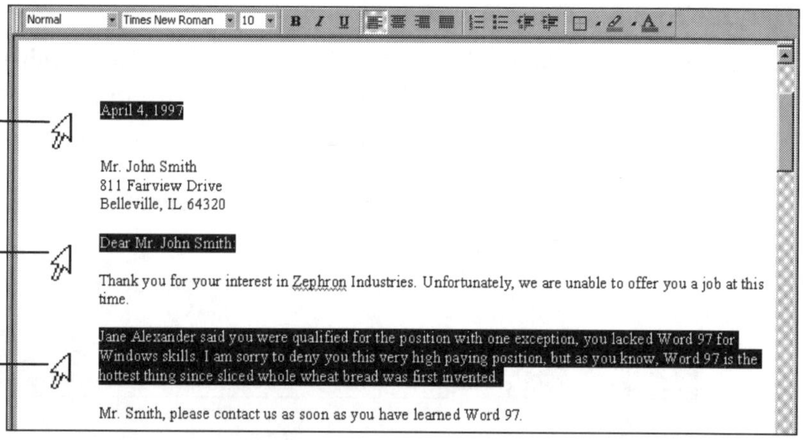

2. Try **dragging** the mouse pointer down in the left margin.

   Be sure to press & hold the left mouse button as you drag and multiple lines will be selected.

3. Try **triple-clicking** the mouse pointer anywhere in the left margin.

   The entire document will become selected. Triple-clicking can be tricky, so you may need to try it several times.

4. **Deselect** the document by **clicking** anywhere on the selected text.

Selecting a Word

You can select a word by double-clicking it.

Hands-On 3.10 – Select words

1. **Double-click** the I-Beam on **any word** in the Hands-On Lesson 3 letter.
2. **Double-click** a **different word** and notice that the previous word has been deselected.
3. **Select five different words** one after another by **double-clicking** them.
4. **Deselect** the last word you selected by **clicking** the I-Beam anywhere outside of it.

Another Way to Select Paragraphs

You can select a paragraph by triple-clicking the I-Beam anywhere within the paragraph. A paragraph can be as short as one line or it can contain several lines of text.

Hands-On 3.11 – Select paragraphs

1. **Triple-click** the I-Beam on any paragraph and the entire paragraph will be selected.
2. Practice using all of the selection techniques you have learned thus far.

Drag Selecting

Drag selecting is the most basic mouse selecting technique and it will work with all Windows programs. This book has a heavy emphasis on drag selecting because it is a fundamental technique.

Hands-On 3.12 – Drag selecting

1. Use the following steps to drag select a phrase.

❶ *Position the I-Beam here just in front of* **Thank you**.

❷ ***Press & hold*** *the left mouse button, then* ***drag*** *to the* ***right*** *until the phrase,* ***Thank you for your interest*** *is selected.*

❸ ***Release*** the ***mouse button*** *and the text will remain selected.*

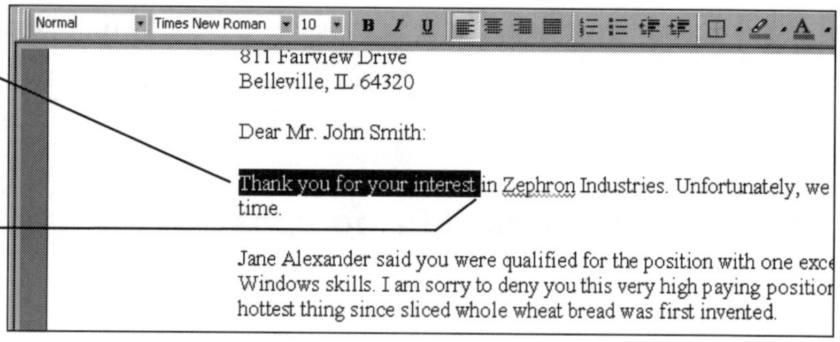

2. **Click & hold** the I-Beam anywhere in the second paragraph (the large paragraph that begins with *Jane Alexander*), then **drag** the mouse up, down, left, right and in any other direction that you may think of.

   Notice how the selection block expands and contracts as you move the mouse.

3. **Release** the mouse button and the text will remain selected.

4. **Deselect** the text by **clicking** the I-Beam just outside of it.

5. Position the I-Beam anywhere on the name **Jane Alexander** and drag the mouse to the right.

   Notice that entire words are selected once the selection includes more than one word. This feature is nice because it simplifies the process of selecting several whole words.

6. Take two minutes to practice selecting text using the drag technique.

7. Take five minutes to practice selecting text using all the techniques you have learned thus far.

   You will get extensive practice selecting text throughout this course.

Deleting and Replacing Text

Text can be easily deleted by first selecting it and then tapping the Delete key. Text can also be replaced by first selecting it and then typing new text.

You can also use the Delete and Backspace keys as well as several different keystroke combinations to rapidly delete text. It is usually easier to use the keystrokes when deleting small amounts of text such as a few characters. Likewise, it is usually easier to use the selecting method when deleting larger blocks of text such as whole words and sentences.

Hands-On 3.13 – Edit the letter

In this exercise, you will use the mouse to select and delete text from the letter. The required editing changes are shown on the next page of this book.

Delete several words

1. Look at the next page and notice that **Mr.** must be deleted from the inside address.
2. **Select** the word **Mr.** by **double-clicking** the I-Beam on it.
   Notice that Word does not select the period after Mr.
3. **Tap** [Delete] to delete the selected text.
   Notice that a period and the blank space after it have been left behind. It is usually desirable to have the punctuation mark left behind. However, it is not beneficial in this case.
4. **Tap** [Delete] **twice** to remove the period and the blank space.
5. Now **delete** the word **Mr.** from the salutation, **Dear Mr. John Smith:**.
   Look at the following page and notice that Smith and the blank space in front of Smith need to be deleted from the salutation. Also, notice that the colon after Smith should not be deleted. Word automatically deletes the blank space in front of a selected word when you delete the word. However, Word will not remove the punctuation mark (a colon in this case).
6. **Select** the word **Smith** by **double-clicking** it.
7. **Tap** [Delete] and Smith and the blank space in front of it will be removed.
   In the next two steps, you will select a word. You will type a new word, which will automatically replace the selected word.

Select a word and type a replacement word

8. **Select** the word **said** in the first line of the second paragraph by **double-clicking** it.
9. **Type** the word **indicated**.
   *Notice that **indicated** replaced **said** and Word maintained the proper spacing between the words.*
10. Look at the illustration on the following page and notice that the word **were** needs to be replaced by the word **are**.
11. **Select** the word **were**, then type **are**.

Continued...

12. Complete the editing changes shown below.

April 4, 1997

~~Mr.~~ John Smith
811 Fairview Drive
Belleville, IL 64320

Dear ~~Mr.~~ John ~~Smith~~:

Thank you for your interest in Zephron Industries. Unfortunately, we are unable to offer you a job at this time.

indicated **are**
Jane Alexander ~~said~~ you ~~were~~ qualified for the position with one exception, you lack~~ed~~ Word 97 for Windows skills. I am sorry to deny you this very high paying position, but as you know, Word 97 is the hottest thing since sliced whole wheat bread was first invented.

me
~~Mr.~~ John ~~Smith~~, please contact ~~us~~ as soon as you have learned Word 97.

Regards,

Bill Brown
Manager, Human Resources

Xx:Hands-On Lesson 3

13. Click the Save button to update the changes.

14. Feel free to print the letter by **clicking** the Print button.

The Print button prints all pages of the document without asking you for any input. You should ask your instructor if it is OK to print. You will learn about additional print options as you progress through this book.

More Practice with Undo and Redo

Word records every action you take. This allows you to reverse those actions at a later time. Both Undo and Redo have a Down Arrow button next to them that displays a list of all preceding actions. You can undo or redo any action by choosing it from the list. You can also undo and redo multiple actions by drag selecting them on the list.

Hands-On 3.14 – Use Undo and Redo

In this exercise, you will make several changes to the letter. You will use Undo to cancel each change immediately after you make it.

1. Delete any word in the letter.
2. **Click** Undo and the word will be restored.
3. **Select** any paragraph, then **tap** Delete to remove the paragraph.
4. **Click** Undo to restore the paragraph.
5. **Click** Redo and the paragraph will vanish again.
   Redo always reverses the most recent undo.
6. **Click** Undo again to restore the paragraph.
7. Practice deleting text and then restoring it with Undo.
   Make sure you use Undo immediately after making a deletion.
8. Practice using both the Undo and Redo buttons.

Undoing and Redoing Multiple Actions

The down arrow buttons next to Undo and Redo display lists of the most recent actions. You can reverse any of the last 99 actions by choosing them from the lists.

Hands-On 3.15 – Undo and Redo multiple actions

1. Use the following steps to delete three items.

❶ ***Click** the **down arrow button** next to Undo and a list of all preceding actions will be displayed. Don't worry if your list does not match the list in this illustration.*

❷ *Use the scroll bar to browse through the list of actions. Scroll to the top of the list when you are finished browsing and make a mental note of the first three or four actions on the list.*

❸ ***Tap** the **Esc** key to close the list.*

❹ ***Select** the **month** and then **delete** it.*

❺ ***Select** the word **Dear**, then **delete** it.*

❻ ***Select** this **paragraph**, then **delete** it.*

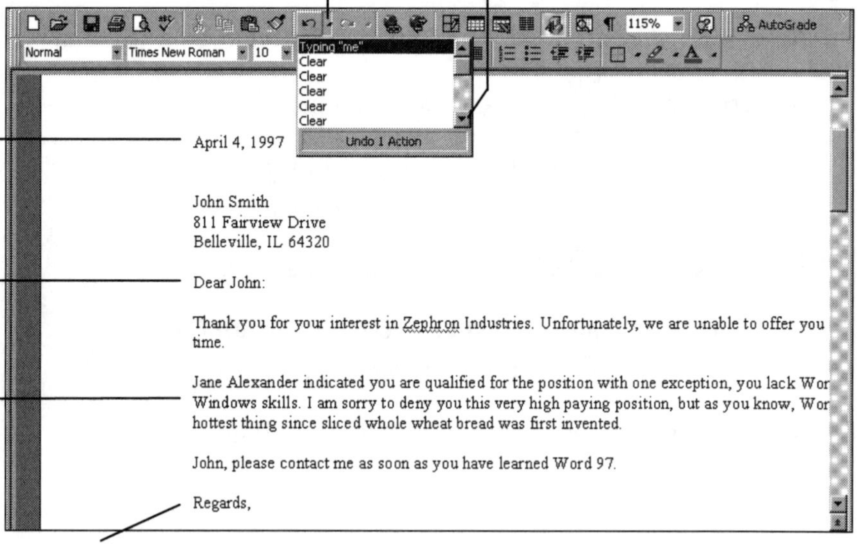

❼ *Position the insertion point in front of the word **Regards** and **type** the word **Best**, so that the complimentary close becomes Best Regards.*

In the preceding steps, you deleted three separate items and you typed new text. You will see these four actions on the Undo Actions list in the steps on the following page.

Continued...

2. Use the following steps to Undo the last four actions.

❶ ***Click this button*** *and notice there are four new actions at the top of the list. Your most recent action was typing the word "Best" so it appears on top of the list. Each action is given a descriptive name to help identify it.*

❷ *Position the mouse pointer on the first action,* ***Typing "Best"****, then* ***drag*** *the mouse* ***down*** *until the first four actions are selected as shown here.*

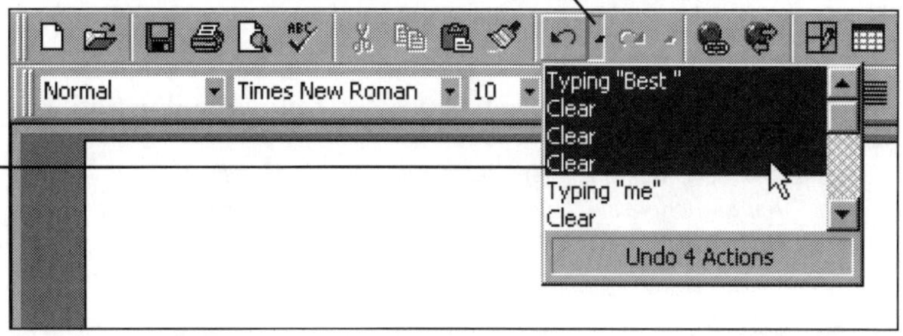

❸ ***Release*** *the* ***mouse button*** *and the four actions will be undone. Your document should be exactly as it was prior to making the changes.*

3. Feel free to experiment with Undo and Redo. Use the down arrow next to Redo to redo several actions at once.

Keep in mind that you must use undo one or more actions before you can use Redo. Also, don't be concerned if you change your letter and are unable to recover from the changes. You saved and printed the letter in an earlier exercise, so you can always recover it (provided you don't save the unwanted changes).

4. When you have finished experimenting, choose **File→Close** from the menu bar.

5. **Click** the **No** button if Word asks you to save the changes.

You can always close without saving to eliminate changes that have occurred since the last save. The exercise on the next page will instruct you to open the letter. You will notice that the most recent changes have not been saved.

6. Finally, notice that there is no document in the document window.

The document window always has this appearance when all documents have been closed.

Opening Files

The Open File dialog box lets you retrieve a document from a disk into the computer's memory. You can edit the document once it has been opened.

Hands-On 3.16 – Open the Hands-On Lesson 3 document

1. Choose **File→Open...** from the menu bar or **click** the Open button on the Standard toolbar. Take a few moments to study the following illustration but don't perform the steps yet.

You can click this list and choose a disk drive. *This button moves you up one level in the file hierarchy.* *This button launches your Web browser.* *Use these buttons to create and access your favorite folders.* *These buttons change the way the files are displayed in the dialog box.*

You can select a filename or folder from this list.

You can also type the desired filename in this box.

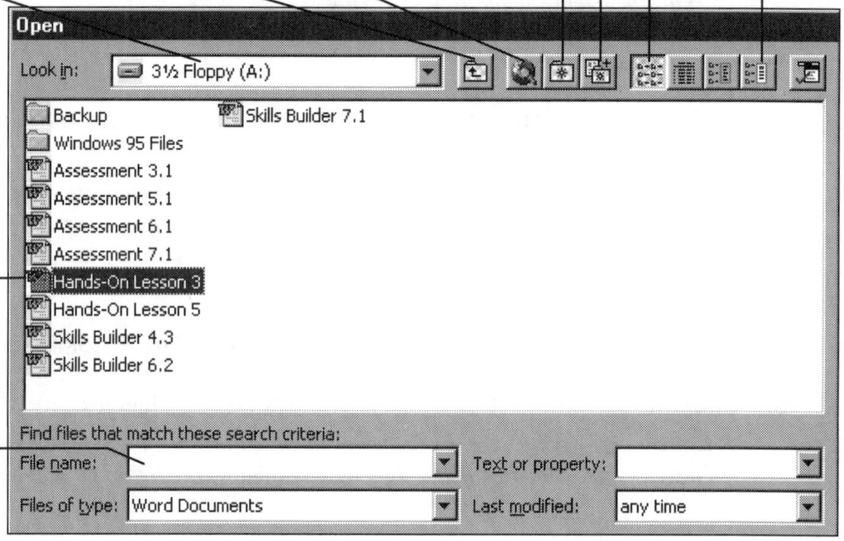

2. Use the following steps to open the Hands-On Lesson 3 document.

❶ *Choose the disk drive that your diskette is in. It is most likely in 3 ½ Floppy [A:].*

❷ *Choose* ***Hands-On Lesson 3.***

❸ ***Click*** *the* ***Open*** *button.*

Note: *You can also open a workbook by double-clicking it on the list. This saves you the effort of having to click the Open button.*

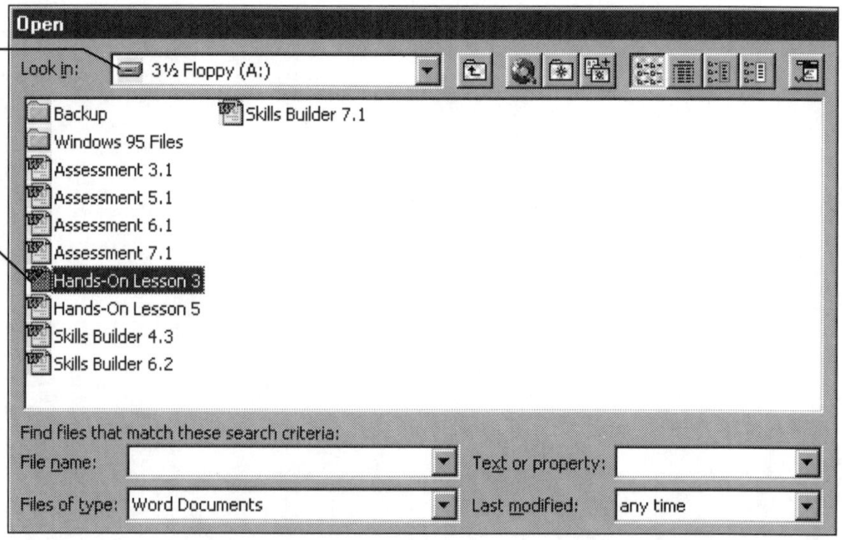

3. Take a few moments to scroll through the letter and notice that the most recent changes **were not** saved (because you closed without saving). You will exit from Word on the next page.

Exiting From Word

You should always exit from Word when you have finished using the program. If you have one or more open documents that have not been saved recently, then Word will ask if you wish to save them.

Hands-On 3.17 – Exit from Word

1. Choose **File→Exit** from the menu bar.

   Word will close and the Windows desktop will appear. Word did not ask you to save the letter because you did not change it after opening it in the previous exercise.

   Now continue with the questions and exercises on the following pages.

Concepts Review

True / False

1.	The insertion point is automatically repositioned when you scroll through a document.	1. **T F**
2.	The Enter key is used to end one paragraph and begin another.	2. **T F**
3.	The Show/Hide button is used to display symbols such as paragraph marks.	3. **T F**
4.	The OVR button toggles Word between insert and overwrite modes.	4. **T F**
5.	A single word can be selected by clicking once on the word.	5. **T F**
6.	The Undo button lets you reverse only the last three changes.	6. **T F**
7.	Paragraph marks cannot be deleted once they have been inserted in a document.	7. **T F**
8.	Word 97 restricts filenames to just eight characters.	8. **T F**
9.	The Backspace key deletes the character to the right of the insertion point.	9. **T F**
10.	Overwrite mode is the default editing mode in Word.	10. **T F**

Multiple Choice

1. What is clicking?
   a) Pressing and holding a mouse button.
   b) Moving a mouse across a mouse pad.
   c) Gently tapping the mouse on the mouse pad.
   d) Pressing and releasing a mouse button. ( )

2. Which shape does the mouse pointer have when it is in the text area?
   a) Right pointing arrow
   b) I-Beam
   c) Left pointing arrow
   d) None of the above. ( )

3. How many characters can you use when naming a file in Word 97?
   a) 8
   b) 32
   c) 255
   d) Unlimited ( )

4. Which of the following methods can be used to select a paragraph?
   a) Double-click anywhere in the paragraph
   b) Triple-click anywhere in the paragraph
   c) Triple-click anywhere in the left margin
   d) None of the above ( )

5. What is happening if your existing text is disappearing as you type new text?
   a) You are in overwrite mode
   b) You are in insert mode
   c) You are tapping the delete key by accident
   d) None of the above. ( )

Skills Builder 3.1

1. Start Word and type the block style letter shown below. Only tap Enter as indicated.

> Today's Date [Enter]
> [Enter]
> [Enter]
> [Enter]
> Melissa Thompson[Enter]
> 810 Ivanhoe Way[Enter]
> Urbana, IL 61801[Enter]
> [Enter]
> Dear Melissa:[Enter]
> [Enter]
> I wanted to take this opportunity to thank you for sending me the software. [Enter]
> [Enter]
> I have put your program to good use. As you know, application programs can increase a person's productivity tremendously. Your program has allowed me to manage my schedule much more effectively.[Enter]
> [Enter]
> I am enclosing the $45 fee that you requested.[Enter]
> [Enter]
> Please send me a receipt. Thank you for your assistance.[Enter]
> [Enter]
> Regards,[Enter]
> [Enter]
> [Enter]
> [Enter]
> Bill Mitchell [Enter]

2. Position the insertion point after the period in the first paragraph (the paragraph that begins with, **I wanted to take this opportunity...**).

3. **Tap** the [SpaceBar] and then type the sentence, **I appreciate the overnight delivery.**
   The sentence will be added to the end of the paragraph.

4. Add the sentence, **The program is also a lot of fun!** to the end of the second paragraph.

5. Use the Show/Hide [¶] button to display the paragraph marks in the document.

6. Position the insertion point at the end of the sentence that reads **I am enclosing the $45...** and **tap** the [Delete] key twice.
   This will remove two paragraph marks and the third and fourth paragraphs will be combined.

7. Now position the insertion point just in front of the phrase **Thank you...** in the combined paragraph and **tap** [Enter] **twice** to create a new paragraph.

8. Use the Show/Hide [¶] button to turn off the symbols.

9. Print [Print button] the document.

10. Choose **File→Close** from the menu bar and save the document as **Skills Builder 3.1**.

Skills Builder 3.2 – Create a Modified Block Style Letter

A modified block style letter has the same elements and similar formatting as a block style letter. The difference is that with the modified block style the date, complimentary close, signature and signature block begin at the center of the lines.

In Word, the default page width is 8.5", so the center of the page is at 4.25". The default left and right margins are 1.25". This means there are 3" between the left margin and center of the page. In this exercise, you will use the Tab key to move the insertion point to the center of the page. The insertion point moves ½" each time the Tab key is tapped. For this reason, you will tap the Tab key six times (1/2" * 6 = 3") to move the insertion point to the center of the line.

1. **Click** the New button on the Standard toolbar.

   You use the New button to open an empty document window.

2. Type the following modified block style letter.

   Tap the Tab key six times to begin the date and other elements at the center. Also, tap Enter the correct number of times between paragraphs as you did with the other letters in this lesson.

Today's Date

Jessica Simms
811 Fairview Drive
Kansas City, MO 64106

Dear Jessica:

I am pleased to inform you that you had excellent scores on all of your placement tests. You scored 98% on the word processing test, 97% on the spreadsheet test and 99% on the secretarial procedures test. These scores were far above average and are a testament to the quality vocational training program you recently completed.

I am pleased to offer you employment with Wilkinson Legal Services at this time. Sarah Adams is looking forward to working with you should you decide to accept our offer.

I know you have several other job offers and I hope you will give Wilkinson serious consideration. Sarah has already expressed an interest in having you train our staff members due to your excellent knowledge in Word and Excel. You will certainly have a bright future at Wilkinson.

Jessica, please contact me soon. We look forward to having you as part of the Wilkinson team.

Sincerely,

Cynthia Lentz
Director, Human Resources

Xx:Skills Builder 3.2

3. **Close** the document and **save** it as **Skills Builder 3.2**.

Assessment 3.1

1. **Open** the document named **Assessment 3.1** and make the editing changes shown below.

> May 15, 1997
>
> **Wanda**
> Ms. ~~Amy~~ Chung
> Deep Sea Adventures
> 130 Ocean View Drive
> San Diego, CA 92158
>
> **Wanda**
> Dear ~~Amy~~:
>
> **all** **tiger**
> I recently participated in your ~~two~~ day shark adventure and I landed a 6-foot shark. This was ~~definitely~~ one of the most exciting adventures of my life.
>
> **that**
> ~~The reason~~ I'm writing you ~~is~~ to request information on other adventures your company offers. Please send me literature as soon as possible.
>
> Thank you for your assistance.
>
> Betty Simms
> 890 Fairmont Lane
> San Diego, CA 92158

2. Add the following sentence to the end of the first main paragraph.

   I was so excited that I had difficulty sleeping for two nights.

3. Add the following sentence to the end of the third paragraph.

   I look forward to hearing from you soon.

4. Insert the phrase **Satisfied Customer** on a new line below the name Betty Simms.

   The new line should be inserted between the signature line (Betty Simms) and the address line (890 Fairmont Lane).

5. **Print** the document, then **close** it and **save** the changes.

Assessment 3.2

1. Use the following guidelines to create the block style letter shown below.
    - Tap Enter the correct number of times between paragraphs. Use the spacing conventions discussed for block style letters at the beginning of this lesson.
    - Type accurately because your document will be checked for accuracy.
    - Type the date shown in the letter (not today's date).

May 19, 1997

Mr. Jeremy Jackson
The Atlas Tire Company
124 West Oak Lane
Downey, CA 90241

Dear Jeremy:

Thank you for the excellent advice on adding Super Track Plus tires to my four wheel drive vehicle. I now have excellent traction especially in wet weather.

I would like to know when I can expect the rebate you promised me. I mailed in my rebate coupon last month and I have yet to hear from the company. Do rebates normally take this long? Please contact me as soon as possible at (510) 232-3344. Thank you for your assistance.

Sincerely,

Miranda Johnson

2. **Print** the letter.
3. **Close** the letter and **save** it as **Assessment 3.2**.

4 Creating a Memorandum and Press Release

Objectives:

- Create an interoffice memorandum and press release
- Insert the date and time
- Insert symbols
- Display, hide and move toolbars
- Format text
- Use the highlight tool and animation
- Use various view modes
- Use the Zoom Control
- Insert and remove page breaks
- Use the Format Painter

The Project – Creating a Memorandum and Press Release

In this lesson, you will create a memorandum and accompanying press release. You will use a hard page break to separate the two pages. You will learn proper techniques for formatting professional business memorandums. You will also learn how to format text, copy text formats, insert the date as a field and insert symbols. Finally, you will use special effects such as highlighting and animation to draw attention to a document. The memorandum and press release that you will create in the main part of this lesson are shown below.

Memorandum

Date: April 11, 1997

To: Bill Watson

Cc: John Smith, Debra Livingston

From: Lashanda Robertson

Re: Flexico® press release

I have attached a press release to announce the launch of our new FlexMax™ line of fabrics. Please review the press release and let me know if you have comments or suggestions. I will submit this press release to the media organizations early next week.

Flexico®, Inc.
Press Release
Flexico Announces FlexMax™ Active Wear

San Francisco, Ca. - Today's Date - ***Flexico, Inc.*** today announced the ***FlexMax***™ fabric for active wear. This revolutionary fabric is designed by ***Flexico*** and allows for maximum range of motion while providing support, comfort and moisture protection. ***FlexMax***™ fabric is ideally suited for active wear such as biking, hiking and aerobics attire. Many major active wear manufacturers have already committed to using this revolutionary new fabric.

Delivery and Availability
FlexMax™ products are expected to reach retailers shelves by the third quarter of this year. Look for the distinctive ***Flexico***® logo and the ***FlexMax***™ trademark. ***FlexMax***™ products will be available at most quality sporting goods stores.

Founded in 1988, ***Flexico***® is a leading manufacturer of fabrics for active wear and outdoor activities. ***Flexico***® fabrics are used in fine active wear products worldwide.

Memorandum Styles

Overview

There are a variety of acceptable memorandum styles in use today. Many new formats have emerged since the widespread use of computer and word processing technology. The style discussed below is a traditional memorandum style with minimal formatting. All memorandum styles contain the same elements but with varied formatting.

Traditional Memorandum Style

A phrase such as ***Memorandum*** *or* ***Interoffice Correspondence*** *is positioned* ***1"*** *down. The phrase is either left or center aligned and it is followed by a triple space.*

Lead words such as Date: and To: appear next. Double space between lines with lead words. Triple space between the last lead line and the body of the memo.

The body of the memo comes next followed by a double space.

Reference initials and other elements are positioned here.

Memorandum

Date: April 11, 1997

To: Bill Watson

From: Lashanda Robertson

Re: Flexico®™ press release

I have attached a press release to announce the launch of our new FlexMax line of fabrics. Please review the press release and let me know if you have comments or suggestions. I will submit this press release to the media organizations early next week.

xx:filename
Attachments

Inserting the Date and Time

Word lets you rapidly insert the current date and/or time into a document. The date and time are inserted at the insertion point. Word lets you insert the date and time using several different formats. For example, the date could be inserted as 4/25/97, April 25, 1997 or 25 April, 1997.

The date and time can be inserted as text or fields

You can insert the date and time as **text** or as **fields**. Inserting the date as text has the same effect as typing the date into the document. Fields, however, are updated whenever the document is opened or printed. For example, imagine you create a document on April 25, 1997 and you insert the date as a field. If you open the document the next day, then the date will automatically be updated to April 26, 1997.

Use caution when inserting the date as a field

You should be cautious when inserting the date as a field especially in legal documents where the date provides an important historical record. You may not want the date to be updated because you will lose the original date that the document was created on. The original date could be important for legal purposes.

Quick Steps: ***Inserting the Date and Time***

To insert the date and/or time

- *Choose Insert→Date and Time... from the menu bar.*
- *Choose a format and click OK.*

Hands-On 4.1 – Create a memorandum

In this exercise, you will create a memorandum. You will use the **Insert→Date and Time...** command to automatically insert the date and you will use the Tab key to align text in the memorandum.

Begin typing and insert the date

1. **Start Word** or **click** the New button if you are already in Word.
2. Type the word **Memorandum** and **tap** Enter **three times**.
3. Type **Date:** and **tap** the Tab key.
   You will insert the date in the next step.
4. Choose **Insert→Date and Time...** from the menu bar.
   Notice the various date and time formats. If the date and time are not accurate on your computer, then you will need to change them. You should ask your instructor for assistance with this process.
5. Make sure the ☑ Update automatically box is checked at the bottom of the dialog box.
   This option instructs Word to insert the date as a field.
6. Choose the **3rd date format** on the list and **click OK** to insert today's date.

Continued...

Type the remainder of the memorandum

7. Now type the remainder of the memorandum as shown below.

   Make sure you triple space after the Re: line and double space between all other paragraphs. Also, use the Tab key to line up the phrases after the To:, Cc:... lead words. Your completed memorandum should match the memorandum shown below.

Memorandum

Date: Today's Date

To: Bill Watson

Cc: John Smith, Debra Livingston

From: Lashanda Robertson

Re: Flexico press release

I have attached a press release to announce the launch of our new FlexMax line of fabrics. Please review the press release and let me know if you have comments or suggestions. I will submit this press release to the media organizations early next week.

8. **Click** the Save button and save the memorandum as **Hands-On Lesson 4.**

   You will continue to enhance the memorandum throughout this lesson.

Inserting Symbols

Word provides over 1,000 symbols that can be inserted in documents. These symbols are inserted with the **Insert→Symbol...** command.

Hands-On 4.2 – Insert the Registered ® and Trade Mark ™ symbols

1. Position the insertion point to the right of the word Flexico on the Re: line of the memo.

   You will insert a Registered Trademark ® symbol in the next few steps. A registered trademark gives a company the exclusive right to use a trademark (Flexico in this case) nationwide.

2. Choose **Insert→Symbol...** from the menu bar.

3. Use the following steps to insert the Registered ® symbol.

❷ ***Scroll*** *to the bottom of the list and* ***click Wingdings****.*

❶ ***Click here*** *to see a list of the available Word symbol sets.*

❸ *Try clicking various symbols in the Windings set and the selected symbol will get magnified (like the* ❶ *symbol shown below). You could insert the symbol at this point, however, we are interested in the Registered symbol.*

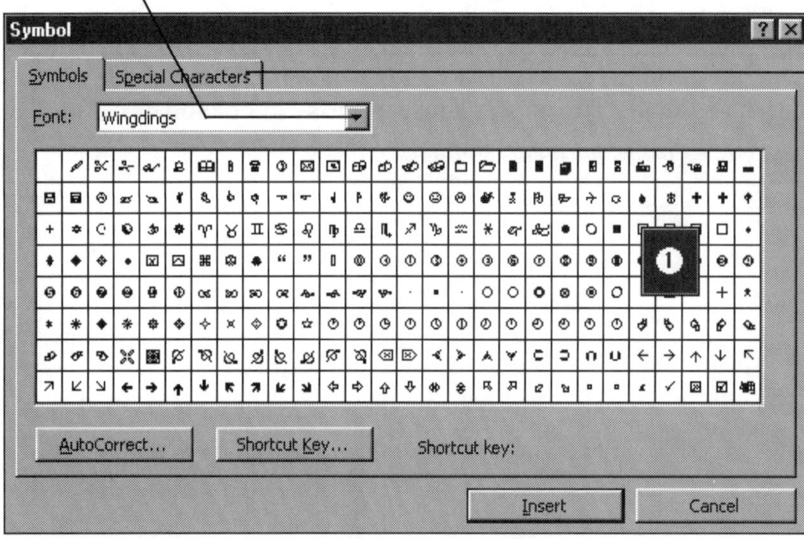

❹ ***Click*** *the* ***Special Characters*** *tab. This tab contains frequently used symbols.*

❺ ***Choose*** *the* ***Registered*** *symbol and* ***click*** *the* ***Insert*** *button.*

Notice the Registered ® symbol appears in your document and the Symbol dialog box remains open. Word leaves the dialog box open in case you wish to insert additional symbols.

4. **Click** the insertion point to the **right of** the word **FlexMax** in the main paragraph (you may need to drag the dialog box out of the way in order to see the word).

5. **Insert** the **Trademark ™** symbol.

   The Trademark symbol indicates that a company claims a phrase or icon as their trademark but they have not received federal protection (indicated by the Registered ® symbol).

6. **Click** the **Close** button to close the dialog box.

7. **Click** the Save button to save the changes.

Formatting Text

Word lets you change the appearance of text by formatting it in various ways. You can change the size, typeface, style and color of text. You can set formats before typing the text or you can apply formats to existing text. The typeface determines the basic shape of text. The size is measured in points where one point is equal to 1/72". The following examples show the Times New Roman and Arial typefaces in various sizes with and without the bold style.

Times New Roman 12 Points

Times New Roman Bold 12 Points

Times New Roman Bold 18 Points

Arial 12 Points

Arial Bold 12 Points

Arial Bold 18 Points

What Are Fonts and Where Do They Come From?

A font is a combination of typeface, size and style. For example, Arial Bold 12 point is a font. Fonts come from several sources including your printer, the Windows operating system and your application programs such as Word.

Printer fonts are known as **hard fonts**. Some printers have a wider selection of fonts than others do. Using printer fonts may reduce the portability of your documents. This is because few printers use the same fonts, so your documents may print differently on other printers.

The Windows operating system provides True Type fonts. True Type fonts are graphically created, so they can be scaled to any point size. You should use True Type fonts whenever possible because they are available on nearly all Windows based computers. This will make your documents portable, which will allow you to print them on any printer.

Using the Formatting Toolbar

The Formatting toolbar lets you rapidly specify a typeface and size for text as well as the Bold, Italics and Underline text styles. You will format the memorandum in the exercise on the following page.

Hands-On 4.3 – Format the Flexico memorandum

The Flexico memorandum should still be in the document window from the last exercise.

Format the heading

1. **Select** the heading **Memorandum** at the top of the document by **double-clicking** it.
2. Use the following steps to format the heading.

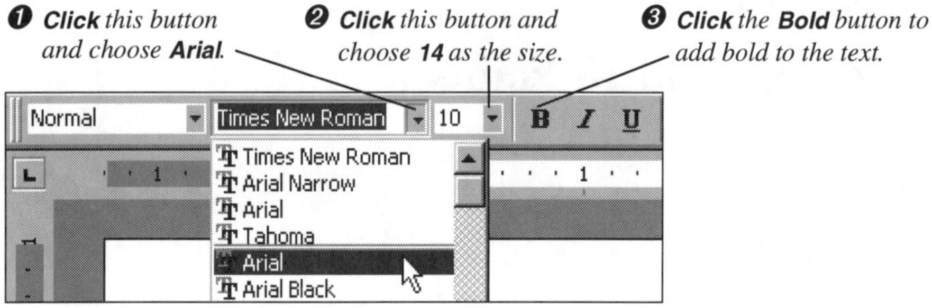

Notice the Arial typeface is listed twice on the list in the illustration above. The most recently used typefaces appear above the horizontal line (just above Tahoma in the illustration) on the typeface list. This makes it easy for you to choose a typeface over-and-over.

3. **Click** anywhere outside of the text to deselect it and you will be able to see the formatting.

Increase the point size for the rest of the memo

4. **Select** the remainder of the memo (from Date: downward) by **dragging** in the left margin.
5. Set the size to **11** point and then **click anywhere** in the document to deselect the text.

Format the lead words on the next five lines

6. **Select** the lead word **Date:** (and the colon after date).

   The best way to do this is to drag the mouse from right to left over the text. Be careful not to select the date. You only want to select the lead word Date:.

7. Set the font to **Arial Bold**.
8. **Format** the next four lead words **To:**, **Cc:**, **From:** and **Re:** as **Arial Bold**.
9. **Save** the changes and continue with the next topic.

View Modes

Word lets you work with documents in several different view modes: normal; page layout; outline; online layout; print preview and full screen. You can edit and modify documents in any view mode. The most common view modes can be accessed through the View option on the menu bar or by clicking the view buttons on the left end of the horizontal scroll bar.

Page Layout View

Page layout view displays your document almost exactly as it will print. This is known as near **WYSIWYG** (What You See Is What You Get). The following illustration shows a document in page layout view. Notice that the pages resemble sheets of paper. Also notice that page numbers and a footer appear at the bottom of the page. You will learn about page breaks later in this lesson. Page numbering and footers are discussed in Labyrinth Publications *Off to Work with Word 97* book.

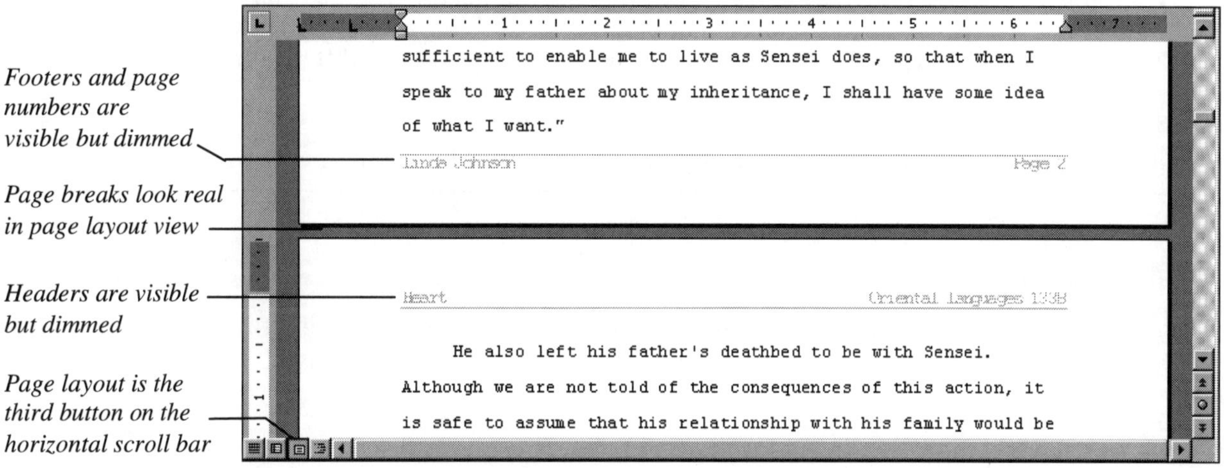

You can scroll to the bottom of the page

Word displays the entire page in page layout view even if a large portion of the page is blank. You can use the scroll buttons to scroll through the entire page even if the bottom portion is blank.

Hands-On 4.4 – Switch to page layout view

1. Notice the location of the Page Layout button in the illustration above.
2. **Click** the Page Layout button on the horizontal scroll bar (or choose View→Page Layout if you have trouble locating the button).

   This may not change the view because you may already have been in page layout view. Notice that the button is pushed in. This means that page layout view is in effect. Notice the large amount of empty space on the page. This empty space is always visible in page layout view.
3. Scroll down until the bottom of the page is visible.
4. Now scroll up until the top of the page is visible.

   You will experiment with normal view in the next exercise.

Normal View

Normal view imitates a WYSIWYG environment although it is not true WYSIWYG. Text and graphics will look exactly like they do in page layout view but some features such as page numbers and headers and footers will not display. Also, the empty space at the bottom of pages will not display.

Normal view may speed up your computer

Normal view may be useful if you have an older computer. This is because your computer does not have to work as hard in normal view and it may become more responsive.

Hands-On 4.5 – Switch to normal view

1. **Click** the Normal View button (it is the leftmost button on the horizontal scroll bar).
2. **Scroll** up and down and you will notice the text area appears quite different in normal view.
3. **Click** the Page Layout button to switch back to page layout view.
   Use page layout view from now on unless you are instructed otherwise.

Other Views

There are several other useful view modes in Word 97. You can get more information on the various views by using Word 97's online Help. You will do this in the following exercise.

Hands-On 4.6 – Use Help

1. Choose **Help→Contents and Index** from the menu bar.
2. If necessary, **click** the **Index tab**.
3. Type **viewing** in the box with the number 1 in front of it.
4. **Double-click** the **viewing documents** topic that appears.
5. **Double-click** the **Different ways to view a Word document** topic that appears.
6. **Click** the yellow and red hyperlink **Online layout view** buttons that are below the various topics and help screens will appear.
7. **Click** the Close button at the top-right corner of the Help window when you have finished.

Using the Zoom Control

Word's zoom control feature lets you change the magnification of the document. Zooming changes the size of text and graphics on the screen but it does not affect the size of printed text and graphics. You can zoom from 10% to 500%. The following illustration shows the Flexico document with a 150% zoom.

You can type a zoom percentage into this box and tap Enter, or...

you can click this button and select an option from the drop down menu.

Notice how large the text appears. However, it will print in the normal size.

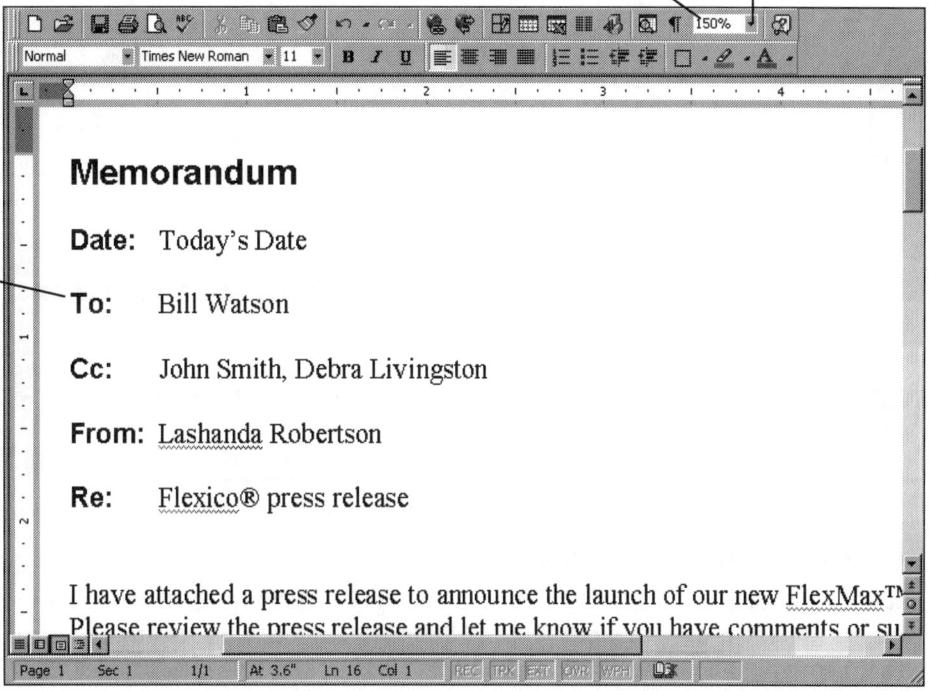

Hands-On 4.7 – Experiment with the zoom control

1. Use the following steps to experiment with the zoom control.

   ❶ ***Click** in this box, **type 123** and then **tap Enter**. This will adjust the zoom to 123% of normal.*

   ❷ ***Click** the Zoom Control button and choose **150%**.*

   ❸ ***Click** this button again and choose **Page Width**. Page Width adjusts the zoom to the width of the page.*

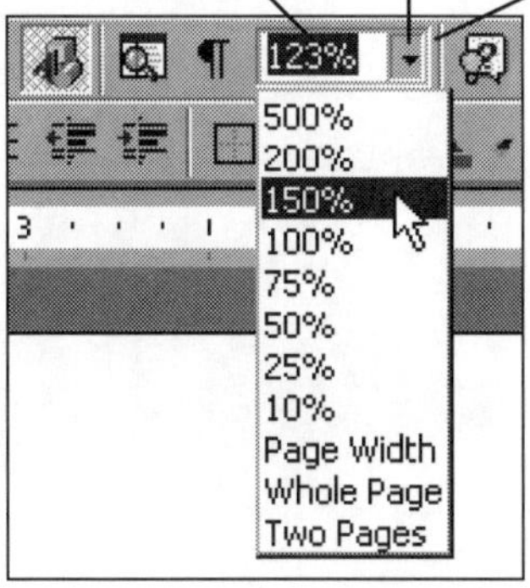

2. Use the Zoom Control button to select the following three zoom modes: **Whole Page**; **75%;** and finally **Page Width**. Feel free to experiment with the zoom control.

Page Breaks

Soft Page Breaks

When text is being typed and the insertion point reaches the bottom of the page, Word breaks the page and begins a new one. These automatic page breaks are called **soft page breaks**. The following illustration shows the document window with a soft page break separating two pages. Notice that the text is a long continuous stream that is naturally broken by the soft page break.

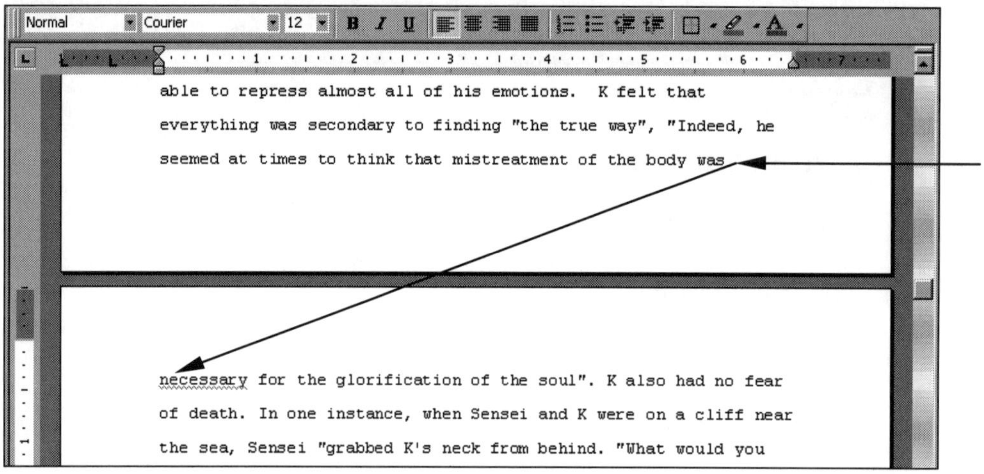

Notice how the text flows continuously from one page to another with a soft page break.

Soft page breaks are dynamic

The location of soft page breaks change as text is added to or deleted from a document. This dynamic behavior makes it easy to work with multiple page documents. Soft page breaks are useful if you aren't concerned with where the page break occurs (like in a novel for example). You will experiment with soft page breaks later in this course.

Hard Page Breaks

You can begin a new page at any time by inserting a hard page break. The location of hard page breaks is fixed. Hard page breaks remain in the same location regardless of how a document changes. The illustration below shows a document with a hard page break. Notice how the top page ends prematurely.

A hard page break looks like a soft page break.

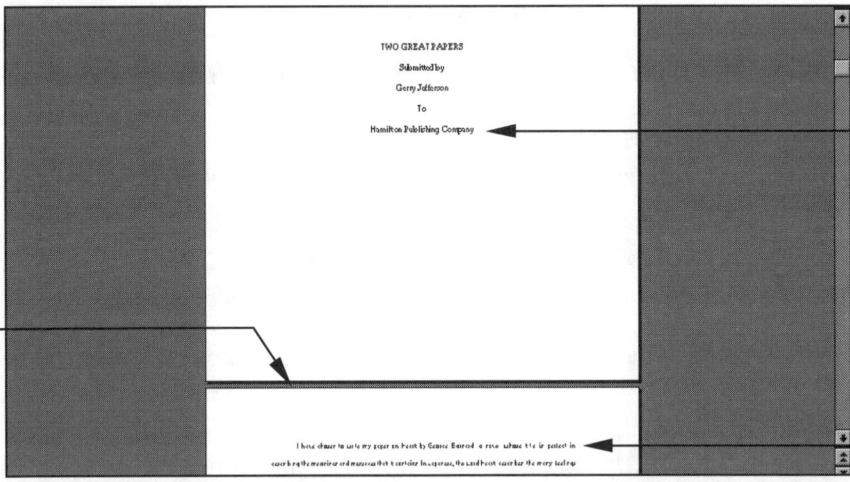

Notice how this page ends abruptly

and

this page begins.

Quick Steps: **Inserting Hard Page Breaks**	
To insert a hard page break	
Keyboard method	***Menu bar method***
• *Press Ctrl + Enter*	• *Choose Insert→Break* • *Choose Page Break and click OK*

Removing a Hard Page Break

A hard page break can be removed by positioning the insertion point above the break and tapping Delete. You can also position the insertion point below the break and tap BackSpace. In normal view, you can position the insertion point directly on the page break and then delete it. These concepts are discussed in the following illustrations.

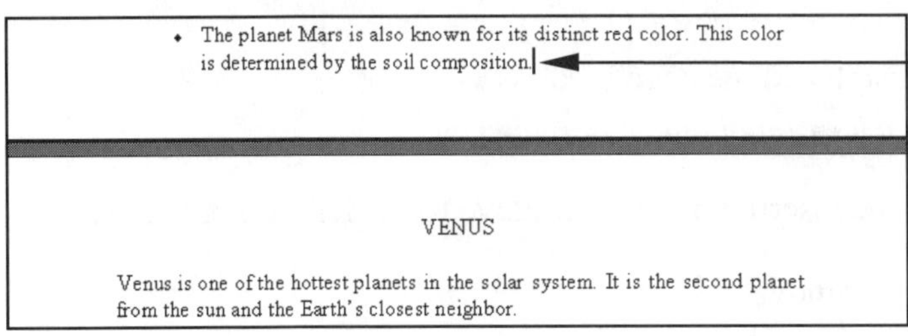

This page break can be deleted by positioning the insertion point above the break and tapping the Delete key.

In normal view, the page break can be deleted by positioning the insertion point on it and then tapping Delete.

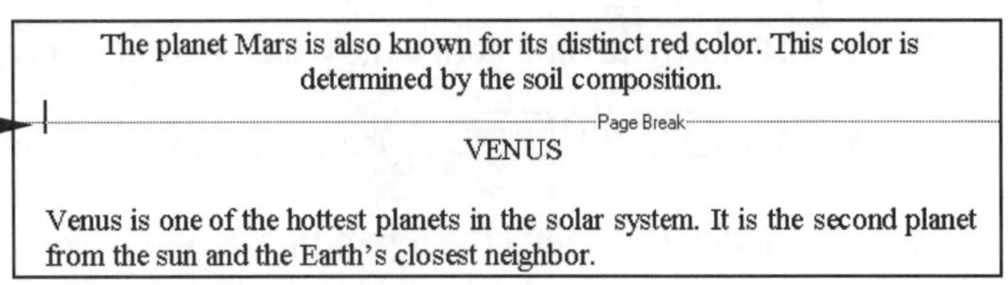

Hands-On 4.8 – Add a page break to the Flexico memorandum

Switch views and insert a page break

1. Make sure you are in page layout view.
2. Position the insertion point at the end of the main paragraph (to the right of the period).
3. Choose **Insert→Break...** from the menu bar.
   Notice there are several types of breaks. You will work with section breaks later in this course.
4. Make sure Page Break [Page break] is chosen and **click OK**.
   You should be able to see the bottom half of page 1 and the top of page 2.
5. Look at the Status bar at the bottom of the screen and it will show the insertion point is on Page 2.

Remove the page break

6. Use the mouse to **Scroll** to the top of the document and notice the first page is still intact.
7. **Scroll** down until the page break is visible.
   You should also be able to see the insertion point at the top of the second page.
8. **Tap** the BackSpace key and the page break will be removed.
9. Try scrolling down to the second page and you will notice it has been removed.

Use the Ctrl + Enter keystroke to reinsert the break

10. **Scroll** up and make sure the insertion point is at the end of the main paragraph.
11. **Press** Ctrl + Enter to reinsert the page break.
    This shortcut keystroke is useful to remember because page breaks are inserted often.

Switch to normal view and delete the page break

12. **Click** the Normal View button.
13. **Scroll** up until both the main paragraph and the page break is visible.
    Notice that the page break appears as a horizontal line in normal view.
14. **Click** anywhere on the page break and the insertion point will move to the left end of the break.
15. **Tap** the Delete key and the break will be removed.
16. Switch back to Page Layout view.
17. **Scroll** down and notice the page break is gone.
18. Use the Ctrl + Enter keystroke combination to reinsert the break.
19. **Scroll** down until the top of the second page is visible and continue with the next exercise.

Hands-On 4.9 – Type the press release

1. Type the press release shown below onto the second page of the document. Use the **Insert→Date and Time...** command to insert Today's Date as shown in the first main paragraph below. Use the **Insert→Symbol...** command to insert the Registered® and TradeMark™ symbols as shown. You can keep the Symbols dialog box open while you insert the ® and ™ symbols in various locations. However, you must click at each location that you wish to insert the symbols prior to clicking the Insert button on the dialog box.

> Flexico®, Inc.
> Press Release
> Flexico® Announces FlexMax™ Active Wear
>
> San Francisco, Ca. - Today's Date - Flexico®, Inc. today announced the FlexMax™ fabric for active wear. This revolutionary fabric is designed by Flexico and allows for maximum range of motion while providing support, comfort and moisture protection. FlexMax™ fabric is ideally suited for active wear such as biking, hiking and aerobics attire. Many major active wear manufacturers have already committed to using this revolutionary new fabric.
>
> Delivery and Availability
> FlexMax™ products are expected to reach retailers shelves by the third quarter of this year. Look for the distinctive Flexico® logo and the FlexMax™ trademark. FlexMax™ products will be available at most quality sporting goods stores.
>
> Founded in 1988, Flexico® is a leading manufacturer of fabrics for active wear and outdoor activities. Flexico® fabrics are used in fine active wear products worldwide.

2. Save the changes and continue with the next exercise.

Hands-On 4.10 – Use the Font dialog box to format text

In this exercise, you will use the Font dialog box to add color and animation to the press release. The Font dialog box provides several options that are not available on the Formatting toolbar.

Format the heading lines and add color to them

1. **Select** the heading lines on the press release by dragging in the left margin as shown below.

2. Choose **Format→Font...** from the menu bar.

3. Use the steps on the following page to format the text.

Continued...

❶ ***Scroll** through the list of typefaces by tapping the **up arrow** and **down arrow** keys on the keyboard. Choose your favorite typeface and notice it is displayed in the Preview window.*

❷ *Choose* **Bold.**

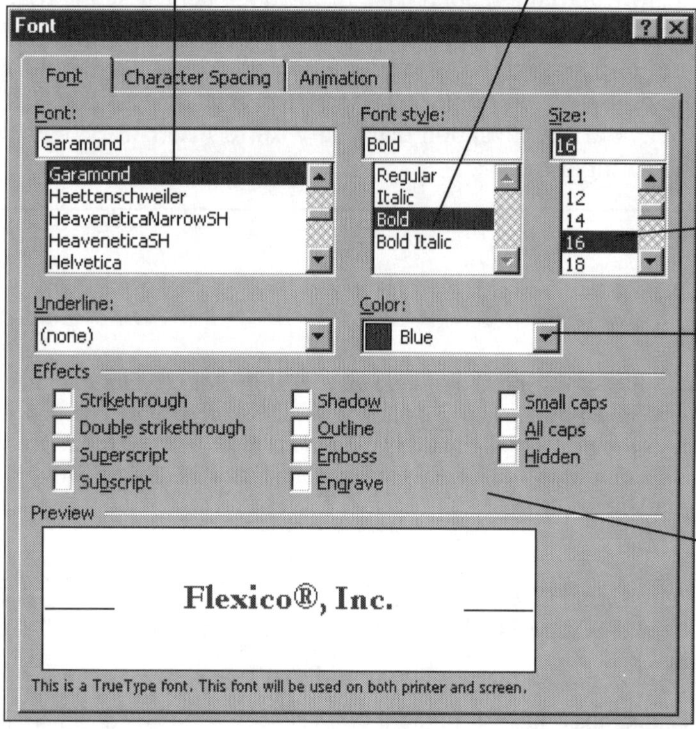

❸ ***Scroll** through the size list and choose **16**.*

❹ ***Click here** and choose your favorite color. The color will display on your screen, however, it will only print in color if you have a color printer.*

❺ *Feel free to choose an effect.*

❻ ***Click** **OK.***

4. **Click** outside of the selected text and you will be able to see the formatting.

   You can usually format text with the Formatting toolbar. However, sometimes you will want an effect that is only available through the Font dialog box.

Use animation

5. **Select** the third line in the heading (Flexico Announces FlexMax…).
6. Choose **Format→Font...** and **click** the **Animation** tab on the dialog box.
7. Choose an animation effect such as **Blinking Background** and **click OK**.

   Animation is useful if you are using Word to create a Web page or some other type of online document. In this example, the press release could be posted on the World Wide Web. The animation would be an effective way to draw attention to the announcement.

8. Feel free to keep the animated effect or click Undo to cancel it.

Use the Formatting toolbar

9. **Select** the phrase **San Francisco, Ca. - Today's Date** in the first paragraph.
10. **Click** the Bold button on the Formatting toolbar.
11. **Select** the phrase **Flexico, Inc.** which is just to right of the phrase you just bolded.
12. **Click** both the Bold and Italics buttons on the Formatting toolbar.
13. Save the changes to your document and continue with the next topic.

The Format Painter

The Format Painter lets you copy text formats from one location to another. This can be an effective way to format text. The Format Painter helps you create consistent formatting throughout a document.

Quick Steps: *Copying Text Formats*

To copy text formats with the Format Painter

- *Position the insertion point anywhere on the text with the format you wish to copy.*
- *Click the Format Painter button or double-click it if you wish to copy to more than one location.*
- *Select the text that you wish to copy the formats to.*
- *If you double-clicked in the first step, then click the Format Painter button when you are finished.*

Hands-On 4.11 – Copy text formats in the memorandum

Copy a format to one location

1. **Click** anywhere on the **Flexico, Inc.** phrase in the large paragraph.

   In the previous exercise, you formatted that phrase with bold and italics. You must position the insertion point on the text whose formats you wish to copy before clicking the Format Painter.

2. **Click** the Format Painter and the pointer will become a paintbrush.

   In the next step, you will click once on the word you wish to copy the formats to. You only need to click a word once and the formats will be copied to it. You can also copy formats to phrases and paragraphs by using any of the selection techniques you have learned.

3. **Click** the word **FlexMax** that is just to the right of the phrase Flexico, Inc.

   FlexMax should be formatted with bold and italics. Notice that the paint brush icon is no longer attached to the mouse pointer. You clicked the Format Painter button just once, so you can only copy the formats to one other location. You must double-click the Format Painter if you wish to copy the formats more than once.

Copy the format to several locations

4. Make sure the insertion point is somewhere on the formatted word FlexMax.
5. **Double-click** the Format Painter.
6. **Click** the word **Flexico** in the second line of the paragraph.

   Notice the paint brush icon is still attached to the pointer.

7. **Click** the word **FlexMax** in the third line.
8. Now **click** every occurrence of **FlexMax** and **Flexico** in the main paragraphs.
9. When you have finished, **click** the Format Painter to turn it off.
10. Feel free to format the document in any way you desire.
11. When you have finished, choose **File→Close** from the menu bar and save the changes.

    Continue with the end-of-lesson questions and exercises on the following pages.

Concepts Review

True / False

1. Word lets you display a maximum of two toolbars on the screen. 1. **T F**
2. Toolbars are fixed on the screen and their positions cannot be changed. 2. **T F**
3. The zoom control changes the size of printed text. 3. **T F**
4. The Formatting toolbar can be used to set all text formats. 4. **T F**
5. Normal view is a full WYSIWYG view. 5. **T F**
6. An older computer may have better performance if Normal view is used. 6. **T F**
7. The Format Painter button copies text formats. 7. **T F**
8. One point is equal to 1/36". 8. **T F**
9. Hard page breaks remain in place until they are deleted. 9. **T F**
10. You can remove a hard page break in both Normal and Page Layout views. 10. **T F**

Multiple Choice

1. In order to copy text formatting to several locations in a document, you must:
   a) Click the Format Painter button and then select the desired text.
   b) Double-click the Format Painter button and then select the desired text.
   c) Use the Copy button.
   d) This cannot be done in Word. ( )
2. Which of the following statements most accurately describes hard page breaks?
   a) Hard page breaks remain in place until they are deleted.
   b) Hard page breaks are inserted by the user.
   c) Hard page breaks are inserted by pressing Ctrl + Enter.
   d) All of the above. ( )
3. Which of the following view modes most closely resembles a WYSIWYG mode?
   a) Page Layout
   b) Normal
   c) Zoom
   d) None of the above. ( )
4. What is the percentage range of the zoom control?
   a) 25% - 200%
   b) 10% - 500%
   c) 25% - 500%
   d) None of the above. ( )
5. Which of the following procedures can be used to remove a hard page break?
   a) Switch to Page Layout view, position the insertion point directly on the break and Tap Insert.
   b) Switch to Normal view, position the insertion point directly on the break and Tap Backspace. ( )
   c) Switch to Normal view, position the insertion point directly on the break and Tap Delete.
   d) All of the above.

Skills Builder 4.1

In this exercise, you will create the document shown below. This document uses several typefaces and point sizes. The indicated fonts should be available on your computer. If they are not available, then substitute fonts that are available to you.

1. **Click** the New button.
2. Set the font to **Arial 16 Bold**.
3. Type **Peterson's Pet Supply**, then **tap** Enter **twice**.
4. Set the font size to **12** and **click** the Italics button.
5. Type, ***Is Having A***, then **click** the Italics button to turn off italics.
6. **Tap** Enter **twice**.
7. Continue entering text and changing typefaces and sizes until the document shown below is complete. Tap Enter twice after completing each line.

   Your completed document should closely match the document shown below.

8. Close the document and save it as **Skills Builder 4.1**.

Arial Bold 16 →	**Peterson's Pet Supply**
Arial Bold Italic 12 →	***Is Having A***
Arial Bold 20 →	**Big Fish Sale**
Times New Roman 8 →	Small Gold Fish Just .59
Times New Roman 12 →	Medium Gold Fish Just .79
Times New Roman 14 →	Large Gold Fish Just $1.29
Times New Roman 20 →	Huge Gold Fish Just $3.59
Times New Roman 10 →	LEGAL DISCLAIMER: We take no responsibility for the safety and/or well being of your fish. If your cats get them or your kids flush them, well, bye-bye fishy. The good news is, with these prices, you can keep your cats fat, your kids entertained and still have a bowl of bug-eyed fish to enjoy.

Skills Builder 4.2

In this exercise, you will create the memorandum below. You will add color to the memorandum with the Font Color button. You will also use Word's highlighting tool to highlight text.

1. Start a new document and change the **point size** to **12.**

2. Type the following memorandum.

   You will need to tap the Tab key once or twice in order to line up the text to the right of the lead words. Notice this memorandum uses the phrases Interoffice Correspondence and Subject (instead of Memorandum and Re). These are both appropriate conventions for memorandums.

Interoffice Correspondence

Date: Today's Date

To: Jason Alexander

From: Tamika Jackson

Subject: Monthly sales meeting

Our monthly sales meeting will be held in the conference room at 10:00 on Thursday, July 24. Please bring your sales forecast for August and any important accounts that you wish to discuss. I will give you a presentation on our new products that are scheduled for release in September. I look forward to seeing you then.

Xx:Skills Builder 4.2

Add color and highlighting

3. Select the title Interoffice Correspondence and increase the size to **16**.

4. **Click** the Font Color drop-down button on the right end of the Formatting toolbar.

5. Choose your favorite color.

   Notice that the color you chose is now displayed on the button.

6. **Select another phrase** and apply the same color to it by **clicking** the Font Color button.

7. **Select** the **Subject: line** and **click** the Highlight button on the Formatting toolbar.

8. **Click** anywhere **outside the text** and the highlight will be visible.

   Notice that highlighting is an effective way to draw attention to text. Feel free to use the drop-down button to the right of the highlight button to apply different highlight colors or to remove highlights. However, you must have the desired text selected before using this or any other formatting options.

9. **Close** the document when you have finished and **save** it as **Skills Builder 4.2**.

Skills Builder 4.3

In this exercise, you will open a document on your exercise diskette. The document contains four paragraphs with one formatted phrase in each paragraph. You will use the Format Painter to copy the formats to other phrases.

1. **Open** the document named **Skills Builder 4.3** on your exercise diskette.

   The document has four paragraphs. The phrase Flexico, Inc. is formatted differently at the beginning of each paragraph. You will paint the Flexico, Inc. formatting onto the words Flexico, Tempest and Flexico, Inc. within each paragraph.

2. **Click** the insertion point on the phrase ***Flexico, Inc.*** at the beginning of the first paragraph.

3. **Double-click** the Format Painter button.

4. **Click** the paintbrush on the word **Flexico** in the middle of the first line.

   Notice that a single word is painted when you click on that word. The pointer should still have the paintbrush shape because you double-clicked in step 3.

5. **Click** the paintbrush on the word **Tempest** near the beginning of the second line.

   The formatting will be copied to that word.

6. Continue **clicking** the words Tempest and Flexico in the **first paragraph only** but stop when you get to the phrase Flexico, Inc. which is near the end of the paragraph.

7. Use the mouse to **drag** the paintbrush over the phrase Flexico, Inc.

   The formatting should be copied to that phrase.

8. **Click** the Format Painter button to turn it off.

   The formatted paragraph should closely match the following paragraph.

Flexico, Inc. is proud of its newest product lines. ***Flexico*** strives to improve its products and with the new ***Tempest*** line, ***Flexico*** has proven itself as the industry leader. ***Flexico*** has a tradition of affordable quality. This tradition and the ***Tempest*** products will help ***Flexico, Inc***. remain the industry leader.

9. **Click** the insertion point on the phrase, **Flexico, Inc.** at the beginning of the second paragraph.

10. **Double-click** the Format Painter button and then copy the format to the words, Flexico, Tempest and Flexico, Inc. in the second paragraph.

11. **Click** the Format Painter button when you have finished, then paint the third and fourth paragraphs using the same techniques. Use Undo if you make mistakes.

12. **Close** the document and save the changes when you have finished.

Assessment 4.1

1. **Click** the New button to open a new document window.
2. Use the following guidelines to create the memorandum shown below. You must use these guidelines in order to get full credit for this assessment.
    - Use a Times New Roman 10-point font for all text except for the bolded title and lead words. The title **Memorandum** should have an Arial Bold 12-point font. The lead words, Date:, To:, Cc:, From: and Subject: should have an Arial Bold 10-point font.
    - Insert today's date as a field.
    - Make sure you use the correct number of hard returns between paragraphs.
    - Tap the Tab key **once** to align the text to the right of each lead word.

Memorandum

Date: Today's Date

To: Steve Ellison

Cc: Tina Litton, Ralph Warren

From: Paula Lark

Re: Expense Reports

Please have your staff submit their expense reports by the 10th of each month. As you know, we have limited staff in the accounting department. Late expense reports create confusion and make it difficult for us to do our jobs. I would truly appreciate your support and follow through on this matter.

Please contact me if you have questions.

3. **Print** the memorandum.
4. Choose **File→Close** from the menu bar and **save** the document as **Assessment 4.1**.

Assessment 4.2

1. **Click** the New button to open a new document window.
2. Use the following guidelines to create the two-page memorandum shown below and on the following page. You must use these guidelines in order to get full credit for this assessment.
   - Use a Times New Roman 11-point font for all text except for the bolded titles and lead words. The titles **Interoffice Correspondence** and **Belmont Shores Proposal – Outstanding Issues** should have an Arial Bold 14-point font. The lead words, Date:, To:, From: and Subject: should have an Arial Bold 11-point font.
   - Use bold to highlight the items on the issues list as shown on the next page.
   - Insert today's date as a field.
   - Make sure you use the correct number of hard returns between paragraphs.
   - Use the Tab key to align the text to the right of each lead word. You will need to use two tabs on most lines and one on the last line.
   - Insert a hard page break immediately to the right of the word Document, which is the last word on page 1.

Interoffice Correspondence

Date: Today's Date

To: Wanda Allison

From: Jackson Jones

Subject: Proposal deadline

I spoke with Bill Nicholson today and he informed me that January 23rd is the deadline for proposal submissions. This is two weeks earlier than we had initially planned, so we must make every effort to complete the proposal by that date. I would like to meet with your staff next Monday to discuss our strategy. Please let me know which time will be best for you. I will require one hour of your time.

I have attached a list of outstanding issues that need to be addressed prior to the proposal deadline. Please develop an action plan for these issues prior to our meeting. Thank you.

Attachment: Outstanding Issues Document

Continued...

Belmont Shores Proposal - Outstanding Issues

I have composed the following list of issues that must be addressed prior to the submission of our proposal. Each item is equally important to our success. I encourage everyone on your staff to work hard on these issues so that we may resolve them in time.
Develop a reference list
Complete the portfolio
Receive bids from all subcontractors
Receive regulatory approval from the state
Complete environmental impact study
Develop 5-year budget forecast

3. **Print** the memorandum.
4. Choose **File→Close** from the menu bar and **save** the document as **Assessment 4.2**.

5 Professional Writing and Editing Tools

Objectives:

- Use automatic spelling and grammar checking
- Use the spelling and grammar checker
- Use word count
- Use the thesaurus
- Use find and replace
- Go to a specific page
- Open a recently used document

The Project – Editing a Report

In this lesson, you will open an eight-page report from your exercise diskette. You will use Word 97's writing tools to "clean up" the document. You will check the document for spelling and grammar. You will also replace words and phrases with the Find and Replace commands. The thesaurus will be used to improve the clarity of the writing. Finally, you will use the Go To command to rapidly go to a specific page. The following illustration shows the document you will work with. The document contains several underlined words and phrases. You will use Word 97's writing tools to correct these and other errors.

The Washington Witchcraft Triales

The village of Washington, Massachusetts experienced one of the strangest events in history between the months of February and September 1692. During these eight months, the village experienced widespread accusations of witchcraft and sorcery. Initially, the problems afflicted a few individuals but they soon grew to affect the entire community. These accusations resulted in over 100 arrests and 19 executions.

Witchcraft and witchtrials had been around for centuries in Europe but they had never occurred in such large numbers in the colonies. The widespread accusations resulted in the establishment of a special court just to deal with the the accused witches. THis court accepted strange evidence and tried people from all aspects of society.

The village of Washington, Massachusetts was founded in 1626 by the Massachusetts Bay Company. The village grew as more settlers came to the New World from Europe. The community

Spell Check Concepts

Word checks a document for spelling errors by comparing each word to the contents of a dictionary. The dictionary contains a large number of commonly used words. The spell checker also looks for double words such as **the the**, words with numbers such as ***93budget*** and certain types of capitalization errors.

The speller also uses a custom dictionary

Word actually compares your document with two (or more) dictionaries: the main dictionary and one or more custom dictionaries. Custom dictionaries contain words such as last names or company names that may not be in a normal dictionary. You can add words to a custom dictionary during a spell check. This is beneficial because the speller will skip over these words once they have been added to the custom dictionary. You can even create new custom dictionaries or purchase dictionaries with specific terminology such as medical or legal jargon.

Automatic Spelling and Grammar Checking

Word 97 automatically checks spelling and grammar as you type. Each word is checked for spelling errors after you complete it. Likewise, each sentence is checked for grammar after you complete the sentence. Word "flags" spelling and grammar errors with wavy red and green underlining. You can immediately correct errors by right-clicking on them and choosing options on the pop up menu that appears.

Hands-On 5.1 – Use automatic spell checking

Correct spelling errors

1. Open the document named **Hands-On Lesson 5** on your exercise diskette.

   This document has plenty of spelling and grammar errors for you to correct.

2. Notice the word Triales in the title has a wavy red underline.

   Misspelled words are identified by wavy red underlines.

3. **Right-click** the word **Triales** and the pop up menu shown below will appear.

   Take a few moments to study the following illustration.

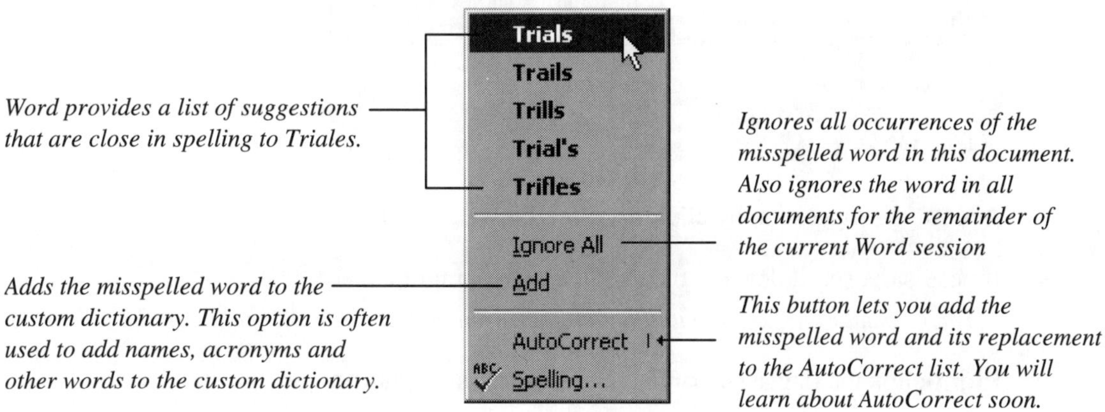

4. Choose **Trials** from the top of the list as shown above.

   Trials will replace the word Triales.

Continued...

5. If necessary, **scroll down** until the word **witchtrials** is visible at the top of the second paragraph.
   It should also have a wavy red underline because it is misspelled.

6. **Right-click** the word **witchtrials** and notice that Word has no spelling suggestions.
   This word needs to have a space between witch and trials.

7. Use the **left** mouse button to **click** the insertion point between witch and trials as shown below.

   witchtrials

8. **Tap** the SpaceBar to complete the change.

Correct double word and capitalization errors

9. If necessary, **scroll down** until the 4th line of the second paragraph is visible.
   This line has both double word and capitalization errors.

10. **Right-click** the double word **the the**.

11. Choose **Delete Repeated Word** from the pop up menu.

12. **Right-click** the word **THis** towards the end of the line.

13. Choose **This** from the pop up menu.
    As you can see, the spell checker looks for spelling, double words and capitalization errors.

Hands-On 5.2 – Use automatic grammar checking

1. If necessary, **scroll down** until the 1st line of the third paragraph is visible.
   Notice that nearly the entire first sentence is underlined. The automatic grammar checker has determined that this sentence has a grammar problem.

2. **Right-click** the sentence and the pop up box shown below will appear.
   In this case, the grammar checker has proposed an excellent suggestion.

3. **Accept** the suggestion by **clicking** it (as shown above).

4. If necessary, scroll down to the middle of the paragraph.
   The grammar checker should flag another grammar error in the middle of the fourth sentence.

5. **Right-click** the flagged **error** and **choose the suggestion**.
   In these examples, the grammar checker provided excellent suggestions. However, the grammar checker is not perfect. In fact, it often proposes incorrect grammar! So be careful and use the grammar checker with caution.

Using the Spelling and Grammar Dialog Box

The Spelling and Grammar dialog box is useful when you are spell checking and/or grammar checking a large document. It also provides access to customization options. For example, you use the Spelling and Grammar dialog box to choose a customized dictionary for the spell checker and to choose the writing style for the grammar checker. The Spelling and Grammar dialog box is displayed with the **Tools→Spelling and Grammar** command or by clicking the Spelling and Grammar button on the Standard toolbar.

Hands-On 5.3 – Use the Spelling and Grammar dialog box

1. **Click** the Spelling and Grammar button on the Standard toolbar.
   The spell check will begin and the speller should stop on the word WAs in the third paragraph.
2. Take a few moments to study the following illustration.

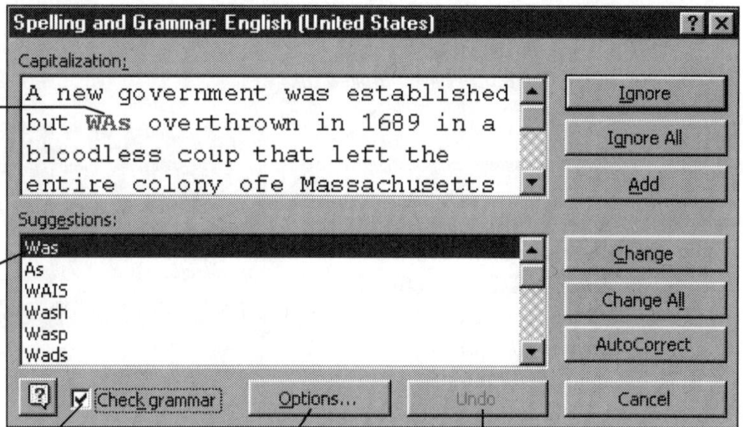

If Word has no valid suggestions, then select the highlighted word or phrase here and type a replacement word or phrase.

You can choose a suggestion from this list and click the Change button.

This box turns on grammar checking when using this dialog box. However, it does not affect automatic grammar checking.

Change the custom dictionary, writing style and other options.

This button lets you Undo the last spelling or grammar correction.

3. Use the following guidelines to spell check and grammar check the remainder of this document.
   - Assume that all names such as Ethel Kelly are spelled correctly.
   - Use the Ignore All button to skip over the names.
   - Use your best judgment to determine the correct spelling of all misspelled words.
   - Use your best judgment to determine the correct grammar if Word reports grammar errors. Skip over grammar errors if you are unsure of how to resolve them.
4. **Click** the **OK** button when the spell check is complete.
5. **Click** the Save button to update the changes.
   Leave the document open because you will continue to use it.

Thesaurus

The thesaurus can help improve your vocabulary by providing lists of synonyms (words with the same meaning) for a selected word. The Thesaurus will sometimes provide antonyms (words with the opposite meaning) as well. To use the thesaurus you must click on a word and use the **Tools→Language→Thesaurus** command.

Hands-On 5.4 – Use the thesaurus

In this exercise, you will use the Thesaurus to replace a word in the Hands-On Lesson 5 document. The document should still be open from the preceding exercise.

1. **Scroll** up and **click** the word **experienced** in the first line of the first paragraph.
2. Choose **Tools→Language→Thesaurus...** from the menu bar.
3. Use the following steps to explore the Thesaurus dialog box.

❶ *Notice **experienced** is the word that is currently being looked up.*

❷ *A list of synonyms (words with the same meaning) is displayed here.*

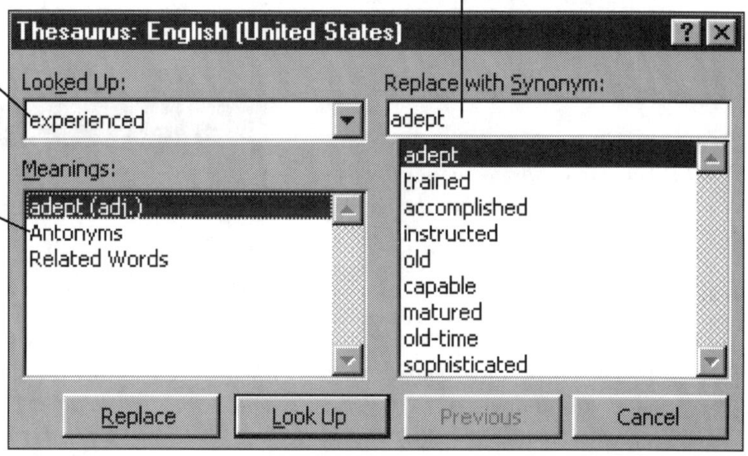

❸ ***Click** here on the word **Antonyms**. The synonym list will be replaced with an antonym list (words with the opposite meaning).*

❹ ***Click** the **Cancel** button because there weren't any good synonyms on the synonym list.*

4. **Click** the word **Witchcraft** in the title.
5. Choose **Tools→Language→Thesaurus...** from the menu bar.
   The word sorcery should be at the top of the synonym list.
6. **Click** the **Replace** button and Witchcraft will be replaced by Sorcery.
   Notice that Word capitalized Sorcery because Witchcraft was capitalized.
7. Now use the Thesaurus to change **Sorcery** back to **Witchcraft**.
8. Feel free to experiment with the Thesaurus.
9. Continue with the next topic when you have finished experimenting.

The Find Command

Word has a powerful Find command that lets you search for words, phrases and other combinations of characters. You can also use find to search for formatting such as bold or italics and to search for objects such as paragraph marks and page breaks. Find is often the fastest way to move to a specific location in a document. You display the Find dialog box with the **Edit→Find** command.

Hands-On 5.5 – Use the Find command

Find the word February

1. Position the insertion point at the top of the document and make sure that no text is selected.
2. Choose **Edit→Find...** from the menu bar.
3. Use the following steps to find the word February.

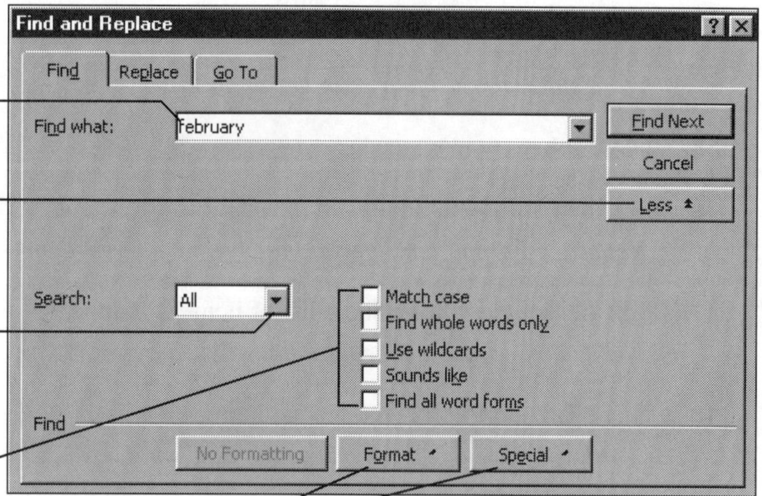

Word should find and select the word February in the second line of the first paragraph.

Find another word

4. **Click** in the **Find what** box, delete february and **type WITCH** (in capital letters) in its place.
5. **Click** the **Find Next** button.

   Notice that WITCH was found even though it is part of the word witchcraft. Also, you typed WITCH in capital letters, yet it was still found. By default, Find is not case sensitive and it doesn't care if you enter a whole word or part of the word. You will change this, however, in the next few steps.

Try to find WITCH in all capital letters

6. **Click** the Match case check box.

   This box instructs Word to only find occurrences of the search string with the same matching case.

7. **Click** the **Find Next** button and Word will tell you the search item was not found.

   The word WITCH does not occur in this document in all capital letters.

Continued...

8. **Click** the **OK** button on the message box.

9. **Click** the **Match Case** check box to remove the check.

Find witch as a whole word only

10. **Click** the 

check box.

11. **Click** the **Find Next** button and Word will find the word witch.

12. **Click Find Next** again and Word will find the next occurrence of witch.

    Word will not find words like witchcraft and witchtrials because you told it to look only for whole words. Also notice that Word is ignoring the case because the Match Case box is not checked.

13. **Click** the 

box to remove the check.

Search for text formats and use other Find options

14. **Click** the button 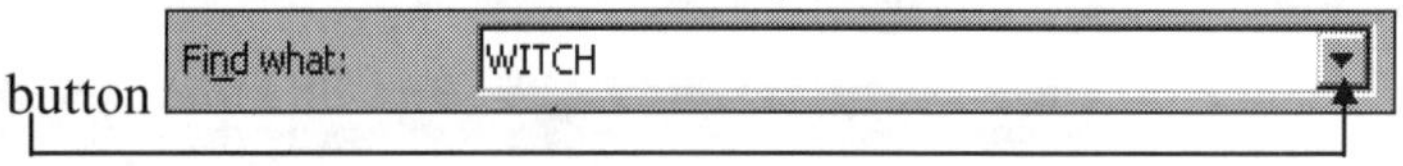

on the Find what box.

    Word stores the last four searches on this list.

15. Choose **february** from the list.

16. **Click** the **Find Next** button and the next occurrence of february will be found.

    *Notice the **Format** and **Special** buttons at the bottom of the dialog box.*

17. **Click** the **Special** button and a list of items will appear.

    You can search for any item (although you have not learned how to use these items yet).

18. Choose **Tab Character** (the second item on the list).

    Word will place a ^t character in the Find what box. This character tells Word to search for a tab.

19. **Click Find Next**.

    Word will select the space at the front of a paragraph. The space was created by a tab.

20. **Click** the **Find Next** button again and word will go to the next tab space.

21. **Click** the **Format** button at the bottom of the dialog box.

    The Format button lets you search for specific fonts, paragraph formats and other items.

22. Choose **Font...** from the list.

23. Choose **Bold** from the Font Style list and **click** the **OK** button.

    *The words **Format: Bold** should appear below the Find what box.*

24. **Remove** the **^t** character from the Find what box, then **click** the **Find Next** button.

    Word should select part of the title because it is in bold.

25. **Click** the **Cancel** button to discontinue the find procedure.

    You will learn how to Find and Replace text in the next topic. Leave the document open because you will continue to use it.

Replacing Text

The Replace command lets you search for a phrase and replace it with a different phrase. For example, suppose you have typed a letter to Alice Jones only to discover that she spells her first name as Alyce. You could replace Alice with Alyce throughout the entire document.

Hands-On 5.6 – Use the Replace command

1. Position the insertion point at the top of the document in front of the title.

   Notice that the title reads The Washington Witchcraft Trials.... *The word Washington needs to be replaced with Salem. Also notice that Washington has a capital W.*

2. Choose **Edit→Replace...** from the menu bar.

   This is the same dialog box you used with the Find command but the Replace tab is active.

3. **Click** the **No Formatting** button at the bottom of the dialog box.

   This turns off the bold setting that you searched for in the previous exercise.

4. Use the following Hands-On Illustration to find the word washington and replace it with salem.

   ❶ *Type* ***washington*** *in lowercase.*

   ❷ *Type* ***salem*** *in lowercase.*

   ❸ ***Click Find Next.***

   ❹ ***Click Replace.***

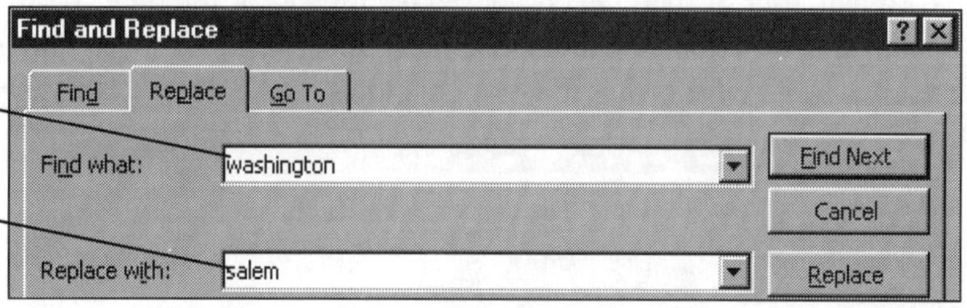

   Notice that Washington was replaced by Salem (you may need to scroll up to see this). Washington was capitalized so Word also capitalized Salem.

5. **Click** the **Replace** button **two** more times to make two more replacements.

6. Now **Click Replace All** and Word will replace all occurrences of Washington with Salem.

7. **Click OK** on the message box that appears.

   Be careful with Replace All because you may make accidental replacements. For example, if you replace ***cat*** *with* ***dog****, then words like* ***cat****apult may become* ***dog****apult. Use the Find Whole Words Only option if the word you are replacing might be part of a larger word (like cat and catapult).*

8. Use **Replace All** to make the replacements shown in the following table. There is no need to use the Find Whole Words Only box because these names are not likely to be part of a larger word.

Find	Replace with	Number of replacements that Word should make
Bill Phips	William Phips	2
Donna Good	Dorsa Good	1
Buffrows	Burroughs	4

9. **Click** the **Find tab** on the dialog box and search for Buffrows, Bill Phips or Donna Good. Do they still exist in the document?

10. **Close** the **dialog box** but leave the document open because you will continue to use it.

Word Count

The word count feature counts the number of words, sentences, paragraphs and several other items in the current document. This feature is often used by word processors that bill clients by the word or page.

Hands-On 5.7 – Use word count

1. Make sure there are no words selected in the document.
2. Choose **Tools→Word Count...** from the menu bar.

   Word will analyze the document and it will display the statistics.
3. Take a few moments to study the results, then **click** the **Close** button.
4. **Close** the document and **save** the changes.

Opening the Most Recently Used Documents

Word lists four or more recently used documents at the bottom of the File menu. You can open any of these documents by choosing them from the File menu. This is the fastest and most efficient way to open documents. The following illustration shows four documents listed at the bottom of the File menu.

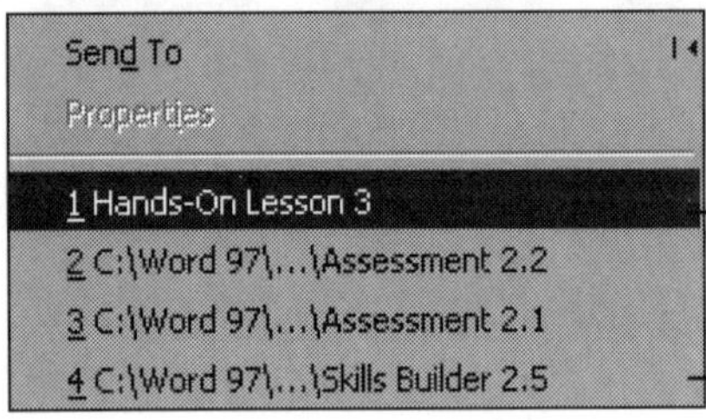

The four most recently opened documents are displayed at the bottom of the file menu. You can open one of these documents by choosing it from the menu.

Hands-On 5.8 – Open the Hands-On Lesson 5 document

1. Choose **File** from the menu bar.

   Notice the four most recently used documents are listed at the bottom of the menu. The Hands-On Lesson 5 document should be at the top of the list because you used it in the previous exercise.
2. Choose **Hands-On Lesson 5** from the list and the document will open.
3. Try to open some of the other files that are listed on the File menu.

   You may not be able to open them if other students created them. This is because the files will be on their diskettes and not yours.
4. Close any documents you just opened except for Hands-On Lesson 5.

   You will continue to use the document in the next exercise.

The Go To Command

The *Go To* command lets you rapidly move the insertion point to a specific page in a document. Go To is the third tab on the Find and Replace dialog box. You can rapidly display the Go To tab on the Find and Replace dialog box by using the techniques in the following Quick Steps table.

Quick Steps: ***Going to a Specific Page***
To Go To a specific page
• *Press Ctrl + G*
or
• *Double-click the Page Number section of the Status bar.*
• *Enter the desired page number and click OK.*

Hands-On 5.9 – Go to a page

Use the Ctrl + G command

1. **Press** Ctrl + G and the Go To tab of the Find and Replace dialog box will appear.

   Notice that you can use this shortcut keystroke to initiate Find and Replace as well.

2. Type **4** into the **Enter page number** box and **click** the **Go To** button.

   The insertion point should move to the top of page 4.

3. **Click** the **Close** button on the dialog box.

Use the Status bar

4. Display the Find and Replace dialog box by **double-clicking** the status bar as shown below.

   Double-click anywhere on this part of the status bar.

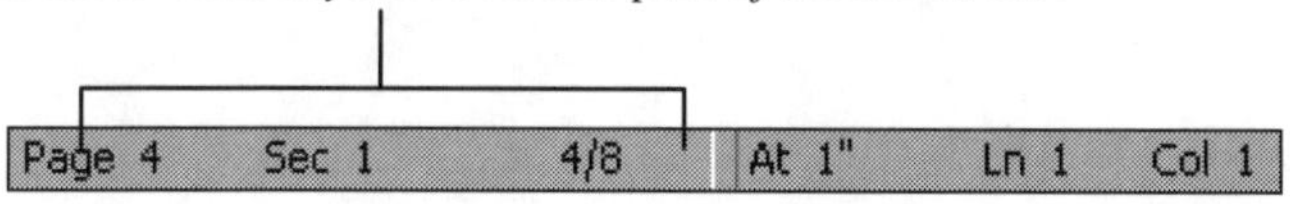

   Notice that the dialog box lets you GoTo other locations such as Sections, Lines etc. In this course, we will only focus on going to pages.

5. Type **6** into the **Enter Page Number** box and then **click** the **Go To** button.

6. **Click** the **Close** button.

   You have learned two methods for displaying the Go To dialog box. You should focus on using the method that is easier for you to remember.

7. **Close** the document and continue with the end-of-lesson questions and exercises.

Concepts Review

True / False

1. Word marks words it thinks are misspelled with a wavy red underline. 1. **T F**
2. You can correct a misspelled word by first clicking it with the left mouse button. 2. **T F**
3. The Ignore All command ignores a misspelled word for the current spell check only. 3. **T F**
4. The grammar checker always provides correct suggestions. 4. **T F**
5. You can search for a phrase by using the Edit→Find command. 5. **T F**
6. The Edit→Replace command lets you search for text and replace it with other text. 6. **T F**
7. Word displays the names of the last four open documents at the bottom of the File menu. 7. **T F**
8. The Go To command can be initiated by pressing Alt + G. 8. **T F**
9. The thesaurus lets you find and replace misspelled words. 9. **T F**
10. The spell checker finds certain types of capitalization errors. 10. **T F**

Multiple Choice

1. Which of the following actions will let you use the thesaurus on a word?
   a) Click on the word and choose Edit→Thesaurus.
   b) Choose Tools→Language→Thesaurus.
   c) Click on the word and then choose Tools→Language→Thesaurus.
   d) None of the above. ( )
2. Which command initiates the Word Count tool?
   a) Tools→Word Count
   b) Edit→Word Count
   c) Format→Word Count
   d) None of the above. ( )
3. Which of the following statements is true?
   a) The spell checker uses only a main dictionary unless your document is in Spanish.
   b) The spell checker uses a custom dictionary only for legal documents.
   c) The spell checker uses a main and custom dictionary for all spell checks.
   d) None of the above. ( )
4. The Go To dialog box can be displayed by pressing Ctrl + G and by double-clicking the Page number section of the Status bar. Which of the following commands can also be used to display the Go To dialog box?
   a) Format→Go To.
   b) Edit→Go To. ( )
   c) File→Go To.
   d) None of the above.
5. Which of the following statements is true?
   a) The sun rises in the East and sets in the West.
   b) The Earth revolves around the sun.
   c) The Oakland Raiders are the greatest football team ever.
   d) All of the above. ( )

Skills Builder 5.1

In this exercise, you will type the letter shown below. You will use the Find and Replace command later in this exercise to replace certain words.

1. Start a new document and set the font to **Times New Roman 12**.

2. Type the letter shown below. You can type today's date or insert it as a field. Use Word's automatic spell checking and grammar checking while you are typing the letter. Do not format the letter with bold and italics yet. You will be instructed to add bold and italics in step 3.

> Today's date
>
> Mr. Juan Lopez
> Editor in Chief
> Birds of Prey Magazine
> 1450 Parker Lane
> Ventura, CA 93003
>
> Dear Mr. Lopez:
>
> I recently subscribed to *Birds of Prey* magazine and I am enjoying it immensely. Your monthly tips have been especially useful. I have spotted over 20 new species in my local area since I first subscribed to *Birds of Prey*. **Keep up the good work!**
>
> One thing that I would like to see more of in *Birds of Prey* is recommendations on bird watching sites in the Western United States. I am especially interested in bald eagles and golden eagles. I would appreciate any suggestions you may have.
>
> Sincerely,
>
> Your Name

3. Use the Formatting toolbar to add **bold** and **italics** to various phrases as shown above.

4. Choose **Edit→Replace...** from the menu bar.

5. Replace all occurrences of **Birds of Prey** with **Bird Watcher**.
   Word should automatically italicize the phrase Bird Watcher because Birds of Prey was italicized.

6. Make sure there are no spelling errors in the document.

7. **Close** the document and **save** it as **Skills Builder 5.1**.

Skills Builder 5.2

In this exercise, you will modify the letter you created in the previous exercise.

1. Choose **File** from the menu bar, then choose **Skills Builder 5.1** from the bottom of the menu.

   *Use this technique when you want to open the four most recently used documents. Imagine you want to use a phrase other than **bird watching sites** in the second paragraph. Can you think of a replacement word for **watching**? Fortunately, the thesaurus is always close at hand. You will use the thesaurus in the next few steps to find a substitute for watching.*

2. **Click** anywhere on the word **watching** in the second paragraph.

3. Choose **Tools→Language→Thesaurus...** from the menu bar.

   *You should see several good synonyms including **viewing**.*

4. **Choose any synonym** from the list and **click** the **Replace** button.

5. Use the thesaurus to find replacements (choose any replacements) for the two words shown below.

Word	Location in the document
useful	Second sentence of the first paragraph
appreciate	Last sentence of the second paragraph

6. **Click** the insertion point on the word **recently** at the beginning of the first paragraph.

7. Choose **Tools→Language→Thesaurus...** from the menu bar and notice the thesaurus proposes several phrases that can be used in place of recently.

8. Choose **not long ago** and **click Replace**.

9. Now restructure the sentence to make it grammatically correct.

   *You will need to **delete** the word **I** from the beginning of the sentence and re-insert it after the phrase **not long ago**, then capitalize the word not.*

10. **Close** the letter and **save** the changes.

Assessment 5.1

1. **Open** the document on your exercise diskette named **Assessment 5.1**.

2. **Spell check** the document. Use your best judgment to determine which replacement words to use for incorrectly spelled words. Assume all names are spelled correctly.

3. Use Find and Replace to make the following replacements. Also, write the number of replacements in the third column of the table.

Word	Replace with	Number of replacements
Mary	Chitra	
arthritis	cancer	

4. **Print** the document when you have finished.

5. **Close** the document and **save** the changes.

6 Creating a Simple Report

Objectives:

- Understand basic report formats
- Understand paragraph concepts
- Change paragraph alignment
- Set line spacing
- Select an entire document
- Indent paragraphs
- Use the horizontal ruler

The Project – Creating a Simple Report

In this lesson, you will create a report using a traditional report format. You will format the report by changing line spacing, indents and other options. The report you will create is shown below.

COMPUTER TECHNOLOGY IN THE 21ST CENTURY

Our society has changed from a manufacturing oriented society to an information society. Those with access to capital had power in the early 1900's. In the 21st century, however, power will come from access to information. The amount of worldwide information is growing at a rapid pace. Computer technology is responsible for much of this growth but it can also help us manage the information.

Information management is an important use of computer technology. Daryl Richardson of Harmond Technology describes four other reasons why the average person may want to acquire above average knowledge of computers.

> Computer skills are becoming more important in the business world. Many companies need employees with excellent computer skills.
>
> The Internet and other information resources provide access to a global database of information.
>
> Computer skills can often simplify one's personal life. Computers can be used for entertainment, to manage finances and to provide a stimulating learning tool for children.
>
> Using computers can provide a sense of accomplishment. Many people suffer from "computerphobia." Learning to use computers often creates a feeling of connection with the information age.

Report Styles

Overview

There are a variety of acceptable report styles. The style shown below is a traditional report style. Other report styles are used for research papers and other types of documents.

Traditional Report Style

The report title begins 2" from the top of the page. The title is typed in uppercase and is centered on the line. You can also format the title to make it stand out.

Tap Enter four times between the title and body of the report.

Double-space the body paragraphs.

Quotations and other text you wish to emphasize are single-spaced and indented one inch on the left and right. You should double-space (by tapping Enter twice) between quotes.

COMPUTER TECHNOLOGY IN THE 21ST CENTURY

Our society has changed from a manufacturing oriented society to an information society. Those with access to capital had power in the early 1900's. In the 21st century, however, power will come from access to information. The amount of worldwide information is growing at a rapid pace. Computer technology is responsible for much of this growth but it can also help us manage the information.

Information management is an important use of computer technology. Daryl Richardson of Harmond Technology describes four other reasons why the average person may want to acquire above average knowledge of computers.

> Computer skills are becoming more important in the business world. Many companies need employees with excellent computer skills.
>
> The Internet and other information resources provide access to a global database of information.
>
> Computer skills can often simplify ones personal life. Computers can be used for entertainment, to manage finances and to provide a stimulating learning tool for children.
>
> Using computers can provide a sense of accomplishment. Many people suffer from "computerphobia." Learning to use computers often creates a feeling of connection with the information age.

Paragraph Concepts

The word **paragraph** has a special meaning in Word. A paragraph is any text, graphics or other objects that are followed by a paragraph mark ¶. You can change the appearance and behavior of paragraphs by formatting them. For example, you can change the line spacing and indents as shown on the previous page.

Paragraph formats are copied to new paragraphs when Enter is tapped

Word copies the current paragraph's formats to the new paragraph that is created when you tap Enter. This is convenient because you can format one paragraph and the formatting is applied to new paragraphs as you type them.

Paragraphs must be selected before you can format them

You can rapidly format one or more existing paragraphs by first selecting them. Word applies the same formats to all paragraphs in a selection. You can format a single paragraph by positioning the insertion point anywhere within the paragraph. Positioning the insertion point within a single paragraph is equivalent to selecting it. The following illustrations discuss these concepts.

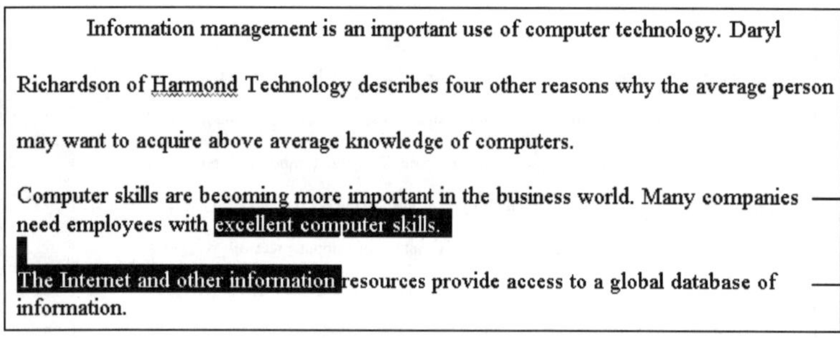

Information management is an important use of computer technology. Daryl Richardson of Harmond Technology describes four other reasons why the average person may want to acquire above average knowledge of computers.

Computer skills are becoming more important in the business world. Many companies need employees with excellent computer skills.

The Internet and other information resources provide access to a global database of information.

These paragraphs are partially selected, so they are the only paragraphs that will be affected by paragraph format commands. You only need to select part of a paragraph prior to formatting it.

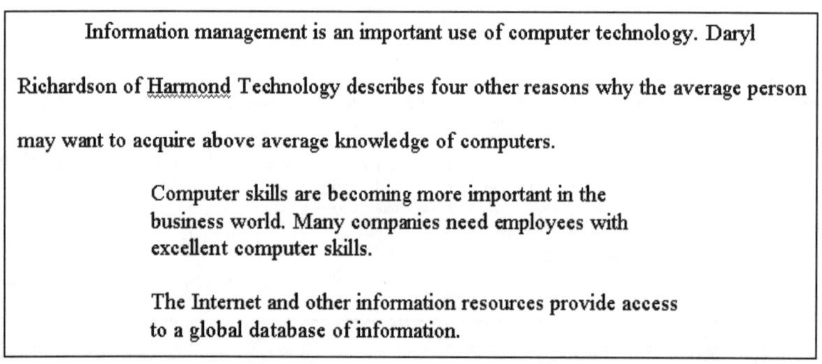

Information management is an important use of computer technology. Daryl Richardson of Harmond Technology describes four other reasons why the average person may want to acquire above average knowledge of computers.

Computer skills are becoming more important in the business world. Many companies need employees with excellent computer skills.

The Internet and other information resources provide access to a global database of information.

The Indent command was issued, so only the selected paragraphs were indented.

Aligning Text

Word makes it easy to align paragraphs horizontally. Text can be left or right aligned, centered or justified. The default setting is for left alignment. The following illustrations show the paragraph alignment options. Take a few moments to read the text in the illustrations as it provides details on the alignment options.

> *This text is* **center aligned.**
> *Notice that each line is centered horizontally.*
> *This option is often used on titles.*

Center alignment

> *This text is* **right aligned.**
> *Each line is flush with the right margin.*
> *This is often referred to as flush right.*

Right alignment

> *This is an example of* **left alignment.** *Notice how each line is aligned with the left margin. Also, notice the text is not aligned with the right margin. Left alignment is the default in Word.*

Left alignment

> *This text is* **justified.** *Each line (except the last one) is flush with both the left and right margins. Justified text may create large gaps between words when used with short lines (such as those created by narrow columns).*

Justified

Paragraph formats affect the entire paragraph

The entire paragraph is formatted when you issue a paragraph formatting command. For this reason, you cannot mix alignments such as left, center and right on the same line unless you use a feature such as tables. You will learn how to work with tables later in this book.

Hands-On 6.1 – Center align a title

In this exercise, you will center a report title and experiment with the paragraph alignment options.

1. Open a New document.
2. **Tap** Enter **six** times.

   Look at the Status bar and notice the ***At 1.9"*** *indicator. This shows that the insertion point is 1.9" from the top of the page. Report titles are positioned about 2" down from the top of the page.*
3. Look at the Formatting toolbar and the Align Left button should be depressed.

   Left alignment is usually the default setting in Word.
4. **Click** the Center button.

   Notice the button becomes depressed and the insertion point moves to the center of the line.
5. Set the font to **Arial Bold 12.**
6. Turn on CapsLock by **tapping** the **CapsLock** key.
7. Type **COMPUTER TECHNOLOGY IN THE 21ST CENTURY** and **tap** Enter.

   Word's AutoCorrect feature should convert the ST in 21st to a superscript format. Also, notice that center alignment is still in effect. This is because paragraph formats (center alignment) are copied to the next paragraph when Enter is tapped.

Continued...

8. **Click** the Align Left button.

9. **Turn off CapsLock** and then **tap** Enter **three** more times.
   You should quadruple space after report titles.

Experiment with the alignment options

10. **Click** anywhere on the **title** that you just created.

11. Try clicking the Left, Center and Right alignment buttons.
    The entire paragraph will move to the left, center or right. Paragraph formats (such as alignment) affect the entire paragraph.

12. Change the alignment back to **center**.

13. Now move the insertion point down to the last blank line you just created.

14. Save the document as **Hands-On Lesson 6** and continue with the next topic.

Line Spacing

Line spacing determines the amount of vertical space between lines in a paragraph. The default line spacing is single. Word lets you set double-spacing and several other options including multiple spacing. Multiple spacing lets you precisely control the line spacing by setting multiples such as 1.3 or 2.4.

Line spacing is measured in points

Word measures line spacing in points where one point is equal to 1/72". Word makes a single spaced line slightly larger than the largest character in the line. For example, if you are using a 12-point font, then single line spacing is slightly larger than 12 points.

Quick Steps: ***Line Spacing***	
To set line spacing	
Paragraph dialog box method	***Shortcut keystroke method***
• *Select the desired paragraphs.* • *Choose Format→Paragraph and set the desired line spacing.*	• *Select the desired paragraphs.* • *Press Ctrl + 1 to set single spacing, Ctrl + 5 for 1.5 spacing or Ctrl + 2 for double spacing.*

Hands-On 6.2 – Change line spacing

In this exercise, you will change the line spacing to double and you will type two paragraphs.

Set the spacing

1. Make sure the insertion point is on the 3rd blank line below the title.

2. Set the font to **Times New Roman 12** and **turn off** bold.

3. Choose **Format→Paragraph...** from the menu bar.

Continued...

4. Notice the Line Spacing section of the dialog box.

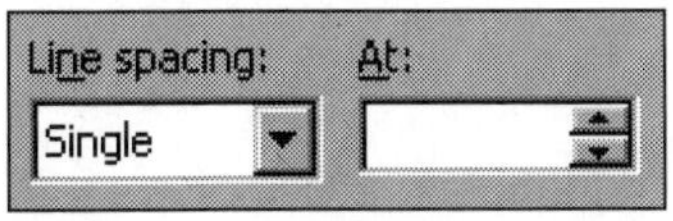

5. **Click** the Line spacing drop-down button and notice the various options.

6. Choose **Double** from the list and **click OK**.

7. **Tap** the Tab key once to create a ½" indent at the start of the paragraph.

8. Now type the following paragraph but only tap Enter after the last line in the paragraph.
   The lines will be double-spaced as you type them.

> Our society has changed from a manufacturing oriented society to an information society. Those with access to capital had power in the early 1900's. In the 21st century, however, power will come from access to information. The amount of worldwide information is growing at a rapid pace. Computer technology is responsible for much of this growth but it can also help us manage the information.

9. Make sure you tap Enter after the last line, then **tap** Tab once and type the following paragraph.
   Notice the double spacing has been carried to the new paragraph.

> Information management is an important use of computer technology. Daryl Richardson of Harmond Technology describes four other reasons why the average person may want to acquire above average knowledge of computers.

Set the line spacing to single

10. Make sure the insertion point is at the end of the paragraph you just typed and tap Enter.

11. Choose **Format→Paragraph...** from the menu bar and set the line spacing to **single**.

12. Now type the paragraphs on the following page. Make sure you **tap Enter twice between paragraphs**. There is no need to use the Tab key at the start of these paragraphs.

Continued...

Computer skills are becoming more important in the business world. Many companies need employees with excellent computer skills.

The Internet and other information resources provide access to a global database of information.

Computer skills can often simplify one's personal life. Computers can be used for entertainment, to manage finances and to provide a stimulating learning tool for children.

Using computers can provide a sense of accomplishment. Many people suffer from "computerphobia." Learning to use computers often creates a feeling of connection with the information age.

13. Save the changes to your document and continue with the next topic.

The Select All Command

You can rapidly select an entire document by triple clicking in the left margin area or by choosing Edit→Select All from the menu bar. This can be convenient if you are trying to format an entire document.

Hands-On 6.3 – Change the alignment of all paragraphs

In this exercise, you will experiment with the alignment options.

1. Choose **Edit→Select All** from the menu bar.
2. **Click** the Justify button on the Formatting toolbar.
3. **Scroll** through the document and notice that all paragraphs are now flush with both the left and right margins.
4. Now **Scroll** to the top of the document and **click** anywhere **on the title**.
5. **Click** the Center button to re-center the title.
6. Now continue with the next topic.

Indenting Paragraphs

Indenting creates space between text and the left and right margins. The **left** and **right indents** are the most widely used types of indent. These indents move paragraphs in from the left or right margins. This lets you set text off from the margins as shown in the following illustration.

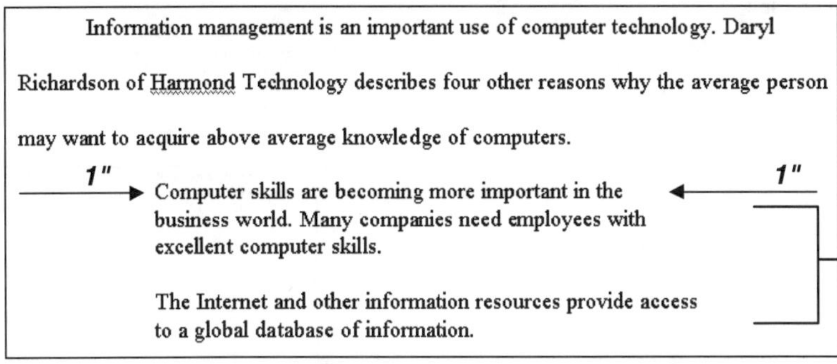

These paragraphs are indented 1" from the left and right margins.

You can set left indents with the Formatting toolbar

The Increase Indent and Decrease Indent buttons on the Formatting toolbar make it easy to change the left indent. These buttons increase or decrease the left indent to the nearest tab stop. The default tab stops are set every ½", so the indent changes ½" each time you click the buttons.

Hands-On 6.4 – Experiment with left indents

Indent one paragraph

1. **Click** on one of the single spaced paragraphs you just typed.
2. **Click** the Increase Indent button near the right end of the Formatting toolbar.
   The paragraph should be indented 1/2" on the left.
3. **Click** the Decrease Indent button to remove the indent.

Indent several paragraphs

4. Use the mouse to select any portion of two or more paragraphs.
5. **Click** Increase Indent twice to create a 1" left indent on each of the selected paragraphs.
6. Now **click** Decrease Indent twice to remove the indents.
   Leave the document open because you will continue to use it.

The Horizontal Ruler

You can set indents, margins and tab stops by dragging markers on the horizontal ruler. This is convenient because you can see the result as you make changes. The horizontal ruler is positioned just below the toolbars. You can display or hide the ruler with the **View→Ruler** command. The following illustration shows the ruler and the various indent markers.

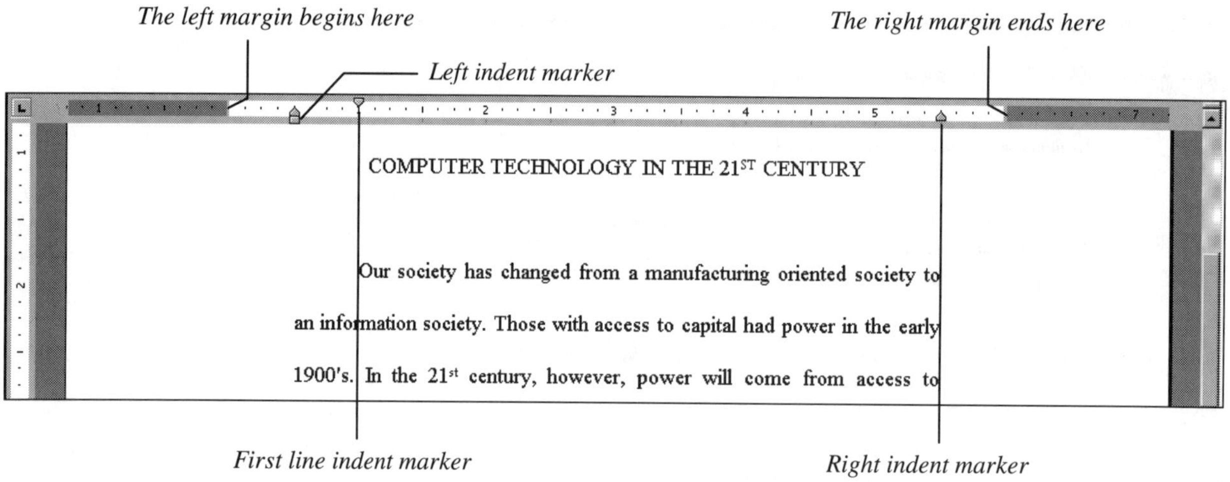

Hands-On 6.5 – Display the horizontal ruler

1. If necessary, use the **View→Page Layout** command to switch to Page Layout view.
2. If necessary, use the **View→Ruler** command to display the horizontal ruler.
3. Use the Zoom Control on the Standard toolbar to zoom to **Whole Page**.
   Notice the ruler shrinks to fit the new zoom percentage.
4. Zoom back to **Page Width**.
5. Notice the indent markers on the ruler.
   Your markers will be in different positions from those shown in the illustration above. You will use these markers in the next exercise.

Indenting Paragraphs with the Ruler

You can indent selected paragraphs by dragging the indent markers on the ruler. Paragraphs can be indented on the left, right or both sides. You can also indent just the first line of paragraphs. This is similar to using a Tab at the start of a paragraph, however, first-line indents let you indent a precise distance. Another advantage in using first-line indents is you can indent several paragraphs at once. Indent markers are discussed in the following table.

You can set...	By dragging the following marker
First-line indents	
Hanging indents	← Top triangle
Left indents	← Bottom square
Right indents	(On the right end of the ruler)

Hands-On 6.6 – Set indents with the ruler

Set left and right indents for the single spaced paragraphs

1. **Scroll down** until the four single spaced paragraphs at the bottom of your document are visible.
2. Select all four paragraphs by dragging the mouse pointer in the left margin. The selection should match the following example.

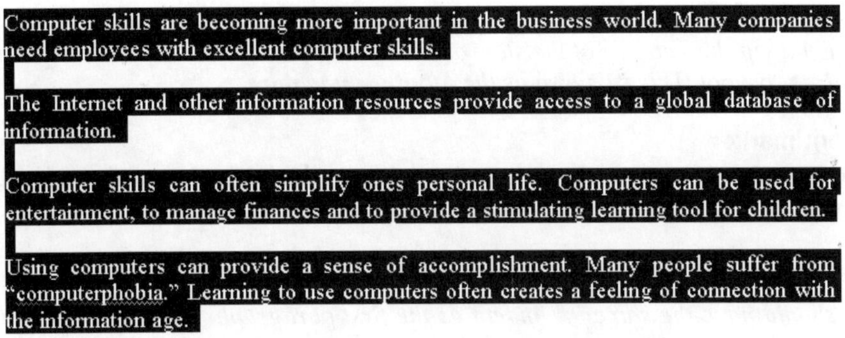
Computer skills are becoming more important in the business world. Many companies need employees with excellent computer skills.

The Internet and other information resources provide access to a global database of information.

Computer skills can often simplify ones personal life. Computers can be used for entertainment, to manage finances and to provide a stimulating learning tool for children.

Using computers can provide a sense of accomplishment. Many people suffer from "computerphobia." Learning to use computers often creates a feeling of connection with the information age.

3. Use the following steps to adjust the left and right indents.

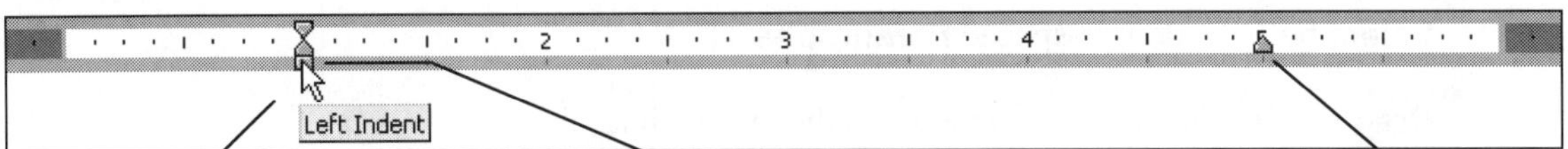

❶ *Position the pointer on the Left Indent marker (the bottom box). A yellow Left Indent tip will appear as shown here.*

❷ *Drag the marker from the margin to the 1" position as shown here. Both triangles should move with the box.* ***Use Undo if you make a mistake.***

❸ ***Drag** the **Right Indent** marker from the right margin to the **5"** position.*

The paragraphs should now be indented 1" on both sides.

Hands-On 6.7 – Convert tab stops to first-line indents

In this exercise, you will remove the tabs from the two paragraphs at the top of the document. Then you will use first-line indents to indent the first line of each paragraph.

1. **Scroll** to the top of the document.
2. If necessary, click the Show/Hide ¶ button to display the symbols.

   In the next step, you are instructed to remove the tab → symbol from the start of the first paragraph. You should have inserted the tab when you created the paragraph. It is possible that your paragraph will not have a tab → symbol (even if it is indented). Skip the next step if there is no tab → symbol.

3. Use the following steps to remove the tab symbol at the start of the first main paragraph.

   ❶ ***Click*** *to the left of the tab symbol.* → Our·society·has·chang

   society.·Those·with·access·to·

   ❷ ***Tap*** *the* ***Delete*** *key.*

   The space created by the tab should be removed from the first line.

Use the Tab key to create a first-line indent

4. Make sure the insertion point is at the start of the paragraph and **tap** the (Tab) key.

   The first line will be indented ½" although you won't see a tab → symbol. The first-line indent marker should have moved to the ½" position on the ruler. Word 97 automatically creates a first-line indent when you tap the Tab key at the start of an ***existing*** *paragraph. This has the same effect as inserting a tab → symbol. This is known as the AutoIndent feature.*

Drag a first-line indent marker

5. Use the technique in step 3 to remove the tab → symbol from the beginning of the second double-spaced paragraph.
6. Now drag the first-line indent marker (the top triangle) to the ½" position on the ruler.

   The paragraph should have the same ½" indent as the first paragraph. As you can see, there are several ways to indent the first line of a paragraph.

Adjust the first-line indents

7. **Select** both the double-spaced **paragraphs**.
8. **Drag** the first-line indent marker to the left or right.

   The first-line indent of both paragraphs will be adjusted.

Adjust the left indent

9. Make sure the paragraphs are still selected and **drag** the **left** (bottom square) indent marker.

   Both the hanging indent and first-line indent markers will move together. The hanging indent affects all lines in the paragraph except for the first line. The left indent affects all lines in the paragraph because it moves both the first-line indent marker and the hanging indent marker.

10. Feel free to experiment with indents, then **close** the document and **save** the changes.

Concepts Review

True / False

1.	Paragraph formats are carried to the next paragraph whenever Enter is tapped.	1. **T F**
2.	You must select all text in a paragraph in order to apply paragraph formats to the paragraph.	2. **T F**
3.	The Increase Indent button changes the right indent.	3. **T F**
4.	The Decrease Indent button changes the right indent.	4. **T F**
5.	Paragraphs can be indented by using the ruler bar.	5. **T F**
6.	The Ctrl + 2 keystroke combination can be used to set double-spacing.	6. **T F**
7.	The Ruler bar is displayed with the Edit→Ruler command.	7. **T F**
8.	Paragraph formats can be applied to part of a paragraph (not the entire paragraph).	8. **T F**
9.	First-line indents only affect the first line of each selected paragraph.	9. **T F**
10.	The title begins 2” from the top of the page in a traditional report style.	10. **T F**

Multiple Choice

1. Which of the following statements most accurately describes paragraph formats?
   a) Paragraph formats affect the entire paragraph.
   b) Paragraph formats are carried to the next paragraph when Enter is tapped.
   c) Paragraph formats can be applied to several paragraphs with one command.
   d) All of the above. ( )

2. What will happen if you tap the Tab key at the beginning of an existing paragraph?
   a) The left indent will increase.
   b) The first-line indent will increase.
   c) A tab symbol will be inserted.
   d) None of the above. ( )

3. Which of the following line space settings can be used?
   a) 1.3
   b) 1.8
   c) 2.0
   d) All of the above. ( )

4. Which of the following actions should you take if you want to adjust the right indent of three paragraphs?
   a) Drag the right indent marker.
   b) Select the paragraphs and then drag the right indent marker.
   c) Select the paragraphs and tap the Tab key.
   d) All of the above. ( )

5. Which of the following techniques can be used to adjust the right indent of a selected paragraph?
   a) Click the Increase Indent button.
   b) Click the Decrease Indent button.
   c) Drag the Right-indent marker on the Ruler.
   d) All of the above. ( )

Skills Builder 6.1

In this exercise, you will use indented paragraphs to create the document shown below.

Create the title and main paragraph

1. Start a new document, **click** the Center button and set the font to **Arial 14 Bold**.
2. Type the title shown below and then set the font to **Arial 11** (no bold).
3. **Tap** Enter **four times** and then change the alignment to Align Left.
4. **Press and hold** the Ctrl key and **tap** the number **2**.

   This shortcut keystroke will turn on double-spacing. You may want to remember this keystroke if you use double-spacing often. This shortcut is listed in the quick reference guide of this book.

5. Type the double-spaced paragraph shown below and **tap** Enter **once** at the end of the paragraph.

Use the Paragraph dialog box

6. Choose **Format→Paragraph...** from the menu bar.
7. Set the line spacing to **single**, the left and right indents to **1"** and **click OK**.

   The Paragraph dialog box is useful if you are trying to set several options or when you want to precisely adjust line spacing, indents and other options.

8. **Click** the Italics button and type the three quotations shown below.

   Double-space between quotations by tapping Enter twice and use bold to emphasize the author's names. The single spacing and indents will be carried to each new paragraph as you type.

Famous American Quotes

Quotations have the power to inspire and define moments in our history. They are a window into the minds and lives of great people. Famous Americans certainly have contributed their share of famous quotes.

There was never yet an uninteresting life. Such a thing is an impossibility. Inside of the dullest exterior, there is a drama, a comedy, and a tragedy. - ***Mark Twain***

We hold these truths to be sacred and undeniable; that all men are created equal and independent, that from that equal creation they derive rights inherent and inalienable, among which are the preservation of life, and liberty, and the pursuit of happiness. - ***Thomas Jefferson***

I think, at a child's birth, if a mother could ask a fairy godmother to endow it with the most useful gift, that gift would be curiosity. - ***Eleanor Roosevelt***

9. **Close** the document and **save** it as **Skills Builder 6.1**.

Skills Builder 6.2

In this exercise, you will open a report on your exercise diskette. You will adjust the line spacing and indents for the entire document.

Adjust the first-line indent and line spacing

1. **Open** the document named **Skills Builder 6.2**.
2. Use the Zoom Control [88%] to switch to a **Whole Page** zoom.
3. Select the entire document by **triple-clicking** in the left margin or choosing **Edit→Select All**.
4. **Drag** the First Line Indent marker on the ruler to the **.5"** position.

   This will indent the first line of all paragraphs by ½" (including the title).
5. Set the line spacing to **double**.

Format the title and credit line

6. Use the Enter key to push the title down to approximately the 2" position.
7. Center align the title.

   Look at the ruler bar and you will notice that the first-line indent marker is at the ½" position. This will cause the title to be slightly off center.
8. Set the first-line indent for the title paragraph to zero.
9. Format the title as **Arial Bold 14**.
10. **Click** on the **credit line** at the bottom of the document (the line that reads, Taken from *The Forest People* – Colin M. Turnbull).
11. Set the first-line indent to zero.
12. Right align the paragraph.

    The paragraph should be flush with the right margin.
13. **Close** the document and **save** the changes.

Skills Builder 6.3

Not all reports require the strict formality that you have used thus far in this lesson. In this exercise, you will use the multiple line spacing option to set a line spacing of 1.3 and create the document shown below. The multiple line spacing option lets you precisely control line spacing.

1. Create the document shown below. **Don't** format the text with fonts, line spacing or indents at this point. However, **do** double-space between paragraphs and center align paragraphs as shown. Also, triple-space after the date and after the first body paragraph.
2. Now format the text with whichever fonts and sizes you desire.
3. Select all paragraphs from the body paragraph below the date to the end of the document.
4. Choose **Format→Paragraph...** and set the line spacing to a **multiple** of **1.3** as shown below.

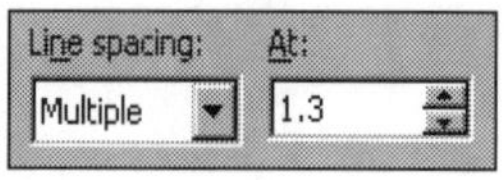

5. Select the last three paragraphs (the paragraphs with information on the cast members). Set the left indent of these paragraphs to ½" using either the ruler or the Paragraph dialog box.
6. You completed document should closely match the document shown below.

The West Coast Playhouse

Presents

An Evening with Mabel

Today's Date

This fabulous play has been entertaining audiences since its opening night on March 1, 1993. The cast is first class and the ambience is magical. You will find this play delightfully humorous and deeply moving. Please enjoy this wonderful performance.

The Cast

Rebecca Thomas – Rebecca is a graduate of the Smithton School of Dramatic Arts. Rebecca has played lead roles in 17 theatrical productions. She has also appeared on Saturday Night Live and other television productions.

Jim Oliver – Jim is a recent graduate with a major in drama. Jim was voted the best overall actor in his graduating class and he has won numerous other awards. We are confident that you will find Jim's performance truly memorable.

Clara Boyd – Clara recently moved here from London, England where she specialized in Shakespearean theatrical performances. Clara is also a world-class pianist.

7. **Close** the document and **save** it as **Skills Builder 6.3**.

Assessment 6.1

1. **Open** the document named **Assessment 6.1**.
2. Format the document until it matches the document shown on the following page. The required formatting changes are shown in the illustration below.
3. **Print** the document.
4. **Close** the document and **save** the changes.

Center and Bold Tap Enter four times after

```
Reinforcers vs. Rewards and Punishments
```

Double space these paragraphs and set first-line indents to .5"

```
Rewards, like reinforcers, are stimuli that increase the frequency
of behavior. However, rewards are also considered pleasant events.
Skinner preferred the concept of reinforcement to that of reward
because reinforcement does not suggest trying to "get inside the
head" of an organism (person or lower animal) to guess what it would
find pleasant or unpleasant.
Punishments are aversive events that suppress or decrease the
frequency of the behavior they follow. Punishment can rapidly
suppress undesirable behavior and may be warranted in emergencies
such as when a child tries to run out into the street. But many
learning theorists agree that punishment is usually undesirable,
especially in rearing children, for reasons such as the following:
```

Single space but use Enter to double space between and set left and right Indents to 1"

```
Punishment does not in and of itself suggest an alternative,
acceptable form of behavior.
Punishment can create anger and hostility. Adequate punishment will
almost always suppress unwanted behavior-but at what cost? A child
may express accumulated feelings of hostility against other
children.
Punishment may overgeneralize. The child who is punished severely
for bad table manners may stop eating altogether. Overgeneralization
is more likely to occur when children do not know exactly why they
are being punished and when they have not been shown alternative,
acceptable behaviors.
```

Double space First-line Indent .5"

```
It is usually preferable to focus on rewarding children for
desirable behavior than to punish them for unwanted behavior. By
ignoring their misbehavior, or by using time out from positive
reinforcement, we can consistently avoid reinforcing misbehavior.
```

Reinforcers vs. Rewards and Punishments

Rewards, like reinforcers, are stimuli that increase the frequency of behavior. However, rewards are also considered pleasant events. Skinner preferred the concept of reinforcement to that of reward because reinforcement does not suggest trying to "get inside the head" of an organism (person or lower animal) to guess what it would find pleasant or unpleasant.

Punishments are aversive events that suppress or decrease the frequency of the behavior they follow. Punishment can rapidly suppress undesirable behavior and may be warranted in emergencies such as when a child tries to run out into the street. But many learning theorists agree that punishment is usually undesirable, especially in rearing children, for reasons such as the following:

> Punishment does not in and of itself suggest an alternative, acceptable form of behavior.
>
> Punishment can create anger and hostility. Adequate punishment will almost always suppress unwanted behavior-but at what cost? A child may express accumulated feelings of hostility against other children.
>
> Punishment may overgeneralize. The child who is punished severely for bad table manners may stop eating altogether. Overgeneralization is more likely to occur when children do not know exactly why they are being punished and when they have not been shown alternative, acceptable behaviors.

It is usually preferable to focus on rewarding children for desirable behavior than to punish them for unwanted behavior. By ignoring their misbehavior, or by using time out from positive reinforcement, we can avoid reinforcing misbehavior.

7 Introduction to Desktop Publishing

Objectives:

- Work with Drawing Objects
- Use WordArt
- Move object anchors
- Create drop caps
- Insert and format clip art
- Use AutoShapes
- Use text boxes
- Format drawing objects
- Use paragraph spacing
- Create page borders

The Project – Creating a Flyer

In this lesson, you will receive an introduction to desktop publishing using Word 97. Desktop publishing is the process of creating graphic designs using desktop computers. Word 97 makes desktop publishing fun and easy. Everyone from beginners to advanced users will find something exciting in Word 97. You will create the flyer shown below as you progress through this lesson. You will use many exciting graphic design tools including TextArt, AutoShapes, drop caps and text boxes.

Drawing Objects

Office 97 has an excellent set of drawing tools that let you create lines, arrows, rectangles, callouts, WordArt and many other objects. These objects are easy-to-use and a lot of fun! The drawing objects are particularly useful for creating flyers and other types of graphic documents.

Working with drawing objects

You create drawing objects by choosing the desired object from the Drawing toolbar and then dragging the mouse in the document. Drawing objects can also be edited and formatted after they have been created.

Hands-On 7.1 – Use WordArt

In this exercise, you will use WordArt. WordArt lets you create stylized text in a variety of shapes, colors and formats.

Insert a WordArt object

1. Locate the Drawing button on the Standard toolbar. This button displays or hides the Drawing toolbar that is shown below. The Drawing toolbar is usually docked at the bottom of the screen. If necessary, click the Drawing button to display the Drawing toolbar. The following illustration discusses the layout of the Drawing toolbar.

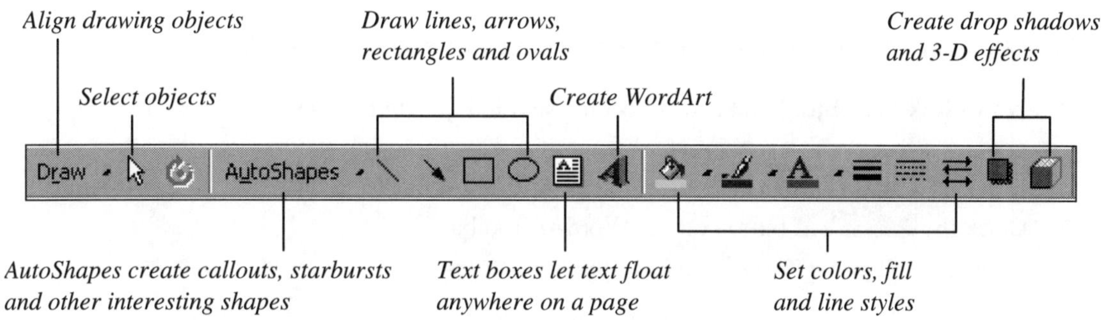

2. **Click** the WordArt button on the Drawing toolbar.
   The WordArt Gallery dialog box appears.
3. Choose a WordArt style (the project in this lesson uses the style in the fourth-column, fourth-row) and **click OK**.
   The Edit WordArt Text dialog box appears. This box lets you type and format the WordArt text.
4. **Type** the phrase **Shop Till You Drop**.
5. Feel free to choose a typeface (the project in this lesson uses Impact) and **click OK**.
   The WordArt object is inserted in your document and the WordArt toolbar appears. Be aware that your WordArt text may look different from the example in this book if you changed the typeface.

Continued...

Size and position the WordArt object

You can edit drawing objects in a variety of ways. In the next few steps, you will change the size and position of the WordArt object. Notice the object has sizing handles (small squares) on its edges. You change the size of objects by dragging the sizing handles. Sizing handles appear whenever an object is selected (as your WordArt object is now). You select an unselected object by clicking it once. Once a WordArt object is selected, you can change the object with the buttons on the WordArt toolbar.

6. Use the following steps to position and size the object.

❶ ***Widen** the **object** slightly by **dragging** a side-sizing handle.*

❷ *Position the mouse pointer on the object and drag it to the top of the document as shown here. Position the object about 2" from the top and center it horizontally. Use the horizontal ruler to help you align the object horizontally.*

7. Click anywhere **outside of the object** and it will become deselected.

8. Now **click the object** and it will become selected (sizing handles will appear).

Edit the object

9. Click the Edit Text... button on the WordArt toolbar.

The Edit WordArt Text dialog box appears.

10. Click to the right of the phrase Shop Till You Drop and type an exclamation point **!**.

The completed phrase should now read Shop Till You Drop!.

11. Click OK to complete the change.

12. Experiment with the buttons on the WordArt toolbar.

The object must be selected (with sizing handles) in order to edit it. Don't be afraid to make mistakes. Use UnDo if you make a mistake or wish to reverse an action.

13. Save the document as **Hands-On Lesson 7** and continue with the next topic.

Object Anchors

Objects are designed to "float over the text" in a document. This allows you to superimpose objects on top of text. However, every object is **anchored** to a paragraph. Objects move with the paragraph they are anchored to. As the document changes, the object retains the same position relative to the paragraph to which it is anchored. You can always move an object by dragging it to a new location. An object will anchor itself to a different paragraph whenever it is moved.

Hands-On 7.2 – Move the object and change the anchor

In this exercise, you will change the paragraph that the WordArt object is anchored to.

Display the anchor symbol

1. **Click** anywhere **outside** the WordArt **object** to deselect it.

   The insertion point will be positioned at the top of the document.

2. **Tap** Enter **four** times.

   The object should move down each time you tap Enter. This is because it was anchored to the first paragraph mark which has now been pushed down four times.

3. **Click** the Show/Hide ¶ button on the Standard toolbar.

4. **Click** once on **the object** to select it and an anchor symbol will appear to the left of the last paragraph mark.

   The object is anchored to that paragraph.

Move the object and change the anchor position

5. **Drag** the object **up** until the anchor is positioned to the left of the first paragraph mark.

   Now the object will move only when the first paragraph mark moves. In a moment, you will add additional paragraphs to the bottom of the document and the object will not move. Keep in mind that you normally do not have to be concerned with anchors. The purpose of this exercise is to help you understand what is going on "behind the scenes". When working with documents, you can move an object without being concerned about the anchor.

6. Now **click** the insertion point in front of the **last paragraph mark**.

7. **Tap** Enter **four** more times and continue with the next topic.

Drop Caps

Word's Drop Caps feature lets you easily create large drop-down capitals at the beginning of paragraphs. You create drop caps with the **Format→Drop Cap** command.

Hands-On 7.3 – Create a drop cap

Create the drop cap

1. Change the font **Bookman Old Style 16**.
2. Type the following paragraph.

> Jane's Designer Headwear is having a sale. Stop by our Marina store from 9:00 – 5:00, July 16 for incredible savings on designer headwear. All headwear will be reduced by at least 50%. Don't miss this once per year opportunity. Our Marina store is located at 455 Beach Drive in Ocean City.

3. Make sure the insertion point is positioned somewhere in the paragraph.
   The insertion point can be positioned anywhere in the paragraph when creating a drop cap.
4. Choose **Format→Drop Cap...** from the menu bar.
5. Take a few moments to study the dialog box options but do not change them.
6. Choose the Dropped  style and **click OK**.
   Notice the drop cap has a border surrounding it and sizing handles.
7. **Click** anywhere in the paragraph and the drop cap border will disappear.

Remove and restore the drop cap

8. Choose **Format→Drop Cap...** from the menu bar.
9. **Choose** the **None** option and **click OK**.
   As you can see, removing a drop cap is just as easy as creating it.
10. **Click** Undo  to restore the drop cap and continue with the next topic.

Using Clip Art

Word 97 lets you insert clip art anywhere in a document. You can use clip art that is provided with Office 97 or you can insert your own clip art (such as a company logo). Clip art is inserted with the **Insert→Picture** command.

Microsoft Office Clip Gallery

Microsoft provides a number of clip art objects with Office 97. These clip art objects are installed as part of Office 97. All Office 97 programs (including Word) can use the clip art. Office 97 also has a Clip Gallery that helps you manage the clip art and other graphics on your system. You will use the Clip Gallery to insert clip art in the following exercise.

Hands-On 7.4 – Insert clip art

Turn to the front of this lesson and notice the clip art object of the "man with many hats" at the bottom of the document. You will insert this object in the following steps.

1. **Position** the insertion point at the end of the large paragraph and **tap** Enter once.

   When you insert the clip art in the next step, it will be anchored to the new paragraph.

2. Choose **Insert→Picture...** from the menu bar.

   Notice the Clip Art and From File options. The Clip Art option displays the Clip Gallery dialog box. The Clip Gallery is a convenient way to organize and manage your clip art. The From File option lets you insert pictures that are located on any disk drive on your system.

3. Choose **Clip Art...** and use the following steps to insert an image.

➊ *Notice the dialog box tabs. The Clip Gallery lets you organize clip art, pictures (such as scanned in pictures), sound and video. You can use any of these elements in Office 97 documents. Make sure the Clip Art tab is chosen.*

➋ *Notice the clip art is organized in categories.* ***Choose*** *the* ***All Categories*** *option to see all clip art.*

➌ ***Scroll*** *down the clip art list and* ***choose*** *the* ***man with hats*** *image. (Choose another image if the man with hats is not available.)*

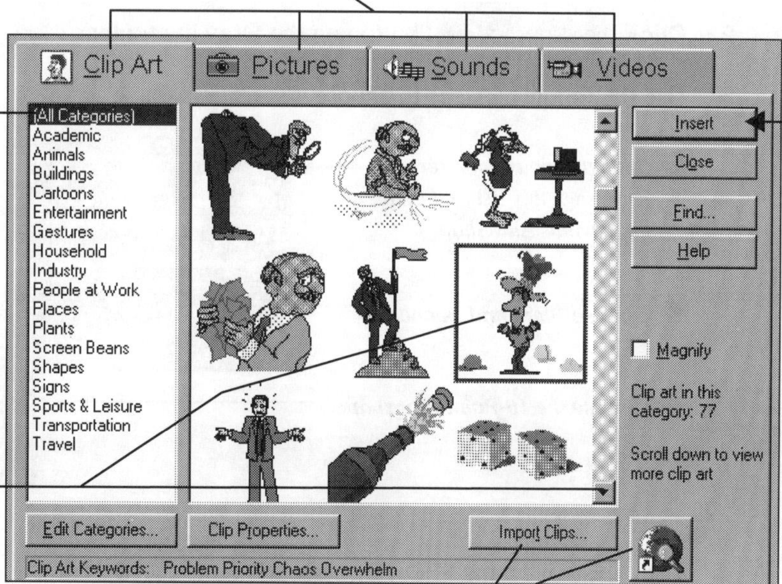

These buttons let you add clips to the gallery. The Connect to Web button sends you to a page on Microsoft's World Wide Web site. You can download clip art from Microsoft's Web site into the gallery. You must have an Internet connection and a Web browser to use this feature.

➍ ***Click*** *the* ***Insert*** *button.*

Continued...

Word will insert the picture and the Picture toolbar will appear. If the picture toolbar didn't appear, then you can display it with the View→Toolbars command.

Change the zoom percentage and move the picture

Notice the picture has sizing handles (small squares) on its edges. You change the size of pictures by dragging the sizing handles. This is the same technique you used to change the size of the WordArt object. You can also move pictures by dragging them to the desired location.

4. Use the **Zoom Control** to switch to a **whole page** zoom.

   You will need to switch zoom percentages often when doing desktop publishing. In this situation, you will need to see the whole page so that you can position the picture in the correct location.

5. **Drag** the picture **down** towards the bottom center of the page.

   Check the project page at the start of this lesson for the correct position.

6. **Click** on the **blank line** below the main paragraph and continue with the next topic.

AutoShapes

AutoShapes are a new feature in Office 97. AutoShapes include a variety of fun shapes to enhance the appearance of your documents. The shapes include starbursts, callouts, banners and more.

Hands-On 7.5 – Create AutoShapes

In this exercise, you will create starburst and cloud AutoShapes. The Zoom Control should still be set to Whole Page.

1. Make sure the insertion point is positioned on the blank line below the large paragraph.

2. **Click** the AutoShapes button on the Drawing toolbar.

3. Use the following steps to choose a starburst shape.

❶ ***Slide*** *the mouse pointer up-and-down this list and notice the various AutoShapes.*

❷ ***Choose Stars and Banners.***

❸ ***Choose*** *the* ***16-Point Star*** *shape.*

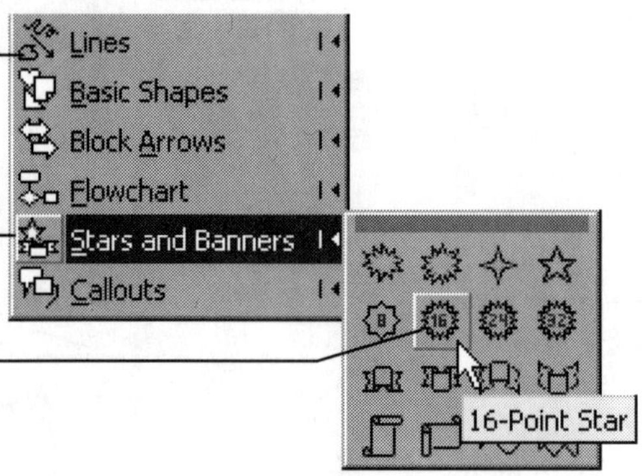

4. Use the steps on the following page to create the starburst.

Continued...

❶ *Position the mouse pointer here and* **drag up to the right** *until the starburst has approximately this shape and size.*

❷ **Release** *the mouse button and the starburst will be created. You will add text to the starburst later.*

Use the following steps to create a callout

5. **Click** the AutoShapes button and **choose Callouts**.
6. Choose the Cloud Callout shape (fourth button on the top row).
7. Use the following step to create the callout.

   Use Undo if you make any major mistakes. Don't be concerned if your callout is slightly different from the example shown here. You will learn how to format the callout in the following topics.

❶ *Position the mouse pointer here and* **drag up to the right** *until the callout has approximately this shape and size.*

Continued...

Add text to the callout and then format the text

One of the benefits of callouts is you can type text directly in the callout. Other AutoShapes, such as the starburst you created earlier, lack this ability.

8. Set the Zoom Control to **Page Width**.
9. If necessary, scroll down until the callout is visible.
10. **Click inside** the callout **cloud** and type the phrase **I'll Take**.
11. **Tap** Enter and then type the phrase **All of Them**.
12. **Select** both of the paragraphs that you just typed.
13. Set the font to **Bookman Old Style 16** and add color to the text with the Font Color button.
    Choose another font if Bookman is not available and use any color you desire.
14. Now Center Align the paragraphs.
15. **Click** anywhere **outside the callout** and it should closely match the following example.

Change the position, size, fill and line color

16. Use the following steps to format the callout.

❶ ***Click anywhere** on the callout, and then **click any edge**. The pattern on the edge will change to indicate the callout is selected. (You must click an edge before you can size, move and format callouts.)*

❷ *Use the Fill Color button on the Drawing toolbar to add a fill (background) color. Use the Line Color button to add the same line color that you used for the text inside the callout.*

❸ ***Drag** any sizing handle to change the size.*

❹ ***Drag** any edge to move the callout.*

❺ ***Drag** the yellow anchor point to change the anchor position.*

17. Save the changes and continue with the next topic.

Text Boxes

Text boxes are one of the most important drawing objects. Text boxes let you position text anywhere on a page. You can use text boxes to superimpose text on top of other text or on top of pictures and other types of graphics.

Hands-On 7.6 – Create a text box

In this exercise, you will use a text box to superimpose the phrase Designer Brands over the starburst that you created earlier in this lesson.

1. If necessary, scroll up until the starburst is visible.
2. **Click** the Text Box button on the Drawing toolbar.
3. Use the following step to create the text box.

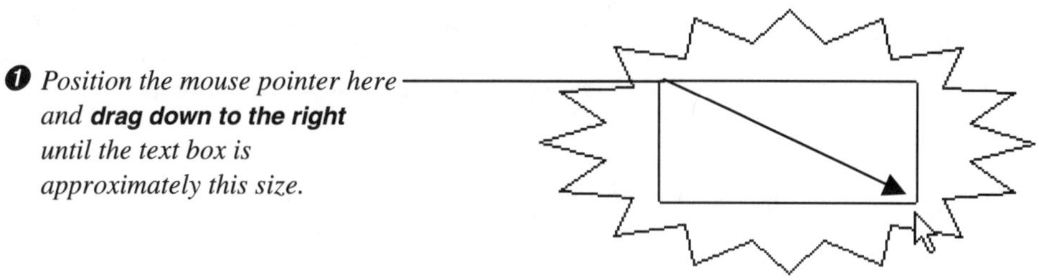

4. **Type** the word **Designer** in the text box and then tap Enter.
5. **Type** the word **Brands**.
6. **Select** both of the paragraphs that you just typed.
7. Set the font to **Arial Bold 14.**
8. If necessary, adjust the width and/or height of the text box and starburst.
   The text should fit in the box without wrapping and the text box should fit inside of the starburst.
9. Select the text in the text box and use the Font Color button to add color to it.
   You should be able to apply the same color that you used for the callout by clicking the face of the button. This is because the last color used is displayed on the face of the button.
10. Now Center Align the paragraphs.
11. **Click** anywhere **outside the textbox**.
    The text box and starburst should closely match the following example. However, your text box may not have a border surrounding it. It may also have a fill pattern. You will adjust these options soon.

Formatting Drawing Objects

You have already formatted the callout in a previous exercise by changing the line color and adding a fill color. However, Word 97 provides many other formatting options. You can use buttons on the Drawing toolbar to change the line style and other options. In addition, you can **right-click any drawing object** and a dialog box will appear with all available formatting options for that object.

Hands-On 7.7 – Use the Formatting dialog box

In this exercise, you will remove the line from the text box that was created in the previous exercise. You will also change the line color and fill pattern of the starburst.

1. Use the following step to select the text box.

❶ ***Click** any **edge** of the **text box** and a thatched border and sizing handles will appear. (You can click an edge even if the box does not have a border.)*

2. Use the following step to display a formatting dialog box for the text box.

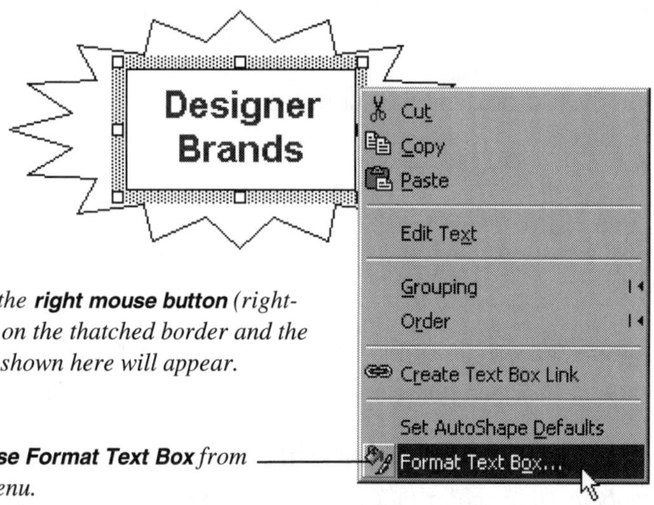

❶ ***Click** the **right mouse button** (right-click) on the thatched border and the menu shown here will appear.*

❷ ***Choose Format Text Box** from the menu.*

3. Take a few moments to **click** the various dialog box **tabs** and study the available options.

   Most of the options are available for all drawing objects. However, a few are unique to text boxes and certain other types of drawing objects.

4. **Click** the **Colors and Lines** tab.

5. Use the following steps to set the fill color and line color.

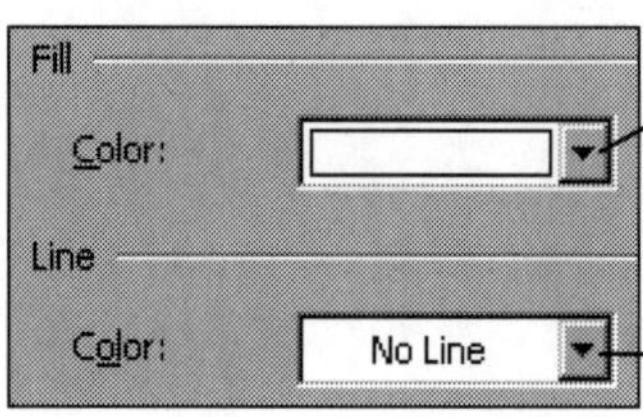

❶ *If necessary, **click** the **Color** **button** and **choose white**. If the fill color of the text box is the same as the background color (white in this case) then the text will appear to float over the background object.*

❷ ***Click** the **Line Color button** and **choose No Line**.*

Continued...

6. **Click OK** and the line should be removed from the text box.

Format the starburst

7. **Click** anywhere **on the Starburst** and sizing handles will appear.
8. **Click** the Line Style button on the Drawing toolbar.
9. Choose a **1 ½** pt line style.

   The starburst should now have a much thicker line.
10. Use the Line Color button on the Drawing toolbar to apply the same line color to the starburst as you used for the cloud callout.

Format the cloud callout

11. Select the cloud callout by clicking it once.
12. Use the Line Style button to apply a **1 ½ pt** line to the cloud callout.
13. Save the changes and continue with the next topic.

Additional Drawing Object Techniques

The following table lists a variety of techniques you can use with drawing objects.

Technique	How to do it
Select multiple objects	Click Select Objects and drag over the desired objects.
Use the keyboard to select multiple objects	Press the Shift key and click the desired objects.
Draw perfect horizontal, vertical or 45 degree lines	Press the Shift key while drawing a line or arrow line.
Draw perfect squares	Press the Shift key while using the Rectangle tool.
Draw perfect circles	Press the Shift key while using the Oval tool.
Copy objects with the mouse and keyboard	Press the Ctrl key while dragging the desired objects.
Change alignment, order and other options	Use the Draw button on the Drawing toolbar.

Hands-On 7.8 – Experiment with drawing objects

1. Take a few minutes to experiment with the various drawing objects.

   Try using the techniques in the table above. Also, experiment with the various buttons on the Drawing toolbar especially the AutoShapes. You will almost certainly find other AutoShapes that are fun and interesting to use. Continue with the next topic when you have finished.

Paragraph Spacing

The Spacing Before and Spacing After options on the Paragraph dialog box let you precisely control the spacing before and after paragraphs. These options are quite useful in desktop publishing where spatial arrangements are important. You use these options as an alternative to the Enter key. The Enter key creates a large amount of space between paragraphs. Sometimes, a smaller space is more appealing visually and may be necessary. You use the **Format→Paragraph** command to display the Paragraph dialog box.

Paragraph spacing is different from line spacing

Line spacing affects the spacing within and after a paragraph. Paragraph spacing, however, has no impact on lines within a paragraph. Paragraph spacing only changes the spacing before or after a paragraph.

In the following exercise, you will change the spacing before the phrase **I'll Take** in the cloud callout. This will allow you to precisely control the vertical position of the text within the callout. The following illustration shows the text in the callout box before and after paragraph spacing has been applied. Notice the text has been pushed down slightly in the second illustration.

Spacing Before 0

Spacing Before 6 pt

Hands-On 7.9 – Change the paragraph spacing in the callout

1. **Click** anywhere on the phrase **I'll Take** in the callout.
2. Choose **Format→Paragraph...** from the menu bar.
3. Set the paragraph spacing before to **6 pt** as shown below.

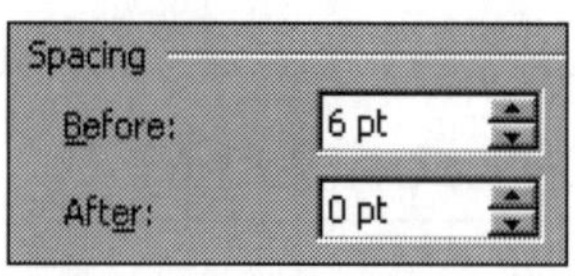

4. **Click OK** and the text within the callout should be pushed down slightly.
5. If necessary, continue to adjust the paragraph Spacing Before until the text is centered within the callout as shown in the illustration above.

   Now continue with the last topic in this lesson.

Page Borders

Word 97 lets you apply borders to pages. To apply a border to a page, you must have the insertion point somewhere on the page. The border is applied to all pages in the document unless the document is divided into sections (sections are not discussed in this course). You use the **Format→Borders and Shading** command to apply page borders.

Hands-On 7.10 – Apply a page border

1. **Click** anywhere **on** the **main paragraph** in your flyer.

   You must make sure that no objects are selected before issuing the Borders and Shading command.

2. Choose **Format→Borders and Shading...** from the menu bar.

3. Use the following steps to create a page border.

   ❶ ***Click** the **Page Border** tab.*

   ❷ ***Choose** the **Box** setting.*

   ❸ ***Choose** a **color**.*

   ❹ ***Choose** a **2 ¼ pt** width.*

   ❺ *Feel free to check out the Art option. This option lets you create a border that is composed of symbols.*

   ❻ ***Click OK** to apply the border.*

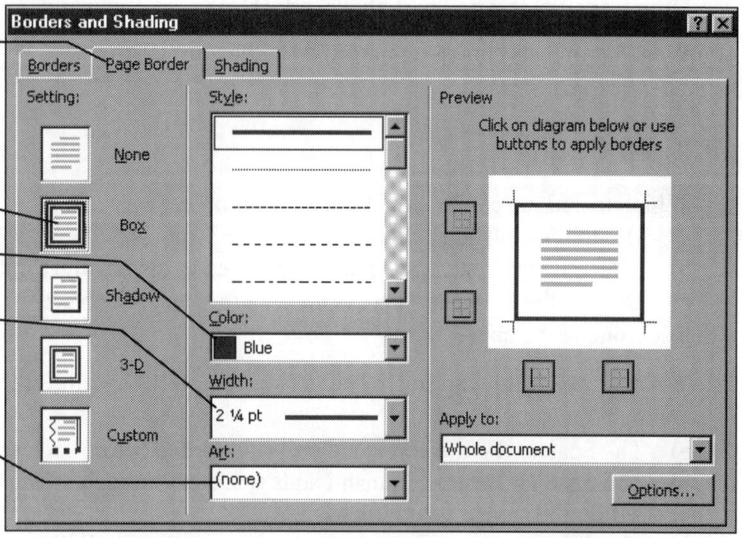

   You should now have an attractive border around the entire page. Word places the border approximately ½" from the edges of the page. Keep in mind that you can always remove a border by issuing the Format→Borders and Shading command and choosing the None option.

4. At this point, your completed flyer should match the flyer shown at the start of this lesson.

5. Feel free to **print** the flyer, however, the colors will only print if you have a color printer.

6. **Close** the document when you have finished and **save** the changes.

7. Continue with the end-of-lesson questions and exercises on the following pages.

Concepts Review

True / False

1.	The alignment buttons on the Formatting toolbar cannot be used to align text in a text box.	1. **T F**
2.	You can change the size of pictures after they have been inserted.	2. **T F**
3.	You can display the Format dialog box for an object by right-clicking a border of the object.	3. **T F**
4.	The Drawing button displays and hides the Drawing toolbar.	4. **T F**
5.	You cannot format text within a callout box.	5. **T F**
6.	The Select Objects tool lets you select multiple drawing objects.	6. **T F**
7.	The Paragraph Spacing Before and After commands can be used as an alternative to the Enter key when creating space between paragraphs.	7. **T F**
8.	Text boxes can be used to superimpose text on other text or objects.	8. **T F**
9.	Drop Caps are inserted with the Insert→Drop Cap command.	9. **T F**
10.	WordArt objects cannot be moved once they are inserted.	10. **T F**

Multiple Choice

1. Which technique can be used to display an object's anchor?
   a) Use the Show/Hide button to display the symbols and then select the desired object.
   b) Select the desired object. There is no need to display the symbols.
   c) Display the symbols. There is no need to select the object.
   a) None of the above. ( )

2. Which of the following statements most accurately describes the Paragraph Spacing Before command?
   a) The Spacing Before command only adds space before each selected paragraph.
   b) The Spacing Before command adds space before each selected paragraph and to each line within the selected paragraphs. ( )
   c) The Spacing Before command adds space before and after each selected paragraph.
   d) None of the above.

3. Which command displays the Borders and Shading dialog box?
   a) Format→Paragraph
   b) Edit→Borders and Shading
   c) Format→Borders and Shading
   d) None of the above. ( )

4. Which command is used to insert a WordArt object?
   a) Insert→WordArt
   b) Click the WordArt button on the Drawing toolbar
   c) Format WordArt
   d) None of the above. ( )

5. Which keyboard key is used to select multiple drawing objects?
   a) Shift
   b) Alt
   c) Ctrl
   d) None of the above. ( )

Skills Builder 7.1

In this exercise, you will open a document on your exercise diskette. You will insert clip art images into the document. You will also change the wrapping options on the clip art to embed it within the paragraphs.

Insert a picture and reduce the size

1. **Open** the document named **Skills Builder 7.1**.
2. Choose **Insert→Picture→Clip Art** from the menu bar.
3. **Choose** the **stop sign** picture as shown on the next page (choose another picture if the stop sign is not available) and **click OK**.

   The picture will be quite large and it will appear to "take over" the document.
4. Use the Zoom Control to switch to a **Whole Page** zoom.
5. Reduce the size of the picture until it is approximately the same size as shown on the next page.

   The picture may move to an unusual location on the page. Do not be concerned if this happens.

Change the wrapping options

The wrapping options let you control the behavior of pictures and other objects in relation to the paragraphs that they are attached to. You will change the wrapping option in the next few steps.

6. **Right-click** (click the right mouse button) on the **picture** and choose **Format→Picture...** from the pop up menu.

   You can always format objects by using the right-click technique.
7. **Click** the **Wrapping** tab.
8. Choose **Through** as the Wrapping style and **Both sides** as the Wrap to option as shown below.

   Take a moment to study the other wrapping options. The illustrations in the dialog box show the way text will wrap around a picture using the various styles.

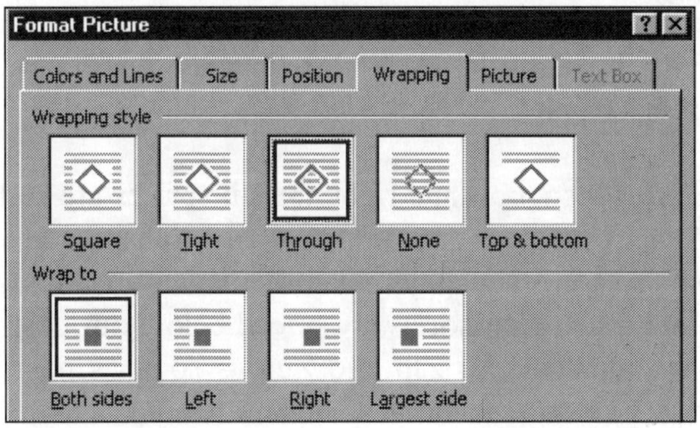

9. **Click OK** to complete the change.

Position and size the picture

10. Now **drag** the picture into the **center of** the **first paragraph** as shown on the following page. If necessary, reduce the size of the picture until it has the position and size shown. You may want to set the **Zoom Control** back to **Page Width**.

    Notice how the wrapping options you set force the text to wrap around the box.

Continued...

11. Now fine-tune the position of the picture by **pressing and holding** the Ctrl key while you **tap** the **arrow keys** on the keyboard.

    You can always precisely position drawing objects and pictures using these keystrokes.

Create a drop cap

12. Make sure the insertion point is somewhere in the first paragraph.

13. Choose **Format→Drop Cap...** from the menu bar.

14. Choose **Dropped** as the Position, set the Lines to drop to **2** and **click OK**.

    The Drop Cap will be slightly smaller than the drop cap you created earlier in this lesson. This is because you reduced the Lines to drop to 2.

Insert a picture in the second paragraph

15. **Click** anywhere in the **second paragraph** and insert the picture of the ribbon as shown below.

16. Reduce the size of the picture as shown.

17. Use the **right-click** technique to display the Format Picture dialog box.

18. Set the Wrapping style to **Through** and the Wrap to option to **Right** and **click OK**.

19. **Drag** the picture to the beginning of the second paragraph and **adjust the size** as shown below. You can fine tune the position of the picture using the **Ctrl + arrow** key method discussed above.

    The completed document should closely match the document shown below.

20. **Close** the document and **save** the changes.

Stop what you are doing! Zen Electronics is having a sale. We are growing rapidly and cannot keep up with customer demand. Our sales keep climbing upward and we must move to a larger store where we can stock more merchandise. We are selling everything in our store at rock bottom prices to reduce our moving costs. This incredible sale will last for two weeks beginning this Saturday. We must sell everything! You should Zip over to Zen if you are in the market for electronics.

Computers have always been our hottest products and right now the prices are so hot that we're afraid the cabinets might melt. Computers can be difficult to transport because of the delicate components inside, so we are practically giving them away. All name brand PCs printers, modems, software and other accessories are priced below our cost. This is no joke. We are actually selling PCs below our cost! So Zip into Zen as soon as possible and speak with one of our excellent customer service representatives. At Zen, we are known for our blue ribbon support.

Skills Builder 7.2

1. Create the flyer shown below. Use WordArt to create the Protected Wetlands title. The clip art image of the bird is in the Word Clip Gallery. Use any page border thickness and style that you desire. Create the drop cap as shown. Use whichever font sizes and typefaces you desire.

2. **Close** the document and **save** it as **Skills Builder 7.2**.

Protected Wetlands

Keep Out!

This land is owned and protected by the East Bay Preservation Society. Only qualified members of the Preservation Society are allowed to enter. Please do not litter or disturb wildlife in any way.

For More Information

Call 1-510-237-3233

Assessment 7.1

1. **Open** the document named **Assessment 7.1**.

   In this assessment, you will modify the document until it matches the document below.

2. Use the following instructions to modify the document. You must follow these instructions exactly as stated in order to get full credit for this assessment.
   - Do not add any new text or paragraphs to the document.
   - **Add drop caps** to the two main paragraphs as shown. The drop caps should occupy three lines as shown.
   - **Insert** a **picture** in the second paragraph as shown. Try to use the clock picture shown here. Use a substitute if the picture shown is not available. You must set the wrapping style to **Through** and the wrap to option to **Both sides**. This technique was discussed in Skills Builder 7.1. Reduce the size of the picture until it fits in the paragraph as shown.

3. **Print** the document when you have finished.

4. **Close** the document and **save** it as **Assessment 7.1**.

Bay Area Bicycles is closing its original store at 1600 Fairview Drive in San Francisco. This is a result of overwhelming demand for our fine bicycles and other products. We will be moving to our new location at 11240 Wesley Avenue in San Francisco. Everything must go in order to reduce our moving costs. Bicycles are expensive to transport because of the large amount of time and money required protecting them from damage. For this reason, we must sell everything!

There has never been a better time to buy from Bay Area Bicycles. This is the best time ever to buy a bicycle, skateboard or surfboard. Many of our prices are actually below the manufacturers suggested price. You simply will not believe the quality products that you can buy at incredibly low prices. So, hurry down to Bay Area Bicycles because the clock is ticking.

Assessment 7.2

In this assessment, you will create the flyer shown on the following page. In the first three steps, you are instructed to change the margins. Changing the margins allows you to place more or less text and graphics on a page.

1. Choose **File→Page Setup…** from the menu bar.

2. **Click** the **Margins tab** on the File Page Setup dialog box.

3. Set all four margins (top, bottom, left and right) to **1.5"** and **click OK**.

4. Use the following instructions to create the flyer. You must follow these instructions exactly as stated in order to get full credit for this assessment.
    - Set the font to **Times New Roman 24**.
    - **Tap** Enter exactly **five** times and type the first paragraph shown on the following page.
    - **Tap** Enter **twice** after the first paragraph and then **type** the **second paragraph**. Do not tap Enter after the second paragraph and do not type any additional text or use any additional hard returns in the document.
    - Add drop caps to the two main paragraphs as shown. The drop caps should occupy two lines as shown.
    - Add the WordArt object to the top of the document as shown. Use the 4th WordArt style in the top row of the WordArt Gallery. Insert the WordArt object in the blank space at the top of the document. **Do not insert any new hard returns in the document or you will lose credit!**
    - Insert the picture shown at the bottom of the document on the following page. Try to use the picture shown on the following page but use a substitute if the picture shown is not available. Adjust the size and position of the picture as shown. There is no need to set wrapping or any other options for this picture. Once again, do not insert any additional hard returns.
    - Add a 3 pt blue page border as shown. Use the Box style for the border.

5. **Print** the document when you have finished.

6. **Close** the document and **save** it as **Assessment 7.2**.

Congratulations Vickie

Vickie Johnson is retiring after 25 years at Velcor and it's about time she had a party. The theme of this celebration is Sailing Away.

We need volunteers and fresh ideas to help make this the celebration of a lifetime for Vickie. Please call June Roberts at 234-9900 if you are interested in volunteering your time.

Unit Three

Excel 97

8 Creating and Editing a Simple Worksheet

Objectives:

- Create a simple worksheet
- Understand workbook and worksheet concepts
- Display, hide and move toolbars
- Enter text and numbers
- Edit cell entries
- Select cells
- Align cell entries
- Use AutoSum
- Open and close workbooks

What is Microsoft Excel?

Microsoft Excel is an electronic spreadsheet program that makes working with numbers a pleasure instead of a chore. Excel has powerful features to let you enter and edit text and numbers, perform an endless variety of calculations, produce charts and other reports and make informed financial decisions. Excel is the most widely used spreadsheet program in both homes and businesses.

Why Use Excel?

Excel provides a number of important features and benefits that make it a smart choice to use.

1. IntelliSense Technology - Excel's IntelliSense technology includes many automated tools to assist you in entering, editing and analyzing data. This speeds up the process of creating worksheets, so that you can focus on analysis and other tasks.
2. GUI - Excel's Graphical User Interface is so easy to use that even beginning computer users find it simple. The interface reduces the need to memorize commands and it will make you more productive.
3. Charting - Have you heard of the expression **"a picture speaks a thousand words"**? This is especially true with financial or numeric data. Excel's powerful charting and formatting features let you display your data in a powerful and convincing graphic format.
4. Widely used - Excel is the most widely used spreadsheet software. Excel is the right choice if you are trying to develop marketable skills and find employment.
5. Integration with other Office programs - Excel is part of the Microsoft Office suite of programs which also include Word, Access and PowerPoint. The ability to exchange data with these programs is one of the most powerful and attractive features of Excel.

It's Time to Learn Excel!

It's time to put your fears behind and learn this wonderful program. You will be amazed at the power and simplicity of Excel and how easy it is to learn. The knowledge you are about to gain will give you a marketable skill and make you the master of Excel.

The Project - Diane's Cafe

In this lesson, you will develop a worksheet for Diane's Café. Diane needs to track the weekly various menu items, so that she can better plan her inventory purchases. You will enter data inc text and numbers. You will compute Totals using the AutoSum button on the toolbar and you the worksheet columns. You will also learn some preliminary techniques and concepts such as starting Excel, using toolbars and scrolling. You will create the following worksheet as you progress through this introductory lesson.

	A	B	C	D	E	F	G	H
1	Diane's Café - Weekly Sales Data							
2								
3			Wednesday	Thursday	Friday	Saturday	Sunday	
4	Soups							Totals
5		Vegetable	3	10	12	15	16	56
6		Chicken	4	8	10	13	14	49
7		Split Pea	6	13	15	18	19	71
8		Total	13	31	37	46	49	176
9								
10	Salads							
11		Mixed Greens	2	5	4	10	8	29
12		Cobb	3	7	5	12	10	37
13		Spinach	4	8	11	14	14	51
14		Fruit & Nut	2	3	5	5	3	18
15		Total	11	23	25	41	35	135
16								
17	Entrees							
18		Chicken Kiev	3	5	5	6	8	27
19		Pot Roast	6	1	2	3	7	19
20		Fish	8	2	3	4	5	22
21		Total	17	8	10	13	20	68
22								
23	Dessert							
24		Apple Pie	3	6	8	7	2	26
25		Key Lime Pie	5	3	2	2	1	13
26		Pecan Pie	2	2	6	8	3	21
27		Total	10	11	16	17	6	60

Starting Excel

There are several ways to start Excel. The three most common methods are listed below.

- Click the Start button and choose Microsoft Excel from the Programs menu.
- Click a desktop shortcut for the Excel program (if a shortcut is on the desktop).
- Click the Microsoft Excel button on the Microsoft Office toolbar (if it is displayed).

Hands-On 8.1 - Start Excel

In this exercise, you will start the Excel program.

1. Start your computer and the Windows desktop will be displayed.
2. **Click** the Start button and choose **Programs**.
3. Choose **Microsoft Excel** from the Programs menu.

   The Excel program will load and the Excel window will appear. Don't be concerned if your window appears different from the example shown below.

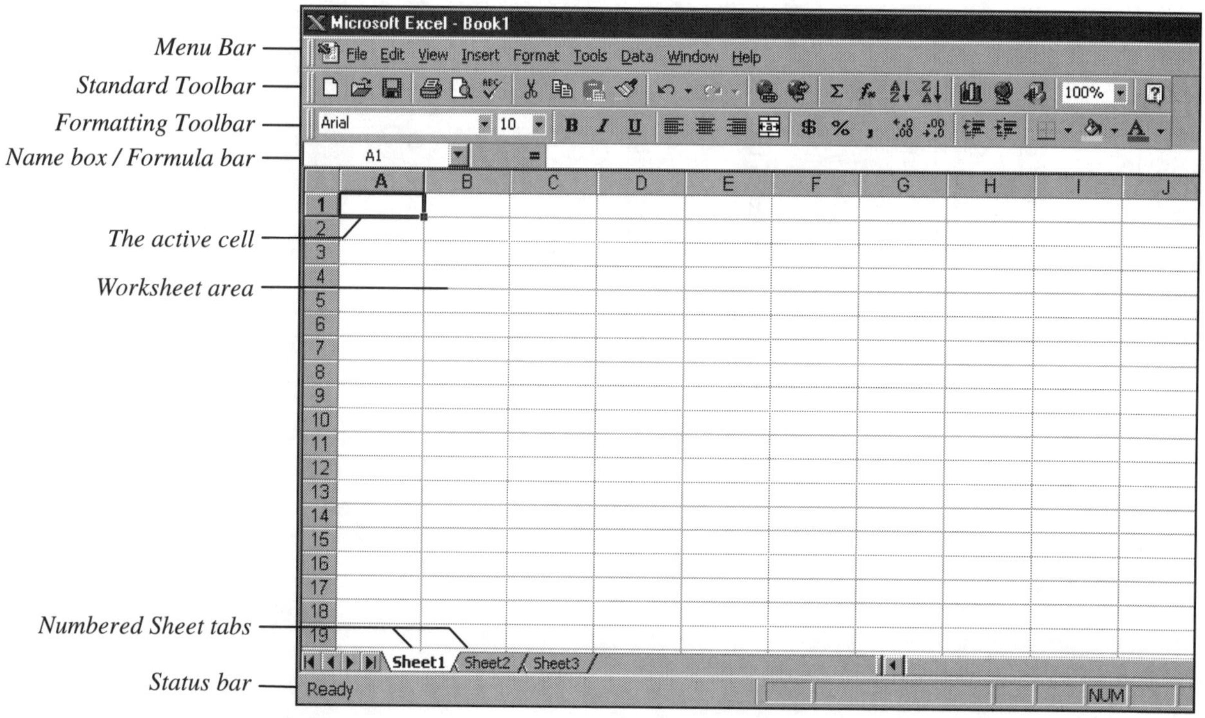

Workbooks and Worksheets

Excel displays a blank **workbook** the moment you start the program. A workbook is composed of **worksheets**. This is similar to a paper notebook that has many sheets of paper. You enter text and numbers and insert formulas, charts and other objects in the worksheets. Excel provides 3 worksheets in a new workbook. However, you can increase this number and have up to 255 worksheets in one workbook.

A worksheet is composed of rows and columns

A worksheet has a grid structure with horizontal rows and vertical columns. The intersection of each row and column is a **cell**. The worksheet actually has 256 columns and 65,536 rows although only a small number of the rows and columns are visible in the worksheet window. Each cell has a **reference** that is the column letter followed by the row number. For example, A1 is the reference of the cell in the top left corner of the worksheet. So we refer to this cell as cell A1.

Moving the Highlight and Scrolling

A thick line known as the highlight surrounds the active cell. You can make a cell active by clicking it with the mouse or by using the keyboard. Changing the active cell is important because data is entered into the active cell. You can also use the vertical and horizontal scroll bars to scroll through the worksheet. However, you must position the highlight in the desired cell after scrolling. The following table lists several important keystroke commands that are used to move the highlight and thus make a cell active.

Use these keys	To move the highlight like this
→ ← ↑ ↓	One cell to the right, left, up or down
Home	Column A of the active row
Ctrl + Home	Cell A1
PageDown	Down one screen
PageUp	Up one screen

Hands-On 8.2 - Move the highlight and check out the Excel window

In this exercise, you will use the mouse and keyboard to move the highlight around the worksheet.

Click in the desired cell

1. Slide the mouse and the pointer will have a thick cross ✥ shape when it is in the worksheet area.
2. **Click** the pointer on **any cell** and the highlight will move to that cell.
3. Move the highlight **five times** by clicking in various cells.

Use the keyboard to move the highlight

*In the next few steps, you will move the highlight with the keyboard. You can use the keys on the main part of your keyboard or on the Numeric keypad at the bottom right corner. Keep in mind, however, that you must have the Num Lock key turned **off** if you want to move the highlight with the Numeric keypad. The word NUM will disappear from the Status bar when Num Lock is turned off.*

Continued...

4. Use the arrow → ← ↑ ↓ keys to position the highlight in **cell F10**.

5. **Tap** the Home key and the highlight will move to cell A10.

   The Home key always moves the highlight to column A in the active row.

6. **Press** Ctrl + Home to move the highlight to Cell A1.

7. **Tap** the PageDown key two or three times.

   Notice that Excel displays the next twenty or so rows each time you tap PageDown.

8. **Press & Hold** the ↑ key until the highlight is in cell A1.

Use the scroll bars

9. **Click** the Scroll Right ▶ button on the horizontal scroll bar until columns AA and AB are visible.

   Excel labels the first 26 columns A - Z and the next 26 columns AA - AZ. A similar labeling scheme is used for the remaining columns.

10. Take a few minutes to practice scrolling and moving the highlight.

Explore the Excel window

11. Use the following steps to explore the Excel window.

❶ *Notice the Name box on the Formula bar (don't worry if your Formula bar is not displayed. You will learn to display and hide the Formula bar soon.) The Name box displays the name or reference of the active cell.*

❷ ***Click** the **Sheet2** tab and another blank worksheet will be displayed.*

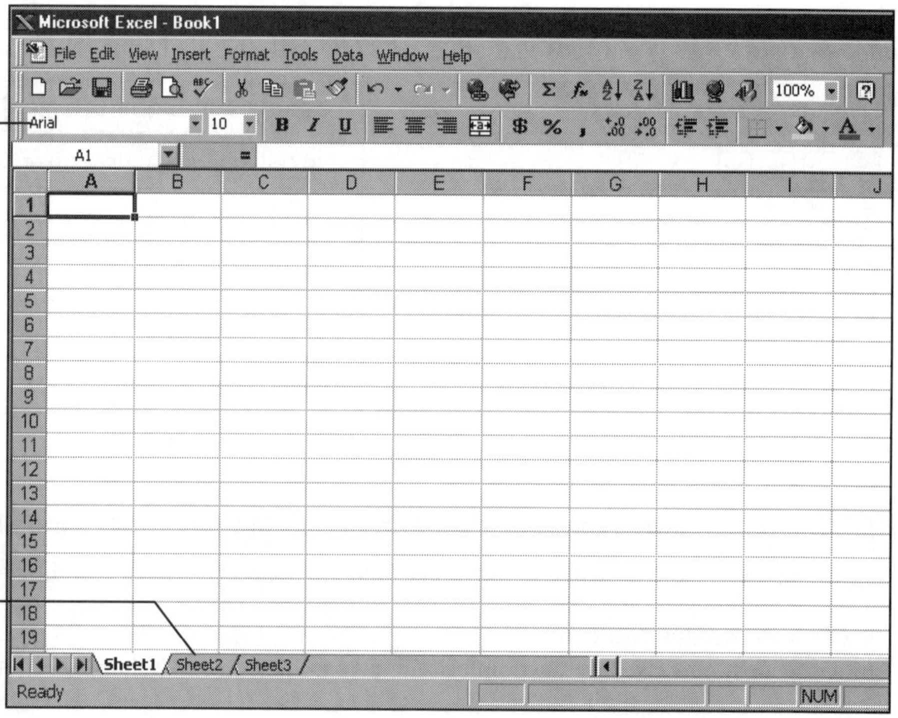

❸ ***Click** the **Sheet1** tab.*

12. **Press** Ctrl + Home to move the highlight to cell A1.

Entering Data

You can begin entering data the moment Excel is started. Data is entered into the active cell (the cell with the highlight). You can enter text, numbers or formulas into cells. Text and numbers are used for different purposes in a worksheet. Text is used for descriptive headings and entries that require alphabetic characters or a combination of alphabetic and numeric characters. Numbers can be calculated using formulas. Excel recognizes the data you enter and it decides whether the entry is text, a number or a formula. Text and number entries are discussed in detail below and on the following pages.

Entering Text

An entry is considered to be text whenever it contains alphabetic characters or spaces. Excel left aligns text entries in cells although you can change the alignment to center or right. The following table shows several examples of text entries. Notice that each example contains at least one alphabetic character or a space.

Examples of text entries	
1996 Budget	555 9090
Q1	Bicycle Sales

Long text entries

Text entries are often too long to fit in a cell. These entries are known as **long entries**. Excel uses the following rules when deciding how to display long entries.

1. If the cell to the right of the long entry is empty, then the long entry is displayed over the adjacent cell.
2. If the cell to the right of the long entry is **not** empty, then Excel shortens or **truncates** the display of the long entry.

Keep in mind that Excel does not actually change the long entry, it simply truncates the display of the entry. You can resolve this situation by widening the column that contains the long entry.

Deleting and Replacing a Cell's Content

You can delete the content of a cell by making the cell active (clicking the cell) and then tapping the Delete key. Likewise, you can replace the content of a cell by clicking the cell and entering the new data.

Undo and Redo

Excel's **Undo** button lets you reverse your last 16 commands or actions. You can reverse simple actions such as accidentally deleting a cell's content or you can reverse more complex actions such as deleting an entire row. You can Undo most commands or actions. However, there are a few commands that cannot be undone such as deleting entire worksheets, printing and saving workbooks.

Excel also has a **Redo** button that reverses Undo. Use Redo when you Undo actions but then decide that you want to go through with them after all. You will probably love Redo if you have a difficult time making up your mind.

The arrow buttons to the right of Undo and Redo let you Undo or Redo multiple actions. In fact, you can Undo or Redo up to 16 actions! You will use Undo, Redo and the arrow buttons soon.

Hands-On 8.3 - Entering text

In this exercise, you will begin creating a worksheet for Diane's Café. Diane needs to track the weekly sales of her various menu items, so that she can better plan her inventory purchases. You will create a worksheet for this purpose.

Type a long text entry and check out the Formula bar

1. Make cell **A1** active by clicking the mouse pointer ✥ in it.
2. Type, **Diane's Cafe - Weekly Sales** (don't try to format the text) and **tap** Enter.

   The text should be entered in the cell and the highlight should move down to cell A2. Excel moves the highlight down when you tap Enter because most people enter data column-by-column. Notice that the entry displays over cells B1 and C1. The long entry would not display over these cells if they contained data.
3. **Click** the mouse pointer ✥ in cell A1 and the Formula bar will have the appearance shown below.

   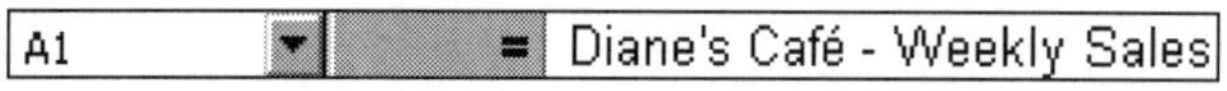

   *Notice that the Formula bar displays the name of the active cell (A1) and the cell's content. In this example, the cell's content is the title **Diane's Café - Weekly Sales**. The title is a long entry because it is wider than cell A1. Cells B1 and C1 are empty, so the long entry is displayed over them. Keep in mind; however, that the entire entry belongs to Cell A1. This concept will be demonstrated in the next few steps.*

Delete the entry and use Undo and Redo

4. **Tap** the Delete key and the entire entry will be deleted.

   Notice the entire entry was deleted because it belonged to cell A1.
5. **Click** the Undo button to restore the entry.
6. **Click** the Redo button and the entry will be deleted again.

   Redo always reverses Undo.
7. **Click** Undo again to restore the entry.

Verify that the entry belongs to cell A1

8. **Tap** the → key to make cell B1 active.
9. Look at the Formula bar and you will see that cell B1 is empty.

   Once again, the long entry belongs to cell A1 even though it is displayed over cells B1 and C1.

Type additional text entries

10. Use the arrow → ← ↑ ↓ keys to position the highlight in cell **C3**.
11. Type **Wednesday** and **tap** → once.

    Notice the entry is completed and the highlight moves to cell D3. You can always use the arrow keys to complete an entry and move the highlight in the desired direction.

Continued...

12. Type **Thursday** in cell D3 and **tap** →.

Notice that the display of Wednesday is shortened or truncated. A long entry is always truncated when the cell to the right contains text or a number.

13. Enter the remaining text entries as shown below.

Use Undo if you make a mistake. Also, you can change any entry by clicking in the desired cell and retyping the entry.

	A	B	C	D	E	F	G
1	Diane's Café - Weekly Sales						
2							
3			Wednesda	Thursday	Friday	Saturday	Sunday
4	Soups						
5		Vegetable					
6		Chicken					
7		Split Pea					
8		Total					
9							
10	Salads						
11		Mixed Greens					
12		Cobb					
13		Spinach					
14		Fruit					
15		Total					
16							
17	Entrees						
18		Chicken					
19		Pot Roast					
20		Fish					
21		Total					
22							
23	Dessert						
24		Apple Pie					
25		Key Lime Pie					
26		Pecan Pie					
27		Total					

You will continue to enhance your worksheet in the next exercise.

Entering Numbers

Numbers can only contain the digits 0 - 9 and a few other characters. Excel right aligns numbers in cells although you can change the alignment to center or left. The following table discusses the characters you can use when entering numbers.

Characters which can be used in numbers
Digits 0 - 9
The following characters: + - ( ) , / $ % .

Don't type commas, dollar signs or other number formats

It isn't necessary to type commas, dollar signs or other number formats when entering numbers. It is easier to just enter the numbers and then use Excel's formatting commands to add the desired number format. You will learn how to format numbers soon.

Do type decimal points and minus signs

You should always type a decimal point if the number you are entering requires one and a minus sign (or parenthesis) if the number is negative.

The Confirm and Cancel Buttons

In the previous exercise, you used Enter and the arrow keys to complete an entry and move the highlight. The Confirm button on the Formula bar can also be used to complete an entry. Also, you can cancel an entry before completing it by clicking the Cancel button on the Formula bar or by tapping the Esc key.

Hands-On 8.4 – Entering numbers

In this exercise, you will add numbers to the worksheet.

Use the Confirm button

1. Position the highlight in cell **C5**.
2. Type **3** but **don't** tap Enter or the arrow keys.
3. Look at the Formula bar and notice the Cancel and Confirm buttons.
   These buttons appear when you begin entering data in a cell or when you edit data.
4. **Click** the Confirm button to complete the entry.
   Notice the highlight remains in cell C5. It is preferable to complete entries with the keyboard when building a worksheet. This is because the highlight automatically moves to the next cell. The Confirm button is actually most useful when editing entries.

Use the Cancel button and the Esc key

5. Position the highlight in cell **C6** and type **4** (but don't confirm the entry).
6. **Click** the Cancel button on the Formula bar to cancel the entry.

Continued...

7. Type **4** again but this time **tap** the (Esc) key on the keyboard.

The Escape key has the same effect as the Cancel button.

8. Type **4** once again and **tap** the (↓) key.

Notice the number is right aligned in the cell.

9. Enter the remaining numbers as shown below.

Keep in mind that some of the numbers you enter will cause entries in column B to be truncated. You will solve this problem by widening column B later in this exercise.

	A	B	C	D	E	F	G
1	Diane's Café - Weekly Sales						
2							
3			Wednesda	Thursday	Friday	Saturday	Sunday
4	Soups						
5		Vegetable	3	10	12	15	16
6		Chicken	4	8	10	13	14
7		Split Pea	6	13	15	18	19
8		Total					
9							
10	Salads						
11		Mixed Gre	2	5	4	10	8
12		Cobb	3	7	5	12	10
13		Spinach	4	8	11	14	14
14		Fruit	2	3	5	5	3
15		Total					
16							
17	Entrees						
18		Chicken	3	5	5	6	8
19		Pot Roast	6	1	2	3	7
20		Fish	8	2	3	4	5
21		Total					
22							
23	Dessert						
24		Apple Pie	3	6	8	7	2
25		Key Lime I	5	3	2	2	1
26		Pecan Pie	2	2	6	8	3
27		Total					

10. Take a few minutes to check the accuracy of your text and numbers.

It is very important to be accurate when entering data in worksheets. Excel's formulas, charts and other features are of no use unless your data is accurate.

You will learn how to save the workbook on the next page.

Saving a Workbook

One important lesson to learn is to **save your workbooks frequently!** Power outages and careless accidents can result in lost data. The best protection is to save your workbooks every 10 or 15 minutes and after making significant changes. It is recommended that you understand the concepts of files, folders and pathnames before attempting this exercise. These and many other essential Windows 95 concepts are discussed in Labyrinth Publications, ***Laying a Foundation with Windows 95*** textbook.

The Save and Save As Commands

Excel provides several commands that let you save documents. The **Save** command saves the current workbook onto a disk. If the workbook had previously been saved, then Excel replaces the old version of the workbook with the new edited version. If the workbook is new, then Excel displays the **Save As** dialog box. The Save As dialog box lets you name the workbook and it lets you specify the disk drive and folder that you wish to save it to. You can also use Save As to make a copy of an existing workbook by saving the workbook under a new name.

Excel 97 supports long filenames

Excel 97 supports long filenames. You can use up to 255 characters when naming a workbook in Excel 97. This is a huge improvement over the 8 character limitation in some earlier versions of Excel.

Hands-On 8.5 – Save the workbook

In this exercise, you will save the workbook. Your instructor will probably want you to use the diskette that is provided with this course. You will probably be saving workbooks onto the A: disk drive.

1. Choose **File→Save...** from the menu bar and the **Save As** dialog box will appear.
2. Use the following steps to save the workbook.

❶ ***Click here*** *and choose the disk drive with your exercise diskette. It is most likely 3 ½ Floppy [A:].*

❷ *Notice that Excel proposes the Filename,* ***Book1****.*

❸ *Type the name* ***Hands-On Lesson 8*** *and it will replace Book1. (If you switched disk drives, then you may need to click in the File name box, delete the name Book1 with the Delete and/or Backspace keys, then type the new name.)*

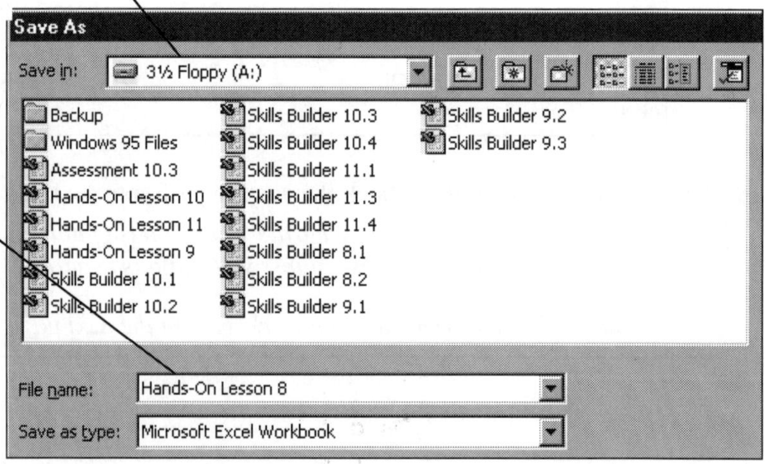

❹ ***Click*** *the* ***Save*** *button.*

Notice the workbook was saved and it also remains on the screen. You will continue to use the workbook throughout this lesson.

Editing Cell Contents

You can edit the active cell by clicking in the Formula bar and making the desired changes. You can also double-click a cell and then edit the contents directly in the cell. This technique is known as in-cell editing.

It may be easier to retype the entry

Editing a cell is beneficial if the entry is long and retyping it would be time consuming. Editing can also be beneficial with complex formulas and other functions that are difficult to recreate. However, it is usually easier to just replace an entry if the entry is small and requires little typing.

Using the Delete and Backspace Keys

You can use the Delete and Backspace keys to delete characters from an entry. The following table discusses the Delete and Backspace keys.

This key	Deletes like this
Delete	Character to the right of the insertion point.
BackSpace	Character to the left of the insertion point.

Hands-On 8.6 – Edit entries

The Hands-On Lesson 8 workbook should be open from the previous exercise.

Use the Formula bar to Edit the title

1. **Click** cell **A1**.

2. Use the following steps to edit cell A1 using the Formula bar.

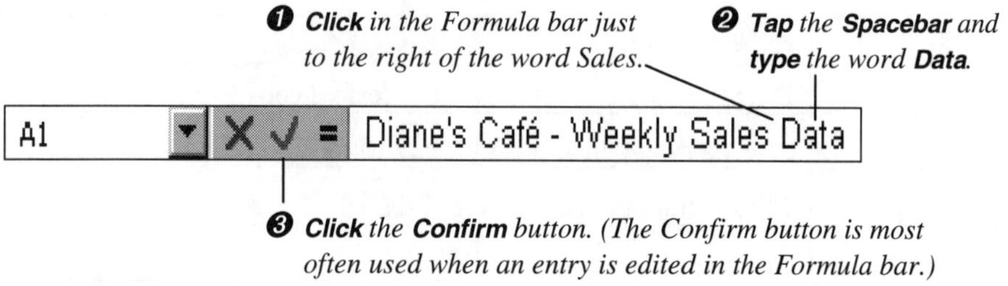

Use in-cell editing

3. **Double-click** cell **B14** (the cell with the word Fruit).

4. Use the mouse or the → key to position the flashing insertion point to the right of the word Fruit.

5. **Tap** the SpaceBar once and type **& Nut**.

6. **Tap** Enter or **click** the Confirm button to complete the change.
   *The entry should now read **Fruit & Nut** (although the entry may be slightly truncated).*

7. Change the entry in cell **B18** to **Chicken Kiev** and cell **A23** to Dessert**s** (plural).

8. **Click** the Save button to update the changes.
   The Save button automatically saves changes to a workbook that has previously been saved.

Selecting Cells

There are many ways to **select** cells in Excel. When you select cells, you are telling Excel which cells you wish to perform a command on. You can move, copy, delete, format and perform numerous other operations on selected cells. You can select with both the mouse and the keyboard.

Ranges

A range is a rectangular group of cells. Earlier in this lesson, you learned that each cell has a reference. For example, A1 refers to the first cell in a worksheet. Likewise, a range reference specifies which cells are included in the range. The range reference includes the first and last cells in the range separated by a colon (:). For example, the range C3:G3 includes all cells between C3 and G3. The following illustration shows several ranges and their corresponding range references. Notice that the ranges appear in black with white text (or reverse video as it is often called).

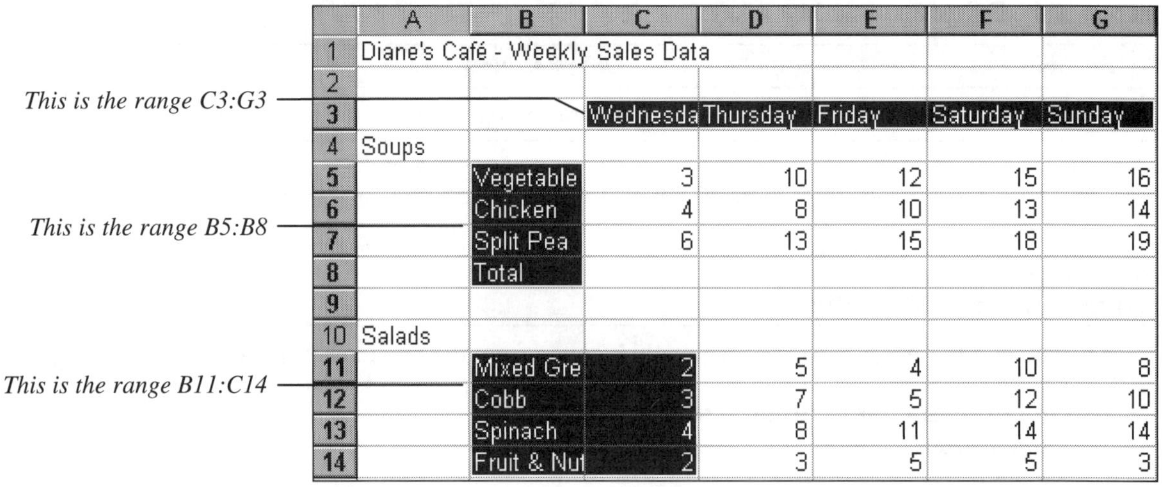

The following table describes the various methods of selecting cells in Excel.

Method	How to do it
Select a range	Drag the mouse pointer over the desired cells.
Select several ranges	Select a range, then press Ctrl while selecting additional ranges.
Select an entire column	Click a column heading (e.g. A).
Select an entire row	Click a row heading (e.g. 1).
Select multiple columns or rows	Drag the mouse pointer over the desired column or row headings.
Select an entire worksheet	Click the Select All button at the top left corner of the worksheet.
Select using the Shift key	Position the highlight in the first cell you wish to select, then press & hold Shift and click the last cell in the range. You can also press & hold Shift while tapping the arrow keys on the keyboard.

Hands-On 8.7 – Practice selecting

Drag-select and deselect

1. Position the mouse pointer ✥ on cell **C3**.
2. **Press & Hold** the left mouse button and **drag** to the right until the range C3:G3 is selected.

Continued...

3. **Deselect** the cells by **clicking** anywhere in the worksheet.

Select multiple ranges

4. **Select** the range **C3:G3** as you did in steps 1 and 2.

5. **Press & Hold** the Ctrl key while you select the range **B5:B8** as shown on the previous page.

   Both the C3:G3 and B5:B8 ranges should be selected. The Ctrl key lets you select more than one range at the same time.

6. **Press & Hold** while you select the range **B11:C14** as shown on the previous page.

   There should now be three ranges selected as shown on the previous page.

7. **Deselect** the ranges by **releasing** the Ctrl key and **clicking** anywhere in the worksheet.

Select entire columns and rows

8. Use the following series of steps to select various rows and columns.

❶ ***Click here*** *on the Column A heading and the entire column will become selected.*

❷ *Position the mouse pointer on the Column C heading, then* ***drag*** *to the right until columns C, D and E are selected. Column A will be deselected.*

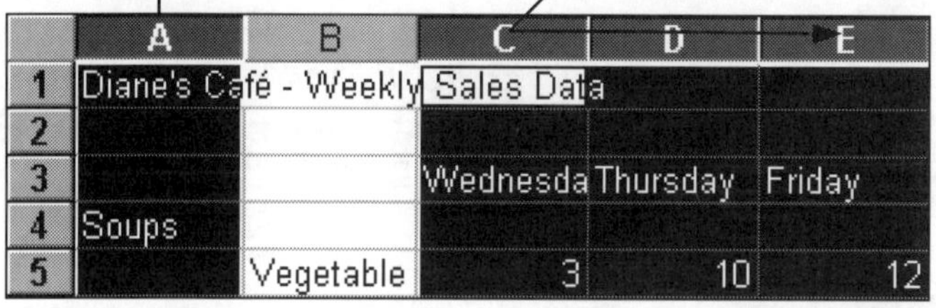

❸ ***Click*** *the* ***Select All*** *button to select the entire worksheet.*

❹ ***Click*** *the* ***Row 4 heading*** *to select row 4.*

❺ ***Drag*** *the mouse pointer* ***down*** *over the row 10 - 15 headings to select those rows.*

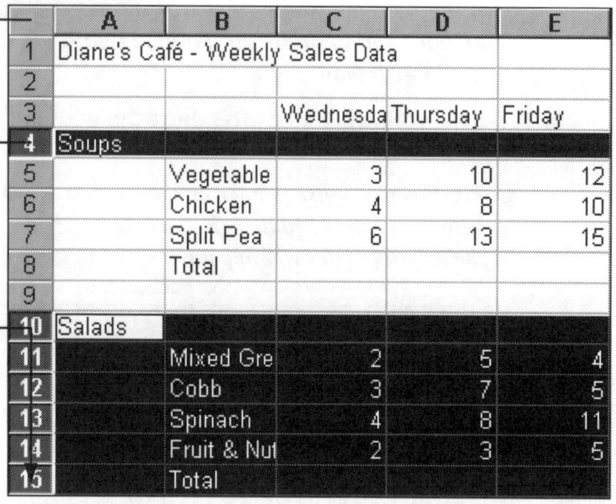

Use the Shift key methods

9. **Click** cell **B5**.

10. **Press & Hold** the Shift key, then **click** cell **G8** to select the range B5:G8.

11. **Click** cell **B11**.

12. **Press & Hold** the Shift key, then **tap** → five times and ↓ four times.

    The range B11:G15 should be selected. Notice that the Shift key methods give you precise control when selecting. You should use the Shift key methods if you find it difficult to select with the mouse.

13. Take five minutes to practice selecting ranges, rows and columns.

Aligning Cell Entries

Excel makes it easy to align text and numbers within cells. Entries can be left, right or center aligned. You already learned that text entries are automatically left aligned and numbers are automatically right aligned. The alignment buttons on the Formatting toolbar let you change the default alignments as shown below.

Friday	Friday	Friday
Left aligned	Center aligned	Right aligned

Hands-On 8.8 – Align text entries and widen a column

In this exercise, you will align the entries in row 3. You will also widen columns B and C.

Select a range and change the alignment

1. **Select** the range **C3:G3** as shown below.

2. **Click** the Align Right button on the Formatting toolbar.

   Each entry in the range (except Wednesday) should be right aligned. Wednesday does not appear right aligned because it is too wide for the cell. You will change the width of column C in a moment.

3. Take a few moments to practice aligning entries in other cells or ranges. Use the Undo button after making each change.

Adjust the width of columns B and C

In the next few steps, you will adjust the width of columns B and C. This section provides a brief introduction to adjusting column widths. A complete discussion of adjusting column widths is given in a later lesson.

4. Use the following steps to adjust the width of column B.

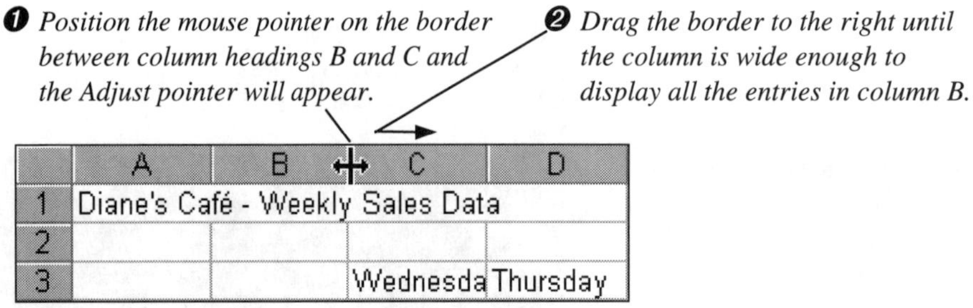

5. Widen column C until the word Wednesday is completely visible in cell C3.

   You will need to drag the border between column headings C and D.

6. **Click** the Save button to save the changes.

Continue with the topic on the next page where you will learn to use the AutoSum button.

The AutoSum Button

The power of Excel becomes apparent when you begin using formulas and functions. The most common type of calculation is when a column or row of numbers is added or **summed**. In fact, this type of calculation is so common that Excel provides the AutoSum [Σ] button specifically for this purpose.

Quick Steps: ***Using AutoSum***
To use AutoSum
• *Click the cell where you want the Total to appear or select a range of cells where you want Totals to appear.*
• *Click the AutoSum [Σ] button.*
• *Confirm [✓] the entry.*

Hands-On 8.9 – Use AutoSum to compute the column totals

In this exercise, you will use AutoSum to compute the Totals. Keep in mind that this section provides an introduction to formulas. You will learn more about formulas as you progress through this course.

Compute one column Total at a time

1. **Click** cell **C8**.
2. **Click** AutoSum [Σ].
3. Use the following steps to check out the formula and confirm the entry.

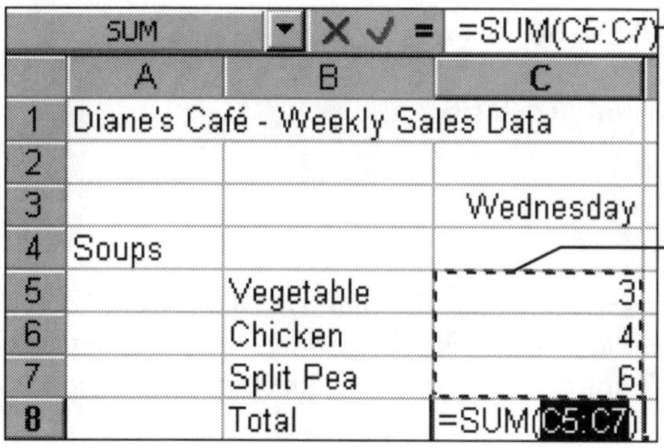

❶ **Notice** *that Excel proposes the formula =SUM(C5:C7) in cell C8 and in the Formula bar. All formulas begin with an equal = sign. SUM is a built-in function that adds up the numbers in a range (in this example the range is C5:C7).*

❷ **Notice** *the flashing marquee that surrounds the range C5:C7. AutoSum assumes you want to sum up all cells above C8 until the first empty cell is reached. The marquee identifies this range of cells.*

❸ **Click** *the Confirm [✓] button on the Formula bar to complete the entry.*

The Total should be 13.

4. **Click** cell **D8**.
5. **Click** AutoSum [Σ], then **click** Confirm [✓].
6. Use the preceding technique to compute the column Totals in cells **E8**, **F8** and **G8**.

Continued...

Compute an entire row of column Totals with one command

7. **Select** the range **C15:G15** as shown below.

   This range will contain the column Totals for row 15.

8. **Click** AutoSum.

   The column Totals should automatically be computed. AutoSum only displays the marquee and requires confirmation when you are computing a single Total.

9. Use the preceding steps to compute the column Totals in rows **21** and **27**.

Make column H a Totals column

10. **Click** cell **H4**, type the word **Totals** and Confirm the entry.

11. Use the Align Right button to right align Totals.

12. **Click** cell **H5**.

13. **Click** AutoSum and Excel assumes you want to add the cells to the left of H4 as shown below.

	A	B	C	D	E	F	G	H
1	Diane's Café - Weekly Sales Data							
2								
3			Wednesday	Thursday	Friday	Saturday	Sunday	
4	Soups							Totals
5		Vegetable	3	10	12	15	16	=SUM(C5:G5)

14. Confirm the entry and the row Total should be **56**.

15. Use the preceding steps to compute the row Total in cell **H6**.

Override the range that AutoSum proposes

16. **Click** cell **H7**, then **click** AutoSum.

    Notice that Excel assumes you want to sum the cells H5 and H6 that are above H7. This assumption is incorrect. The reason Excel made this assumption is there were two cells above H7, which is enough to make a range. Excel will always propose a column summation if it has a choice between a column and row summation.

17. Use the following steps to override the range that AutoSum is proposing.

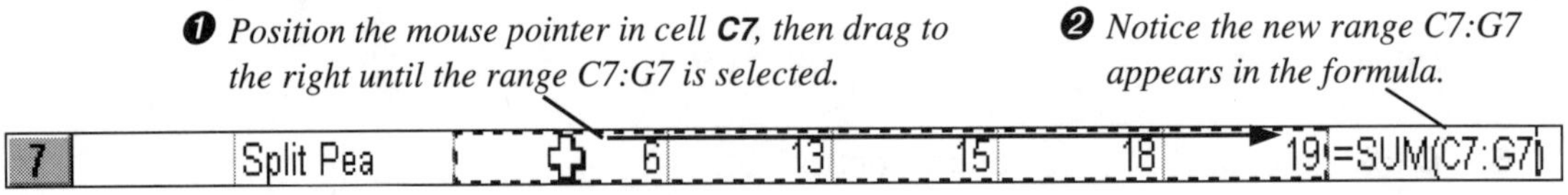

18. **Confirm** the entry and the row Total should be 71.

19. Use the preceding technique to compute the row Total in cell **H8** (the Total should equal 176).

    Actually, you could have accepted the formula that AutoSum proposed for cell H8. In this case, the column and row summations would have been the same.

Continued...

Sum the row Totals one range at a time

You can eliminate the problem of AutoSum proposing the wrong formula by summing a range of row Totals with one command. This is the same technique you used to sum the column Totals.

20. Select the range **H11:H15** as shown below.

	A	B	C	D	E	F	G	H
9								
10	Salads							
11		Mixed Greens	2	5	4	10	8	
12		Cobb	3	7	5	12	10	
13		Spinach	4	8	11	14	14	
14		Fruit & Nut	2	3	5	5	3	
15		Total	11	23	25	41	35	

21. Click AutoSum Σ.

The five row Totals should automatically be computed.

22. Use the preceding steps to compute the row Totals for the ranges **H18:H21** and **H24:H27**.
Your completed worksheet should match the worksheet shown below.

	A	B	C	D	E	F	G	H
1	Diane's Café - Weekly Sales Data							
2								
3			Wednesday	Thursday	Friday	Saturday	Sunday	
4	Soups							Totals
5		Vegetable	3	10	12	15	16	56
6		Chicken	4	8	10	13	14	49
7		Split Pea	6	13	15	18	19	71
8		Total	13	31	37	46	49	176
9								
10	Salads							
11		Mixed Greens	2	5	4	10	8	29
12		Cobb	3	7	5	12	10	37
13		Spinach	4	8	11	14	14	51
14		Fruit & Nut	2	3	5	5	3	18
15		Total	11	23	25	41	35	135
16								
17	Entrees							
18		Chicken Kiev	3	5	5	6	8	27
19		Pot Roast	6	1	2	3	7	19
20		Fish	8	2	3	4	5	22
21		Total	17	8	10	13	20	68
22								
23	Desserts							
24		Apple Pie	3	6	8	7	2	26
25		Key Lime Pie	5	3	2	2	1	13
26		Pecan Pie	2	2	6	8	3	21
27		Total	10	11	16	17	6	60

Continue with the next page where you will learn how to close and save the workbook.

Closing a Workbook

You can close a Workbook by choosing **File→Close** from the menu bar. Excel will prompt you to save the workbook if it is new or if you have changed it since the last time you saved it.

Hands-On 8.10 – Close the workbook

1. Choose **File→Close** from the menu bar.
2. **Click** the **Yes** button when Excel asks if you want to save the changes.

   Hands-On Lesson 8 should have been the only open workbook. The Excel window changes when you close the last open workbook as discussed in the following illustration.

Most commands on the pull-menus are unavailable when all workbooks have been closed.

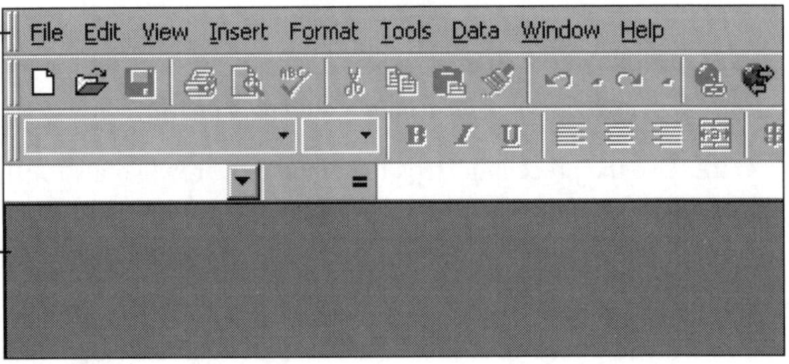

No worksheets are visible when all workbooks have been closed.

Your Excel window will most likely have the appearance shown in the preceding illustration. Don't be concerned if you still have an open workbook. You will learn to open new and existing workbooks and exit from Excel in the following sections.

Creating a New Workbook

You can create a new empty workbook at anytime by clicking the New button on the Standard toolbar.

Hands-On 8.11 – Create a New Workbook

1. **Click** the New button.

   A new empty workbook should appear. You could use this workbook to create a new worksheet, however, you will close this workbook in the next step.

2. Choose **File→Close** from the menu bar.

   The workbook is empty, so Excel will close it without asking you to save it.

Opening Existing Workbooks

The **Open** dialog box lets you open a workbook from a disk into the computer's memory. You can edit the workbook once it has been opened.

Hands-On 8.12 – Open the Hands-On Lesson 8 workbook

1. Choose **File→Open...** from the menu bar or **click** the Open button on the Standard toolbar. Take a few moments to study the following illustration but don't perform the steps yet.

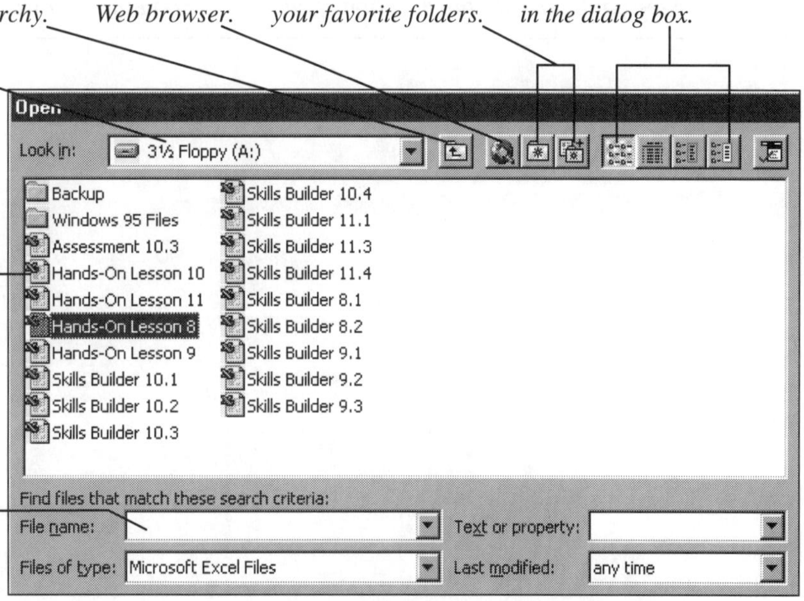

2. Use the following steps to open the Hands-On Lesson 8 workbook.

❶ ***Click here** and choose the disk drive that your diskette is in. It is most likely in 3 ½ Floppy [A:].*

❷ *Choose the **Hands-On Lesson 8** workbook.*

❸ ***Click** the **Open** button.*

***Note:** You can also open a workbook by double-clicking it on the list. This saves you the effort of having to click the Open button.*

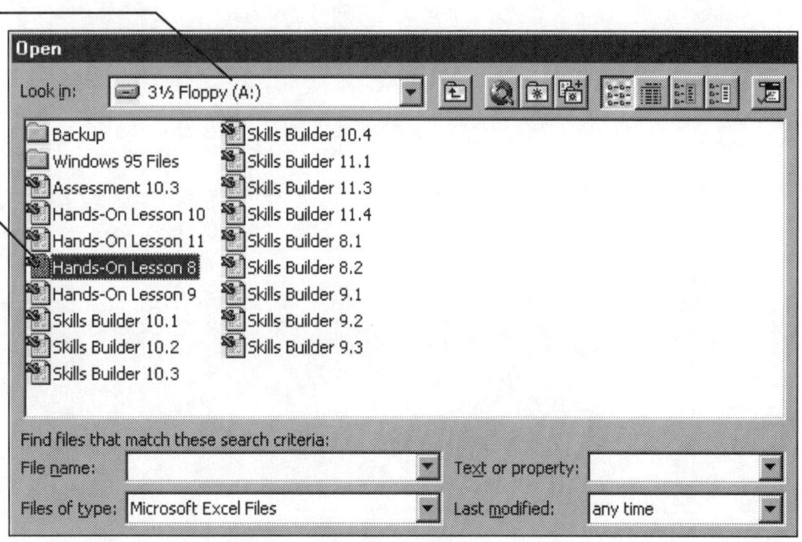

3. Take a few moments to scroll through the worksheet and you should notice that the most recent changes have been saved. You will exit from Excel on the next page.

Exiting From Excel

You should always exit from Excel when you have finished using the program. If you have one or more open workbooks and they have not been saved recently, then Excel will ask if you wish to save them.

Hands-On 8.13 – Exit from Excel

1. Choose **File→Exit** from the menu bar.

   The Excel program should close automatically and the Windows desktop should be displayed. Excel did not ask you to save the Hands-On Lesson 8 workbook because you did not change it after opening it in the previous exercise.

   Now continue with the questions and exercises on the following pages.

Concepts Review

True / False

1. Each workbook can have a maximum of one worksheet. 1. **T F**
2. A worksheet is composed of horizontal rows and vertical columns. 2. **T F**
3. Toolbars can be moved in the Excel window. 3. **T F**
4. Text entries can contain spaces. 4. **T F**
5. Numbers can only contain the digits 0 - 9 and not other characters. 5. **T F**
6. The Undo button lets you reverse up to the last 16 changes. 6. **T F**
7. A colon **:** is used to separate the beginning and ending cells in a range reference. 7. **T F**
8. You can select an entire row by clicking the row header. 8. **T F**
9. When given a choice, AutoSum will always sum the numbers to the left of the active cell instead of summing the numbers above the active cell. 9. **T F**
10. The New 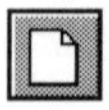 button lets you open an existing workbook. 10. **T F**

Multiple Choice

1. Which of the following keystrokes will always move the highlight to cell A1?
   a) Home.
   b) Ctrl + PageUp.
   c) Ctrl + Home.
   d) Ctrl + Insert. ( )
2. What happens when you enter a number in a cell that already has a text entry?
   a) The number replaces the text entry.
   b) Excel rejects the number and keeps the text entry intact.
   c) The cell contains both the number and text entry.
   d) The computer overheats and begins smoking. ( )
3. What happens when you insert an entry in the cell to the **right** of a long text entry?
   a) The display of the long entry is truncated.
   b) The long entry is permanently changed.
   c) It has no effect on the long entry.
   d) None of the above. ( )
4. What happens when you insert an entry in the cell to the **left** of a long text entry?
   a) The display of the long entry is truncated.
   b) The long entry is permanently truncated.
   c) It has no effect on the long entry.
   d) None of the above. ( )
5. Which button is used to confirm an entry?
   a) 
   b) 
   c) 
   d) None of the above. ( )

Skills Builder 8.1

In this exercise, you will open and edit a workbook. The purpose of this exercise is to demonstrate that sometimes it is easier to replace entries while other times it is easier to edit them.

Open a workbook and replace several entries

1. **Start Excel** and **click** the Open button on the Standard toolbar.
2. Navigate to your exercise diskette and **double-click** the workbook named **Skills Builder 8.1**.
3. **Click** cell **A4**.
4. Type **Ralph** and **tap** Enter.

   Notice it was easy to replace the entry because the name Ralph is easy to retype.
5. Replace the name **Calvin** in cell **A6** with the name **Steven**.

Use the Formula bar to edit several entries

6. **Click** cell **C4**.
7. **Click** in the Formula bar just in front of the telephone prefix 222.
8. **Tap** Delete **three times** to remove the prefix.
9. Type **333** and Confirm the entry.
10. Change the area code in cell **C8** from 714 to **814**.

Use in-cell editing to edit several entries

11. **Double-click** cell **D4**.

    The flashing insertion point should appear in the cell.
12. Use the → or ← keys to position the insertion point in front of the word **Lane**.
13. Use the Delete key to remove the word **Lane**.
14. Type **Dam** (as in holds back water) and Confirm the entry.
15. Edit the next five addresses using either the Formula bar or in-cell editing. The required changes are shown in bold in the following table.

Cell	Make these changes
D5	2900 **Carlton** Drive, San Mateo, CA 94401
D6	**2300** Palm Drive, Miami, FL 33147
D7	888 Wilson Street, **Concord**, CA **94518**
D8	320 Main Street, **Pittsburgh**, PA 17951
D9	132nd Street, Los Angeles, CA **90045**

16. When you have finished, choose **File→Close** from the menu bar and **click** the **Yes** button when Excel asks if you wish to save the changes.

Skills Builder 8.2

In this exercise, you will open and edit a workbook. You will use AutoSum to compute totals and you will use the alignment buttons to align entries.

Open a workbook and compute the Totals

1. **Click** the Open button on the Standard toolbar.

2. Navigate to your exercise diskette and **double-click** the workbook named **Skills Builder 8.2**.

3. **Click** cell **C10**.

4. **Click** AutoSum.

   Notice that Excel proposes the formula =SUM(C8:C9). Excel proposes this incorrect formula because there are empty cells in the range you need to sum. You will correct this by selecting the correct range in the next step.

5. **Drag** the mouse pointer over the range **C5:C9** as shown below.

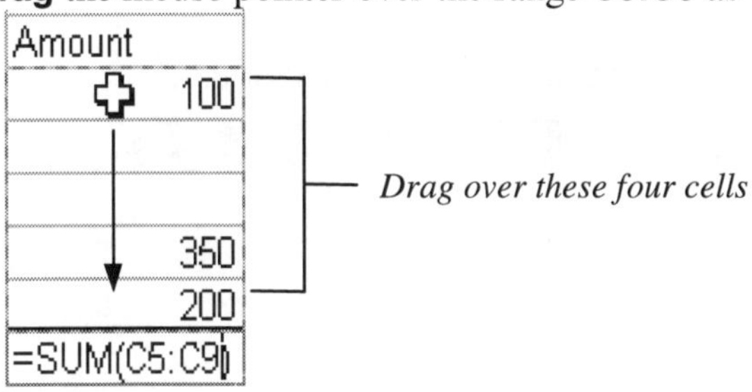

6. Confirm the entry and the total should equal **650**.

7. Use the preceding steps to compute the totals in cells **E10**, **G10** and **I10**.

   You may need to scroll to the right to see column I.

Align the entries

8. Use the following steps to align the cell entries for Q1.

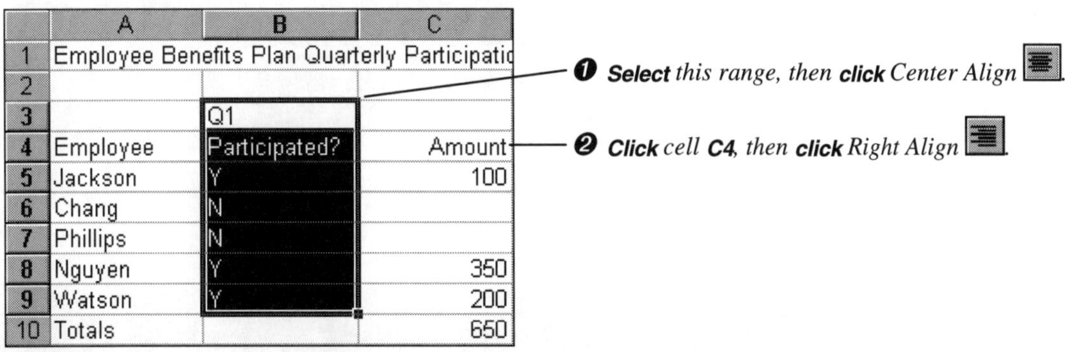

9. **Align** the entries for **Q2**, **Q3** and **Q4** as you just did for Q1. **Hint:** Use the Ctrl key to select multiple ranges that require the same alignment and align them with one command. You will also need to **right align** the word **Amount** in cells **E4**, **G4** and **I4**.

10. **Close** the workbook when you have finished and **save** the changes.

Assessment 8.1

1. Open a New workbook.
2. Use the following guidelines to create the worksheet shown below.
   - You will need to widen some of the columns to prevent the long entries from being truncated.
   - Use formulas to compute the Totals. Be careful because the rows and columns contain blank cells. You will need to manually override the ranges that AutoSum proposes.
   - Align the text entries in row 3 as shown.

Your completed worksheet should match the worksheet shown below.

3. **Click** the Print button on the Standard toolbar when you have finished.
   The Print button prints the entire worksheet.
4. **Close** the workbook when you have finished and **save** it as **Assessment 8.1**.

	A	B	C	D	E	F	G
1	Diane's Café - Employee Hourly Time Log						
2							
3	Employee	Wednesday	Thursday	Friday	Saturday	Sunday	Totals
4	Mary Johnson	6.5		5	6.5	4	22
5	Cliff Packard	4	6	6.5	6.5	4	27
6	Helen Martinez	4	6	6.5	6.5		23
7	Sarah Stonestown		4	4	4		12
8	Totals	14.5	16	22	23.5	8	84

9 Expanding on the Basics

Objectives:

- Use the Office Assistant
- Use the fill handle
- Work with formulas
- Format text and numbers
- Use the Merge and Center button
- Indent text entries
- Use the Format Painter
- Use Print Preview and the Print dialog box

The Project - Donna's Deli

In this lesson, you will help Donna Prusko develop an income and expense-tracking sheet for her new vegetarian health food business - Donna's Deli. Donna has recently given up a dead end job to pursue her dream and passion - a deli that serves delicious health-conscious food at reasonable prices. However, Donna realizes that the health of her business is just as important as the health of her customers. For this reason, she wants to develop a worksheet to track her income and expenses. The worksheet will use formulas to determine both gross and net profits and it will compute an important financial ratio. You will develop the worksheet shown below as you progress through this lesson.

	A	B	C	D	E	F
1	**Donna's Deli - Income and Expense Worksheet**					
2						
3			Quarterly Income			
4		Q1	Q2	Q3	Q4	
5	Dine-in Sales	21,000	23,000	28,000	42,000	
6	Take-out Sales	12,000	16,000	25,000	56,000	
7	Subtotal	**$33,000**	**$39,000**	**$53,000**	**$98,000**	
8						
9	Tips	2,500	2,700	3,000	4,500	
10	Sublease	500	500	500	500	
11	Subtotal	**$3,000**	**$3,200**	**$3,500**	**$5,000**	
12	Total Income	**$36,000**	**$42,200**	**$56,500**	**$103,000**	
13						
14			Quarterly Expenses			
15		Q1	Q2	Q3	Q4	
16	Rent	3,000	3,000	3,000	3,000	
17	Utilities	400	310	290	380	
18	Marketing	800	800	800	800	
19	Salaries	12,000	12,000	14,000	14,000	
20	Supplies	15,000	15,500	18,000	24,000	
21	Equipment	6,000	2,000	1,000	-	
22	Total Expenses	**$37,200**	**$33,610**	**$37,090**	**$42,180**	
23						
24	Gross Profit	**($1,200)**	**$8,590**	**$19,410**	**$60,820**	
25	Net Profit	**($1,200)**	**$8,590**	**$16,499**	**$45,615**	
26	Gross Profit vs. Income	**-3%**	**20%**	**34%**	**59%**	

The Office Assistant

Microsoft Office 97 has an interactive Help feature known as the Office Assistant. The Office Assistant provides tips and suggestions and it also lets you locate Help topics by typing questions in plain English. The Office Assistant monitors your activities and provides suggestions whenever it assumes you need assistance. You can display or hide the Office Assistant as discussed in the following Quick Steps.

Quick Steps: Displaying and Hiding the Office Assistant

To display the Office Assistant

- *Click the Office Assistant button on the Standard toolbar.*

To hide the Office Assistant

- *Click the Close button at the top right corner of the Office Assistant.*

Hands-On 9.1 – Check out the Office Assistant

1. Start Excel.
2. **Click** the Office Assistant button on the right end of the Standard toolbar.
   An animated paper clip or some other assistant will appear. There are several different assistants with different personalities. However, they all provide the same interactive assistance.
3. **Click** the **Tips** button on the yellow command area and a Tip of the Day will appear.
   Reading the daily tips can be an effective way to enhance your Excel skills.
4. **Click** the **Close** button at the bottom right corner of the tip.
5. Use the following steps to search for a Help topic.

❶ ***Click*** *anywhere on the assistant and the yellow command area will reappear.*

❷ *Type* ***Learn about the Fill*** *Handle in this box.*

❸ ***Click*** *the Search button and the Assistant will display a list of Help topics.*

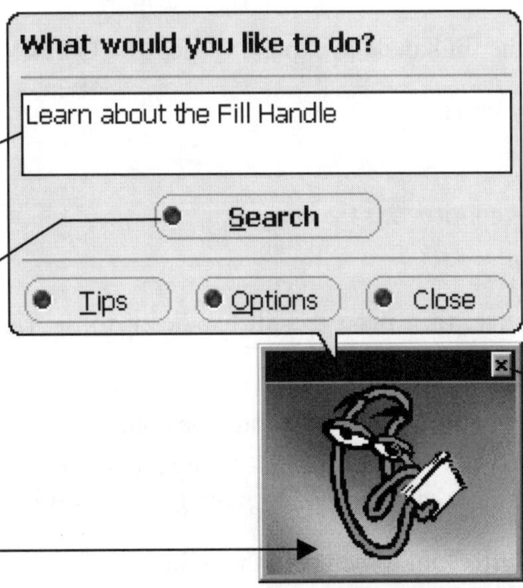

❹ ***Click*** *the* ***blue button*** *to the left of any of the Help topics and a Help screen will appear.*

❺ *Take a minute to read the Help topic, then click the Close button at the top-right corner of the Help screen.*

❻ *Finally,* ***click*** *the Close button on the Assistant.*

Feel free to use the Office Assistant whenever you have a question or are unsure how to complete a procedure. The Assistant can be very helpful once you learn to use it properly. Also, you can close the Assistant at any time by clicking the Close button.

The Fill Handle

A small black square is always visible at the bottom right corner of the active cell or the active range. This square is called the **fill handle**. The fill handle can be used to copy the content of the active cell to adjacent cells. The fill handle can also be used to enter common series such as days of the week or months of the year. You can also use the fill handle to expand a repeating series of numbers such as 5, 10, 15, 20 etc.

Hands-On 9.2 – Use the fill handle to expand a series and copy cells

1. Open the workbook named **Hands-On Lesson 9** from your exercise diskette.

Use the fill handle to expand the Q1 series

2. **Click** cell **B4**.

   Notice that cell B4 contains the heading Q1. Excel recognizes Q1 as the beginning of the series Q1 - Q4. You will expand the series by dragging the fill handle in the next step.

3. Use the following steps to expand the Q1 - Q4 series.

   ❶ *Position the mouse pointer on the bottom right corner of the cell and a black cross will appear.*

   ❷ **Drag** *to the right over the next three cells and a shaded rectangle will appear.*

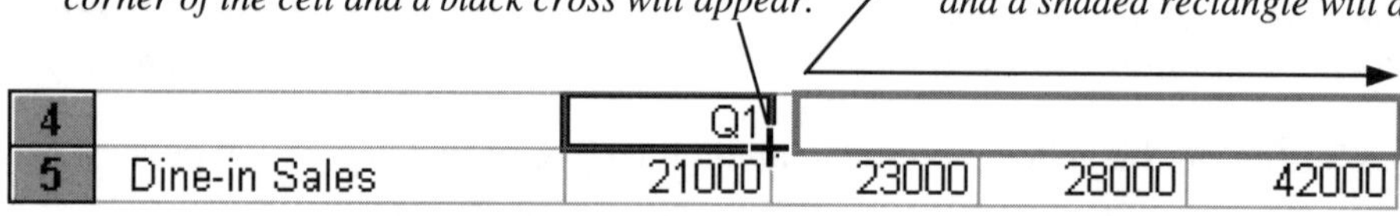

   ❸ *Release the mouse button and the series will be expanded to Q1 - Q4.*

   Excel recognizes Q1 and several other entries such as a day of the week (Saturday) or a month (January) as the beginning of a series. You can always expand the series using the technique shown above. Also, notice that Excel right aligned the headings Q2 - Q4 because Q1 was right aligned.

4. **Click** cell **B15** and use the fill handle to expand Q1 to Q1 - Q4 as you did in the previous step.

Use the fill handle to copy cells

5. **Click** cell **B7**.

6. **Click** AutoSum and confirm the entry.

   The Subtotal should equal 33000.

7. Make sure cell B7 is active, then **drag** the fill handle + to the right until the shaded rectangle is over cells C7, D7 and E7.

8. **Release** the mouse button and the formula should be copied to those cells.

   Notice that Excel determines whether it should copy the cell or expand a series. Excel will always copy the cell unless the cell represents the beginning of a series as explained above.

9. **Click** cell **B11** and use **AutoSum** to compute the Subtotal.

10. Use the fill handle to copy the formula in cell B11 to cells C11, D11 and E11.

11. Use these techniques to compute the **Total Expenses** in row **22** (not Total Income in row 12).

    Keep in mind that it would have been easier to select the four cells in these examples and use AutoSum to automatically compute the totals. However, there are times when it is beneficial to use the fill handle to copy cells as you will see in the next topic.

Formulas

You already learned how to compute totals with the AutoSum button. The AutoSum button provides a convenient method for summing a range of numbers. The summation of a range is the most common type of formula. However, you will need to use many other types of formulas in Excel. In fact, many worksheets such as financial models require hundreds or even thousands of complex formulas! You can manually enter formulas as you will do in this section or you can use Excel's Function Wizard to assist you in creating formulas and functions.

Always begin formulas with an equal = sign

It is recommended that you always begin formulas with an equal = sign. You can also begin formulas with a plus + or minus – sign, however, it is better to adopt one method. This way, you will know that the first step in creating a formula is to always use an equal = sign.

Formulas can include cell and range references

You already used the AutoSum button to create formulas such as =SUM(C3:E3). The formula in this example contains the range reference (C3:E3). Formulas derive their power from the use of cell and range references. There are two important benefits to using references in formulas.

1. Since the formula refers to a cell or a range of cells, the formula results are automatically recalculated when the data is changed in the referenced cell(s).
2. The formula can be copied (as you did with the fill handle) to other cells.

Formulas can include arithmetic operators and spaces

Formulas can include the standard arithmetic operators shown in the following table. You can also use spaces within formulas to improve the appearance and readability of the formula. Notice that each formula in the table begins with an equal = sign. Also, keep in mind that each formula would be entered in a cell and the resulting calculation would be displayed in that cell.

Operator	Example	Comments
+ (addition)	=B7 + B11	Adds the values in cells B7 and B11.
- (subtraction)	=B7 - B11	Subtracts the value in B11 from B7.
* (multiplication)	=B7 * B11	Multiplies the values in B7 and B11.
/ (division)	=B7 / B11	Divides the value in B7 by the value in B11.
^ (exponentiation)	=B7 ^ 3	Raises the value in B7 to the third power (B7*B7*B7).
% (percent)	=B7 * 10%	Multiplies the value in B7 by 10% (.10).
( ) (calculations)	=B7 / (C4-C2)	Parentheses change the order of calculations. In this example, C2 would be subtracted from C4 and then B7 would be divided by the result.

Hands-On 9.3 – Manually enter formulas

In this exercise, you will enter two formulas in the Hands-On Lesson 9 worksheet.

Compute the Total Income in cells B12 and C12

1. **Click** cell **B12**.
2. Type **=B7+B11** and **click** the Confirm button.

   The result should be 36000. This is the summation of the two Subtotals in cells B7 and B11.
3. **Click** cell **C12.**
4. Type **=C7+C11** and **click** the Confirm button and the result should be 42200.

Relative cell references

All formulas use relative cell references unless you specifically instruct Excel to use an absolute reference (absolute references are not discussed in this course). Relative references make it easy to copy formulas to other cells. For example, cell C12 contains the formula =C7+C11. If this formula is copied to cell D12, then the formula in D12 will become =D7+D11. The references to cells C7 and C11 are updated to reflect the new location of the formula.

Point Mode

One potential danger that can occur when typing formulas is that you will accidentally type the wrong cell reference. This is easy to do especially if the worksheet is complex and contains large numbers of cells. **Point mode** can help you avoid this problem. With point mode, you can insert a reference in a formula by clicking or dragging the desired cell(s). You will use this technique in the following exercise.

Hands-On 9.4 – Use point mode and copy a formula with the fill handle

In this exercise, you will complete the last two formulas in row 12.

Create a formula using point mode

1. **Click** cell **D12**.
2. Type an equal = sign.

   Notice Excel begins building the formula by entering the equal = sign in the Formula bar.
3. **Click** cell **D7**.

   Notice that Excel adds the reference D7 to the formula in the Formula bar.
4. Type a plus **+** sign (try tapping the plus + key on the Numeric keypad).
5. **Click** cell **D11**.

   The Formula bar should contain the completed formula =D7+D11.
6. Confirm the entry and the total should be 56500.

Continued...

Copy the formula with the fill handle

7. Make sure the highlight is in cell **D12**, and then **drag** the **fill handle** + one cell to the right.

   The formula should be copied to cell E12 and the result should be 103000.

8. **Click** cell **E12** and notice the formula in the Formula bar.

   The formula should be =E7+E11. The references were updated to reflect the new formula location.

The Edit Formula Button and the Formula Palette

You can begin a formula by clicking the Edit Formula button on the Formula bar. This has the same effect as tapping the equal = key on the Numeric keypad. Excel also displays a Formula Palette whenever the Edit Formula button is clicked. The Formula Pallete can assist you in creating and editing formulas.

Hands-On 9.5 – Use the Edit Formula button to create additional formulas

1. If necessary, scroll down until rows 12 - 26 are visible.

2. **Click** cell **B24**.

   Cell B24 will contain the Gross Profit. The Gross Profit is calculated as the Total Income in cell B12 minus the Total Expenses in Cell B22.

3. **Click** the Edit Formula button on the Formula bar.

   Excel will enter an equal = sign in the Formula bar and the Formula Palette will appear below the Formula bar. You will see the result of your formula in the palette as you build it using point mode.

4. **Click** cell **B12** and the Formula Palette will indicate a result of 36000.

5. Type a minus **-** sign, then **click** cell **B22**.

6. Confirm the formula by **clicking** the **OK** button on the Formula Palette.

   The Gross Profit should equal –1200 or (1200). Excel may be set-up on your computer to display negative numbers with parenthesis instead of minus signs. This is a common convention that many accountants use. As you can see, Donna's Deli is not profitable in the first quarter.

7. Copy the formula to the next three cells by **dragging** the fill handle + to the right.

   The completed row should match the row shown below.

24	Gross Profit	-1200	8590	19410	60820

Calculate Net Profit by multiplying Gross Profit * Tax Rate

*You will calculate the Net Profit in the next few steps. You will use a simplified Net Profit calculation that is the Gross Profit minus income taxes. We will make the assumption that Donna will pay no taxes in Q1 and Q2 because she lost money in Q1 and her gross profit was only $8,590 in Q2. Furthermore, we will assume that Donna's tax rate will be 15% for Q3 and 25% for Q4. The formula is, Net Profit = Gross Profit * (1- Taxrate). For example, if the tax rate is 15%, then Donna will keep 85% of her Gross Profit. So the Net Profit = Gross Profit * .85.*

8. **Click** cell **B24**.

Continued...

Look at the Formula bar and notice the Gross Profit is calculated as B12 - B22. The Gross Profit and Net Profit will be the same in Q1 since Donna will not pay any income tax. In the next few steps, you will attempt to copy the gross profit formula from cell B24 to cell B25.

9. Use the following step to copy the formula from cell B24 to B25.

24	Gross Profit	($1,200)
25	Net Profit	

❶ *Drag the fill handle down to cell B25 and the Net Profit will equal 0.*

10. **Click** cell **B24** and notice the Gross Profit formula in the Formula bar is =B12-B22.

11. Now **click** cell **B25** and notice the Net Profit formula is =B13-B23.

12. Look at cells **B13** and **B23** in the worksheet and you will notice they are empty.

    The result of the formula is 0 because cells B13 and B23 are empty. This example demonstrates that you must be careful when copying formulas. Excel updated the cell references when you copied the formula. This produced an incorrect result.

13. **Click** Undo to reverse the copy procedure.

14. **Click** cell **B25** and enter the formula **=B24**.

    This simple formula makes cells B24 and B25 equal to one another.

15. **Click** cell **C25** and enter the formula **= C24**.

    Once again, the Net Profit and Gross Profit should be equal in Q2.

16. **Click** cell **D25** and enter the formula **=D24 * 85%**.

    The result should be 16498.5. We are assuming a tax rate of 15% in Q3, so Donna gets to keep 85% of her gross profit.

17. **Click** cell **E25** and enter the formula **=E24 * 75%**.

    The result should be 45615. Keep in mind that you can either type the formulas or use point mode and the Formula Palette. From this point forward, you will be instructed to enter a formula and you should use whichever method works best for you.

Calculate the ratios in row 26 by dividing the Gross Profit by the Total Income

Donna wants to determine the ratio of Gross Profit to Total Income or GP/TI. This ratio is important in determining the health of a business. This ratio is one indicator that will show Donna how fast she can grow her business by reinvesting the money she earns. This ratio will show Donna the amount of profit she will earn from each dollar of product she sells.

18. **Click** cell **B26** and enter the formula **=B24/B12**.

    The result should be -0.03333. You will convert this number to a percentage later in this lesson.

19. Use the fill handle to **copy** the formula **to** cells **C26**, **D26** and **E26**.

    The results should match the results shown below.

26	Gross Profit vs. Income	-0.03333	0.203555	0.34354	0.590485

20. **Click** cell **C26** and notice the formula =C24/C12.

    Once again, Excel updated the cell references when the formula was copied. In this case, it is good that the references were updated because the formula now refers to the correct Gross Profit and Total Income in cells C24 and C12.

21. **Click** the Save button to save the changes to the worksheet.

Number Formats

Excel lets you format numbers in a variety of ways. The number formats change the way numbers are displayed in the worksheet. The following table discusses the most common number formats.

Number Format	Description
General	Numbers have a General style when they are first entered. The General style does not apply any special formats to the numbers.
Comma	The Comma format inserts a comma between every third digit in the number. An optional decimal point with decimal places can also be displayed.
Currency	The Currency format is the same as the Comma format except a dollar $ sign is placed in front of the number.
Percent	A percent % sign is inserted to the right of the number. The number is multiplied by 100 and the resulting percentage is displayed in the cell.

The following table provides several examples of formatted numbers.

Number you enter	Format	How the number is displayed
1000.984	General	1000.984
1000.984	Comma with 0 decimal places Comma with 2 decimal places	1,000 1,000.98
1000.984	Currency with 0 decimal places Currency with 2 decimal places	$1,000 $1,000.98
.5366	Percent with 0 decimal places Percent with 2 decimal places	54% 53.66%

Setting Number Formats with the Formatting Toolbar

The Fc-rmatting toolbar has several buttons that let you apply the Currency, Comma and Percent number formats or styles as they are called. These are the most common types of number styles. The Formatting toolbar also has buttons that let you increase or decrease the number of decimal places. The following illustration discusses the various number formatting buttons on the Formatting toolbar.

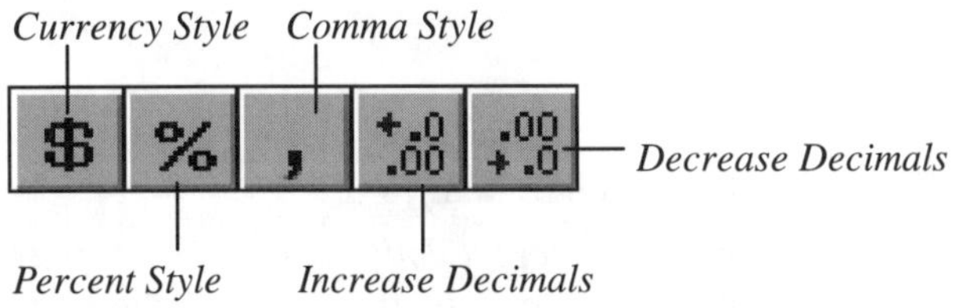

Increasing and decreasing the decimals does not change the actual number

The Increase and Decrease decimal buttons change the number of displayed decimals. For example, you could enter the number 100.37 and then format it as Currency with 0 decimal places. The number would then be displayed as $100. However, the actual number would remain 100.37. The number 100.37 would be used in any calculations that refer to that cell.

Hands-On 9.6 – Format numbers

In this exercise, you will format numbers with buttons on the Formatting toolbar.

Apply the Currency Style to the first Subtotal row

1. **Scroll up** until the top row of the worksheet is visible.
2. **Select** the **four Subtotals in row 7** (but **be careful not to use the fill handle**).

   *The fill handle is **not** used to select cells. It is only used to copy cells or to expand a series. Make sure your pointer has the thick cross ✥ shape whenever you wish to select cells (like now).*

3. **Click** the Currency Style $ button and the cells should be formatted as shown below.

7	Subtotal	$ 33,000.00	$ 39,000.00	$ 53,000.00	$ 98,000.00

   Notice that the Currency Style adds a dollar sign in front of the number and a comma between every third digit. It also adds a decimal point with two decimal places. Excel should also have widened the columns to accommodate the additional characters and numbers. Also notice that the formatted numbers are shifted slightly to the left and do not line-up with the numbers above them. You will adjust the alignment later in this lesson.

Decrease the decimals

4. Make sure the four cells you just formatted are selected.
5. **Click** the Decrease Decimal button **twice** to remove the decimal display.

   Notice the dollar signs $ are positioned on the left side of the cells. Once again, you will adjust this alignment later in the lesson.

6. **Select** the Subtotal and Total Income cells in rows 11 and 12 as shown below.

11	Subtotal	3000	3200	3500	5000
12	Total Income	36000	42200	56500	103000

7. **Click** the Currency Style $ button, then decrease the decimals to 0.
8. Format the numbers in rows **22**, **24** and **25** as **Currency** with **0** decimals.

Apply the Comma Style

9. **Select** the numbers in rows **5** and **6**.
10. **Click** the Comma Style , button, then decrease the decimals to 0.

    Notice the Comma Style is similar to the Currency Style except a dollar sign is not displayed. Also notice that the numbers now line-up with the Currency formatted numbers in the Subtotal row.

11. Format the numbers in the ranges **B9:E10** and **B16:E21** as **Comma** with **0** decimals.

Apply the Percent Style to the last row

12. **Select** the numbers in the last row of the worksheet.
13. **Click** the Percent Style % button.

    The numbers should be formatted as Percent with 0 decimal places. The Percent Style does not display decimals because it is usually better to display percentages without decimals. You can always use the Increase Decimal button to display decimals if desired. You will learn more about number formats in the next section.

Setting Number Formats with the Format Cells Dialog Box

The Format Cells dialog box provides additional number formats that are not available on the Formatting toolbar. You can format numbers in virtually any manner by first selecting them and then using this dialog box. You can even create your own customized number formats to suit your needs.

Dollar signs $ can have a fixed or floating format

The dollar signs $ in the Hands-On Lesson 9 worksheet currently have a fixed format. In other words, they are fixed on the left side of the cells. You can use the Format Cells dialog box to change the dollar sign format to floating. The floating format positions the dollar signs just to the left of the numbers. You will use this technique in the following Hands-On exercise.

Hands-On 9.7 – Change the dollar $ signs to floating and explore the dialog box

1. **Select** the numbers with the Currency format in row 7.
2. Choose **Format→Cells...** form the menu bar.
3. Make sure the Number tab is active at the top of the dialog box.
4. Notice the Custom option is chosen at the bottom of the Category list.

   The Custom option is chosen because you modified the Currency Style when you decreased the decimal places in the previous exercises. You created a custom number format when you did this.

5. Use the following steps to format the numbers with floating dollar $ signs.

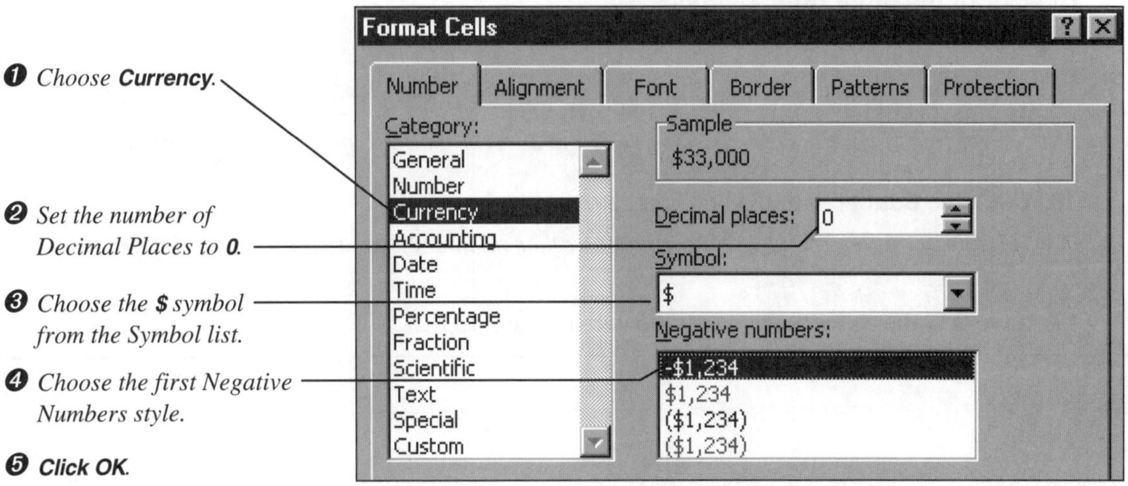

Notice that the dollar signs are now floating just in front of the numbers. The Currency Style creates floating dollar signs. Also, notice that the numbers are now shifted slightly to the right and they no longer line-up with the numbers above them. This is because of the Negative Numbers option you set. The Negative Numbers option impacts the alignment of the numbers. You will adjust the Negative Numbers option in the next step.

Continued...

Adjust the Negative Numbers option

6. Make sure cells **B7:E7** are still selected, then choose **Format→Cells...** form the menu bar.

7. Notice the various Negative Numbers formats.

   The formats that are red in color will cause negative numbers to display in red. This is a convention that many accountants like to use. Also notice that some of the formats have parenthesis around them. Once again, many accountants like negative numbers to be displayed with parenthesis instead of a minus sign as shown in the first format.

8. Choose the third Negative Numbers format **($1,234)** and **click OK**.

   The numbers should now be aligned with the numbers above them. Just remember that the Negative Numbers formats determine how the numbers line-up on the right side or with the decimal points.

Check out the Accounting Style

9. Make sure cells **B7:E7** are still selected, then choose **Format→Cells...** form the menu bar.

10. Choose the **Accounting** option.

11. Make sure the Symbol type is set to **$** and the **Decimal Places** are set to **0**.

12. **Click OK** and the dollar $ signs will once again have a fixed placement on the left side of the cells.

    Notice that this was how the numbers were formatted when you clicked the Currency Style button on the toolbar and decreased the decimals. The Currency Style button actually applies the Accounting Style to the numbers. The Accounting Style positions the dollar signs on the left side of the cell with a fixed format.

13. **Click** Undo  to restore the Currency Style.

Check out the other number styles

14. Choose **Format→Cells...** form the menu bar.

15. Take a few minutes to browse through the various number styles in the Category list.

    Feel free choose a style and then read the description that appears at the bottom of the dialog box.

16. **Click** the **Cancel** button when you have finished exploring.

    Later in this lesson, you will format the other numbers that currently have dollar signs.

17. Save  the changes and continue with the next topic.

Merging Cells

Excel's Merge cells option lets you merge one or more cells together. Merged cells behave as one large cell. This allows you to align text within the merged cell. You can merge cells vertically or horizontally.

The Merge and Center Button

The Merge and Center button merges selected cells and changes the alignment of the merged cell to center. This technique is often used to center a heading across columns. The following example shows a heading that is centered across columns B through E.

The Quarterly Income heading is centered above columns B through E.

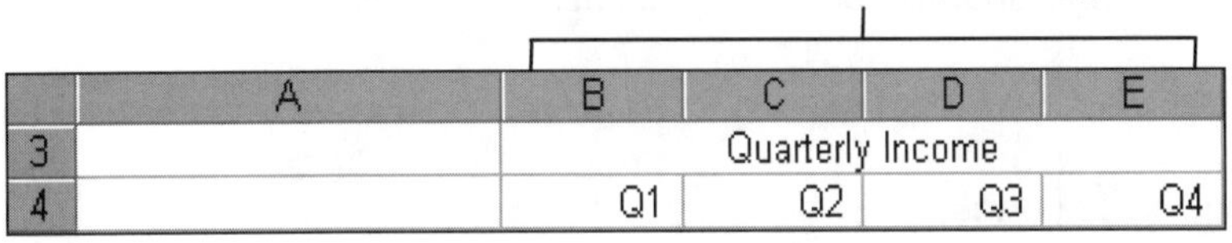

Hands-On 9.8 – Center headings across columns

1. **Select** the range **B3:E3** as shown below.

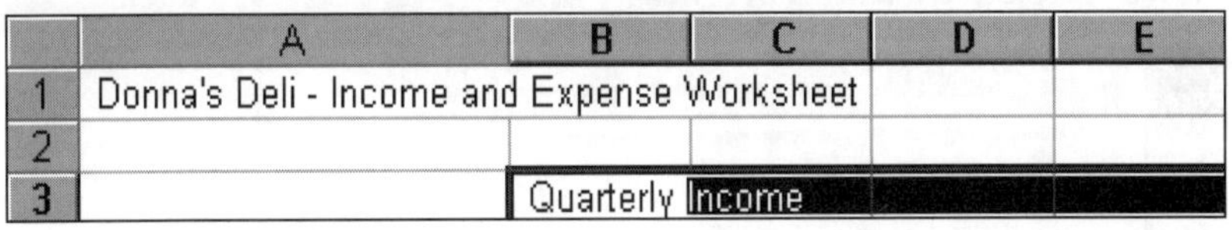

Notice that this range includes the heading you wish to center (Quarterly Income) and the range of cells you wish to center this heading in (B3:E3).

2. **Click** the Merge and Center button (near the middle of the Formatting toolbar).

   Notice the cells have been merged together and the Center button is depressed.

3. **Click** the Align Left button and the entry will move to the left side of the merged cell.
4. **Click** the Center button to re-center the entry.
5. Choose **Format→Cells...** from the menu bar.
6. **Click** the Alignment tab on the Format Cells dialog box.

   Notice the Merge cells *box is checked. This box is checked whenever cells are merged.*

7. Remove the check from the Merge cells box and **click OK**.
8. **Click** anywhere to deselect the cells and notice they are no longer merged.
9. **Click** Undo to restore the merging.
10. **Select** the range **B14:E14**.
11. **Click** the Merge and Center button to center the Quarterly Expenses heading.

Indenting Text

The Increase Indent and Decrease Indent buttons on the Formatting toolbar let you indent text entries from the left edge of the cell. This can be useful in showing that one entry is subordinate to another.

Hands-On 9.9 – Indent text entries

1. **Click** cell **A5**.
2. **Click** the Increase Indent button **twice**.

   Notice the Dine-in Sales entry is indented slightly each time you click the button.
3. **Click** the Decrease Indent once.
4. **Click** cell **A6** and increase the indent **once**.

Indent multiple entries

5. **Select** cells **A9** and **A10**.
6. **Press & Hold** the Ctrl key and select the range **A16:A21**.

   The cells you should have selected are shown below.

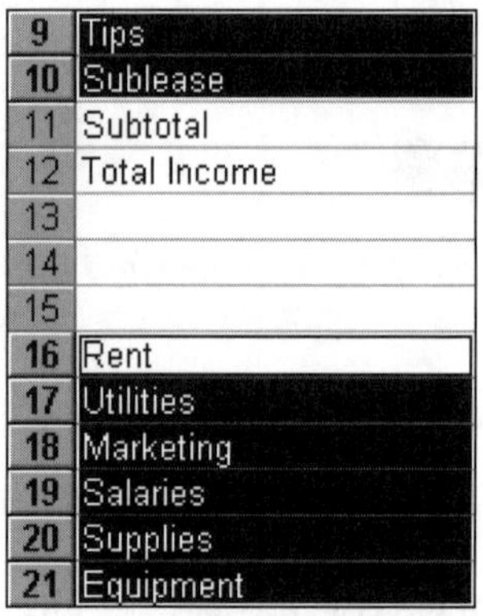

7. Increase the indent **once**.

Formatting Text and Numbers

The Formatting toolbar has several buttons that let you format text and numbers. You can change the size and typeface of text. You can also change the color of text and add bold, italics and underlining to text.

Hands-On 9.10 – Formatting text and numbers

Change the typeface and size and add Bold

1. **Click** cell **A1**.

2. Use the Formatting toolbar and the following steps to format the title.

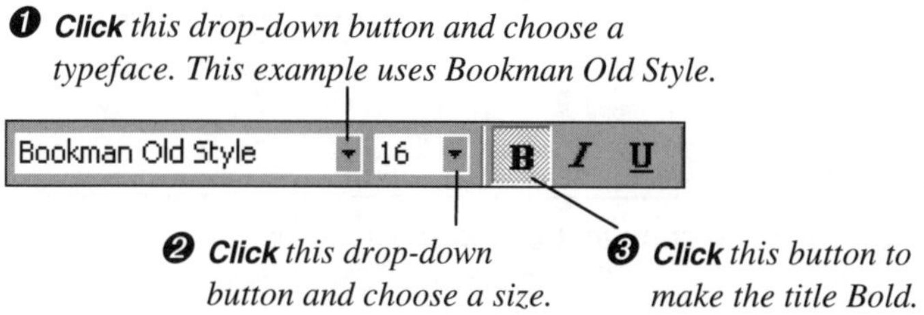

Notice that the entire title is formatted. Once again, the entire title belongs to cell A1 even though it is displayed over the adjacent cells.

Change the color

3. **Click** the Font Color drop-down button on the right end of the Formatting toolbar.

4. Choose your favorite color.

   Notice that the color you chose is now displayed on the button. You can now apply the same color to other cells by selecting the cells and then clicking the button.

Apply the same color to another cell

5. **Click** cell **B3**.

   Cell B3 is now part of the large merged cell in the range B3:E3.

6. **Click** the Font Color button and the same color will be applied to Quarterly Income.

7. Increase the size of Quarterly Income to **12** and make it **Bold**.

Format the Q1-Q4 headings

8. **Select** the **Q1 - Q4** headings in row 4.

9. Apply any formats you desire to Q1 – Q4.

   You will use the Format Painter to copy text and number formats in the next topic.

The Format Painter

The Format Painter button on the Standard toolbar lets you copy text and number formats from one cell to other cells. This can be an effective and efficient way to format cells. Another benefit of the Format Painter is it helps create consistent formatting throughout a workbook.

Quick Steps: *Copying Text and Number Formats*

To copy text and number formats with the Format Painter

- *Click the cell whose formats you wish to copy.*
- *Click the Format Painter or double-click if you wish to copy the formats to more than one location.*
- *Select the cells that you wish to copy the formats to.*
- *If you double-clicked in the first step, then click the Format Painter button when you are finished.*

Hands-On 9.11 – Copy text and number formats

In this exercise, you will use the Format Painter to copy text and number formats.

Copy text formats

1. **Click** cell **B3** (the merged cell with the Quarterly Income heading).
2. **Click** the Format Painter and the PaintBrush pointer should appear.
3. **Click** cell **B14** (the merged cell with the Quarterly Expenses heading).
   The text formats should be copied to that heading.
4. **Click** cell **B4**.
   This cell should contain the heading Q1.
5. **Click** the Format Painter.
6. **Select** the range **B15:E15** as shown below and the format will be copied to those cells.

15		Q1	Q2	Q3	Q4

Copy number formats

7. **Select** the cells that contain numbers in row 7 and add Bold to the numbers.
8. **Click** cell **B7**.
   Notice that this cell (and the rest of the numbers in row 7) has a Currency Style with the dollar sign floating just in front of the number. You will use the Format Painter to copy both the number and text formats to the numbers in rows 11 and 12 and rows 22-25. Notice that these rows currently have a fixed dollar sign on the left edge of the cell.
9. **Double-click** the Format Painter.
10. **Select** the range **B11:E12** as shown below and the formats will be copied to those cells.

11	Subtotal	$3,000	$3,200	$3,500	$5,000
12	Total Income	$36,000	$42,200	$56,500	$103,000

Continued...

11. **Select** the range **B22:E26** as shown below and the formats will be copied to those cells.

22	Total Expenses	$37,200	$33,610	$37,090	$42,180
23					
24	Gross Profit	($1,200)	$8,590	$19,410	$60,820
25	Net Profit	($1,200)	$8,590	$16,499	$45,615
26	Gross Profit vs. Income	($0)	$0	$0	$1

12. **Click** the Format Painter to turn it off.

    Notice that you had to turn the Format Painter off this time because you double-clicked it initially. Also, notice the Percent number style in row 26 has been removed. Be careful when you are trying to copy text formats but not number formats. In this example, you wanted to copy the bold text style to row 26 but not the Currency Style. Keep in mind that the Format Painter copies both text and number formats.

13. **Select** the numbers in row 26 and use the Percent Style button to reapply the Percent Style.

14. Feel free to format the worksheet in any way that you feel looks attractive.

    When formatting a worksheet, try to format the items you wish to draw attention to.

15. Turn to the second page of this lesson and take a look at the completed worksheet. The numbers and formats should match the worksheet you have developed.

16. Save the changes and continue with the next topic.

Print Preview and the Print Dialog Box

You have been printing with the Print button thus far in this course. The Print button sends the entire worksheet to the printer. Excel also has a Print dialog box which provides several printing options and lets you manage your print jobs. The Print Preview feature lets you preview a worksheet prior to printing it. The worksheet appears almost exactly as it will appear when it is printed. Print Preview can save paper and wear and tear on your printer. It can also save you time and help you avoid printing worksheets that aren't quite ready to be printed.

Hands-On 9.12 – Use Print Preview and the Print dialog box

Use Print Preview

1. **Click** the Print Preview button on the Standard toolbar (5th button from the left).

   The Print Preview window will appear. The colored text in your worksheet will appear in black if you do not have a color printer. You can only print colored text if you have a color printer.

2. Zoom in by **clicking** the mouse pointer (it will look like a magnifying glass) on the worksheet.

3. Use the vertical scroll bar to **scroll** up and down.

   Notice that Print Preview displays the worksheet almost exactly as it will print. Print Preview is very close to full WYSIWYG (What You See Is What You Get). Also, notice the Zoom option on the Print Preview toolbar. You just used the Zoom option by clicking on the worksheet. You will learn how to use the Setup and Margins options later in this course. Also notice the Print button. You could use this button to print the worksheet. However, we will delay printing for now.

4. **Click** anywhere on the worksheet to zoom back out.

5. **Click** the **Close** button to return to the normal worksheet view.

Check out the print range

6. If necessary, scroll to the right until you see a vertical dashed line in your worksheet.

   The line should be located between columns G and H. This line represents the right edge of the first printed page. This line appears after you use Print Preview or after you print the worksheet.

7. **Scroll** down until you see a horizontal dashed line in your worksheet.

   The line should be located around row 50. This line represents the bottom of the first page.

Continued...

Check out the Print dialog box

8. Choose **File** from the menu bar.

Notice that Print Preview can also be chosen from the File menu (but don't do it).

9. Choose **Print...** and the Print dialog box will display.

10. Take a few moments to study the following illustration.

This button lets you choose a print driver (although you probably won't need to). A print driver lets Excel communicate with your printer.

You can print multiple copies of a worksheet by entering a number here.

These buttons let you choose which worksheets in the workbook you want to print. The Selected Sheets option is chosen because you are only using one worksheet (Sheet1). The Selection option lets you print only the cells that are currently selected in the worksheet.

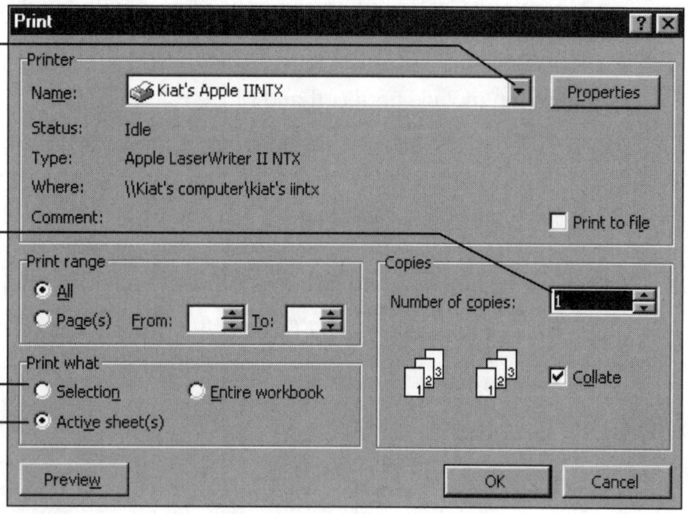

11. Click OK to print the entire worksheet.

Keep in mind that you did not have to use the Print dialog box to print this worksheet. The Print  *button would have worked just fine for this worksheet. The Print dialog box becomes more useful with large worksheets or when you have special printing needs.*

Print a selected range

12. Select the range **A1:E12**.

You will print just this income part of the worksheet in the next few steps.

13. Choose **File→Print...** from the menu bar.

14. Choose the Selection 

option and **click OK**.

15. Retrieve your printout from the printer and you will see that only the selected range was printed.

16. Feel free to experiment with the print options.

17. Close the workbook and **save** the changes when you have finished.

Now continue with the end-of-lesson questions and exercises on the following pages.

Concepts Review

True / False

1. The Office Assistant  button is used to display the Office Assistant. 1. **T F**
2. The fill handle cannot be used to copy formulas. 2. **T F**
3. The Merge and Center button can only be used with numbers. 3. **T F**
4. Formulas must always begin with an open parenthesis (. 4. **T F**
5. Formulas can include both cell and range references. 5. **T F**
6. The * is used to represent multiplication in formulas. 6. **T F**
7. Point mode can be used to insert cell and range references in formulas. 7. **T F**
8. The Comma number style inserts a dollar sign in front of the number. 8. **T F**
9. You can set a typeface and size for both text and numbers. 9. **T F**
10. The Format Painter copies text formats but not number formats. 10. **T F**

Multiple Choice

1. What should you do before clicking the Merge and Center button?
   a) Click the cell that contains the entry you wish to center.
   b) Select the cells you wish to center the entry across while making sure the entry is included in the selection.
   c) Select the entire row that contains the entry you wish to center. ( )
   d) None of the above.
2. Which of the following symbols can be used to begin a formula?
   a) +
   b) -
   c) =
   d) All of the above. ( )
3. Which of the following characters can be used in formulas?
   a) +
   b) %
   c) blank space
   d) All of the above. ( )
4. How would the number 10000.367 be displayed if you format it as comma with 2 decimals?
   a) 10,000.38
   b) $10,000.38
   c) 10,000
   d) None of the above. ( )
5. How is the dollar sign positioned with the Accounting number style?
   a) Floats to the immediate left of the number.
   b) Fixed on the left edge of the cell.
   c) The Accounting style does not place a dollar sign in front of the number.
   d) It depends on whether the number has a decimal point. ( )

Skills Builder 9.1

In this exercise, you will open a home budget worksheet on your exercise diskette. You will format the worksheet until it matches the worksheet shown at the end of this exercise.

Open the workbook and center the title

1. **Open** the workbook named **Skills Builder 9.1** on your exercise diskette.
2. Widen column A until the text entries in that column are visible.
3. **Select** the range **A1:G1** as shown below.

1	1996 Home Budget						

4. **Click** the Merge and Center button to center 1996 Home Budget above the worksheet.

Use the fill handle to copy headings

5. **Select** the heading **January** in cell **B3 and** the **empty cell** to the right of January.
6. **Drag** the fill handle + over the **next four cells** to the right and Excel will expand the series.

   Excel assumes you want the series January - March with an empty cell between each month. This is a correct assumption and the result is shown below.

3		January		February		March

7. **Select** cells **B4** and **C4** (the Budget and Spent cells).
8. **Drag** the fill handle + over the next four cells to the right and Excel will copy cells B4 and C4 to those cells.

   You should now have three sets of Budget Spent cells.

Center the month headings across columns

9. **Select** the **January** heading and the **blank cell** to the right of it.
10. **Click** Merge and Center to center January over the Budget and Spent columns.
11. **Center** the **February** and **March** headings over their Budget and Spent columns.
12. **Select row 4** and right align the Budget and Spent headings.

Compute all three Subtotals with a single command

In the next two steps, you will use the Ctrl key to select multiple ranges.

13. **Select** the range **B9:G9** (the cells where the Subtotals in row 9 will be placed).
14. **Press & Hold** the Ctrl key while you **select** the ranges **B14:G14** and **B19:G19**.

    You should now have all three of the Subtotal ranges selected.

15. **Click** AutoSum Σ and all three Subtotal rows will be computed.

Compute the Totals and Differences

16. **Click** cell **B21**.
17. Enter the formula **=B9+B14+B19** and confirm the entry.

    You can type the formula or use Point Mode.

Continued...

18. Use the **fill handle** ✛ to copy the formula across the row.

19. Click cell **B22**.

This cell will contain the Difference between the January Budget and January Spent in row 21.

20. Enter the formula **=B21-C21**.

The result should be 158.

21. Compute the Differences in cells **D22** and **F22**.

The results should be 118 and -739. You may want to use some trick or shortcut to enter these formulas. For example, you may want to use the fill handle to copy the formula in cell B22 across and then delete the formulas in cells C22, E22 and G22.

Format the numbers then copy the number formats

22. Select the **Subtotal** numbers in **row 9**.

23. Click the Currency button.

24. Click the Decrease Decimal button **twice** to reduce the decimals to 0.

If you want the dollar $ signs to float next to the numbers, then make sure the cells are selected and use the Format→Cells... command. Choose the Currency style and set the number of decimal places and other options as desired.

25. Click cell **B9**.

26. Double-click the Format Painter button.

27. Drag the mouse pointer over the Subtotal numbers in row 14, then row 19, and finally drag over the Total and Difference numbers in the last rows.

The Currency format should be copied to the numbers in those rows.

28. Click the Format Painter to turn it off.

Format the text

29. Click cell **A1** (the large merged cell).

30. Set the point size to **16** and use **Bold** and a color to make the title stand out.

31. Format the headings in rows **3** and **4** in any way you feel looks attractive.

32. Format the first Subtotal row with an attractive size, color and typeface.

33. Use the Format Painter to copy the formats from the Subtotal row to the other Subtotal rows.

34. Format the Total and Differences rows with an attractive size, color and typeface.

Continued...

Change the numbers and watch the formulas recalculate

35. Click cell **G5**.

This cell contains the amount of money that was spent on the mortgage. Imagine you have an adjustable rate mortgage and the monthly payment just went up. You will change the number in cell G5 in the next step. Keep an eye on the Totals and Differences formulas at the bottom of the worksheet when you change the number. The formulas will automatically recalculate the numbers.

36. Type **1075** and Confirm ✓ the entry.

The new Total in cell G21 should be 2879 and the new difference in cell F22 should be -814.

37. Your worksheet should match the example below (although the formatting may be different). For example, your dollar signs $ may be fixed on the left edges of the cells.

38. Close the worksheet when you have finished and **save** the changes.

	A	B	C	D	E	F	G
1	1996 Home Budget						
2							
3		January		**February**		**March**	
4		Budget	Spent	Budget	Spent	Budget	Spent
5	Mortgage	1000	1000	1000	1000	1000	1075
6	Insurance	200	200	0	0	0	0
7	Phone	60	75	60	80	60	145
8	Utilities	100	78	100	120	100	95
9	**Subtotal**	**$1,360**	**$1,353**	**$1,160**	**$1,200**	**$1,160**	**$1,315**
10							
11	Clothing	100	54	100	0	100	234
12	Entertainment	120	80	120	90	120	245
13	Food	235	220	235	190	235	250
14	**Subtotal**	**$455**	**$354**	**$455**	**$280**	**$455**	**$729**
15							
16	Car Insurance	180	180	0	0	0	0
17	Car Maintenance	50	0	50	67	50	435
18	Car Payment	400	400	400	400	400	400
19	**Subtotal**	**$630**	**$580**	**$450**	**$467**	**$450**	**$835**
20							
21	**Grand Total**	**$2,445**	**$2,287**	**$2,065**	**$1,947**	**$2,065**	**$2,879**
22	**Differences**	**$158**		**$118**		**-$814**	

Skills Builder 9.2

In this exercise, you will open a worksheet on your exercise diskette. You will format the worksheet until it closely matches the worksheet shown below.

1. **Open** the workbook named **Skills Builder 9.2**.
2. **Merge and Center** the title **Corporate Budget** across columns A-E.
3. Use the fill handle + to expand the series Q1 to Q1 - Q4.
4. **Right align** the headings **Q1 - Q4.**
5. **Compute** the **Subtotals** and **Total**.
6. **Widen** column A until the entries in column A are visible.
7. **Format** the **numbers** as shown below.

   You will need to use the Format→Cells command to format the Subtotals and Totals as Currency with zero decimals. Format the remaining numbers as Comma with 0 decimals.
8. Format the **title** and **headings** with attractive text formats.
9. Format the **Subtotal** rows with **Italics** as shown.
10. Format the **Total** row with **Bold** and **Italics** as shown.
11. **Close** the workbook and **save** the changes when you have finished.

	A	B	C	D	E
1	Corporate Budget				
2					
3		Q1	Q2	Q3	Q4
4	Marketing	1,234,890	2,346,890	2,156,580	1,900,890
5	Sales	2,316,780	2,145,670	2,134,670	2,145,760
6	*Subtotal*	*$3,551,670*	*$4,492,560*	*$4,291,250*	*$4,046,650*
7					
8	Manufacturing	8,909,800	8,769,870	7,869,870	9,878,760
9	Distribution	3,456,570	3,245,670	2,314,560	3,897,860
10	*Subtotal*	*$12,366,370*	*$12,015,540*	*$10,184,430*	*$13,776,620*
11					
12	Customer Support	93,450	72,150	63,670	93,670
13	Human Resources	65,640	87,890	65,670	86,780
14	*Subtotal*	*$159,090*	*$160,040*	*$129,340*	*$180,450*
15					
16	***Total***	***$16,077,130***	***$16,668,140***	***$14,605,020***	***$18,003,720***

Skills Builder 9.3

In this exercise, you will open a workbook on your exercise diskette. You will format the worksheet until it closely matches the worksheet shown below.

1. **Open** the workbook named **Skills Builder 9.3**.
2. **Merge and Center** the title **Q2 Sales Volume Comparison** across columns A-E.
3. Use the fill handle to expand the series Store 1 to Store 1 - Store 4 in rows 3, 8, and 13.
   As you can see, the fill handle can be used to expand many types of series.
4. **Right Align** the headings **Store 1 - Store 4.**
5. **Left Align** the **dates** in column A.
6. **Widen** column A until the entries in column A are visible.
7. **Format** the **numbers** in rows 4, 5, 9, 10, 14 and 15 as **Comma** with **0** decimals.
8. **Click** cell **B6**.
   In the next step, you will enter a formula that computes the Percentage Increase. This formula uses parenthesis to change the order of calculations. The Percentage Increase is calculated as the April 92 sales minus April 91 sales and this difference is then divided by the April 91 sales. The formula is (B5 - B4)/B4.
9. Enter the formula **=(B5 - B4)/B4**.
10. Use the fill handle to copy the formula across the row.
11. Enter similar formulas in cells **B11** and **B16** and then copy the formulas across the rows.
12. Format the numbers in the Percentage Increase rows as Percent with **2** decimals.
13. Format the worksheet in any way you feel looks attractive.
14. The completed worksheet should match the worksheet shown below.
15. **Close** the workbook and **save** the changes when you have finished.

	A	B	C	D	E
1	***Q2 Sales Volume Comparison***				
2					
3		Store 1	Store 2	Store 3	Store 4
4	April-91	13,234,657	34,789,564	23,000,908	65,908,456
5	April-92	14,456,900	40,987,560	28,546,905	70,987,235
6	Percentage Increase	**9.24%**	**17.82%**	**24.11%**	**7.71%**
7					
8		Store 1	Store 2	Store 3	Store 4
9	May-91	18,985,342	40,234,908	24,234,908	45,003,345
10	May-92	19,234,987	41,210,908	24,400,098	46,989,456
11	Percentage Increase	**1.31%**	**2.43%**	**0.68%**	**4.41%**
12					
13		Store 1	Store 2	Store 3	Store 4
14	Jun-91	24,234,980	65,230,980	18,230,350	51,006,983
15	Jun-92	25,235,908	66,234,908	27,908,990	58,231,900
16	Percentage Increase	**4.13%**	**1.54%**	**53.09%**	**14.16%**

Assessment 9.1

In this assessment, you will develop the worksheet shown below to track customer credit line payments.

1. Open a New workbook.
2. Create the worksheet shown below. You must use formulas in columns D and F and row 11. Make sure the formula results match the worksheet below. Format the numbers and text as shown.
3. Use **Print Preview** when you have finished and **print** the worksheet when it is completed.
4. **Close** the workbook and **save** it as **Assessment 9.1**.

	A	B	C	D	E	F
1	**Donna's Deli - Customer Credit Lines**					
2						
3	Customer	Previous Balance	New Charges	Subtotal	Payment Amount	New Balance
4	George Lopke	100	50	150	150	0
5	Wanda Watson	230	85	315	315	0
6	Alicia Thomas	58	100	158	100	58
7	Bill Barton	60	35	95	0	95
8	Latisha Robertson	140	80	220	0	220
9	Amy Chang	200	150	350	350	0
10	Dan Long	90	65	155	100	55
11	***Total Credit***	***$878***	***$565***	***$1,443***	***$1,015***	***$428***

Assessment 9.2

1. Create the following worksheet. You must use formulas in rows 10 and 11 and columns E and F. You will need to figure out which formulas to use to get your worksheet to match the worksheet shown below. Format the worksheet as shown.
2. **Print** the worksheet, then **close** it and **save** it as **Assessment 9.2**.

	A	B	C	D	E	F
1	Donna's Deli - Customer Survey Results					
2						
3	Category	January	February	March	Total	Average
4	Flavor	4.80	4.75	4.80	14.35	4.78
5	Service	4.60	4.50	4.70	13.80	4.60
6	Nutritional Value	4.95	4.95	4.83	14.73	4.91
7	Presentation	4.20	4.35	4.30	12.85	4.28
8	Price	4.20	4.20	4.45	12.85	4.28
9	Convenience	4.30	4.40	4.20	12.90	4.30
10	Total	27.05	27.15	27.28	81.48	
11	***Average***	***4.51***	***4.53***	***4.55***	***13.58***	

10 Powerful Features and Automated Tools

Objectives:

- Use online Help
- Use AutoCorrect and AutoComplete
- Understand function concepts
- Create functions with the Function box
- Create functions with the Paste Function box
- Use the AVERAGE, MIN and MAX functions
- Use Cut, Copy and Paste
- Use drag & drop and drag & copy
- Add borders and colors to cells
- Use AutoFormat
- Use the Zoom Control

The Project - Centron Cellular Commission Report

In this lesson, you will develop a commission report for Centron Cellular. Centron's National Sales Manager wants statistical information on the commissions that her sales reps are receiving. You will use the AVERAGE, MIN and MAX functions to compute these numbers. You will use many other Excel features including online Help, Cut, Copy and Paste and the AutoFormat command. You will develop the following worksheet as you progress through this lesson.

	A	B	C	D	E	F	G
1	Centron Cellular						
2							
3	Region 1						
4	**Sales Rep**	*Jan Sales*	*Jan Comm*	*Feb Sales*	*Feb Comm*	*March Sales*	*March Comm*
5	**Branston**	32000	4800	32000	4800	23000	3450
6	**Barton**	15000	2250	32000	4800	23890	3583.5
7	**Alexander**	45000	6750	8900	1335	43000	6450
8	**Aliotto**	23000	3450	19000	2850	10900	1635
9	**Chin**	34000	5100	34000	5100	32000	4800
10	**Total**		22350		18885		19918.5
11	**Average**		4470		3777		3983.7
12	**Maximum**		6750		5100		6450
13	**Minimum**		2250		1335		1635
14							
15							
16	Region 2						
17	**Sales Rep**	*Jan Sales*	*Jan Comm*	*Feb Sales*	*Feb Comm*	*March Sales*	*March Comm*
18	**Richardson**	18000	2700	54000	8100	36790	5518.5
19	**Thomas**	12000	1800	35900	5385	45678	6851.7
20	**Carter**	56000	8400	34900	5235	72490	10873.5
21	**Williams**	39000	5850	54000	8100	21000	3150
22	**Jones**	23000	3450	89000	13350	38900	5835
23	**Total**		22200		40170		32228.7
24	**Average**		4440		8034		6445.74
25	**Maximum**		8400		13350		10873.5
26	**Minimum**		1800		5235		3150

Using Online Help

Excel's online Help puts a complete reference book at your fingertips. Help is available for just about any topic you can imagine. It is important that you know how to use online Help because Microsoft and other software publishers no longer provide reference manuals with their software. The reference manuals are now integrated into online Help.

The key to online Help is finding the desired Help topic

Your goal when using online Help is to locate a Help topic. The Help feature has several different methods you can use to locate topics. All Help topics have key words that identify them. For example, a Help topic that discusses copying cells can probably be located by using the key words **copying cells**. Regardless of which search method you use, the goal is to locate a topic. Once you locate the desired topic, you can display it and follow the instructions in the topic.

Help is consistent across Office applications and Windows

Online Help works the same way in Windows, Excel, Word and other Microsoft applications. The following table describes the various search methods that can be used to locate Help topics.

Search Method	Description
Contents	The Contents method is useful if you are trying to locate a topic but you aren't really sure how to describe it. The Contents method lets you navigate through a series of categories until the desired topic is located.
Index	The Index method lets you locate a topic by typing key words. An alphabetically indexed list of topics is displayed from which you can choose the desired topic. This method is most useful if you know the name of the topic or feature that you need assistance with.
Find	The Find method searches inside of the Help topics for the key words you enter. This provides an in-depth search and lets you locate topics that you may not be found using the other search methods.
Office Assistant Search	The Office Assistant Search lets you locate topics by typing questions in plain English. You used the Office Assistant Search in the previous lesson. The results are usually quite good although the Office Assistant often returns a broad range of topics.

Hands-On 10.1 – Experiment with online Help

Use an Index search

1. Start Excel and choose **Help→Contents and Index** from the menu bar.

   The Help Topics dialog box will appear. Notice the Contents, Index and Find tabs at the top of the dialog box. This dialog box lets you search for all Help topics.

2. **Click** the **Index tab** and use the steps on the next page to get help on a topic called AutoComplete.

   You will use AutoComplete and AutoCorrect in this lesson.

Continued...

❶ *Type **Auto** here. (Notice that Help displays a list of topics beginning with the word Auto. The Index is the fastest way to locate a topic if you know the name of the feature or topic you are looking for.)*

❷ *Choose **AutoComplete** and **click** the **Display** button at the bottom of the dialog box (or double-click AutoComplete).*

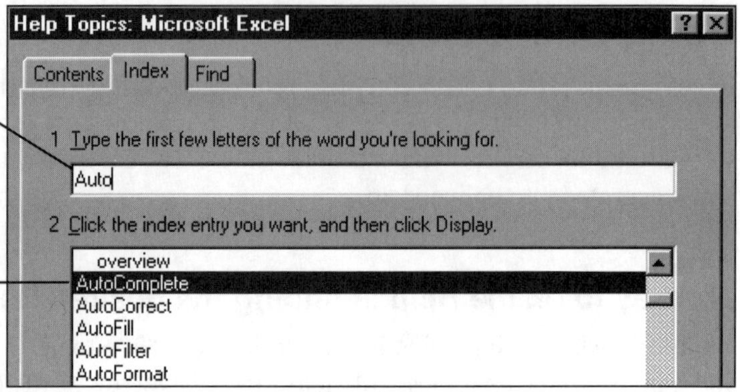

Excel will display a list of topics that are related to the AutoComplete feature.

3. Choose **Quickly fill in repeated entries in a column** and **click** the **Display** button.
   You could also have double-clicked the topic.

4. Take a moment to read the Help topic.

5. **Click** anywhere in the Excel worksheet area and notice the dialog box remains open.
   Help topics remain "on top" to allow you to work while reading the topic.

6. **Click** the Help Topics [Help Topics] button on the dialog box.
   The Help Topics dialog box will reappear.

7. Take 15 minutes to experiment with the Help feature. Try using the Find and Contents search method techniques. Experiment and explore until you are comfortable using Help.

8. **Close** the Help Topics dialog box when you have finished experimenting.

The What's This? Option

The What's This? option on the Help menu is used to get descriptions of buttons, menu items and other screen objects. The What's This? option is useful if you are trying to figure out how a button or other object is used.

Hands-On 10.2 – Use the What's This? option

1. Choose **Help→What's This?** from the menu bar.

2. **Click** any button on the toolbars and a description will pop up.

3. **Read** the description, then **click anywhere** in the worksheet to close the description.

4. Choose **Help→What's This?**, then choose **Format→Cells...** from the menu bar.
   Notice that you can use What's This? to get descriptions of buttons and menu bar commands.

5. **Close** the description by clicking in the worksheet.
   Feel free to experiment with the What's This? option.

Getting Assistance with Data Entry

Excel's AutoCorrect and AutoComplete features provide assistance with entering text.

Using AutoCorrect

Excel's AutoCorrect feature can improve the speed and accuracy of entering text. AutoCorrect is most useful for replacing abbreviations with a full phrase. For example, you could set up AutoCorrect to substitute ***as soon as possible*** whenever you type ***asap***. AutoCorrect also automatically corrects common spelling errors. For example, the word ***the*** is often misspelled as ***teh*** and the word ***and*** is often misspelled as ***adn***. These and other common spelling mistakes are built into Excel as AutoCorrect entries. AutoCorrect also capitalizes the first letter in the names of days and it corrects words that have two initial capital letters by switching the second letter to lowercase.

Expanding AutoCorrect entries

AutoCorrect goes into action each time you type a word in a text entry and tap the Spacebar and when you complete a text entry. The word or entry you type is compared to all entries in the *AutoCorrect table*. The AutoCorrect table contains a list of words and their replacement phrases. If the word you type matches an entry in the AutoCorrect table, then a replacement phrase from the table is substituted for the word. This is known as expanding the AutoCorrect entry.

Using AutoComplete

The AutoComplete feature is useful if you want the same entry repeated more than once in a column. If the first few characters you type match another entry in the column, then AutoComplete will complete the entry for you. Of course, you can override AutoComplete by typing the remainder of the entry yourself.

Hands-On 10.3 – Use AutoCorrect and AutoComplete

In this exercise, you will open a workbook from your exercise diskette. You will experiment with AutoCorrect and AutoComplete and you will create a new AutoCorrect entry.

Use AutoCorrect to correct misspelled words

1. Open the workbook named **Hands-On Lesson 10.**
2. **Click** cell **A1**.
3. Type **adn** (that's adn not and) and **tap** Enter.
   Excel should correct the misspelling and enter the word and in the cell.
4. **Click** cell **A1**.
5. Type, **This adn that**.
   Notice that Excel corrected the misspelling again after you typed adn and tapped the Spacebar.

Create a new AutoCorrect entry

6. **Tap** Enter then choose **Tools→AutoCorrect...** from the menu bar.

Continued...

7. Use the following Hands-On Illustration to create a new AutoCorrect entry.

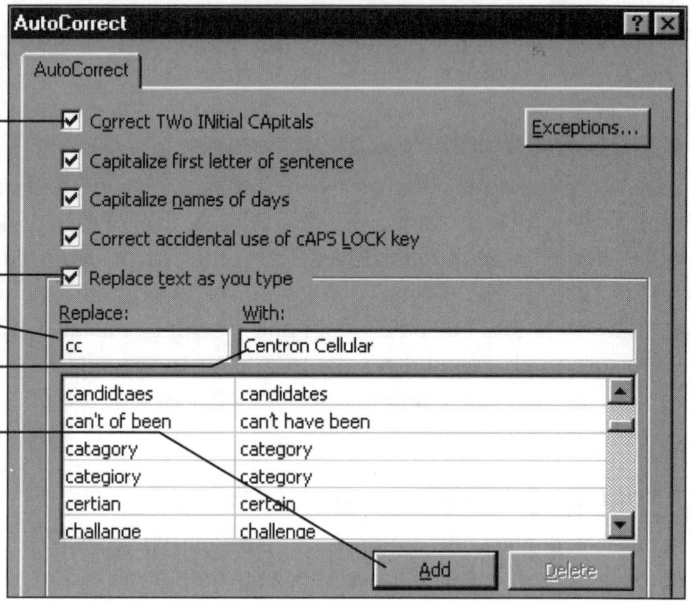

❶ *Notice these check boxes. These boxes instruct AutoCorrect to automatically make the specified corrections in your worksheets.*

❷ *Type* **cc** *in the Replace box.*

❸ *Type* **Centron Cellular** *in the With box.*

❹ **Click** *the* **Add** *button to add the entry to the list.*

❺ *Feel free to* **scroll** *though the list and you will see hundreds of AutoCorrect entries.*

❻ ***Click OK.***

8. **Click** cell **A1**.

9. Type **cc** and **tap** Enter.

   AutoCorrect should replace cc with Centron Cellular. Notice that you can use AutoCorrect as a type of shorthand. AutoCorrect can replace abbreviations with phrases you use often such as your company name or address.

Delete the AutoCorrect entry

10. Choose **Tools→AutoCorrect...** from the menu bar.

11. **Scroll** through the list of AutoCorrect entries and choose the **cc**, **Centron Cellular** entry.

12. **Click** the **Delete** button, then **click OK**.

Use AutoComplete

13. **Click** cell **A5**.

14. Type **Branston** and **tap** Enter.

15. Type the letter **B** in cell A6 and AutoComplete will display the word Branston in the cell.

    You could accept this proposal by confirming the entry, however, you will type a different entry.

16. Type **arton** (to make the entry Barton) and **tap** Enter.

    AutoComplete will constantly try to assist you in completing entries. You can ignore AutoComplete and continue typing your entries or confirm the entries that AutoComplete proposes.

17. Enter the following Sales rep names into the next three cells.

7	Alexander
8	Aliotto
9	Chin

Continue with the next topic. You will continue to enhance the worksheet throughout this lesson.

Functions

Excel has over 400 built-in **functions** that perform a variety of calculations. You already used the SUM function in the previous lessons. In this lesson, you will use the MAX, MIN and AVERAGE functions.

Function Syntax

Functions must be constructed using a set of basic rules or they will not work properly. These rules are known as the syntax. The good news is that most functions have the same syntax and the syntax is very easy to use and remember. The following illustration discusses the syntax of the SUM function. This syntax also applies to the MIN, MAX and AVERAGE functions, which you are about to learn.

Always begin functions with an equal = sign unless they are embedded in a larger formula.

=SUM(B5:B9)

The function name always follows the equal = sign.

A set of parentheses always surrounds the argument. The argument is usually a range of cells as in this example.

=SUM(A5,A10,B5:B9)

If an argument has more than one parameter, then commas must separate the parameters. In this example, cells A5 and A10 would be added to the range B5:B9.

Hands-On 10.4 – Manually enter the AVERAGE function

In this exercise, you will manually enter the AVERAGE function.

Do a little detective work and use AutoSum

1. Notice the worksheet has a January Commissions column (Jan Comm).
   The commissions are calculated with a simple formula.
2. What is the commission rate that the sales reps are being paid?
   You can find this out by clicking a commission cell in Column C and checking out the formula.
3. **Click** cell **C10**.
4. **Click** AutoSum and Confirm the entry.
   The Total Commissions for January should be 20550.
5. Look at the Formula bar and notice the function =SUM(C5:C9) that AutoSum placed in the cell.
   The SUM function uses the standard function syntax discussed above.

Type the AVERAGE function

6. **Click** cell **C11**.
7. Type the function **=AVERAGE(C5:C9)** and Confirm the entry.
   The result should be 4110. This is the average of the values in the range C5:C9. Notice the syntax is the same as the SUM function except you used the function name AVERAGE instead of SUM.

The Function Box

The Function Box appears on the left end of the Formula bar whenever the Edit Formula button is clicked. The Function Box has a drop-down button that shows the 10 most recently used functions. Excel displays the Formula Palette whenever you choose one of these functions from the Function Box. The Formula palette then provides assistance in creating functions.

Hands-On 10.5 – Use the Function Box and Formula palette

In this exercise, you will use the Function Box to create the MAX and MIN functions.

Use the Function Box to create the MAX function

1. **Click** cell **C12**.
2. **Click** the Edit Formula button on the Formula bar.
3. Use the following steps to explore the Function Box.

❶ ***Click*** *this drop-down button and a list of the 10 most recently used functions will appear.*

❷ *Notice the most recently used function (in this case AVERAGE) appears on the face of the Function Box and at the top of the list.*

❸ *Also notice that the MAX function appears on the list shown here. It may also appear on your list. You could choose MAX at this point, however, you will choose the MAX function using the More Functions... option in the next step. This will show you how to choose a function even if it is not on the 10 most recently used functions list.*

❹ ***Choose More Functions...***

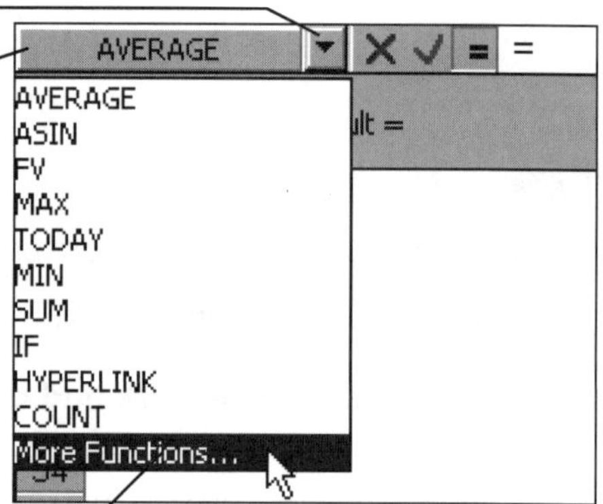

The Paste Function dialog box will appear. The Paste Function dialog box provides access to all 400+ functions in Excel. This dialog box can also be displayed by clicking the Paste Function button on the Standard toolbar (but don't do it).

4. Use the following steps to choose the MAX function.

❶ *Notice the functions are organized into categories. The functions for the selected category are displayed on the right.*

❷ ***Choose*** *the* ***Statistical*** *category.*

❸ ***Scroll down*** *through the list of Function names and choose* ***MAX****.*

❹ ***Click OK****.*

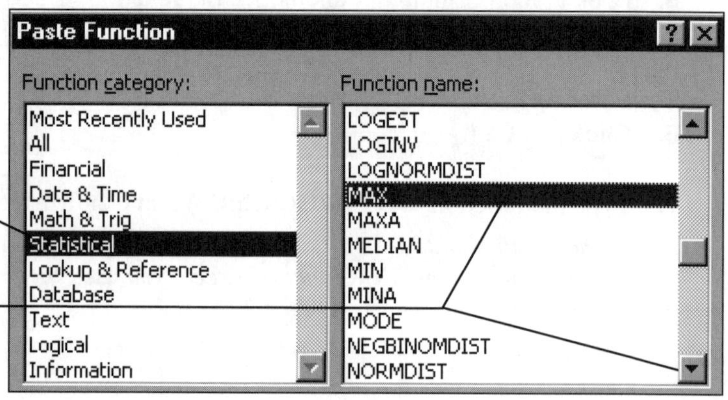

Continued...

Notice the MAX(C11) function appears in the Formula palette. This is the correct function, however, the range C11 is incorrect. You could type the correct range C5:C9 in the Formula palette or the Formula bar. However, you will use another technique in the following steps.

5. Use the following step to minimize the Formula palette so that you can see the worksheet.

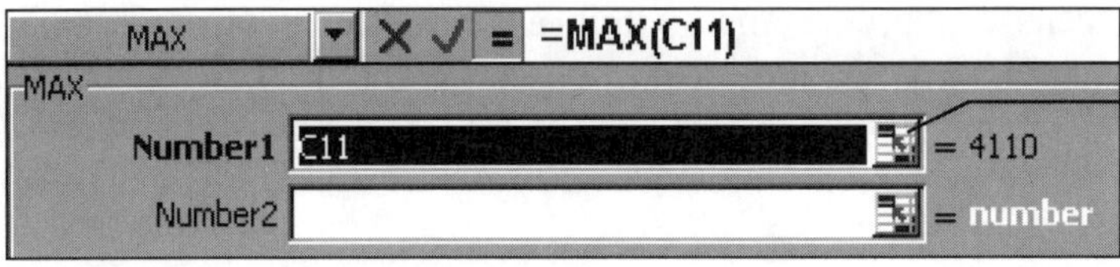

❶ *Click this button at the end of the Number 1 box and the Formula palette will be minimized.*

6. Use the following step to select the appropriate range of cells and redisplay the Formula palette.

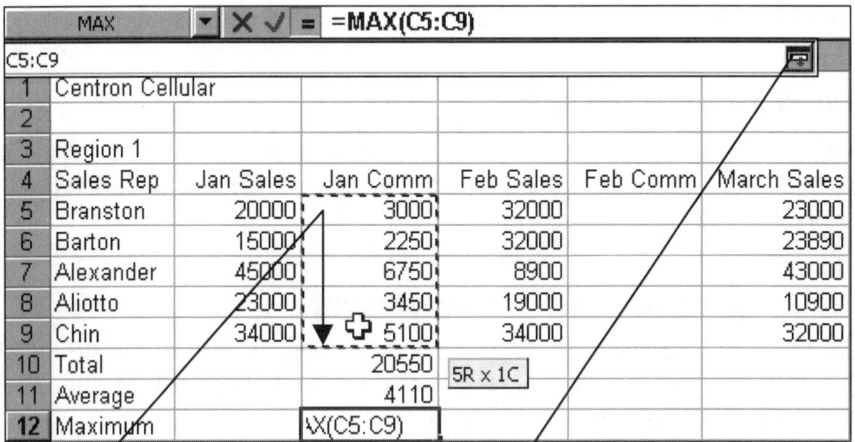

❶ ***Drag** the mouse over the range **C5:C9** as shown here.*

❷ ***Click** this button to restore the Formula palette.*

Take a moment to check out the formula in the Formula bar. It should be =MAX(C5:C9).

7. Complete the function by **clicking OK** on the Formula palette (the result should be 6750).

Use point mode to create the MIN function in cell C13

8. **Click** cell **C13** and type **=min(**

   You can type a function in lowercase and Excel will convert it to uppercase when you confirm the entry. Also, you must always type the opening parenthesis when entering a function in point mode.

9. **Drag** the mouse down the range **C5:C9**.

10. Type a closing parenthesis **)** and your formula should be =min(C5:C9).

11. Confirm ✓ the entry and the result should be 2250.

   In this exercise, you used three different methods to create functions. In the future, use whichever method you find easiest and which gives you the most accurate results.

Change the values and watch the formulas recalculate

You may be wondering why you used the MIN and MAX functions in this worksheet. It is easy to see which sales rep had the minimum and maximum commissions for a month. The benefit of using the functions is when the values change or when there are a large number of rows. The functions are dynamic and they will automatically recalculate the SUM, AVERAGE, MAX and MIN values.

12. **Click** cell **B5** and change the sales number from 20000 to **32000**.

   Notice how the functions recalculate the numbers. The topics on the following pages will teach you several new ways to move and copy cells.

Using Cut, Copy and Paste

Excel has several features that let you move and copy text, numbers and graphics from one location to another. You already used the fill handle to copy a cell's content to adjacent cells. The fill handle is limited in this respect because it can only be used to copy to adjacent cells. Excel also supports drag & drop, which is best for moving or copying cells a short distance within a worksheet. Cut, copy and paste is usually best for moving or copying cells a long distance within a worksheet or between worksheets or workbooks.

Cut, Copy and Paste

Cut, copy and paste is available in most Windows programs. With cut, copy and paste, you can copy cells within a worksheet, between worksheets and workbooks and even between programs.

The Windows clipboard makes it possible

The Windows clipboard is a part of the computer's memory where cut and copied objects are temporarily stored. All Windows programs have access to the clipboard. The Paste command copies the clipboard's contents into the current worksheet.

The clipboard contents are replaced with each new cut

The clipboard contents are replaced whenever new objects are cut or copied. You can paste the clipboard content over and over again as long as you do not issue a new Cut or Copy command. This is convenient if you wish to paste multiple copies of the objects.

Hands-On 10.6 – Use copy and paste

In this exercise, you will use the Copy and Paste commands to copy formulas and text.

Copy the commission formula to cell E5

1. **Click** cell **C5**.
2. Take a moment to study the formula in the formula bar.

   Your objective is to copy this formula to the February and March commission columns. This cannot be done with the fill handle because those cells are not adjacent to cell C5.
3. **Click** the Copy button on the Standard toolbar.

   Notice the flashing marquee in cell C5. This indicates the sales commission formula is on the clipboard and ready to be pasted.
4. **Click** cell **E5**.
5. **Click** the Paste button.

   The formula should be pasted and it should calculate the commission as 4800. The flashing marquee in cell C5 indicates the formula is still available for pasting into other cells.

Paste the formula into a range of cells

6. **Select** the range **E6:E9**.
7. **Click** the Paste button to paste the formula.

   You can always copy a single cell to a range of cells (as in this example).

Continued...

8. **Select** the range **G5:G9** and paste the formulas into those cells.

   Once again, you can continue to paste as long as the marquee is flashing.

9. **Tap** the Esc key on the keyboard and the marquee will stop flashing.

   You can always turn off the flashing marquee with the Escape key.

10. **Click** any cell that you just pasted into and notice the formula in the formula bar.

    Excel updates the references in the formulas to reflect the new formula locations.

Use the Ctrl key to paste into two separate ranges

11. **Click** cell **C10**.
12. **Click** the Copy button.
13. **Click** cell **E10**.
14. **Press & Hold** the Ctrl key and **click** cell **G10**.

    Both cells E10 and G10 should be selected.

15. **Click** the Paste button to paste the formula into both cells.
16. Use the preceding technique to copy the AVERAGE, MAX and MIN functions from column C to columns E and G.

Copy the heading rows for Regions 1 to Region 2

17. **Select rows 3** and **4** by dragging over the row headings as shown below.

3	Region 1						
4	Sales Rep	Jan Sales	Jan Comm	Feb Sales	Feb Comm	March Sales	March Comm

18. **Click** the Copy button.
19. **Click** cell **A16**.

    In the next step, you will paste the range to cell A16. You should paste a large range like this to one cell (A16 in this case). When you do this, Excel will use A16 as the starting location of the pasted range. You must be careful because the pasted range will overwrite any cells that are in its way.

20. **Click** the Paste button.

    In the next exercise, you will continue to copy cells with the drag & drop technique. For now, continue with the data entry task below.

21. Enter the following Sales rep names into the range **A18:A22**.

18	Richardson
19	Thomas
20	Carter
21	Williams
22	Jones

22. Change the heading for the second region from Region 1 to **Region 2**.

Drag & Drop

Drag & drop can be used to move or copy selected cells from one location to another. This produces the same result as cut, copy and paste. However, drag & drop may be more efficient if you are moving or copying a short distance within the same worksheet.

Use the Ctrl key to drag and copy

You drag & drop selected cells by pointing to any border of the selection and then dragging the selection to the desired location. You can make a copy of the selected cells by pressing & holding the Ctrl key while you drag & drop the selection. This is known as drag & copy. When using drag & copy, it is important to release the mouse button before the Ctrl key. Otherwise, your copy will become a move.

Hands-On 10.7 – Use drag & drop

In this exercise, you will use drag & drop to copy text and formulas in the worksheet.

Move the formula row headings to Region 2

1. Use the following Hands-On Illustration to drag & drop text entries.

❶ ***Select*** *the range* ***A10:A13****.*

❷ ***Point*** *to the bottom border of the range and the pointer will become an arrow. You can actually point to any border when using drag & drop.*

❸ ***Drag*** *the mouse* ***down*** *until the shaded box is positioned just below the names in Region 2.*

❹ ***Release*** *the mouse button and the range will be moved.*

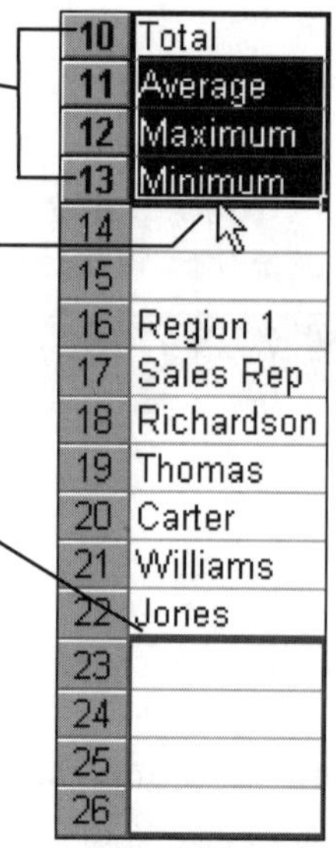

Notice how easy it was to move the cells using drag & drop. You should focus on using drag & drop if the move is a short distance within the same worksheet. Unfortunately, you should have copied the cells instead of moving them. You will correct this in the next few steps.

2. **Click** Undo to reverse the move.

3. **Press & Hold** the Ctrl key while you drag & drop the cells as you did in the Hands-On Illustration above. **Make sure you release the mouse button first, then release Ctrl!** You will notice the mouse pointer has a plus sign attached to it to indicate a copy is being performed.

   Excel should copy the cells to the range A23:A26.

Continued...

Use drag & copy to copy the formulas

4. Use the following Hands-On Illustration to copy the January Commission formulas to Region 2.

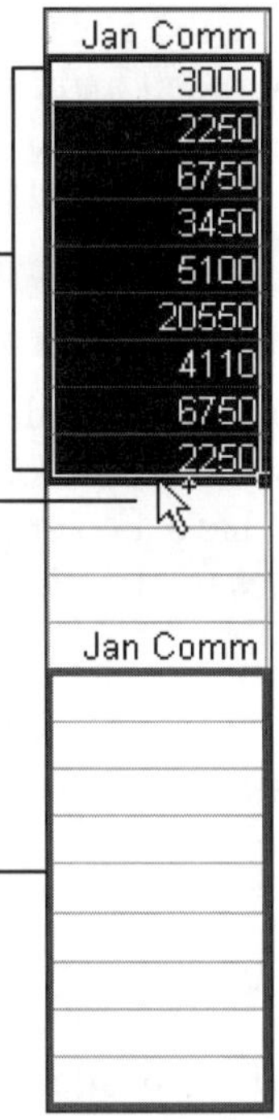

❶ ***Select** the range **C5:C13**.*

❷ ***Point** to the bottom border of the range and **press & hold Ctrl**. The pointer will have + sign attached to it.*

❸ ***Drag** the mouse **down** until the shaded box is positioned just below the Jan Comm heading.*

❹ ***Release** the **mouse button first**, then release **Ctrl**.*

5. Use drag & copy to copy the February and March commission formulas to Region 2.

6. Save the changes.

At this point, your worksheet should match the worksheet shown below.

	A	B	C	D	E	F	G
1	Centron Cellular						
2							
3	Region 1						
4	Sales Rep	Jan Sales	Jan Comm	Feb Sales	Feb Comm	March Sales	March Comm
5	Branston	32000	4800	32000	4800	23000	3450
6	Barton	15000	2250	32000	4800	23890	3583.5
7	Alexander	45000	6750	8900	1335	43000	6450
8	Aliotto	23000	3450	19000	2850	10900	1635
9	Chin	34000	5100	34000	5100	32000	4800
10	Total		22350		18885		19918.5
11	Average		4470		3777		3983.7
12	Maximum		6750		5100		6450
13	Minimum		2250		1335		1635
14							
15							
16	Region 2						
17	Sales Rep	Jan Sales	Jan Comm	Feb Sales	Feb Comm	March Sales	March Comm
18	Richardson	18000	2700	54000	8100	36790	5518.5
19	Thomas	12000	1800	35900	5385	45678	6851.7
20	Carter	56000	8400	34900	5235	72490	10873.5
21	Williams	39000	5850	54000	8100	21000	3150
22	Jones	23000	3450	89000	13350	38900	5835
23	Total		22200		40170		32228.7
24	Average		4440		8034		6445.74
25	Maximum		8400		13350		10873.5
26	Minimum		1800		5235		3150

Adding Borders and Color to Cells

You can add borders and color to cells with the Borders and Fill Color buttons on the Formatting toolbar. Each cell has a top, bottom, left and right border. You can apply borders and color to an individual cell or to a range of cells. You can also apply borders and color by choosing Format→Cells… from the menu bar and then using the Format Cells dialog box.

Borders and color are printed when the worksheet is printed

Excel displays gridlines in the worksheet to show you the cell borders. However, the gridlines are not printed when the worksheet is printed. Borders and color, on the other hand, are printed. Keep in mind that your worksheets will print in color only if you have a color printer. If you use colors and you do not have a color printer, then the colors will print in shades of gray that are proportionate to the color density.

Hands-On 10.8 – Add borders and color

Make the title stand out

1. **Select** the range **A1:G1** in row 1 and click the Merge and Center button.
2. Make sure the range is still selected, then **click** the Borders drop-down button and the borders box will appear.
3. Use the following steps to put a thick border around the range.

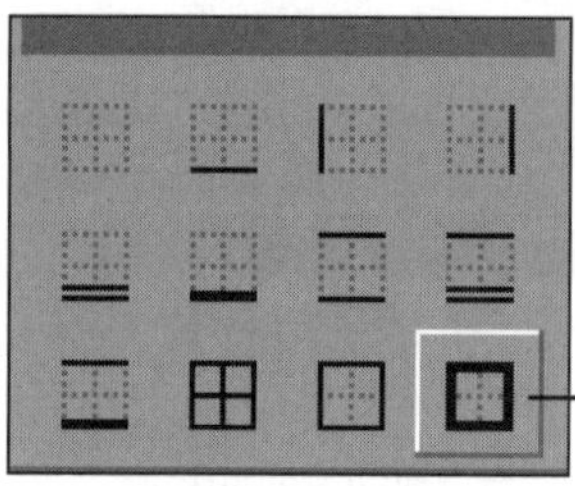

❶ *Take a moment to study the various border styles. The first style removes borders. Notice the other styles place thin, thick or double lines on various borders.*

❷ *Choose this option to put a thick border around the selected cells.*

4. Make sure the range is still selected, then **click** the Fill Color drop-down button.
5. Choose your favorite color.
6. Make sure the range is still selected, then **click** the Font Color drop-down button.
7. Choose your favorite color, then **click** outside the range and you will be able to see the formats.

   The lines on the top and left sides of the range may not be visible because the column and row headings are blocking them. Notice that the color button determined the fill color of the cells while the Font Color button determined the color of the text or numbers within the cell. Also notice that the colors and line style you chose now appear on the face of the buttons. You could now apply these same colors and line style to other selected cells by clicking the buttons.
8. **Click** the Print Preview button.
9. **Click** the mouse pointer on the worksheet to zoom in.

   You should now be able to see the lines on the top and left sides of the range. However, the colors will not be visible if you have a black and white printer. Print Preview is very accurate and it will show you the color or gray shades that will be printed.

Continued...

Add borders to all sides of all cells

10. Click the **Close** button to exit from Print Preview.

11. Select the range **A2:G26**.

This range represents all cells in the active worksheet area except for the title row.

12. Click the Borders drop-down button.

13. Choose the All Borders style, which is the second style on the bottom row.

14. Click Print Preview.

Do you like having lines on every border of every cell? Many people find this to be busy and distracting. You will correct this by changing the pattern in the next step.

Remove the borders

15. Close the **Print Preview** window.

16. Make sure the range **A2:G26** is still selected.

17. Click the Borders drop-down button and choose the Thick Outline style.

18. Click Print Preview and you will notice the inside borders have not been removed.

19. Close the **Print Preview** window.

20. Click the Borders drop-down button and choose the No Lines button (first button).

This will remove the lines from the selected range.

21. Click the Borders drop-down button again and choose the Thick Outline style.

22. Click Print Preview to check out the results, then **close** Print Preview.

Add color to one row and use the Format Painter to copy the format to other rows

23. Select the range **A10:G10** (all the cells in row 10).

24. Use the Fill Color button to add the color of your choice.

25. Use the Font Color button to change the font color.

26. Double-click the Format Painter.

27. Paint the cells in **rows 12**, **23** and **25**.

This will format every other formula row. This way, the various formulas are clearly differentiated.

28. Click the Format Painter to turn it off.

29. Take 10 minutes to play around with the Borders, Color and Font Color buttons.

30. Save the changes and continue with the next topic.

The AutoFormat Command

The Format→AutoFormat command lets you choose from a variety of predefined formats. The predefined formats automatically apply number formats, borders, colors, font colors, font sizes and other formats. You may be pleasantly surprised when you see the professional formatting that AutoFormat can apply.

You must select a range before using AutoFormat

You must select a range or AutoFormat will not work. You may want to select all cells in the worksheet or a smaller range, as you will do in the following exercise.

Hands-On 10.9 – Use AutoFormat

Use AutoFormat on Region 1

1. **Select** the range **A3:G13** which includes all cells for Region 1.
2. Choose **Format→AutoFormat...** from the menu bar.
3. Use the following Hands-On Illustration to format the range.

❶ ***Click*** *the* ***Options>>>*** *button and check boxes will appear or disappear at the bottom of the dialog box. These boxes let you decide which formats you want AutoFormat to adjust. Make sure all the boxes are checked.*

❷ ***Scroll*** *through the list and choose various formats. The format you choose will display in the Sample window.*

❸ *Scroll to the top of the list and choose* ***Classic 3****.*

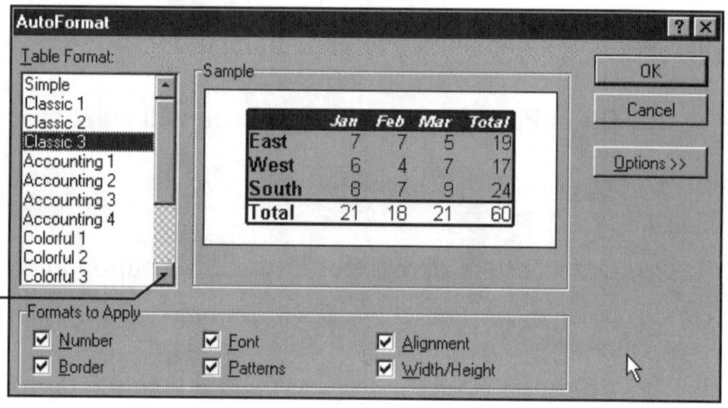

4. **Click OK** then **click** in an open part of the worksheet and check out the results.

   You will notice that AutoFormat adjusted virtually every format. Notice that AutoFormat was intelligent enough to detect the rows that have formulas and it formatted those rows in a different manner than the body and header rows. AutoFormat makes its formatting decisions by detecting which rows and columns have text, numbers and formulas.

Remove the AutoFormatting

5. **Select** the range **A3:G13** (the range you just used AutoFormat on).
6. Choose **Format→AutoFormat...** from the menu bar.
7. **Scroll** to the bottom of the Formats list and choose **None**.
8. **Click OK** and the formats will be removed.

   You can use AutoFormat to remove formats that were applied manually or with AutoFormat.

9. Experiment with AutoFormat. Format the Region 1 cells four times using a different AutoFormat each time. Finally, choose your favorite format and then apply it to Region 2.
10. Save the changes and continue with the next topic.

Using the Zoom Control

Excel's zoom control lets you change the magnification of the worksheet. Zooming changes the size of the worksheet on the screen, however, it does not affect the size of the printed worksheet. You can zoom from 10% to 400%. The following illustration shows the Hands-On Lesson 10 worksheet with a 200% zoom. Keep in mind that your worksheet may have a different number of columns and rows displayed than shown here. This is because your monitor may be a different size.

You can type a zoom percentage into this box and tap Enter, or…

you can click this button and select an option from the drop-down menu.

Notice how large the text and cells appear in this example.

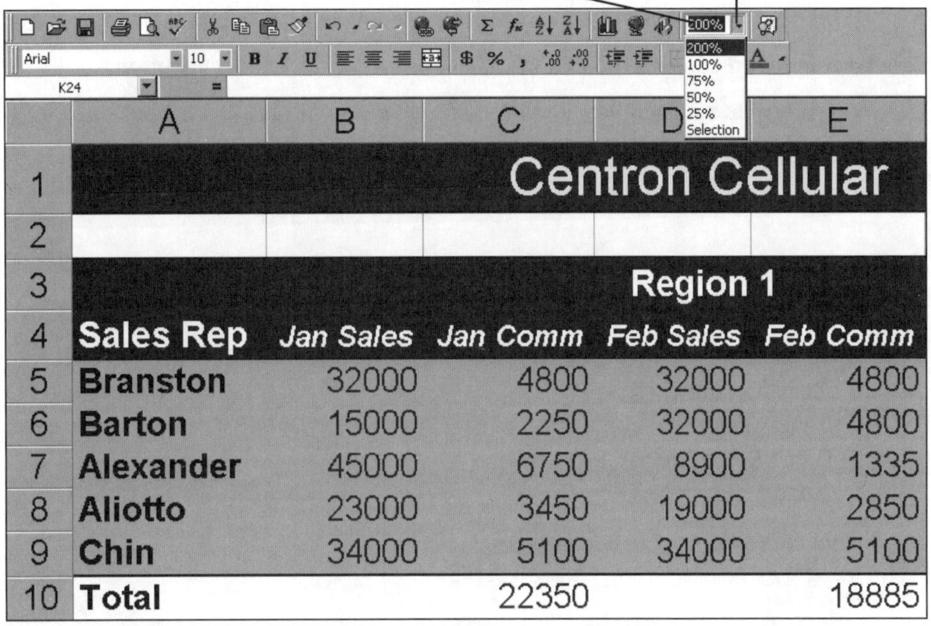

Hands-On 10.10 – Experiment with the Zoom Control

1. Use the following steps to adjust the Zoom Control.

   ❶ ***Click** in the Zoom Control box, type **150** and tap **Enter**. You can zoom to any percentage between 10% and 400% by typing a number and tapping Enter.*

   ❷ ***Click** the Zoom Control button and choose **200%**.*

   ❸ *Zoom to 100%.*

2. **Select** the range **A4:C13**.

   Imagine that you want to analyze just the January sales numbers. You can use the Zoom Control to get a close up view of just this range.

3. **Click** the Zoom Control button and choose **Selection**.

   Excel will zoom to the maximum percentage possible for that selection.

4. Feel free to experiment with the Zoom Control then **close** the workbook and **save** the changes.

Concepts Review

True / False

1. An Index search is the best Help search method if you know the name of the topic or feature. 1. **T F**
2. The Office Assistant lets you type help questions in plain English. 2. **T F**
3. AutoCorrect entries are expanded when the Spacebar is tapped or entry is confirmed. 3. **T F**
4. You must accept an AutoComplete entry that Excel proposes. 4. **T F**
5. MIN and MAX are examples of functions. 5. **T F**
6. A function's arguments are always surrounded by quotation marks "". 6. **T F**
7. The clipboard contents are deleted whenever you click the Paste button. 7. **T F**
8. You can paste a copied formula into multiple cells with one paste command. 8. **T F**
9. Borders and colors are printed when the worksheet is printed. 9. **T F**
10. The Zoom Control can zoom to a maximum of 400%. 10. **T F**

Multiple Choice

1. Which command displays the AutoCorrect dialog box?
   a) Format→AutoCorrect
   b) Tools→AutoCorrect
   c) Edit→AutoCorrect
   d) None of the above. ( )
2. Which button is used to add borders to cells?
   a) 
   b) 

   c) 
   d) None of the above. ( )
3. Which key should you press if you want drag & drop to copy instead of moving?
   a) Shift
   b) Alt
   c) Ctrl
   d) None of the above. ( )
4. Which command is used to display the AutoFormat dialog box?
   a) Tools→AutoFormat
   b) Format→AutoFormat
   c) Format→Cells
   d) None of the above. ( )
5. Which of the following magnification ranges does the Zoom Control let you use?
   a) 10% to 400%
   b) 10% to 200%
   c) 25% to 200%
   d) 25% to 400% ( )

Skills Builder 10.1

In this exercise, you will develop the worksheet shown at the bottom of this page.

1. Open the workbook named **Skills Builder 10.1**.

2. **Select** the range **A1:E2** as shown below.

	A	B	C	D	E
1	Quality Greeting Cards - 1996 Customer Complaints				
2		Christmas	Easter	Valentines	Thanksgiving

3. **Click** the Copy button.

4. **Click** cell **A10**, **click** the Paste button then change 1996 in the pasted heading to **1995**.

5. **Select** the range **A3:A8** as shown below.

3	Boston
4	Los Angeles
5	New York
6	St. Louis
7	Total
8	Average

6. **Click** Copy, **click** cell **A12**, then **click** the Paste button.

7. Use AutoSum Σ to compute the Totals in rows **7** and **16**.

8. **Click** cell **B8** and enter the function **=AVERAGE(B3:B6)**.

9. Use the Copy and Paste buttons to copy the AVERAGE function across rows 8 and 17.

   You can copy this function to both rows 8 and 17 because the function computes the average of a range of 4 cells and that is the formula that is required in both rows 8 and 17.

10. **Click** cell **B20** and enter the formula **=B7-B16**.

11. **Copy** this formula **across row 20**.

12. Enter a formula in cell **B21** that computes the difference between the Averages for 1996 and 1995, then copy the formula across row 20.

13. Your completed worksheet should match the worksheet shown below. **Close** the workbook and **save** the changes when you have finished.

	A	B	C	D	E
1	Quality Greeting Cards - 1996 Customer Complaints				
2		Christmas	Easter	Valentines	Thanksgiving
3	Boston	27	43	14	34
4	Los Angeles	31	47	19	39
5	New York	35	51	24	44
6	St. Louis	39	55	29	49
7	Total	132	196	86	166
8	Average	33	49	21.5	41.5
9					
10	Quality Greeting Cards - 1995 Customer Complaints				
11		Christmas	Easter	Valentines	Thanksgiving
12	Boston	19	31	16	24
13	Los Angeles	22	34	18	26
14	New York	25	37	20	28
15	St. Louis	28	40	22	30
16	Total	94	142	76	108
17	Average	23.5	35.5	19	27
18					
19	Differences Between 1996 and 1995				
20	Totals	38	54	10	58
21	Averages	9.5	13.5	2.5	14.5

Skills Builder 10.2

In this exercise, you will open a workbook on your exercise diskette. You will then use AutoFormat to apply an attractive format to the worksheet.

Use AutoFormat

1. **Open** the workbook named **Skills Builder 10.2**.
2. **Select** the range **A1:E16** which includes all cells in the worksheet.
3. Choose **Format→AutoFormat...** from the menu bar.
4. Choose the **List 2** style and **click OK**.
5. **Click** outside the worksheet and you will be able to see the format.
   The format looks good although it would be nice to have a more distinctive title row. You can format the Worksheet with AutoFormat and then add your own formatting enhancements.

Manually change the format of the title row

6. **Select** the range **A1:E1** and use Merge and Center to center the title.
7. Increase the size of the title to **14** point.
8. **Click** outside the worksheet and you will be able to see the format.
9. **Close** the workbook and **save** the changes.

Skills Builder 10.3

In this exercise, you will open a workbook and you will use copy & paste to copy text and formulas.

1. **Open** the workbook named **Skills Builder 10.3**.
2. **Select** the range **A3:E4** which includes all the text entries in rows 3 and 4.
3. Copy the cells to the clipboard.
4. **Click** cell **A10** and Paste the entries above the second set of numbers.
   Notice the text formats (including the coloring) were copied with the text.
5. **Click** cell **A17** and Paste the entries above the third set of numbers.
6. Change the headings to **February** and **March** for the second and third sets of numbers.
7. **Select** the range **A5:A8** which includes the names and word Totals in column A.
8. **Copy** the selection to the clipboard, then Paste it to cells **A12** and **A19**.
9. **Copy** the **formulas** from the Totals row below the first set of numbers and Paste them below the second and third sets of numbers.
10. **Close** the workbook when you have finished and **save** the changes.

Skills Builder 10.4

In this exercise, you will open a workbook and compute averages using three methods. You will compute the averages manually using a formula with parentheses that change the order of calculations. You will also enter AVERAGE functions with multiple parameters within the argument.

Manually compute the Average New Orders in row 18

1. **Open** the workbook named **Skills Builder 10.4**.
2. **Click** cell **B18**.
3. Type the formula **=(B4+B9+B14)/3** into cell B18 and Confirm the entry.

   The result should be 193.333... Notice the formula you entered includes parentheses ( ). The parentheses change the order of calculations. They instruct Excel to add cells B4, B9 and B14 and then divide the result of that summation by 3. Without the parentheses, Excel would first divide cell B14 by 3 and then it would add the result to B4 + B9. This would produce a very different result and you would not receive the average you are trying to compute. Keep in mind that the AVERAGE function does this work for you. This formula was entered manually to demonstrate the way an average is computed and to show how parentheses are used to change the order of calculations.
4. Use the fill handle + to copy the formula across row 18.

Compute the Average Exchanges in row 19 by typing the AVERAGE function

5. **Click** cell **B19**.
6. Type the function **=average(b5,b10,b15)** and Confirm the entry.

   The result should be 23.3333. Once again, you can type the function name and arguments in lowercase and Excel will convert them to uppercase. Notice the function you entered has three parameters within the argument. In this function, the parameters are cell references and commas separate them. Most functions let you have multiple arguments within the parentheses and commas always separate the arguments. In this example, the function simply computes the average of cells b5, b10 and b15.
7. Use the fill handle + to copy the formula across row 19.

Compute the Average Returns in row 20 by using point mode with the AVERAGE function

8. **Click** cell **B20**.
9. Type ***=average(***
10. **Click** cell **B6**.

    The reference B6 will be added to the function in the Formula bar.
11. Type a comma **,** then **click** cell **B11**.
12. Type a comma **,** then **click** cell **B16**.
13. Type a closing parentheses **)** and Confirm the entry.

    The result should be 8.3333. Once again, using point mode is usually beneficial because it reduces errors by preventing you from typing the wrong cell reference.
14. Use the fill handle + to copy the formula across row 20.
15. **Select** the cells in rows **18**, **19** and **20** and decrease the decimals to **2**.
16. **Close** the workbook and **save** the changes.

Assessment 10.1

1. Use the following guidelines to create the worksheet shown below.
   - Use formulas to compute the Interest Charge in column E and the New Balance in Column F. The formulas are as follows.
     - Interest Charge = 1.5% * (Beginning Balance - Payments)
     - New Balance = Beginning Balance + Purchases - Payments + Interest Charge

     Notice that you must use parenthesis in the Interest Charge formula to change the order of calculations. You want Excel to subtract the Payments from the Beginning Balance and then multiply the result by 1.5%. Also, don't be confused and try to type the words Beginning Balance etc. in the formulas. You should use the appropriate cell references in the formulas.
   - Format rows 5, 10, 11 and 12 with the Currency formatting as shown.
   - Format the title and header rows as shown.
   - Compute the Totals in row 10 and use the MAX and MIN functions to compute the Highest and Lowest numbers in rows 11 and 12.
2. **Print** the worksheet when you have finished.
3. **Close** the worksheet and **save** it as **Assessment 10.1**.

	A	B	C	D	E	F
1	Bill's Hot Tubs - Accounts Receivable Report					
2						
3		**Beginning**			**Interest**	
4	**Customer**	**Balance**	**Purchases**	**Payments**	**Charge**	**New Balance**
5	Zelton	$2,000	$2,300	$1,000	$15	$3,315
6	Ranier	2450	1000	2450	0	1000
7	Worthington	5400	2190	3000	36	4626
8	Alonzo	3400	500	3400	0	500
9	Barton	100	3400	100	0	3400
10	***Totals***	***$13,350***	***$9,390***	***$9,950***	***$51***	***$12,841***
11	***Highest***	***$5,400***	***$3,400***	***$3,400***	***$36***	***$4,626***
12	***Lowest***	***$100***	***$500***	***$100***	***$0***	***$500***

Assessment 10.2

1. Use the following guidelines to create the worksheet shown at the bottom of this page.
   - Enter all the numbers and text as shown. Use the copy & paste or drag & drop techniques to copy the text or numbers whenever possible. For example, all three of the Wilson family children were paid the same allowances in all four years. Therefore, you can enter the data in row 5 and copy row 5 to rows 10 and 15.
   - Use Increase Indent to indent the Allowance, Saved and Interest Earned entries as shown.
   - Calculate the Interest Earned with the formula **Interest Earned = Saved * Interest Rate**. Use the Interest Rates shown in the following rate table. You will notice that the interest rates change from year to year.

1992	1993	1994	1995
3.5%	4.5%	6.5%	6.5%

   - Widen the columns as necessary and format the worksheet with bold, italics and the Currency format as shown.

2. You completed worksheet should match the worksheet shown below.
3. **Print** the worksheet, then **close** it and **save** it as **Assessment 10.2**.

	A	B	C	D	E	F
1	Wilson Family Allowances					
2						
3		1992	1993	1994	1995	
4	Jason					Total Interest
5	Allowance	260	300	300	340	
6	Saved	120	110	200	220	
7	***Interest Earned***	***4.2***	***4.95***	***13***	***14.3***	***$ 36.45***
8						
9	Cindy					
10	Allowance	260	300	300	340	
11	Saved	120	110	200	220	
12	***Interest Earned***	***4.2***	***4.95***	***13***	***14.3***	***$ 36.45***
13						
14	Betty					
15	Allowance	260	300	300	340	
16	Saved	130	290	280	310	
17	***Interest Earned***	***4.55***	***13.05***	***18.2***	***20.15***	***$ 55.95***
18						
19	**Total Family Interest 1992 - 1995**					**$ 128.85**

Assessment 10.3

1. **Open** the workbook named **Assessment 10.3**.
2. Use the **Classic3** AutoFormat style to format the worksheet as shown below.
3. **Print** the worksheet, then **close** it and **save** the changes.

	A	B	C	D	E	F	G
1	Diane's Café - Employee Hourly Time Log						
2							
3	**Employee**	*Wednesday*	*Thursday*	*Friday*	*Saturday*	*Sunday*	*Totals*
4	**Mary Johnson**	6.5		5	6.5	4	22
5	**Cliff Packard**	4	6	6.5	6.5	4	27
6	**Helen Martinez**	4	6	6.5	6.5		23
7	**Sarah Stonestown**		4	4	4		12
8	**Totals**	14.5	16	22	23.5	8	84

11 Creating an Impact with Charts

Objectives:

- Use more than one worksheet
- Rename worksheets
- Insert a chart as a separate worksheet
- Embed a chart in a worksheet
- Create column, line and pie charts
- Edit and format charts
- Change the location of charts
- Print charts

The Project - AutoSoft Sales Report

In this lesson, you will help AutoSoft - a young and rapidly growing software company - analyze their annual sales. The executives at AutoSoft want charts that compare sales in the various quarters, a growth trend for the year and the contributions of each sales rep to the total company sales. You will create three charts that will provide an impressive solution to this request. The three charts you will create are shown below.

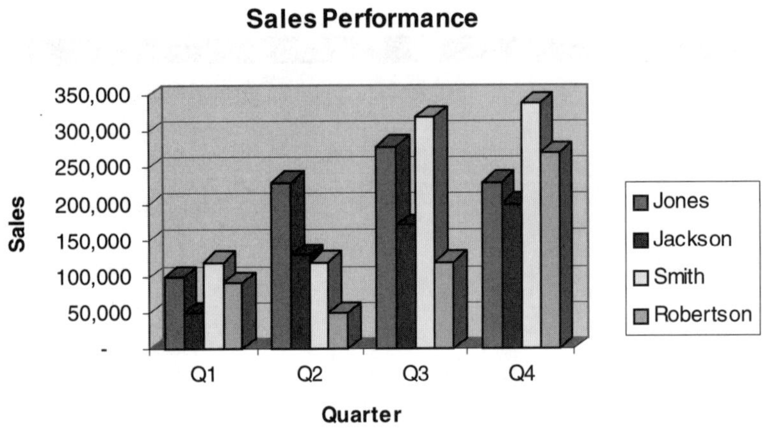

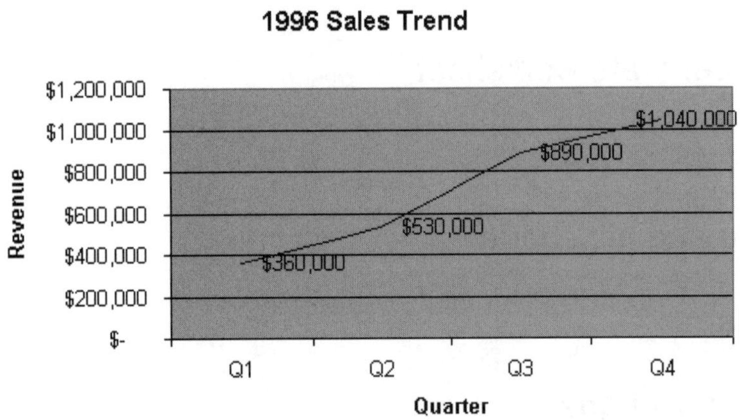

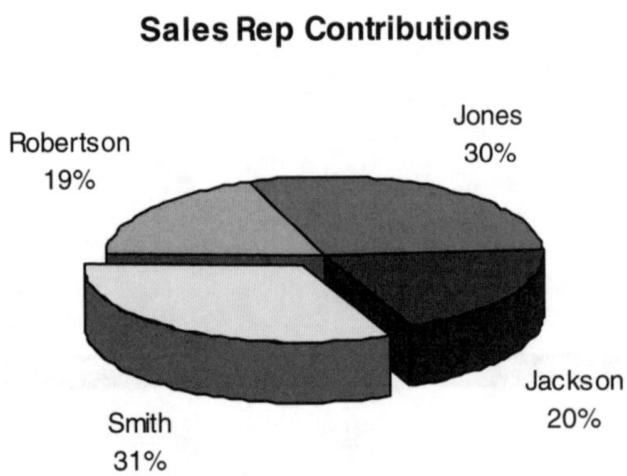

Using More than One Worksheet

Excel lets you have up to 255 worksheets in a workbook. Excel initially provides 3 worksheets in a new workbook, however, you can add additional worksheets up to the maximum of 255. A tab at the bottom of the worksheet identifies each worksheet.

Sheets can be renamed, inserted, deleted and moved

You can rename any worksheet by double-clicking the worksheet tab and typing the desired name on the tab. This lets you give meaningful names to worksheets so that you can easily identify them. You can also insert and delete worksheets and move them to different positions in the worksheet order. This gives you the flexibility to modify your workbooks as your needs change. The following table discusses the procedures that are used to rename, insert, delete, move and activate worksheets.

To	Use this procedure
Rename a worksheet	Double-click the worksheet tab and type the new name on the tab.
Insert a worksheet	Click a worksheet tab and choose Insert→Worksheet.
Delete a worksheet	Click the desired worksheet tab, choose Edit→Delete Sheet and click OK.
Move a worksheet	Drag the worksheet tab to the desired position in the worksheet order.
Activate a worksheet	Click the worksheet tab.

Hands-On 11.1 – Rename a worksheet and experiment

1. **Open** the workbook named **Hands-On Lesson 11.**
2. **Double-click** the Sheet1 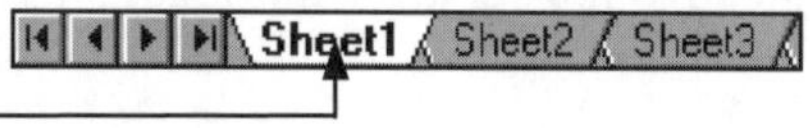 tab at the bottom of the screen.
3. **Type** the name **Sales** and it will replace the name Sheet1.
4. **Click** anywhere in the worksheet to complete the renaming.
5. Position the mouse pointer on the **Sales** sheet tab. **Drag** the tab until the black triangle is to the right of the 4th sheet tab as shown below.

6. **Release** the mouse button and the Sales sheet will be repositioned.
7. **Drag** the **Sales** sheet back until it is positioned to the left of Sheet 2.
8. **Click** the **Sheet 4** tab and choose **Edit→Delete Sheet** from the menu bar.
9. **Click OK** to complete the deletion.
10. Try to **click** Undo and notice the sheet cannot be restored.

    Worksheets are permanently deleted when you issue the Edit→Delete Sheet command. The only way to recover a deleted sheet is to close the workbook without saving it and then reopen it.

11. **Click** the **Sales** sheet tab to make the sales sheet active and continue with the next topic.

Working with Charts

It is often easier to understand numerical data if it is presented in a chart. Excel lets you create and modify a variety of charts. Excel provides 14 major chart categories and each category has several variations to choose from. Excel literally has a chart for every occasion. The following illustration provides examples of charts you can create in Excel.

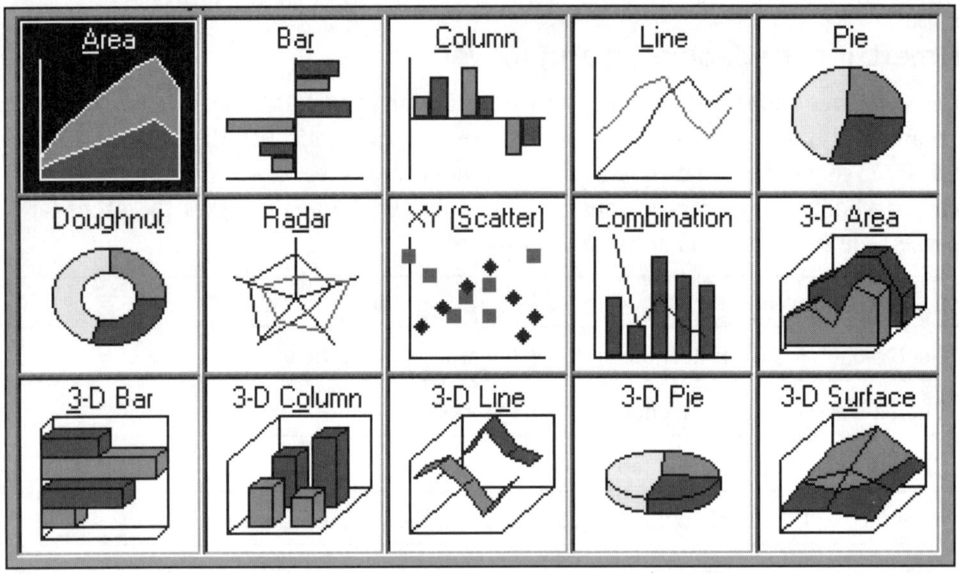

Charts can be embedded in a worksheet or placed on a separate sheet

You can place a chart on the same worksheet that contains the data the chart was created from. This is known as embedding the chart. You can also place a chart on a separate worksheet. This prevents the chart from cluttering the worksheet that contains the data and it allows you to easily print the chart. Charts are always linked to the data they were created from. A chart is automatically updated when the data changes.

Each chart type is designed for a specific purpose

Each chart type presents data in a different manner. You can present the same data in completely different ways by changing the chart type. For this reason, you should always use the chart type that most effectively conveys your data.

Creating Charts

Excel's **Chart Wizard** guides you through each step of chart creation. You can also edit and enhance a chart after it has been created.

The most important step is selecting the correct data

The first step in creating a chart is to select the data you want included in the chart. Many beginners find this step to be the most difficult. This is because they are unsure how Excel will interpret the selected data. You will receive step-by-step guidance on selecting data as you progress through this lesson.

Column and Bar Charts

Column charts compare values (numbers) by using vertical bars. Bar charts use horizontal bars. Each column or bar represents a value from the worksheet. Bar and column charts are most useful for comparing sets of values.

Column and bar charts have a category and value axis

The horizontal line that forms the base of a column or bar chart is called the **category axis**. The category axis typically measures units of time such as days, months or quarters. The vertical line on the left side of a column or bar chart is known as the **value axis**. The value axis typically measures values such as dollars. Most chart types (including column and bar charts) have a category and value axis. The following illustrations show the column chart you will create in the next few exercises. The illustrations show the objects that are present on most column charts and the corresponding data that was used to create the chart. Take a few minutes to study these illustrations carefully.

	A	B	C	D	E
1	Autosoft 1996 Quarterly Sales				
2					
3		Q1	Q2	Q3	Q4
4	Jones	100,000	230,000	280,000	230,000
5	Jackson	50,000	130,000	170,000	200,000
6	Smith	120,000	120,000	320,000	340,000
7	Robertson	90,000	50,000	120,000	270,000
8					
9	Total	$ 360,000	$ 530,000	$ 890,000	$ 1,040,000

The chart below was created using the selected data shown here. Notice the Total row was not included in the selection. The column chart compares the sales numbers for the individual quarters but it does not include the Total sales in row 9.

This is the vertical value axis. The numbering scale (0 - 350,000) was created by Excel after it determined the range of values that were included in the chart.

Notice the chart has a chart title (Sales Performance), a value axis title (Sales) and a Category axis title (Quarter). The Chart Wizard lets you specify the titles when you create the chart.

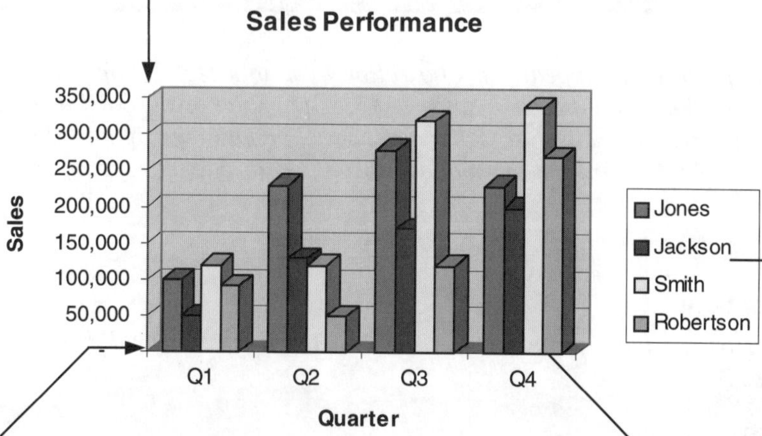

This is a legend that identifies the various columns. Notice the legend text (Jones, Jackson, Smith and Robertson) was taken from the first column of the selected worksheet cells (shown above).

This is the horizontal category axis. Notice the category axis labels (Q1, Q2, Q3 and Q4) were taken from row 3 of the selected worksheet cells (shown above).

Notice the chart columns. They represent the various data series. The first data series is the Jones' numbers in row 4. The first column in each quarter represents the Jones' numbers.

Hands-On 11.2 – Create a column chart on a separate sheet

The Hands-On Lesson 11 worksheet should still be open from the previous exercise.

Create the chart

1. **Select** the range **A3:E7** as shown on the previous page.
2. **Click** the Chart Wizard button on the Standard toolbar.

   The Chart Wizard - Step 1 of 4 dialog box will appear.

3. Use the following steps to explore the dialog box.

❶ *Check out the various chart types by clicking the options on the Chart type list.*

❷ ***Choose** the **Column** type when you have finished exploring. Also, make sure the first sub-type is chosen on the right side of the dialog box.*

❸ ***Press and hold** the mouse pointer on this button to see a Sample of your chart.*

❹ ***Click** the **Next** button.*

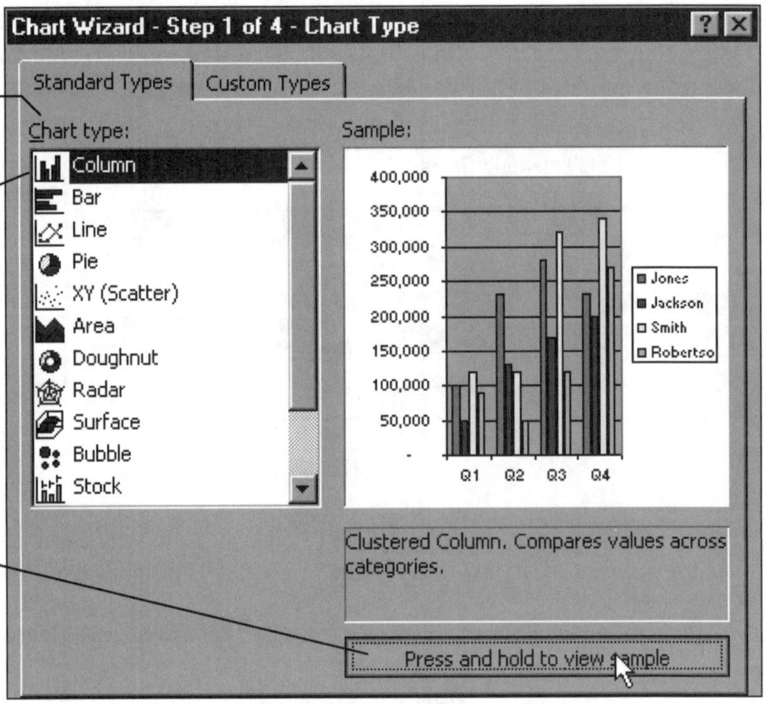

The Chart Wizard - Step 2 of 4 box will appear. This box allows you to select a different range of cells. Notice that the range in the dialog box is =Sales!$A$3:$E$7. Sales is the worksheet name and the dollar signs indicate these are absolute cell references. For now, just ignore the dollar signs and think of the range as A3:E7. You will learn about absolute cell references soon.

4. The range Sales!$A$3:$E$7 is correct, so **click** the Next > button.

Check out the various chart options

The Step 3 dialog box has 6 tabs that let you set various chart options. You will explore these options in the next few steps.

5. Notice the options on the Titles tab.

   You will add titles to a chart in the next exercise.

6. **Click** the **Axes tab.**

   The options on the Axes tab let you hide the labels on the category axis and value axis. You will almost always want to leave these options set to the default settings.

Continued...

7. **Click** the **Gridlines** tab.

   Gridlines help identify the values in the chart. Your chart should have Major gridlines for the value axis displayed. These are the horizontal lines across the chart.

8. Feel free to click the various gridlines boxes and notice how they appear in the Preview box.

9. **Click** the **Legend** tab.

   Notice the legend on the right side of the Preview box. The Legend identifies the various columns. For example, the columns for Jones are identified by a color that also appears in the legend.

10. **Remove** the **check** from the **Show legend box** and the legend will vanish.

11. **Click** the **Show legend box** again to redisplay the legend.

12. **Click** the **Data Labels** tab.

    Data labels are printed at the top of the columns. They identify the exact value of the column.

13. **Click** the **Show Value** option and values will appear at the top of each column.

    The numbers will be very crowded in the Preview box.

14. **Click** the **Show Label** option, then **click** the **None** option to remove the data labels.

15. **Click** the **Data Table** tab.

16. **Click** the **Show data table** check box and a table will appear below the Preview chart.

17. Take a moment to check out the data table, then **remove** the **check** from the Show data table box.

18. **Click** the Next > button and the Step 4 of 4 dialog box will appear.

19. **Click** the As new sheet: option.

    This option instructs Excel to create the chart on a separate chart sheet.

20. **Click** the Finish button.

    Look at the sheet tabs and notice the chart has been created on a new sheet named Chart1. The Chart1 sheet is inserted immediately to the left of the Sales sheet.

21. **Click** the Print Preview button.

    Notice the chart occupies the entire page in a landscape orientation. Charts that are created as separate sheets are large and easy-to-view, however, they lack titles and other descriptive text.

Delete the Chart1 sheet

22. **Click** the **Close** button on the Print Preview toolbar.

23. Choose **Edit→Delete Sheet** and **click OK**.

    Continue with the next Hands-On exercise where you will create an embedded chart.

Hands-On 11.3 – Create an embedded chart

In this exercise, you will use the Chart Wizard to create an embedded 3-D Column chart. An embedded chart is placed in the worksheet next to the data it is created from.

Start the Chart Wizard and define the chart area

1. Make sure the range A3:E7 is still selected.
2. **Click** the Chart Wizard button on the Standard toolbar.
3. Choose the 4th sub-type from the right side of the dialog box.
   This is the Clustered column with a 3-D visual effect as shown below.

4. **Click** the Next > button, then **click** Next > again on the Step 2 of 4 box.
5. **Click** the **Titles tab** and use the following steps in the Step 3 of 4 box.

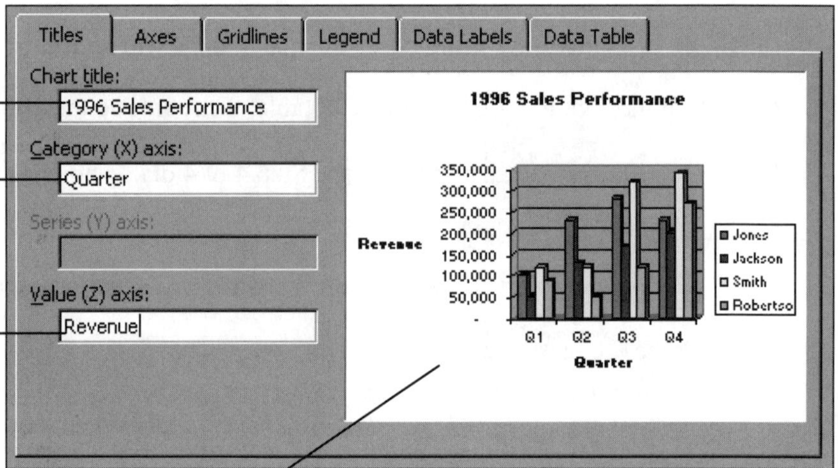

❶ *Enter the titles shown here.*

❷ *Notice the position of the various titles in the preview window.*

6. **Click** the Next > button.
7. Leave the chart location set to ⊙ As object in: on the Step 4 of 4 box and **click** Finish.
   Excel will embed the chart in your worksheet. The Chart toolbar will most likely appear as well. Continue with the next topic where you will learn how to move and size a chart.

Moving and Sizing Embedded Charts

Excel lets you move and size charts after they have been created. Excel considers the entire chart to be an object. You can easily move and resize objects using standard mouse techniques.

You must select the chart before you move or size it

You select a chart by clicking anywhere in the **Chart Area** . The Chart Area is the area just inside the border of the chart where there are no objects. Tiny squares called **sizing handles** appear on the corners and four sides of a selected chart. A chart is also automatically selected immediately after it is created. The following table discusses the move and size procedures.

To	Do this
Move a chart	Drag it to a new location.
Change the size	Drag any sizing handle.

Hands-On 11.4 – Move and size the chart

Move and size the chart

1. **Deselect** the chart by **clicking** anywhere outside of it.

   The sizing handles will vanish.

2. Use the Zoom Control to zoom to 50% [50%] of normal.

   This will give you plenty of room to move and size the chart.

3. Use the following steps to move and size the chart.

❶ ***Click*** *in the Chart Area (an open part of the chart) and the sizing handles will reappear.*

❷ *Position the mouse pointer in the Chart Area, then drag the chart to a new location.*

❸ ***Point*** *to a corner sizing handle and the Adjust pointer will appear.*

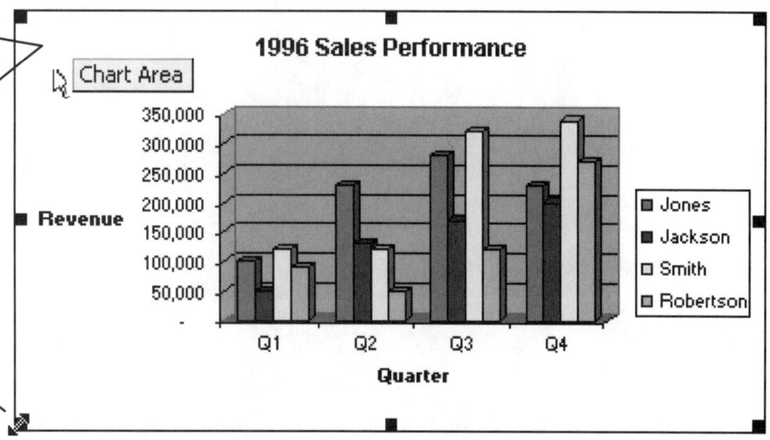

❹ ***Drag*** *the sizing handle to change both the width and height.*

❺ *Move and size the chart until both the chart and the worksheet data are visible.*

Change the data and watch the chart change

4. **Click outside the chart** to deselect it, then **Zoom** to **100%**.

5. Take a few minutes to study your chart and the worksheet data that was used to create it.

Continued...

6. **Click** cell **B4**.

7. Enter the number **300000** (that's five zeros) and watch the first column in the chart rise.

   Charts are linked to the worksheet data. They always reflect changes in the data even if they are placed in a separate chart sheet.

8. **Click** cell **B4** again and enter the number **1000000** (that's six zeros).

   Notice that 1000000 is much larger than the other numbers in the worksheet. Notice how the other columns are very small and it is difficult to determine their values in the chart. The large number changes the scale of the value axis so much, that it makes the chart difficult to interpret.

9. **Click** cell **B4** again and enter the number **100000** (that's five zeros).

10. Save  the changes and continue with the next topic.

The Chart Toolbar

The Chart toolbar has several buttons to help you format charts. The Chart toolbar can be displayed by right-clicking on any toolbar and choosing Chart from the shortcut menu. You will display the Chart toolbar in the following exercise.

Hands-On 11.5 – Use the Chart toolbar

Display the Chart toolbar

1. **Right-click** on any toolbar and a shortcut menu will appear.

   All toolbars that are currently displayed will have a check mark next to them.

2. If Chart is already checked, close the menu by clicking in the worksheet. Otherwise, choose **Chart** and the Chart toolbar will appear.

   The Chart toolbar may be anchored above the worksheet or it may float in the worksheet area.

Use the Chart Type drop-down list to choose a chart type

3. Select the chart by **clicking** anywhere in the Chart Area (an open part of the chart).

   Most of the buttons on the Chart toolbar will now become available.

4. Use the following steps to explore the Chart toolbar and change the chart type.

❶ ***Notice*** *the Object list and Format button. These tools are used to format chart objects. You will use these tools in the next exercise.*

❷ ***Click*** *the Chart Type drop-down button. This option lets you select from a variety of standard chart types.*

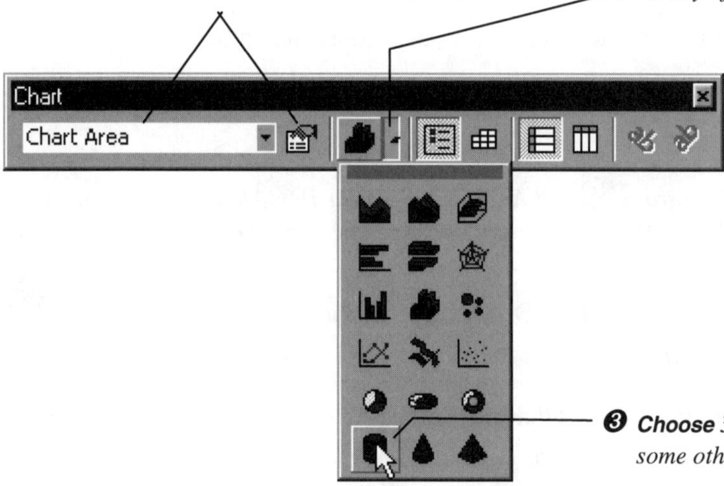

❸ ***Choose*** *3-D Cylinder or some other chart type.*

5. Feel free to experiment with the options on the Chart Type drop-down list.

   However, you won't be able to choose the 3-D Column Chart that you originally had. In the next few steps, you will use another technique to choose your original 3-D Column Chart.

Use the Chart menu to choose a chart type

6. Make sure your chart is still selected, and then notice the menu bar at the top of the Excel window.

   The Menu bar should have a Chart option. The Menu bar usually has a Data menu, however, a Chart menu appears whenever a chart is selected. The Chart menu gives you access to the Chart Wizard dialog boxes. These are the same dialog boxes that appear when you create a chart with the Chart Wizard. This gives you complete control over chart properties such as the chart type.

Continued...

7. Choose **Chart→Chart Type...** from the menu bar.
   Notice the dialog box provides access to all chart types.

8. Choose **Column** from the top of the Chart Type list and choose the **4th sub-type** on the right side of the dialog box.

9. **Click OK** to restore your original column chart.

Explore the remaining buttons on the Chart toolbar

10. **Click** the Legend button on the Chart toolbar to turn off the legend.

11. **Click** the Legend button again to restore the legend.

12. **Click** the Data Table button to add a data table to the chart.

13. **Click** Data Table again to turn off the table.

14. **Click** the By Column button (two buttons to the right of the Data Table button).
    Notice Excel displays the sales rep names along the horizontal (category) axis and the Quarters in the legend box. The sales for each rep are now grouped into one set of columns. This gives you a different view of the same data.

15. **Click** the By Row button to switch to the original view.

16. **Click** anywhere on the chart title and it will become selected as shown below.

    Notice the Angle Text Downward and Angle Text Upward buttons are now available. You can use these buttons to change the angle and appearance of certain objects such as titles.

17. Feel free to experiment with the Angle Text Downward and Angle Text Upward buttons.
    You will proably find the angled text buttons of limited use because of the length of the title.

18. Remove the angle effect from the title by **clicking** whichever Angle Text button is currently acitve.
    You will learn how to format and change the various chart objects in the following topics.

Editing and Formatting Chart Objects

Excel lets you edit and format objects within charts. You can delete or move objects, change the color of objects and perform other editing and formatting actions.

You must select the object you want to format

You select an object by clicking it or choosing it from the Objects [Chart Title ▾] list. You can format the object once it is selected.

Editing and Formatting Titles

You can edit the text in any chart title. You can also change the font, size and color of titles. The following table discusses the procedures for editing and formatting chart titles.

To	Do this
Edit a title	Select the title, pause and then click the title again to position the insertion point within the title. Make the desired editing changes.
Format the font, size and color	Use the Font, Size and Font Color buttons on the Formatting toolbar.

Hands-On 11.6 – Edit and format the titles

Edit the Chart title

1. Make sure the Chart Title is selected as shown below.

   1996 Sales Performance

2. Position the mouse pointer on the title and the pointer will have an I-Beam shape.
3. **Click** the I-Beam just in front of the word **Performance**.
4. Type the word **Rep** to make the title 1996 Sales Rep Performance.

   You can edit a title in the Formula bar or directly in the title box (as you just did).

Replace the Revenue title

5. **Click** the **Revenue** title (the title on the left side of the chart) and type **Sales**.

   The word Sales will appear in the Formula bar.

6. Confirm the entry and the title will become Sales.

Format the titles

7. **Click** the Chart Title (1996 Sales Rep Performance) and it will become selected.
8. Use the Formatting toolbar [Arial ▾] [12 ▾] [B] [I] [U] to format the title as desired.
9. Use the Font Color button to add color to the title.

   Be careful not to use the Fill Color button. The Fill Color button will add color to the background of the title but not to the text.

10. Format the Value Axis title (Sales) and the Category Axis title (Quarter) as desired.

Hands-On 11.7 - Use the Object list and Format buttons on the Chart toolbar

Add color to the Chart Area

1. **Click** the **Chart Title** (1996 Sales Rep Performance) and it will become selected.

2. Use the following steps to further understand the Chart toolbar.

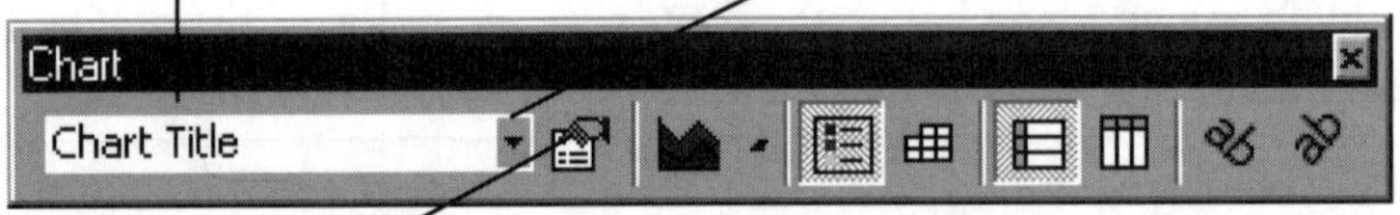

3. **Click** the **Patterns tab** and notice you can format either the Border or the Area.

4. **Choose any color** in the Area section and **click OK**.
   The color you chose will fill the Chart Area and provide a colored background for the chart.

Change the orientation of the value axis title

5. **Click** the value axis title (Sales) and it will become selected.

6. **Click** the Format button on the Chart toolbar.
   A dialog box with formatting options for titles will appear.

7. **Click** the Alignment tab.

8. Use the following step to adjust the orientation.

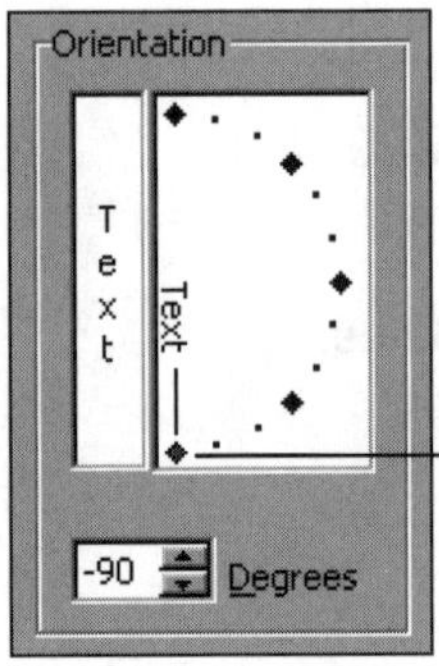

9. **Click OK** and the title will have a vertical orientation.
   This will allow the chart columns to expand horizontally.

10. Feel free to edit any chart object by clicking on it and then using the Format button on the Chart toolbar.

11. When you have finished experimenting, save the changes and continue with the next topic.

Line Charts

Line charts are useful for comparing trends over a period of time. For example, line charts are often used to show stock market and economic activity where the upward or downward trend of the data is important.

Line charts also have a category and value axis

Line charts have a category axis and value axis, as do column charts. Most of the objects on line charts such as the legend, titles, and axis labels are used in the same way as with column charts. The illustration below shows the line chart you will create next. The chart depicts the trend in quarterly sales throughout the year. Take a moment to study the illustration and the accompanying worksheet.

3		Q1	Q2	Q3	Q4
4	Jones	100,000	230,000	280,000	230,000
5	Jackson	50,000	130,000	170,000	200,000
6	Smith	120,000	120,000	320,000	340,000
7	Robertson	90,000	50,000	120,000	270,000
8					
9	Total	$ 360,000	$ 530,000	$ 890,000	$ 1,040,000

The chart below was created using the selected data shown here. Notice the data is in two separate ranges. You will use the Ctrl key to select these non-contiguous ranges. This will let you chart just the Totals for each quarter and the Q1-Q4 labels.

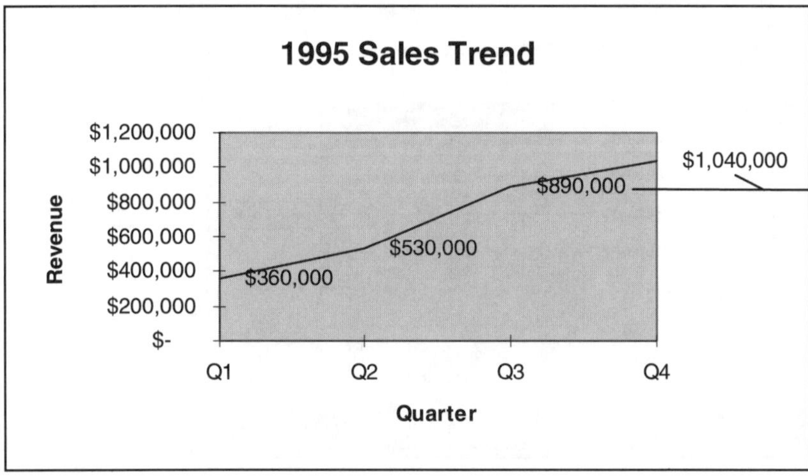

*These numbers are known as **data labels**. They show the exact value of the various data points. You can use Data Labels with any type of chart.*

Notice the line chart makes it quite clear that the sales volume had an upward trend throughout the year.

Hands-On 11.8 – Create a line chart

In this exercise, you will create a line chart in the Sales sheet. When you are finished, the Sales sheet will contain the data and both the column and line charts.

Reduce the size of the column chart to make room for the line chart

1. **Click** the column chart once to select it.
2. **Drag** a corner sizing handle until the chart is very small (approximately 1" by 1").
   You can always restore the size at a later time.
3. Move the chart to the top edge of the screen (just to the right of the worksheet data).
   You can move the chart by dragging it with the mouse.
4. **Click** outside the chart to deselect it.

Continued...

Select the data

5. Use the following Hands-On Illustration to select the data.

3		Q1	Q2	Q3	Q4
4	Jones	100,000	230,000	280,000	230,000
5	Jackson	50,000	130,000	170,000	200,000
6	Smith	120,000	120,000	320,000	340,000
7	Robertson	90,000	50,000	120,000	270,000
8					
9	Total	$ 360,000	$ 530,000	$ 890,000	$ 1,040,000

❶ *Use the mouse to select the range* ***A3:E3*** *as shown here.*

❷ ***Press & Hold*** *the* ***Ctrl*** *key on the keyboard while you select the range* ***A9:E9*** *as shown here.*

Use the Chart Wizard

6. Click the Chart Wizard button.

7. Choose the Line (Line) chart type and the 1st sub-type.

8. Click Next > **twice** and then enter the titles in the Step 3 of 4 box as shown below.

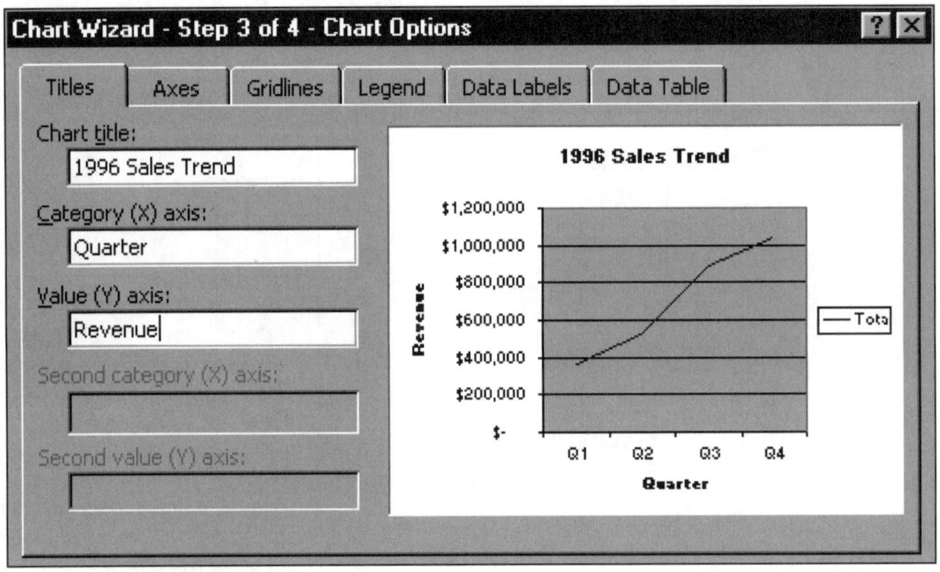

9. Click the Finish button.

There was no need to click Next on the Step 4 of 4 box because we want the chart embedded in the current worksheet. Keep in mind that you can click Finish at any step in the Chart Wizard.

10. Take a few moments to study your chart, and then continue with the next topic.

Editing Charts with the Chart Wizard

The Chart Wizard can be used to edit charts after they have been created. You can set any chart option just as you would when creating a chart. Earlier in this lesson, you used the Chart option on the menu bar to display the Chart Wizard dialog boxes and edit a chart. The difference between that technique and the Chart Wizard technique, is the Chart Wizard technique guides you through the four or five steps of editing a chart just as it does when you create a new chart.

Inserting Data Labels

Excel can display **data labels** at any **data point**. Data points occur at the top of columns or at the locations where a line chart changes. Data labels display the exact values of the data points. Data labels are most effective when there are only a few data points. A chart may be cluttered if you use data labels and there are too many columns or lines.

Hands-On 11.9 – Insert data labels in the line chart

1. **Click** anywhere in the Chart Area of the line chart.
2. **Click** the Chart Wizard button.
3. **Click** Next > **twice** and then **click** the **Data Labels** tab.
4. Choose the Show value option and **click** the Finish button.
   Excel displays data labels at the points that correspond to the numbers in Row 9.
5. Feel free to format the line chart in any way you desire.
6. When you have finished, **click** outside the chart to deselect it.
7. Increase the size of the column chart you created earlier and position both charts at any location you desire.
8. Save the changes and continue with the pie chart topic on the next page.

Pie Charts

Pie charts are useful for comparing parts of a whole. For example, pie charts are often used in budgets to show which part of the budget is being allocated for various purposes.

You typically select two sets of data when creating a pie chart. You select the values that make up the parts of the pie and labels that identify the categories. The following illustrations show a 3-D pie chart and the worksheet data you will use in the following exercises. Notice the worksheet has an extra column added to it. You will create this column in the next exercise.

3		Q1	Q2	Q3	Q4	Total
4	Jones	100,000	230,000	280,000	230,000	840,000
5	Jackson	50,000	130,000	170,000	200,000	550,000
6	Smith	120,000	120,000	320,000	340,000	900,000
7	Robertson	90,000	50,000	120,000	270,000	530,000

The names in column A will become labels on the pie slices. The numbers in column F will determine the size of the slices.

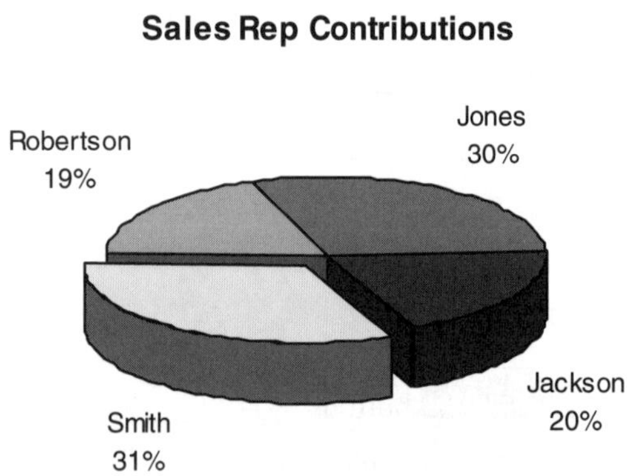

Excel calculates the percentages based upon the numbers you select. Notice that the Smith slice is "exploded" out from the pie.

Hands-On 11.10 – Create a pie chart on a separate chart sheet

In this exercise, you will create a 3-D pie chart. You will instruct Excel to insert the pie chart in a new worksheet. The Hands-On Lesson 11 workbook should still be open.

Add a Total column

1. **Click** cell **F3** and enter the word **Total** (you may need to move the column or bar chart).
2. **Select** the range **F4:F7** and use AutoSum to compute the Totals for column F.

   Notice these totals calculate the total annual sales for each sales rep. Your Totals should match those shown above.

Create the chart on a separate chart sheet

3. **Select** the ranges **A4:A7** and **F4:F7** as shown above (you will need to use the Ctrl key when selecting the second range).
4. **Click** the Chart Wizard button.
5. Choose the Pie Pie chart type and the 3-D sub-type.
6. **Click** Next > **twice** and the Step 3 of 4 box will appear.

Continued...

7. If necessary, **click** the **Titles tab** and enter the title **Sales Rep Contributions** as the Chart title.

8. **Click** the **Legend tab** and remove the check from the [Show legend] box.
   The legend won't be needed because you will add data labels in the next step.

9. **Click** the **Data Labels tab** and choose the [Show label and percent] option.
   Each pie slice should have the sales rep name and percentage of the total sales displayed.

10. **Click** [Next >] and the Step 4 of 4 box will appear.

11. **Click** the [As new sheet:] button, and then **click** the [Finish] button.

12. Look at the sheet tabs and notice the chart has been created on a new sheet named Chart2.

13. **Double-click** the **Chart2** sheet tab and the Chart2 text will become selected.

14. Type **Pie Chart** as the new sheet name.

Exploding Pie Slices and Changing the 3-D View

You can make a pie slice stand out from the rest of the pie by **exploding** the slice. Exploding simply means to draw the slice out from the pie. Excel also lets you rotate a pie chart to draw attention to a particular part of the pie.

Hands-On 11.11 – Explode one slice and change the 3-D Rotation and Elevation

Explode the Smith slice

1. **Click** anywhere on the pie and the entire pie will become selected.

2. Now **click** once on the **Smith** slice and it will be the only selected slice.

3. Use the following step to explode the Smith slice.

❶ *Position the mouse pointer on the Smith slice and drag it out of the pie as shown here.*

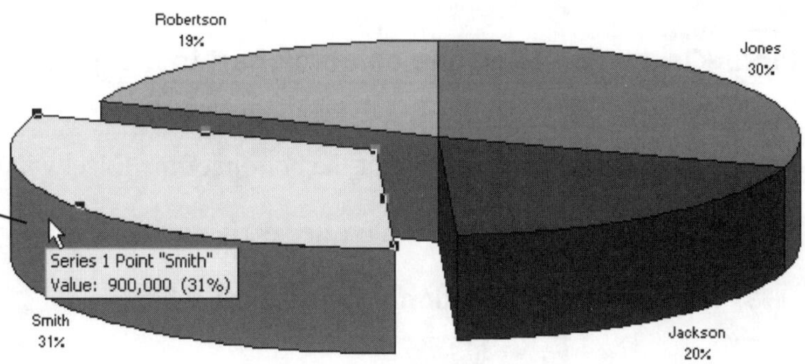

Explode all of the slices

4. **Drag** the Smith slice back into the pie until the pie is whole again.

5. **Click** outside of the pie to deselect it.

Continued...

6. **Click** anywhere on the pie and the entire pie will become selected.
7. **Drag** any slice out of the pie and all of the pie slices will become exploded.
8. **Release** the mouse button and all slices will be exploded.
9. Now explode just the Smith slice again.
   You will need to make the pie whole again by dragging a slice back to the center. All slices will move to the center when you do this. Then you can explode the Smith slice.

Change the 3-D Rotation and Elevation

10. Make sure the pie is selected, and then choose **Chart→3-D View...** from the menu bar.
11. Use the following steps to adjust the rotation and elevation.

❶ ***Click*** *this button until the Elevation box reads* **25**.

❷ ***Click*** *this button until the rotation box reads* **320**.

❸ ***Click OK*** *and notice how the pie orientation changes.*

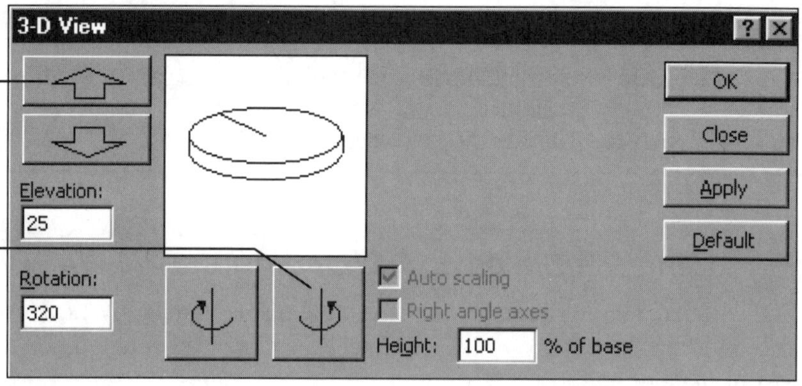

12. Feel free to experiment with the 3-D View and other options on the Chart menu.
13. Save your worksheet when you have finished and continue with the next topic.

Changing the Chart Location

You can move an embedded chart to a separate chart sheet and vice-versa. This is easily accomplished by selecting the chart and using the **Chart→Location...** command on the menu bar.

Hands-On 11.12 – Move the column chart to a separate chart sheet

In this exercise, you will move the column chart from the Sales sheet to a separate chart sheet.

1. **Click** the **Sales sheet tab** at the bottom of the Excel window.
2. **Click** the column chart you created earlier in this lesson.
3. Choose **Chart→Location...** from the menu bar.
4. Choose the As new sheet: option.
5. **Click OK** and the chart will be placed on a separate chart sheet.
6. Change the name of the new sheet to **Column Chart**.
7. Feel free to experiment with charts, and then **close** the workbook and **save** the changes.

Concepts Review

True / False

1. A workbook can have a maximum of 16 worksheets. 1. **T F**
2. You can rename a worksheet by first double-clicking the sheet tab. 2. **T F**
3. Embedded charts are updated when the worksheet data changes. 3. **T F**
4. Charts on a separate chart sheet are not updated when the worksheet data changes. 4. **T F**
5. Column charts are most useful for comparing the parts of a whole. 5. **T F**
6. Column charts have a category and value axis. 6. **T F**
7. The Chart Wizard can only be used to create embedded charts. 7. **T F**
8. The Chart menu on the menu bar is only available when a chart is selected. 8. **T F**
9. You must select a chart before you can move or resize it. 9. **T F**
10. A chart has a portrait orientation when it is first created on a separate chart sheet. 10. **T F**

Multiple Choice

1. Which procedure would you use to change the position of a worksheet in the sheet order?
   a) Double-click the sheet tab then drag the tab to the desired location.
   b) Click the sheet tab and choose Edit→Move sheet from the menu bar.
   c) Drag the sheet tab to the desired location.
   d) None of the above. ( )
2. Which command would you use to move an embedded chart to a separate sheet?
   a) Edit→Move chart
   b) Chart→Location
   c) Chart→Move
   d) This cannot be done ( )
3. Which chart would be best for showing a trend over a period of time?
   a) Line chart
   b) Bar chart
   c) Column chart
   d) Pie chart ( )
4. Which technique can be used to insert Data Labels after a chart has been created?
   a) Select the chart and click the Data Labels button on the Chart toolbar.
   b) Select the chart and choose the Insert→Data Labels command.
   c) Select the chart, choose Chart→Options, and then click the Data Labels tab.
   d) Data labels cannot be inserted after a chart has been created. ( )
5. Which technique can be used to explode a single pie slice?
   a) Select the chart, click anywhere on the pie and drag the slice.
   b) Click the chart, click the pie, click the desired slice, and then drag it.
   c) Click the chart, double-click the pie and drag the slice.
   d) None of the above. ( )

Skills Builder 11.1

In this exercise, you will create a column chart to display student enrollments at a university.

Enter the years in column A by expanding the series

1. **Open** the workbook named **Skills Builder 11.1**.

   Notice the enrollment data has been completed in column B but the years have not been completed in column A. Notice the first two years 1980 and 1981 form the beginning of the series 1980 - 1996. The best way to expand this series is with the fill handle.

2. **Select** cells **A4** and **A5**.

3. **Drag** the fill handle + down to row 20 to expand the series.

4. Left align the years in column A.

Create the chart

5. **Select** the range **A3:B20**.

   This range includes the enrollment data and the Year and Total Enrollment labels.

6. **Click** the Chart Wizard button.

7. Choose the Column Column chart type and the first sub-type.

8. **Click** Next > and the Step 2 of 4 box will appear.

   Take a moment to study the step 2 dialog box and you will notice a problem. Excel is interpreting the years 1980 – 1996 as numbers and it is plotting them as a data series in the chart. The years are the short columns to the left of the tall-thin enrollment data columns. The years should actually be displayed as labels on the horizontal category axis. You will correct this in the next few steps.

9. **Click** the **Series tab** on the dialog box.

   The Series tab lets you modify the data series that are plotted in the chart.

10. Use the following step to remove the year columns.

❶ **Choose Year** *from the Series list.*

❷ **Click** *the* **Remove** *button.*

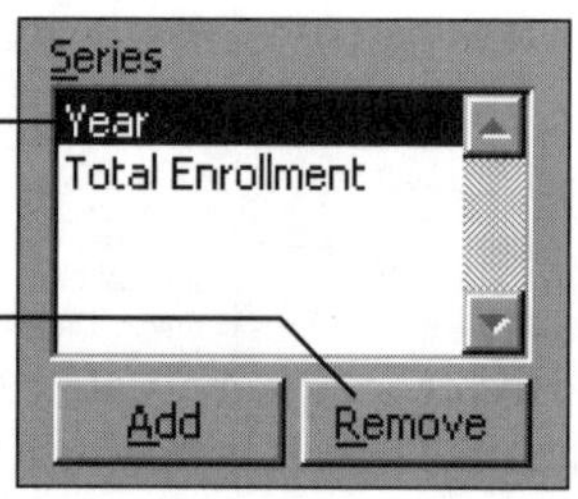

In the next few steps, you will add the years as Category axis labels.

11. **Click** in the Category (X) axis labels box.

12. Select the years 1980 – 1996 in the worksheet as shown on the following page.

    The Source Data dialog box will temporarily close as you select the data.

Continued...

The Category (X) axis labels box should now match the following example.

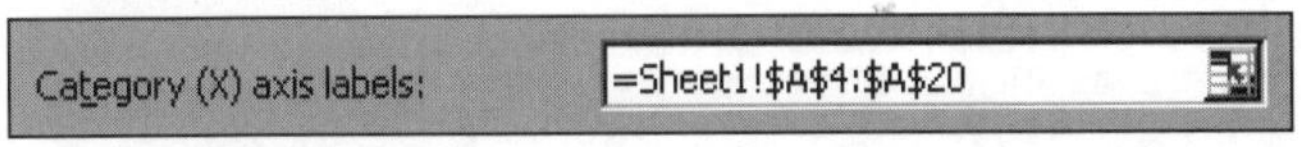

Notice that the dates are now displayed in an angled fashion on the Category axis.

13. **Click** Next > to continue with step 3 of 4.

14. **Click** the **Titles tab** and type the title **Student Enrollments** in the Chart title box.

15. **Click** the **Legend tab** and **remove** the legend.

16. **Click** Finish to complete the chart.

    Take a few moments to study your worksheet and chart. Make sure you understand the relationship between the worksheet data and the chart.

Convert the chart to a line chart

Imagine you are interested in seeing only the trend in enrollments as opposed to the enrollments in individual years. You can easily convert this chart to a line chart.

17. Make sure the chart is selected.

18. **Click** the Chart Type button on the Chart toolbar and choose Line Chart from the list.

    Your chart should be converted to a line chart.

Format the chart title

19. **Click** the **Student Enrollments** chart title.

20. Use the Font Color button to add your color of choice to the title.

21. Feel free to format the chart and title in any other way you desire.

22. When you have finished, **close** the workbook and **save** the changes.

Skills Builder 11.2

In this exercise, you will create a chart for Holy Donuts. The chart will show the various types of donuts that make up the sales volume at Holy Donuts. What type of chart do you think you will use? Well a donut chart what else!

Create the worksheet

1. If necessary, open a New Workbook and create the worksheet shown below. Format the numbers in column B as Comma with 0 decimals.

	A	B	C
1	**Holy Donuts Product Analysis**		
2			
3	**Type of Donut**	**Total Number Sold**	
4	Creme Filled	12,000	
5	Frosted	10,500	
6	Nut Covered	2,300	
7	Glazed	7,000	
8	Old Fashioned	4,500	

Create the chart

Doughnut charts function much like pie charts because they are used to compare parts of a whole. Therefore, the data is selected, as it would be for a pie chart.

2. **Select** the donut data in the range **A4:B8**.
3. **Click** the Chart Wizard button.
4. Choose **Doughnut** as the Chart type and choose the **first sub-type**.
5. **Click** Next > **twice** and the Step 3 of 4 dialog box will appear.
6. **Click** the **Titles** tab and enter the Chart title **Donut Analysis**.
7. **Click** the **Legend tab** and remove the check from the Show Legend box.
8. **Click** the **Data Labels tab** and choose the **Show label and percent** option.
9. **Click** the Finish button.

Remove the border from the chart

10. Make sure the chart is selected and **click** the Format button on the Chart toolbar.
11. Make sure the Patterns tab is active and set the Border option to None.
12. **Click OK** and the border should be removed.

Change the color of the percentages and labels

13. **Click** any of the labels or percentages (such as Glazed 19%) and the entire group will be selected.
14. Use the Font Color button on the Formatting toolbar to apply a striking color such as red.
15. Feel free to modify your chart by changing the color of the donut slices or other objects. This is easily accomplished by clicking the object, clicking the Format button and choosing the desired options from the dialog box. Finally, **close** the workbook and **save** it as **Skills Builder 11.2**.

Skills Builder 11.3

In this exercise, you will create four pie charts to illustrate employee expenses for Hollywood Productions - a motion pictures production company. The pie charts will show how employee costs are divided between departments and how each department's employee costs are allocated. You will create each chart on a separate chart sheet.

Create the company pie chart

1. **Open** the workbook named **Skills Builder 11.3**.

2. Use the following Hands-On Illustration to select two ranges.

3		Marketing	Production	Finance
4	Salaries	3,400,000	4,500,000	1,200,000
5	Benefits	1,292,000	1,980,000	336,000
6	Travel	1,700,000	1,500,000	120,000
7	**Total**	**$ 6,392,000**	**$ 7,980,000**	**$ 1,656,000**

❶ *Use the mouse to select the range* ***B3:D3*** *as shown here.*

❷ ***Press & Hold*** *the* ***Ctrl*** *key and select the range* ***B7:D7****.*

3. **Click** the Chart Wizard button and create the following pie chart on a **separate chart sheet**.

   Make sure the chart type, title, and labels match the following example. Also notice the example does not have a legend.

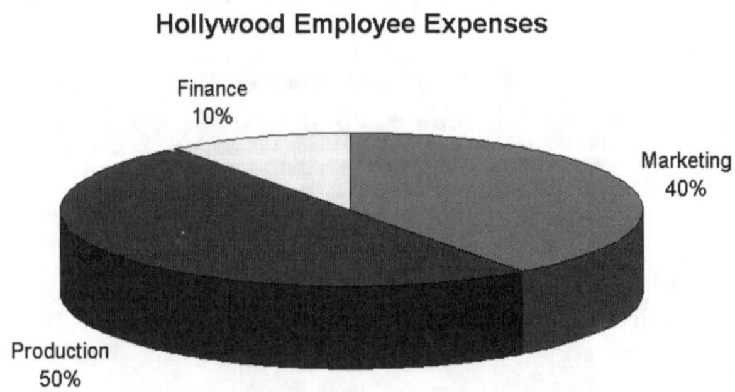

4. **Double-click** the **Chart1** sheet tab and change the sheet name to **Hollywood Chart**.

   Notice you can use long names when naming sheets.

5. Rename Sheet1 as **Employee Expense Data**.

Create a separate pie chart for the Marketing department

6. **Select** the range shown below.

3		Marketing	Production	Finance
4	Salaries	3,400,000	4,500,000	1,200,000
5	Benefits	1,292,000	1,980,000	336,000
6	Travel	1,700,000	1,500,000	120,000
7	**Total**	**$ 6,392,000**	**$ 7,980,000**	**$ 1,656,000**

7. **Click** the Chart Wizard button and create a pie chart on a **separate chart sheet**. Use the same chart type and labels as the previous chart but use the title **Marketing Employee Costs**.

8. Rename the sheet as **Marketing Chart**.

9. **Click** the **Employee Expense Data** sheet tab to return to that sheet.

Continued...

Create pie charts for the Production and Finance departments

10. Use the techniques in this exercise to create the same style pie charts for the Production and Finance departments. Create each chart on a separate chart sheet using the techniques in this exercise. Use the chart titles and sheet names shown in the table below. Also, you should select data for the Production department chart as shown below. You will need to decide how to select the data for the Finance department (although that should be an easy decision to make).

Chart	Use this title	Use this sheet name
Production	Production Employee Costs	Production Chart
Finance	Finance Employee Costs	Finance Chart

3		Marketing	Production	Finance
4	Salaries	3,400,000	4,500,000	1,200,000
5	Benefits	1,292,000	1,980,000	336,000
6	Travel	1,700,000	1,500,000	120,000
7	**Total**	**$ 6,392,000**	**$ 7,980,000**	**$ 1,656,000**

Rearrange the sheet tabs

11. Use the following steps to move the Employee Expense Data sheet tab.

❶ *If necessary, use the tab scrolling buttons until the Employee Expense Data tab is visible.*

❷ **Drag** *the* **Employee Expense Data** *tab to the left until it is in front of the Hollywood Chart tab. You may need to drag part way, use the left tab-scrolling button and then continue dragging.*

Explode the pie slices and increase the elevation

12. Click the **Hollywood Chart** tab to activate it.

13. Click once on the pie, pause, then **click** the **Production** slice (the largest slice).

14. Drag the slice out slightly to explode it.

15. Choose **Chart→3-D View...** from the menu bar.

16. Increase the Elevation  to **25** and **click OK**.

17. Click the **Marketing Chart** sheet tab.

18. Explode the **Salaries** slice (the largest slice) and increase the **Elevation** to **25**.

19. Explode the largest slice and increase the Elevation to **25** for the **Production** and **Finance** charts.

20. Take a few minutes to click the various sheet tabs and check out your charts.

21. Feel free to format and enhance your charts in any way.

22. Close the workbook when you have finished and **save** the changes.

Skills Builder 11.4

In this exercise, you will create a pie chart that shows the budget allocation for a school district. You will also learn how to print an embedded chart.

Open the workbook and create a pie chart

1. **Open** the workbook named **Skills Builder 11.4**.
2. **Select** the data shown below.

4	Facilities	3,500,000
5	Employee Costs	4,500,000
6	Transportation	540,000
7	Students	2,300,000
8	Equipment	1,200,000

3. Use the Chart Wizard to create the **embedded** pie chart below. Make sure you include the chart title and increase the elevation as shown. Also, remove the chart border and legend as shown.

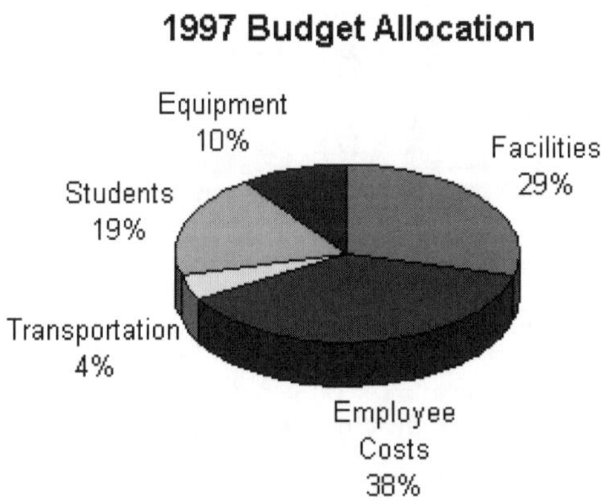

Use Print Preview for the chart only

4. Make sure the chart is selected and **click** Print Preview.

   Notice the chart is displayed on a full page in landscape orientation. This is the same result as when you use Print Preview with a separate chart sheet. You can always use this technique to print embedded charts as separate objects. Just remember to select the desired chart prior to printing or using Print Preview.

5. **Close** Print Preview.
6. **Close** the workbook and **save** the changes.

Skills Builder 11.5

In this exercise, you will create a worksheet and line chart to track the trends in a stock portfolio.

1. Open a New Workbook.

2. Use the following guidelines to create the worksheet shown below.
   - Notice that the dates in cells A4 and A5 form the beginning of a series. You can enter these dates, select them and then drag the fill handle down to cell A11 to complete the series.
   - Columns B-D contain mixed numbers (whole numbers and fractions). Just type the numbers exactly as shown with a space between the whole numbers and the fractions.
   - Widen columns B-D as necessary.

	A	B	C	D
1	My Stock Portfolio - 8 Week Trends			
2				
3		Silicon Technology	Dakota Mining	Anderson Diesel
4	9/6/97	58 1/2	32	45
5	9/13/97	59	31	43
6	9/20/97	56	28	45
7	9/27/97	59	30 1/8	48
8	10/4/97	63	33	49
9	10/11/97	68	34	47
10	10/18/97	70	34	42
11	10/25/97	69	36 1/2	38

3. **Select** the range **A3:D11** (all active cells except for the title).

4. Use the Chart Wizard to create the embedded line chart shown below. Make sure you have the same titles and legend as shown.

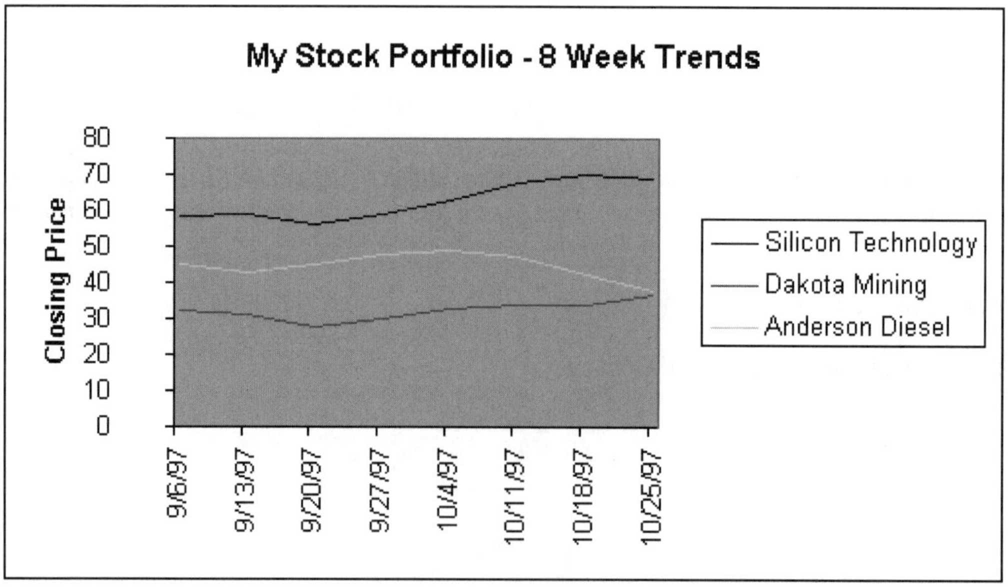

5. **Close** the workbook and **save** it as **Skills Builder 11.5**.

Assessment 11.1

1. **Click** the New Workbook button.

2. Create the worksheet shown below.

	A	B	C	D
1	SysTech 12 Month Stock Performance			
2	March 1, 1996 - February 28, 1997			
3				
4	Date	Stock Price		
5	3/1/96	78		
6	4/1/96	82.6		
7	5/1/96	83		
8	6/1/96	78.6		
9	7/1/96	72		
10	8/1/96	62		
11	9/1/96	65.8		
12	10/1/96	72.6		
13	11/1/96	85		
14	12/1/96	86		
15	1/1/97	90		
16	2/1/97	92		

3. Use the worksheet data to create the chart shown below on a **separate chart sheet**. Make sure you use the data labels and title as shown.

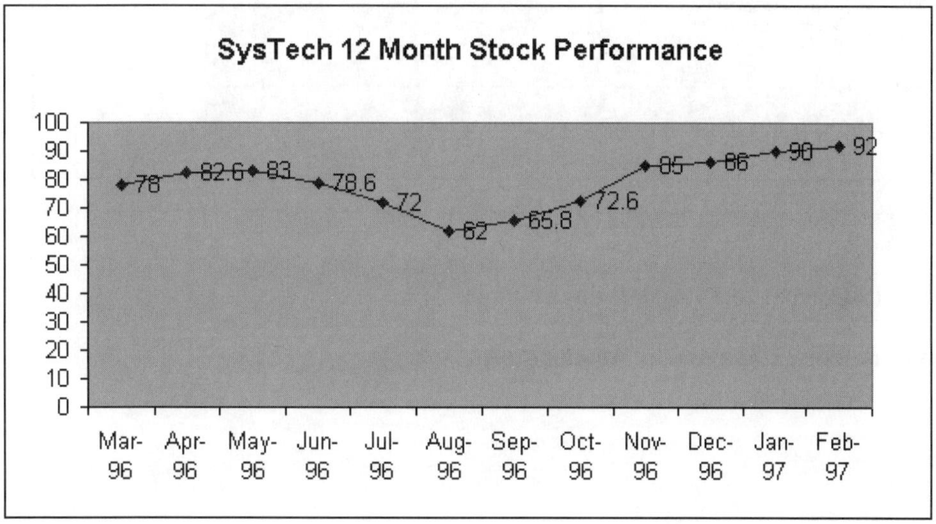

4. Rename the Chart1 sheet as **12 Month Chart**.

5. Rename the Sheet1 sheet as **12 Month Data**.

6. **Print** both the **worksheet** and **chart**.

7. **Close** the workbook and **save** it as **Assessment 11.1**.

Assessment 11.2

1. Create the worksheet and embedded column chart shown below. Notice the column chart is two-dimensional. The Differences in row 6 are simply the budget numbers minus the spent numbers. Notice the negative differences dip below the X axis in the chart.

	A	B	C	D	E	F	G	H
1	**Personal Budget Analysis (January 97 - June 97)**							
2								
3		Jan	Feb	Mar	Apr	May	Jun	
4	Budget	5000	5500	5000	5300	5300	5500	
5	Spent	4500	6000	4750	6200	4900	5500	
6	Difference	500	-500	250	-900	400	0	

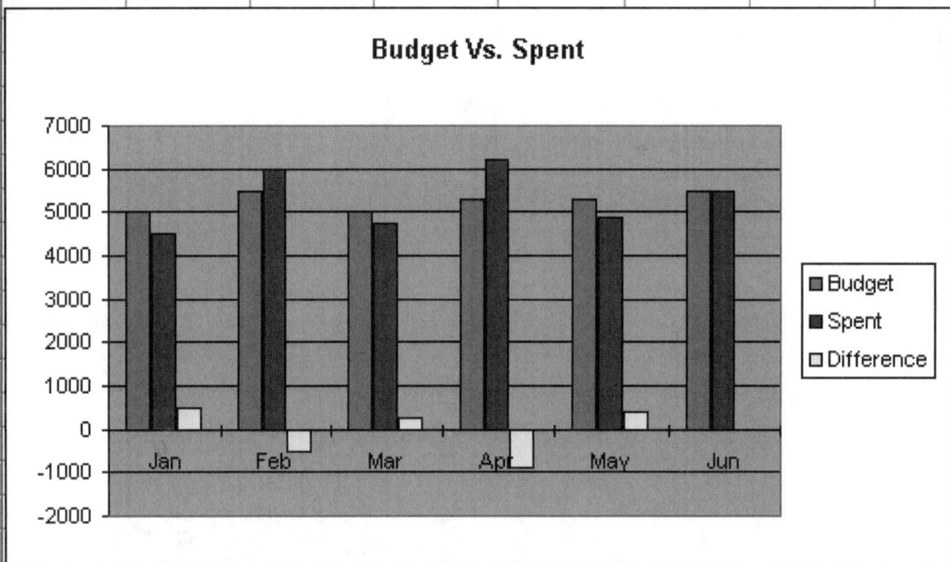

2. **Print** the worksheet and column chart on one page.

3. **Close** the workbook and **save** it as **Assessment 11.2**.

12 Integration: Word, Excel and the Web

Objectives:

- Learn about integration concepts
- Learn about object linking and embedding
- Link a worksheet to a Word document
- Create and use hyperlinks
- Use Excel's Internet tools
- Run Web queries

The Project – A Letter to a Financial Planner

In this lesson, you will help Shirley Washington compose a letter to Cindy Wilson, her financial planner. Cindy assists Shirley with long term planning, goals and objectives. However, Shirley has elected to manage her stock portfolio on her own using Microsoft Excel. Shirley sends Cindy a quarterly letter that details the holdings in her portfolio. You will help Shirley link the portfolio worksheet to the quarterly letter. This way, any changes made to the portfolio worksheet will automatically be reflected in the letter. The letter and linked worksheet that you will create are shown below.

Today's Date

Ms. Cindy Wilson
Wilson Financial Planning
500 Kellogg Avenue
Anaheim, CA 92807

Dear Cindy:

I have included an Excel worksheet containing my current stock portfolio. Please review my portfolio and compare it to the previous quarter.

Company	Symbol	Number of Shares	Purchase Price	Initial Value	Current Price	Current Value	Gain/Loss
IBM	IBM	500	30	15,000	94	47,000	32,000
Apple	AAPL	500	27	13,500	16	8,000	(5,500)
GM	GM	1000	39	39,000	57	57,000	18,000
Digital	DEC	300	72	21,600	38	11,400	(10,200)
Totals				$89,100		$123,400	$ 34,300
Average							$ 8,575

Please contact me if you have any questions. I look forward to hearing from you soon.

Best regards,

Shirley Washington

Integrating Office Applications

Microsoft Office 97 is composed of five main applications: Outlook; Word; Excel; PowerPoint and Access. The true power of Office 97 is in the integration of the programs. The old adage -The whole is greater than the sum of the parts- is especially relevant with Office 97. Office 97 has a variety of techniques and tools to let you share data between applications. Integration occurs between a **source** document and a **destination** document. For example, you may want an Excel worksheet to appear in a Word document. In this case, the Excel worksheet is the source document and the Word letter is the destination document. The following table lists the three most common integration methods.

Integration method	Description
Copy and paste	With copy and paste, the source document becomes part of the destination document. If you copy an Excel worksheet to a Word document, then the worksheet is converted to a Word table. You can edit the table in Word but it has no effect on the original Excel worksheet. Also, any formulas in the table will not be recalculated if the numbers in the table are changed.
Copy and embed	With copy and embed, the Excel worksheet becomes part of the Word document and it remains as a worksheet. You can edit the worksheet within Word using Excel's features. The worksheet formulas are recalculated if you change the numbers from within Word. However, the worksheet does not change in Word if you make changes to the original worksheet in Excel.
Copy and link	With copy and link, the Excel worksheet does not become part of the Word document. It appears to be part of the Word document, however, it is linked to the original Excel worksheet. Changes you make to the original worksheet in Excel are reflected into the Word document as well.

Hands-On 12.1 – Create a stock portfolio workbook

In this exercise, you will develop a stock portfolio worksheet for Shirley Washington. In a later exercise, you will link the worksheet to a Word document.

1. Start a new workbook and enter the data shown below. You will need to use the Alt + Enter keystroke combination to create the multi-line entries. Simply type the first line of the multi-line entry, press Alt + Enter and type the second line.

	A	B	C	D	E	F	G	H
1	Company	Symbol	Number of Shares	Purchase Price	Initial Value	Current Price	Current Value	Gain/Loss
2	IBM	IBM	500	30		94		
3	Apple	AAPL	500	27		16		
4	GM	GM	1000	39		57		
5	Digital	DEC	300	72		34		
6	Totals							
7	Average							

Continued...

Create the formulas

2. Create formulas in the worksheet as discussed below.
   - Calculate the Initial Value in the range E2:E5 as the Number of Shares * Purchase Price.
   - Calculate the Current Value in the range G2:G5 as the Number of Shares * Current Price.
   - Calculate the Gain/Loss in the range H2:H5 as the Current Value – Initial Value.
   - Calculate the totals in cells E6, G6 and H6 and the average in cell H7.

3. Format the values and narrow the columns as shown below. At this point, your worksheet should match the worksheet below.

	A	B	C	D	E	F	G	H
1	Company	Symbol	Number of Shares	Purchase Price	Initial Value	Current Price	Current Value	Gain/Loss
2	IBM	IBM	500	30	15,000	94	47,000	32,000
3	Apple	AAPL	500	27	13,500	16	8,000	(5,500)
4	GM	GM	1000	39	39,000	57	57,000	18,000
5	Digital	DEC	300	72	21,600	34	10,200	(11,400)
6	Totals				$89,100		$122,200	$ 33,100
7	Average							$ 8,275

Format the worksheet with AutoFormat

4. **Select** the range **A1:H7**.

5. Choose **Format→AutoFormat...** from the menu bar.

6. Choose the **Classic 3** style and **click OK**.

7. If necessary, widen the columns slightly until the worksheet is formatted as shown below.

	A	B	C	D	E	F	G	H
1	**Company**	**Symbol**	***Number of Shares***	***Purchase Price***	***Initial Value***	***Current Price***	***Current Value***	***Gain/Loss***
2	**IBM**	**IBM**	500	30	15,000	94	47,000	32,000
3	**Apple**	**AAPL**	500	27	13,500	16	8,000	(5,500)
4	**GM**	**GM**	1000	39	39,000	57	57,000	18,000
5	**Digital**	**DEC**	300	72	21,600	34	10,200	(11,400)
6	**Totals**				$89,100		$122,200	$ 33,100
7	**Average**							$ 8,275

8. Save the workbook as **Hands-On Lesson 12.**

Hands-On 12.2 – Create the Word document

In this exercise, you will create the Microsoft Word document shown below. The Excel worksheet will eventually be linked to this letter.

1. Start Microsoft Word and a blank new document will appear.
2. Set the font to **11** point.
3. Type the letter shown below.

   Don't be concerned if your text wraps at a different location than shown below.

> Today's Date [Enter]
> [Enter]
> [Enter]
> [Enter]
> Ms. Cindy Wilson [Enter]
> Wilson Financial Planning [Enter]
> 500 Kellogg Avenue [Enter]
> Anaheim, CA 92807 [Enter]
> [Enter]
> Dear Cindy: [Enter]
> [Enter]
> I have included an Excel worksheet containing my current stock portfolio. Please review my portfolio and compare it to the previous quarter. [Enter]
> [Enter]
> Please contact me if you have any questions. I look forward to hearing from you. [Enter]
> [Enter]
> Best regards, [Enter]
> [Enter]
> [Enter]
> [Enter]
> Shirley Washington [Enter]

4. Save the document to your exercise diskette as **Cindy Wilson Letter**.

   Leave the document open because you will continue to use it.

Object Linking and Embedding

Object linking and embedding or OLE allows you to tie applications together. A description of both linking and embedding was given in the table at the beginning of this lesson. In the following exercise, you will link the Cindy Wilson letter to the stock portfolio worksheet.

> **Quick Steps: Integrating Applications**
>
> ***To copy and paste between applications***
> - *Select the desired data in the source application and click the Copy button.*
> - *Switch to the destination application and click the Paste button.*
>
> ***To copy and embed between applications***
> - *Select the desired data in the source application and click the Copy button.*
> - *Switch to the destination application and choose Edit→Paste Special.*
> - *Choose the Paste option, choose Microsoft Excel worksheet object and click OK.*
>
> ***To copy and link between applications***
> - *Select the desired data in the source application and click the Copy button.*
> - *Switch to the destination application and choose Edit→Paste Special.*
> - *Choose the Paste link option, choose Microsoft Excel worksheet object and click OK.*

Hands-On 12.3 – Link the worksheet to the letter

In this exercise, you will link the stock portfolio worksheet to the letter.

1. **Switch to Excel** by clicking the Microsoft Excel button on the Windows 95 taskbar.
2. **Select** the range **A1:H7**.
3. **Click** the Copy button.
4. **Switch to Word** by clicking the Microsoft Word button on the Windows 95 taskbar.
5. **Click** in the **blank line** between the two main paragraphs as shown below.

   I have included an Excel worksheet containing my current stock portfolio. Please review my portfolio and compare it to the previous quarter.

   Click here —— |

   Please contact me if you have any questions. I look forward to hearing from you soon.

6. Choose **Edit→Paste Special...** from the menu bar.
7. Choose the Paste link: option.
8. Choose **Microsoft Excel Worksheet Object** from the As list and **click OK**.

   The worksheet will be inserted. Notice the worksheet has sizing handles surrounding it. This is because you inserted it as a Microsoft Excel object and it is linked to the original worksheet. The only way you can edit the object is from within Excel. You can activate Excel by clicking the Excel button on the Taskbar or you can double-click the object in the Word document. Any changes you make to the object in Excel will be reflected in the Word document.

Continued...

Edit the worksheet in Excel

Notice the current price in cell F5 is 34. Imagine the share price has increased between the time you created this letter and the time you are ready to send it. You will make this adjustment by editing the worksheet in Excel.

9. **Double-click** the **worksheet** in the Word document and Excel will be activated.

   Notice the toolbars and all other screen elements belong to Excel.

10. **Tap** the Esc key on the keyboard to turn off the flashing marquee.

11. Change the value in cell F5 to **38**.

    The formulas in the worksheet will recalculate.

12. **Click** the **Microsoft Word button** on the Windows 95 taskbar.

    Notice the value in cell F5 has been updated to 38 and the formulas have been recalculated. This is because the Excel worksheet was inserted as a link. Any changes made in the worksheet will be reflected in the Word document.

13. Feel free to enhance the Word document in any way you feel is necessary.

    You may want to insert a hard return above the worksheet to push it down slightly.

Hyperlinks

Office 97 lets you insert hyperlinks in Excel worksheets and other office documents. A hyperlink sends you to another location whenever it is clicked. You can jump to a location within the same worksheet, to another worksheet, to a document in another program and even to the World Wide Web. Hyperlinks are a powerful way to tie your documents and applications together.

Quick Steps: ***Inserting Hyperlinks***
To insert a hyperlink • *Choose Insert→Hyperlink...* • *Specify the filename of a file or the URL of a Web address in the Insert Hyperlink box and click OK.*

Hands-On 12.4 – Insert a hyperlink in the worksheet

In this exercise, you will insert a hyperlink in the stock portfolio worksheet. This link will open the Cindy Wilson Letter whenever it is clicked. This way, you can easily open the letter whenever you update the portfolio worksheet and wish to update the letter as well.

1. If necessary, switch to Microsoft Word.

2. Choose **File→Exit** and **save** the changes to the Cindy Wilson Letter.

3. **Switch to Excel** and **click** cell **A12**.

   You will insert the hyperlink in this cell.

4. Choose **Insert→Hyperlink...** from the menu bar.

Continued...

5. **Click** the **Browse** button and **navigate to your floppy diskette**.

6. **Locate** the **Cindy Wilson Letter** document and **double-click** it.

   The pathname of the file will appear in the Link to file or URL box. If you were linking to a Web page, then you would have a Web URL such as http://www.labyrinth-pub.com (the Web site of Labyrinth Publications).

7. Notice the Named location in file box.

   This box lets you specify a location within a file such as a cell or named range in a worksheet or a bookmark in a Word document. You will leave this box empty because the Cindy Wilson Letter is quite small. Going to a specific location in a small document has little practical use.

8. **Click OK** to complete the hyperlink.

   Your hyperlink should appear in blue and be underlined.

Activate the link

9. Position the mouse pointer over cell A12 and it will have a pointing finger shape.

   The pointer always has this shape when it is over a hyperlink.

10. Now **click** the hyperlink in cell **A12**.

    Microsoft Word will start and the Cindy Wilson Letter will open.

11. Feel free to insert a hyperlink in the Cindy Wilson Letter that points to the Excel worksheet.

    This way, you can easily move back and forth between these related documents.

12. **Close Microsoft Word** and **save** any changes you have made to the Cindy Wilson Letter.

Excel and the Web

Office 97 has a number of new features that let you connect to the world. Excel 97 is the first version of Excel that lets you access the wealth of information and data on the Internet. The following table discusses the new Internet related features in Office 97.

Feature	Description
Web toolbar	The Web toolbar lets you launch your Web browser and browse the Web from within Excel and other Office 97 applications. The Web toolbar is displayed with the **View→Toolbars** command.
HTML file creation	The **File Save as HTML** command launches an HTML wizard. This wizard guides you through the process of converting a worksheet to HTML format. Once this has been accomplished, you can post the worksheet on a corporate intranet or on the World Wide Web. An intranet is a large network within a company.
Web queries	Web queries let you download data from the Internet into an Excel worksheet.

More on Web Queries

Web queries let you download data from the Internet into an Excel worksheet. This powerful capability can be used to download stock prices, currency exchange rates and other types of data. Web queries are also a powerful way for employees to access data on corporate Intranets.

Excel 97 provides several Web queries

Excel 97 has several Web queries that are already set up for you. These queries are all designed to download stock market data and they are excellent for Web query demonstrations. Setting up Web queries is a rather involved task, so you will use one of the built-in Excel queries in the following exercise.

Hands-On 12.5 – Run a Web query

In this exercise, you will run a Web query that downloads up to 20 stock quotes at once. You will download the latest stock prices for the four stocks in Shirley Washington's portfolio. Keep in mind that this exercise will only work if you have a Web browser and an Internet connection.

1. If necessary, log on to your Internet service provider.

   This step shouldn't be necessary if you are in a computer lab with a permanent Internet connection.

2. If necessary, start Excel and open the Hands-On Lesson 12 workbook.

3. **Click** the **Sheet2** tab.

   You will download the stock quotation into this sheet.

4. Choose **Data→Get External Data→Run Web Query...** from the menu bar.

   The Queries folder should appear in the Look in box with four stock related Web queries listed. These queries are provided as part of Excel 97.

5. Choose **Multiple Stock Quotes by PC Quote, Inc** and **click** the **Get Data** button.

6. **Click OK** on the Returning External Data to Microsoft Excel dialog box.

   The Enter Parameter Value box appears. This is where you list the stock symbols.

7. Carefully type **IBM AAPL GM DEC** and **click OK**.

   You must type a space between each set of symbols. Depending on the speed of your Internet connection, the Web query may require a minute or more to run. The downloaded data will have a format similar to the following example. This data is updated constantly throughout the business day. You can always download "fresh" stock data using this technique.

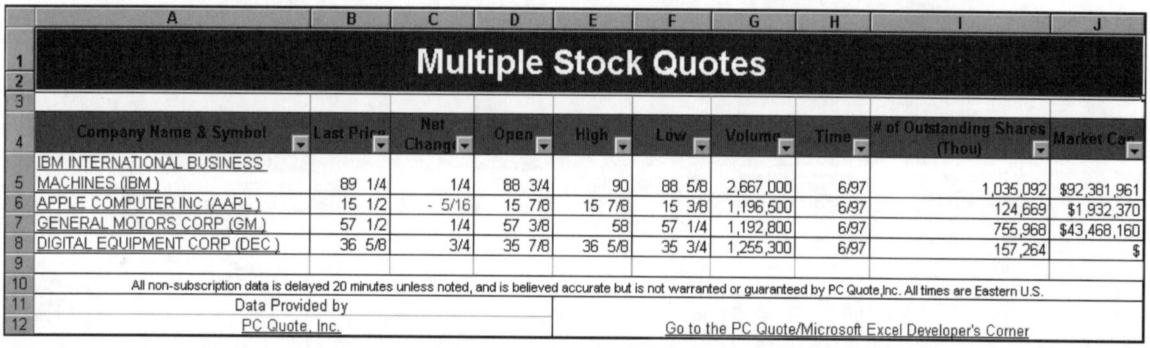

	A	B	C	D	E	F	G	H	I	J
1–2	Multiple Stock Quotes									
3										
4	Company Name & Symbol	Last Pric	Net Chang	Open	High	Low	Volume	Time	# of Outstanding Shares (Thou)	Market Ca
5	IBM INTERNATIONAL BUSINESS MACHINES (IBM)	89 1/4	1/4	88 3/4	90	88 5/8	2,667,000	6/97	1,035,092	$92,381,961
6	APPLE COMPUTER INC (AAPL)	15 1/2	- 5/16	15 7/8	15 7/8	15 3/8	1,196,500	6/97	124,669	$1,932,370
7	GENERAL MOTORS CORP (GM)	57 1/2	1/4	57 3/8	58	57 1/4	1,192,800	6/97	755,968	$43,468,160
8	DIGITAL EQUIPMENT CORP (DEC)	36 5/8	3/4	35 7/8	36 5/8	35 3/4	1,255,300	6/97	157,264	$
9										
10	All non-subscription data is delayed 20 minutes unless noted, and is believed accurate but is not warranted or guaranteed by PC Quote,Inc. All times are Eastern U.S.									
11	Data Provided by									
12	PC Quote, Inc.			Go to the PC Quote/Microsoft Excel Developer's Corner						

8. Feel free to enter the latest stock prices in your portfolio worksheet.

9. Try running the other built-in Web queries.

10. **Close** the workbook when you have finished and **save** the changes.

Concepts Review

True / False

1. Changes made to an Excel worksheet that is embedded in a Word document are reflected in the Word document. 1. **T F**
2. Changes made to an Excel worksheet that is linked to a Word document are reflected in the Word document. 2. **T F**
3. Hyperlinks can only be used to link documents that are created using the same application. 3. **T F**
4. Hyperlinks are underlined and usually appear in a blue color. 4. **T F**
5. Web queries can download data from the Internet. 5. **T F**

Multiple Choice

1. Which command is used to initiate object linking and embedding?
   a) Edit→Paste
   b) Insert→Paste
   c) Edit→Paste Special
   d) Insert→Paste Special ( )
2. Which command is used to create hyperlinks?
   a) Insert→Hyperlink
   b) Edit→Hyperlink
   c) Tools→Hyperlink
   d) Edit→Paste Special→Hyperlink ( )
3. Which command is used to display the Web toolbar?
   a) Insert→Web toolbar
   b) View→Toolbars
   c) View→Web Toolbar
   d) None of the above. ( )

Unit Four

Access 97

13 Creating Tables and Entering Data

Objectives:

- Understand database concepts
- Learn about the objects in an Access database
- Create tables
- Enter and edit data
- Set data types and field properties
- Set primary keys
- Work with Datasheet view and Design view
- Change the structure of tables
- Adjust column widths
- Print tables
- Use the Table Wizard

What is Microsoft Access?

Microsoft Access is a relational database management system that lets you store, organize and manage information. Access is a powerful and flexible program that can handle virtually any data management task. For example, you can use Access to keep a simple contact list or you can develop a full-featured order entry and database management system. Access gives anyone with a personal computer the ability to organize and manage data in a sophisticated manner.

Access is an integral part of Office 97

Access is an integral part of the Office 97 suite of software tools. Access plays a pivotal role in Office 97 because it is the data storage and management tool. You can share Access data with Word, Excel and PowerPoint. For example, you can merge a Word form letter with an Access database to produce a mass mailing. You can also export Access data to Excel and then use the calculating and charting capabilities of Excel to analyze the data.

Access provides the key for accessing data in Office 97

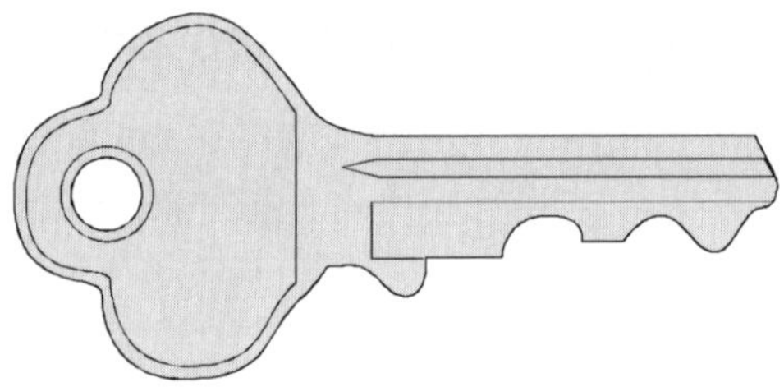

The Project – The Pinnacle Pet Car Database

In this lesson, you will begin developing a database for the Pinnacle Pet Care pet clinic. You will set up two Access tables and enter data in the tables. All data in an Access database is stored in tables. You will continue to develop the Pinnacle Pet Care system throughout this course. By the time you have finished, you will have developed a sophisticated application that is customized to the needs of Pinnacle Pet Care. One of the tables and several other objects from the Pinnacle Pet Care system are shown below.

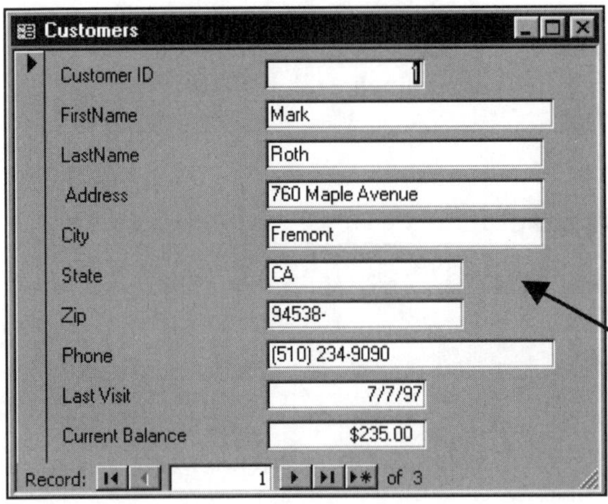

You can create forms to display records and to enter data into tables.

In Access, all data is stored in tables.

Customer ID	FirstName	LastName	Address	City	State	Zip	Phone	Last Visit	Current Balance
1	Mark	Roth	760 Maple Avenue	Fremont	CA	94538-	(510) 234-9090	7/7/97	$235.00
2	Tony	Simpson	312 York Lane	Richmond	CA	94804-	(510) 238-2233	9/7/97	$185.00
3	Jason	Jones	2233 Crystal Street	San Mateo	CA	94403-	(415) 312-2312	7/5/97	$48.00

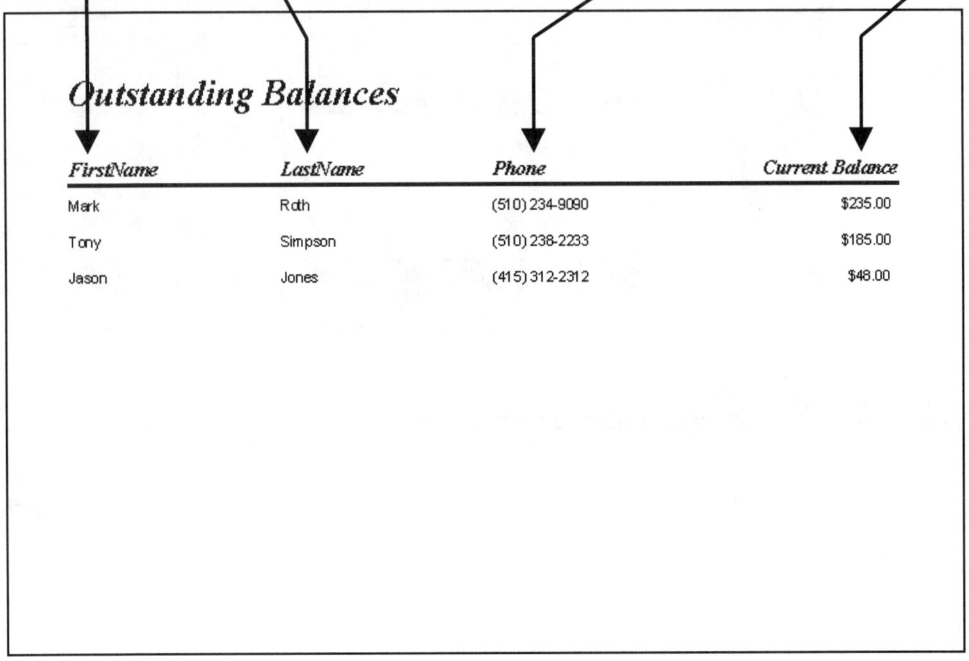

You can create reports using data from your tables.

Starting Access and Creating a New Database

There are several ways to start Access. The three most common methods are listed below.

- Click the Start button and choose Microsoft Access from the Programs menu.
- Click a desktop shortcut for the Access program (if a shortcut is on the desktop).
- Click the Microsoft Access button on the Microsoft Office toolbar (if it is displayed).

Once Access is started, you can create a new database by choosing the Blank Database radio button and clicking OK. Access will prompt you to save the new database and give it a name.

Hands-On 13.1 - Start Access and create a new database

1. Start your computer and the Windows desktop will be displayed.
2. **Click** the Start button and choose **Programs**.
3. Choose **Microsoft Access** from the Programs menu.

   Access will start and the Access window will appear. Don't be concerned if your window appears different from the example shown here.

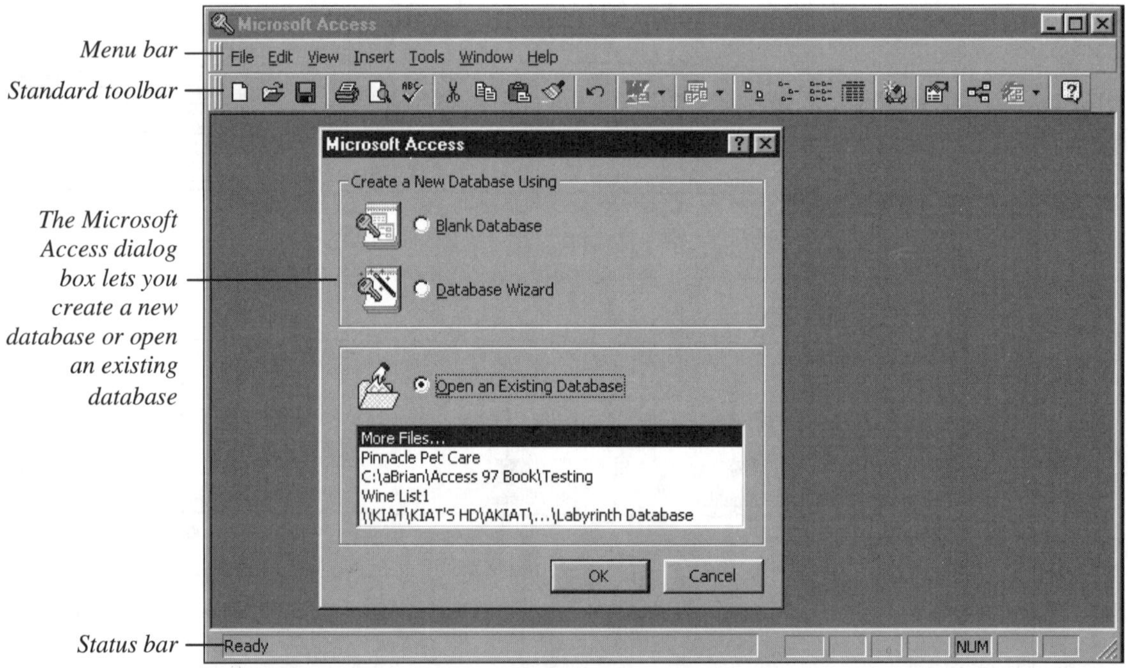

4. **Click** the Blank Database radio button and **click OK**.

Continued...

5. Use the following steps to name the new database and to save it to your exercise diskette.

❶ ***Click here*** *and choose the disk drive with your exercise diskette. It is most likely 3 ½ Floppy [A:].*

❷ *Notice that Access proposes the filename* ***db1****.*

❸ *Type the name* ***Pinnacle Pet Care*** *and it will replace db1. (If you switched disk drives, then you may need to click in the File name box, delete the name db1 with the Delete and/or Backspace keys, then type the new name.)*

❹ ***Click*** *the* ***Create*** *button.*

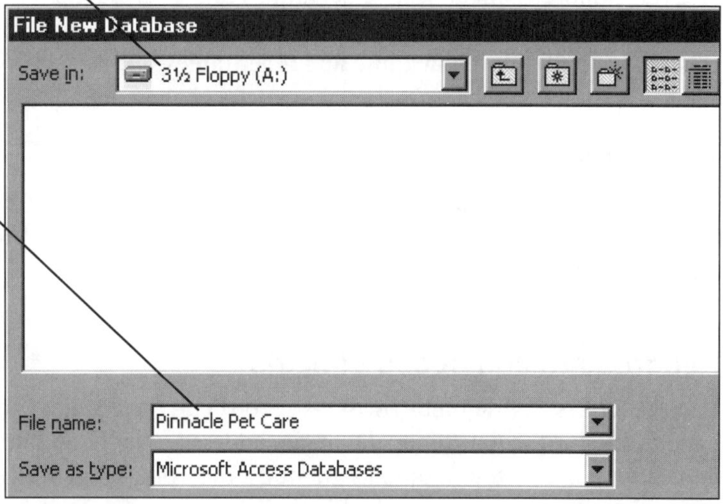

The Access database window will appear.

6. Use the following steps to explore the database window.
You will create a table in the next exercise.

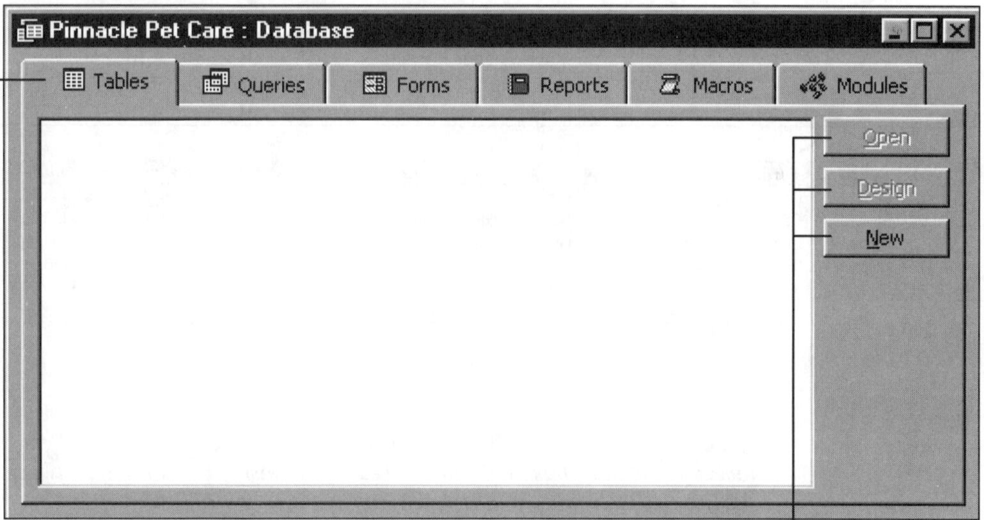

❶ *Notice the six tabs in the Access window. These tabs represent the six types of objects that you can create in an Access database. The objects you create will be displayed under the various tabs.*

❷ *These buttons let you open objects, change the design of objects and create new objects.*

Working with Access Tables

In Access, data is stored in tables. Tables are used to organize data so that it can easily be retrieved at a later time. A simple database may have one or two tables while a sophisticated database may have dozens or even hundreds of tables. A separate table is used for each type of related data. For example, your Pinnacle Pet Care database will initially have a table for customers and a table for pets. Later in this course, you will learn how these and other tables interact with one another.

Tables are composed

Tables are composed of rows where each row is a record. For example, your Pinnacle Pet Care database will have a Customer table that contains all of the customer information as shown below. Each row in the Customer table will contain the data for one customer.

Records are composed of fields

Each record is divided into fields. A record can have many fields. For example, the Customers table will have fields for the Customer ID, name, address, telephone number, etc. In Access, each column in a table is a field. Take a few moments to study the following illustration. The illustration shows the first two tables that you will create in the Pinnacle Pet Care database.

The Customers table contains one row/record for each customer. All of the data for a customer is stored in one row.

The records are composed of fields.

Customer ID	FirstName	LastName	Address	City	State	Zip	Phone	Last Visit	Current Balance
1	Mark	Roth	760 Maple Avenue	Fremont	CA	94538-	(510) 234-9090	7/7/97	$235.00
2	Tony	Simpson	312 York Lane	Richmond	CA	94804-	(510) 238-2233	9/7/97	$185.00
3	Jason	Jones	2233 Crystal Street	San Mateo	CA	94403-	(415) 312-2312	7/5/97	$48.00

Pet ID	Pet Name	Pet Type	Breed	Sex	Color	Date of Birth	Last Visit	Expenditures	Number of Visits	Customer ID
CT02	Max	Cat	Unknown	Male	White	1/7/86	9/7/97	$1,450.55	20	2
CT16	Stripes	Cat	Tortoise shell	Male	Black and brown	10/8/90	7/15/97	$450.00	9	3
DG12	Wolfy	Dog	German Shepherd	Male	Brown	6/6/91	7/15/97	$450.00	7	3
DG13	Dillon	Dog	Mutt	Male	Black	10/5/94	7/7/97	$150.55	8	1
RB23	Bugs	Rabbit	Jack	Unknown	Brown	6/7/95	9/7/97	$600.50	4	2
CT92	Tony	Cat	Unknown	Male	Brown with black stripes	4/3/97	7/7/97	$145.00	6	1

Notice that the Customer ID field appears in both the Customers and Pets tables. Eventually, this field will be used to establish a relationship between the two tables. Establishing relationships between tables is what gives Access and other relational database systems their power and flexibility.

Setting up Tables

In Access, you can set up tables in Design view or with the Table Wizard. In Design view, you specify the field names, the data type of each field and any other parameters as needed. Design view lets you precisely determine the characteristics of each field. The Table Wizard automates the process of creating a table by letting you choose from a set of predefined fields. The Table Wizard lacks the flexibility of Design view, however, it is often useful for beginning Access users. Besides, you can always switch to Design view to modify a table that has been set up with the Table Wizard. Access gives you complete control in setting up and modifying tables and other Access objects.

Field Names

Each field in an Access table is identified by a unique name. The name can be **up to 64 characters** in length and can contain letters, numbers, spaces and most punctuation marks. Field names cannot contain periods, exclamation marks and a few other characters.

Data Types

Each field is assigned a data type that determines the type of data the field may contain. Common data types are text, number, currency and date. Text fields can contain any type of characters. Access also lets you set the size of text fields. The default size is set to 50 characters but you can increase or decrease the size as desired. Fields with a Number data type can only contain numbers. Number fields can be used in calculations. Currency fields also contain numbers but Access formats the numbers with currency symbols. Finally, date fields can only contain dates.

Quick Steps: ***Setting up Tables in Design View***

To set up a table

- *Click the Tables tab in the Access Database window.*
- *Click the New button.*
- *Choose Design View from the New Table dialog box and click OK.*
- *Type a field name in the Field Name column of the table that appears.*
- *Choose a Data Type for the new field and type a description if desired.*
- *Repeat the last two steps for all desired fields.*

Hands-On 13.2 – Set up a table in Design view

In this exercise, you will begin setting up the Pets table for the Pinnacle Pet Care database.

1. Use the following steps to display a new table in Design view.

❶ *Make sure the Tables tab is chosen.*

❷ ***Click** the **New** button.*

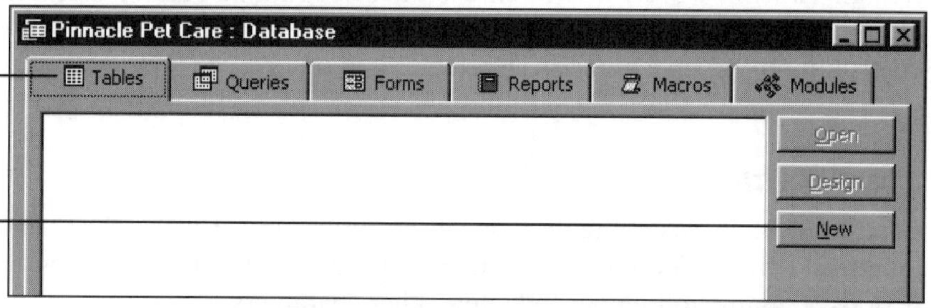

❸ *Choose **Design View**.*

❹ ***Click OK**.*

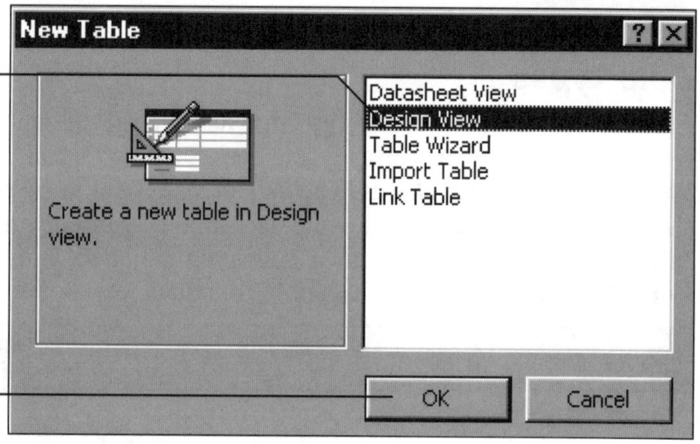

2. Use the following step to maximize the Table1 window that appears.

❶ *If necessary, **click** the **Maximize** button on the Table1 window.*

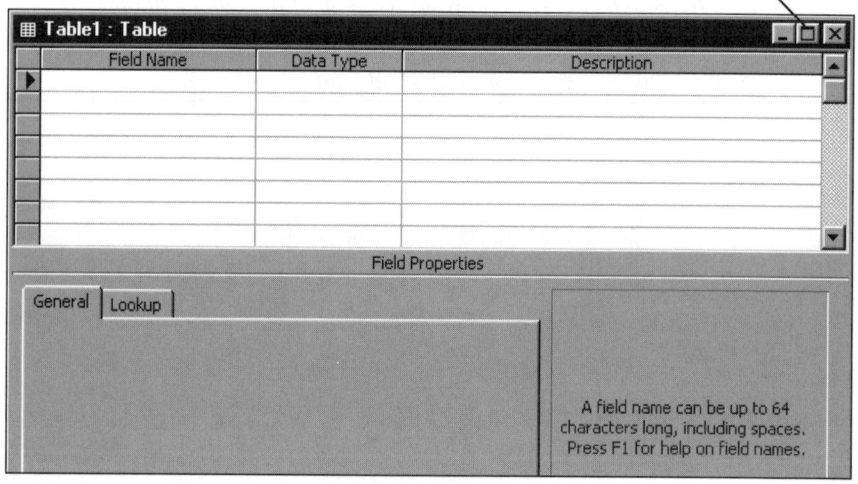

Now continue with the next exercise where you will define the fields for the table.

Hands-On 13.3 – Define fields

Define text fields

1. Use the following steps to define a text field.

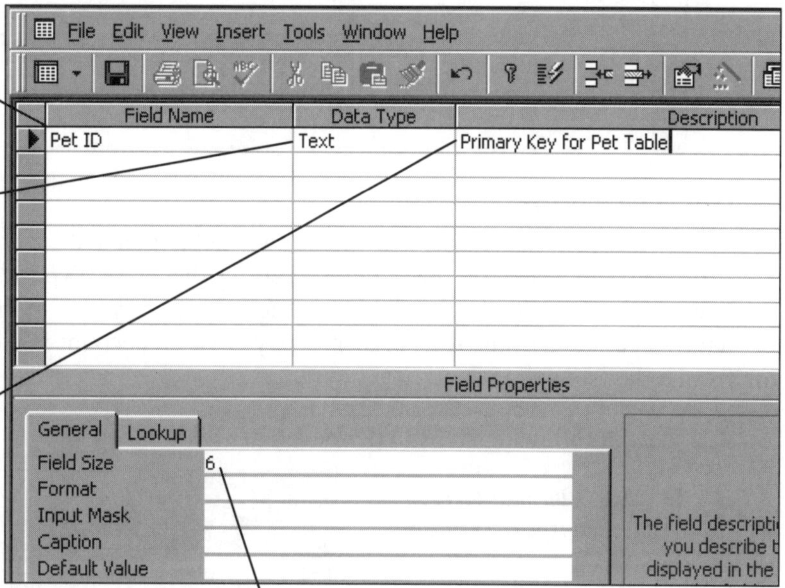

❶ *Type **Pet ID** as the field name.*

❷ ***Tap** the **Tab** key to move to the Data Type box. Notice the Data Type is set to Text. This is the correct setting because the Pet ID will be composed of letters and numbers. The Text data type is used if the field contains text or a combination of text and numbers.*

❸ ***Tap** the **Tab** key to move to the Description box and type the description shown here. You will learn about primary keys later in this lesson.*

❹ ***Click** in the Field Size **box** and change the size from 50 to **6**. It is OK to reduce the size of the Pet ID field because the ID for each pet will contain a maximum of six characters. The Field Properties section of the dialog box reflects the properties of the current field (Pet ID). You will learn more about these properties as you progress through this course.*

You have just defined a field in your database. You will enter data into this field and other fields later in this lesson. You will use a data entry mode known as Datasheet view to enter the data. Currently, you are working in Design view, which allows you to define a table. The Text field type that you chose for the Pet ID field will allow you to enter any type of data in the field. However, the Pet ID for each pet will be restricted to six characters.

2. Use the following steps to define another text field.

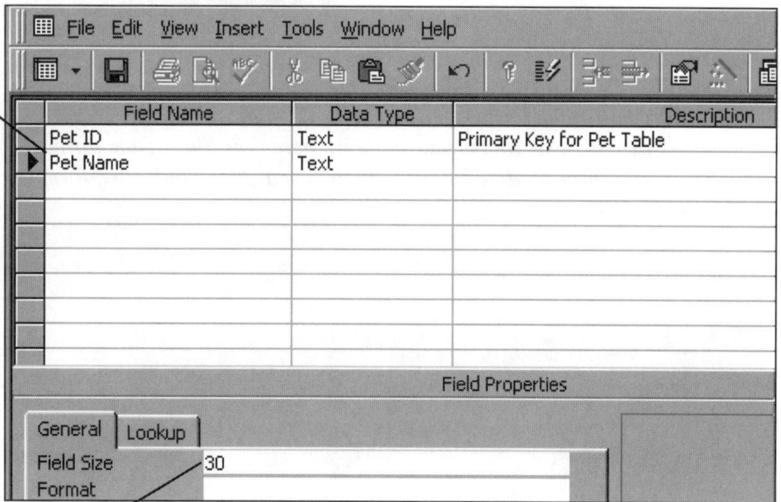

❶ ***Click** in the next Field Name box and type **Pet Name**. The Pet Name field will contain the names of the pets.*

❷ ***Tap** the **Tab** key and Text will appear as the default Data Type. Leave the Data Type set to Text and do not enter a description for this field. Descriptions are optional and are only used when necessary.*

❸ ***Click** in the **Field Size box** and change the size to 30 as shown here.*

Continued...

3. Use the steps in the preceding illustration to create the next four fields as shown in the following illustration. Set the Field Size to **30** for all of the fields except the Sex field. Set the size of the **Sex** field to **10**.

Field Name	Data Type	Description
Pet ID	Text	Primary Key for Pet Table
Pet Name	Text	
Pet Type	Text	
Breed	Text	
Sex	Text	
Color	Text	

Define date fields

In the next few steps, you will define two fields that will eventually contain dates. You will set the Data Type to Date for these fields. Setting the Data Type to Date is useful because Access will identify the contents of the fields as dates. Dates can be used in calculations. For example, you can have Access determine the number of days that an account is past due by subtracting the invoice date from today's date.

4. Use the following steps to define a date field.

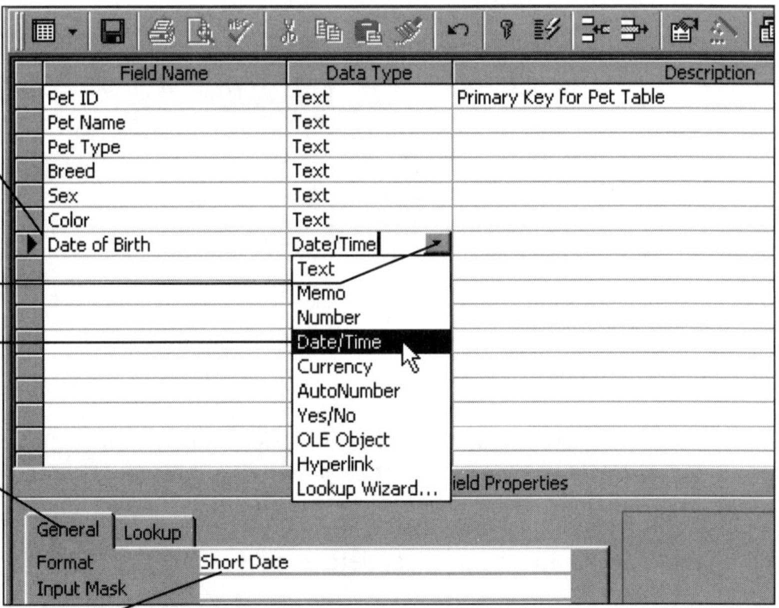

❶ ***Click*** *in the next Field Name box and type* ***Date of Birth****.*

❷ ***Tap*** *the* ***Tab*** *key and* ***click*** *the* ***drop-down button*** *in the Data Type box. A list of data types will appear as shown here.*

❸ ***Choose Date/Time*** *from the drop-down list.*

❹ *Notice the Field Properties section does not contain a Field Size box. You cannot set the field size for date fields. The options on the Field Properties list change for each field type.*

❺ ***Click*** *in the Format box,* ***click*** *the drop-down ▾ button and then choose* ***Short Date*** *as shown here. The Short Date format will force all dates in the field to appear in the indicated format.*

Continued...

5. Now define another date field named Last Visit as shown in the following illustration. Set the Format to Short Date as shown at the bottom of the illustration.

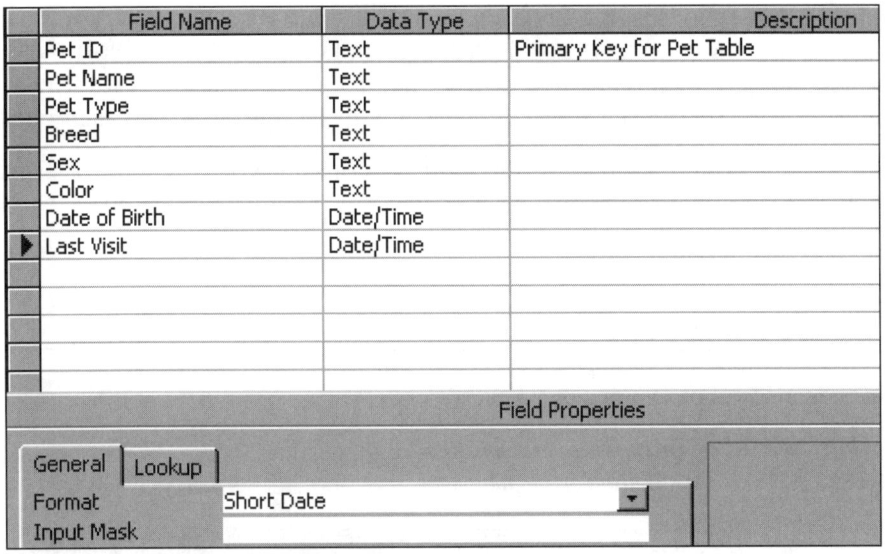

Define currency and number fields

In the next few steps, you will define two more fields. You will set the Data Type to Currency for one of the fields and Number for the other. Currency and number fields can be used in calculations. Furthermore, fields that are formatted with the Currency data type will display a dollar sign, a decimal point and decimals whenever you enter data into the field.

6. Use the following steps to define the Expenditures and Number of Visits fields.

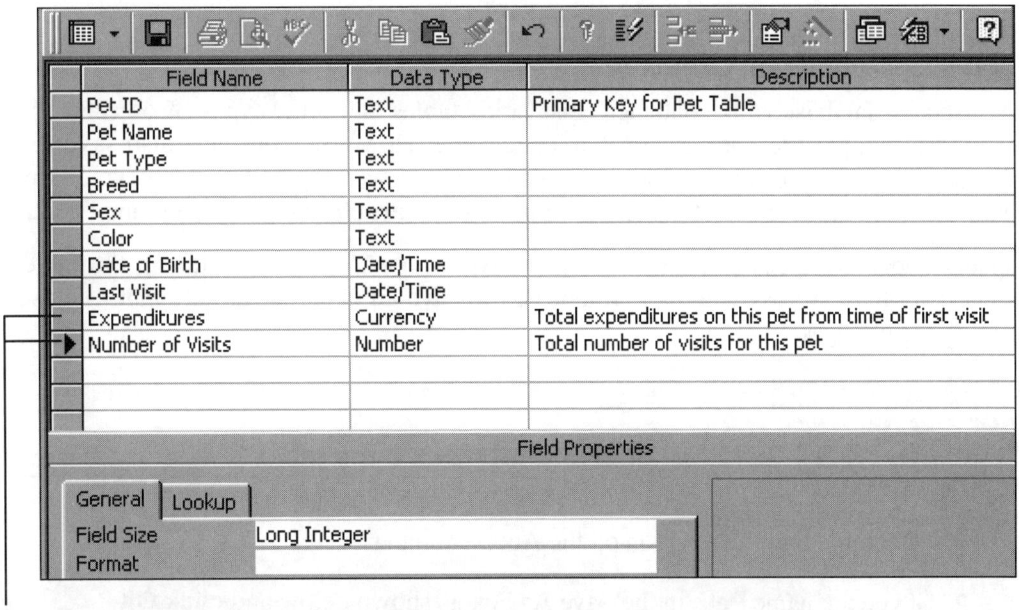

➊ ***Define** the **Expenditures** and **Number of Visits** fields as shown here. Set the Data Types as shown and enter the descriptions as shown. Leave the Field Properties at the bottom of the dialog box set to the default settings. Number fields normally have a Field Size of Long Integer as shown here. Keep in mind that choosing Field Properties can be an involved process that requires extensive knowledge of Access. In fact, these and other Access settings are most often used by professional database programmers.*

7. Now continue with the next topic where you will define a primary key for the table.

Choosing a Primary Key

Every Access table must have one field defined as the primary key. **The primary key field uniquely identifies each record in the table.** For this reason, each record must have a unique entry in the primary key field. Most tables use numbers or codes in the primary key field. For example, the Pet ID field will be the primary key in the table you just set up. Each pet will have a unique ID that identifies it in the table. You specify a primary key by clicking in the desired field while in Design view and then clicking the Primary Key button on the Access toolbar. Access will also prompt you to choose a primary key field if you close a table that has not been assigned a primary key.

Hands-On 13.4 – Choose a primary key

1. Use the following steps to choose a primary key.

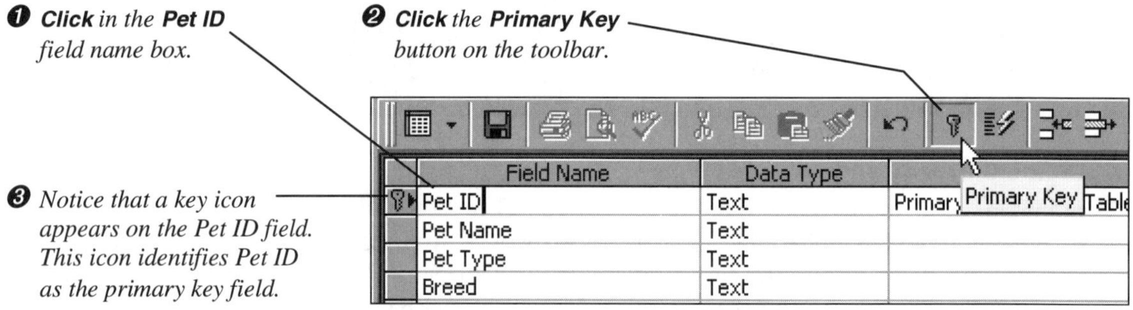

Saving Database Objects

An Access database is a "container" that holds tables and other types of objects. The entire database is saved as a single file onto a hard disk or diskette. However, you must also save the objects within the database. You give database objects names when you save them. This helps you identify the objects at a later time. A database object name can be up to **64 characters** in length and may contain letters, numbers, spaces and other types of characters. You save an open object by clicking the Save button on the Access toolbar. Access will also prompt you to save an object if you attempt to close the object without saving the changes.

Hands-On 13.5 – Save the table and then close the table

1. **Click** the Save button on the Access toolbar.
2. Type the name **Pets** in the Save As box as shown below and **click OK**.

Continued...

3. Now use the following illustration to close the table.

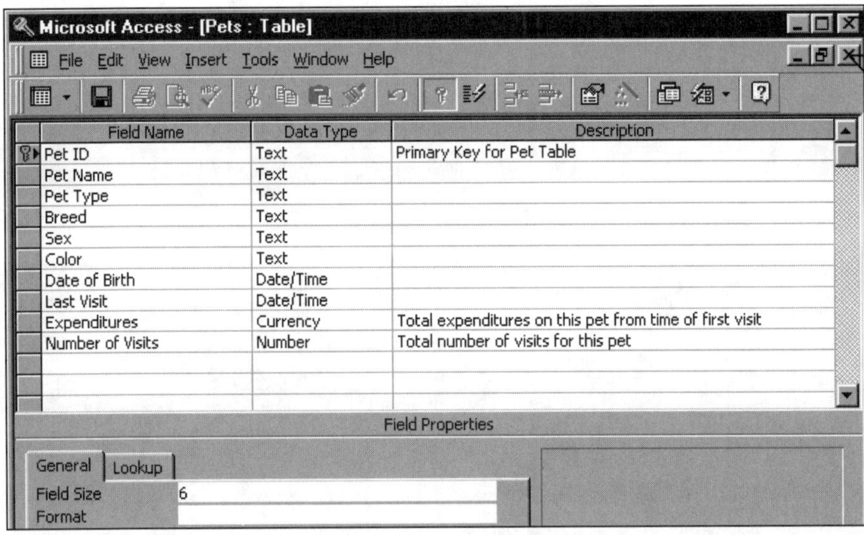

❶ *Notice there are two Close buttons in the Access window. The top button is used to close the entire Access program while the bottom button is used to close the open object (a table in this case).*

❷ ***Click** the **bottom Close button** and the table will close.*

A "Pets icon" will appear below the Tables tab in the Access window. You have completed the process of setting up a table. At this point, you could set up additional tables or other types of objects. However, you will enter data into the Pets table in the next exercise. To accomplish this, you will use Datasheet view.

Entering Data in Datasheet View

In the previous exercises, you used Design view to set up an Access table. Design view lets you define or modify the fields in a table. However, to enter data into a table you must open the table in Datasheet view or switch to Datasheet view from Design view. You open a table in Datasheet view by choosing the table in the Access window and clicking the **Open button** on the Tables tab. You can switch between Datasheet and Design views by choosing the desired view from the Access **View** menu or by clicking the Datasheet View or Design View buttons on the Access toolbar.

Hands-On 13.6 – Enter data

1. Use the following steps to open the Pets table in Datasheet view.

❶ *Make sure the Pets table icon is selected in the Tables tab.*

❷ ***Click** the **Open** button.*

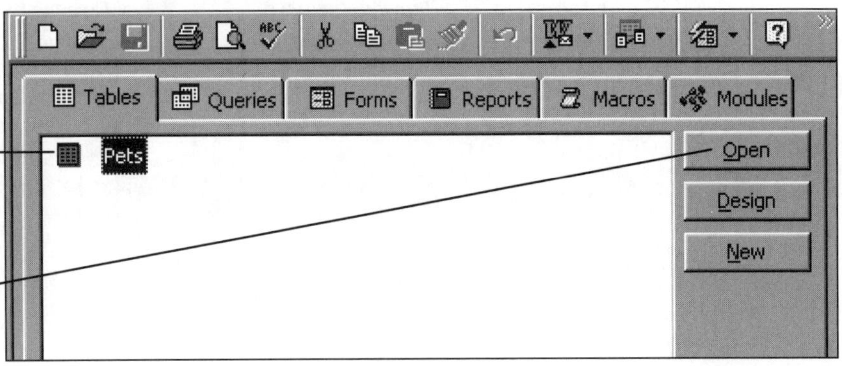

Continued...

2. Use the following illustration to explore the Datasheet view window. Keep in mind that your window may have different dimensions than the example shown here.

❶ *Notice that many of the toolbar buttons are different from those in the Design view window.*

❷ *Notice that the various field names are displayed as column headings.*

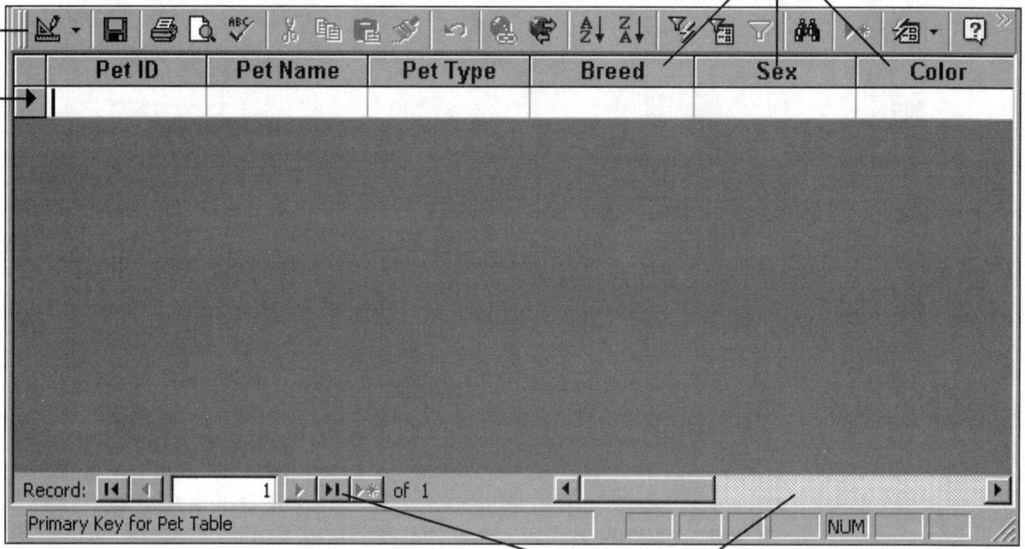

❸ *Data is entered into the rows (although you will only see one row at this point). Each row is a record. For example, each row will contain all of the data for one pet. You use the Tab key to move the insertion point from one field to the next within a row (or you can click in the desired row/field).*

❹ *The record selection buttons and the horizontal scroll bar are used to move between records and to scroll from left to right through the fields.*

3. Use the following steps to begin entering a record.

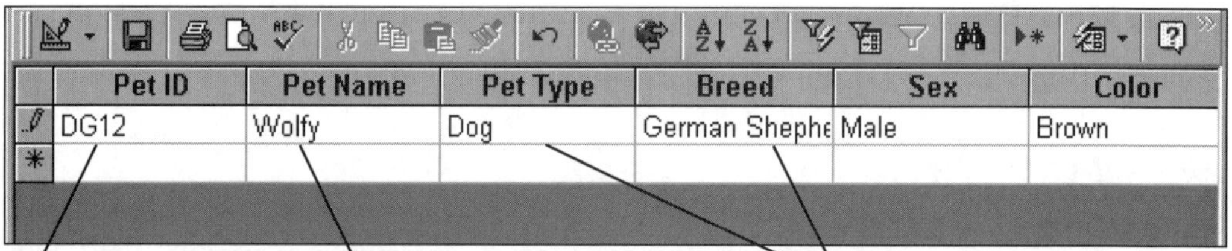

❶ ***Type DG12*** *as the Pet ID and Access will add a new row in preparation for the next record.*

❷ ***Tap*** *the* ***Tab*** *key to move to the next field and* ***type*** *the pet name* ***Wolfy****.*

❸ *Continue entering the data shown here using the Tab key to move between fields. When you get to the Breed field,* ***type*** *the name* ***German Shepherd*** *even though the text is wider than the column. Access will scroll the column thus allowing you to enter the text. If necessary, use the horizontal scroll bar to scroll to the right until the Color field is visible. In the next few steps, you will enter data in the remaining fields.*

Continued...

4. Use the following step to display the remaining fields.

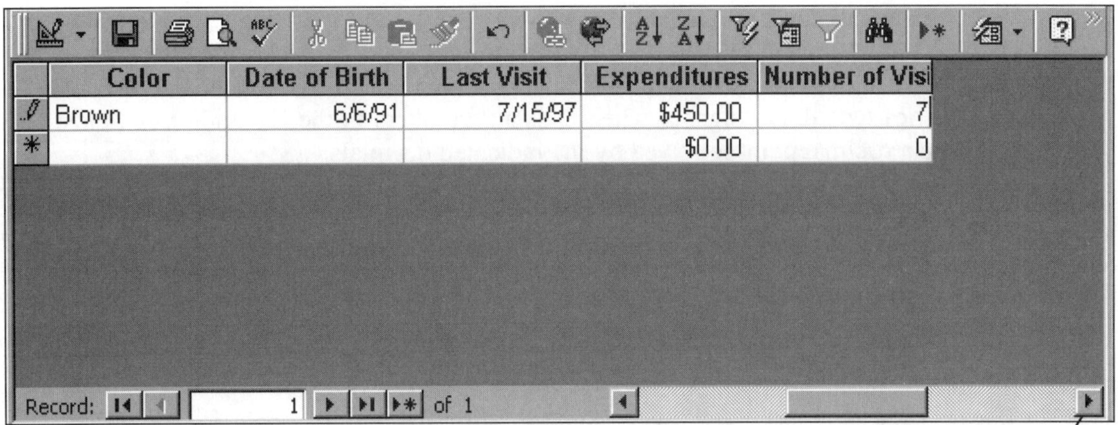

❶ *Use the horizontal scroll bar to scroll to the right until the fields shown here are visible.*

5. Use the following steps to enter data in the remaining fields.

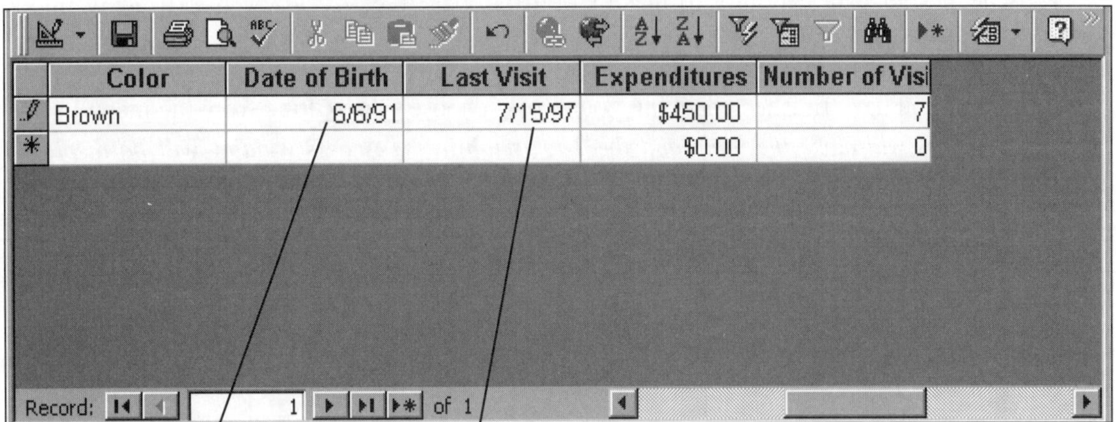

❶ *Make sure the insertion point is in the Date of Birth field and type* ***6/6/91****. Access will prompt you with an error message if you attempt to enter a number (or text) that is not a valid date. For this reason, you must use the forward slashes / while entering dates or enter dates using another valid date format such as 6-Jun-91.*

❷ ***Tap*** *the* ***Tab*** *key and enter* ***7/15/97*** *in the Last Visit field.*

❸ ***Tap*** *the* ***Tab*** *key and* ***type 450*** *in the Expenditures field.* ***Tap tab again*** *and Access will format the number with a dollar sign $, a decimal place and two zeros to the right of the decimal. Access formats the number this way because you chose the Currency format for this field when you set up the table.*

❹ *Type* ***7*** *in the Number of Visits field and then* ***tap Tab*** *to move to the Pet ID field in the next record.*

Also notice that Access right-aligned the dates and numbers in the last four fields. Access always right-aligns entries that can be used in calculations.

Continued...

6. Now use the following guidelines to enter the records shown below into the table.
   - Use the Tab key to move between fields.
   - Make sure you use forward slashes / when entering the dates.
   - **Do not** type dollar signs $ when entering numbers in the Expenditures fields. However, **do** type a decimal point followed by the indicated decimals.

Pet ID	Pet Name	Pet Type	Breed	Sex	Color	Date of Birth	Last Visit	Expenditures	Number of Visits
DG13	Dillon	Dog	Mutt	Male	Black	10/5/94	7/7/97	150.55	3
CT89	Puffy	Cat	Siamese	Female	White with patches	12/12/96	7/7/97	30.00	1
RB23	Bugs	Rabbit	Jack	Unknown	Brown	6/7/95	9/7/97	600.50	4
CT02	Max	Cat	Unknown	Male	White	1/7/86	9/7/97	1450.55	20
CT16	Stripes	Cat	Tortoise shell	Male	Black and brown	10/8/90	7/15/97	450	9

7. Check your data carefully to make sure it is error free! Accuracy is extremely important when performing data entry.

8. When you have finished checking your work, choose **File→Close** from the menu bar.

   Access will close the table and the Tables tab in the Access window will be displayed. You can always close an open object with either the File→Close command or by clicking the Close ☒ button (as you did in an earlier exercise). Notice that Access did not prompt you to save the table. Access automatically saves data that you enter into a table.

Changing the Structure of a Table

You can make changes to the structure of a table after it has been set up. For example, you may need to change the size or name of a field or add a new field. You make structural changes to a table in Design view. You can open the desired table in Design view or switch between Datasheet and Design views by clicking the Datasheet View or Design View buttons on the Access toolbar.

Changing the structure of a table may impact the data

You must be careful when changing the structure of a table especially if data has already been entered into the table. For example, imagine that a field has a length of 30 and you have already entered records into the table. If you reduce the field length to 20, then you may delete up to 10 characters from some records. Access will usually provide a warning message if you attempt to change a field and the change has the potential of destroying data.

Setting the Default Value of Fields

In the following exercise, you will modify the Number of Visits field by changing the default value to 1. Access lets you set a default value for fields. The default value is automatically entered in new records when you enter data in Datasheet view. This can be convenient if a field is typically set to a certain value. For example, you will set the default value of the Number of Visits field to 1. Pets will be entered into the database when they make their first visit to the clinic. By setting the Number of Visits field to 1, you will be able to skip over the field when entering the data for a new pet.

Hands-On 13.7 – Modify a field, add a field and switch views

1. Make sure the Pets icon is selected in the Access window and **click** the Design button.
   The Pets table will open in Design view.
2. Use the following steps to change the default value for the Number of Visits field.

*❶ **Click** anywhere in the **Number of Visits row** (you may need to scroll down).*

*❷ Change the Default Value to **1**.*

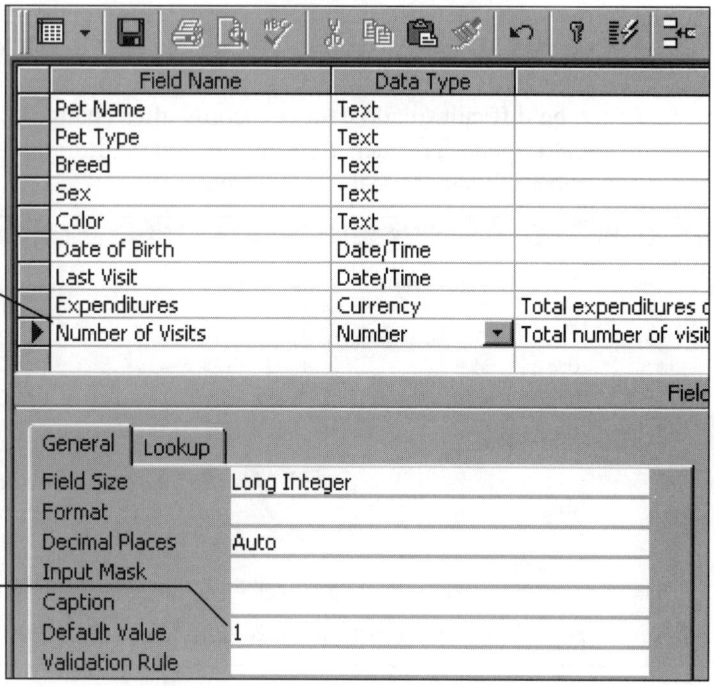

Continued...

Add a field

In the next few steps, you will add a Customer ID field to the table. The Customer ID field will eventually link the Pets table to a Customers table.

3. Use the following steps to add the Customer ID field.

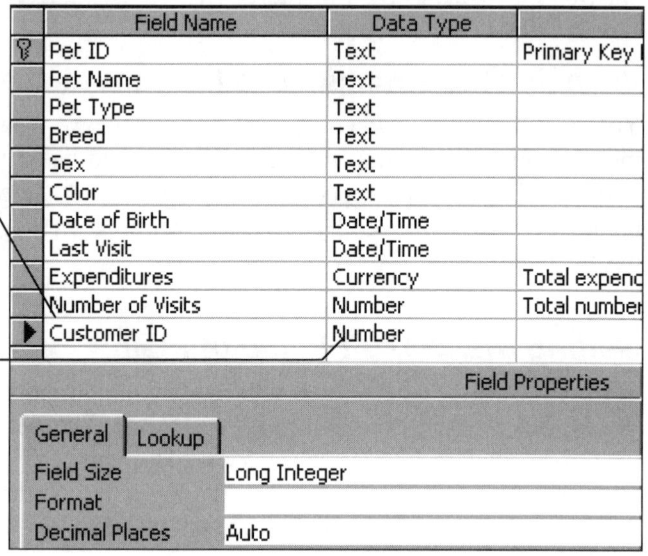

❶ ***Click** in the box below Number of Visits and type the name **Customer ID**. Make sure you include a space between Customer and ID. The space is necessary because the name will eventually need to match the name in the Customers table.*

❷ *Set the Data Type to **Number** as shown here.*

❸ *Take a moment to check the spelling of every field name. Make sure the spelling is correct and matches the spelling of the field names in this illustration. It is important that the field names be spelled correctly because they will be used in other objects throughout this course.*

Switch views and add Customer ID numbers to the records

4. **Click** the Datasheet View button on the left end of the Access toolbar and then **click** the **Yes** button when Access asks if you want to save the table.

   Notice that the order of the records has changed in the table. The records should now be sorted in alphabetical order based upon the primary key field. The records were sorted when you closed the table and then reopened it. One of the benefits of choosing a primary key field (such as Pet ID) is that Access will sort the records based upon the primary key field.

5. Now add the Customer ID's shown below into the table. Make sure you enter the correct Customer ID in each record. You may need to scroll to the left and right in the table to ensure that the correct Customer ID has been entered for each Pet ID. As you can see from this example, it can be difficult to add data to records after changing the structure of a table. For this reason, you should spend as much time as necessary designing and planning a database to minimize the number of changes that are required.

Pet ID	Pet Name	Pet Type	Breed	Sex	Color	Date of Birth	Last Visit	Expenditures	Number of Visits	Customer ID
CT02	Max	Cat	Unknown	Male	White	1/7/86	9/7/97	$1,450.55	20	2
CT16	Stripes	Cat	Tortoise shell	Male	Black and brown	10/8/90	7/15/97	$450.00	9	3
CT89	Puffy	Cat	Siamese	Female	White with patches	12/12/97	7/7/97	$30.00	1	1
DG12	Wolfy	Dog	German Shepherd	Male	Brown	6/6/91	7/15/97	$450.00	7	3
DG13	Dillon	Dog	Mutt	Male	Black	10/5/94	7/7/97	$150.55	3	1
RB23	Bugs	Rabbit	Jack	Unknown	Brown	6/7/95	9/7/97	$600.50	4	2

❶ *Make sure that each Pet ID has the correct Customer ID.*

6. Leave the view set to Datasheet view and continue with the next topic.

   You will add a record and make other changes in the next exercise.

Finding, Editing and Selecting Records

Access provides several toolbar buttons and a set of navigation buttons to let you locate, edit and delete records. The following table and illustration provide an overview of these buttons.

This button...	Has this function
Find	Lets you go to a record by searching for a phrase.
New Record	Moves the insertion point to a new empty record at the end of the table.
Delete Record	Deletes the current record.

The following navigation buttons can also be used at the bottom of the Access window.

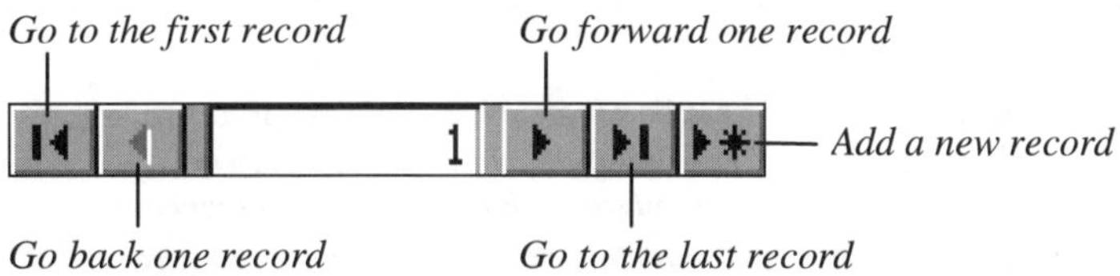

Notice that the Back One Record button is "ghosted out" in the illustration. This is because the insertion point is in record 1 as shown in the center of the navigation bar. Since the insertion point is in record 1, there is no record to go back to.

Hands-On 13.8 – Edit records

The Pets table should be in Datasheet view from the previous exercise.

Add a record

1. **Click** the New Record button on the Access toolbar.
   The insertion point will move to a new record at the end of the table.
2. Enter the following data into the new record.

Pet ID	Pet Name	Pet Type	Breed	Sex	Color	Date of Birth	Last Visit	Expenditures	Number of Visits	Custo mer ID
CT92	Tony	Cat	Unknown	Male	Brown with black stripes	4/3/97	7/7/97	145	6	1

Use the navigation buttons

3. Use the illustration on the following page to go to various records.

Continued...

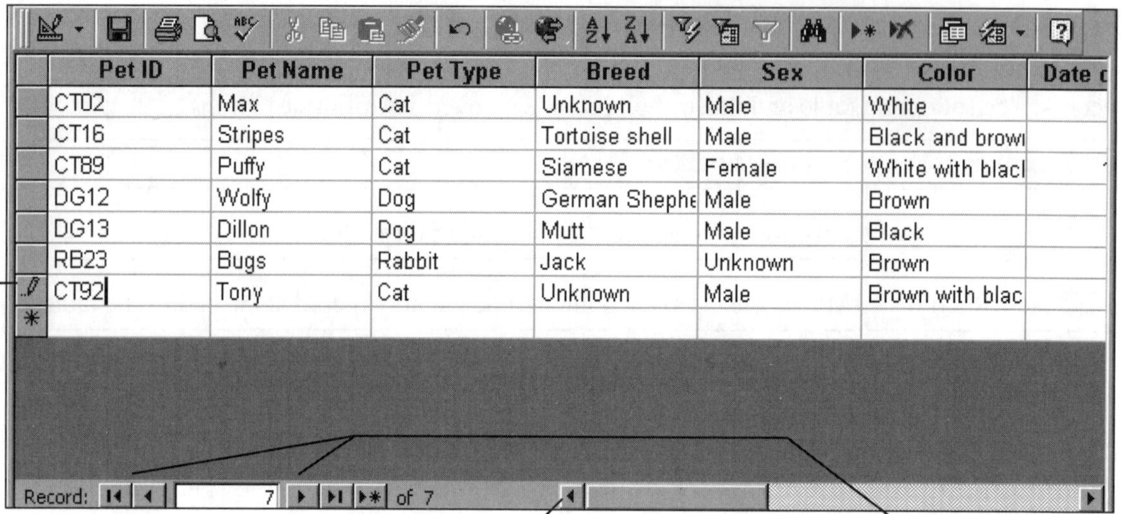

❶ *Notice the pencil icon shown in this illustration. The pencil icon indicates that the current record is being edited.*

❷ *If necessary,* **scroll** *to the* **left** *until the Pet ID field is visible.*

❸ **Click** *the various* **navigation buttons** *to browse through the records. The navigation buttons are useful when you have a large database with many records.*

4. Use the following illustration to delete a record.

❶ **Click** *the* **square box** *to the left of the CT89 record and the record will become selected. The vertical column of boxes to the left of the records is called the Selection bar.*

❷ **Click** *the* **Delete Record** *button on the Access toolbar.*

❸ **Click** *the* **Yes** *button on the warning box that appears to confirm the deletion.*

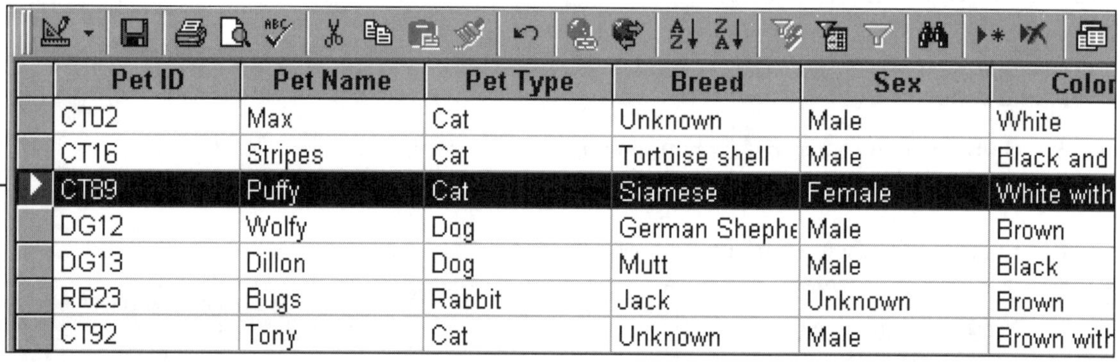

In the preceding steps, you selected the CT89 record prior to deleting it. You could actually have deleted the record by clicking anywhere in the CT89 row and then clicking the Delete Record button. The Selection bar is most useful when you want to delete or perform some other action on multiple records. You can select multiple records by dragging the mouse down the selection bar.

Find a record

5. **Click** on **any Pet ID** in the Pet ID column.

   In the next few steps, you will search for Pet ID's. You must have the insertion point somewhere in the column that you wish to search through prior to initiating the search.

6. **Click** the Find button on the Access toolbar.

Continued...

7. Use the following steps to conduct the search.

❶ *Notice the Title bar indicates that you are searching for a Pet ID.*

❷ *Type* **ct92** *in the Find What box.*

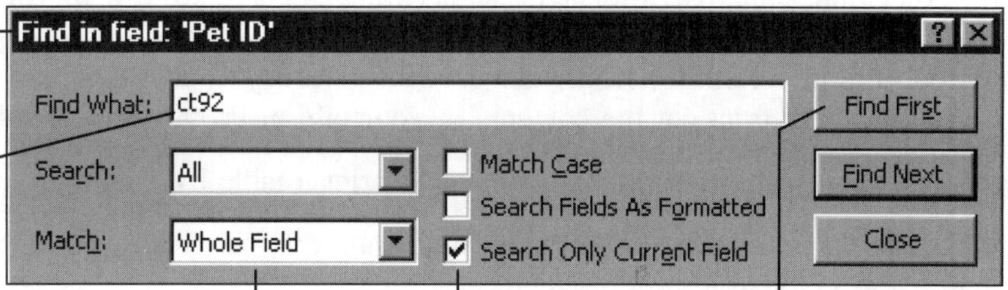

❸ *Notice the drop-down boxes and check boxes. These boxes let you control the search. For example, the Match Case box should be unchecked for the current search as shown here. This is because you typed the search string in lowercase (ct92) but the actual Pet ID in the database is CT92. Access will find the Pet ID because the Match Case box is unchecked.*

❹ ***Click*** *the* ***Find First*** *button and Pet ID CT92 will become selected.*

8. Use the preceding steps to find Pet ID **DG12**.

   Keep in mind that the Find feature is most useful when you have a large database and the item you are searching for is not visible on the screen.

9. **Click** the **Close** button on the Find dialog box.

10. Leave the Access window in Datasheet view and continue with the next topic.

Printing Tables

It is very important that you enter data accurately. There are few things more upsetting to customers and other business contacts than misspelling their names and making other types of data entry errors. For this reason, it is important to check your data for accuracy after it has been entered. Perhaps the best way to check data is to print out the contents of your tables. Proofreading hard copy (paper printout) is usually the best way to spot errors. You can easily print a table by clicking the Print button on the Access toolbar or by issuing the **File→Print** command. You may also want to use the Print Preview button to preview a table prior to printing it.

Adjusting Column Widths

You may need to adjust the width of the columns in a table in order to see the entire contents of table cells on a printout. You can use several techniques to adjust column widths as discussed in the following table.

To do this...	Use this technique
Manually adjust column widths	Drag the border between two column headings
Set column widths to fit the widest entry in a column	Double-click the border between two column headings
Set a precise column width	Choose Format→Column Width and enter the desired width

Changing the Margins and Page Orientation

Many tables are quite wide and they may not fit on a page. Fortunately, most printers can print text vertically in **portrait** orientation or horizontally in **landscape** orientation. The following illustration shows both portrait and landscape orientations. You set the orientation of a page by issuing the **File→Page Setup** command, clicking the Page tab and choosing the desired orientation. You can also adjust the page margins in the Page Setup dialog box.

Hands-On 13.9 – Widen columns, set the orientation and print the table

1. Choose **File→Page Setup...** from the Access menu bar.
2. Make sure the Margins tab is active and set all four margins to **.25"** (that's .25 not 25).
3. **Click** the **Page tab** and choose the Landscape radio button.
4. **Click OK** to complete the changes.
5. Use the following steps to manually adjust the width of the Pet ID column.

❶ Position the mouse pointer on the border between the Pet ID and Pet Name column headings and the Adjust pointer will appear.

*❷ **Drag** the border to the **left** until the Pet ID column is just wide enough to display the heading and entries.*

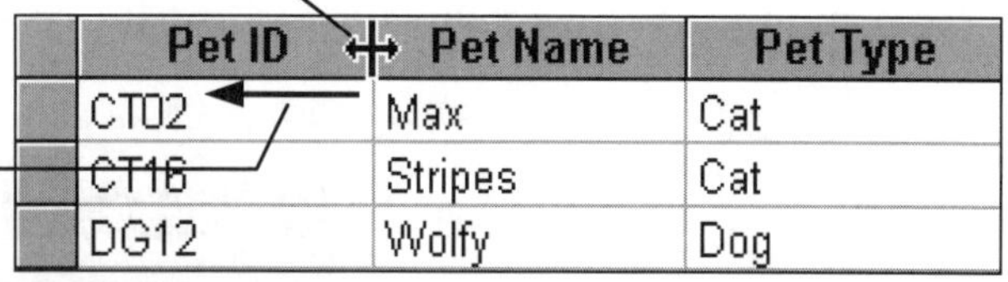

6. Now use the following steps to automatically fit a column to the widest entry in the column.

*❶ Position the mouse pointer on the border between the Pet Name and Pet Type columns and **double-click**. This technique can be tricky, so keep trying until the Pet Name column shrinks to fit the heading.*

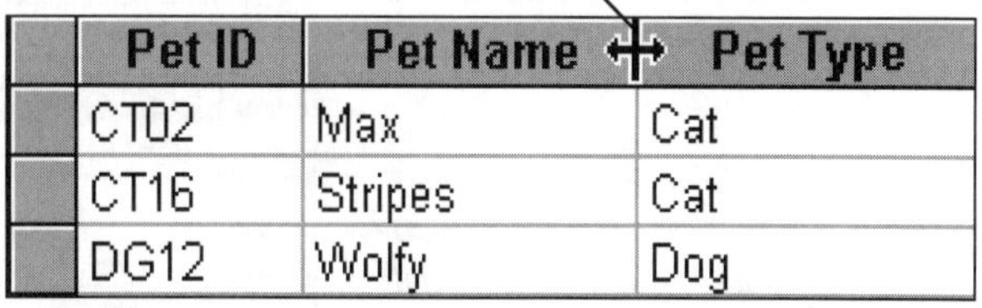

7. Use the double-click technique to minimize the width of all columns in the table. You can accomplish this by double-clicking the borders between all columns. You can also minimize all column widths by first dragging the mouse pointer across all of the column headings. This will select the columns. You can then double-click the border between any two of the selected column headings and all of the column widths will be minimized.

Print the table

8. **Click** the Print Preview button on the Access toolbar.
9. **Zoom in** by clicking the mouse pointer (it will look like a magnifying glass) on the table.
10. If necessary, **scroll left** or **right** to view all cells in the table.
11. **Click** on the **table again** to zoom out.
12. Feel free to print the table by clicking the Print button.
13. **Click** the **Close** button on the Print Preview toolbar when you have finished.
14. Now close the table by choosing **File→Close** from the Access menu bar.
15. **Click** the **Yes** button when Access asks if you want to save the changes.

In the next topic, you will set up another table using the Table Wizard.

The Table Wizard

Access provides a Table Wizard to help you set up tables. The Table Wizard provides predefined tables with fields that are most likely required for that type of table. However, many people prefer to set up tables without the assistance of the Table Wizard. In the next exercise, you will use the Table Wizard to set up a Customers table. This way, you will have experience setting up tables manually and with the Table Wizard. In the future, you can use whichever method best suits your needs. To start the Table Wizard, you **click** the **New** button on the Tables tab and **double-click** the **Table Wizard** option.

Hands-On 13.10 – Use the Table Wizard

The Tables tab should be displayed in the Access window from the previous exercise.

1. **Click** the **New** button on the right-side of the Access window.
2. **Double-click** the **Table Wizard** option in the New Table box.
3. Use the following steps to begin setting up a table.

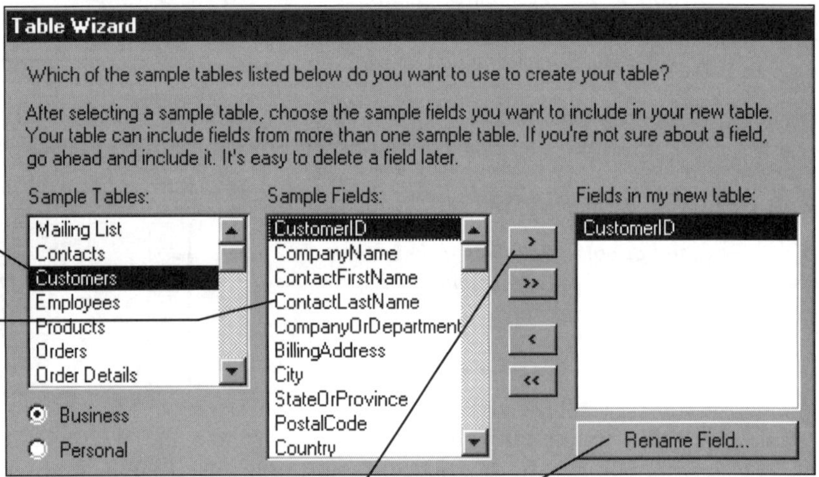

❶ ***Choose** the **Customers** sample table.*

❷ *Notice the list of Sample Fields for the Customers table. Each sample table contains a different set of sample fields.*

❸ *Make sure the **CustomerID** field is selected in the Sample Fields list and **click** this Add button. The CustomerID field will move to the **Fields in my new table list** as shown here.*

❹ ***Click** the **Rename Field** button and **insert** a **space** in the name to make it **Customer ID**, then **click OK**. This is necessary so that the spelling of the field name matches the Customer ID field in the Pets table.*

4. Now add the **ContactFirstName**, **ContactLastname**, **BillingAddress**, **City**, **StateOrProvince**, **PostalCode** and **PhoneNumber** fields by choosing them one at a time and then clicking the Add Field [>] button. Change the names of the fields as you add them as follows.

Change...	To
ContactFirstName	FirstName
ContactLastName	LastName
BillingAddress	Address
City	Leave as is
StateOrProvince	State
PostalCode	Zip
PhoneNumber	Phone

Continued...

5. If you mistakenly added a field, then you can remove it by choosing it from the **Fields in my new table list** and clicking the Remove Field < button. Your completed **Fields in my new table list** should match the following example.

6. **Click** the Next > button at the bottom of the dialog box.
   The next screen will propose the table name Customers and offer to set the primary key for you.
7. Leave the options set as they are by **clicking** the Next > button.
   The next screen will ask you about relationships between tables.
8. Leave the option set to **not related to Pets** by **clicking** the Next > button.
   The next screen will ask how you wish to display the completed table.
9. Choose the Modify the table design. option and **click** the Finish button.
   Access will create the table for you and display it in Design view. Leave the table open, as you will modify it in the next exercise.

Hands-On 13.11 – Modify the structure of the table

Many Access users use the Access wizards (such as the Table Wizard) to set up tables and other objects. Then they modify the objects to suit their particular needs. In this exercise, you will use this approach by modifying the structure of the Customers table.

1. Use the following illustration to explore the table you just created.

❶ *Notice that the Data Type of the Customer ID field has been set to AutoNumber. The AutoNumber field type is often used with primary key fields. AutoNumbering automatically assigns sequential numbers (beginning with 1) to the AutoNumber field of records as you add records to a table. For example, the first customer you add will be assigned a Customer ID of 1 while the next customer will be assigned the Customer ID 2, etc.*

❷ ***Click** anywhere on the **Address field** and then change the field size from 255 to **50** at the bottom of the dialog box.*

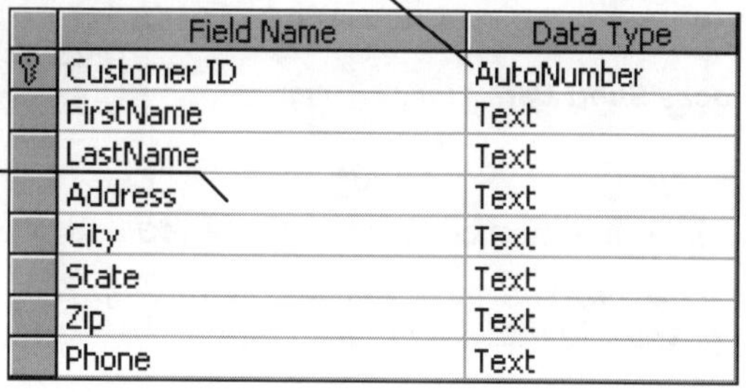

Continued...

2. Use the following illustration to change the default value of the State field.

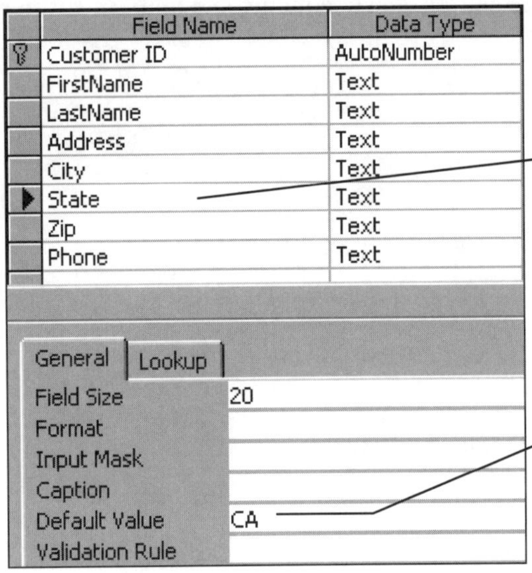

❶ ***Click** anywhere on the **State field**.*

❷ *Change the default value to **CA** (even if you do not live in California). Each new record that you add to the database will display CA as the default state.*

3. Use the following illustration to check out the Input Mask property for the phone field.

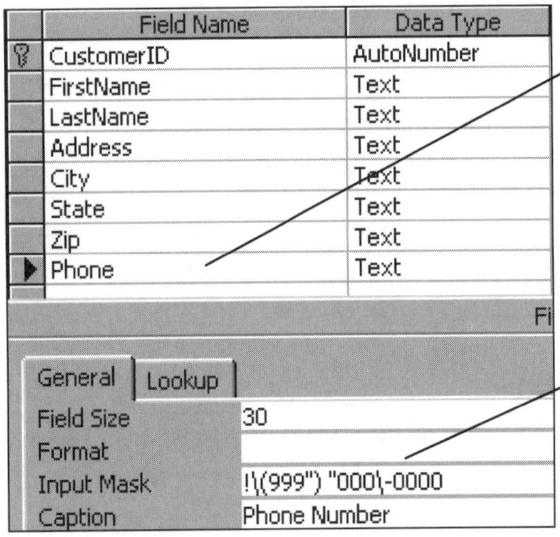

❶ ***Click** anywhere on the **Phone field**.*

❷ *Notice these characters in the Input Mask box. An input mask displays characters in a field to assist you in entering data. For example, the input mask shown here will display parentheses as you enter data in the Phone field. The parentheses are displayed so that you know where to type the area code. The input mask can also restrict the characters that you are allowed to enter in a field. For example, some input masks will only let you enter the digits 0-9. The Table Wizard set up this Input Mask for the Phone field. However, you can apply input masks to fields by choosing the desired mask in the Input Mask box. However, you would need to install the Input Mask Wizard in Microsoft Office before doing this.*

Add new fields

4. Use the following steps to insert a new date field.

❶ ***Click** below the Phone field and **type Last Visit**.*

❷ ***Click** in the Data Type box and **choose Date/Time** from the drop-down list.*

❸ ***Choose Short Date** as the Format.*

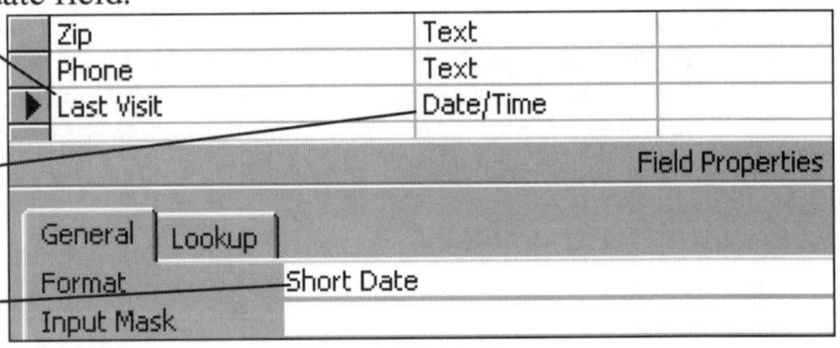

5. Now add a field named **Current Balance** and set the Data Type to **Currency**.

At this point, you have finished setting up the Customers table. Continue with the next exercise where you will add data to the table.

Hands-On 13.12 – Add records and print the table

1. **Click** the Datasheet View button on the toolbar.
2. **Click Yes** when Access asks if you wish to save the table.
   Notice the word (AutoNumber) is selected in the first empty record. This field is formatted with the AutoNumber data type so you will bypass it in the next step. Access will automatically assign the number 1 to the record when you begin entering data in the FirstName field.
3. **Tap** the **Tab** key to bypass the Customer ID field.
4. Type the name **Mark** in the FirsName field and the number 1 will appear in the Customer ID field.
5. **Tap Tab** and type **Roth** in the Lastname field.
6. **Tap Tab** and type **760 Maple Avenue** in the Address field.
7. **Tap Tab** and type **Fremont** in the City field.
8. **Tap Tab** and notice that the State field is set to CA.
   This is because you set CA as the default value for this field.
9. **Tap Tab** to bypass the State field (CA is correct) and type **94538** in the Zip field.
   You will notice that a hyphen appears to the right of the digits. This is because the Zip field has also been formatted with an input mask. The input mask inserts a hyphen between the first five and last four digits (if you use nine digits).
10. **Tap Tab** to bypass the last four digits of the zip code.
11. Type the area code **510** in the Phone field and the input mask will surround the number with parenthesis.
    Once again, the input mask is hard at work formatting your entry.
12. Complete the phone number by typing **2349090**.
    Access will format the number by inserting a hyphen between the 4 and the 9.
13. **Tap Tab** and type **7/7/97** in the Last Visit field.
14. **Tap Tab** and type **235** in the Current Balance field.
15. Now add the following two records to the table.
    The AutoNumber feature will insert numbers in the Customer ID field so just tap Tab when you reach that field.

Custo mer ID	FirstName	LastName	Address	City	State	Zip	Phone	Last Visit	Current Balance
2	Tony	Simpson	312 York Lane	Richmond	CA	94804	(510) 238-2233	9/7/97	185
3	Jason	Jones	2233 Crystal Street	San Mateo	CA	94403	(415) 312-2312	7/15/97	48

Continued...

Print the table

16. Adjust the width of all columns to fit the widest entry/heading in the columns. You can accomplish this by double-clicking the borders between the column headings. You can also select all of the columns by dragging the mouse pointer across the column headings and then double-clicking the border between the column headings of any two selected columns.
17. Use the **File→Page Setup** command to set all four margins to **.5"**.
18. Set the orientation to **Landscape** using the Page tab in the Page Setup dialog box.
19. **Click OK**, use **Print Preview** to preview the table and then print the table if desired.
20. **Close Print Preview** and feel free to experiment with any of the topics that you have learned in this lesson.
21. **Close** the **table** when you have finished experimenting and save any changes.
22. Close Access by choosing **File→Exit** from the Access menu bar.
23. Now continue with the end-of-lesson questions and exercises on the following pages.

Concepts Review

True / False

1. An Access database can have a maximum of 1 table. 1. **T F**
2. Datasheet view is used to set up the structure of tables. 2. **T F**
3. If you are in Design view and you want to switch to Datasheet view, then you must close the table and reopen it in Datasheet view. 3. **T F**
4. A database is like a container because it can hold several types of objects including tables. 4. **T F**
5. Changing the structure of a table will never result in lost data. 5. **T F**
6. Print Preview lets you preview prior to printing. 6. **T F**
7. The page orientation can be changed with the File→Print command. 7. **T F**
8. Portrait orientation causes a table to print horizontally on a page. 8. **T F**
9. The Table Wizard is used to automate data entry in a table. 9. **T F**
10. Fields with a Number data type can contain both text and numbers. 10. **T F**

Multiple Choice

1. What is the maximum number of characters that a field name may contain?
   a) 8
   b) 32
   c) 64
   d) 255 ( )

2. What function does the  button serve?
   a) Adds a new record to the table
   b) Makes a field a primary key
   c) Deletes a record ( )
   d) Adds bold to text

3. Which of the following buttons switches you from Design view to Datasheet view?
   a) 
   b)  ( )
   c) 
   d) None of the above

4. What is the first step that you should take if you want to delete a record?
   a) Click in the desired record or select it
   b) Click the Delete Record button on the toolbar
   c) Narrow the column
   d) Delete all text from the cells ( )

5. Which of the following commands is used to change the page orientation?
   a) File→Print
   b) File→Page Setup
   c) Format→Page Orientation ( )
   d) Format→Print Preview

Skills Builder 13.1

In this exercise, you will set up a new database for the Tropical Getaways travel company. Tropical Getaways is an exciting new travel company that specializes in inexpensive vacations to tropical locations worldwide. You have been asked to set up a database that tracks clients and trips. In this exercise, you will create the first table for the database.

1. **Start Access**, choose the **Blank Database** option and **click OK**.
2. Assign the name **Tropical Getaways** to your new database and save it on your exercise diskette.
   The Tables tab should be displayed in the Tropical Getaways window.
3. **Click** the **New** button on the right-side of the window and then **double-click** the **Design View** option to begin setting up a new table in Design view.
4. Type **Customer ID** as the first field name and **tap** the **Tab** key.
5. **Click** the drop-down button in the Data Type box and choose **AutoNumber**.
   Access will automatically assign sequential Customer ID's when you enter data in this table.
6. **Click** the Primary Key button on the toolbar to make Customer ID the primary key.
7. Set up the remainder of this table using the field names, data types and options shown in the following table. Keep in mind that you have already set up the Customer ID field.

Field Name	Data Type	Field Size	Primary Key	Description
Customer ID	AutoNumber		Yes	
FirstName	Text	30		
LastName	Text	30		
Address	Text	50		
City	Text	30		
State	Text	2		
Zip	Text	5		
Profile	Text	20		The profile indicates the category of trips the customer prefers

8. When you have finished, **click** the Datasheet View button on the Access toolbar.
9. **Click Yes** when Access asks if you wish to save the table.
10. Type the name **Customers**, **click OK** and then enter the following four records. The Customer ID numbers should be entered automatically because Customer ID has an AutoNumber data type.

Customer ID	FirstName	LastName	Address	City	State	Zip	Profile
1	Debbie	Thomas	450 Crestwood Lane	Austin	TX	78752	Adventure
2	Wilma	Boyd	855 State Street	Richmond	NY	12954	Leisure
3	Ted	Wilkins	900 C Street	Fort Worth	TX	76104	Adventure
4	Alice	Simpson	2450 Ridge Road	Fort Worth	TX	76105	Family

11. When you have finished, choose **File→Close** from the Access menu bar to close the table.
    Access automatically saves the data you entered. You will set up another table in the next Skills Builder exercise.

Skills Builder 13.2

In this exercise, you will set up another table for the Tropical Getaways database. The Table tab should be displayed in the Access widow from the preceding exercise.

1. **Click** the **New** button on the right-side of the window and then **double-click** the **Design View** option to begin setting up a new table in Design view.
2. Set up the table using the following structure.

Field Name	Data Type	Field Size / Format	Primary Key	Description
Trip ID	Text	8	Yes	Four to eight character unique identifier for each trip
Customer ID	Number	Long Integer		ID number from Customers table
Destination	Text	50		
Category	Text	30		All trips have a category such as Adventure, Leisure etc.
Departure Date	Date/Time	Short Date		
Return Date	Date/Time	Short Date		
Cost	Currency			

3. Switch to **Datasheet view** and **save** the **table** with the name **Trips**.
4. Enter the following data into the Trips table. Do not type the dollar signs $ and commas when entering the Cost numbers. Access will add the dollar signs and commas for you because you chose the Currency data type when setting up the Cost field.

TripID	Customer ID	Destination	Category	Departure Date	Return Date	Cost
Adv01	1	Kenyan Safari	Adventure	8/5/94	9/4/94	$6,600
Lei01	2	Caribbean Cruise	Leisure	9/19/95	9/28/95	$2,390
Adv02	1	Amazon Jungle Trek	Adventure	8/7/95	9/14/95	$7,765
Fam01	4	Orlando	Family	3/4/96	3/10/96	$3,400

5. **Close** the **Trips** table when you have finished.

   The Table tab should now display both the Customers and Trips table icons. Continue with the next exercise where you will print the Customers table.

Skills Builder 13.3

The Tropical Getaways database should be open and the Customers and Trips tables should be visible in the Tables tab of the Access window.

1. **Double-click** the **Customers** table to open it in Datasheet view.
   You can always open a table in Datasheet view by double-clicking it.
2. **Adjust** the widths of all **columns** to display the widest entries in the columns.
3. Use the Print Preview button to preview the table.
4. **Zoom in** on the table by clicking anywhere on it.
5. Feel free to **print** the table and check your data for accuracy.
6. **Close Print Preview** when you have finished and then **close** the **table**.
7. Now **open** the **Trips** table and **adjust** the **column widths** to fit the widest entries.
8. **Print** the table and check your data for accuracy.
9. **Close** the **table** when you have finished.
10. Finally, exit from Access by choosing **File→Exit** from the menu bar.

Assessment 13.1

In this assessment, you will begin creating a database for Classic Cars. Classic Cars is an organization devoted to tracking, categorizing and preserving classic automobiles. You will begin by creating tables to track collectors and cars.

1. Start Access and create a new database named **Classic Cars**.
2. Create a new table with the following structure.

Field Name	Data Type	Field Size	Primary Key	Description
Collector ID	AutoNumber		Yes	
FirstName	Text	30		
LastName	Text	30		
Address	Text	50		
City	Text	30		
State	Text	2		
Zip	Text	5		
Era of Interest	Text	20		This field identifies the time period that the collector is most interested in
Collection Size	Number	Long Integer		Number of cars in collection

3. Enter the following records into the table and name the table **Collectors**.

Collector ID	FirstName	LastName	Address	City	State	Zip	Era of Interest	Collection size
1	Cindy	Johnson	4220 Edward Street	Northlake	IL	60164	1950's	42
2	Tammy	Olson	1200 Big Pine Drive	Moses Lake	WA	98837	1960's	6
3	Ed	Larkson	2300 Watson Street	Cainesville	OH	43701	Early 1900's	34
4	Bob	Barker	6340 Palm Drive	Rockridge	FL	32955	1950's	7

4. **Adjust** the width of all **columns** to fit the largest entry/heading in the columns.
5. Use Print Preview to **preview** the table. If necessary, switch the orientation to landscape and reduce the margins until the table fits on one page.
6. **Print** the table.
7. **Close** the **table** when you have finished and save any changes that you have made.

Continued...

8. Create another new table with the following structure.

Field Name	Data Type	Field Size / Format	Primary Key	Description
Car ID	Text	15	Yes	Up to 15 characters to uniquely identify each car
Collector ID	Number	Long Integer		ID number from Collectors table
Year	Text	20		
Make	Text	30		
Model	Text	50		
Color	Text	30		
Condition	Text	30		
Value	Currency			Estimated value

9. Enter the following records into the table and name the table Cars.

Car ID	Collector ID	Year	Make	Model	Color	Condition	Value
CJ01	1	58	Chevrolet	Corvette	Red and white	Mint	$65,000
TO05	2	62	Chevrolet	Corvette	Blue	Excellent	$30,000
CJ22	1	59	Ford	Thunderbird	Tan	Good	$20,000
BB03	4	58	Chevrolet	Corvette	Black	Excellent	$35,000

10. **Adjust** the width of all **columns** to fit the largest entry/heading in the columns.

11. Use Print Preview to **preview** the table.

12. **Print** the table.

13. **Close** the **table** when you have finished and save any changes that you have made.

14. **Exit** from **Access** when you have finished.

14 Forms and Reports

Objectives:

- Create forms
- Use the AutoForm tool
- Use forms to delete records
- Create reports
- Use the Report Wizard
- Copy objects
- Delete objects

The Project – Enhancing the Pinnacle Pet Care Database

In this lesson, you will enhance the Pinnacle Pet Care database with forms and reports. You will create forms that will make it easy to view, enter and edit data in the Customers and Pets tables. You will also create reports to present your data in a variety of ways. The form and report that you will create for the Customers table are shown below.

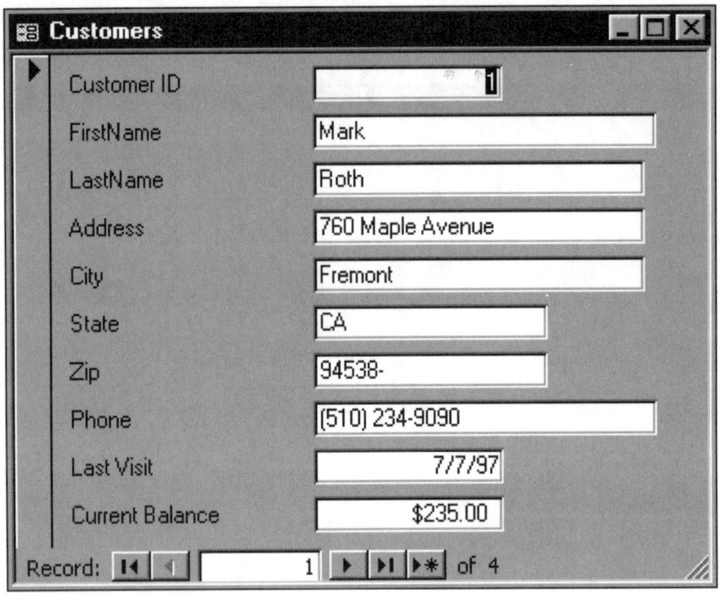

Form for Customers table

Outstanding Balances report for Customers

Outstanding Balances

FirstName	*LastName*	*Phone*	*Current Balance*
Mark	Roth	(510) 234-9090	$235.00
Tony	Simpson	(510) 238-2233	$185.00
Jason	Jones	(415) 312-2312	$48.00
Jacob	Samuels	(404) 367-8002	$250.50

Forms

In the previous lesson, you learned that an Access database is composed of various objects. A form is a type of object that lets you view, edit and enter data. The benefit of a form is that it allows you to focus on a single record in the database. This is in contrast to Datasheet view where you are able to view many records at the same time. The following illustration discusses a form for the Customers table in the Pinnacle Pet Care database. You will create this form in the next exercise.

Notice the form displays one complete record from the database. Forms let you focus on a single customer, pet, etc.

Fields such as Phone, Last Visit and Current Balance are automatically formatted with symbols (as they are in Datasheet view).

The form also contains navigation buttons to let you browse through the database.

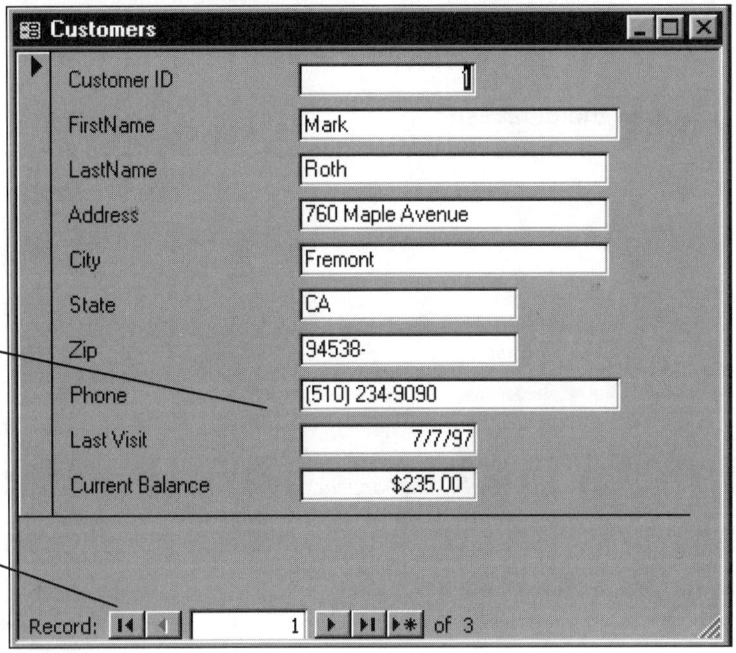

The AutoForm Tool

You can use the AutoForm tool to automatically create a simple form for any table. The form in the example above was created with the AutoForm tool. The following Quick Steps discuss the process of creating forms with the AutoForm tool.

Quick Steps: *Using the AutoForm Tool*

To create a form using the AutoForm tool

- *Open the desired database.*
- *Make sure the Tables tab is active in the database window.*
- *Choose the desired table.*
- *Click the New Object drop-down button on the right-end of the Access toolbar.*
- *Choose AutoForm from the drop-down list.*
- *Close the form when you have finished using it and assign it a name.*

You can also create more complex forms using a form Design view or with a Form Wizard. However, these techniques are not discussed at this time.

Hands-On 14.1 – Open the Pinnacle Pet Care database and use the AutoForm tool

In this exercise, you will open the Pinnacle Pet Care database from your exercise diskette. You will enhance this database throughout this course. If you have not satisfactorily completed the Hands-On exercises in the previous lesson, then ask your instructor to copy the file named Pinnacle Pet Care – Lesson 14 to your exercise diskette. This file provides the Pinnacle Pet Care database in the state it should be in after completing Lesson 13. If necessary, your instructor can provide you with files to give you a fresh starting point whenever you begin a new lesson in the Access unit of this book.

Open the database

1. Start Access and use the illustration below to open the Pinnacle Pet Care database.

❶ *If the Pinnacle Pet Care database is listed in the dialog box that appears, then choose it from the list as shown here and* ***click OK****. If it is not listed, then skip this illustration and continue with step 2.*

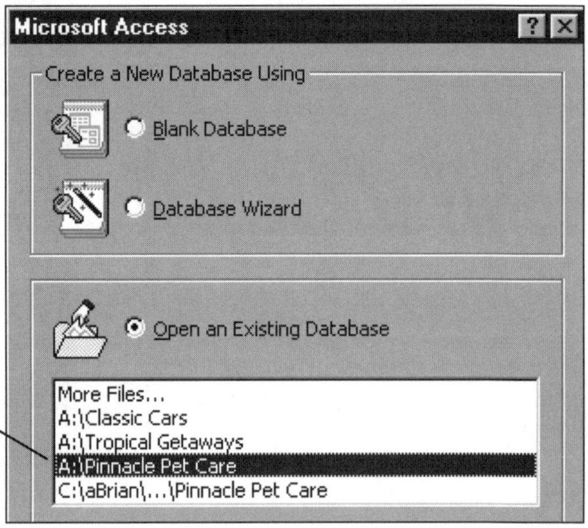

2. If the Pinnacle Pet Care database was not listed as shown above, then click the Cancel button on the dialog box, click the Open button on the Access toolbar, navigate to your exercise diskette and open the Pinnacle Pet Care file.

Create a form for the Customers table

3. Use the following illustration to create a form for the Customers table.

❶ *Choose* ***Customers*** *in the Tables tab. You must choose the desired table before creating a form.*

❷ ***Click*** *the* ***drop-down button*** *on the New Object button and* ***choose AutoForm*** *as shown here.*

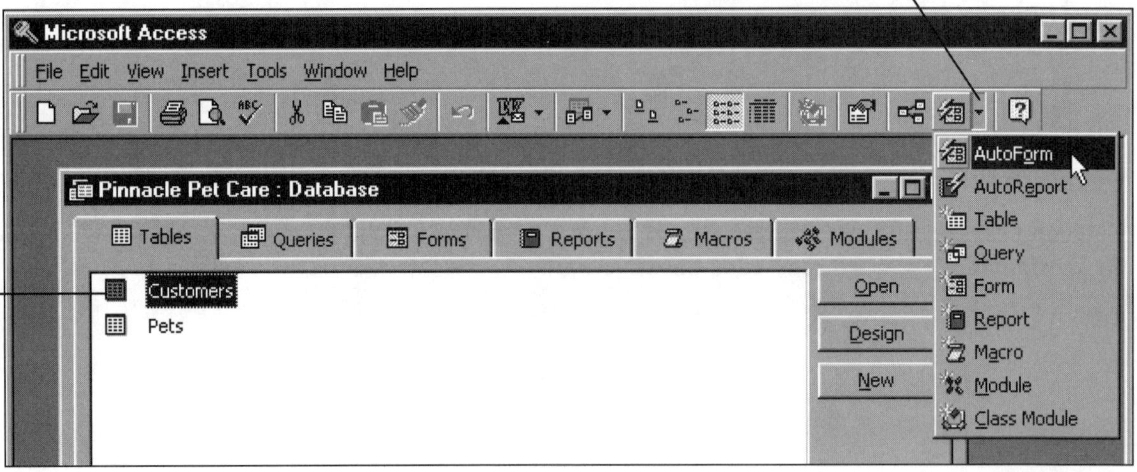

Continued...

Access will create the form and the Mark Roth record will be displayed. This is because the Mark Roth record is the first record in the table.

4. Feel free to browse through the records by clicking the navigation buttons at the bottom of the dialog box.

5. Use the following illustration to prepare to enter a new record.

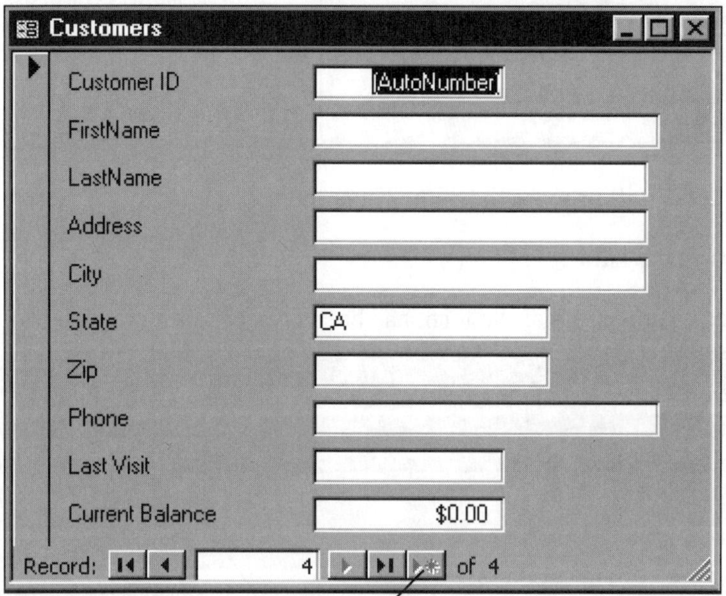

❶ ***Click** the **New Record button** and a new record will appear as shown here.*

❷ ***Tap** the **Tab key** to bypass the Customer ID field and move the insertion point to the FirstName field.*

6. Use the following illustration to enter a new record.

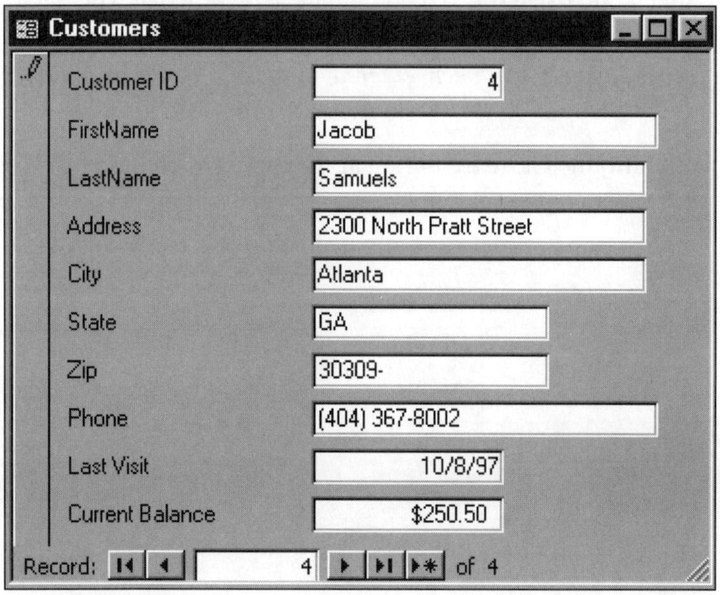

❶ ***Enter** the **data** shown here using the **Tab** key to move from one field to the next. Notice that you must change the entry in the state field from CA to GA. You can always change the default value for a record by typing a new value. You set the default value to CA when you created the table in the previous lesson. Also, the dollar sign will not appear in the Current Balance field until you go to another field or record after typing the entry in the Current Balance field.*

Continued...

Close the form, save the form and then reopen it

In the next few steps, you will close the form and assign a name to it. You name forms as you name tables and all other database objects.

7. Use the following illustration to close the form.

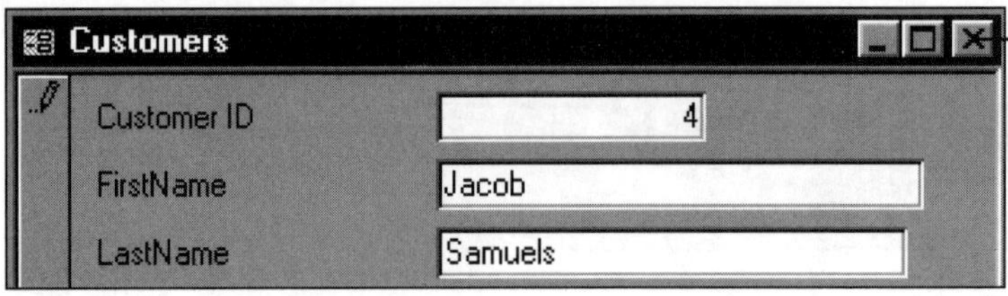

❶ ***Click** the **Close button** on the form and Access will ask if you want to save the form.*

8. **Click** the **Yes** button and Access will propose the name Customers.

9. **Click** the **OK** button to confirm the name.

10. Use the following illustration to confirm that the form has been created and to reopen it.

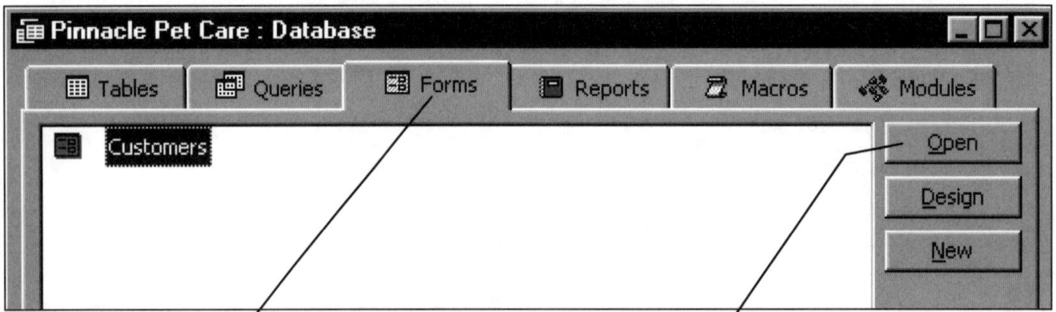

❶ ***Click** the **Forms** tab in the dialog box and the Customers form will be visible as shown here.*

❷ ***Click** the **Open** button to open the Customers form (or double-click the form).*

11. Browse through the records and notice that the Jacob Samuels record that you just added is visible as the last record.

    The data you entered for Jacob Samuels has been entered into the Customers table. The form provides an attractive interface for data entry and for viewing the contents of the table.

12. Now close the form again by **clicking** the Close ☒ button at the top-right corner of the form.

Hands-On 14.2 – Create a form for the Pets table

1. **Click** the **Tables tab** in the Access window and choose the Pets table.
2. **Click** the New Object drop-down button (near the right end of the Access toolbar) and choose **AutoForm**.

   Access will create the form based upon the fields in the Pets table.
3. **Click** the New Record button on the navigation bar at the bottom of the form.
4. Enter the following two records.

Pet ID	Pet Name	Pet Type	Breed	Sex	Color	Date of Birth	Last Visit	Expenditures	Number of Visits	Customer ID
DG24	Ben	Dog	Terrier	Male	Black	6/1/92	10/8/97	480	3	4
DG25	Spike	Dog	Chow	Male	Brown	4/3/84	10/8/97	890	12	4

5. **Click** the Close button on the form when you have finished entering the data.
6. **Click Yes** when Access asks if you want to save the form.
7. **Click OK** on the Save As box to accept the name Pets.
8. **Click** the **Forms tab** in the Access window and both the Customers and Pets form icons should be visible.
9. Now continue with the next topic where you will use the form to delete a record.

Deleting Records with Forms

You can delete a record while using a form by first navigating to the desired record. Once the desired record is displayed in the form, you can click the Delete Record button on the toolbar.

Hands-On 14.3 – Delete a record

1. **Double-click** the **Pets** icon in the Forms tab and the Pets form will open.
2. **Click** the New Record button on the Pet form navigation bar.
3. Type **SN01** as the Pet ID and **tap** the **Tab** key.
4. Type **Slinky** as the Pet Name and **tap** the **Tab** key.
5. Type **Snake** as the Pet Type.
6. It turns out that snakes are not allowed in the Pinnacle Pet Care clinic, so **click** the Delete Record button on the Access toolbar.
7. **Click Yes** to confirm the deletion.
8. Now close the form by **clicking** the Close button at the top-right corner of the form.

Reports

Access lets you create reports to present your data in a variety of ways. You can specify the fields that you wish to include in reports and you can format reports using built-in report styles. In the next exercise, you will create the report that is shown below. Notice that the report lists just four fields from the Customers table.

Outstanding Balances

FirstName	*LastName*	*Phone*	*Current Balance*
Mark	Roth	(510) 234-9090	$235.00
Tony	Simpson	(510) 238-2233	$185.00
Jason	Jones	(415) 312-2312	$48.00
Jacob	Samuels	(404) 367-8002	$250.50

Reports can be complex

In this lesson, you will use a Report Wizard to create simple reports like the report shown above. However, Access reports can be quite complex. For example, reports can include calculated fields that add columns of numbers and grouping levels that organize records in various ways. Access gives you the flexibility to create a "report for every occasion."

The AutoReport Tool and the Report Wizard

In the previous exercises, you used the AutoForm tool to create forms. The AutoForm tool creates a form using all of the fields from a table. This is acceptable, because you will normally want all of the fields to be placed on a form. Reports, on the other hand, usually require a subset of the fields from a table. For example, the report shown above uses just four fields from the Customers table. The AutoReport tool inserts all fields from a table into a report and thus it has limited use. Fortunately, Access provides a Report Wizard that gives you flexibility when setting up reports. The Report Wizard lets you choose the fields to include in the report. The Report Wizard also lets you specify a variety of formatting options. In the next exercise, you will use the Report Wizard to create the report shown above.

Quick Steps: ***Using the Report Wizard***

To create a report using the Report Wizard

- *Open the desired database.*
- *Click the Reports tab in the Database window.*
- *Click the New button on the Database window.*
- *Choose Report Wizard.*
- *Choose the desired table or query that you wish to base the report on from the drop-down list at the bottom of the dialog box and click OK.*
- *Follow the Report Wizard steps to create the desired report.*

Hands-On 14.4 – Use the Report Wizard

1. **Click** the Reports tab in the Access window and then **click** the New button.
2. Use the following illustration to initiate the Report Wizard.

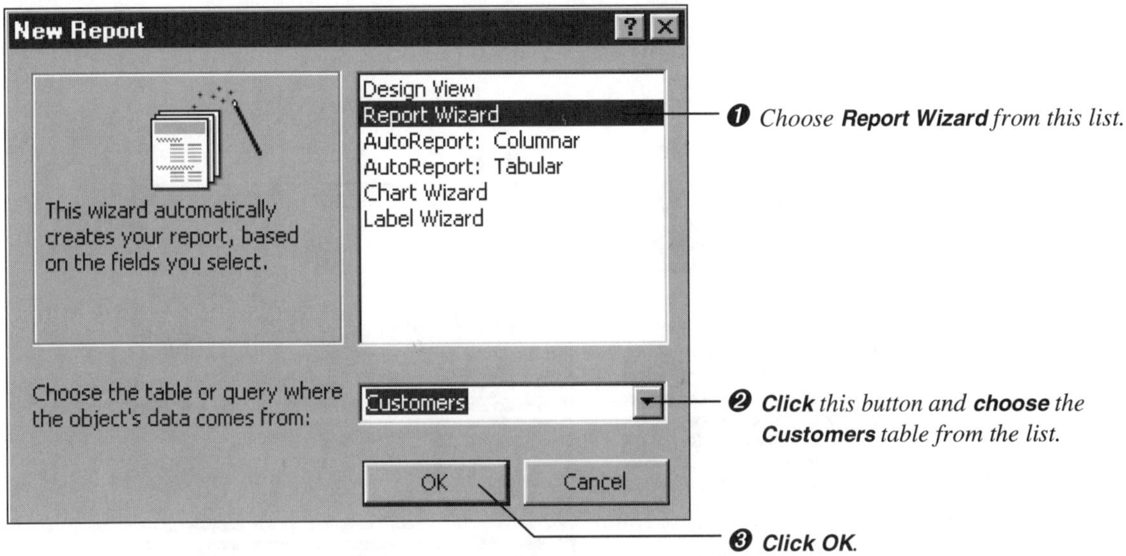

3. The first Report Wizard screen will appear asking you to choose the fields that you wish to include in the Report.
4. Use the following steps to choose the FirstName field.

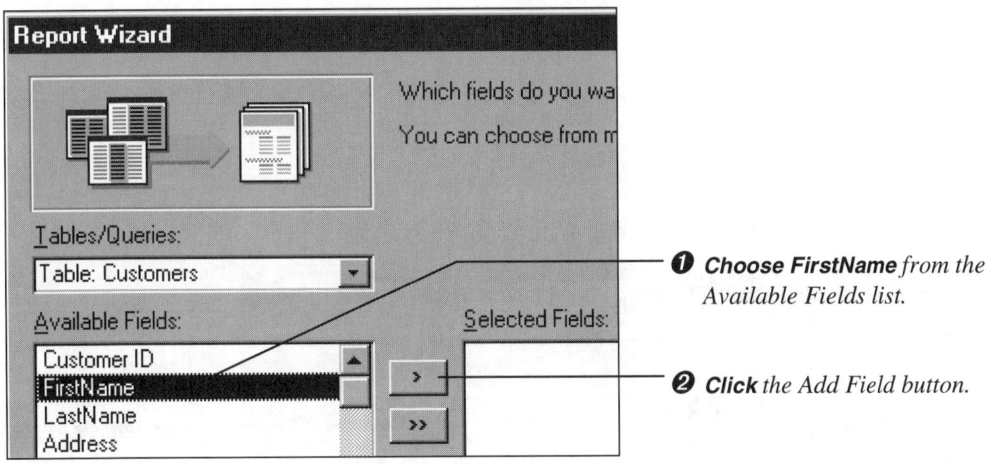

5. Now add the LastName, Phone and Current Balance fields. The completed Selected Fields list should match the following example.

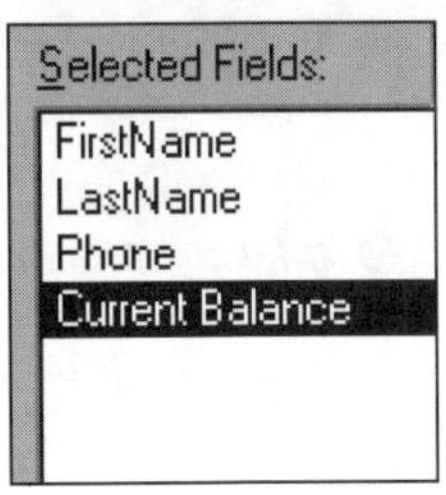

Continued...

6. **Click** the Next > button.
   The next screen will ask if you want grouping levels.

7. **Click** the Next > button to bypass the grouping level screen.
   The next screen will ask if you want to sort the records in the report.

8. **Click** the Next > button to bypass the sorting screen.
   The layout screen will appear.

9. Make sure the layout options are set as shown below.

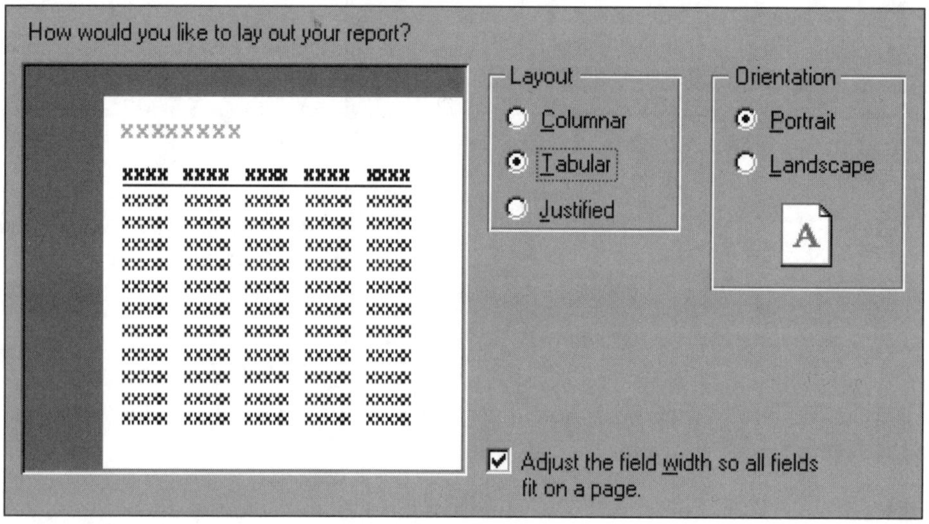

10. **Click** the Next > button.
    The next screen will ask which style you want.

11. Choose **Corporate** and **click** the Next > button.

12. Use the following steps to set the final options for the report.

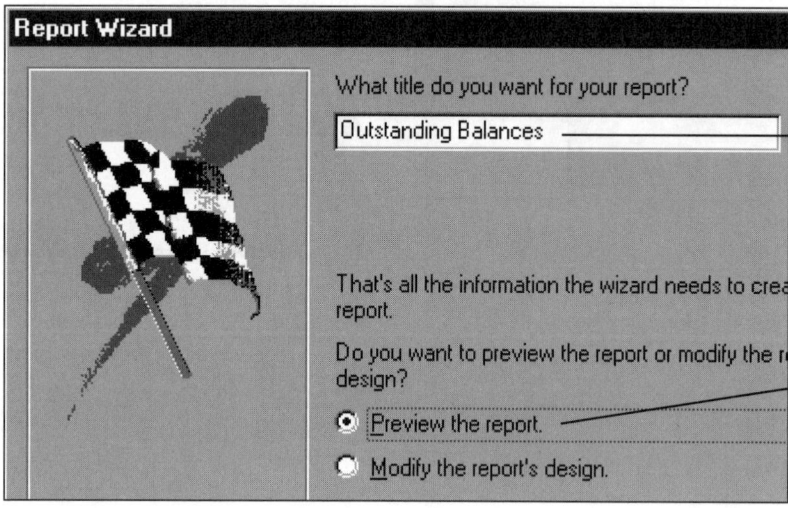

❶ *Type* ***Outstanding Balances*** *as the report title.*

❷ *Make sure the Preview the report option is chosen.*

❸ ***Click*** *the* ***Finish*** *button and the report will be created and displayed in Print Preview.*

Continued...

13. If necessary, maximize the Print Preview window by clicking its Maximize button.

14. Zoom in or out on the report by clicking the mouse pointer anywhere on it.

The top section of your report should match the following example. The bottom of the report will also contain a footer with the date the report was created and page numbering.

Outstanding Balances

FirstName	*LastName*	*Phone*	*Current Balance*
Mark	Roth	(510) 234-9090	$235.00
Tony	Simpson	(510) 238-2233	$185.00
Jason	Jones	(415) 312-2312	$48.00
Jacob	Samuels	(404) 367-8002	$250.50

15. When you have finished previewing your report, **click** the Design View button on the left end of the Print Preview toolbar.

The report will display in Design view with a report header, page header, detail section, etc. You can change the position of objects within a report and add/remove objects while working in Design view. However, you won't work in Design view at this time.

16. **Click** the Print Preview button on the left end of the toolbar to switch back to Print Preview.

17. Feel free to print the report by clicking the Print button on the Print Preview toolbar.

18. Choose **File→Close** from the menu bar to close the report.

The Report will automatically be assigned the name Outstanding Balances and an Outstanding Balances icon will appear in the Reports tab. As you can see from this example, creating simple reports is quite easy if you use the Report Wizard.

19. Now continue with the next exercise where you will create a report to accompany the Pets table.

Hands-On 14.5 – Create a report for the Pets table

1. Make sure the Reports tab is active and **click** the New New button.
2. Choose **Report Wizard** from the dialog box that appears and then choose **Pets** from the drop-down list near the bottom of the dialog box.
3. **Click OK** and the Available fields screen will appear.
4. Add the **Pet Name**, **Pet Type**, **Expenditures** and **Number of Visits** fields to the Selected Fields list as shown below.

5. **Click** the Finish button to accept all of the remaining default settings and the completed report shown below will appear.

   Keep in mind that you can click Finish at any time while using a Wizard.

Pets

Pet Name	*Pet Type*	*Expenditures*	*Number of Visits*
Wolfy	Dog	$450.00	7
Dillon	Dog	$150.55	3
Bugs	Rabbit	$600.50	4
Max	Cat	$1,450.55	20
Stripes	Cat	$450.00	9
Tony	Cat	$145.00	6
Ben	Dog	$480.00	3
Spike	Dog	$890.00	12

6. Notice the alignment of the fields within the columns as shown above.

   The fields have the same left or right alignment in the report as they do in the table that the report is based upon.

7. Close the report by choosing **File→Close** from the menu bar.

   The Reports tab should now have an Outstanding Balance report and a Pets report. You can preview a report at any time by double-clicking the desired report in the Reports tab or by choosing the desired report and clicking the Preview button.

Copying and Deleting Objects

You can make copies of tables, forms, reports and other types of objects. Copying an object can be useful if you intend to modify the object. By making a copy, you will have a backup of the object in case you damage the original. You copy objects with the **Copy and Paste** buttons on the Access toolbar.

You can also delete objects from an Access database. However, you must be careful when deleting objects because they are permanently deleted from the database. Deleting objects can be useful especially when using Wizards and tools like AutoForm. If you make a mistake or are unhappy with the results that one of these automated tools produces, then you can delete the object and start over. You delete an object by selecting it in the database window and choosing **Edit→Delete** from the menu bar.

Hands-On 14.6 – Copy a report and then delete the copy

Copy a report

1. Choose the **Pets** icon in the Reports tab and **click** the Copy button on the toolbar.
2. **Click** the Paste button on the toolbar and the Paste As box will appear.
3. Type **Copy of Pets** in the Paste As box and **click OK**.
   The Copy of Pets report will appear in the Reports tab.
4. **Double-click** the **Copy of Pets** report and it will open.
   Notice this report is identical to the Pets report.
5. Close the report by choosing **File→Close** from the menu bar.

Delete the report

6. Make sure the Copy of Pets report is chosen in the Reports tab.
7. Choose **Edit→Delete** from the menu bar.
8. **Click Yes** to confirm the deletion.
   Keep in mind that you can delete a report (or other object) whenever you want to "get a fresh start." This technique is useful when using wizards and other automated tools. You may need to use this technique in the Skills Builder and Assessment exercises on the following pages. You will create several reports in these exercises that are more complex than the reports that you just created. If you make mistakes, remember to delete the report and recreate it with the Report Wizard.
9. Now close the Pinnacle Pet Care database by choosing **File→Close** from the menu bar.

Concepts Review

True / False

1. Forms can be used to enter data into a table. 1. **T F**
2. The main benefit of forms is that they allow you to view several records simultaneously. 2. **T F**
3. The navigation buttons at the bottom of a form can be used to move between records. 3. **T F**
4. Forms to not display currency symbols $ and other formatting characters. 4. **T F**
5. The AutoForm tool is initiated by choosing File→AutoForm from the menu bar. 5. **T F**
6. The AutoForm tool creates a form for the table that is selected in the Tables tab of the Access window. 6. **T F**
7. Forms cannot be saved for later use. 7. **T F**
8. The Report Wizard lets you choose the fields that you wish to use in a report. 8. **T F**
9. Reports can be printed. 9. **T F**
10. The Report Wizard lets you choose portrait or landscape orientations. 10. **T F**

Multiple Choice

1. Which of the following buttons is used to initiate the AutoForm tool?
   a) 
   b)  ( )
   c) 
   d) None of the above.

2. Which of the following statements is/are accurate?
   a) Forms can be used to enter records into a table.
   b) Forms can be used to browse through the records in a table.
   c) Forms let you focus on one record at a time.
   d) All of the above. ( )

3. Which of the following commands can you issue through the navigation buttons on a form?
   a) Insert a new record
   b) Delete a record
   c) Change the size of a field
   d) All of the above. ( )

4. Which of the following statements is true?
   a) The Report Wizard lets you choose portrait or landscape orientations.
   b) The Report Wizard lets you choose the fields to include in a report.
   c) The Report Wizard lets you choose a title for the report.
   d) All of the above. ( )

5. The Report Wizard is initiated from which tab in the database window?
   a) Tables tab
   b) Reports tab
   c) Forms tab
   d) Any of the above. ( )

Skills Builder 14.1

The Access window should be open from the previous exercise and all databases should be closed. In this exercise, you will open the Tropical Getaways database from your exercise diskette. You will continue to enhance this database as you progress through the Skills Builder exercises in this course. If you did not accurately complete the Skills Builder exercises in the previous lesson, then ask your instructor to copy the file named **Tropical Getaways – Lesson 14** to your exercise diskette. This file provides the Tropical Getaways database as it should be after completing Lesson 13.

Create a form for the Customers table

1. **Click** the Open button, navigate to your diskette and open the **Tropical Getaways** database.
2. Make sure the **Tables** tab is active.
3. Choose **Customers**, **click** the New Object drop-down button and choose **AutoForm**.

Access will create the form shown below. The form uses all of the fields in the Customers table.

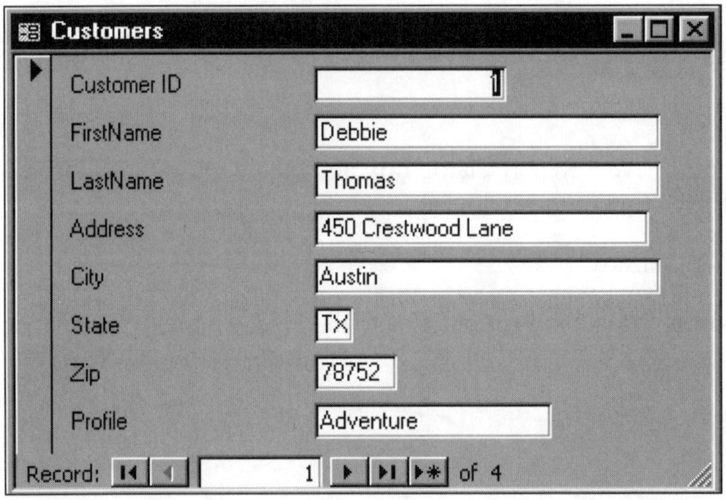

4. **Click** the New Record button on the form's navigation bar and add the following records.

Customer ID	FirstName	LastName	Address	City	State	Zip	Profile
5	Victor	Thomas	2311 Wilmont Street	Danvers	MA	01923	Adventure
6	Lisa	Simms	100 Westside Drive	Batavia	NY	14020	Leisure
7	Ted	Carter	250 Smith Street	Charlton	MA	01507	Family

5. **Click** the Close button on the form and choose **Yes** when Access asks you to save the form.
6. **Click OK** to accept the proposed name Customers.

Create a form for the Trips table

7. Use the AutoForm tool to create a form for the **Trips** table.

Continued...

8. Use the form to add the following records to the Trips table.

TripID	Customer ID	Destination	Category	Departure Date	Return Date	Cost
Adv03	1	Swiss Alps	Adventure	10/10/96	11/5/96	$3,500
Adv04	5	Rocky Mountains	Adventure	5/6/97	5/22/97	$2,190
Adv05	5	Baja California	Adventure	8/8/97	8/18/97	$2,900
Lei02	6	Hawaii	Leisure	2/5/97	2/15/97	$4,500
Fam02	7	Hawaii	Family	3/7/97	3/15/97	$5,300

9. **Close** the **form** and **save** it with the proposed name **Trips**.

   Leave the Tropical Getaways database open because you will continue to use it in the next exercise.

Skills Builder 14.2

In this Skills Builder exercise, you will create reports for the Tropical Getaways database. You will use the sort option in the Report Wizard to sort the records in the reports.

1. **Click** the **Reports tab** in the Tropical Getaways database window.
2. **Click** the New button.
3. Choose **Report Wizard** from the New Report dialog box and then choose the **Customers** table from the drop-down list at the bottom of the dialog box.
4. **Click OK** to initiate the Report Wizard.
5. Add the **FirstName**, **LastName**, **State** and **Profile** fields to the Selected Fields list as follows.

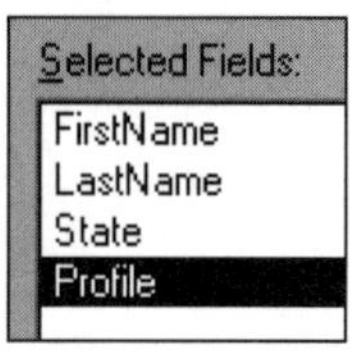

6. **Click** the Next > button **twice** and the sorting screen will appear.
7. **Click** the **drop-down button** on the first sorting box and choose **State** as shown below.

   This will group all records with the same state together in the report. Notice that you could set additional sort options. For example, imagine that you had a large database and you wanted the records sorted first by state and then by zip code within the states. In that situation, you would set the second sort key to zip code.

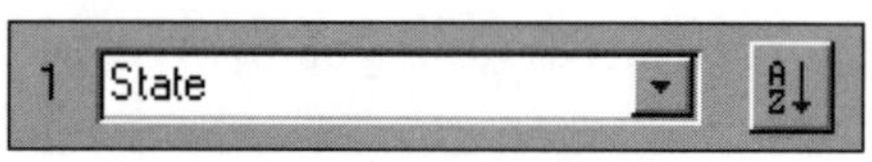

8. **Click** the Next > button **twice** and the report style screen will appear.
9. Choose the **Soft Gray** style and **click** Next >.
10. Type the name **Customer Profiles by State** in the title box of the last screen.
11. **Click** the Finish button to complete the report.

    The completed report is shown on the following page. Notice that the State field appears first in the report and the records for each state are grouped together.

Continued...

Customer Profiles by State

State	FirstName	LastName	Profile
MA	Ted	Carter	Family
MA	Victor	Thomas	Adventure
NY	Lisa	Simms	Leisure
NY	Wilma	Boyd	Leisure
TX	Alice	Simpson	Family
TX	Ted	Wilkins	Adventure
TX	Debbie	Thomas	Adventure

12. **Close** the **report** when you have finished viewing it.

    Access will automatically name the report Customer Profiles by State.

Create a report for the Trips table

13. Now create the report shown below for the Trips table. You will need to start the Report Wizard and choose the appropriate fields from the Trips table. Also, sort the report on the Category field, choose the Soft Gray style and use the title Trips by Category.

Trips by Category

Category	Destination	Cost
Adventure	Baja California	$2,900.00
Adventure	Rocky Mountains	$2,190.00
Adventure	Swiss Alps	$3,500.00
Adventure	Amazon Jungle Trek	$7,765.00
Adventure	Kenyan Safari	$6,600.00
Family	Hawaii	$5,300.00
Family	Orlando	$3,400.00
Leisure	Hawaii	$4,500.00
Leisure	Caribbean Cruise	$2,390.00

14. **Close** the **report** when you have finished viewing it.

    Your Tropical Getaways database should now have two reports: Customer Profiles by State and Trips by Category.

15. Close the Tropical Getaways database with the **File→Close** command.

Assessment 14.1

1. **Open** the **Classic Cars** database.
   You began setting up this database in the assessments in the previous lesson.

2. Use the AutoForm tool to create the form shown below for the Collectors table.

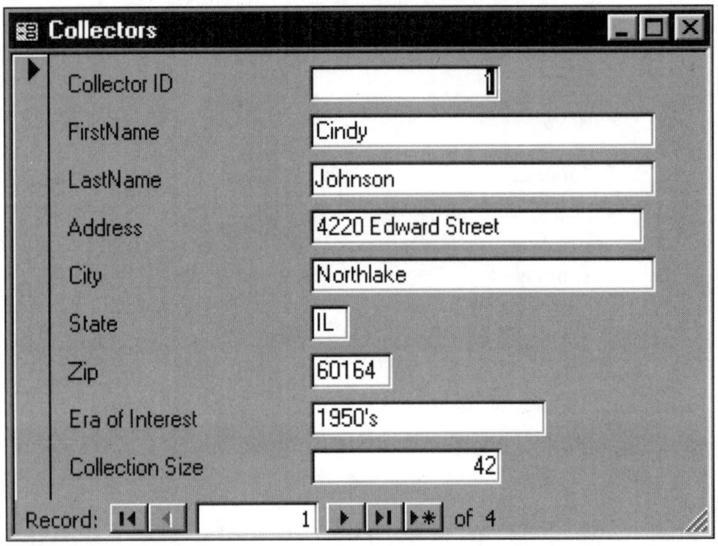

3. Use the form to enter the following new record into the Collectors table.

Collector ID	FirstName	LastName	Address	City	State	Zip	Era of Interest	Collection size
5	Jake	Johnson	840 Edgewood Drive	Arcadia	FL	33821	1920's	3

4. **Close** the **form** and save it with the proposed name **Collectors**.

5. Use the AutoForm tool to create the form shown below for the Cars table.

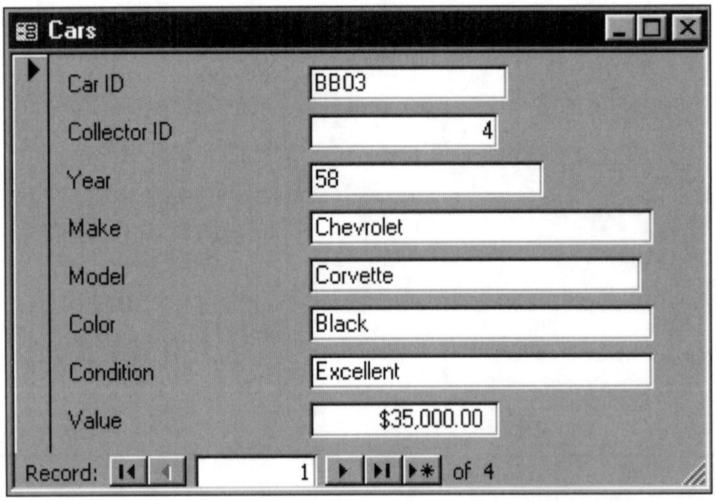

Continued...

6. Use the form to enter the following new records into the table.

Car ID	Collector ID	Year	Make	Model	Color	Condition	Value
CJ04	1	48	Packard	Custom Eight Sedan	White	Fair	$15,000
JJ01	5	27	Ford	Model A	Black	Mint	$75,000
BB04	4	57	Chevrolet	Corvette	Red	Excellent	$42,000

7. **Close** the **form** and save it with the proposed name **Cars**.

8. Create the report shown below for the Collectors table. The report sorts the records by the Era of Interest field and it uses the Compact style. Also notice the title is Era of Interest.

Era of Interest

Era of Interest	FirstName	LastName	Collection Size
1920's	Jake	Johnson	3
1950's	Bob	Barker	7
1950's	Cindy	Johnson	42
1960's	Tammy	Olson	6
Early 1900's	Ed	Larkson	34

9. **Print** the report and then **close** it.

Continued...

10. Create the report shown below for the Cars table. When adding the fields in the first Report Wizard screen, you will need to add them in the order shown on the report. For example, choose the Model field first and click the Add Field button >. Next, choose the Year field and click the Add Field button >. This report is sorted on the Model field and it uses the Compact style.

Models Report

Model	Year	Condition	Color	Value
Corvette	57	Excellent	Red	$42,000.00
Corvette	58	Excellent	Black	$35,000.00
Corvette	62	Excellent	Blue	$30,000.00
Corvette	58	Mint	Red and white	$65,000.00
Custom Eight Sedan	48	Fair	White	$15,000.00
Model A	27	Mint	Black	$75,000.00
Thunderbird	59	Good	Tan	$20,000.00

11. Print the report and then **close** it.

12. Close the Classic Cars **database** when you have finished and continue with the next lesson.

15 Getting Answers with Queries

Objectives:

- Understand query concepts
- Use the query design grid
- Run queries
- Sort query results
- Create criteria to select records
- Create compound criteria
- Create calculated fields
- Use statistical functions
- Use grouping

The Project – Getting Answers in the Pinnacle Pet Care database

The staff at Pinnacle Pet Care needs to have answers to a variety of questions. You will create queries that will provide the answers to these questions. Some of the questions that you will find answers to include the following.

- What is the current balance of each customer in California?
- Which customers have a current balance that is greater than $200?
- Which customers in California have a current balance that is greater than $200?
- What is the average amount of money that customers spend on cats and dogs?

The following illustration shows a query from the Pinnacle Pet Care database, the Customers table from the database and the query results.

Field:	FirstName	LastName	Phone	Current Balance
Table:	Customers	Customers	Customers	Customers
Sort:				Descending
Show:	☑	☑	☑	☑
Criteria:				>200

A query contains fields and criteria that select records from a table.

Customer ID	FirstName	LastName	Address	City	State	Zip	Phone	Last Visit	Current Balance
1	Mark	Roth	760 Maple Avenue	Fremont	CA	94538-	(510) 234-9090	7/7/97	$235.00
2	Tony	Simpson	312 York Lane	Richmond	CA	94804-	(510) 238-2233	9/7/97	$185.00
3	Jason	Jones	2233 Crystal Street	San Mateo	CA	94403-	(415) 312-2312	7/15/97	$48.00
4	Jacob	Samuels	2300 North Pratt Str	Atlanta	GA	30309-	(404) 367-8002	10/8/97	$250.50

FirstName	LastName	Phone	Current Balance
Jacob	Samuels	(404) 367-8002	$250.50
Mark	Roth	(510) 234-9090	$235.00

Access produces query results when the query is run.

What are Queries?

Queries are an essential part of any Access database. Most people use queries to get answers to questions and to extract data from one or more tables in a database. When you run a query, Access creates a temporary table using the fields and criteria you specify in the query. The temporary table is composed of data from one or more tables in your database. The temporary table or "query results" can even be used as the basis for forms and reports. Queries can extract data from more than one table and thus, they give you the ability to produce forms and reports using data from multiple tables.

Select Queries

Select queries are the most common type of query. Select queries let you selectively extract data from one or more tables in a database. When designing select queries, you specify the fields that you wish to include in the query results. You can also specify **criteria** that are used to select records from the table(s) in your database. The following illustration shows the Customers table from the Pinnacle Pet Care database and the results of running a query. Take a few moments to read the text in the illustration.

Customer ID	FirstName	LastName	Address	City	State	Zip	Phone	Last Visit	Current Balance
1	Mark	Roth	760 Maple Avenue	Fremont	CA	94538-	(510) 234-9090	7/7/97	$235.00
2	Tony	Simpson	312 York Lane	Richmond	CA	94804-	(510) 238-2233	9/7/97	$185.00
3	Jason	Jones	2233 Crystal Street	San Mateo	CA	94403-	(415) 312-2312	7/15/97	$48.00
4	Jacob	Samuels	2300 North Pratt Str	Atlanta	GA	30309-	(404) 367-8002	10/8/97	$250.50

Customers Table

A query is run that instructs Access to only choose the FirsName, LastName, Phone and Current Balance fields from the Customers table for those customers with a Current Balance > $200.

FirstName	LastName	Phone	Current Balance
Jacob	Samuels	(404) 367-8002	$250.50
Mark	Roth	(510) 234-9090	$235.00

The query produces the results shown here. Notice that the query results only includes the specified fields for customers with a Current Balance > $200.

Setting Up Queries

You can use the **Query Wizard** to assist you in setting up queries or you can set them up yourself using the **query design grid**. The design grid gives you complete flexibility in determining the tables, fields and options you wish to include in the query. The following Quick Steps show you how to display the Query window and how to add tables to the query. You must add table(s) to the Query window so that you can use the desired fields from the table(s) in the query.

Quick Steps: Adding Tables to the Query Window

To add tables to the Query window

- *Open the desired database and make sure the Queries tab is active in the database window.*
- *Click the New button.*
- *Choose Design View from the New Query box and click OK.*
- *Choose a table that you want the query to extract data from in the Show Table box and click Add.*
- *Add any other tables that you want the query to extract data from.*
- *Click the Close button on the Show Table box.*

Hands-On 15.1 – Display the query design grid and add a table

In this exercise, you will begin setting up a query. You will display the Query window and you will add the Customers table in the Pinnacle Pet Care database to the Query window.

Display the Query window

1. Start Access and **open** the **Pinnacle Pet Care** database.
2. **Click** the **Queries tab** in the Database window.
3. **Click** the New button and the New Query dialog box will appear.
4. Choose **Design View** and **click OK**.

   The Query window will appear and the Show Table dialog box will be displayed. The Show Table dialog box lets you choose the table(s) that you wish to use in the query. In this exercise, you will add just the Customers table to the Query window.

5. Choose **Customers** and **click** the **Add** button.

   A Customers field list will appear above the design grid. The field names in the list are taken from the Customers table. In a moment, you will use the Customers field list to add fields to the query.

6. **Click** the **Close** button on the Show Table dialog box.

   You won't be using the Pets table in this exercise.

Set up the window

7. Make sure the Access window is maximized and the Query window is maximized within the Access window. If you see a Maximize button at the top-right corner of either the Access or Query windows, then click it to maximize the window.
8. Use the following illustration to adjust the size of the design grid and the Customers field list.

❶ *Position the mouse pointer on the top border of the design grid and a double-headed arrow will appear as shown here.*

❷ *Drag the border down to allocate more space to the top-half of the window as shown here.*

❸ *If possible, drag the bottom border of the Customers field list down until all field names are visible as shown here.*

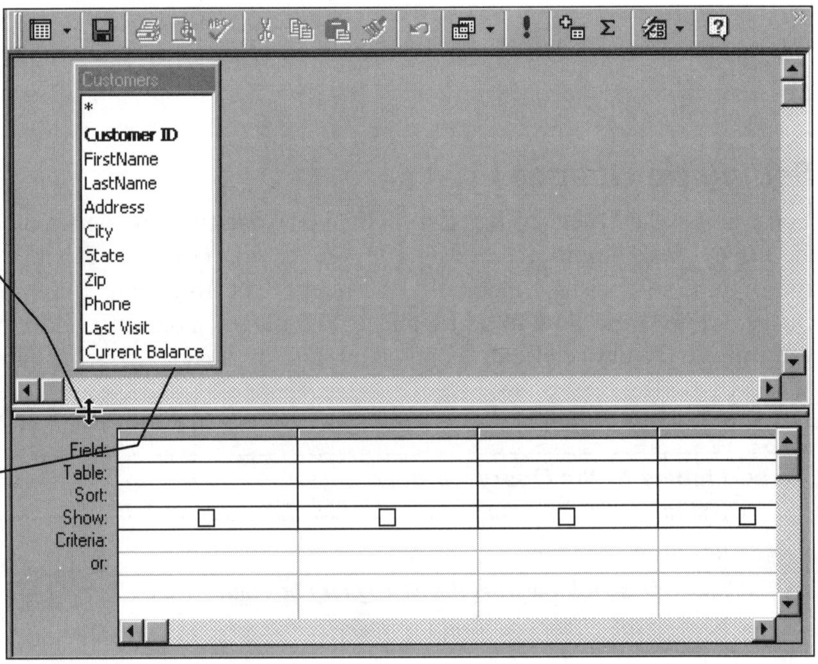

The Design Grid

The design grid appears when you begin setting up a new query. The design grid lets you specify the fields to include in the query. You can also use the design grid to specify criteria and other parameters that affect the output of the query. The following illustration discusses the layout of the design grid and the query output for the sample query shown in the illustration. You will develop the query that is shown in the illustration as you progress through the next few exercises.

Fields such as FirstName, LastName, Phone and Current Balance are added to the columns of the design grid. These fields will be displayed in the query results.

The Table row indicates the table that each field is taken from. In this example, all fields are taken from the Customers table.

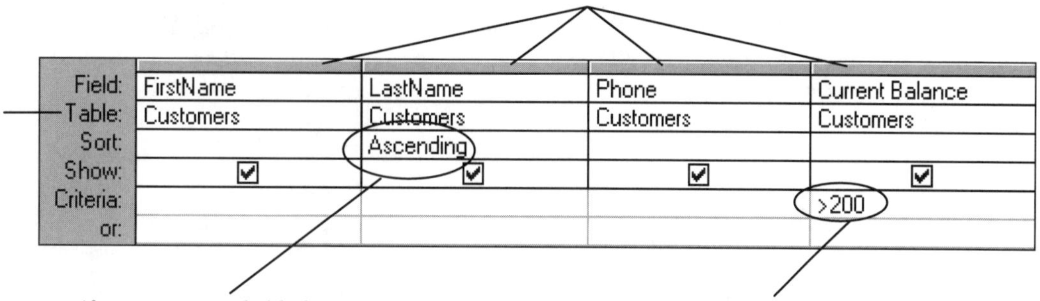

The Sort row lets you specify one or more fields for sorting the selected records. In this example, the query results will be sorted in Ascending order (A-Z) by the LastName field.

You can use criteria to select records from the table(s). In this example, only customer records with a Current Balance greater than $200 will be selected.

The query displays customer records with a Current Balance greater than $200. Only the fields specified in the query are displayed.

FirstName	LastName	Phone	Current Balance
Mark	Roth	(510) 234-9090	$235.00
Jacob	Samuels	(404) 367-8002	$250.50

Adding Fields to the Design Grid

The first step in defining a query is to add fields to the design grid. The fields you add to the design grid will determine the fields that are displayed in the query results. Once you have added fields to the design grid, you can specify sorting options, criteria and other options that affect the query output. The following table discusses the techniques you can use to add fields to the design grid.

Technique	Description
Double-click	You can add a single field to the design grid by double-clicking the desired field in the field list.
Drop-down list	You can add a single field by clicking in a field cell, clicking the drop-down button that appears in the cell and then choosing the desired field from the drop-down menu.
Drag	You can add a single field or multiple fields to the design grid by dragging them from a field list to the desired cell in the design grid. You can select multiple fields prior to dragging them by pressing and holding the Ctrl key while clicking the desired field names in the field list.
All fields	You can add all fields to the design grid by double-clicking the asterisk * symbol at the top of the desired field list.

Hands-On 15.2 – Add fields to the design grid

1. Use the following illustration to add the FirstName field to the design grid.

➊ ***Double-click*** *the* ***FirstName*** *field in the field list and it will appear in the first cell of the design grid as shown here.*

➋ *Notice the* ***Table*** *row specifies that the field is taken from the Customers table. Knowing which table the field is taken from can be important especially when the same field name is used in more than one table.*

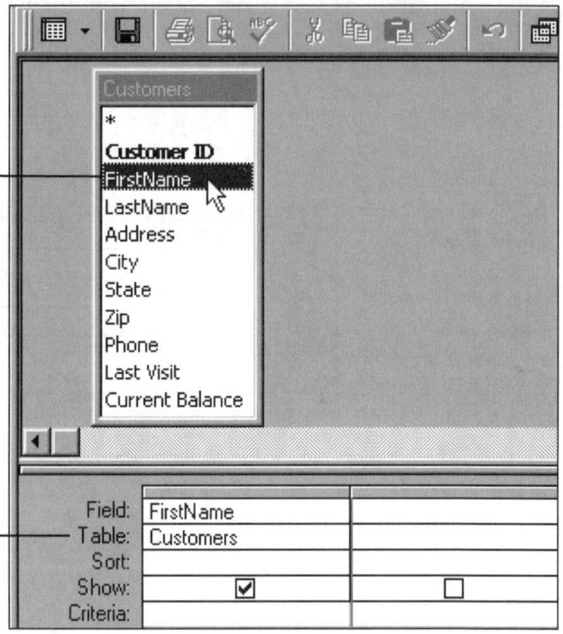

2. Now **add** the **LastName**, **Phone** and **Current Balance** fields to the design grid by double-clicking them on the field name list. The design grid should match the following illustration when you have finished adding the fields.

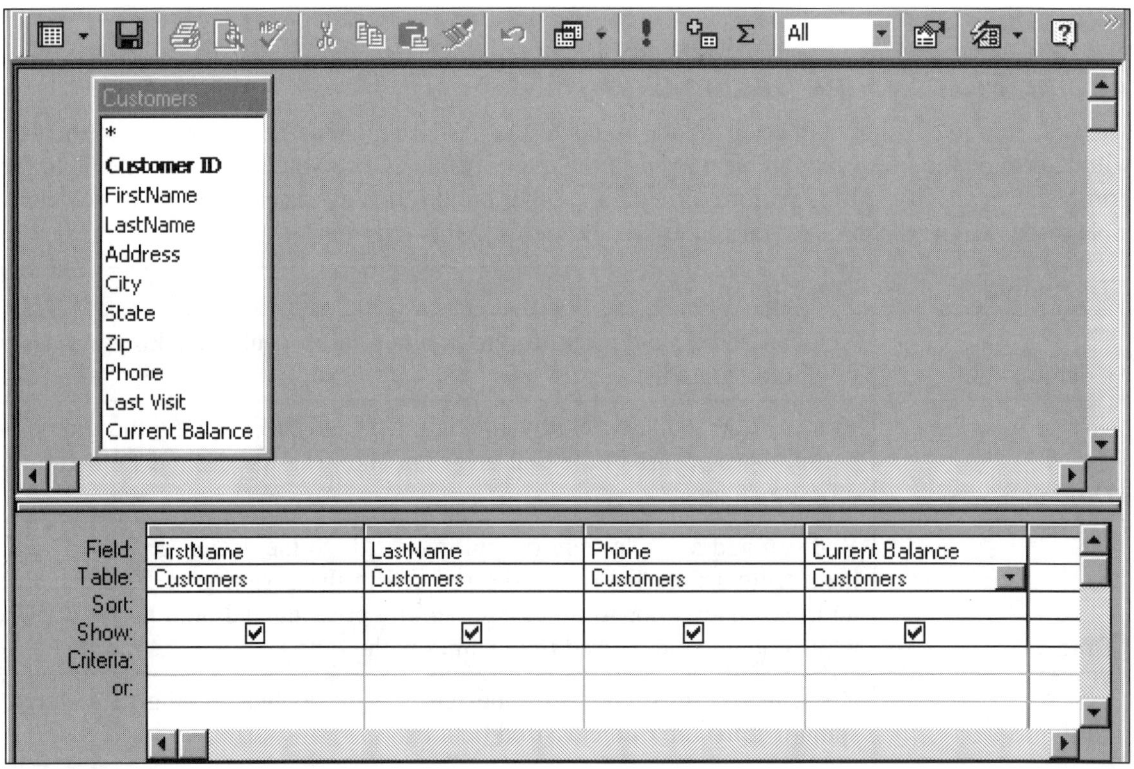

Removing Fields From the Design Grid

You can remove fields from the design grid by clicking in the desired column and choosing **Edit→Delete Columns** from the menu bar. You may need to remove fields from time-to-time as you develop queries. Remember to use this technique if you make a mistake and add an incorrect field to the design grid.

Hands-On 15.3 – Delete a field and then add it using a new technique

1. **Click** anywhere **in** the **Current Balance column** in the design grid.
2. Choose **Edit→Delete Columns** from the menu bar and the field will be removed.
3. Use the following illustration to add the Current Balance field back to the design grid using the drop-down list technique.

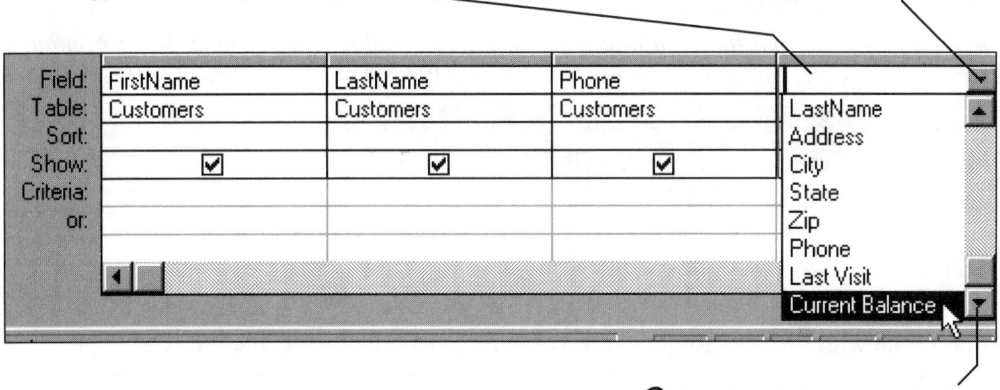

The Current Balance field should be returned to the grid as shown in the illustration at the bottom of the previous page. As you can see, there are several ways to add fields to the design grid. Once again, feel free to remove fields from the design grid whenever you make a mistake or wish to change the order of the fields in the grid.

Running Queries

You can run a query by clicking the Run button on the Access toolbar. When you run a query, Access selects records and fields from tables in your database and displays the results in a datasheet. You can simply view the datasheet or print it if desired. The query results will always reflect the current data from the database.

Editing Data in a Datasheet

When you run a query, Access displays a datasheet with records and fields from the database. The resulting datasheet is connected to the underlying table(s) that the query is based upon. If you edit data in the datasheet, then the data in the underlying tables is changed as well. However, most queries are only used for viewing selective data.

Hands-On 15.4 – Run the query

1. **Click** the Run button on the Access toolbar.

   The query will run and the resulting datasheet shown below will appear. Keep in mind that your query is quite basic. The query simply displays four fields from every record in the Customers table.

FirstName	LastName	Phone	Current Balance
Mark	Roth	(510) 234-9090	$235.00
Tony	Simpson	(510) 238-2233	$185.00
Jason	Jones	(415) 312-2312	$48.00
Jacob	Samuels	(404) 367-8002	$250.50

2. Now continue with the next topic where you will learn how to sort the query results.

Sorting the Results

You can instruct Access to sort the rows in the resulting datasheet using one or more fields as sort keys. For example, you may want to view the resulting datasheet with the largest current balances displayed first. You sort query results by setting the sort box to Ascending or Descending for one or more fields in the design grid. If you set the sort box for more than one field, then the first field is used as the primary sort key followed by the next field and so on.

Hands-On 15.5 – Sort the results

The resulting datasheet should be displayed from the previous exercise.

1. Notice that the records in the datasheet do not appear to be sorted in any particular order.

   However, the records are actually sorted on the Customer ID field, which is the primary key for the Customers table. In the next few steps, you will sort the records based upon the LastName field. You will run the query again and the resulting datasheet will be organized with the Jones record first followed by the Roth record and so on.

2. **Click** the Design View button on the left end of the Access toolbar.

   The Query window and the design grid will reappear. You can always use the view button to switch back and forth between datasheet and design views.

3. Use the following illustration to set a sort key.

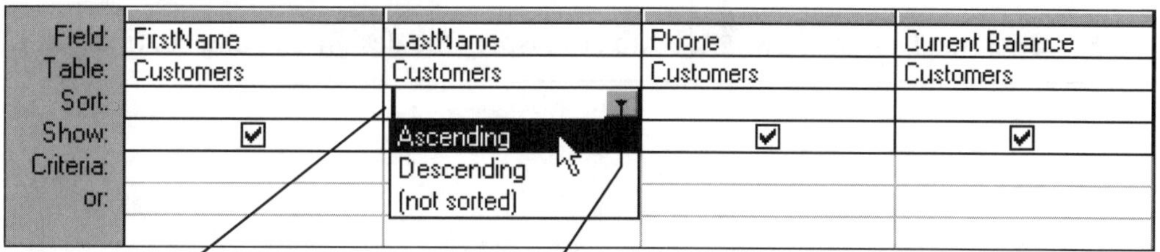

❶ ***Click** in the **Sort box** for the **LastName** field.*

❷ ***Click** the **drop-down button** and choose Ascending from the list as shown here. The word Ascending will appear in the Sort box.*

4. **Click** the Run button and the resulting datasheet shown below will appear.

   Notice that the records are sorted based upon the LastName field.

FirstName	LastName	Phone	Current Balance
Jason	Jones	(415) 312-2312	$48.00
Mark	Roth	(510) 234-9090	$235.00
Jacob	Samuels	(404) 367-8002	$250.50
Tony	Simpson	(510) 238-2233	$185.00

5. **Click** the Design View button to display the design grid.

Continued...

6. Use the following illustration to remove the LastName sort key and to set the sort order to descending based upon the Outstanding Balance field.

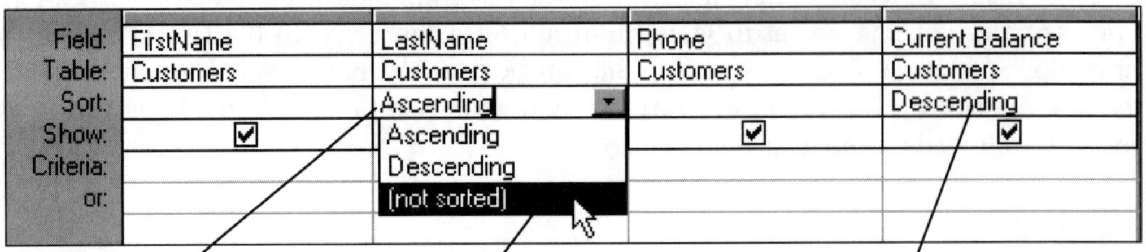

❶ ***Click** in the **Sort box** for the **LastName** field.*

❷ ***Click** the drop-down **button** and choose **(not sorted)** as shown here. The Sort box will be cleared.*

❸ *Choose **Descending** as the sort order for the Current Balance field.*

7. **Click** the Run button and the resulting datasheet shown below will appear.
   Notice that the records with the largest Current Balance are displayed first.

FirstName	LastName	Phone	Current Balance
Jacob	Samuels	(404) 367-8002	$250.50
Mark	Roth	(510) 234-9090	$235.00
Tony	Simpson	(510) 238-2233	$185.00
Jason	Jones	(415) 312-2312	$48.00

8. **Click** the Design View button to display the design grid and continue with the next topic.

Using Criteria to Select Records

One of the most important benefits of queries is they let you select records by specifying **criteria**. This gives you the ability to extract the data you desire from a database. For example, you may want to know how many customers have an outstanding balance that is greater than $200. Or perhaps you are interested in viewing only those records where the state is equal to CA (California). These and other questions are easily answered by specifying criteria in the query design grid.

Equality Criteria

You can instruct Access to choose only those records where a field has a specific value. For example, you may want to display only those records where the state field is equal to CA. You accomplish this by entering the desired value that you want the field to equal in the Criteria row of the design grid. The following illustration shows how this is accomplished.

Field:	FirstName	LastName	Phone	Current Balance	State
Table:	Customers	Customers	Customers	Customers	Customers
Sort:				Descending	
Show:	☑	☑	☑	☑	☑
Criteria:					CA
or:					

This is the Criteria row.

Entering CA in the State Criteria box instructs Access to display only those records where the state is equal to CA.

As expected, only records where the state = CA are displayed when the query is run.

FirstName	LastName	Phone	Current Balance	State
Mark	Roth	(510) 234-9090	$235.00	CA
Tony	Simpson	(510) 238-2233	$185.00	CA
Jason	Jones	(415) 312-2312	$48.00	CA

Comparison Criteria

You can use the comparison operators > (greater than), < (less than), >= (greater than or equal to), <= (less than or equal to) and NOT (not equal to) to specify criteria as well. Access will display only those records that match the criteria. For example, placing the criterion >200 in the Current Balance field instructs Access to only display records where the Current Balance is greater than 200.

The Show Check Box

The Show row in the design grid contains a check box ☑ for each field. You can prevent a field from being displayed in the query results by removing the check from the Show box. This can be useful in many situations. For example, in the illustration above, the State field is used to select only records where the state is equal to CA. The State field must be present in the design grid in order to specify this criteria. However, you may not want the State field to be displayed in the query results. You could prevent the State field from being displayed in the query results by removing the check from the State field in the design grid.

Hands-On 15.6 – Use criteria

The design grid should be displayed from the previous exercise.

Use an equality criterion

1. **Double-click** the **State field** on the Customers field list to add the field to the design grid.
   The State field should be in the fifth column of the design grid as shown below.

2. Use the following illustration to set a criterion for the State field.

Field:	FirstName	LastName	Phone	Current Balance	State
Table:	Customers	Customers	Customers	Customers	Customers
Sort:				Descending	
Show:	☑	☑	☑	☑	☑
Criteria:					CA
or:					

❶ ***Click** in the **Criteria box** for the **State** field.*

❷ *Type **CA** as shown here. You can type it in uppercase (CA) or lowercase (ca).*

❸ ***Click** in the box below CA and Access will surround CA with quotation marks **"CA"**. The quotation marks indicate that this is a text criterion (as opposed to a number or date).*

3. **Click** the Run button.
   The three records with the State field equal to CA will be displayed as shown on the previous page.

4. **Click** the Design View button to display the design grid.

Use comparison criteria

5. Use the following illustration to create a greater than comparison criterion for the Current Balance field.

Field:	FirstName	LastName	Phone	Current Balance	State
Table:	Customers	Customers	Customers	Customers	Customers
Sort:				Descending	
Show:	☑	☑	☑	☑	☑
Criteria:				>200	

❶ ***Click** in the **Criteria box** for the Current Balance field and type **>200** as shown here.*

❷ ***Click** in the Criteria box for the State field and **delete** the **"CA"** criterion as shown here.*

6. **Click** the Run button and the results shown below will appear.
   Notice that the current balance is greater than $200 for each selected record.

FirstName	LastName	Phone	Current Balance	State
Jacob	Samuels	(404) 367-8002	$250.50	GA
Mark	Roth	(510) 234-9090	$235.00	CA

7. **Click** the Design View button again to display the design grid.

8. Change the >200 criterion to **<200** and **run** the **query** again.
   Only records with current balances that are less than $200 will be displayed.

Continued...

Uncheck the Show box for the State field

In the next few steps, you will prevent the State field from displaying in the results by removing the check from the Show box.

9. **Click** the Design View button to display the design grid.
10. Use the following illustration to set up the query.

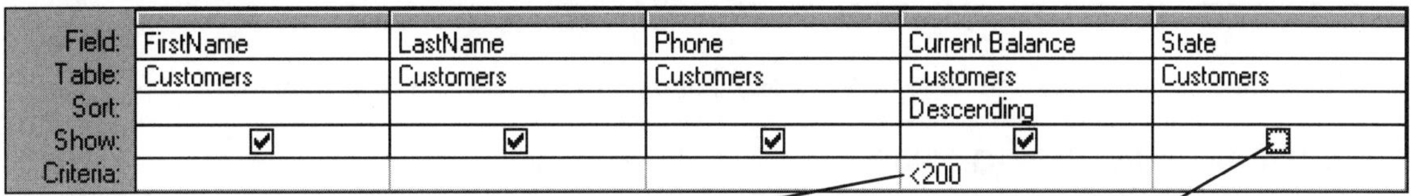

❶ *Make sure the Current Balance criteria is set to <200 as shown here.*

❷ ***Click*** *the Show* ***check box*** *for the State field and the check will be removed as shown here.*

11. **Click** the Run button and the State field will no longer be visible in the results.
12. Take 10 minutes to experiment with the query you have been using. Try entering various criteria and perhaps adding and removing fields from the design grid.
13. Continue with the next topic when you have finished experimenting.

Clearing the Design Grid

You can clear all entries from the design grid with the **Edit→Clear Grid** command. This command can be used to give you a "fresh start" when working in the design grid.

Hands-On 15.7 – Clear the grid and use the asterisk to add all fields to the grid

1. If necessary, click the Design View button to display the design grid.
2. Choose **Edit→Clear Grid** to remove all fields from the grid.
3. Use the following illustration to add all fields from the Customers table to the design grid.

❶ ***Double-click*** *the* ***asterisk*** ** at the top of the Customers field list.*

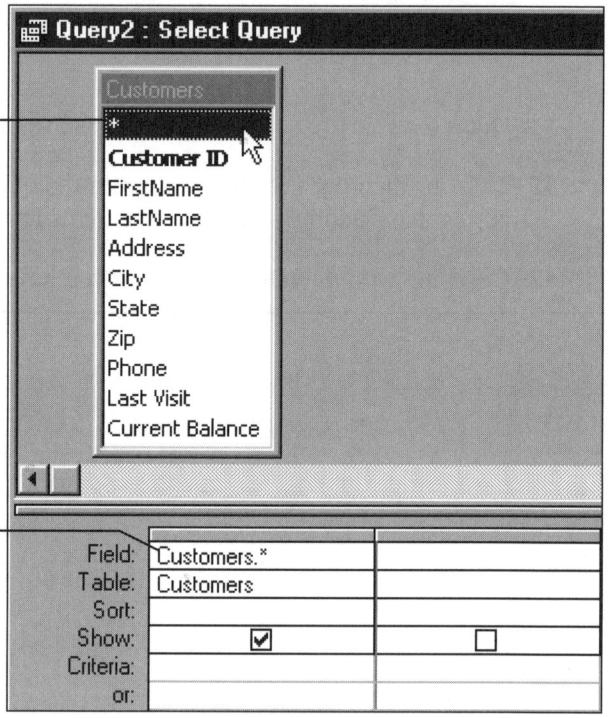

❷ *Notice that a Customers.* entry is inserted in the grid. This entry indicates that all fields from the Customers table will be displayed when the query is run.*

4. **Click** the Run button and all records from the Customers table should be displayed.

Use a criterion to select records

In the next few steps, you will add the Current Balance field to the design grid and specify a criterion for that field.

5. **Click** the Design View button to display the design grid.

Continued...

6. Use the following steps to add the Current Balance field to the grid and to specify a criterion.

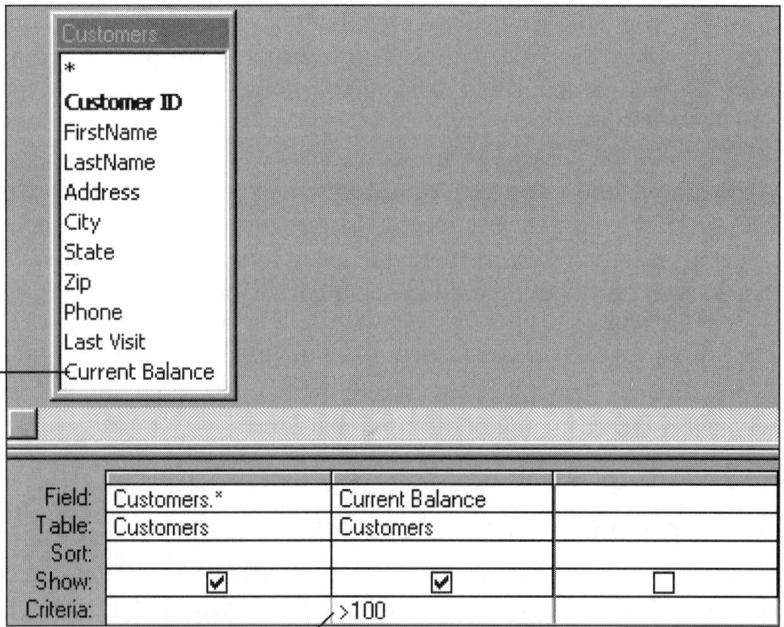

❶ ***Double-click** the **Current Balance** field on the Customers field list. The Current Balance will be added to the design grid as shown in the lower section of this illustration.*

❷ *Enter the expression **>100** in the Criteria box of the Current Balance field.*

7. Run the query and the results shown below will be displayed.

Notice that the query results contains a Customers.Current Balance field and a Field0 field on the right-end of the datasheet. This unusual nomenclature was used because the Current Balance field was included twice in the query design grid. It was included once as part of the Customers. entry and again as a separate field in the second column. Access cannot display the same field name twice in a table or datasheet. Therefore, Access changed the names of the column headings in the query results because it could not display the Current Balance heading twice. You will correct this by removing the check from the Show box in the next few steps.*

Customer ID	FirstName	LastName	Address	City	State	Zip	Phone	Last Visit	Customers.Curre	Field0
1	Mark	Roth	760 Maple Avenue	Fremont	CA	94538-	(510) 234-9090	7/7/97	$235.00	$235.00
2	Tony	Simpson	312 York Lane	Richmond	CA	94804-	(510) 238-2233	9/7/97	$185.00	$185.00
4	Jacob	Samuels	2300 North Pratt Str	Atlanta	GA	30309-	(404) 367-8002	10/8/97	$250.50	$250.50

8. Switch to Design View and remove the check from the Show box for the Current Balance field. The design grid should match the following example.

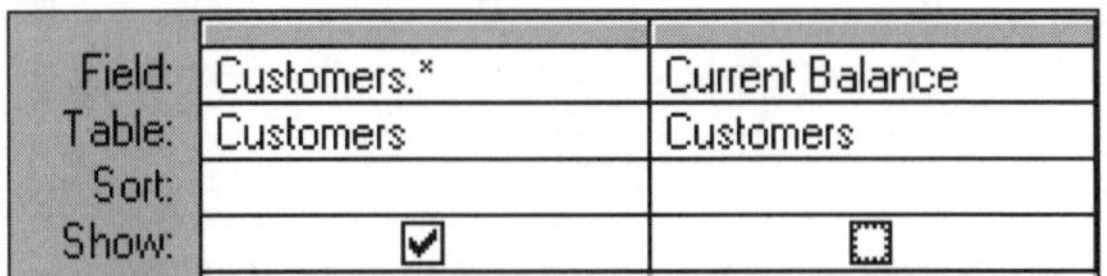

9. **Run** the **query** and only one Current Balance field will be visible.

Notice that only records with a Current Balance >$100 are displayed.

Close the query and save it

In the next few steps, you will close the query and save it. You can save queries for later use as you can save any other object in an Access database.

10. Choose **File→Close** from the menu bar and **click** the **Yes** button to save the query.

11. **Type** the name **Current Balance** in the Save As box and **click OK**.

Compound Criteria

Thus far, you have worked with relatively simple queries that contained at most one criterion. However, there are times that you will need to use more than one criterion. Criteria that are composed of two or more criteria are known as compound criteria. There are two types of compound criteria; AND criteria and OR criteria.

AND criteria allow you to select records based on logical AND expressions. In the next exercise, you will use AND criteria to select records in the Pets table. For example, you will use an AND expression to select all records where the pet type is dog **and** the number of visits is greater than 5. With AND criteria, Access will only select records when all of the criteria are true.

OR criteria allow you to select records based on logical OR expressions. For example, you will use an OR expression to select all records where the pet type is dog **or** the pet type is cat. With OR criteria, Access will select records if any of the criteria are true.

Setting up Compound Criteria

You set up compound criteria in the design grid. AND criteria are set up by placing the various criteria in different fields within the same Criteria row. OR criteria are set up by placing the various criteria on different rows within the design grid. The following illustration discusses the compound criteria that you will set up in the next exercise.

Field:	Pet Name	Pet Type	Last Visit	Expenditures	Number of Visits
Table:	Pets	Pets	Pets	Pets	Pets
Sort:					
Show:	☑	☑	☑	☑	☑
Criteria:		"dog"			>5

*In this example, the criteria "dog" and >5 are on the same Criteria row. This creates an AND condition. Only records where the Pet Type = dog **and** the Number of Visits > 5 will be chosen.*

Field:	Pet Name	Pet Type	Last Visit	Expenditures	Number of Visits
Table:	Pets	Pets	Pets	Pets	Pets
Sort:					
Show:	☑	☑	☑	☑	☑
Criteria:		"dog"			
or:		"cat"			

*In this example, the criteria are on different rows within the Pet Type field. This creates an OR condition as indicated by the **or** heading at the left end of the second row. All records where the Pet Type = dog **or** the Pet Type = cat will be chosen.*

Hands-On 15.8 – Use compound criteria

In this exercise, you will set up a new query using the Pets table from the Pinnacle Pet Care database. You will use compound criteria to query the database in various ways.

Set up the query window

1. Make sure the Queries tab is active in the Pinnacle Pet Care database window.
2. **Click** the New button and the New Query dialog box will appear.
3. Choose **Design View** and **click OK**.
4. Choose **Pets** from the Show Table box and **click** the **Add** button.
5. **Click** the **Close** button on the Show Table dialog box.
6. If necessary, maximize the query window. Also, you may want to adjust the size of the design grid and the Pets field list to allow you to see the entire content of the Pets field list. You used this technique in the first exercise in this lesson with the Customers field list.

Create an AND criterion

7. **Double-click** the **Pet Name**, **Pet Type**, **Last Visit**, **Expenditures** and **Number of Visits** fields on the Pets field list to add those fields to the design grid.
8. Enter the criteria shown below into the Pet Type and Number of Visits boxes in the Criteria row.

Field:	Pet Name	Pet Type	Last Visit	Expenditures	Number of Visits
Table:	Pets	Pets	Pets	Pets	Pets
Sort:					
Show:	☑	☑	☑	☑	☑
Criteria:		"dog"			>5

9. **Click** the Run button and the query results shown below will be displayed.

   Notice that both records have Dog as the Pet Type and the Number of Visits is greater than 5.

Pet Name	Pet Type	Last Visit	Expenditures	Number of Visits
Wolfy	Dog	7/15/97	$450.00	7
Spike	Dog	10/8/97	$890.00	12

Create an OR criterion

10. Switch to Design View and **remove** the **>5** criteria from the Number of Visits criteria box.
11. **Add** the **cat** criterion to the row below the "dog" criterion as shown below.

   When using OR criteria, you can use as many rows as necessary. Each row that you add creates one more condition in the OR expression.

Field:	Pet Name	Pet Type	Last Visit	Expenditures	Number of Visits
Table:	Pets	Pets	Pets	Pets	Pets
Sort:					
Show:	☑	☑	☑	☑	☑
Criteria:		"dog"			
or:		"cat"			

Continued...

12. Click the Run button and the query results shown below will be displayed.

Notice that all of the records have a Pet Type of Dog or Cat.

Pet Name	Pet Type	Last Visit	Expenditures	Number of Visits
Wolfy	Dog	7/15/97	$450.00	7
Dillon	Dog	7/7/97	$150.55	3
Max	Cat	9/7/97	$1,450.55	20
Stripes	Cat	7/15/97	$450.00	9
Tony	Cat	7/7/97	$145.00	6
Ben	Dog	10/8/97	$480.00	3
Spike	Dog	10/8/97	$890.00	12

Use a combination of AND and OR compound criteria

13. Switch to Design View but do not change the "dog" and "cat" criteria.

14. Add the **>5** criteria to the Number of Visits field as shown below.

This compound criteria will choose all records where the Pet Type is dog ***and*** *the Number of Visits is greater than 5* ***OR*** *the Pet Type is cat* ***and*** *the Number of Visits is greater than 5.*

Field:	Pet Name	Pet Type	Last Visit	Expenditures	Number of Visits
Table:	Pets	Pets	Pets	Pets	Pets
Sort:					
Show:	☑	☑	☑	☑	☑
Criteria:		"dog"			>5
or:		"cat"			>5

15. Click the Run button and the query results shown below will be displayed.

Pet Name	Pet Type	Last Visit	Expenditures	Number of Visits
Wolfy	Dog	7/15/97	$450.00	7
Max	Cat	9/7/97	$1,450.55	20
Stripes	Cat	7/15/97	$450.00	9
Tony	Cat	7/7/97	$145.00	6
Spike	Dog	10/8/97	$890.00	12

16. Switch back **to design view** and take 10 minutes to experiment with compound criteria.

Be creative and query the Pets table for answers to any questions that may come to mind.

17. When you have finished experimenting, choose **File→Close** from the menu bar and **click** the **Yes** button when Access asks if you want to save the query.

18. Type the name **Compound Criteria** in the Save As box and **click OK**.

19. Now continue with the next topic where you will continue to develop your querying skills.

Calculated Fields

Access lets you create calculated fields within queries. Calculated fields perform calculations using values from other fields within the query or from fields in the underlying table(s). For example, in the next exercise, you will set up a new query that is based upon the Pets table. The Pets table contains an Expenditures field that represents the total expenditures for a particular pet and a Number of Visits field that represents the total number of visits by that pet. You will create a calculated field within the query named Expenditures Per Visit. The Expenditures Per Visit will be calculated as the Expenditures divided by the Number of Visits. The following illustration shows the design grid with the Pet Name and Pet Type fields and the Expenditures Per Visit calculated field.

Expenditures Per Visit is a calculated field and it is too wide to be completely visible in the cell. The complete content of the cell is **Expenditures Per Visit: [Expenditures]/[Number of Visits].**

Field:	Pet Name	Pet Type	Expenditures Pe
Table:	Pets	Pets	
Sort:			
Show:	☑	☑	☑
Criteria:			

The following illustration discusses the syntax that must be used with calculated fields.

A descriptive name for the calculated field is entered into an empty Field cell. You can use spaces in the name as shown here.

A colon : must follow the name. The colon identifies the field as a calculated field.

*An expression follows the colon. The expression can include field names, numbers and operators such as +, -, * and /. The various parts of the expression are surrounded with brackets.*

Expenditure Per Visit: [Expenditures]/[Number of Visits]

The Zoom Dialog Box

Calculated field expressions can be quite long and complex. For this reason, you may not be able to see the entire expression as you enter it in a cell. Fortunately, Access provides a Zoom command that displays a Zoom dialog box. You can enter the desired expression into the Zoom dialog box. This way, you can see the entire expression as it is entered. In the following exercise, you will use the Zoom dialog box to enter an expression. You display the Zoom dialog box by **right-clicking** the cell where the expression will be entered and choosing **Zoom...** from the pop up menu.

Hands-On 15.9 – Create a calculated field

The Queries tab should be visible in the Database window from the previous exercise.

1. Set up a **new query** in Design view and **add** the **Pets table** to the query.
2. **Close** the **Show Tables** dialog box.
3. **Add** the **Pet Name** and **Pet Type** fields to the design grid.

Continued...

4. Use the following illustration to display the Zoom dialog box.

❶ **Click** *in the empty field cell to the right of Pet Type.* ❷ **Click** *the* **right** *mouse button (right-click) and the menu shown here will pop up.* ❸ *Choose* **Zoom** *from the menu.*

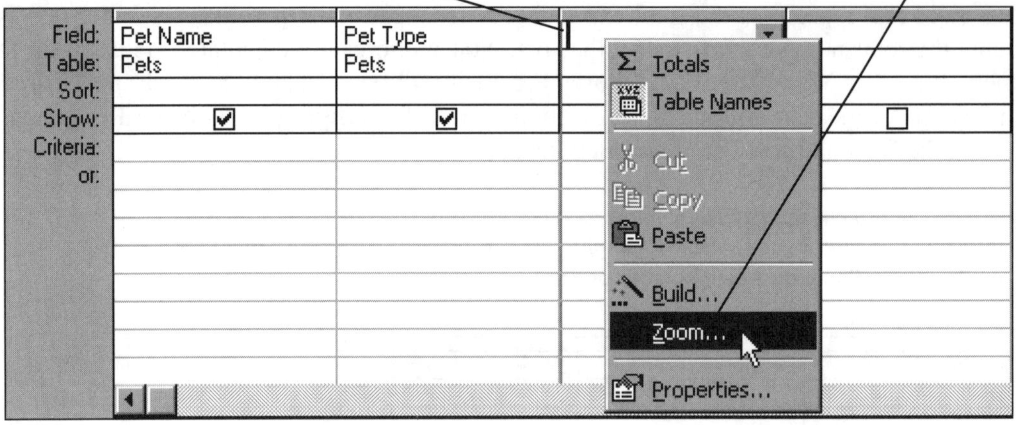

5. Enter the calculated field expression shown below into the dialog box. Make sure you enter the expression exactly as shown. In particular, make sure you use a colon **:** (not a semicolon ;), correctly spell the field names, use the correct open and closed brackets [ ] and use the forward slash / symbol to represent division. Access is leniant when it comes to spaces, so you can omit the spaces that come after the colon and before and after the forward slash / if you desire.

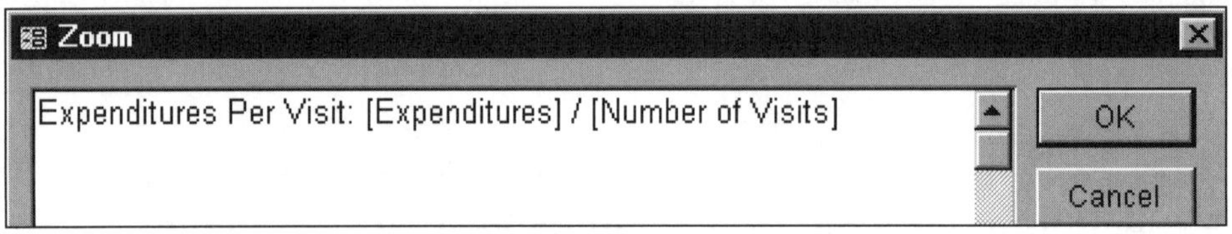

6. **Click OK** to insert the expression in the field.

7. Use the left arrow and right arrow keys on your keyboard to scroll through the expression within the cell. Make sure the syntax is correct as shown above. If necessary, you can edit the expression within the cell or redisplay the Zoom dialog box and make any necessary changes.

8. **Click** the Run button and the query results shown below will be displayed.

   The numbers shown in the Expenditures Per Visit field represent the average expenditure for each pet on each visit. Notice the excessive number of decimal places that are displayed in the calculated field. In the next exercise, you will reduce the number of displayed decimals by changing one of the properties of the Expenditures Per Visit field.

Pet Name	Pet Type	Expenditures I
Max	Cat	72.5275
Stripes	Cat	50
Tony	Cat	24.1666666667
Wolfy	Dog	64.2857142857
Dillon	Dog	50.1833333333
Ben	Dog	160
Spike	Dog	74.1666666667
Bugs	Rabbit	150.125

9. Switch to Design View and continue with the next topic.

Setting Properties

Access lets you set properties for fields, calculated fields and other types of Access objects. The property settings for number fields determine the format of the numbers including the number of displayed decimals. In the following exercise, you will use properties to format the Expenditures Per Visit calculated field. You display the Properties dialog box by choosing the desired object and clicking the Properties button on the Access toolbar.

Hands-On 15.10 – Set the Format property for the Expenditures Per Visit field

The query design grid should be displayed from the previous exercise.

1. **Click** in the **Expenditures Per Visit box** and then **click** the Properties button on the toolbar.

   The Field Properties dialog box will appear.

2. Use the following steps to set the format of this field to Currency.

   When the query is run, the Currency format will display a dollar sign and two decimals in the Expenditures Per Visit field.

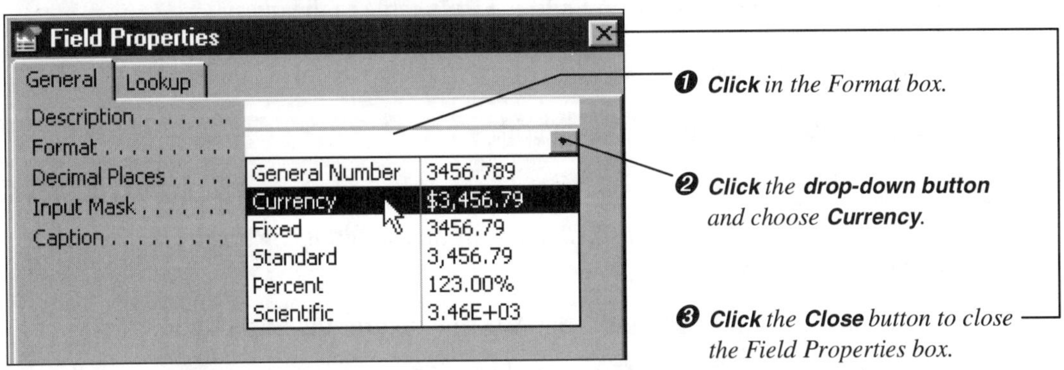

3. **Click** the Run button.

   The numbers in the Expenditures Per Visit field should now be formatted with the currency format, which includes a dollar sign $ and two decimals.

4. Switch to Design View.

Enter a criterion

5. **Click** in the Criteria box for the Pet Type field and type **dog** as shown below.

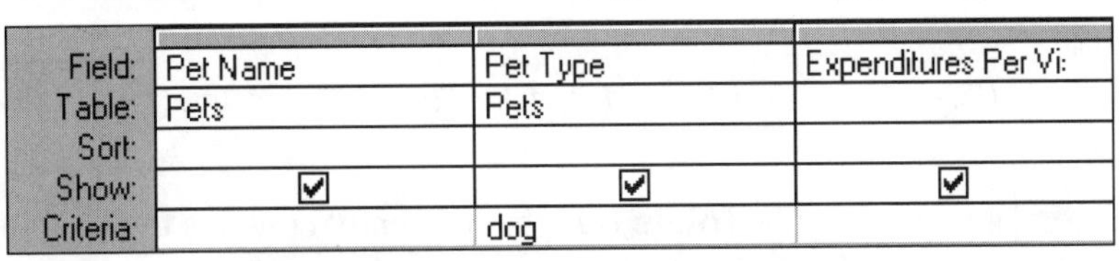

6. **Click** the Run button.

   The Pet Name, Pet Type and Expenditures Per Visit will be displayed for records where the Pet Type is Dog. As you can see, Access allows you to combine criteria, calculated fields and other parameters within a query.

7. Choose **File→Close** to close the query and **save** it with the name **Expenditures Per Visit**.

Statistical Functions

Access provides built-in statistical functions that make it easy to compute statistical information for fields in a query. The built-in statistical functions include Sum (summation), Avg (average), Min (minimum), Max (maximum) and Count. For example, you could use the Avg function to compute the average expenditures on pets or you may want to use the Count function to count the number of Dogs that attend the Pinnacle Pet Care clinic.

The Total Row

To use the statistical functions, you must first click the Totals button to display a Total row in the query design grid. Once the Total row is displayed, you can choose statistical function(s) for the desired field(s) in the query. Queries that use statistical functions will normally have just one or two fields.

Hands-On 15.11 – Use statistical functions

The Queries tab should be visible in the Database window from the previous exercise.

1. Set up a new query in Design view and **add** the **Pets** table to the query.
2. **Close** the **Show Tables** dialog box.
3. **Add** the **Expenditures field** to the design grid.
4. **Click** the Totals button on the toolbar and a Total row will appear below the Table row.
   The Total row lets you choose statistical functions and set grouping for fields. You will learn about grouping later in this lesson.
5. Use the following illustration to choose the Avg function for the Expenditures field.

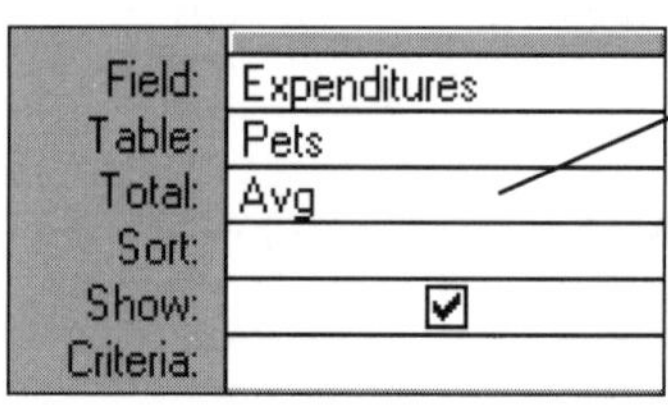

❶ **Click** *in the Total box and a drop-down button will appear.*

❷ **Click** *the* **drop-down button** *and choose* ***Avg.***

When you run the query, Access will determine the average expenditure for all pets. Access will display a single cell in the resulting datasheet that contains the result of the average calculation.

6. **Click** the Run button
   The result should be $577.08. In other words, each pet has been responsible for an average of $577.08 in revenue.
7. Switch to Design View and **click** in the **Totals box** that currently contains the Avg function.
8. **Click** the **drop-down button**, **scroll up** to the top of the list and **choose Sum**.
9. Run the query again and this time the result should be $4,616.60.
   This number represents the summation of the expenditures for all pets.
10. Switch to Design View and continue with the next topic.

Using Criteria with Statistical Functions

You can combine criteria with statistical functions to refine your statistical calculations. For example, imagine that you are interested in determining the total expenditures for dogs at Pinnacle Pet Care. The answer can be found by summing the Expenditures of all records where the Pet Type is dog. The following illustration shows how this is expressed in the design grid.

The Expenditures field uses the Sum function.

The Pet Type field is added to the design grid and the Where function is chosen in the Total cell.

Field:	Expenditures	Pet Type
Table:	Pets	Pets
Total:	Sum	Where
Sort:		
Show:	☑	☐
Criteria:		dog

The word dog is entered in the criteria cell for the Pet Type field.

These settings will sum the expenditures of all records where the Pet Type is equal to dog.

Hands-On 15.12 – Use criteria with statistical functions

1. **Double-click** the **Pet Type field** on the Pets field list to add it to the design grid.
2. Use the following illustration to specify criteria for the Pet Type field.

Field:	Expenditures	Pet Type
Table:	Pets	Pets
Total:	Sum	Where
Sort:		
Show:	☑	☐
Criteria:		dog

❶ **Click** *in the* **Total box**, **click** *the* **drop-down button** *that appears,* **scroll to the bottom** *of the list and* **choose Where** *as shown here.*

❷ **Click** *in the Criteria box and type* **dog**.

3. **Run** the **query** and the result should be $1,970.55.
   This number represents the total expenditures on dogs.
4. Switch back to **Design view** and continue with the last topic in this long lesson.

Using Grouping with Statistical Functions

The Total row in the design grid has a Group By option that can be used in conjunction with statistical functions. If you choose Group By for a field and run the query, then Access will group all records together that have the same value in the Group By field. For example, if the Pet Type field is set to Group By, then all records that have cat as the pet type will be in one group and all records that have dog as the pet type will be in another group. If you are performing a statistical calculation as well, then the statistical calculation will be performed on each group. For example, if you use the Sum function to calculate the expenditures for the groups mentioned above, then the total expenditures for cats will be calculated, as will the total expenditures for dogs.

Hands-On 15.13 – Use the Group By setting

1. Use the following illustration to set grouping for the Pet Type field.

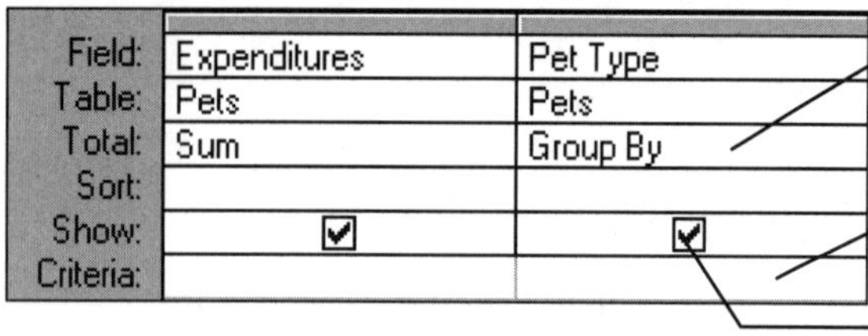

❶ ***Click** in the **Total box**, **click** the **drop-down button**, **scroll up** and choose **Group By**.*

❷ ***Click** in the **Criteria box** and **delete** the **dog** criteria.*

❸ *Make sure the Show box is checked as shown here.*

2. **Run** the **query** and the results shown below will appear.

   The results represent the total expenditures for each type of pet.

SumOfExpend	Pet Type
$2,045.55	Cat
$1,970.55	Dog
$600.50	Rabbit

3. Switch back to Design view.
4. Take 15-30 minutes to practice all of the querying techniques you have learned in this lesson.
5. When you have finished experimenting, **close** the **query** and **save** it with the name **Expenditures by Pet Type**.
6. Now use the **File→Close** command again to close the Pinnacle Pet Care database.
7. Continue with the end-of-lesson questions and exercises on the following pages.

Concepts Review

True / False

1.	Criteria determine the records that are selected in a query.	1.	**T**	**F**
2.	The query design grid is where you define a query.	2.	**T**	**F**
3.	You can add fields to the design grid by double-clicking the desired fields on the field list(s) above the design grid.	3.	**T**	**F**
4.	You can add all fields to the design grid by double-clicking any field in the field list.	4.	**T**	**F**
5.	Changing data in the datasheet that a query produces has no impact on the underlying data in the table(s) that the query is based upon.	5.	**T**	**F**
6.	Queries can only be sorted in ascending order.	6.	**T**	**F**
7.	You must type criteria in the same case (uppercase or lowercase) as the data in the tables you are querying or Access will not select the desired records.	7.	**T**	**F**
8.	If a field has been entered into the design grid, then there is no way to prevent the field from displaying in the query results.	8.	**T**	**F**
9.	The two types of compound criteria are Sum and Avg.	9.	**T**	**F**
10.	The Zoom dialog box can be used to enter expressions in calculated fields.	10.	**T**	**F**

Multiple Choice

1. Which of the following commands can be used to remove fields from the design grid?
   a) Field→Remove
   b) Edit→Delete Columns
   c) Edit→Delete Rows
   d) File→Delete Columns

   ( )

2. Which of the following buttons is used to run a query?
   a) 
   b) 
   c) 
   d) None of the above

   ( )

3. Which of the following symbols is used to represent **greater than** in query criteria?
   a) <
   b) >
   c) <=
   d) >=

   ( )

4. Which of the following commands is used to clear the design grid?
   a) File→Clear All
   b) File→Clear Grid
   c) Edit→Clear Grid
   d) The grid cannot be cleared

   ( )

5. Which symbol(s) must be placed after the field name when creating a calculated field?
   a) A colon :
   b) A semicolon ;
   c) Parenthesis “ “
   d) Brackets [ ]

   ( )

Skills Builder 15.1

In this exercise, you will use comparison criteria and compound criteria to query the Customers table in the Tropical Getaways database.

1. **Open** the **Tropical Getaways database** on your exercise diskette and **click** the **Queries tab**.
2. **Click** the [New] button.
3. Choose **Design View** and **click OK**.
4. Choose **Customers** in the Show Table box and **click** the **Add** button.
5. **Click** the **Close** button to close the Show Table dialog box.
6. If necessary, **maximize** the **Query window** and adjust the height of the design grid and the Customers field list box.
7. **Add** the **FirstName**, **LastName** and **Profile** fields to the design grid by double-clicking them on the Customers field list.
8. Type the word **adventure** in the Criteria box of the Profile field as shown below.

Field:	FirstName	LastName	Profile
Table:	Customers	Customers	Customers
Sort:			
Show:	☑	☑	☑
Criteria:			adventure

9. Run  the query and only records with the Adventure profile will be displayed as shown below.

FirstName	LastName	Profile
Debbie	Thomas	Adventure
Ted	Wilkins	Adventure
Victor	Thomas	Adventure

10. Switch back to Design  view.
11. **Add** the **State** field to the design grid.
12. Set the criteria for the State field to TX and the **sort** order of the **LastName** field **to Ascending** as shown below.

Field:	FirstName	LastName	Profile	State
Table:	Customers	Customers	Customers	Customers
Sort:		Ascending		
Show:	☑	☑	☑	☑
Criteria:			"adventure"	TX

13. Run  the query and only records where the profile is Adventure **and** the state is TX will be displayed as shown below.

FirstName	LastName	Profile	State
Debbie	Thomas	Adventure	TX
Ted	Wilkins	Adventure	TX

14. **Close** the **query** and **save** it with the name **Adventure Profiles**.

Skills Builder 15.2

In this exercise, you will use calculated fields in the Tropical Getaways database.

1. Set up a **new query** in Design view and **add** the **Trips table** to the query.
2. **Close** the **Show Tables** dialog box.
3. **Add** the **Destination**, **Category** and **Cost** fields to the design grid.
4. Set the **Sort** box for the **Category** field to **Ascending**.
5. Use the following illustration to display the Zoom box for a new calculated field.

❶ ***Click*** *in the empty field cell to the right of the Cost field.*

❷ ***Click*** *the* ***right*** *mouse button (right-click) and the menu shown here will pop up.*

❸ *Choose* ***Zoom*** *from the menu.*

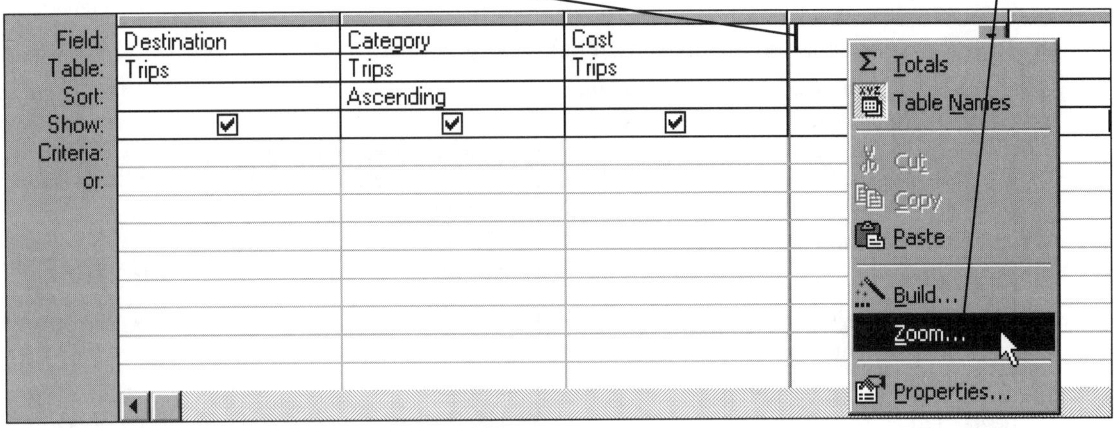

6. Enter the expression shown below into the Zoom box. Make sure you type the expression exactly as shown including the colon **:** after the word Duration.

   When you run the query, this expression will calculate the duration of each trip. You can perform calculations using dates in Access and Excel.

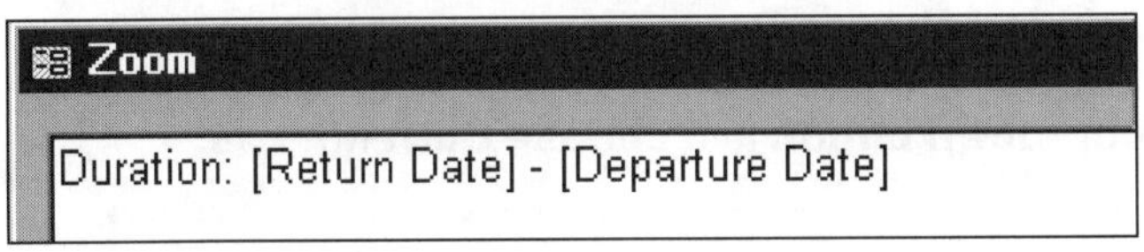

7. **Click OK** and if necessary, use the left arrow and right arrow keys on your keyboard to check your new calculated field for errors. Correct any errors that you find.
8. **Run** the **query** and the results shown below will appear.

Destination	Category	Cost	Duration
Baja California	Adventure	$2,900.00	10
Rocky Mountair	Adventure	$2,190.00	16
Swiss Alps	Adventure	$3,500.00	26
Amazon Jungle	Adventure	$7,765.00	38
Kenyan Safari	Adventure	$6,600.00	30
Hawaii	Family	$5,300.00	8
Orlando	Family	$3,400.00	6
Hawaii	Leisure	$4,500.00	10
Caribbean Cruis	Leisure	$2,390.00	9

Continued...

In the next few steps, you will add another calculated field that computes the average daily cost of each trip. The average daily cost will be calculated as the Cost / Duration. This new calculated field will use the Duration calculated field as part of the calculation. Access allows you to "nest" calculated fields in this manner.

9. Switch to Design view.

10. Click the **empty field cell** to the right of the Duration cell and then **click** the **right** mouse button.

11. Choose Zoom from the pop up menu and enter the expression shown below into the Zoom box.

Zoom

Cost per day: [Cost]/[Duration]

12. Click OK to insert the Cost per day calculated field into the cell.

13. Run the **query** and the results shown below will appear.

Notice that the Cost per day numbers are not formatted with the Currency format. You will correct this in the next few steps.

Destination	Category	Cost	Duration	Cost per day
Baja California	Adventure	$2,900.00	10	290
Rocky Mountair	Adventure	$2,190.00	16	136.875
Swiss Alps	Adventure	$3,500.00	26	134.615384615
Amazon Jungle	Adventure	$7,765.00	38	204.342105263
Kenyan Safari	Adventure	$6,600.00	30	220
Hawaii	Family	$5,300.00	8	662.5
Orlando	Family	$3,400.00	6	566.666666667
Hawaii	Leisure	$4,500.00	10	450
Caribbean Cruis	Leisure	$2,390.00	9	265.555555556

14. Switch to Design view.

15. Right-click on the **Cost per day** field and **choose Properties** from the pop up menu.

16. Click the **Format box**, **click** the **drop-down button** and **choose Currency**.

17. Close ☒ the Properties box.

18. Run the **query** and the Cost per day numbers should be formatted as shown below.

Destination	Category	Cost	Duration	Cost per day
Baja California	Adventure	$2,900.00	10	$290.00
Rocky Mountair	Adventure	$2,190.00	16	$136.88
Swiss Alps	Adventure	$3,500.00	26	$134.62
Amazon Jungle	Adventure	$7,765.00	38	$204.34
Kenyan Safari	Adventure	$6,600.00	30	$220.00
Hawaii	Family	$5,300.00	8	$662.50
Orlando	Family	$3,400.00	6	$566.67
Hawaii	Leisure	$4,500.00	10	$450.00
Caribbean Cruis	Leisure	$2,390.00	9	$265.56

19. Close the **query** and **save** it with the name **Cost per day**.

Skills Builder 15.3

In this exercise, you will create a query to perform statistical calculations in the Tropical Getaways database.

1. Create a new query that uses the Trips table.
2. **Add** the **Cost field** to the design grid.
3. Display the Total row by **clicking** the Totals Σ button on the toolbar.
4. **Choose** the **Avg** function in the **Total box** as shown below.

Field:	Cost
Table:	Trips
Total:	Avg
Sort:	
Show:	☑
Criteria:	

5. **Run** the **query** and the average cost of a trip should be calculated as $4,282.78.
6. Switch to Design view.
7. **Add** the **Category field** to the design grid.

   The Total box will automatically be set to Group By as shown below. When you run the query, the Avg function in the Cost field will calculate the average cost for each category of trip.

Field:	Cost	Category
Table:	Trips	Trips
Total:	Avg	Group By
Sort:		
Show:	☑	☑
Criteria:		

8. **Run** the **query** and the results shown below will appear.

AvgOfCost	Category
$4,591.00	Adventure
$4,350.00	Family
$3,445.00	Leisure

9. **Close** the **query** and **save** it with the name **Cost by Category**.

Skills Builder 15.4

1. Take 30 minutes to experiment with queries in the Tropical Getaways database. Feel free to create as many new queries as desired.
2. When you have finished, close the database and continue with the Assessment exercises on the following page.

Assessment 15.1

1. **Open** the **Classic Cars** database.
2. **Create** a **new query** and **add** the **Collectors table** to the query.
3. Set up the query to produce the resulting datasheet shown below. Notice that this query simply chooses the indicated fields and sorts the records by Collection Size.

FirstName	LastName	Era of Interest	Collection Size
Cindy	Johnson	1950's	42
Ed	Larkson	Early 1900's	34
Bob	Barker	1950's	7
Tammy	Olson	1960's	6
Jake	Johnson	1920's	3

4. **Run** the **query**, **print** the results and then **close** the query and **save** it as **Collection Sizes.**
5. **Create** a **new query** and **add** the **Cars table** to the query.
6. Set up the query to produce the resulting datasheet shown below. Notice that this query only selects records where the Model is Corvette and the Condition is Excellent. The query also sorts the records by Value with the largest values appearing first.

Make	Model	Year	Color	Condition	Value
Chevrolet	Corvette	57	Red	Excellent	$42,000.00
Chevrolet	Corvette	58	Black	Excellent	$35,000.00
Chevrolet	Corvette	62	Blue	Excellent	$30,000.00

7. **Run** the **query**, **print** the results and then **close** the query and **save** it as **Excellent Corvettes.**
8. **Create** a **new query** and **add** the **Cars table** to the query.
9. Set up the query to produce the resulting datasheet shown below. Notice that this query computes the average value of each group of models. In other words, the query groups the records on the Model field and then calculates the average value of each group. The query also sorts the records by Value with the largest values appearing first.

Model	AvgOfValue
Model A	$75,000.00
Corvette	$43,000.00
Thunderbird	$20,000.00
Custom Eight Sedan	$15,000.00

10. **Run** the **query** and then **adjust** the **width of the Model column** as shown above to fit the widest entry in the column. You can accomplish this by double-clicking the border between the Model and AvgOfValue column headings.
11. **Print** the results and then **close** the **query** and **save** it as **Average Value of Model Groups.**
12. **Close** the Classic Cars **database** when you have finished and **exit** from **Access.**

16 Integration: Analyzing Access Data with Excel

Objectives:

- Set up an Access query
- Send the query results to Excel
- Analyze and chart data with Excel

The Project – Analyze Access Data with Excel

In this lesson, you will use the OfficeLinks feature in Access 97 to output data to Excel 97. You will develop an Access query that computes the average expenditures per visit for each pet type in the Pinnacle Pet Care database. You will use the Excel OfficeLink in Access to output the query results to Excel. Once the data is in Excel, you will create a pie chart to compare the average expenditures of the various pet types. The query, Excel worksheet and chart that you will create are shown below.

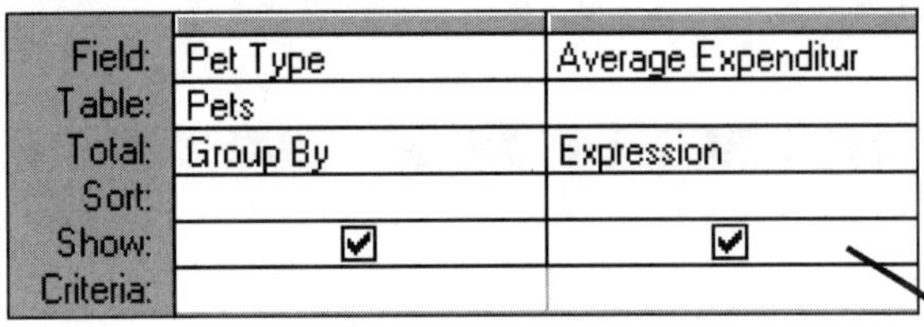

When this Access query is run, the output is sent to Excel and a pie chart is used to analyze and compare the results.

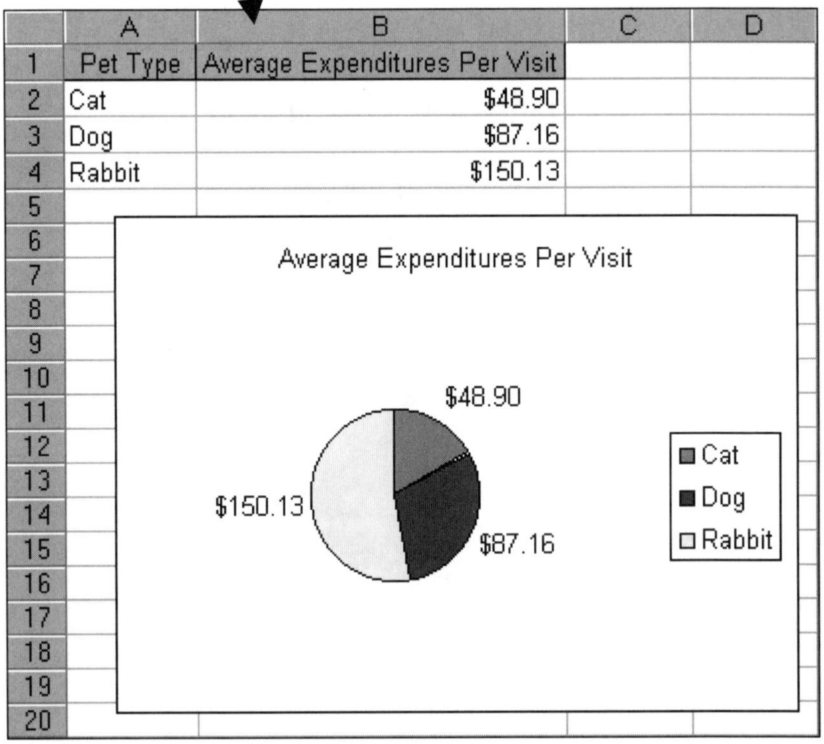

Outputting from Access to Excel

The true power of Office 97 lies in the integration of the various programs. Access provides the database and storage capabilities in Office 97. Access also provides excellent tools for querying a database and generating reports. However, there are times when more sophisticated analysis of data is required. For example, there are times that you may need to perform complex calculations on Access data or create charts from Access data. The best approach in these situations is to output the data to Excel and use the analyzing and charting capabilities of Excel.

Using the Excel OfficeLink with Access

The Access toolbar contains an OfficeLinks button that lets you easily output data from Access to Word 97 and Excel 97. The Excel OfficeLinks button is available whenever a table or query is highlighted in the Access database window. When you click the Excel OfficeLink button, Access opens the highlighted table or runs the highlighted query. Access then opens the Excel program and copies the table data or query results to Excel. You can then use Excel to analyze the data. Changes that are made to the data in Excel have no impact on the original Access data.

Hands-On 16.1 – Set up a query

In this exercise, you will set up a new query in the Pinnacle Pet Care database. The new query will contain a calculated field that computes the average expenditures per visit for each pet type.

Display the Query window

1. Start Access and **open** the **Pinnacle Pet Care** database.
2. **Click** the **Queries tab** in the Database window.
3. **Click** the New button and the New Query dialog box will appear.
4. Choose **Design View** and **click OK**.
5. **Add** the **Pets table** to the query window and then **close** the **Show Table** dialog **box**.
6. **Double-click** the **Pet Type** field in the Pets field list to add that field to the design grid.

Create a calculated field

7. Use the following illustration to display the Zoom dialog box.

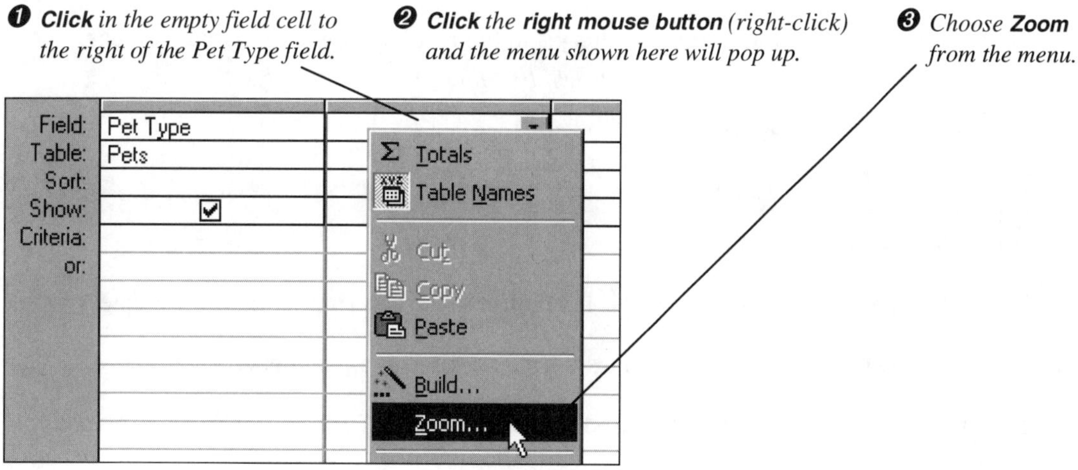

Continued...

8. Enter the calculated field expression shown below into the dialog box. Make sure you enter the expression exactly as shown. In particular, make sure you use a colon **:** (not a semicolon ;), correctly spell the field names, use the correct open and closed parenthesis ( ) and brackets [ ] and use the forward slash / symbol to represent division. This expression will eventually calculate the average expenditures per visit for each pet type.

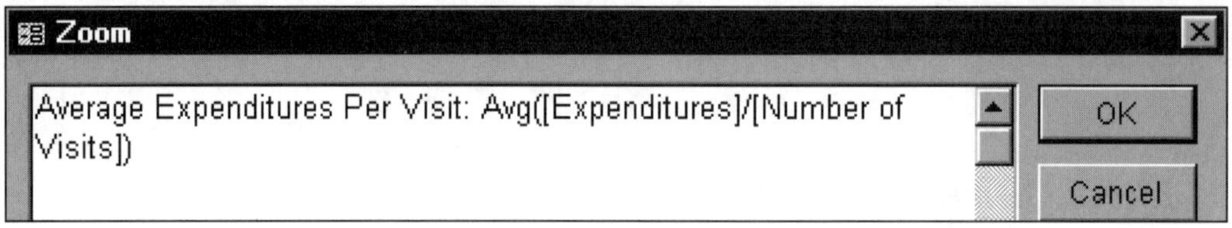

9. **Click OK** to insert the expression in the field.

10. Use the left arrow and right arrow keys on your keyboard to scroll through the expression within the cell. Make sure the syntax is correct as shown above. If necessary, you can edit the expression within the cell or redisplay the Zoom dialog box and make any necessary changes.

Add grouping to the Pet Type field

11. **Click** the Totals button on the toolbar and a Total row will appear below the Table row.

The Total boxes will be set to Group By for both the Pet Type field and the calculated field.

12. Use the following illustration to set the Total box to Expression for the calculated field.

Field:	Pet Type	Average Expenditur
Table:	Pets	
Total:	Group By	Expression
Sort:		
Show:	☑	☑

❶ ***Click** in the **Total box**, **click** the **drop-down button**, **scroll down** and choose **Expression**.*

❷ *At this point, the query design grid should match the example shown here.*

These settings will group the records by Pet Type and calculate the average expenditures per visit for each group. In other words, the average expenditures per visit will be calculated for dogs, cats and other pet types.

13. If necessary, **click** the Properties button on the Access toolbar to display the Field Properties dialog box.

14. **Click in** the **Format box**, **click** the **drop-down button, scroll down** and **choose Currency**.

When the query is run, the resulting numbers will be formatted with dollar signs and two decimals.

15. **Click** the Run button to run the query and the results shown below will appear.

In the next exercise, these same results will be sent to Excel for analysis.

Pet Type	Expenditures I
Cat	$48.90
Dog	$87.16
Rabbit	$150.13

16. **Close** the **query** by clicking the Close button at the top-right corner of the query window.

17. **Click** the **Yes** button when Access asks if you want to save the query.

18. Type the name **Average Expenditures per Visit by Pet Type** in the Save As box, **click OK** and continue with the next exercise where you will output the results to Excel.

Hands-On 16.2 – Output the query results to Excel

1. Use the following illustration to output the query results to Excel.

❶ *Make sure the Average Expenditures per Visit by Pet Type query is highlighted in the database window.*

❷ ***Click** the OfficeLinks **drop-down button** and choose Analyze It with MS Excel as shown here.*

❸ *If Access indicates that the file named **Average Expenditures per Visit by Pet Type** already exists, then click Yes to replace the file.*

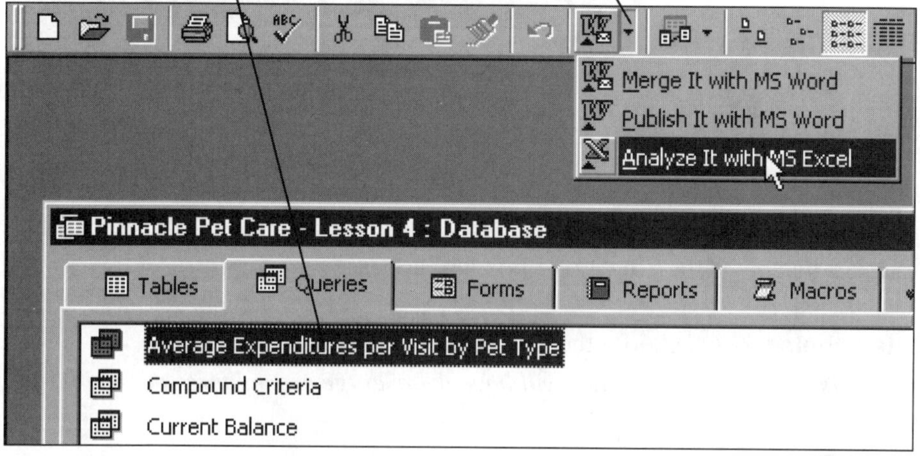

Excel will start and the query results will appear in the Excel window as shown below. Access actually creates an Excel file on the hard disk of your computer system when you output the query. This is why Access may have asked if you wanted to replace the file named Average Expenditures per Visit by Pet Type.

2. Use the following illustration to widen column B in the Excel worksheet.

❶ ***Double-click** the **border** between column headings B and C to widen the column as shown here.*

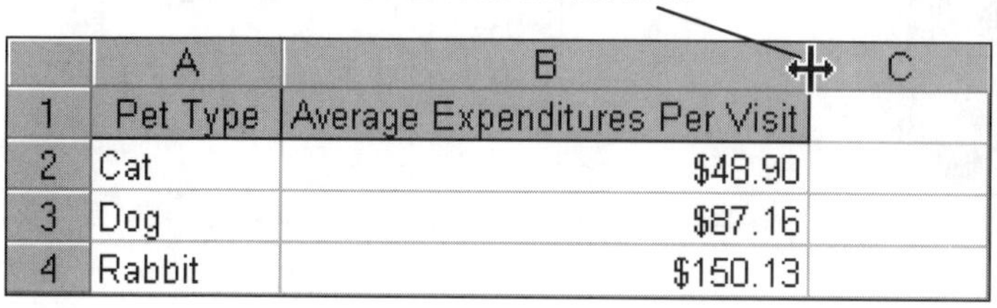

3. Now continue with the next exercise where you will chart the data.

Hands-On 16.3 – Create a pie chart

1. Use the following illustration to select the data prior to creating a pie chart.

   ❶ *Position the mouse pointer on the Pet Type heading and drag down and to the right until the data shown here is selected.*

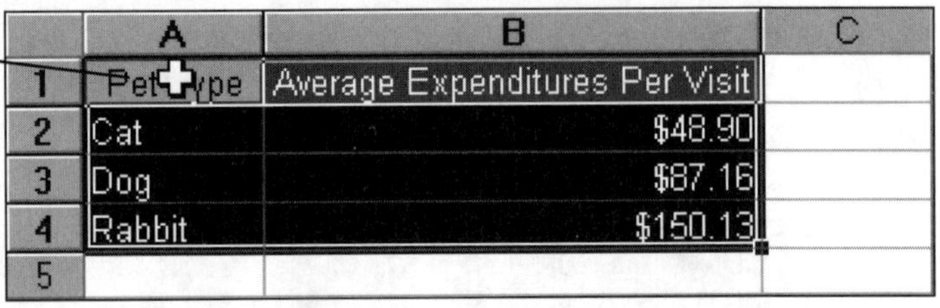

2. **Click** the Chart Wizard button.
3. Choose the Pie chart type and the first sub-type.
4. **Click** Next > **twice** and the Step 3 of 4 box will appear.
5. **Click** the **Data Labels tab** and choose the Show value option.

   When the chart is created, each pie slice will have the average expenditures per visit displayed next to the slice.
6. **Click** the Finish button and the chart will appear in the worksheet as shown below.

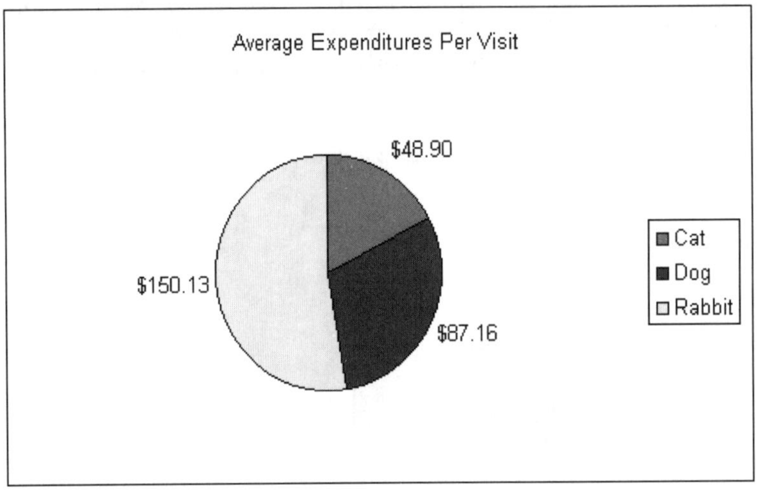

7. Feel free to format and experiment with the chart.

   In the next few steps, you will save the workbook to your exercise diskette.
8. Choose **File→Save As...** from the menu bar.
9. Choose **3 ½ Floppy (A)** from the Save In box and type the name **Hands-On Lesson 16** in the File name box.
10. **Click** the **Save button** to complete the save.
11. Now choose **File→Exit** from the Excel menu bar to close the Excel program. However, leave Access open as you will continue to use Access in the next exercise.

Hands-On 16.4 – Output an entire table to Excel

In this exercise, you will output the entire Pets table to Excel for analysis.

1. **Click** the **Tables tab** in the Access database window.
2. Notice that the OfficeLinks button now has the Excel icon on the face of the button.
   This is because Excel was the last OfficeLink that you used.
3. **Choose** the **Pets table** in the Tables tab and **click** the face of the OfficeLinks button.
   Excel will start and Access will output the entire Pets table to Excel. If Access asks you to save the file, then click Yes to replace the existing pets.xls file.
4. Enter **Total Expenditures** in cell A10, which should be the first empty cell in column A.
5. **Click** cell **I10**, which should be the first empty cell in the Expenditures column.
6. **Click** the AutoSum button and **tap Enter** to compute the total expenditures for all pets.
7. Feel free to create other totals and/or chart any of the data.
8. When you have finished, **close** the **workbook without saving** the changes.
9. Use the **File→Exit** command to close both Excel and Access.

Concepts Review

True / False

1. Office 97 lets you output data from Access to Excel. 1. **T F**
2. Only query results can be output from Access to Excel. 2. **T F**
3. Data that you output to Excel remains linked to the original Access data. 3. **T F**

Multiple Choice

1. Which of the following buttons is the OfficeLinks button?
   a) 
   b) 
   c) 
   d) None of the above.
   ( )

2. What must you do prior to clicking the OfficeLinks button?
   a) Choose the desired table or query in the database window.
   b) Open the desired table or run the desired query.
   c) Print the desired table or query results.
   d) None of the above.
   ( )

Unit Five

PowerPoint 97

17 Creating and Delivering a Presentation

Objectives:

- Understand PowerPoint concepts
- Use design templates
- Create slides
- Work with bulleted lists
- Save a presentation
- Format and move paragraphs
- Use various views
- Create transparencies
- Print slides
- Deliver an electronic presentation

What is PowerPoint?

Microsoft PowerPoint is a presentation graphics program that allows you to easily develop dynamic presentations. Whether you are developing a one-on-one presentation for your supervisor or a sophisticated presentation for a large group, PowerPoint provides the tools to make your presentation a success. PowerPoint lets you output your presentation on transparencies for use with an overhead projector, on 35mm slides for more formal presentations and using a projection device directly from your PC. With PowerPoint 97, you can even create virtual presentations for delivery on the Internet or an Intranet (a network within an organization).

PowerPoint takes care of the design details

PowerPoint provides powerful tools that let you concentrate on the content of your presentation instead of the design details. With PowerPoint's built-in design templates, you can rapidly create colorful and effective presentations. PowerPoint makes it easy to organize your ideas, edit and change a presentation and deliver a presentation with precision and control.

PowerPoint gives your presentation a consistent appearance

PowerPoint's design templates form the foundation of a presentation. The design templates give your presentation an attractive appearance and also create consistency throughout the presentation. Once again, this allows you to focus on the content of your presentation instead of the design.

The Project – The Pinnacle Pet Car Presentation

In this lesson, you will develop a presentation for the Pinnacle Pet Care pet clinic. The managers at Pinnacle Pet Care need to present to a large group at the annual Pet World trade show. The presentation that you develop will introduce Pinnacle to the trade show attendees and entice the attendees with a promotional offer. The presentation will be delivered using a laptop PC attached to a video projection system. Two of the slides from the presentation that you will develop are shown below.

Designing and Delivering an Effective Presentation

Design Tips

Have you ever heard the expression "it isn't what you say it's how you say it?" This old adage remains true even when designing high-tech PowerPoint presentations. The design of your presentation will effect your audience's perception of you and the amount of information they retain. Use the following helpful hints to design effective PowerPoint presentations.

- **Keep it short** – Long presentations tend to lose the audience. Most audiences are lost after just 20 to 30 minutes. Keep your presentation focused and to the point. You can always lengthen your presentation by opening it up to questions after you have finished speaking.
- **Amount of information** – Avoid placing too much information on one slide. Too many words or pictures can distract your audience. If a slide has too much information, then try turning it into two or three slides.
- **Using bullets** – Many PowerPoint slides are set up with bullets. A typical slide should have between three and six bullets. Keep your bulleted phrases as short as possible. If you have too many bullets on a slide, then break the bullets into two columns or create a second slide.
- **Animation and special effects** – PowerPoint lets you use animation and special effects in presentations. Keep in mind that animation and special effects should draw attention to your important points. Don't get carried away with these tools and use them as entertainment. This may be enjoyable but your audience may also miss your point.

Presentation Tips

The manner in which you deliver your presentation is also important. You want the audience to focus on the presentation instead of focusing on you. Use the following helpful hints to deliver effective presentations.

- **Maintain a moderate pace** – Speaking too fast will exhaust your audience and speaking too slow may put them to sleep. Therefore, you should try to maintain a moderate pace.
- **Pauses are important** – Try pausing for five to ten seconds after making important points. This will let your audience rest and give them time to absorb what you have said.
- **Stay still** – Avoid excessive movement while presenting. Movement can be distracting because your audience's attention is drawn to your movements instead of your presentation. Excessive movement may be OK for high energy, motivational presentations but it is a bad approach for most business presentations. The best way to avoid this is to face your audience or maintain a slight angle towards your audience. Avoid moving your feet or rocking on your feet. Move freely from the waist up including your arms and hands. Using your body language to make points is good technique provided you are not "running around the room" while presenting.
- **Speak to your audience** – Always face your audience while speaking. Many presenters speak while facing a white board or projection screen. Your points will definitely be missed if you turn your back to your audience while speaking.

Starting PowerPoint and Setting up a New Presentation

There are several ways to start PowerPoint. The three most common methods are listed below.

- Click the Start button and choose Microsoft PowerPoint from the Programs menu.
- Click a desktop shortcut for the PowerPoint program (if a shortcut is on the desktop).
- Click the Microsoft PowerPoint button on the Microsoft Office toolbar (if it is displayed).

Once PowerPoint is started, you can choose several options from the PowerPoint dialog box that appears. The AutoContent Wizard can be used to automatically set up a presentation containing slides, text and other objects. The Template option can be used to choose a design template. A design template automatically formats slides as you create them. In the following exercise, you will use the Template option to set up a new presentation.

Hands-On 17.1 - Start PowerPoint and set up a new presentation

1. Start your computer and the Windows desktop will be displayed.
2. **Click** the Start button and choose **Programs**.
3. Choose **Microsoft PowerPoint** from the Programs menu.
   PowerPoint will start and the dialog box shown below will appear.
4. Choose **Template** as shown in the following illustration and **click OK**.

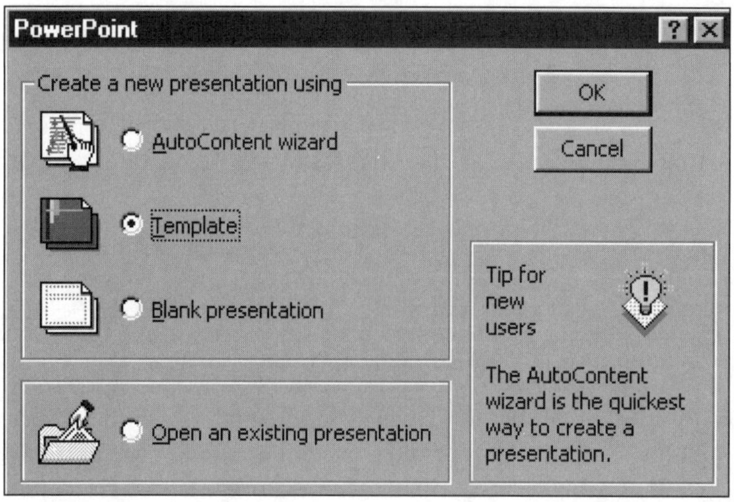

The New Presentation dialog box will appear as shown on the following page. The New Presentation dialog box lets you choose from a variety of templates and pre-existing presentations.

Continued...

5. Use the following illustration to choose a presentation design template.

❶ ***Click** the **Presentation Designs tab** and feel free to **click** the **various designs**. A preview of the selected design will appear in the Preview window.*

❷ ***Choose** the **Contemporary** design and **click OK**. The New Slide dialog box will appear.*

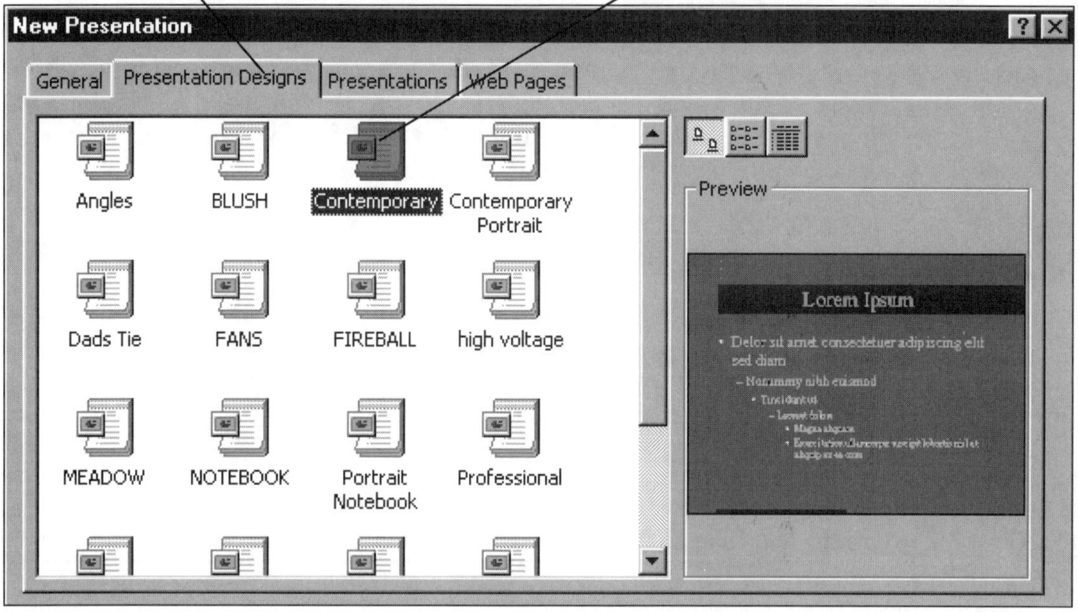

The New Slide dialog box lets you choose an AutoLayout style for each slide in your presentation. You will use this dialog box throughout this lesson as you build your presentation slide-by-slide.

6. Use the following illustration to choose an AutoLayout style.

❶ *Make sure the first AutoLayout style is chosen and **click OK**. The first AutoLayout style is used for the title slide in a presentation. A title slide is typically the first slide in a presentation.*

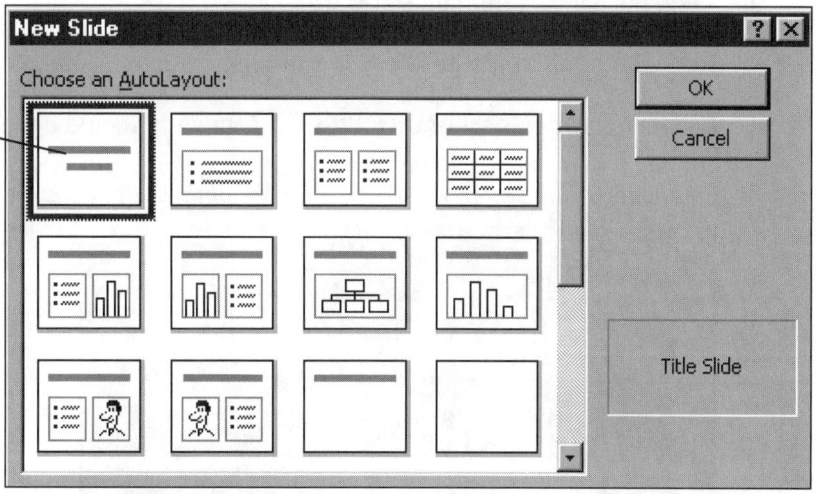

PowerPoint will display a slide with placeholder boxes for a title and subtitle.

7. Continue with the next topic where you will begin developing your presentation.

Creating Slides

PowerPoint presentations are composed of slides. Slides are composed of various objects. Some of the objects that appear on slides include pictures, text boxes and boxes for bulleted lists. PowerPoint gives you complete flexibility to edit, move and size objects and to add and delete objects to or from slides.

Design templates set up slides for you

In the previous exercise, you chose the Contemporary design template when you set up your presentation. Design templates provide a consistent background design for the slides in a presentation. Design templates also position placeholders on slides for titles, text, bulleted lists and other objects. By using design templates, you can literally fill-in the blanks as you create slides.

Title Slides

Most presentations contain a title slide that introduces the presentation to the audience. The title slide typically contains a title, a subtitle and perhaps a graphic such as a company logo. PowerPoint sets up the title slide for you if your presentation uses a built-in design template. You can add text to a title slide by clicking the **placeholder boxes** for the title and subtitle and then typing the desired text.

Hands-On 17.2 – Create the title slide

In this exercise, you will create the title slide for the Pinnacle Pet Care presentation. The presentation should already have been set up in the previous exercise and the title slide should be displayed.

1. **Click** anywhere on the **title box** that contains the text **Click to add title**.

   The box will become selected and the insertion point will be positioned inside the box.

2. **Type** the phrase **Pinnacle Pet Care**.

3. Now **click** the large **sub-title box** and **type** the phrase **Where Pets Get Pampered!**.

4. **Click** on an **open part of the slide** and your slide should have the appearance shown below.

   Notice the color scheme, the globe and the position of the title and sub-title boxes. The Contemporary design template sets up all of these design elements.

5. Now continue with the next topic where you will add additional slides.

Adding New Slides

Currently, your presentation is composed of one title slide. You develop a presentation by adding additional slides and then typing text, inserting graphics and formatting the slides. You add slides to a presentation with the New Slide button on PowerPoint's Standard toolbar or by choosing New Slide from the Common Tasks toolbar.

AutoLayouts

PowerPoint provides a variety of predefined layouts for slides. The layouts include placeholders for text, bulleted lists, pictures, charts and other objects. The easiest way to create a slide is to choose an AutoLayout when adding the slide to the presentation. The AutoLayouts work with the design templates to create consistency throughout the presentation.

Hands-On 17.3 – Display toolbars, add a slide and choose an AutoLayout

In the first few steps of this exercise, you will display toolbars in the PowerPoint window. PowerPoint contains a Common Tasks toolbar that can be useful when developing presentations. The Common Tasks toolbar lets you add slides, change the AutoLayout of existing slides and change the design template for the entire presentation.

1. Choose **View→Toolbars...** from the PowerPoint menu bar and make sure that the Standard, Formatting, Common Tasks and Drawing toolbars are checked as shown below. If these toolbars aren't checked, then use the View→Toolbars... command as many times as necessary until they are checked and displayed. The Common Tasks toolbar should appear as a floating palette somewhere in the PowerPoint window as shown below.

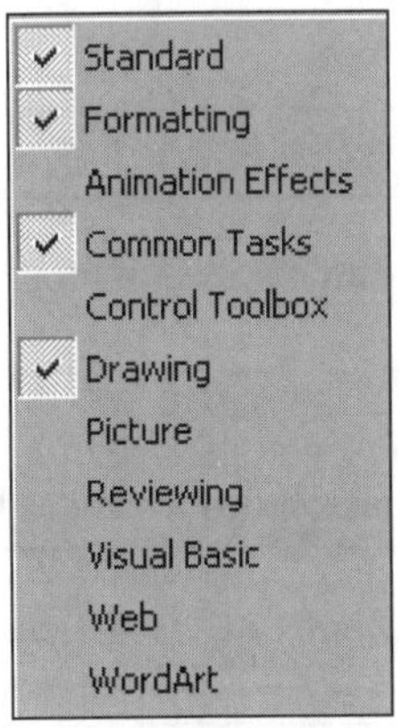

Add a slide

2. Choose **New Slide...** from the Common Tasks toolbar.

   The New Slide dialog box appears with a variety of AutoLayouts. Notice that the AutoLayouts contain placeholders for text, graphics, charts etc. Also notice that the second AutoLayout is already chosen. The Contemporary design template automatically chose this AutoLayout for the second slide (although you can override this decision).

3. **Click OK** to choose the second AutoLayout style.

4. **Click** the **title box** and **type** the phrase **Monthly Events**.

5. Now **click** anywhere in the **large box** with the phrase **Click to add text**.

   In the next exercise, you will type a bulleted list in this box.

Bulleted Lists

PowerPoint makes it easy to create bulleted lists. In fact, many of the AutoLayout slides (such as the slide you just added to your presentation) already have placeholders for bulleted lists. In PowerPoint, bulleted lists can have up to five levels. The following illustration shows a slide with a multi-level bulleted list. You will create this list in the next exercise.

This bulleted list has two levels. A large dot is used for first-level paragraphs and a hyphen is used for second-level paragraphs.

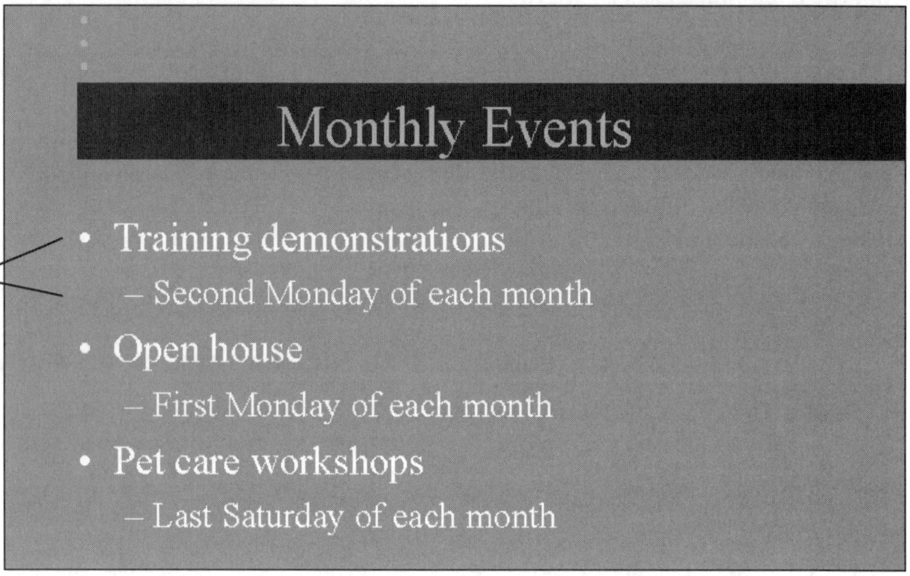

Working with Bulleted Lists

The design template that is in effect automatically formats each paragraph in a bulleted list. The format impacts the bullet style, indentation, font type, font size and other formats for the paragraph. The following table discusses the various techniques that can be used with bulleted lists.

To...	Do this
Turn bullets on and off	Select the desired paragraph(s) and click the Bullets button on the Formatting toolbar.
Promote paragraphs	Select the desired paragraph(s) and click the Promote button on the Formatting toolbar. Promoting reduces a paragraph's indentation level.
Demote paragraphs	Select the desired paragraph(s) and click the Demote button on the Formatting toolbar. Demoting increases a paragraph's indentation level.

Hands-On 17.4 – Create a bulleted list

The insertion point should be within the large placeholder box from the previous exercise.

1. Notice that the first paragraph is already formatted with a bullet.
   The Contemporary design template set up this formatting.
2. Type the phrase **Training demonstrations** and **tap** the **Enter** key.
   PowerPoint will format the new paragraph with the same large bullet. Paragraph formats are carried to new paragraphs when you tap the Enter key.

Continued...

3. Complete the list shown below by typing the indicated text and tapping Enter at the end of each paragraph. However, do not tap Enter after the last paragraph.

   You will demote several of the headings in the next few steps.

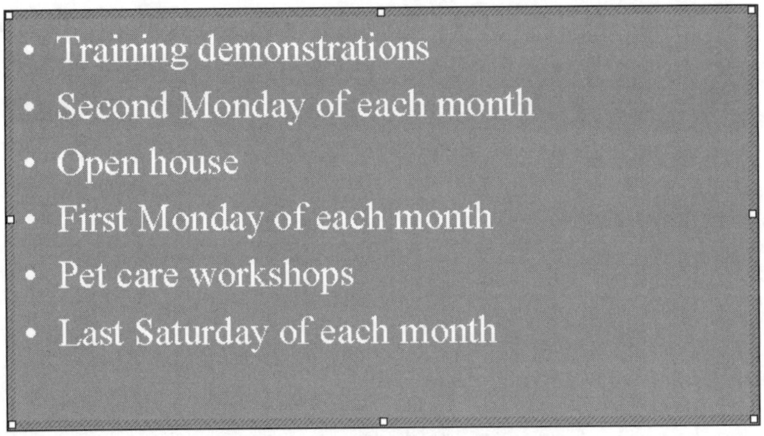

Demote several paragraphs

The most efficient way to create multi-level bulleted lists is to first type the entire list (as you did in the previous step). Once all of the text has been entered, you can promote and demote paragraphs as desired. You use the Promote and Demote buttons to promote and demote selected paragraphs.

4. **Click** anywhere on the **second paragraph** with the text **Second Monday of each month**.

   The flashing insertion point should be positioned on the paragraph text.

5. **Click** the Bullets button on the Formatting toolbar.

   The Bullets button will no longer be recessed and the bullet will be removed from the paragraph. You can always use this technique to remove bullets from paragraphs.

6. **Click** the Bullets button again to reapply the bullet.

7. Now **click** the Demote button on the Formatting toolbar.

   The paragraph will be indented and the bullet style will change to a hyphen.

8. **Click** the Demote button several more times.

   The bullet style will change and the indent will increase each time you click the button. Also, the font size and font style will change with each demotion.

9. Promote the paragraph until it is at the second indentation level with the hyphen bullet style.

10. **Click** anywhere on **the paragraph** with the text **First Monday of each month** and demote the paragraph once.

11. Finally, demote the last paragraph with the text **Last Saturday of each month** and continue with the next exercise.

Moving Between Slides

PowerPoint provides several different views to let you view your presentation in various ways. Currently, you are working in Slide view. Slide view lets you develop and edit a presentation slide-by-slide. While working in Slide view, you use the vertical scroll bar to move between slides. You can drag the scroll box to rapidly move up and down through a presentation or you can use the Previous Slide and Next Slide buttons to move through a presentation slide-by-slide.

Hands-On 17.5 – Add another bulleted slide and move between slides

Add a slide

1. Choose **New Slide...** from the Common Tasks toolbar.
2. Make sure the second AutoLayout is chosen and **click OK**.
3. **Click** the **Title box** and **type** the phrase **Services Provided**.
4. **Click** the **bulleted list box** and **type** the **four bulleted paragraphs** shown below.

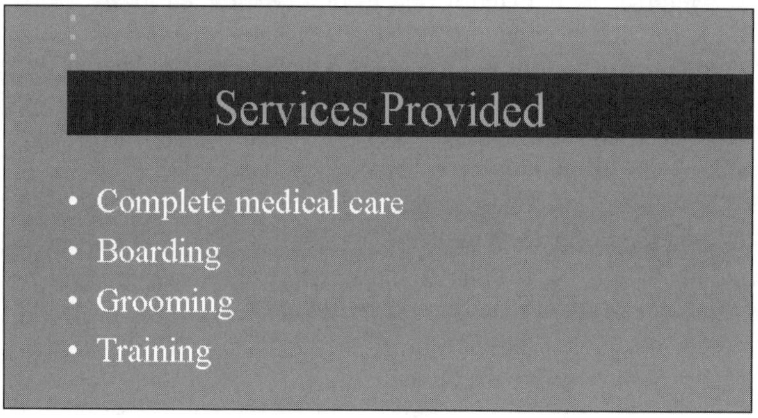

Move between slides

5. **Click** the Previous Slide button (near the bottom of the vertical scroll bar) and the Monthly Events slide will appear.
6. **Click** the Previous Slide button again to view the title slide.
7. **Click** the Next Slide button **twice** to view the Services Provided slide.
8. Feel free to browse through your slides and make any editing changes as necessary.
   You can edit slides at anytime while working in Slide view.

Saving a Presentation

You save a PowerPoint presentation to a storage device as you save any other Office 97 document. The entire presentation is saved as a single file.

Hands-On 17.6 – Save the presentation

1. **Click** the Save button on the Standard toolbar.
2. Use the following steps to save the presentation to your exercise diskette.

   If necessary, obtain a 3 ½" diskette and insert it in the diskette drive.

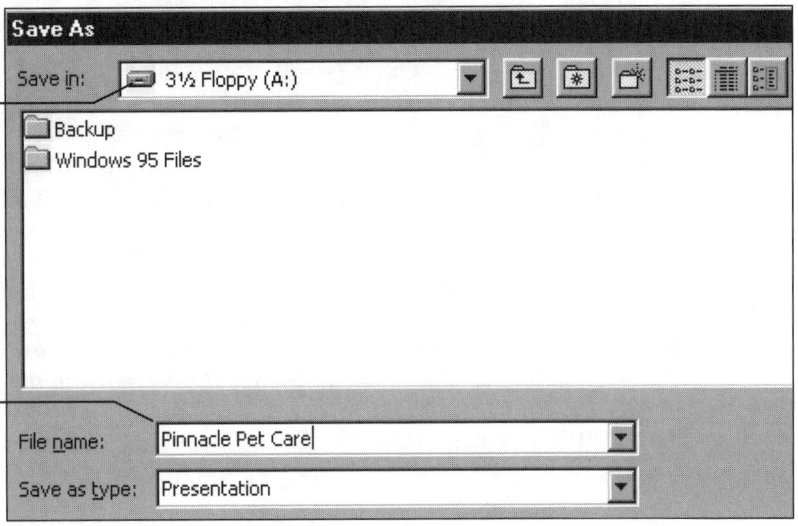

❶ **Click here** *and choose the disk drive with your exercise diskette. It is most likely 3 ½ Floppy [A:].*

❷ **Type** *the name* **Pinnacle Pet Care** *and* **click** *the* **Save** *button.*

Selecting and Moving Paragraphs

PowerPoint lets you rearrange paragraphs and slides in a variety of ways. While working in Slide view, you can move paragraphs by selecting them with the mouse and then dragging them to the desired location. You select paragraphs by dragging the mouse over the desired paragraphs.

Hands-On 17.7 – Add a slide, change the slide AutoLayout and move paragraphs

In this exercise, you will add a new slide to the presentation. You will enter a bulleted list into the new slide. Finally, you will change the AutoLayout for the new slide and rearrange the paragraphs in the bulleted list.

1. Choose **New Slide...** from the Common Tasks toolbar.
2. Make sure the second AutoLayout is chosen and **click OK**.
3. **Click** the **Title box** and **type** the phrase **Products Sold**.
4. **Click** the **bulleted list box** and type the **bulleted paragraphs** shown on the following page.

Continued...

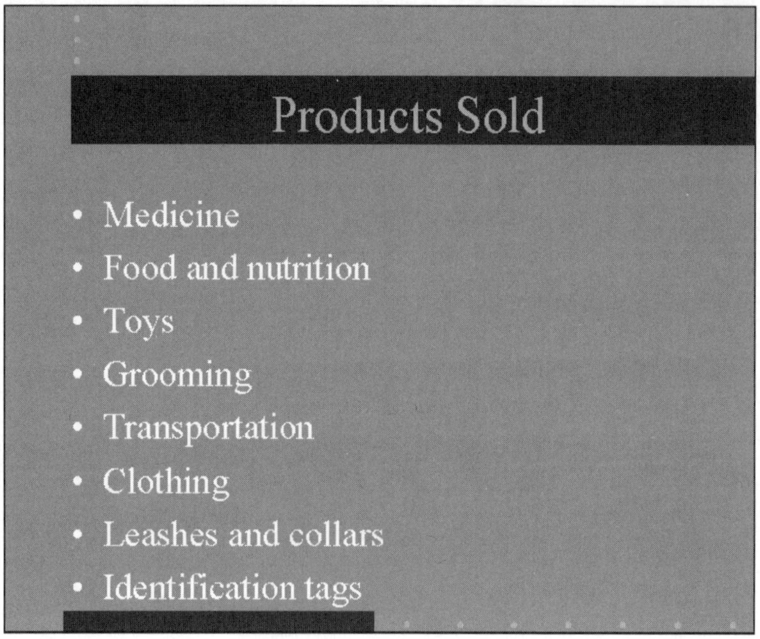

As you can see, the bulleted paragraphs occupy the entire slide. A long list of bulleted paragraphs may appear cluttered and overwhelming to an audience. For this reason, it is usually best to limit the number of bullets in a column to four or five. Another strategy that can be employed is to break the list into two columns. In the next few steps, you will use this technique by choosing a different AutoLayout for the slide. You can change the AutoLayout of a slide after the slide has been created.

5. Choose **Slide Layout...** (not New Slide) from the Common Tasks toolbar.
6. Choose the third AutoLayout 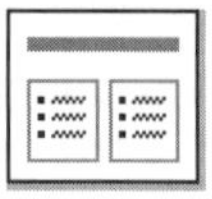 and **click** the **Apply** button.

   PowerPoint will display a second bulleted list column to the right of the first column.
7. Use the following illustration to move the last four bulleted paragraphs to the second column.

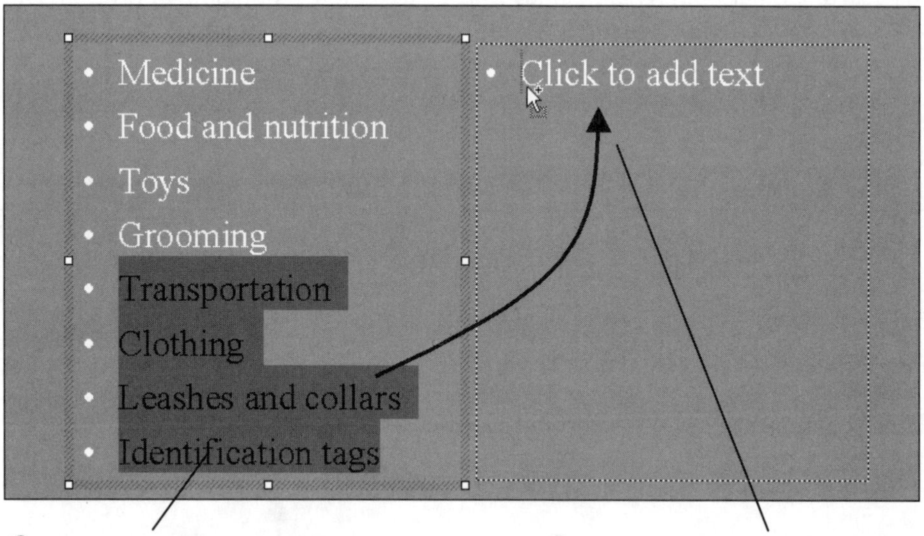

❶ ***Select** the **last four paragraphs** by dragging the mouse over them as shown here and then **release** the **mouse button**.*

❷ *Position the mouse pointer on the selected paragraphs, **drag** them to the second bulleted column and **release** the **mouse button**.*

Continued...

8. **Click** on an **open part of the slide** and the slide should have the appearance shown below.

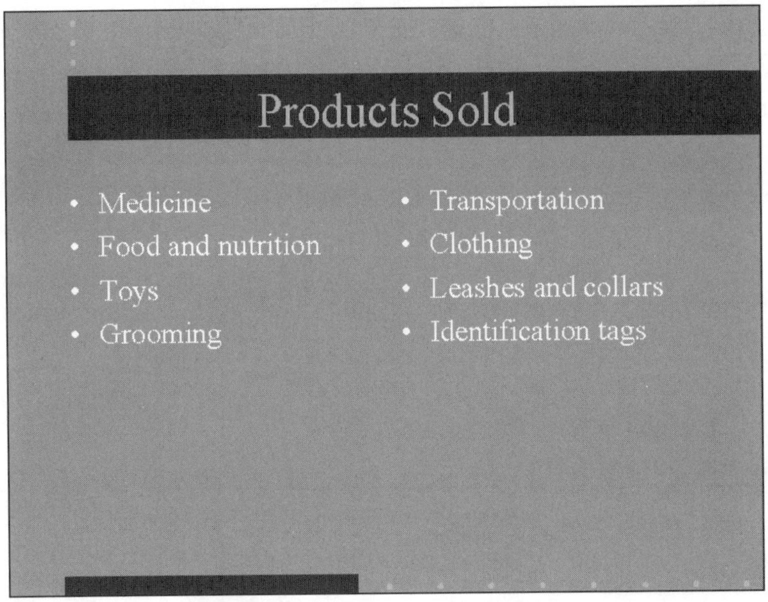

9. **Click** the Save  button to save the changes to your presentation.

Formatting Text

You can format text by using the text formatting tools on PowerPoint's Formatting toolbar. The Formatting toolbar also contains Increase Font Size and Decrease Font Size buttons that let you incrementally increase or decrease the size of selected text.

Paragraph Spacing

The Increase Paragraph Spacing and Decrease Paragraph Spacing buttons let you incrementally increase or decrease the space within and between paragraphs. Increasing the paragraph spacing may make your slides easier to read and understand.

Hands-On 17.8 – Format text and paragraphs

1. Choose **New Slide...** from the Common Tasks toolbar.
2. Choose the second  AutoLayout and **click OK**.
3. **Click** the **Title box** and **type** the phrase **Our Staff**.
4. **Click** the **bulleted list box** and **type** the **three bulleted paragraphs** shown below. Notice that the second paragraph wraps to a second line. PowerPoint will automatically wrap the line for you as you type the text.

*When creating slides, it is important to minimize the amount of information on each slide. The ideal slide contains just a few short bulleted paragraphs. Try to avoid wrapped lines like the second line in the **Our Staff** slide. In the next few steps, you will eliminate the wrapping by reducing the font size of the text. You will also increase the paragraph spacing to "open up the slide." This is necessary for this slide because the lines are long, which gives the slide a cluttered appearance.*

5. **Click** anywhere in the **bulleted list** and the box that surrounds the list will be visible.
6. Use the illustration on the following page to select the box.
   Selecting the box will allow you to format all text and paragraphs at the same time.

Continued...

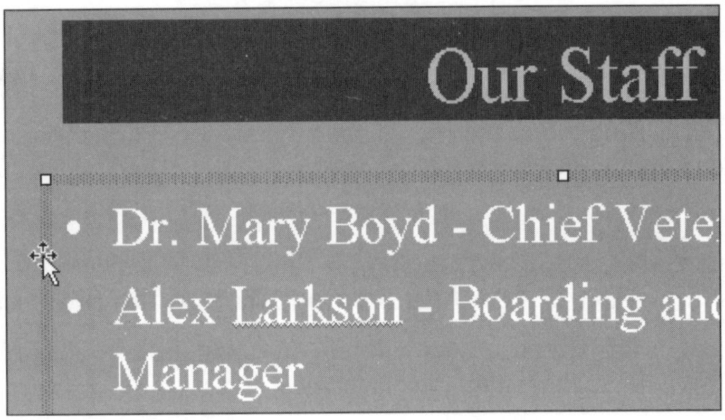

❷ ***Click** the **border** and the border pattern will change from a thatched pattern to a "fine pattern." This means the object is selected. Formatting commands affect all text and paragraphs within a selected object.*

7. **Click** the Decrease Font Size button on the Formatting toolbar.

   This will reduce the font size from 32pt to 28pt. The second paragraph should no longer wrap to a second line.

8. **Click** the Increase Paragraph Spacing button **four times**.

   There should now be more space between the various paragraphs.

9. Feel free to browse through the slides in your presentation and adjust the paragraph spacing and font size as desired.

10. Now continue with the next exercise where you will add another slide to your presentation.

Hands-On 17.9 – Add another slide

1. Use the techniques you have learned thus far to add the following slide to your presentation.

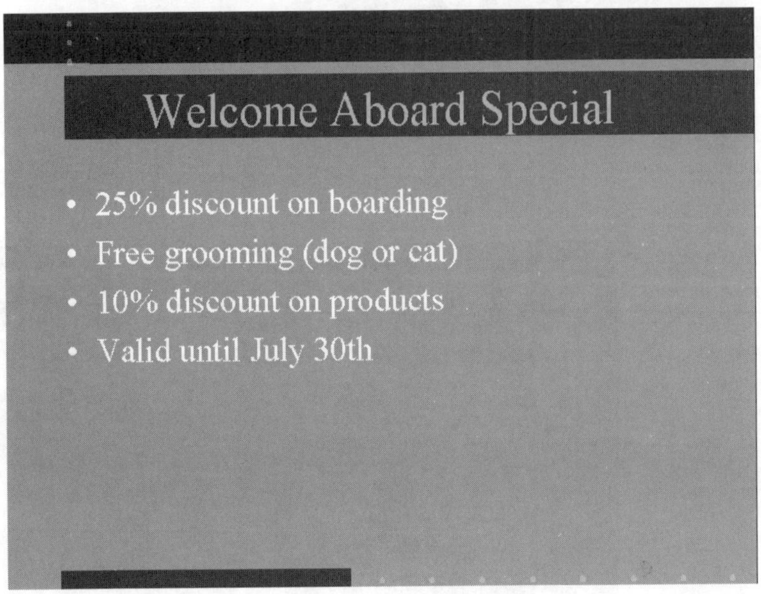

Changing Paragraph Alignment

You use the Left Alignment, Center Alignment and Right Alignment buttons on the Formatting toolbar to change the alignment of paragraphs. The desired paragraphs or the placeholder box containing the paragraphs must be selected before issuing the command.

Hands-On 17.10 – Add the final slide to the presentation

In this exercise, you will add the final slide to your presentation. You will change the alignment of paragraphs within the placeholder box.

1. Choose **New Slide...** from the Common Tasks toolbar.
2. Choose the second AutoLayout and **click OK**.
3. **Click** the **Title box** and **type** the phrase **Pinnacle Pet Care**.
4. **Click** the **bulleted list box** and type the bulleted paragraphs shown below.

5. Use the following illustration to select the placeholder box.

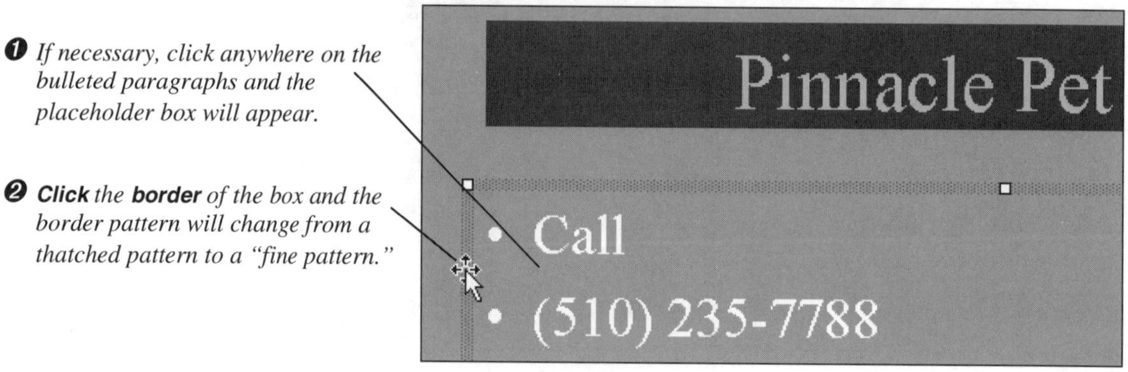

The placeholder box is selected, so any paragraph formatting commands (such as paragraph alignment) will affect all paragraphs in the box.

Continued...

6. **Click** the Bullets button to remove bullets from the paragraphs.
7. **Click** the Center Alignment button to center all paragraphs.

Format individual paragraphs

In the next few steps, you will format individual paragraphs. To accomplish this, you will click on the desired paragraph or select the desired text and then you will issue the desired formatting commands.

8. **Click** anywhere on the word **Call**.
9. **Click** the Decrease Font Size button once to reduce the size to 28.

   If no text is selected, then the Increase Font Size and Decrease Font Size buttons only affect the word with the insertion point.
10. **Select** the entire **telephone number** by dragging the mouse over the number.
11. **Click** the Increase Font Size button **twice** to increase the size to 40.
12. **Decrease** the font size of the word **or** in the third paragraph to **24**.
13. **Decrease** the font size of the fourth paragraph with the phrase **Visit our Web site at** to **28**.
14. **Increase** the font size of the **last paragraph** to **40**.
15. Your completed slide should match the example below.

16. Save the changes to your presentation and continue with the next topic.

PowerPoint Views

Thus far, you have created your presentation using Slide view. Slide view displays one slide at a time, which lets you focus on the development of individual slides. PowerPoint has several other views that are helpful while developing presentations. You switch views by clicking the desired button on the View bar, which is located on the left end of the horizontal scroll bar. You can also switch views by choosing the desired view from the View menu. The various PowerPoint views are discussed in the following table.

View	Description
Slide view	Slide view lets you view and focus on one slide at a time.
Outline view	Outline view lets you develop your ideas and the flow of the presentation. In Outline view, you work with just the text of the presentation.
Slide Sorter view	Slide Sorter view displays all slides in the presentation. Slide Sorter view is useful for rearranging slides.
Notes Page view	Notes Page view lets you develop speaker notes to accompany the presentation.
Slide Show	The Slide Show button lets you run the presentation.

Hands-On 17.11 – Rearrange slides in Slide Sorter view

In this exercise, you will experiment with several views. You will also rearrange the slides using Slide Sorter view.

1. Locate the View bar on the left end of the horizontal scroll bar.
2. **Click** the Outline View button, which is the second button on the View bar.

   Notice that PowerPoint displays your presentation as an outline. Outline view is useful for organizing ideas and rearranging slides. However, you will not use this view at this time.
3. **Click** the Slide Sorter View button, which is the third button on the View bar.

   PowerPoint will display small "thumbnails" of your slides within the PowerPoint window.
4. Use the illustration on the following page to explore the Slide Sorter window and to adjust the zoom control percentage.

Continued...

❶ *Notice the Slide Sorter toolbar that appeared. This toolbar lets you create transitions between slides and other types of special effects. However, you won't use these options at this time.*

❷ ***If necessary**, click this drop-down button and change the zoom percentage until all seven slides are visible. Don't be concerned if your slides have a different arrangement than shown in this illustration.*

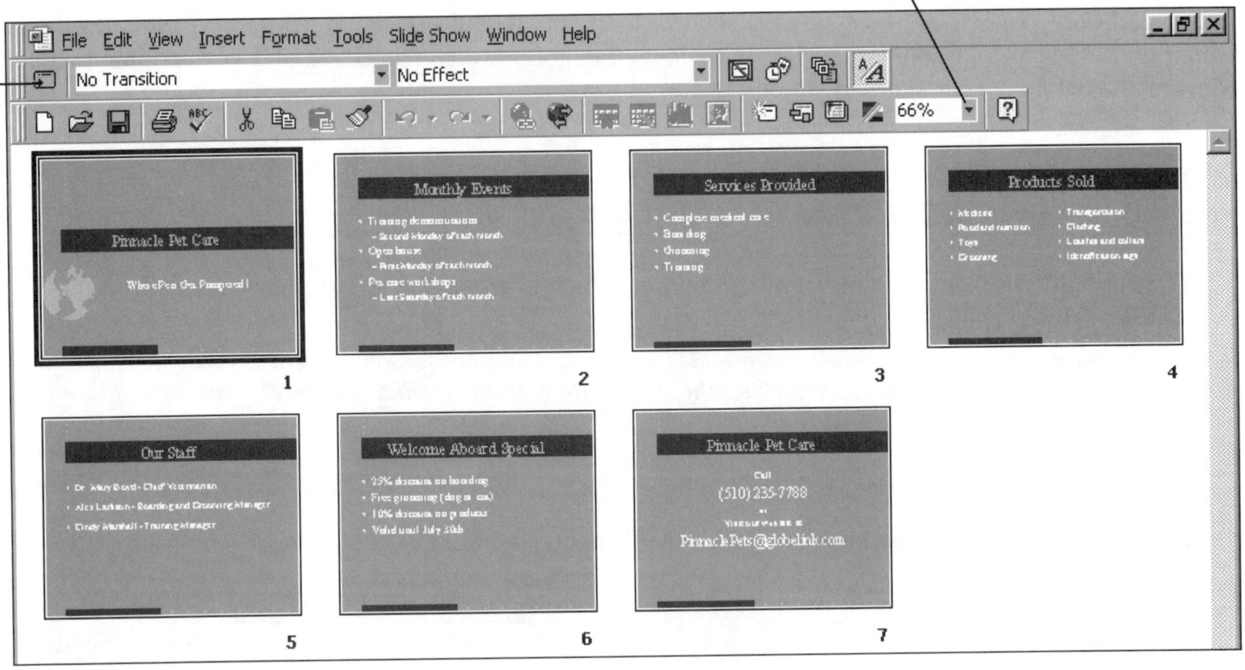

5. Use the following illustration to change the position of the Monthly Events slide from position 2 to position 4.

❶ ***Drag** the **Monthly Events** slide to the left of the Our Staff slide and a large vertical bar will indicate the eventual position of the slide. Don't be concerned if the Our Staff slide is in a different row or column than shown here.*

❷ ***Release** the **mouse button** and the Monthly Events slide will become the fourth slide.*

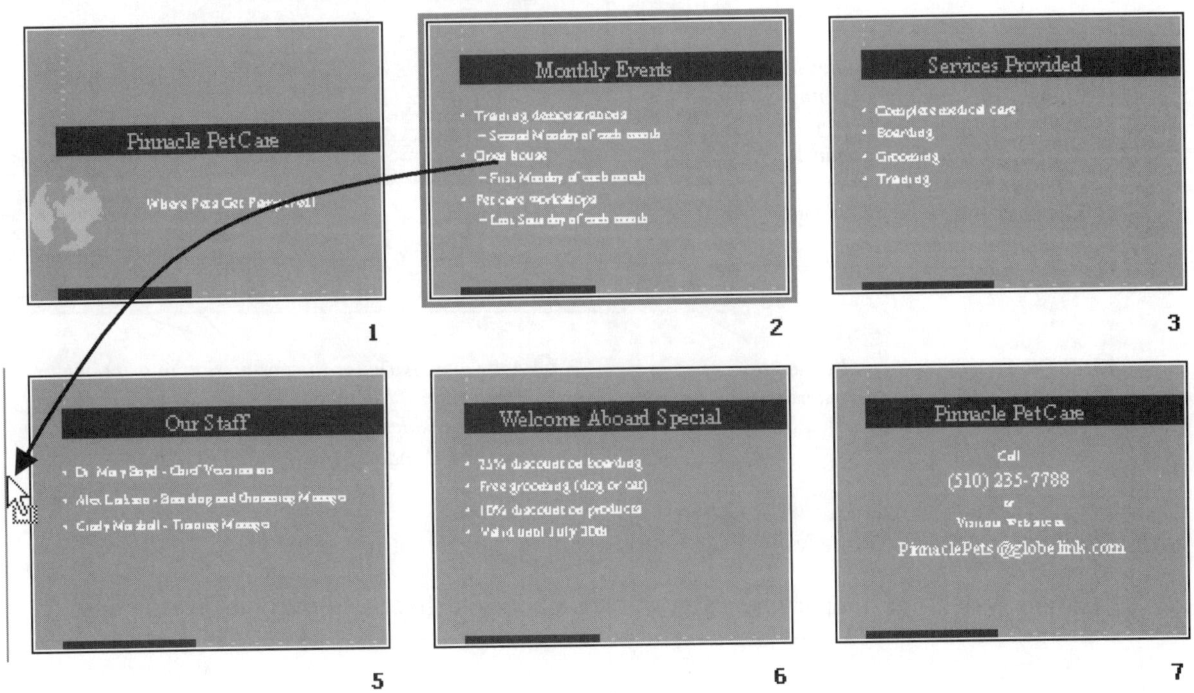

Delivering a Presentation Using Transparencies

There are several ways to deliver a PowerPoint presentation. One method is to create transparencies and use an overhead projector to deliver the presentation. Many laser printers and ink-jet printers let you create transparencies by printing directly onto transparency film. If you are using this technique and your printer can only print black text and gray shades, then you should use the Black and White View button on the Formatting toolbar to view the slides prior to printing. The Black and White View button converts the colors in your slides to various shades of gray.

Hands-On 17.12 – Use Black and White view and print the slides

1. **Click** the Black and White View button, which is just to the left of the Zoom Control on the Formatting toolbar.

   PowerPoint will display all seven slides in black, white and shades of gray. You could print all seven slides at this point by clicking the Print button on the toolbar. However, you will explore the Print dialog box in the next few steps.

2. Choose **File→Print...** form the menu bar.

3. Use the following illustration to explore the Print dialog box.

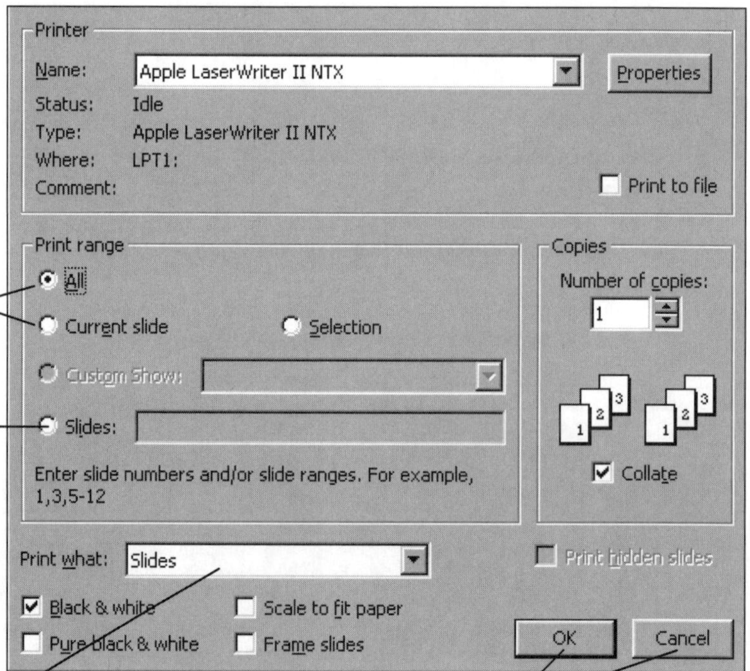

❶ *Notice that you can print all slides or just the current slide using these options.*

❷ *You can print specific slides by clicking this button and typing the desired slide numbers in the Slides box. You use commas to separate the desired slide numbers or a hyphen to indicate a range of slides.*

❸ *The Print what box can be used to print speaker notes and other items.*

❹ *Ask your instructor for permission to print one or more slides. When you are ready to continue, choose the desired printing options and* ***click OK or click Cancel*** *if you decide not to print.*

4. **Click** the Black and White View button again to return to a full color view.

5. Continue with the next topic where you will learn how to deliver an electronic presentation.

Delivering an Electronic Slide Show Presentation

The Slide Show button on the View bar lets you deliver dynamic electronic presentations. You can deliver a presentation using just a personal computer or you can attach a projection device to your PC for presentations to large groups.

Starting a Presentation

You start a presentation from Slide Sorter view by clicking on the slide that you wish to begin the presentation with and then **clicking** the **Slide Show button**. You start a slide show from Slide view by navigating to the desired slide and clicking the Slide Show button.

Displaying Slides and Ending a Presentation

You display the next slide in a presentation by **clicking** the **mouse pointer** anywhere in the PowerPoint window. You can also display the next or previous slides by tapping the **PageDown** and **PageUp** keys on the keyboard. PowerPoint automatically ends a presentation after the last slide has been viewed.

Using the Popup Menu

You can display a popup menu while running a slide show by clicking the Popup Menu button that appears at the bottom left corner of the window. You can also display the popup menu by right-clicking anywhere in the PowerPoint window. The popup menu contains options that let you navigate to various slides, end the slide show and perform other functions.

Hands-On 17.13 – Run the slide show

Your presentation should be displayed in Slide Sorter view from the previous exercise.

1. **Click** the **first slide** in the Slide Sorter window and it will become selected.

   You will start your presentation by displaying the Title slide.

2. **Click** the Slide Show button on the View bar.

   PowerPoint will display your title slide in a full-screen view. All toolbars and other screen objects will be hidden from view.

3. **Click** the mouse pointer **anywhere** on the screen to move to the next slide.
4. Continue to click anywhere on the screen until the last slide with the title Pinnacle Pet Care is displayed.
5. **Click** the **Pinnacle Pet Care slide** and the slide show will end.
6. Make sure the title slide is selected and then **click** the Slide Show button.
7. **Tap** the **PageDown** key **several times** and then **tap** the **PageUp** key **several times**.

   PowerPoint will display the next or previous slide each time you tap these keys.

8. Now **click** the **right mouse button** (right-click) and the popup menu will appear.

Continued...

Notice that the popup menu has options to go to the Next and Previous slides and to end the slide show. The pop up menu also let's you use a Pen tool to draw on the slide and make other enhancements. You will use many of these options as you progress through this course. In the next step, you will use the Go option on the popup menu to go to a specific slide.

9. Choose **Go→By Title→Welcome Aboard Special** from the popup menu as shown below. Depending on the position of your popup menu on the screen, the submenus may open to the left of the main menu.

   PowerPoint will display the Welcome Aboard Special slide. You can always use this technique to rapidly navigate to a specific slide.

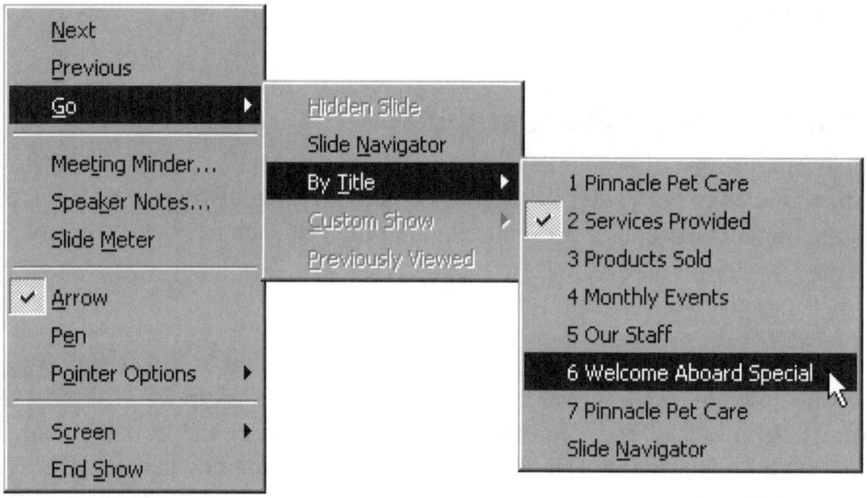

10. **Right-click** on the **current slide** and use the Go menu to go to the **Products Sold** slide.

11. Notice the Popup Menu  button at the bottom-left corner of the window.

    This button can also be used to display the popup menu.

12. **Click** the Popup Menu  button.

13. Choose **End Show** from the bottom of the popup menu to end the slide show.

14. Take 15 minutes to practice running your slide show and experimenting with the various views. Feel free to experiment with the various options on the Slide Show popup menu.

15. When you have finished experimenting, choose **File→Close** from the PowerPoint menu bar to close the Pinnacle Pet Care presentation.

16. Click Yes if PowerPoint asks you to save the changes.

17. Now continue with the end-of-lesson questions and exercises on the following pages.

Concepts Review

True / False

1. PowerPoint's design templates are designed to give presentations a consistent appearance. 1. **T F**
2. A title slide is usually the first slide in a presentation. 2. **T F**
3. AutoLayouts are predefined layouts for slides. 3. **T F**
4. A bulleted list can have a maximum of three levels. 4. **T F**
5. Each slide in a PowerPoint presentation is saved as a separate file. 5. **T F**
6. The horizontal alignment of paragraphs cannot be changed. 6. **T F**
7. Slide view is most useful for organizing ideas. 7. **T F**
8. Slide Sorter view is most useful for focusing on the development of a single slide. 8. **T F**
9. You start a presentation by clicking the Slide Show  button. 9. **T F**
10. You can display a popup menu be clicking the left mouse button anywhere on a slide. 10. **T F**

Multiple Choice

1. Which of the following techniques can be used to add a new slide to a presentation?
   a) Click the New Slide  button on PowerPoint's toolbar.
   b) Choose New Slide from the Common Tasks toolbar.
   c) Both a and b. ( )
   d) None of the above.

2. Which technique can be used to turn off bullets for a single paragraph?
   a) Click on the desired paragraph and click the Bullets button.
   b) Click on any paragraph and click the Bullets button.
   c) Click the placeholder box that contains the bulleted paragraphs and then click the Bullets button. ( )
   d) None of the above.

3. Which of the following buttons is used to promote a bulleted paragraph?
   a) 
   b)  ( )
   c) 
   d) 

4. Which buttons can be used to incrementally increase and decrease paragraph spacing?
   a) 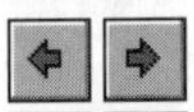
   b) 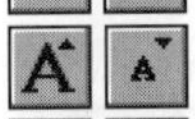 ( )
   c) 
   d) None of the above.

5. Which of the following techniques can be used to move to the next slide in a presentation?
   a) Click anywhere on the current slide.
   b) Tap the PageDown key on the keyboard.
   c) Right-click the current slide and choose Next from the popup menu. ( )
   d) All of the above.

Skills Builder 17.1

In this exercise, you will create a presentation for the Tropical Getaways travel service. The managers at Tropical Getaways need to deliver a presentation to audiences of up to 40 people. The presentation will be used for marketing purposes to sell potential customers a tropical getaway to paradise.

Set up a title slide

1. If the PowerPoint window is still displayed from the previous exercise, then choose File→New... from the menu bar. If PowerPoint is not currently running, then start the program, choose Template from the PowerPoint dialog box and click OK.
2. **Click** the **Presentation Designs tab** in the New Presentation dialog box.
3. Choose the **Contemporary Portrait** design and **click OK**.
4. **Click OK** on the New Slide dialog box to set up the title slide.
5. **Click** the **Title box** and **type** the title **Tropical Getaways**.
6. **Click** the **Subtitle box** and **type** the phrase **Adventures in Paradise**.

   Your completed title slide should match the following example.

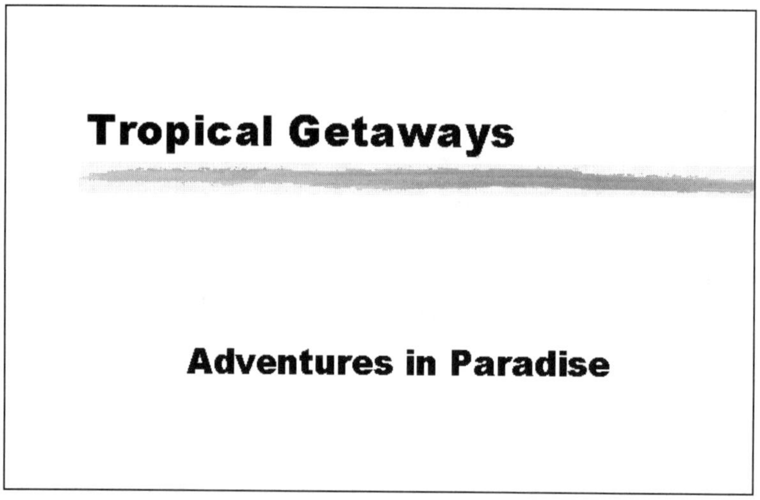

Set up another slide

7. Choose **New Slide...** from the Common Tasks toolbar.
8. **Choose** the **third AutoLayout**  and **click OK**.
9. **Click** the **Title box** and **type** the phrase **Most Popular Destinations**.
10. Add the paragraphs shown on the following page to the bulleted list boxes. You can accomplish this by clicking in the boxes, typing the phrases and tapping Enter.

Continued...

11. **Add another slide** using the **third AutoLayout**.
12. Enter the phrase **Complete Packages** in the title box.
13. Enter the phrase **Packages Include** in the first bulleted list box.
14. **Tap Enter** once and **click** the Demote button.
15. Type the word **Airfare** and **tap Enter**.
16. Complete the slide as shown below.

17. **Add a new slide** to your presentation using the **second AutoLayout**.
18. Enter the title and bulleted lists into your new slide as shown on the following page. You will need to demote the bulleted paragraphs under the headings Package 1 and Package 2. Also, notice that there is a large space above the Package 2 heading. You can create this space by tapping Enter twice after typing the bulleted paragraph with the text **$429 per person**.

Continued...

19. Add the following slide to your presentation using the second AutoLayout.

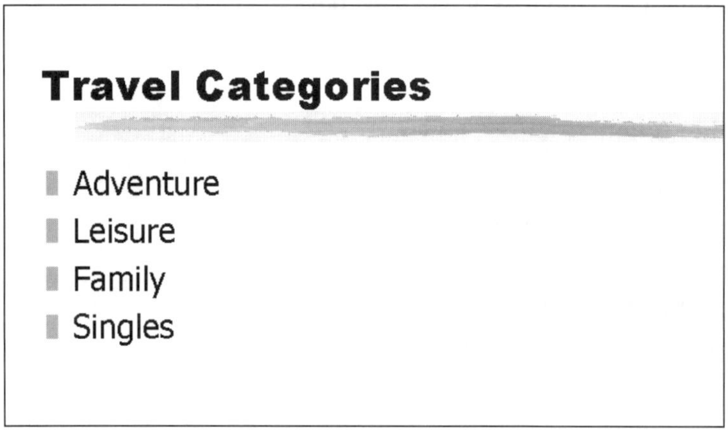

20. Add the following slide using the **Title Slide** AutoLayout. You will need to center align the paragraphs in the subtitle box by selecting them and clicking the Center Alignment button.

Title slides are used quite often as closing slides in presentations.

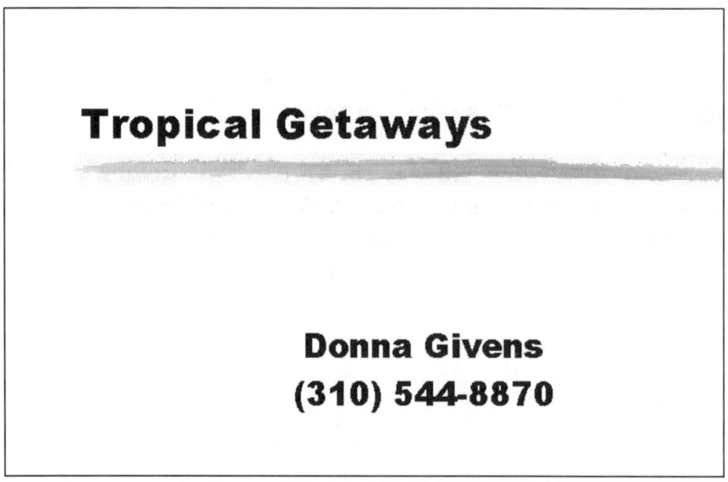

21. Click the Save button and save the presentation to your exercise diskette with the name **Tropical Getaways**.

Skills Builder 17.2

In this exercise, you will reposition one of the slides in the Tropical Getaways presentation.

1. **Click** the Slide Sorter View button to switch to Slide Sorter view.
2. **Drag** the **Travel Categories** slide from position 5 and drop it in position 2 as shown below.

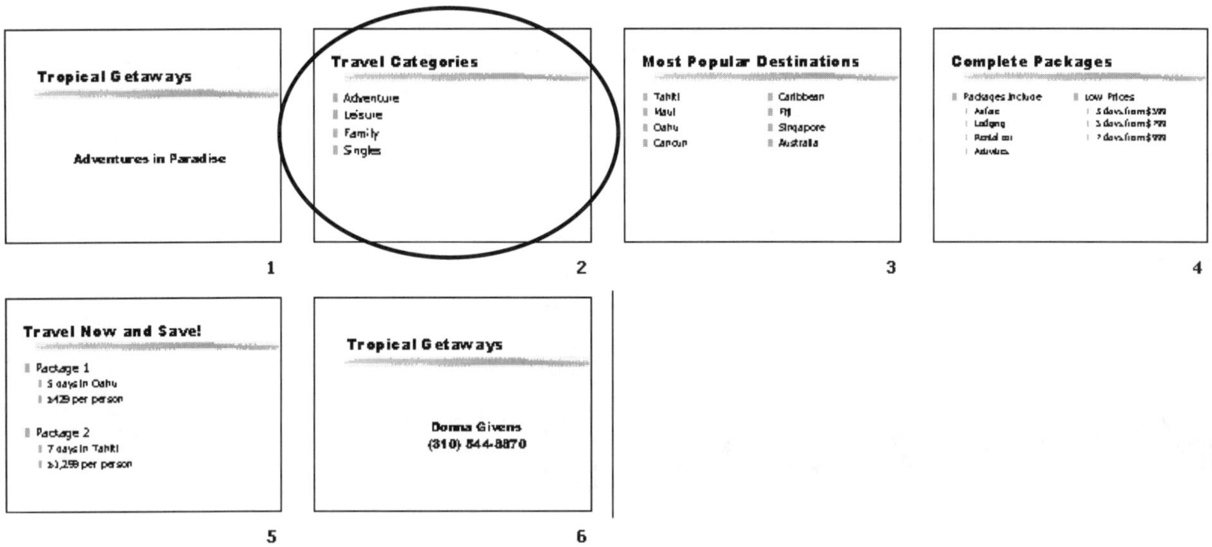

3. Save the change and continue with the next exercise.

Skills Builder 17.3

1. **Click** the **first slide** in the presentation and then **click** the Slide Show button.
2. Click each slide in the presentation until the presentation is complete.
3. Start the presentation again.
4. **Click** the Popup Menu button at the bottom-left corner of the slide.
5. Choose **Go→By Title→Travel Now and Save** to go to the Travel Now and Save slide.
6. Feel free to browse up and down through the slides.
7. Use the Popup Menu button to end the slide show.
8. Choose **File→Close** from the menu bar to close the presentation. Click the Yes button if PowerPoint asks you to save the changes.

Assessment 17.1

In this assessment, you will create a presentation for Classic Cars. Classic Cars is an organization devoted to tracking, categorizing and preserving classic automobiles. The presentation will be given to members of the Classic Cars organization at the annual Classic Cars convention.

1. Choose **File→New...** and **click** the **Presentation Designs tab** in the New Presentation box.
2. **Choose** the **Dads Tie** design and **click OK**.
3. Add the five slides shown below to your presentation and make the following adjustments.
   - Increase the line spacing for the bulleted paragraphs on the Seminar Topics and Collections on Display slides. To accomplish this, select all of the paragraphs and click the Increase Paragraph Spacing button three times.
   - Use the Title AutoLayout style for both the first and last slides.

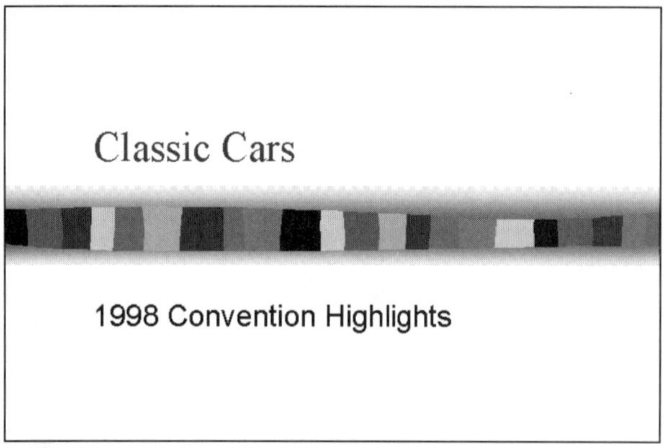

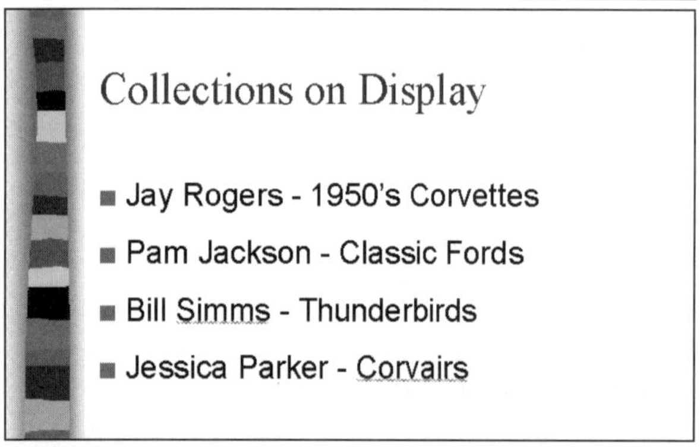

4. Use the Black and White View button to display your presentation in black and white and then print the entire presentation. If necessary, demonstrate your presentation to your instructor. Finally, close the presentation and **save** it with the name **Classic Cars**. If necessary, exit from PowerPoint with the **File→Exit** command.

18 Clip Art, Transitions and Animation

Objectives:

- Use clip art in presentations
- Use the Clip Gallery
- Move and size pictures
- Create transitions between slides
- Select multiple slides in Slide Sorter view
- Use preset text animation
- Create custom animation for text and pictures

The Project – Adding Impact to a Presentation

In this lesson, you will enhance the Pinnacle Pet Care presentation that you created in the previous lesson. You will use clip art to add interest to the presentation. You will also create transitions between slides and use animation to "bring the presentation to life." The following illustration shows a slide from the presentation along with a discussion of the special effects that you will create for the slide.

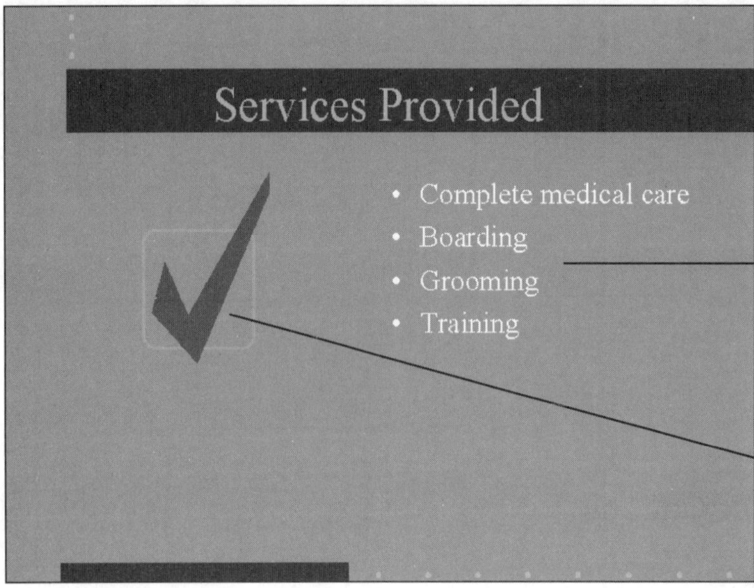

You will animate the paragraphs in the bulleted list by having them "fly in from the left" as they are introduced in the presentation.

You will insert the check mark picture and animate it as well. The picture will "fly in from the left" and it will produce sound as it is introduced.

Using Clip Art

PowerPoint lets you insert clip art in presentations. You can use the clip art that is provided with Office 97 or you can insert your own clip art (such as a company logo). You insert clip art while working in Slide view. Slide view lets you focus on one slide at a time.

Clip art AutoLayouts

PowerPoint has two AutoLayout slides that simplify the task of inserting clip art. The AutoLayout slides contain placeholders for clip art. Clip art is automatically adjusted to the size of a placeholder box when it is inserted. You can actually insert clip art anywhere on a slide. The AutoLayout slides just simplify the process slightly.

The Microsoft Office Clip Gallery

Microsoft provides a variety of clip art objects with Office 97. The clip art objects are installed as part of Office 97. All Office 97 programs (including PowerPoint) can use the clip art. Office 97 also has a Clip Gallery that helps you manage the clip art and other graphics on your system.

You can display the Clip Gallery by double-clicking the clip art icon in an AutoLayout box. You can also display the Clip Gallery by clicking the Insert Clip Art button on the PowerPoint toolbar. You will use the Clip Gallery to insert clip art in the following exercise.

Hands-On 18.1 – Insert clip art in the Pinnacle Pet Care presentation

In this exercise, you will open the Pinnacle Pet Care presentation from your exercise diskette. You will enhance the presentation throughout this lesson. If you **have not** satisfactorily completed the Hands-On exercises in the previous lesson, then ask your instructor to copy the file named Pinnacle Pet Care – Lesson 17 to your exercise diskette. This file provides the Pinnacle Pet Care database in the state it should be in after completing Lesson 17. If necessary, your instructor can provide you with files to give you a fresh starting point whenever you begin a new lesson in this book.

Open the presentation

1. Start PowerPoint and the PowerPoint dialog box should appear as shown below.
2. Choose **Open an existing presentation** as shown below and **click OK**.
   The Open dialog box will appear.

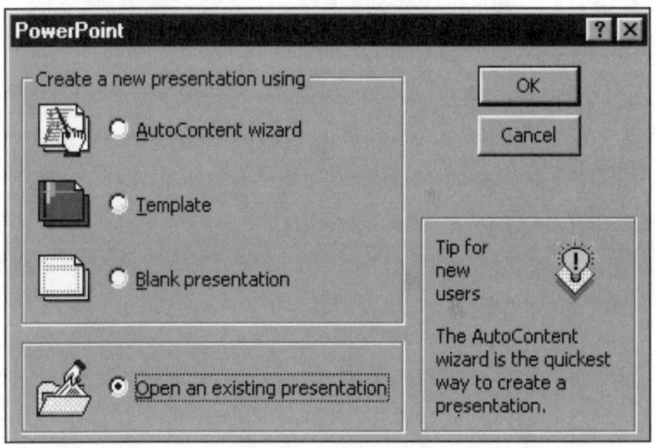

3. Navigate to your exercise diskette, choose the **Pinnacle Pet Care** presentation and **click** the **Open** button.

Continued...

Insert clip art on the title slide

In the next few steps, you will insert a clip art object on the title slide of your presentation. You will size the object and change its position. Later in this lesson, you will animate the object.

4. If necessary, click the Slide view button on the left end of the View bar.
   A single slide will be displayed.
5. If necessary, use the Previous Slide or Next Slide buttons until the title slide is displayed.
   The title slide has the title Pinnacle Pet Care and the subtitle Where Pets Get Pampered!.
6. **Click** the Insert Clip Art button on PowerPoint's Standard toolbar.
7. Use the following illustration to explore the Clip Gallery dialog box and to insert a picture.

❶ *Notice the dialog box tabs. The Clip Gallery lets you organize clip art, pictures (such as scanned in pictures), sound and video. You can use any of these elements in Office 97 documents. Make sure the Clip Art tab is chosen.*

❷ *Notice the clip art is organized in categories.* ***Choose*** *the* ***All Categories*** *option to see all clip art.*

❸ *If necessary, scroll down slightly and* ***choose*** *the* ***rabbit*** *image. (Choose another image if the rabbit is not available.)*

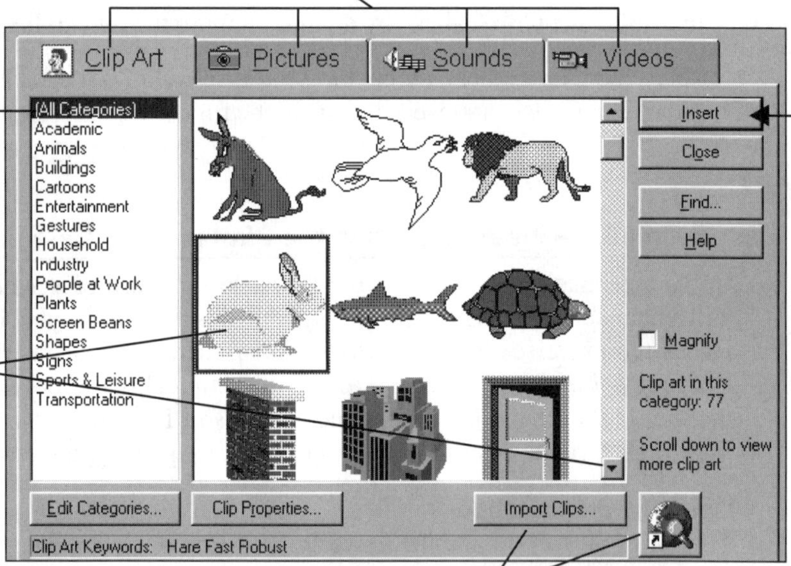

These buttons let you add clips to the gallery. The Connect to Web button sends you to a page on Microsoft's World Wide Web site. You can download clip art from Microsoft's Web site into the gallery. You must have an Internet connection and a Web browser to use this feature.

❹ ***Click*** *the* ***Insert*** *button.*

The rabbit clip art will be inserted in the middle of the slide. The clip art will be quite large as shown in the illustration on the following page.

Continued...

8. Use the following illustration to reduce the size of the picture.

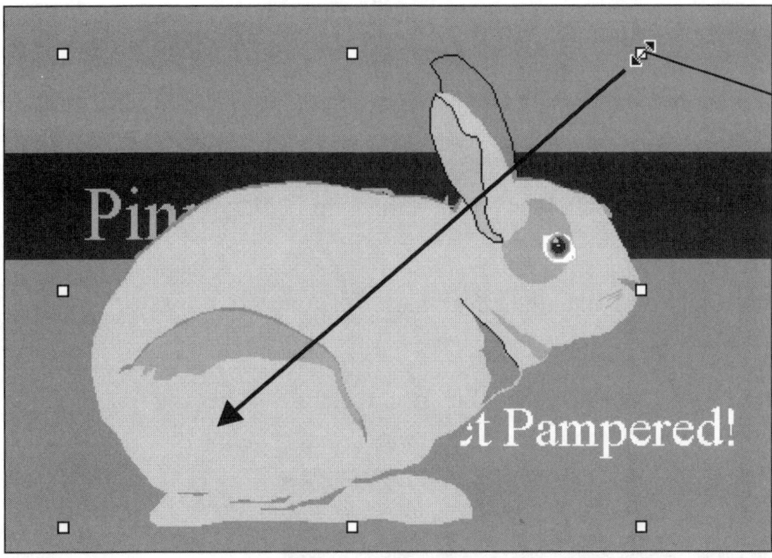

❶ *Position the mouse pointer on a corner-sizing handle and a double-headed arrow will appear.*

❷ **Drag** *the* **corner-sizing handle** *down and left until the picture is about 1" by 1" in size.*

9. Use the following illustration to change the position of the picture.

❶ *Position the mouse pointer on the picture and then* **drag** *the picture to the position shown here.*

Insert clip art on the second slide

In the next few steps, you will insert clip art on the second slide of the presentation. First, however, you will change the AutoLayout for the second slide to a clip art layout. You will then insert the clip art into the clip art placeholder box.

10. Click the Next Slide button on the vertical scroll bar.

The Services Provided slide should be visible.

11. Choose **Slide Layout...** from the Common Tasks toolbar.

The Common Tasks toolbar should be displayed as a floating palette in the PowerPoint window.

Continued...

12. Choose the second AutoLayout style in the last row  and **click** the **Apply** button.

Notice that the bulleted list moves to right-side of the slide and the clip art placeholder appears on the left side. Also notice that an icon and text instructing you to double-click appear in the middle of the clip art placeholder box.

13. Double-click the  icon in the placeholder box and the Clip Gallery dialog box will appear.

14. Scroll through the clip art until you locate the checkmark  clip art.

15. Double-click the checkmark  to insert that clip art in the slide.

Your Services Provided slide should now match the example shown below.

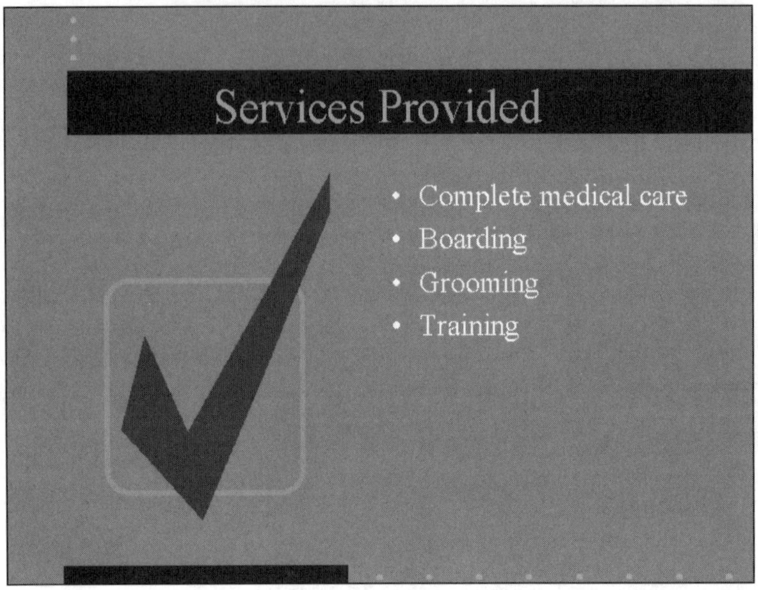

16. Save  the changes to your presentation and continue with the next topic.

Transitions

PowerPoint lets you create transitions between slides in electronic slide shows. For example, the Dissolve transition causes the current slide to slowly dissolve before the next slide is introduced. Transitions can be interesting for the audience to watch and they help create distinct break points between slides. There are 46 transitions that you can use in PowerPoint 97.

Setting up Transitions in Slide Sorter View

Slide Sorter view is the best view to use when setting up transitions. This is because transitions are often applied to multiple slides. Slide Sorter view lets you see all of the slides in your presentation. Keep in mind that you apply transitions to entire slide(s); not to individual objects within slides. Later in this lesson, you will apply custom animation effects to individual objects within slides. Another reason for using Slide Sorter view when setting up transitions is that the Slide Sorter toolbar contains a button and drop-down list to help you apply transitions. The transition controls on the Slide Sorter toolbar are discussed in the following illustration.

This button displays the Slide Transition dialog box, which lets you customize the transitions.

This drop-down button displays a list of transitions that you can apply to selected slides.

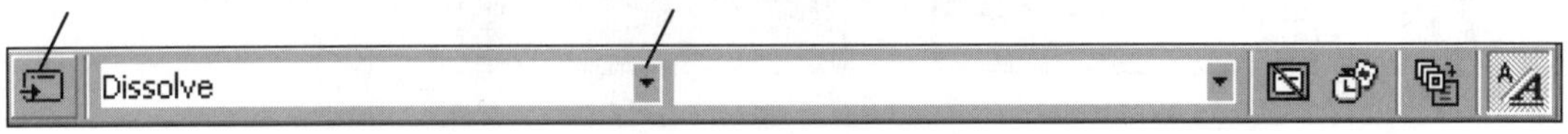

Selecting Multiple Slides in Slide Sorter View

Transitions and other effects are applied to the selected slide(s) in Slide Sorter view. You select a single slide by simply clicking the desired slide. You can select multiple slides by pressing and holding the **Shift** key while clicking the desired slides.

Hands-On 18.2 – Create transitions

In this exercise, you will apply the Dissolve transition to all slides except for the title slide. You will create a more dramatic effect for the title slide at a later time.

1. **Click** the Slide Sorter view button on the View bar.
2. Use the illustration on the next page to select multiple slides and to choose a transition effect.

Continued...

➊ ***Press & hold** the **Shift** key on the keyboard while you **click** slides **2 through 7** (all slides except for the title slide). The slides will become selected as shown here.*

➋ ***Click** the Slide Transition Effects **drop-down button**, **scroll down** through the list and **choose Dissolve** as shown here. The Services Provided slide will briefly demonstrate the Dissolve transition.*

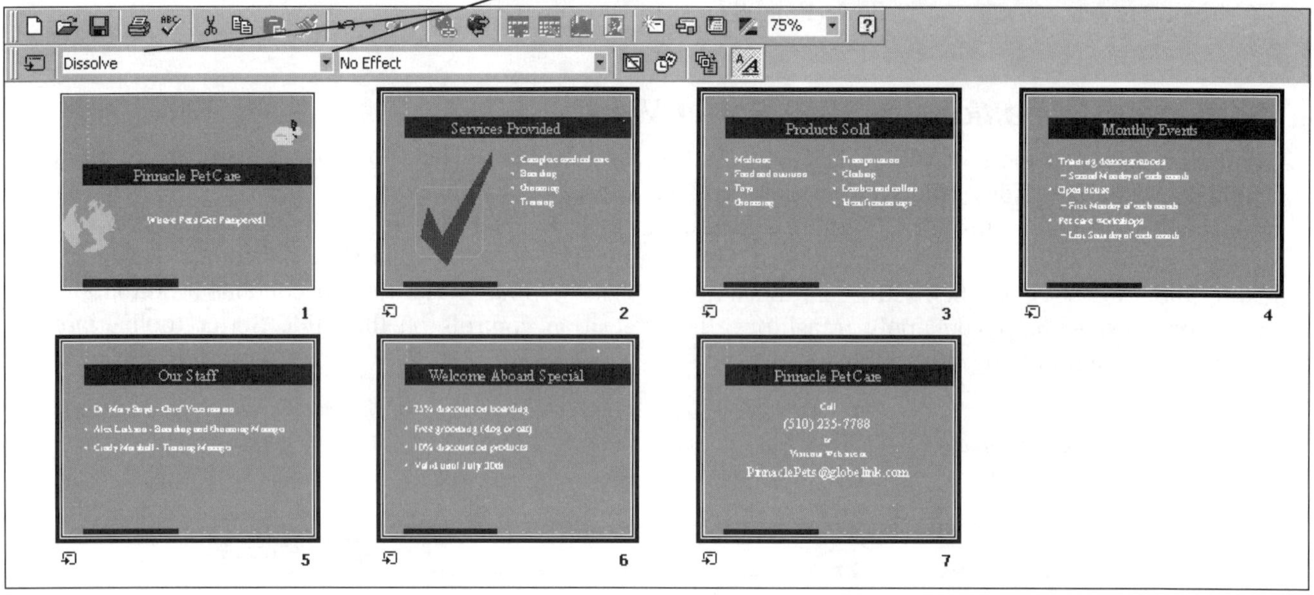

Notice that each of the selected slides has a transition effect icon just below the slide. This icon indicates that a transition effect has been applied to the slide.

Run the presentation

3. **Release** the **Shift key** and **click** the **title slide**.

   At this point, only the title slide should be selected. In the next step, you will run the presentation. Selecting the title slide will force the presentation to begin with that slide.

4. **Click** the Slide Show button on the View bar.

   The title slide will appear without a transition. The title slide would have opened with the Dissolve transition if you had applied the transition to it.

5. **Click** the mouse button and the title slide will dissolve into the Services Provided slide.

6. **Continue to click** the mouse button until the presentation is complete and the Slide Sorter window reappears.

Customize the transition effects

7. **Select** the slides **2 through 7** as you did earlier in this exercise.

8. **Click** the Slide Transition button on the left end of the Slide Sorter toolbar.

   The Slide Transition dialog box appears. This dialog box lets you customize transition effects.

Continued...

9. Use the following illustration to modify the transition effect and to explore the dialog box.

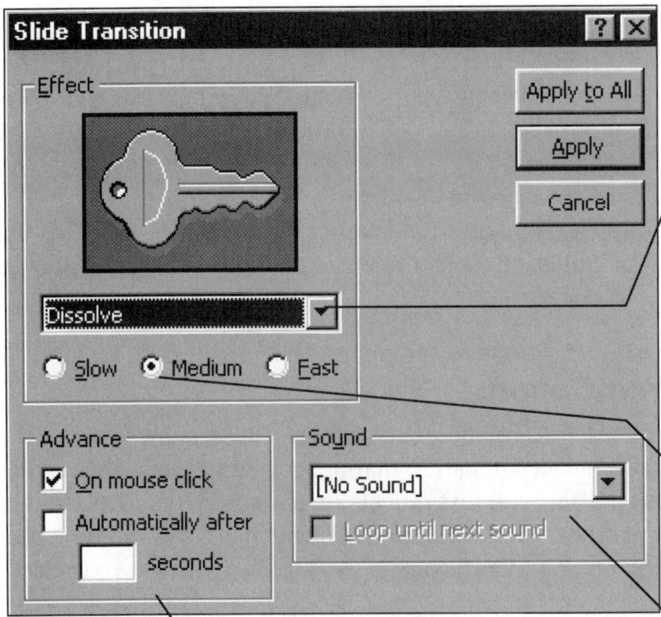

➊ ***Click*** *this* ***drop-down button****.*

➋ ***Tap*** *the* ***DownArrow*** *and* ***UpArrow*** *keys on the keyboard to scroll through the list of transitions. Each transition will preview in the Effect window as you scroll through the list.*

➌ *Now use the mouse to scroll through the list and* ***choose*** *the* ***Dissolve*** *transition.*

➍ ***Click*** *the* ***Medium*** *radio button. This option will slow down the Dissolve effect when you run the presentation.*

➎ *Notice the Advance options. You can have PowerPoint automatically display slides in a presentation by choosing the Automatically after option and setting a second measurement. For example, if you were to set the second option to 10, then PowerPoint would advance to a new slide every 10 seconds.*

➏ *This option allows you to add a sound effect to the transition.*

10. Click the **Apply** (not Apply to All) button to apply the Medium Dissolve effect to the slides.

If you had clicked the Apply to All button, then the effect would have been applied to all slides including the title slide.

11. Click the **title slide** and it will become selected.

12. Click the Slide Show  button on the View bar to begin the slide show.

13. Click the mouse button **repeatedly** until the slide show is complete.

14. Feel free to experiment with the transition effects.

15. Save  the changes and continue with the next topic.

Animating Text

PowerPoint lets you animate text and other objects in a presentation. Text objects include subtitles and bulleted paragraphs. For example, the Fly From Left effect introduces bulleted paragraphs by "flying them in" from the left side of the screen. While delivering your presentation, a new bulleted paragraph is introduced each time you click the mouse button. This allows you to deliver your presentation bullet-by-bullet and to keep your audience engaged.

PowerPoint can also dim a bulleted paragraph as soon as a new paragraph is introduced. This helps keep your audience focused on the most current bullet. You can even use sound effects to add additional impact to a bulleted paragraph when it is introduced.

Using the Text Preset Animation Options

The Slide Sorter toolbar contains a Text Preset Animation drop-down list as shown in the illustration below. This list displays the most common types of animation that are applied to text objects. When you apply animation using this list, the animation affects all text objects on the selected slide(s). You can also apply animation effects to individual paragraphs within a slide by using the Custom Animation dialog box. You will learn about custom animation later in this lesson.

This drop-down button displays a list of animations that can be applied to all text objects on a slide.

Hands-On 18.3 – Add text animation

1. If necessary, click the Slide Sorter view button to switch to Slide Sorter view.
2. **Select** the **title slide** by clicking anywhere on it.
3. Use the following illustration to choose the Spiral effect for the title slide.

   ❶ ***Click** this **drop-down button** on the Slide Sorter toolbar.*

   ❷ ***Scroll down** through the list and **choose Spiral** as shown here.*

   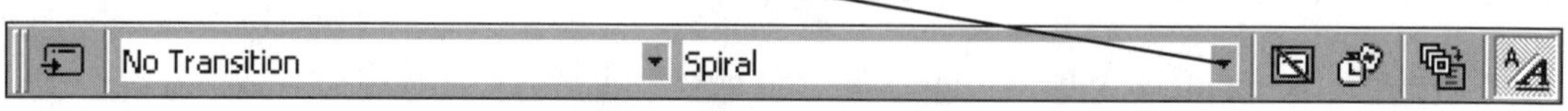

   Notice that the title slide has a text animation effect icon just below the slide. This icon indicates that a text animation effect has been applied to the slide.
4. **Click** the Slide Show button on the View bar.
   *The title slide will appear without displaying the **Where Pets Get Pampered!** subtitle.*
5. **Click** the **mouse button** and the subtitle will spiral into view.
   Later in this lesson, you will add additional enhancements to this effect.
6. **Right-click** anywhere on the presentation and choose **End Show** from the popup menu.
   The Slide Sorter screen should reappear.

Continued...

7. **Select** the **second slide** by clicking anywhere on it.
8. **Press & hold** the **Shift** key while you **click** slides **3 through 6**.
   All slides should be selected except for the title slide and the last slide.
9. Choose the **Fly From Left** text animation effect as shown below.

10. **Select** the **title slide** by clicking it.
11. **Click** the Slide Show button to begin the presentation.
12. **Click** the **mouse button** to introduce the **Where Pets Get Pampered!** subtitle.
13. **Click** the mouse **again** to transition to the Services Provided slide.
    The Dissolve transition will still be in effect.
14. **Click** the mouse **again** and the first bulleted paragraph should "fly in" from the left.
15. **Click again** to introduce the next bullet.
16. **Continue to click** and the next two bullets will be introduced followed by the check mark.
17. **Continue to click** as you progress through the entire presentation.
    Each bulleted paragraph should be introduced sequentially and the Dissolve transition will occur between slides.
18. Continue with the next topic when you have finished.

Custom Animation

The Custom Animation dialog box lets you create animation effects for individual objects within slides. You can animate clip art, text and other types of objects. The Custom Animation dialog box lets you control many aspects of animation including special effects, sounds, timing and other settings.

Applying Custom Animation to Objects

Custom Animation affects individual objects on slides. For this reason, you must be in Slide view before you can display the custom animation dialog box. Slide view displays a single slide and lets you select objects on that slide. You can display the Custom Animation dialog box by **right-clicking** the selected objects and choosing **Custom Animation...** from the popup menu. You can also display the Custom Animation dialog box by choosing **Slide Show→Custom Animation...** from the menu bar.

Animating Clip Art

You can animate clip art in a variety of ways. For example, you can have clip art "fly onto the screen" as you did with bulleted paragraphs. You can also add sound effects when clip art is introduced and control the pace at which the clip art moves.

Hands-On 18.4. – Apply custom animation

In this exercise, you will animate the title slide in the Pinnacle Pet Care presentation.

1. If necessary, end the slide show that you started in the previous exercise.
2. **Click** the Slide View button on the View bar.
3. If necessary, use the Next Slide or Previous Slide buttons to navigate to the title slide.
4. **Click** the rabbit picture and it will become selected.
5. Now **right-click** the selected **picture** and choose **Custom Animation...** from the popup menu.
6. Use the following illustration to set the animation options for the picture.

❶ *If necessary, click the Effects tab.*

❷ ***Click** this button and choose **Crawl From Left**. This is similar to the Fly From Left effect that you used for bullets except that the object will move very slowly.*

❸ ***Click** this button and choose **Hide After Animation**. This setting will cause the rabbit to disappear after if moves across the screen.*

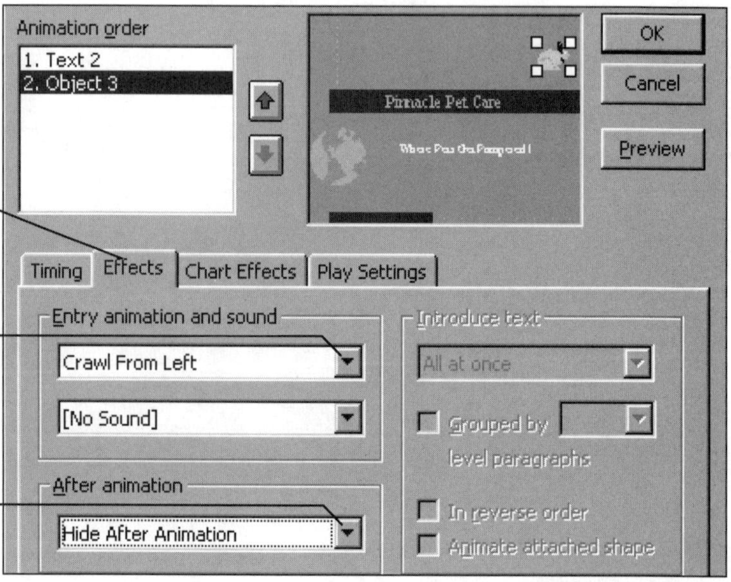

Continued...

7. Leave all other options set as they are and **click OK**.

   You will adjust the timing and other options at a later time.

Animate the subtitle

It is important to immediately grab your audience's attention with your title slide. For this reason, you will continue to enhance the title slide. In the next few steps, you will format the subtitle and add sound to the subtitle animation effect.

8. Use the mouse to **select** the phrase **Where Pets Get Pampered!** in the subtitle box.
9. **Click** the Italics button on the Formatting toolbar.
10. **Click** the Bold button.
11. **Click** the Increase Font Size button **twice**.
12. **Right-click** on the selected text and choose **Custom Animation...** from the popup menu.
13. Use the following steps to set custom animation effects for the subtitle.

❶ *Make sure the Text 2 object appears first in the Animation order as shown here. Use the arrow buttons to the right of the box if it is not first. The animation order determines the order in which the object is animated. In other words, this animation will occur before the rabbit animation.*

❷ ***Click** this **drop-down button** and choose **Whoosh** as the sound effect. However, you will only be able to hear the sound if you have speakers connected to your computer system.*

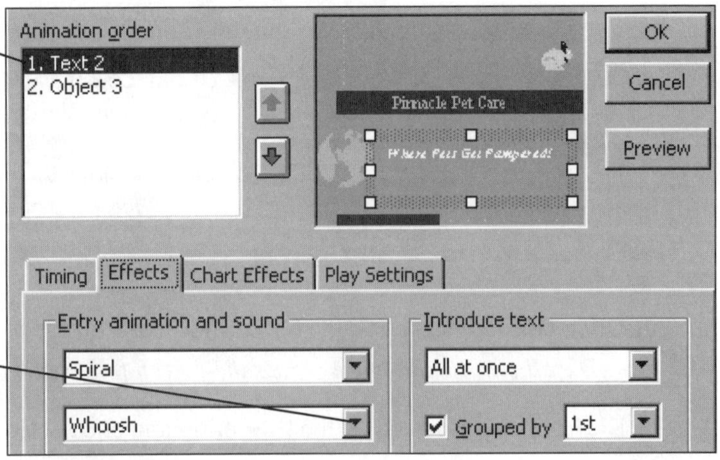

14. Use the following steps to set timing options.

❶ ***Click** the **Timing tab**.*

❷ ***Press and hold** the **Shift** key on the keyboard and **click Object 3** so that both objects are selected. The timing option you set in the next step will now affect both objects.*

❸ ***Click** the **Automatically radio button**. This option will start the animations automatically without you needing to click the mouse.*

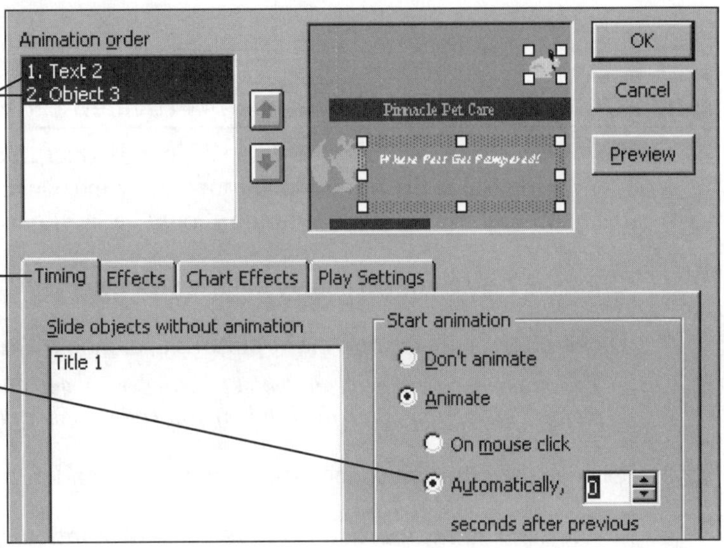

Continued...

15. **Click OK** and then **click** the Slide Show button to begin the presentation.

    The subtitle should automatically spiral into view and you will hear the whoosh sound (if your computer system is equipped with speakers). The rabbit clip art will immediately begin moving across the screen after the subtitle animation is complete. The rabbit should also vanish after it reaches the right-side of the screen.

    The animation order that you just set up may actually be ineffective in a real-world presentation. This is because the moving rabbit will capture the audience's attention. By having it move after the spiraling subtitle, your message about the subtitle may get missed. For this reason, you will change the animation order in the next few steps. The rabbit will begin moving across the screen when the presentation starts, which will give you time to introduce Pinnacle Pet Care. Then the subtitle will spiral into view creating a much more powerful impact.

Change the animation order

16. **Right-click** anywhere on the **title slide** and choose **End Show** from the popup menu.
17. **Right-click** anywhere on the **subtitle** and choose **Custom Animation...** from the popup menu.
18. If necessary, click the Effects tab.
19. Use the following steps to change the animation order.

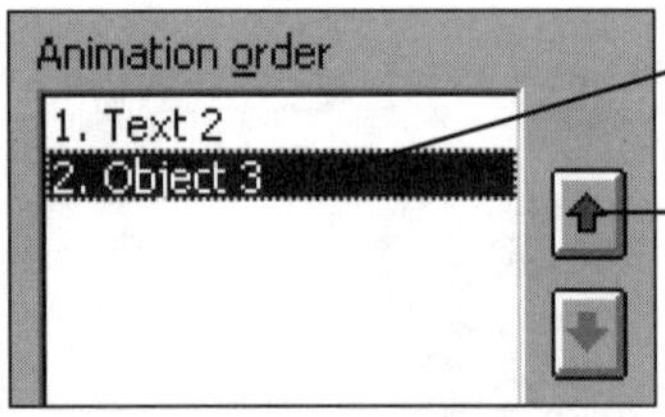

❶ *Choose* **Object 3**, *which is the clip art object.*

❷ **Click** *the* **Move Up button** *to move Object 3 to position 1.*

20. **Click OK** and then **click** the Slide Show button to begin the presentation.

    The clip art should move across the screen followed by the spiraling subtitle.

21. **Right-click** anywhere on the **title slide** and choose **End Show** from the popup menu.

    You will animate other slides in the following exercises.

Hands-On 18.5 – Animate the Services Provided slide

In this exercise, you will add the whoosh sound effect to the clip art on the Services Provided slide. You will also change the timing to automatically introduce the object after the last bulleted paragraph has been introduced. Your presentation should be in Slide view from the previous exercise.

1. **Click** the Next Slide button and the Services Provided slide should be visible.
2. **Right-click** on the **check mark picture** and choose **Custom Animation...** from the popup menu.

   You must right-click on an object in order to get the Custom Animation... option on the popup menu. This option is not available if you right-click on an open part of a slide.

3. Choose the **Whoosh** sound effect from the second drop-down list.
4. **Click** the **Timing tab** and **choose** the **Automatically** option at the bottom of the dialog box. Leave the seconds box set to 0.

Continued...

5. **Click OK** and then **click** the Slide Show button to begin the presentation.
   The presentation will begin with the Dissolve effect and the Services Provided slide.

6. **Click** the **left mouse button four times** to introduce the bulleted paragraphs.
   The check mark will whoosh into view after the fourth bulleted paragraph has been introduced.

7. End the slide show and return to Slide view.

Hands-On 18.6. – Animate the last slide

In this exercise, you will animate the last slide in the presentation.

1. **Click** the Next Slide button until the last slide is visible.

2. **Right-click** the **subtitle box** with the telephone number and choose **Custom Animation...** from the popup menu.

3. Set the entry animation and sound options as shown below.

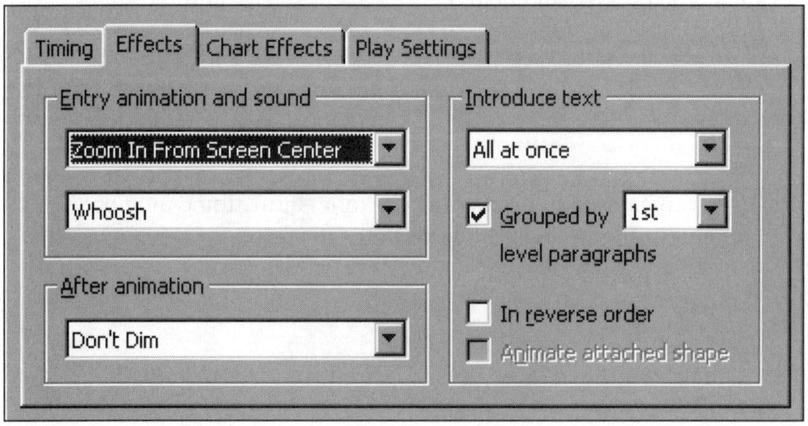

4. **Click** the **Timing tab**.

5. Choose the **Automatically** option at the bottom of the box and leave the seconds box set to 0.

6. **Click OK** and then **click** the Slide Show button to begin the presentation.
   The five paragraphs will whoosh into view one at a time.

7. **Click anywhere** on the slide and the presentation will end.

8. Now use the Previous Slide button to navigate to the title slide (first slide in the presentation).

9. Run the entire presentation from start to finish.

10. Feel free to modify your presentation and experiment with clip art, transitions and animation.

11. **Close** the Pinnacle Pet Care **presentation** when you have finished and **save** the changes.

12. Now continue with the end-of-lesson questions and exercises on the following pages.

Concepts Review

True / False

1. Clip art is inserted while working in Slide Sorter view. 1. **T F**
2. The Clip Gallery can be displayed by clicking the clip art icon in an AutoLayout box. 2. **T F**
3. Transitions are applied to individual objects on slides. 3. **T F**
4. Slide Sorter view is the best view to use when setting up transitions. 4. **T F**
5. You can apply a transition to multiple slides while using Slide Sorter view. 5. **T F**
6. The Slide Sorter toolbar lets you apply both transitions and text effects. 6. **T F**
7. Text objects cannot be animated. 7. **T F**
8. Clicking the mouse can initiate animation steps and transitions. 8. **T F**
9. Customized animations are applied to entire slides. 9. **T F**
10. The Clip Gallery organizes and categorizes clip art. 10. **T F**

Multiple Choice

1. Which of the following keys should be pressed and held if you want to select multiple slides in Slide Sorter view?
   a) Alt
   b) Shift
   c) Ctrl ( )
   d) Enter
2. Which of the following techniques can be used to display the Custom Animation dialog box?
   a) Right-click an open part of a slide while working in slide view.
   b) Right-click an object while working in slide view.
   c) Both a and b.
   d) None of the above. ( )
3. Which of the following effects can be controlled through the Custom Animation dialog box?
   a) Timing
   b) Sound
   c) Motion
   d) All of the above. ( )
4. Which of the following buttons can be used to display the Slide Transition dialog box?
   a) 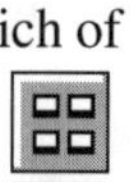
   b)  ( )
   c) 
   d) None of the above.
5. How many different transitions are there in PowerPoint?
   a) 24
   b) 30
   c) 32 ( )
   d) 46

Skills Builder 18.1

In this Skills Builder, you will add clip art to the Tropical Getaways presentation that was developed in the previous lesson. If you did not accurately complete the Skills Builder exercises in the previous lesson, then ask your instructor to copy the file named **Tropical Getaways – Lesson 18** to your exercise diskette. This file provides the Tropical Getaways presentation, as it should be after completing Lesson 17.

1. **Open** the **Tropical Getaways** presentation.
2. If necessary, click the Slide view  button to switch to slide view.
3. Use the Next Slide  button to go to the **second slide** (Travel Categories).
4. Choose **Slide Layout...** from the Common Tasks toolbar.
5. Choose the Text and Clip Art  AutoLayout (first layout in the last row) and **click** the **Apply** button.
6. **Double-click** the clip art  icon in the placeholder box to display the Clip Gallery.
7. **Scroll** through the clip art until you locate the Tennis Player  image.
8. **Double-click** the Tennis Player  to insert that picture in the slide.
   Your Travel Categories slide should now match the example shown below.

9. Use the Next Slide  button to navigate to the **Travel Now and Save!** slide.
10. Change the slide layout to Text and Clip Art  (as you did for the Travel Categories slide).

Continued...

11. Use the following illustration to insert, size and move a clock picture.

❶ ***Insert** the **clock** picture.*

❷ ***Reduce** the **size** of the clock after it is inserted by dragging a corner-sizing handle.*

❸ ***Drag** the clock to the position shown here.*

12. Save the changes to your presentation and continue with the next exercise.

Skills Builder 18.2

In this exercise, you will create transitions in the Tropical Getaways presentation.

1. **Click** the Slide Sorter view button on the View bar.
2. Select slides **2 through 6** by pressing and holding the Shift key while you click the slides.
3. Choose the Cover Down transition effect from the Slide Sorter toolbar as shown below.

4. Save the changes and continue with the next exercise.

Skills Builder 18.3

In this exercise, you will add preset text animation using the Slide Sorter toolbar.

1. **Click** the **title slide** and choose the **Swivel** text animation as shown below.

2. Select slides **2 through 5** and choose the **Fly From Bottom-Right** text animation as follows.

Continued...

3. **Click** the **last slide** and choose the **Zoom in From Screen Center** text animation as shown below.

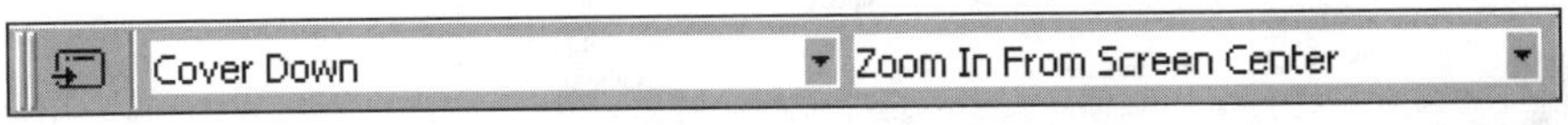

4. **Click** the **title slide** and then **click** the Slide Show button on the View bar.

5. Continuously click the mouse pointer to progress through the presentation.

6. Complete the presentation and you will return to Slide Sorter view.

   You will continue to enhance the presentation by adding custom animation and special effects.

Skills Builder 18.4

Set animation for the title slide

1. **Click** the Slide view button on the View bar.

2. If necessary, use the Previous Slide or Next Slide buttons until the **title slide** is displayed.

3. **Right-click** the subtitle **Adventures in Paradise** and choose **Custom Animation...** from the popup menu.

4. Choose the **Whoosh** sound to accompany the swivel effect.

5. **Click** the **Timing tab** and choose **Automatically**.

6. **Click OK** to complete the settings.

   These settings will cause the subtitle to automatically swivel and whoosh into view when the presentation begins.

Set animation for the Travel Categories slide

7. **Click** the Next Slide button to display the Travel Categories slide.

8. **Right-click** the **Tennis Player** picture and choose **Custom Animation...** from the pop up menu.

9. Choose the **Whoosh** sound, set the timing to **Automatic** and **click OK**.

Set animation for the Complete Packages slide

10. **Click** the Next Slide button **twice** to display the Complete Packages slide.

11. **Right-click** anywhere on the **Packages Include** subtitle and choose **Custom Animation** from the popup menu.

12. Use the illustration on the following page to select both objects and to set animation options.

Continued...

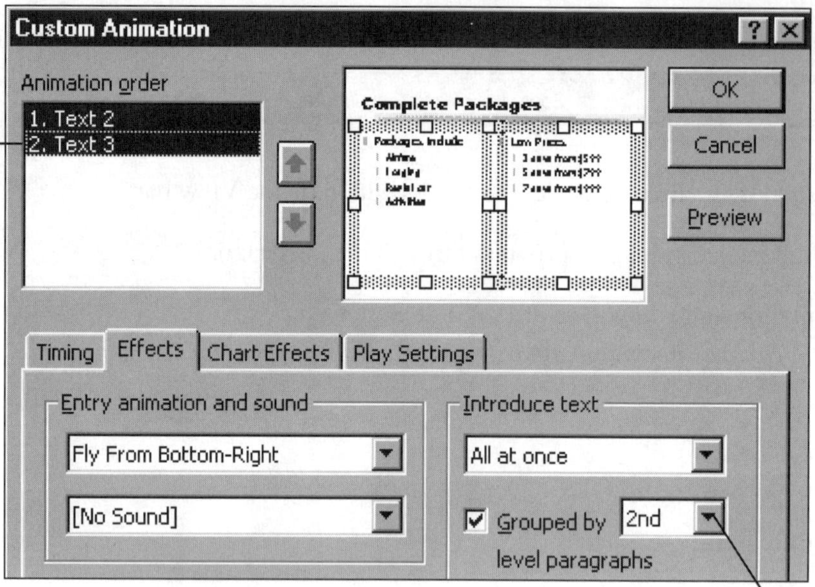

❶ ***Press and hold** the **Shift** key and **click** the **Text 3** item. This will select both placeholder boxes in the Preview window. Any effects that you set will be applied to both objects.*

❷ ***Click** the Grouped by **drop-down button** and choose **2nd**. If this option were set to 1st, then the level one bullet and all level 2 bullets under that bullet would fly onto the screen as a group. By choosing 2nd, the level 2 bullets will fly onto the screen individually each time you click the mouse.*

13. **Click OK** to complete the changes.

14. Use the Previous Slide button to navigate to the **title slide**.

15. **Click** the Slide Show button and progress through the presentation by clicking the mouse.

    Notice the transitions and animation that have been set thus far.

16. Continue clicking and working through the presentation until you have finished viewing the Complete Packages slide.

    Notice how you must click to display the second level bullets.

17. **Right-click** on the current slide and choose **End Show** from the popup menu.

Set animation for the Travel Now and Save! slide

18. Use the Previous Slide or Next Slide buttons to display the **Travel Now and Save!** slide.

    Notice that this slide also has two bullet levels. You will leave the Grouped by option set to 1st for this slide, which will let the 1st and 2nd level bullets fly onto the slide as a group.

19. **Right-click** anywhere on the **Clock** picture and choose **Custom Animation...**.

20. Set the Entry animation and sound options as shown below.

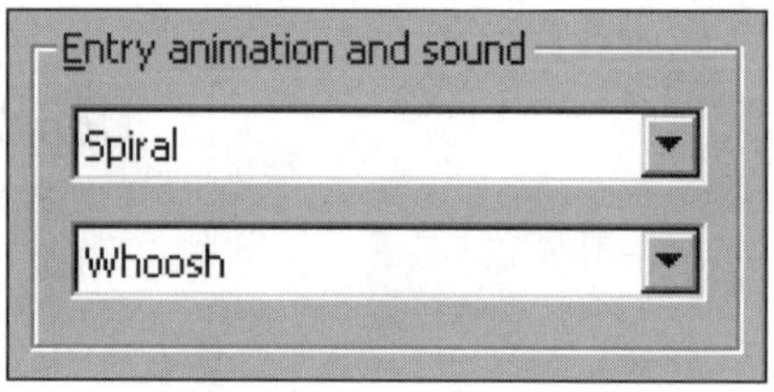

Continued...

21. **Click** the **Timing tab** and choose **Automatically**.

    These settings will cause the clock to spiral onto the slide with a whoosh immediately after the second bullet group is introduced.

22. **Click OK** to complete the changes.

Set animation for the last slide

23. Use the Next Slide button to navigate to the last slide.

24. **Right-click** anywhere on the **subtitle box** with the name Donna Givens and choose **Custom Animation...** from the popup menu.

25. Set the sound option to Camera as shown below.

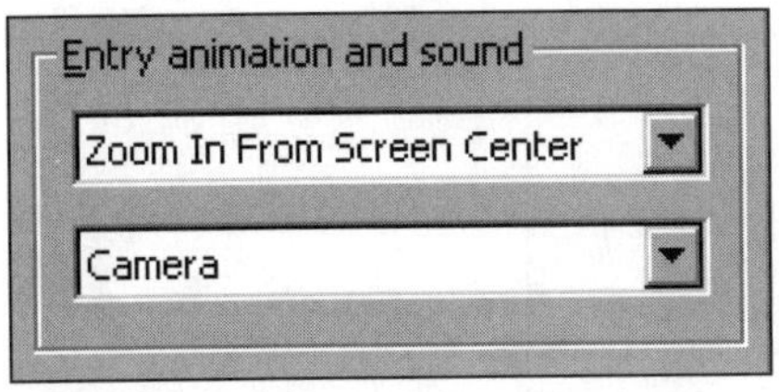

26. **Click** the **Timing tab** and choose **Automatically**.

27. **Click OK** to complete the changes.

Run the show

28. Use the Previous Slide button to navigate to the title slide.

29. **Click** the Slide Show button and progress through the entire presentation.

30. Feel free to experiment with any of the special effects you have used.

    It is important to have a systematic plan when developing presentations. In these Skills Builder exercises, you first added clip art to the presentation. Next, transitions and text affects that affected all bullets on the slide(s) were added. Finally, custom animation was added to individual objects on the slides. This approach allows you to build a presentation layer-by-layer. You should use a similar approach when developing your own presentations.

31. Close the presentation with the **File→Close** command and **save** the changes.

Assessment 18.1

In this assessment, you will add animation effects to the Classic Cars presentation that was developed in the previous lesson.

1. **Open** the **Classic Cars** presentation on your exercise diskette.

Clip Art

2. Add clip art to the second slide (Seminar Topics) as shown below. You will need to change the slide layout for the slide and insert the picture in the placeholder box of the new layout. Reduce the size of the picture after inserting it and adjust the position as shown below. You will also need to reduce the font size of the bulleted paragraphs so that they no longer wrap (as shown below).

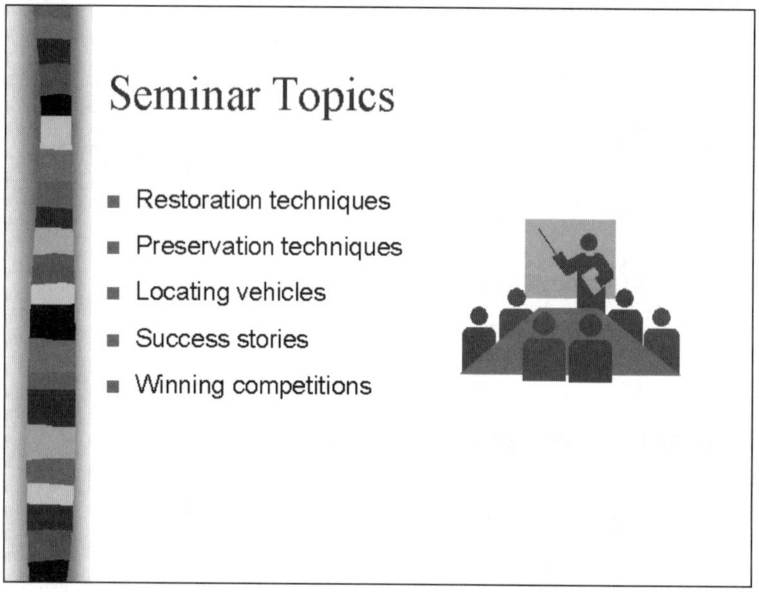

3. Add clip art to the last slide as shown below. There is no need to change the slide layout. Simply insert the picture and size and position it as shown.

Continued...

Transitions and text animation

4. Apply the **Split Vertical Out** transition to slides **2 through 5**.

5. Apply the **Fly From Right** text effect to slides **2 through 4**.

Custom animation – Title slide

6. Animate the **subtitle** on the title slide to **Fly From Left**.

7. Use the **Drive By** sound effect to accompany the Fly From Left effect.

8. Set the timing to **automatic** so that the animation occurs as soon as the presentation is started.

Custom animation – Seminar Topics slide

9. Animate the picture by having it **Fly From Bottom-Left**.

10. Use the **Whoosh** sound effect to accompany the Fly From Bottom-Left effect.

11. Set the animation order so that the **picture** is the **first** object animated.

12. Set the timing to **automatic** so that the picture automatically whooshes into view when the slide is introduced.

13. The animation for the bulleted list should remain as Fly From Right and a bullet should fly each time the mouse is clicked. You may need to check the timing to ensure it is set to **On mouse click** for the bulleted list.

Custom animation – Door Prizes slide

14. Change the **Group by** level to **2nd** so that the 2nd level bulleted paragraphs fly onto the slide one at a time.

Custom animation – Last slide

15. Animate the picture by having it **Crawl From Left**.

16. Set the timing to **automatic** so that the picture automatically crawls into view when the slide is introduced.

Run and demonstrate the presentation

17. Run your presentation when you have finished. Carefully work through the instructions in this exercise until you are confident that your presentation is correct.

18. When you are ready, demonstrate your presentation to your instructor. Your instructor can show you a sample presentation that has the correct pictures and special effects.

19. **Close** your presentation when you have finished and **save** the changes.

19 Integration: Excel and PowerPoint

Objectives:

- Review integration concepts
- Insert an Excel chart in a PowerPoint presentation
- Establish a link between PowerPoint and Excel
- Update a worksheet and notice the changes in PowerPoint

The Project – Presenting for Dollars

In this lesson, you will help Pinnacle Pet Care develop a presentation to the Loan Committee at Bay View Bank. The presentation will contain a chart with financial projections that is linked to an Excel worksheet. The object linking capabilities in Office 97 will automatically update the chart in your PowerPoint presentation whenever data is changed in the Excel worksheet. The Excel worksheet and chart and the linked PowerPoint slide that you will create are shown below.

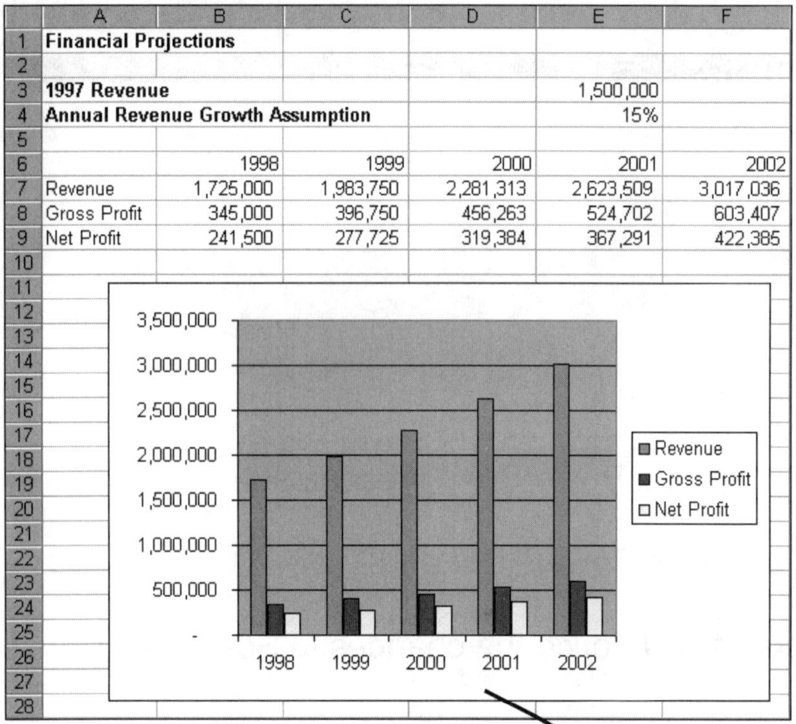

	A	B	C	D	E	F
1	**Financial Projections**					
2						
3	**1997 Revenue**				1,500,000	
4	**Annual Revenue Growth Assumption**				15%	
5						
6		1998	1999	2000	2001	2002
7	Revenue	1,725,000	1,983,750	2,281,313	2,623,509	3,017,036
8	Gross Profit	345,000	396,750	456,263	524,702	603,407
9	Net Profit	241,500	277,725	319,384	367,291	422,385

The Excel chart is pasted into a PowerPoint slide and a link is established. Any changes made to the chart in the worksheet are reflected in the PowerPoint slide.

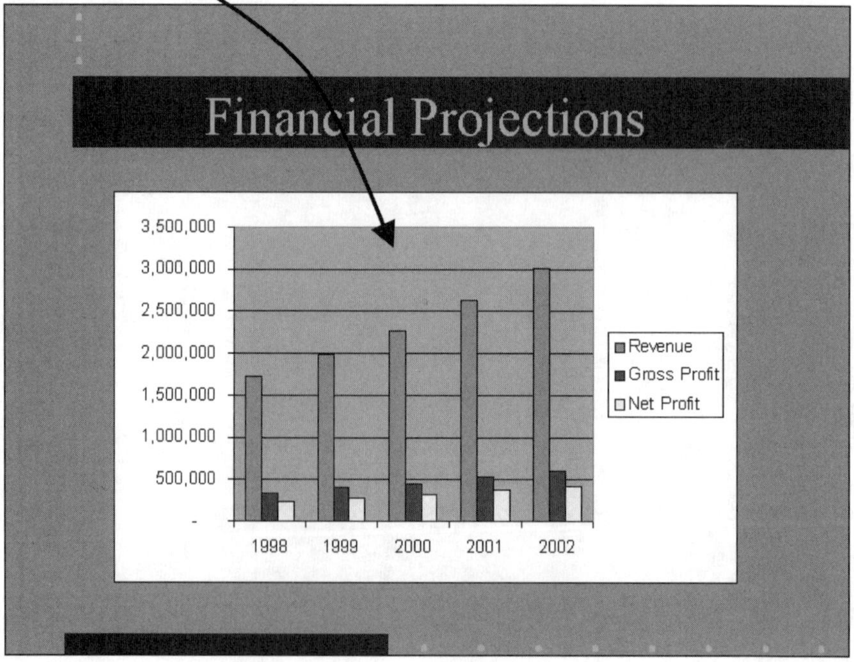

Using Excel Charts in PowerPoint Presentations

PowerPoint 97 contains several AutoLayouts with placeholder boxes for charts. You can create charts in PowerPoint using the Microsoft Graph charting program, or you can create them in Excel and then copy and paste them into your PowerPoint presentations. The copy and paste method may be advantageous because it allows you to take advantage of Excel's powerful analysis and charting capabilities.

Reviewing Object Linking and Embedding

In an earlier integration lesson, you learned that integration occurs between a **source** document and a **destination** document. For example, you may want an Excel chart to appear in a PowerPoint presentation. In this example, the Excel chart would be the source document and the PowerPoint presentation would be the destination document.

Hands-On 19.1 – Create an Excel worksheet

1. Start Excel and enter the data shown in the following worksheet. Make sure you enter the data in the same cells shown in the worksheet.

	A	B	C	D	E	F
1	**Financial Projections**					
2						
3	**1997 Revenue**				1,500,000	
4	**Annual Revenue Growth Assumption**				15%	
5						
6		1998	1999	2000	2001	2002
7	Revenue					
8	Gross Profit					
9	Net Profit					

2. Save the worksheet to your exercise diskette with the name **Hands-On Lesson 19**.

Create the revenue formulas

3. **Click** cell **B7**.

   You will enter a formula in cell B7 that calculates the 1998 revenue as the 1997 revenue plus 15%.

4. Enter the formula **=1500000*(1+E4)**.

   Notice that this formula adds the growth assumption (15%) in cell E4 to the number 1 and multiples that number by one million five hundred thousand. The result should be 1725000. The benefit of referencing cell E4 in the formula is that you can now change the value in E4 and the projected revenue in cell B7 will be recalculated.

5. **Click** cell **C7** and enter the formula **=B7*(1+E4)**.

   The result should be 1983750.

6. Now enter the formulas **=C7*(1+E4)** in cell **D7**, **=D7*(1+E4)** in cell **E7** and **=E7*(1+E4)** in cell **F7**.

   At this point, row 7 in your worksheet should have the following formula results.

6		1998	1999	2000	2001	2002
7	Revenue	1725000	1983750	2281313	2623509	3017036

Continued...

Create the gross profit and net profit formulas

7. **Click** cell **B8** and enter the formula **=B7*.2**.

   This formula assumes that the profit margin will be 20%.

8. Use the fill handle and the following illustration to copy this formula across the row.

   ❶ *Position the mouse pointer on the bottom right corner of the cell and a black cross will appear.*

   ❷ ***Drag** to the right over the next four cells and a shaded rectangle will appear.*

8	Gross Profit	345000				
9	Net Profit					

   ❸ *Release the mouse button and the formula will be copied across the row.*

9. Now **click** cell **B9** and enter the formula **=B8*.7**.

10. Use the fill handle to copy the formula across the row.

    At this point, your worksheet should match the following example.

	A	B	C	D	E	F
1	**Financial Projections**					
2						
3	**1997 Revenue**				1,500,000	
4	**Annual Revenue Growth Assumption**				15%	
5						
6		1998	1999	2000	2001	2002
7	Revenue	1725000	1983750	2281313	2623509	3017036
8	Gross Profit	345000	396750	456262.5	524701.9	603407.2
9	Net Profit	241500	277725	319383.8	367291.3	422385

Format the numbers

11. Use the mouse to select all cells in the range **B7:F9**.

12. **Click** the Comma Style button and then decrease the decimals to 0.

    The numbers in rows 7 through 9 should now be formatted as shown below.

6		1998	1999	2000	2001	2002
7	Revenue	1,725,000	1,983,750	2,281,313	2,623,509	3,017,036
8	Gross Profit	345,000	396,750	456,263	524,702	603,407
9	Net Profit	241,500	277,725	319,384	367,291	422,385

13. Save the changes and continue with the next exercise.

Hands-On 19.2 – Chart the data

In this exercise, you will chart the data that you entered in the previous exercise.

1. **Select** the range **A6:F9** as shown below.

	A	B	C	D	E	F	G
1	**Financial Projections**						
2							
3	**1997 Revenue**				1,500,000		
4	**Annual Revenue Growth Assumption**				15%		
5							
6		1998	1999	2000	2001	2002	
7	Revenue	1,725,000	1,983,750	2,281,313	2,623,509	3,017,036	
8	Gross Profit	345,000	396,750	456,263	524,702	603,407	
9	Net Profit	241,500	277,725	319,384	367,291	422,385	
10							

2. **Click** the Chart Wizard button on the Standard toolbar.
   The Chart Wizard - Step 1 of 4 dialog box will appear.

3. **Click** the Finish button and Excel will create the chart as shown below.
   By clicking the Finish button you accepted all of the default charting options.

	A	B	C	D	E	F
1	**Financial Projections**					
2						
3	**1997 Revenue**				1,500,000	
4	**Annual Revenue Growth Assumption**				15%	
5						
6		1998	1999	2000	2001	2002
7	Revenue	1,725,000	1,983,750	2,281,313	2,623,509	3,017,036
8	Gross Profit	345,000	396,750	456,263	524,702	603,407
9	Net Profit	241,500	277,725	319,384	367,291	422,385

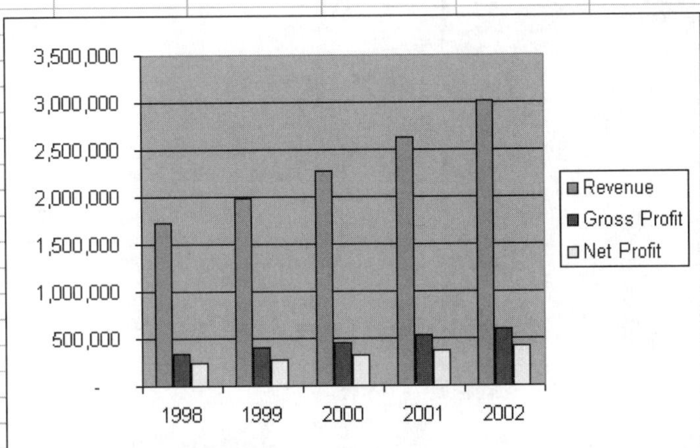

Play what-if analysis

4. **Click** cell **E4** and enter the number **20%**.
   All formulas in the worksheet should recalculate and the chart should be updated. All of the formulas were recalculated because they are dependent upon cell E4.

5. **Change** the number in cell **E4** back to **15%**.

6. **Save** the changes, leave Excel and the workbook open and continue with the next exercise.

Hands-On 19.3 – Set up a PowerPoint presentation

In this exercise, you will set up several slides in a new PowerPoint presentation. In a later exercise, you will paste the Excel chart into the presentation.

1. Start PowerPoint and the PowerPoint dialog box will appear.
2. Choose **Template** from the dialog box and **click OK**.
3. **Click** the **Presentation Designs tab** in the New Presentation dialog box.
4. Choose the **Contemporary** design and **click OK**.
5. Add the following three slides to your new presentation.

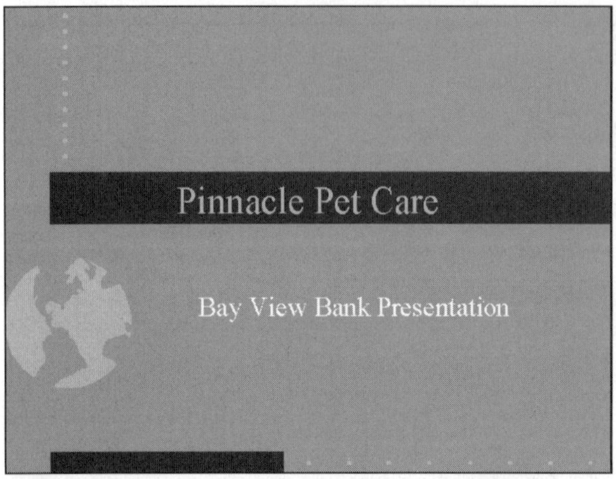

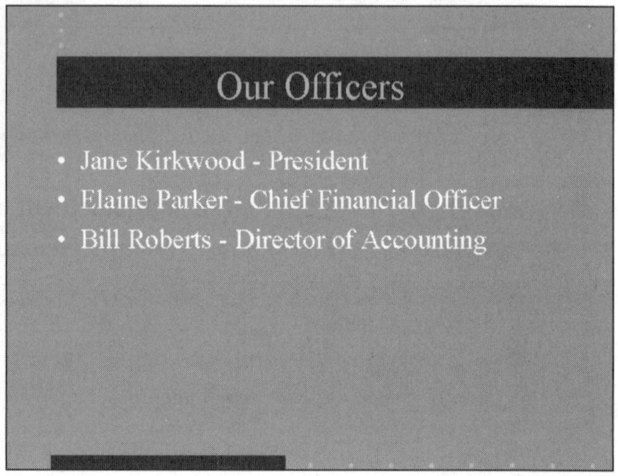

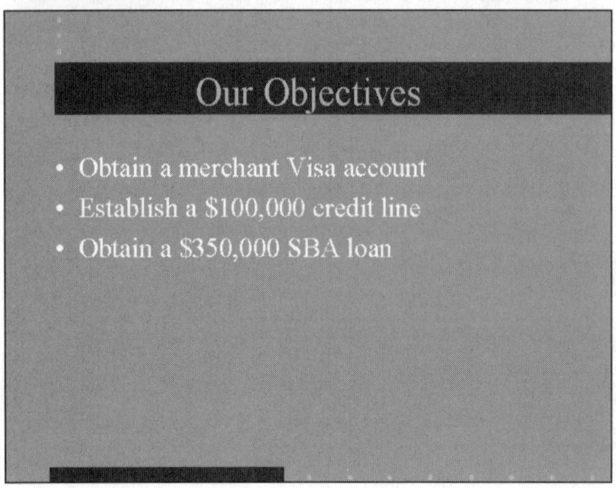

6. **Save** your new presentation with the name **Hands-On Lesson 19**.
   You will continue to enhance the presentation.

Add a chart slide

7. Choose **New Slide...** from the Common Tasks toolbar.
8. Choose the Chart  AutoLayout (fourth AutoLayout on the second row) and **click OK**.
   PowerPoint will insert a title box and a placeholder box for a chart.

Continued...

9. **Click** the **title box** and enter the title **Financial Projections**.

   You could create a chart directly in PowerPoint by double-clicking the chart icon in the chart placeholder box. PowerPoint displays the Microsoft Graph worksheet and toolbar when this is done. However, you will copy and paste the chart from Excel. This way, you can keep your financial data and projections in Excel and continue to use the powerful analysis capabilities of Excel. You will do this in the next exercise.

Hands-On 19.4 – Copy and paste the Excel chart

1. **Switch to Excel** by clicking the Microsoft Excel button on the Windows 95 taskbar.
2. **Click** on a white area of the chart and sizing handles will appear on the outer border of the chart.

   This indicates that the entire chart is selected.
3. **Click** the Copy button on the Excel toolbar.
4. **Switch to PowerPoint** by clicking the Microsoft PowerPoint button on the Windows 95 taskbar.
5. **Click** anywhere on the chart **placeholder box** on the Financial Projections slide and the box will become selected.

   In the next few steps, you will paste the chart into the PowerPoint presentation using the Paste Special command. This will establish a link between the chart in the Excel worksheet and the PowerPoint presentation. The link will automatically update the chart in PowerPoint whenever the chart in Excel changes. You could simply paste the chart using the Paste button; however, it would not be linked to the chart in Excel.
6. Choose **Edit→Paste Special...** and the Paste Special dialog box will appear.
7. Choose the Paste link: option and **click OK**.

   The chart will appear in the PowerPoint slide.
8. Notice that the numbers range from approximately 1,500,000 to 3,000,000.

   These numbers will change when you update the Excel worksheet in the next few steps.

Change the data in Excel and notice the changes in PowerPoint

9. **Switch to Excel** by clicking the Microsoft Excel button on the Windows 95 taskbar.
10. **Click** cell **E4** and change the number to **50%**.

    Notice how the Excel worksheet recalculates all of the formulas and the chart is updated.
11. **Switch to PowerPoint** by clicking the Microsoft PowerPoint button on the Windows 95 taskbar.

    The PowerPoint chart should reflect the same changes that occurred in the Excel chart. Once again, this is because the chart is linked to the Excel worksheet.

Complete the PowerPoint presentation

12. Add the new slide shown on the following page to your PowerPoint presentation.

Continued...

13. Feel free to add clip art, transitions and animation to your presentation.

14. Run your presentation and make any other changes as desired.

15. When you have finished, choose **File→Exit** to close PowerPoint and save the changes to your presentation.

16. Choose **File→Exit** from the Excel menu bar and save the changes to your workbook.

Concepts Review

True / False

1. Charts can be created in PowerPoint using Microsoft Graph. 1. **T F**
2. Excel charts that are inserted in PowerPoint presentations are always linked to the source chart in the Excel worksheet. 2. **T F**
3. If a PowerPoint chart is linked to a chart in an Excel worksheet, then changes in the worksheet chart are reflected in the PowerPoint chart. 3. **T F**

Multiple Choice

1. Which command is used to display the Paste Special dialog box?
   a) Insert→Paste Special
   b) Edit→Paste Special
   c) File→Paste Special
   d) Format→Paste Special ( )
2. Which of the following statements is true?
   a) You thoroughly enjoyed this course.
   b) Your thoroughly enjoyed this computer book.
   c) You are looking forward to learning more about computers.
   d) All of the above. ( )

Index